Inequality

A CONTEMPORARY APPROACH TO RACE, CLASS, AND GENDER

Social stratification is the grouping of people based on income, wealth, political influence, and other characteristics. Widely recognized categories such as upper, middle, and lower class reflect the presence of social stratification in all societies. *Inequality* refers to the inevitable disparities in a person's position in this structure. The research presented in this book ranges from studies of income and wealth disparities to analyses of the nature of the class system.

This textbook reflects a hybrid approach to studying stratification. It addresses the knowledge accumulated by stratification scholars and challenges students to apply this information to their social world. The authors include a wide range of topics and provide current research to round out their discussions. Each chapter includes a list of key concepts, questions for thought, suggested exercises, and multimedia resources.

Lisa A. Keister is Professor of sociology and Director of the Markets and Management Program at Duke University. She conducts research on wealth inequality and asset accumulation and the causes of each. She is the author of *Getting Rich: America's New Rich and How They Got There* (Cambridge, 2005) and *Wealth in America* (Cambridge, 2000). Her research on Chinese corporations and China's economic transition was featured in her book *Chinese Business Groups* (2000) and has appeared in various articles.

Darby E. Southgate is Assistant Professor of sociology at Los Angeles Valley College and a research consultant. Her primary research interests are poverty, education, and culture. Her research investigates the intersection of socioeconomic status, education, and culture. She has authored numerous entries on culture, specifically on music and society. She consults for agencies that aim to reduce homelessness and poverty through education.

Inequality

A CONTEMPORARY APPROACH TO RACE, CLASS, AND GENDER

Lisa A. Keister
Duke University

Darby E. Southgate
Los Angeles Valley College

CAMBRIDGE
UNIVERSITY PRESS

CAMBRIDGE UNIVERSITY PRESS
Cambridge, New York, Melbourne, Madrid, Cape Town,
Singapore, São Paulo, Delhi, Tokyo, Mexico City

Cambridge University Press
32 Avenue of the Americas, New York, NY 10013-2473, USA

www.cambridge.org
Information on this title: www.cambridge.org/9780521680028

First published 2012

Printed in the United States of America

A catalog record for this publication is available from the British Library.

Library of Congress Cataloging in Publication Data

Keister, Lisa A., 1968–
Inequality : a contemporary approach to race, class, and gender / Lisa A. Keister,
Darby E. Southgate.
    p.   cm.
Includes bibliographical references and index.
ISBN 978-0-521-86196-0 (hardback) – ISBN 978-0-521-68002-8 (paperback)
1. Social stratification – United States.   2. Equality – United States.
3. Social classes – United States.   4. Wealth – United States.
5. Poverty – United States.   I. Southgate, Darby E., 1964–   II. Title.
HN90.S6K45   2011
305.5'120973–dc23   2011018856

ISBN 978-0-521-86196-0 Hardback
ISBN 978-0-521-68002-8 Paperback

From LAK to JWM
From DES to AES

Contents

Acknowledgments

We are grateful to several people and organizations that helped us as we conceived of and produced this book. Robert Dreesen and the editorial staff at Cambridge worked with us to complete the book. In the later stages of the project, Rebecca Tippett and Nathan Martin assisted in creating and updating tables.

Three reviewers provided thoughtful, instructive comments on the project at various stages of development. We are thankful for their helpful comments and feel certain that their critiques improved the quality of this book.

Duke, Stanford, and The Ohio State universities provided the space in which we accomplished our work. We are grateful to them and for the assistance of the many people who work there.

Basic Concepts

1 Social Stratification and Opportunities

At the end of a day, Bill and Melinda Gates return to their estate on the shore of Lake Washington near Seattle. They might relax around their indoor/outdoor swimming pool, enjoy a game of tennis or basketball on one of their several athletic courts, or watch a movie in their personal state-of-the-art theater. Their three children can entertain themselves in the trampoline room, which has a 20-foot ceiling, or they might read a book in the family's extensive library. When it is time for dinner, several cooks assist in preparing the meal in one of six kitchens. Other members of the 300-person staff will clean up after dinner, help bathe the children in one of the 24 bathrooms, and put them to bed in one of 7 bedrooms. The Gates's main house comprises 66,000 square feet, making it 33 times the size of the average American house (i.e., about 2,000 square feet). In fact, the Gates's guest room alone is 1,900 square feet and the main reception hall is 2,300 square feet. All of this luxury is not cheap: The house cost more than $97 million to build and the Gates pay approximately $1 million in property taxes on the structure each year. Maintenance costs for salaries and repairs are higher than the total budget of many small American cities.

Across town near downtown Seattle, Brian and Laura Willis have a very different experience when they return home at the end of a day. They live with their three children in a two-bedroom apartment, where the plumbing usually – but not always – works. Because their apartment is in a city-owned low-rent complex, they are seldom a high priority for the landlord's maintenance staff; plumbing repairs and other maintenance issues can take days. Other children live in the complex, but the Willis children typically are not allowed to play outside of their apartment because it is not uncommon for drug dealers to be in the hallways and prostitutes on the street. Brian and Laura try to entertain their children in the evening with games and books. However, almost half of their monthly income goes to pay the rent for their 880-square-foot apartment. After buying groceries, paying utility bills, and occasional visits to a health clinic (health insurance is too expensive), little money remains for clothes, toiletries, furnishings, and other necessities. Toys, games, cable television, family trips to restaurants or the movies, and other forms of entertainment are a rare luxury for the Willis family.

The differences between the lives of these two families are extreme but not unusual. Bill Gates has been the richest person in the world for more than a decade, and his wealth naturally enables him to live an extravagant lifestyle. Yet, he is not alone at the top: There are currently more millionaires and billionaires in America than at any other time in history. The number of billionaires in the United States (i.e., people with more than $1 billion in wealth) increased from slightly more than 80 in the early 1990s to more than 200 by 1998 (Figure 1.1); by 2000, there were 300 billionaires. More recently, this number declined because hard economic times have reduced in value the assets of many of the wealthy; however, the number of billionaires is still more than 200. As the number of billionaires grew, the country's richest families became increasingly richer. The average wealth owned by the Forbes 400 (i.e., the country's 400 richest people) increased dramatically during the 1990s (see Figure 1.1) even net of inflation. The wealth of these families increased slowly through the 1990s and then rose dramatically between 1995 and 2000. In 2000, the average wealth of the Forbes 400 was about $3 billion.

However, not everyone has shared in the growing prosperity experienced by the very wealthy. The gap between rich and poor is enormous and has expanded in recent years, as indicated by two important measures of economic and social well-being: income and wealth. *Income* is money earned from work in the form of wages or salaries, government-transfer payments (e.g., social security payments), and other income, including

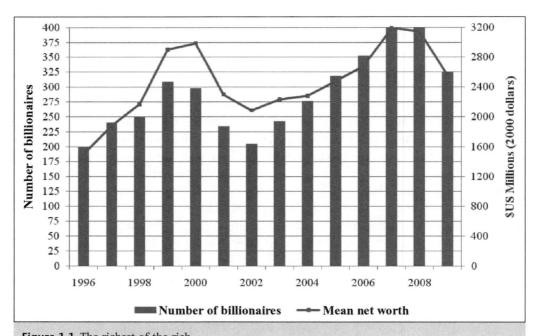

Figure 1.1 The richest of the rich.
Number of billionaires and mean wealth of the "Forbes 400 Richest Americans."
Data source: Forbes Magazine (available at www.Forbes.com, accessed November 2010). Number of individuals in the "Forbes 400 Richest Americans" with a net worth greater than $1 billion (in 2000 dollars) and mean net worth of the full Forbes 400 list (converted to 2000 dollars).

interest and dividends on investments. *Income distribution* is a list of all individuals according to their total income; it reveals the percentage of people at various income levels. *Wealth* is defined by what people own, including homes, savings, investments, real estate, businesses, and vehicles. It is usually measured as *net worth* – that is, the sum of assets less the sum of debts. *Wealth distribution* is a list of all households according to their total wealth. Like income distribution, wealth distribution reveals the percentage of households at various wealth levels. Notice that income is measured for individuals, whereas wealth is measured for households: Income can be attributed to specific people in a household, whereas wealth (e.g., the family home) is usually owned jointly by more than one person.

A review of income distribution reveals that a small percentage of Americans in 2000 earned very high incomes, whereas most people had moderate to low incomes. In 2000, the top 20 percent of income earners earned 50 percent of total income, whereas the bottom 40 percent earned only 12 percent (Figure 1.2). In fact, the richest 1 percent of families earned 20 percent of total income. Inequality in wealth ownership is even more extreme. In 2001, the top 20 percent of wealth owners controlled 84 percent of all household wealth, whereas the bottom 40 percent shared less than 1 percent (Figure 1.3). In the case of wealth, the top 1 percent owned one-third of all assets. For some groups in the distribution, the differences are more startling. In particular, blacks and Hispanics own considerably less wealth than whites. Whereas the median black income is about 60 percent of the median white income, the median net worth for blacks is less than 10 percent of that for whites. Blacks also are more likely than whites to have no wealth or to have more debts than assets (Oliver and Shapiro 1995).

The United States is not alone in this inequality; indeed, it is one trait that nearly all societies share. Among the world's developed countries, however, the U.S. level of

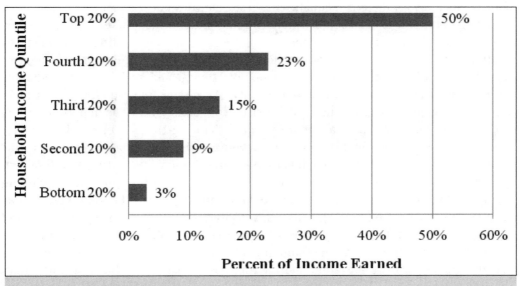

Figure 1.2 Income inequality.
Percentage of income earned, by position in the income distribution.
Data source: U.S. Census Bureau (2008).

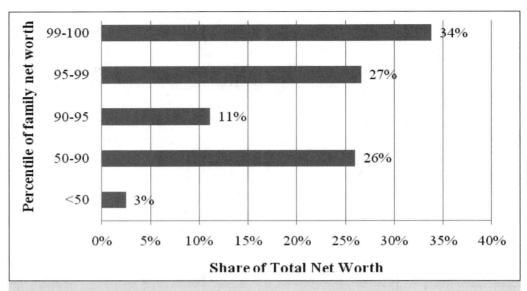

Figure 1.3 Wealth inequality.
Percentage of net worth owned by position in the wealth distribution.
Data source: Survey of Consumer Finance (2007).

inequality in both income and wealth ownership is fairly high. Figure 1.4 shows that high-income U.S. families earn dramatically more than low-income families; the United States is particularly extreme among developed countries on this measure. The top 10 percent of families (by income) in the United States has 5.64 times more income, on average, than the bottom 10 percent. In many developed countries – particularly the countries of Northern Europe, such as Sweden and Finland – the ratio of rich to poor is much lower; there is inequality in these countries but it is not as extreme as in the United States. It is considerably more extreme in the United States than in Canada, its closest developed neighbor. The many possible explanations for differences in stratification across developed countries include historical differences, government policies regarding taxation and redistribution, economic trends, and social and demographic patterns, such as religious ideas about fertility. We discuss these differences in more depth in subsequent chapters; here, their existence is simply noted as important.

Of course, some countries are more unequal than the United States. Many developing countries, for example, have more severe stratification than developed countries, and evidence suggests that inequality initially increases during development. Unfortunately, it can be difficult to obtain accurate data on inequality in developing countries. In Saudi Arabia, for instance, we know about some of the wealthiest people, such as Prince Alwaleed bin Talal Alsaud, who lives even more lavishly than Bill and Melinda Gates. His 317-room palace in Riyadh covers 400,000 square feet and cost nearly $130 million to build. The estate includes luxuries such as a soccer field, other private athletic fields, 8 elevators, more than 500 televisions, and a staff larger than the population of many small cities in Saudi Arabia. It is difficult to compare this standard of living to the average in Saudi Arabia or to specify how much inequality there is because these data are not available from the government. However, we know

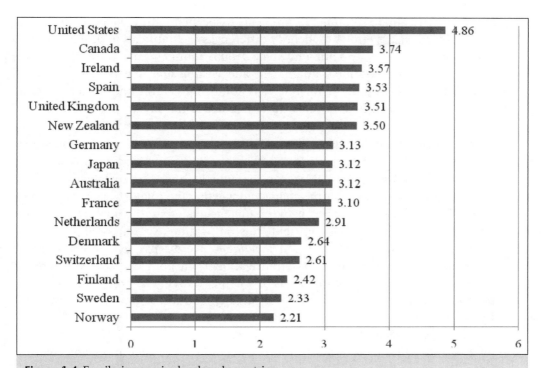

Figure 1.4 Family income in developed countries.
Ratio of the 90th percentile to the 10th percentile (2008).
Data source: Organisation for Economic Cooperation and Development (OECD).

that Saudi Arabia was home to 11 billionaires in 2005 (Forbes 2010). In the same year, the United Nations Development Programme (UNDP) ranked the country very low among developing countries on its human-poverty index, a measure of access to "a long life, knowledge, and a decent standard of living" (UNDP 2004).

Throughout history and in every known society, people and their families have had unequal access to important resources including education, jobs, income, and wealth. As a result, they have had unequal access to the benefits associated with those resources. The previous examples focus on financial inequalities, but differences in *power* and *prestige* are equally extreme throughout the world. Even in societies that have made equality a primary focus, inequality in access to resources including housing, education, and political influence ultimately emerges. In many societies, the reduction of economic and social inequality often is a major objective of social policy, and political leaders routinely appeal to the public sense of social justice to promote all types of initiatives. Although modern societies also spend large amounts to reduce inequality, every known economy still is characterized by some degree of stratification.

Inequality and Stratification: Guiding Questions

This subject of this book is inequality and *social stratification*. The objectives of modern social-stratification research are to describe the origins and nature of inequality, explain the scope of inequality, explore factors that contribute to persistent inequality, and identify and evaluate solutions to problems associated with inequality. Related to these basic objectives are efforts to identify differences in stratification throughout history and in various places, explain why some groups routinely fare better than others on outcomes such as educational attainment and wealth, and understand how much inequality a society is willing to tolerate. The following central questions that guide research on social inequality also guide the remainder of this book:

1. *What is social inequality, and how much inequality is there?* We explore how sociologists and other social scientists define inequality and which types of inequality they consider in their research. We consider whether there are social classes in the United States and other countries today and whether their nature has changed over time. We also draw distinctions between dimensions of stratification (e.g., income and wealth) and factors that contribute to stratification (e.g., race and gender).

2. *Why does inequality exist, and is it inevitable?* We discuss, evaluate, and apply ideas about the nature of social stratification from both classical and modern thinkers. We consider basic questions of whether individual choice and social opportunities explain the persistence of inequality, and we explore whether inequality is inevitable.

3. *Is there an elite class?* We discuss research on the upper class and the elite that proposes the idea that there is more movement into the elite than in previous generations. We discuss the challenges involved in identifying who is in the upper class, "old money" versus "new money," and what it means to be a middle-class millionaire. We describe traits of the upper class (including wealth ownership and debts), and we address how different theoretical approaches account for the upper class.

4. *Who are the people in the remainder of the distribution?* The middle class and poor attract less public attention but, of course, these groups include the bulk of the population. We devote an entire chapter to examining the broad territory between poverty and affluence and to exploring issues (e.g., labor relations and the decline in labor unions) that affect the working poor and middle-class Americans (i.e., neither very rich nor very poor). We then consider issues related to poverty, including what it means to be poor and how social theorists account for persistent poverty.

5. *Is social mobility possible?* We consider income, wealth, and occupational mobility and then explore the factors that facilitate or impede mobility. We discuss the likelihood that people in various segments of the income, wealth, and educational distributions (e.g., the very poor versus the middle class) are able to change positions over time. We also explore whether cultural capital prevents true upward mobility. *Cultural capital* refers to an understanding that people have of the behaviors, skills, and norms that are taken for granted by members of a class. For example, proper behavior at a polo match may be part of the cultural capital of the wealthy, whereas "street smarts" may be part of the cultural capital of those who are relatively poor. Some observers argue that cultural capital prevents true mobility. We also discuss the relative effectiveness of various theories to explain mobility. Finally, although there is limited scholarly research on the subject, we ask whether there is significant downward mobility, how downward mobility changes over time, and what this reverse mobility means for a society.

6. *What role does education have in reproducing or reducing inequality?* We explore the critical role of education in creating and reinforcing patterns of stratification. We discuss trends in educational opportunities and explore the role that education has in critical adult outcomes, such as occupational attainment, income, and wealth accumulation. We also introduce issues of neighborhood-level inequality, such as differences in the resources, quality, and safety of schools. We investigate the degree to which the United States is stratified by education, how this has changed over time, the factors that contribute to continued educational stratification, and the implications of this inequality. We also consider the role of policy interventions (e.g., affirmative-action policies) in abating educational stratification.

7. *How much gender stratification is there and why?* We address many questions related to gender stratification in the United States and other countries. We consider women's roles in society and explore how those roles vary in the United States and other countries. We also discuss issues related to workplace relations, the role of religion in determining women's social positions, the household division of labor, and the changing roles of women in other countries, including transitional economies (e.g., China and countries of the former Soviet Union).

8. *How much racial/ethnic stratification is there and why?* We consider the changing nature of race in the United States and related issues regarding ethnicity. We explore demographic trends and current patterns in racial inequality. We discuss commonly studied minority groups (e.g., African Americans, Hispanics, and Asians) as well as groups that receive less attention (e.g., Native Americans). We also address issues related to race and ethnicity in other countries.

9. *How much inequality is there in other countries?* Related questions include how other countries differ in their levels of inequality and why, whether inequality has changed over time, and what accounts for those differences in changing patterns of inequality. We investigate inequality across and within countries and regions, and we consider significant regional differences in population growth and size, starvation, disease, and conflict.

10. *Are there policies or practices that reduce stratification?* Finally, we discuss public policies that target inequality. We consider the varied constraints that policy makers face when attempting to alleviate inequality and related questions such as welfare policies, policies designed to encourage homeownership, and issues related to taxation and redistribution.

Stratification and Inequality

All societies have individuals and groups that differ in many dimensions. *Social differentiation* refers to the fact that people are not the same within a society. Some traits in which people differ are relatively apparent, such as gender and race. Other differences that are not as easily detected – such as occupation, lifestyle, income, wealth, and political preference – allow people to be categorized into groups with similar people. Occupation, for example, is a major characteristic in which people differ. Because most people are engaged in some form of work for a considerable portion of their lifetime, occupation is a meaningful trait for many (Blau and Duncan 1967; Zhou 2005). The lives of airline pilots, plumbers, nurses, teachers, firefighters, business owners, and salespeople differ significantly. The reality of *social differentiation* does not imply a ranking of these groups, and the term does not suggest that it is better to be in one group than another; it simply means that there are differences. However, stratification and inequality tend to be largely rooted in these social differences.

People differ on many traits, and people tend to agree on the rankings of those traits. *Social stratification* is the ranked ordering of people based on their social and economic traits. In all societies, people have differential access to limited and valuable resources. *Resource access* refers to the notion that social and economic resources are unequally distributed, and the people who occupy privileged positions have access to more desirable resources (e.g., income, wealth, homes, vehicles, education, and jobs). For instance, most societies widely accept the ordering of occupations based on the prestige associated with a certain profession (Duncan 1961; Zhou 2005). When asked to rank occupations, respondents consistently rank physicians higher than taxi drivers; similarly, they rank attorneys higher than secretaries. These are extreme examples but the level of agreement in the rank ordering of occupations is relatively high, even for similar occupations. Clearly, the resources associated with those occupations are at least partially responsible for their relative prestige. Physicians and attorneys typically have higher incomes, more wealth, and greater political influence than taxi drivers and secretaries.

Inequality refers to the fact that there are inevitable disparities in people's positions in these social rankings. Those with relatively privileged positions have benefits that those in lower-ranked positions do not. People with high incomes, for instance, are better able to live in desirable locations, send their children to high-quality schools, and affect political processes in ways that benefit themselves and others like them. *Inequality* usually refers to *inequality of condition* or disparities in the resources, power, and prestige that people or groups currently have. *Inequality of opportunity* is a related concept that refers to disparities in access to important resources such as educational and occupational experiences. When speaking of inequality of opportunity, we usually refer to opportunities that people have beginning early in life (including childhood and early adulthood) that allow them to attend school, find a job, earn an income, and otherwise succeed in life. However, we can consider equality (and inequality) of opportunity at all stages of a person's life to understand why some people are better off than others. Of course, unequal opportunities early in life (e.g., educational opportunities) often translate into unequal opportunities later in life (e.g., income and wealth ownership) that are not easily changed once a certain path has been taken.

Stratification Dimensions

The examples of rich and poor families at the beginning of this chapter highlight the financial aspects of stratification because this dimension is more visible and usually comes to mind when we speak of inequality. Yet, stratification can take many forms. There are three primary dimensions in which people tend to be stratified – economic, prestige, and power – and nearly all forms of stratification can be grouped into one of these basic categories.

First, *economic* or *financial stratification* includes inequality of dimensions related to money, such as income and wealth. *Income* is defined as a flow of money received over time. It usually refers to the money that people receive as wages or a salary in exchange for some form of work. However, income also includes money received from the government as transfer payments, alimony or child-support payments, and interest and dividends on investments. For instance, elderly or disabled people may receive social-security or disability income, and poor families may receive welfare payments and/or food stamps. People who have enough income to save or invest may receive additional income from sources such as interest on a savings account or dividends on stocks, bonds, or mutual funds.

Wealth is the value of the things that people own, including homes, savings, investments, and vehicles. It typically is measured as *net worth*, the sum of assets less the sum of debts. For most families, this includes tangible assets such as their home and vehicles; for other families, it may be vacation homes, other real estate, and business assets. In addition, assets include financial wealth such as checking and savings accounts, stocks, bonds, mutual funds, and certificates of deposit. Debts or liabilities include mortgages on the family home; other mortgages; consumer debt; student, vehicle, and home-equity loans; and other debt to institutional or informal (e.g., family members) lenders. *Financial wealth* is the value of liquid assets such as stocks and bonds, but it does not include housing wealth or the value of business assets or investment real estate. Unlike income, wealth is not used directly to buy necessities such as food and clothing; rather, wealth is the total amount of property owned at a certain point in time.

Income and wealth differences lead to other forms of stratification that also can be considered financial. Inequality in home size or quality, in consumption, and in health care all result directly from differences in income and wealth. Of course, income and wealth do not predict precisely consumption or home quality. For example, people with high incomes may choose not to consume excessively, and people with low incomes may exacerbate their financial difficulties by consuming beyond what they can afford. Many people have both high income and high wealth, but this is not always the case. A surprising number of those who have a high income save very little, thereby accumulating relatively few assets. An attorney who does not save because he is confident that he always can use his legal knowledge to command a high salary has high income and low wealth. There are wealthy people whose assets produce enough interest and dividend income such that they do not need to earn wages or a salary. An entrepreneur whose successful business enabled her to invest well, for instance, may have saved enough so that she can live off of her assets.

Prestige, the second dimension on which people are stratified, refers to the status or esteem associated with certain traits or positions. It is an indicator of the importance or standing that people are afforded by others, and it often reflects the value that others associate with the characteristics of a person, a job, or an achievement. Specialized or unique knowledge, training, and skills often generate prestige because these skills are rare and valuable. Again, occupation provides a useful example. Physicians have high prestige because they have knowledge and skills that are both specialized and relatively rare. Professional athletes and movie stars also may have high prestige if they are particularly skilled in uncommon ways. Prestige often is evident in the deference that people exhibit to those with prestige. Special titles such as *Doctor*, *Sir*, and *Ma'am* are external indicators of prestige differences. For instance, we seldom address people in important political positions by their first name; rather, we use a title such as *President* or *Senator*. Prestige also is evident in the way that people interact with those having higher prestige. For example, meetings tend to occur in the office of the person with the highest prestige. Similarly, in some cultures (particularly in Asia), lower-prestige people may bow lower than higher-prestige people when meeting.

Power, the third general category of stratification, is influence, authority, or persuasion. It is the ability to make others do what one wants, and it is central to all forms of inequality. Those with greater access to economic resources and those with higher prestige tend to be more powerful, and the powerful are able to use their resources or position to affect how others behave. Power also can extend to areas beyond its source. For instance, the president of a company may have power because he has control of resources associated with the company and because he holds a prestigious position. Yet, he may be able to use that power to affect change in areas not directly related to his job as company president (e.g., politics) (Domhoff 2002). As this example suggests, inequality in one dimension often is related to inequality in other dimensions. As a result, the same people tend to rank high in the social-stratification system in multiple dimensions, leading to more pervasive and systemic inequality than expected if only one trait mattered. Of course, high ranking in one dimension does not always imply a high rank in another. A wealthy person who enters a poor neighborhood may find that social relations are important among the residents. Because the wealthy person is a stranger, her money may not buy her prestige. Indeed, she may find that in that neighborhood, her wealth and lack of social connections are a major disadvantage. This is unusual; in most cases, high rank in one dimension is related to high rank in other dimensions.

Who Fits Where?

Many factors – individual, family, and environmental – contribute to social and economic positions. When a person's position in the social structure is primarily the result of individual merit, sociologists term this *achievement*. The idea is that factors such as individual merit, work, and adherence to social norms determine whether people do well. In contrast, when a person's position in the social structure is the result of factors beyond his or her control, sociologists label this *ascription*. Ascription includes characteristics such as race, ethnicity, gender, social class at birth, family size in childhood, and other traits that are primarily inherited. We discuss these in detail in the remainder of this book, but it is worth noting here certain traits that are common causes of inequality.

Race and *ethnicity* are common bases for stratification in the United States. In modern societies in which there are few ethnic differences, the role of race and ethnicity in creating inequality may be diminished. However, race and ethnicity are almost always related to access to resources in social groups. Regardless of the actual association between race and important outcomes, people often expect that race will predict important physical and intellectual capabilities. The expectation that white children perform better academically and black children perform better athletically is not logically associated with race, yet teachers and coaches have been shown to approach students with these expectations. The consequences of these expectations are potentially far-reaching and comprise the subject of an entire chapter. Similarly, immigrant status may affect access to resources and form another basis for inequality. However, immigrants ultimately can assimilate and reduce the effect of foreign nativity on their current well-being.

In addition, *gender* and *sexual preference* are associated with access to important resources in critical ways. Men have long been expected to perform most tasks better than women, regardless of their actual abilities or the logical connection between their gender and the task. For instance, men are expected to be better at fixing cars and performing mathematical tasks and more effective in many occupations. Sexual preference (i.e., heterosexuality or homosexuality) also is correlated with resource access in modern societies. Although awareness of homosexuality has increased and, in some contexts, acceptance also has grown, many people and groups continue to advocate for limiting gay rights (e.g., marriage benefits).

A host of other traits also affect inequality in modern societies. Age, religious affiliation, physical appearance (i.e., attractiveness), handicap (i.e., physical, mental, or emotional), and many other individual traits contribute to a person's access to economic resources, occupational prestige, and power in modern societies. Other traits such as *family structure* (e.g., two parents and their children, a single parent, or a retired couple) and family size may contribute to access to resources. In fact, any individual or family trait that contributes to a person's unique identity also may be a factor for constraining or enhancing access to resources.

Although these factors may be associated with access to resources and, therefore, with a person's social and economic position, they do not necessarily cause inequality. Race, gender, age, and other traits interact in complex ways with one another and with forces external to individuals to shape access to resources. Some factors contribute directly to shaping the resources people have: Inheriting a great fortune naturally increases a person's resources. Other factors contribute indirectly to resources: People who grow up in a large family may complete less education and have fewer resources as a result (Downey 1995). Many traits, such as race and ethnicity, interact with these other factors and the environment in ways that also contribute to resource access. Together, these processes shape a person's access to financial resources, power, and prestige.

Structured Inequality

The fact that people who rank high in one dimension of inequality (e.g., economic resources, prestige, or power) tend to rank high in other dimensions suggests a permanence in social inequality that extends beyond the individuals in the structure. *Structured inequality* refers to the fact that inequality is not arbitrary. Rather, inequality tends to be systematic, and it is usually the case that the same people and groups who have more economic resources also have more prestige and power.

There are two common approaches to thinking about the structure of inequality: categorically and continuously.

Categorical Approach

Many of those who study inequality argue that there are distinct groups in society that can be identified and labeled as upper, middle, lower, professional, and other classes. *Social class* refers to groups of people with relatively similar wealth, income, occupation, and education. The class of people that occupies the most fortunate positions is usually referred to as the *elite* or *upper class*. When we speak of elites, we usually refer to relatively exclusive groups that tend to control financial resources (e.g., companies), have high incomes and great wealth, and enjoy prestigious jobs and political power. At the other end of the spectrum is the *poor class* or *underclass*, which ranks low in most dimensions. Poor people usually have low incomes, low-prestige jobs, and very little power. Between the two extremes are the *middle class* and the *working class*. The middle and working classes are somewhat more difficult to distinguish; but, again, they tend to be groups that are similar in the types of jobs they do and the resources they control. Compared with the middle class, members of the working class tend to occupy lower-skilled jobs that require less education and generate lower incomes. For example, a typical college professor is squarely in the middle class, whereas a groundskeeper at the same college is probably part of the working class. Because the middle class is so broad, the terms *upper-middle class* and *lower-middle class* often are used to characterize different positions within it.

Continuous Approach

Others argue that social class is more accurately considered a continuum along which people are arrayed from lower to upper. This approach suggests that there is a linear progression from very poor to very rich, rather than several ordered groups. Those who think about social class as linear use the term *socioeconomic status* (*SES*), which often is used as a synonym for *class* but has a slightly different meaning. *SES* refers to a value (usually a number) that typically is calculated as the combination of income, wealth, occupational prestige, and education level. When not all of these measures are available, a subset may be used (e.g., only income and education). Regardless of the methodological approach, the underlying notion is that it is difficult to identify clear groups or classes, and a numerical SES value more accurately describes the distribution of people by social and economic position.

Both the categorical and continuous conceptions of class have uses, and we consider each perspective in subsequent chapters. What is important here is that inequality is not random; rather, systematic patterns create and sustain inequality.

Social Mobility

Although it is possible for people to change their social or economic position over time, the majority remain in a relatively constant position during their life. *Social mobility* refers to movement among positions in the social structure, and there is evidence that social mobility is relatively limited. We see this in the similarities between parents and their offspring (even when the offspring become adults) on such measures as income, education, wealth, and occupation. Because people tend to remain in the same class as their parents, it is likely that the nature of inequality will be highly stable over time. There are many explanations for this phenomenon. Some argue that members of the upper class deliberately protect their privileged position by promoting laws and policies that are advantageous to them and by otherwise creating barriers for entry into the upper classes. Alternatively, it is possible that people begin to accept that those who are high in one dimension (e.g., certain occupations) should be high in other dimensions (e.g., high incomes). The expectation that certain traits "go together" makes it acceptable for the same people or groups to rank high in all or many of the dimensions considered important.

Of course, some individuals or groups are upwardly mobile at times. For individuals, it is easy to identify "rags-to-riches" stories. Indeed, some evidence suggests that in modern times, those with better access to educational resources may have opportunities for upwardly mobility (i.e., more income, wealth, and prestige than their parents). This does not imply that upward mobility is easy or even common, only that it is possible. There also are cases in which entire groups have been upwardly mobile. A change in social position for an entire group usually requires some type of change to the rules by which a society operates. The civil rights movement, for example, was an effort to allow blacks and other minorities more opportunities for upward mobility than they had experienced in the past. During the 1950s and 1960s, social movements prompted changes to outlaw segregation of schools and increase employment opportunities to reduce barriers to mobility for minorities. During the 1960s and 1970s, similar changes improved women's access to education, jobs, and related income and power. Although neither movement removed all barriers faced by minorities and women, they are important examples of the types of large-scale changes that are usually necessary to reduce structured inequality and improve social mobility for disadvantaged groups.

Trends in Inequality

Social stratification has been an important part of history in all parts of the world. Throughout most of history, the working classes had limited access to resources and little protection from the harsh policies and practices of the landed classes (i.e., those who control resources such as land and jobs). As a result, the working and poor classes were forced to labor for minimal compensation under dangerous, unhealthy conditions. Table 1.1 shows the percentage of total wealth owned by the top 1 percent (i.e., the wealthiest) of households in the mid-1800s in six U.S. cities. This very small group of households owned as much as half of all assets at that time, leaving only half for the other 99 percent of households to share. Combined with the virtual absence of protection for workers, this created an environment in which the privileges of the wealthy were extremely consequential.

Although conditions such as these are still common in some parts of the world, significant changes occurred in many countries during the twentieth century that involved

Table 1.1 Wealth Inequality before 1900

City	Year	Percentage of Wealth Held by Top 1%
Baltimore	1860	39
Boston	1848	37
New Orleans	1860	43
New York	1845	40
Philadelphia	1860	50
St. Louis	1860	38

Data source: Williamson and Lindert (1980).

creating institutions to protect workers and improve working conditions. This was especially true in the United States, where efforts to ensure that workers received adequate compensation and benefits contributed to rising incomes and reductions in inequality in the two decades following World War II. As a result, household incomes increased significantly and a middle class emerged. During the 1950s, the gap between rich and poor closed and there was speculation that inequality would eventually disappear. The increase in mean and median incomes continued throughout the 1960s and 1970s, and the trend continues today (Figure 1.5).

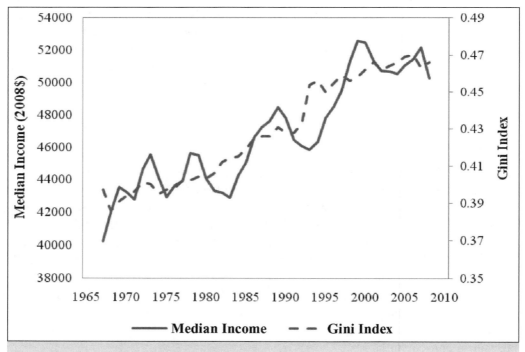

Figure 1.5. Income: Growth and inequality, 1967–2008.
Data source: U.S. Census Bureau (2008).

However, after a short period of declining stratification, inequality began to rise again. This increase is revealed by the *Gini index*, a common indicator of inequality that measures the proportion of income or wealth that must change hands to create perfect equality. Even as incomes rose throughout the 1960s, the Gini index for income grew to remarkably high levels (see Figure 1.5). At the same time, inequality in wealth owner-ship worsened and, by the late 1990s, wealth inequality surpassed what happened during the 1920s (Figure 1.6). Although wealth inequality declined slightly in the early 2000s due to an economic downturn, the trend until that time was toward a widening gap between rich and poor (Danziger and Gottschalk 1993). The increases in inequality oc-curred during a period of economic expansion in the 1990s, including a tripling of gross domestic product (GDP) (i.e., total goods and services that an economy produces). Many observers noted that the wealthiest enjoyed much of the increase in income and wealth that contributes to rising means (Blank 1994). In fact, real wages for many occupations, particularly high-income occupations, actually declined during that time.

Inequality attracts attention because of the remarkable differences between extremely wealthy people, who can spend conspicuously, and the underclass, which includes dis-proportionate numbers of minorities and single parents. Recall the two families described at the beginning of this chapter. Stark differences of this type and over-representation of certain groups among those in more advantaged positions underscore the importance of inequality. Increasing *residential segregation* (i.e., systematic differences in residence by demographic characteristics, such as race) contributes to the visibility of inequality and attracts further attention to the issue (Massey and Denton 1993). Resulting public

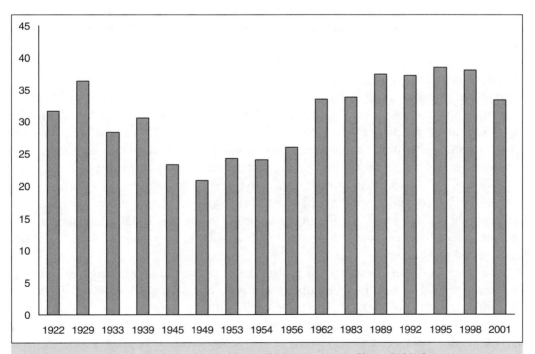

Figure 1.6 Percentage of wealth owned by the wealthiest 1 percent of households from 1922 to 1956. *Data sources:* Estimates for 1922–1956: Lampman (1962); estimates for 1962–2001: Survey of Consumer Finances.

attitudes, however, are not always informed by the facts. For example, it is easy to assume a causal relationship between race or ethnicity and poverty simply because there is a correlation. This book provides the tools to understand and critically evaluate information about inequality to help students arrive at an informed opinion about trends in stratification.

An Analytic Approach to Stratification

Asking and Answering Questions

To understand social phenomena such as inequality, it is useful to understand how sociologists and other social scientists ask and answer questions. An important first principle is the distinction between positive and normative approaches to asking and answering questions. *Positive statements* are objective statements about *what is*. They are statements of fact that can be demonstrated as true or false. Notice that this is a different meaning than the common use of the word (i.e., the opposite of *negative*). In this context, *positive* means factual. For example, a positive statement about inequality would be the following: "Income inequality in the United States has increased significantly in the past five years." The goal of positive social science is to identify, interpret, and understand facts. Consider, for example, the basic question: "How much inequality is there?" A social scientist would approach this question by identifying dimensions in which people are unequal, such as education, income, and wealth ownership. A social scientist would then gather information and data that could be evaluated objectively to draw conclusions about how much more education, income, and wealth some people have than others.

In contrast, *normative statements* are statements about *what should be*. They are not intended to be evaluated as true or false. Rather, the goal is to identify whether facts are acceptable or change is desirable. An example of a normative statement is this: "There is too much income inequality in the United States." A normative approach to answering questions about inequality would involve evaluating issues such as how much inequality our society is willing to tolerate and what might be done to reduce inequality. Legislators, journalists, social commentators, and social activists often use facts produced by positive social scientists to make normative statements, to identify areas in which change is needed, and to specify what type of change is in order. Indeed, understanding the approaches and empirical findings produced by positive social scientists can be a powerful tool for those whose purpose is change; that is, knowing the facts is the first step in changing them.

The basic approach of this book is positive because the majority of research produced in social science is positive. Describing and evaluating facts about social inequality is emphasized in this book. Yet, it is often difficult to answer questions about *what is* without raising questions about *what should be*, particularly in fields such as inequality, in which the realities of stratification imply, for instance, that some people will not have their basic needs met. Thus, although our approach generally is positive, we address issues that are inherently normative as well. In particular, we consider normative questions about how much stratification is acceptable and we discuss the merits of policies designed to change levels of stratification.

Research Approaches

Most social-science research can be grouped into one of three categories: descriptive, causal, and prescriptive. *Descriptive research* explains who, what, when, where, and how, with no effort to identify causes. Descriptive research identifies facts, patterns, and relationships, pointing to facts such as the number of times something happens, how many people are affected, and patterns in how these facts have changed over time. Descriptive research on stratification might estimate the number of families living in poverty, the percentage of wealth owned by the richest families, or the mean education level for people of different races. Social scientists use rigorous methods in analyzing empirical data to describe patterns.

Causal or *explanatory research* attempts to identify, as clearly as possible, which variables lead to change in other variables. Causal research on stratification might attempt to identify the causes of racial or ethnic differences in wealth ownership, gender differences in occupation, or class differences in access to health care. In many cases, related causes that cannot be measured are involved, leaving a degree of doubt about the true causal relationship. For example, it is possible to show that blacks own less wealth than whites, even when other factors such as education, income, and family size are held constant. However, it is impossible to demonstrate with certainty that being black causes low wealth ownership because it is impossible to hold constant all other factors (e.g., influences of family history or deeper psychological considerations) that affect wealth ownership. As in descriptive research, social scientists follow strict rules for analyzing and reporting causal research; journalists and social commentators are less likely to adhere to these standards.

Prescriptive research offers solutions for change. The goal of prescriptive research is to identify and evaluate strategies for altering relationships. Practically, prescriptive research applies knowledge gained through descriptive and causal research to solve problems. Prescriptive research involves action, but this action cannot occur without the underlying descriptive and causal research. For example, prescriptive research on stratification might ask whether job-training programs or limiting the number of months of welfare eligibility are more effective at reducing the length of time people receive welfare. To answer this prescriptive question, however, it is first necessary to predict the results of both job training and time limits, using results of descriptive and causal research, and then to consider the relative merits of the outcomes. Thus, descriptive and causal research are prerequisites for prescriptive research.

In addition, because prescriptive research involves a normative element (i.e., evaluating which outcomes are better), it is less common among social scientists than descriptive and causal research. Rather, public policy researchers and policy makers tend to conduct and use prescriptive research. This is important research and it informs important decisions. However, prescriptive research is clearly distinct from descriptive and causal research.

Next Steps

Developing explanations for social phenomena and conducting reliable empirical research to investigate the validity of the explanations involves stating a clear question, identifying the population of interest, developing a set of logical statements to answer the question, collecting evidence to examine the question, and conducting appropriate statistical analyses of the evidence. This book provides the tools to evaluate the explanations that sociologists have offered for inequality and related patterns. It also is designed to direct students in developing their own explanation of inequality. These skills allow students to (1) better understand published research in this book and findings reported in the news and other sources; (2) formulate opinions and attitudes about social issues; and (3) affect change.

The remaining chapters in this book explore current understanding of social stratification and inequality by focusing on specific themes in the inequality literature. Chapter 2 presents important ideas that sociologists have proposed for understanding stratification. Chapter 3 addresses issues of social class and the structure of inequality. The remaining chapters apply these basic concepts to issues such as how specific social classes differ; the degree to which people can change class; and the role of education, gender, race/ethnicity, culture, and country of origin in shaping these processes. For those who want more detail on how research related to social stratification is conducted, an appendix presents tools for constructing and critiquing social research, developing social theories, collecting empirical evidence, and conducting statistical analyses. This appendix is not a substitute for a course in research methods or statistics, but it provides basic skills for evaluating sociological evidence related to stratification.

Summary

- There is significant social stratification in the United States. There are more millionaires and billionaires now than at any other time in history, but the gap between rich and poor also has grown considerably in recent years. The United States is not unique in being unequal; all societies have some degree of inequality. Compared with many developed countries, however, stratification in the United States is severe. Of course, there are places where stratification is worse than in the United States. In developing countries and regions, for instance, we find even greater stratification, although it often is difficult to verify inequality because data for those areas are limited.
- The aims of research on stratification and inequality are to describe the sources and features of stratification, study the causes of stratification, and identify and evaluate solutions to related problems. Several issues guide the bulk of research on inequality, including whether inequality is inevitable; the dimensions in which people are stratified; whether social classes exist and who is a member of which class; the role that education and other factors have in alleviating or maintaining stratification; how and why some people change their social and economic positions; the role of factors such as gender and race in creating inequality; and the role that government policy has in changing stratification.

- *Social stratification* is the ranked order of people based on their social and economic traits, whereas *inequality* implies that there are nearly always differences in well-being. People tend to be stratified in three dimensions: financial (i.e., income and wealth), prestige, and power. Many traits affect whether people have high or low social and economic positions, including race and ethnicity, gender, sexual preference, age, religion, and physical appearance.

- *Structured inequality* refers to the fact that stratification is not random. Rather, people who have a high rank in one social or economic dimension often rank high in other dimensions as well. The structure of inequality can be understood in two ways. The categorical approach considers distinct groupings or social classes and identifies their role in creating and maintaining inequality. Alternatively, a continuous approach to stratification usually incorporates notions such as SES, which orders people along a continuum from low to high. *Social mobility* refers to movement either between classes or along the continuum.

- This book exposes students to different ways of thinking about social life. It focuses on uncovering and evaluating facts about inequality, exploring and using three types of research in this process. The aim is to provide students with the tools to evaluate the explanations offered about stratification and to allow them to draw their own conclusions about the nature, causes, and consequences of stratification.

Stratification Classics 1. High School Students in the Clarendon Heights Housing Project

In his classic book, *Ain't No Makin' It*, Jay MacLeod (MacLeod 1995) illustrated the complicated process of upward mobility (or lack thereof) when he described the lives of two very different groups of teenagers: One group seemed likely to succeed, the other did not. The setting was Clarendon Heights High School, located in a housing project in Boston; however, the lives that he described are similar in many ways to those of teenagers across the United States and across time.

When MacLeod studied the Clarendon Heights housing project in the early 1990s, it had residential neighborhoods on two sides, a shoe factory on a third side, and a large industrial wasteland on the fourth side. It encompassed six large, three-story buildings and one taller building. The project was relatively small compared with many similar urban housing developments, and it had a few trees and a scattering of grass. Approximately 65 percent of the residents were white, 25 percent were black, and 10 percent were other minorities. Most people in Boston considered Clarendon Heights dangerous because it had been the site of two riots and a gunfight that had killed a policeman and his assailant.

MacLeod described two groups of high school students that differed in their optimism about the future. The "Hallway Hangers" saw little reason to be hopeful, whereas the "Brothers" were relatively optimistic about their potential to succeed. Frankie was the leader of the Hallway Hangers, a group of eight predominantly white boys. He was known to be a good fighter and was missing two front teeth as a result of recent battles. Slick was also a Hallway Hanger, and he was known for his quick wit. He did well in school until he dropped out the year before MacLeod wrote about the neigh-

Box 1.1 The World's Richest People

Who are the richest people in the United States? Each September, *Forbes Magazine* compiles its annual list of the 400 richest Americans. In 2009, the total net worth of the "Forbes 400" was $1.27 trillion, and the minimum to make the list was $960 million. Following are the 10 wealthiest Americans in 2009:

Rank	Name	Net Worth ($ billions)	Age	Residence	Source
1	William Gates III	50.0	53	Medina, WA	Microsoft
2	Warren Buffett	40.0	79	Omaha, NE	Berkshire Hathaway
3	Lawrence Ellison	27.0	65	Redwood City, CA	Oracle
4	Christy Walton	21.5	54	Jackson, WY	Wal-Mart (inherited)
5	Jim C. Walton	19.6	61	Bentonville, AR	Wal-Mart (inherited)
6	Alice Walton	19.3	60	Forth Worth, TX	Wal-Mart (inherited)
7	S. Robson Walton	19.0	65	Bentonville, AR	Wal-Mart (inherited)
8	Michael Bloomberg	17.5	67	New York, NY	Bloomberg L.P.
9	Charles Koch	16.0	73	Wichita, KS	Koch Industries
9	David Koch	16.0	69	New York, NY	Koch Industries

Source: "The 400 Richest Americans 2009" (available at www.Forbes.com, September 30, 2009).

In March 2009, there were 793 billionaires in the world, down from 1,125 the year before the financial crisis and housing-market collapse. Following is a list of the 25 richest billionaires in the world in 2009:

Rank	Name	Net Worth ($ billions)	Age	Source	Citizenship
1	William Gates III	40.0	53	Microsoft	United States
2	Warren Buffett	37.0	79	Berkshire Hathaway	United States
3	Carlos Slim Helú	35.0	69	Telmex, América Móvil	Mexico
4	Lawrence Ellison	22.5	65	Oracle	United States
5	Ingvar Kamprad	22.0	83	IKEA	Sweden
6	Karl Albrecht	21.5	89	Aldi Süd	Germany
7	Mukesh Ambani	19.5	51	Reliance Industries	India
8	Lakshmi Mittal	19.3	58	Arcelor Mittal	India
9	Theo Albrecht	18.8	87	Aldi Nord, Trader Joe's	Germany
10	Amancio Ortega	18.3	73	Inditex Group	Spain
11	Jim C. Walton	17.8	61	Wal-Mart	United States
12	Alice Walton	17.6	60	Wal-Mart	United States
12	Christy Walton	17.6	54	Wal-Mart	United States
12	S. Robson Walton	17.6	65	Wal-Mart	United States
15	Bernard Arnault	16.5	60	LVMH Moët Hennessy • Louis Vuitton	France
16	Li Ka-shing	16.2	80	Cheung Kong Holdings, Hutchison Whampoa	Hong Kong
17	Michael Bloomberg	16.0	67	Bloomberg L.P.	United States
18	Stefan Persson	14.5	61	Hennes & Mauritz	Sweden

Box 1.1 (*continued*)

Rank	Name	Net Worth ($ billions)	Age	Source	Citizenship
19	Charles Koch	14.0	73	Koch Industries	United States
19	David Koch	14.0	69	Koch Industries	United States
21	Liliane Bettencourt	13.4	86	L'Oréal	France
22	Prince Alwaleed bin Talal Alsaud	13.3	54	Kingdom Holding Company, Citigroup	Saudi Arabia
23	Michael Otto	13.2	65	Otto GmbH	Germany
24	David Thomson	13.0	51	The Thomson Corporation	Canada
25	Michael Dell	12.3	44	Dell	United States

Source: Forbes Magazine (available at www.Forbes.com).

Box 1.2 Down with the Ship

Microsoft co-founder Paul Allen spent an estimated quarter of a billion dollars building the 414-foot-long *Octopus*. Equipped with a swimming pool, a music studio, a mini-submarine, and a basketball court that doubles as a helipad, it was the world's biggest private boat at the time of its launching in 2003.

However, even before the *Octopus* had slithered out of the shipyard, another software billionaire, Larry Ellison, was adding an extra 65 feet to a vessel he had under construction. Built in Germany, the 453-foot-long *Rising Sun* made its maiden crossing of the Atlantic in December 2003, coming to roost in St. Thomas, where it has been much ogled and gossiped about.

Now *Rising Sun* is about to be eclipsed by *Platinum*, aka *Golden Star*. Originally commissioned by Prince Jefri Bolkiah of Brunei and completed by Sheikh Mohammed bin Rashid al-Maktoum, the Crown Prince of Dubai, the 525-foot-long *Platinum* is bigger than a World War II destroyer and apparently just about as combat-ready. Its amenities are said to include an airplane hangar, a battery of sophisticated weapons to fend off the paparazzi, garages for jet skis and four-wheel-drive vehicles (which can be taken ashore on special landing craft), and a health spa with a full-time medical staff, in addition to the obligatory mini-submarine. The trickle-down effect has been felt by owners of boats in the 100- to 150-foot range, which are now known as "starter yachts."

A similar process is under way in land vehicles, according to the *Wall Street Journal*'s Robert Frank: "The most expensive Mercedes used to be the CL600, which cost about $100,000 in the late 1990s," he writes. "Last year, the Mercedes group, part of DaimlerChrysler AG, introduced the Maybach 62, which sells for more than $350,000. This year, it started selling the SLR, which is priced at over $450,000 and has a long waiting list. Not to be outdone, Volkswagen AG's Bugatti unit is about to introduce a sports car priced at more than $1 million."

Meanwhile, thanks to the entrepreneurial vision of a Manhattan hair stylist named Orlando Pita, it is possible to spend twice the per capita income of Bangladesh on a haircut. Even some of his competitors think Pita's $800 fee may be a bit stiff. Kenneth Battelle, who runs the Kenneth Salon in the Waldorf-Astoria and has put scissors to the locks of Jacqueline Kennedy, Brooke Astor, Lauren Bacall, and Marilyn Monroe over the years, calls it "an ego trip." The objection does not seem to trouble Mr. Pita. "The luxury market is not about needs or 'Is it worth it?'" he says. "It's about 'What can I spend?'"

Source: Article by Jim Lardner, reprinted from www.inequality.org.

Box 1.3 Poverty Budget

A family of four (i.e., two adults and two children) earning less than $21,027 is considered to be living in poverty. In 2008, 37 million Americans – nearly one in eight – were living below the official poverty line. How far does a budget of $21,027 go today?

Amount	Expense
$6,456	**Housing:** A family living in poverty spends an average of $538 per month on basic shelter.
$4,559	**Transportation:** The average cost of owning, repairing, insuring, and fueling a used car is a minimum of $380 per month.
$4,071	**Food:** Even with public assistance such as food stamps and charitable donations, families living in poverty spend $339 per month on food, which is approximately $2.79 per person per day.
$2,748	**Utilities:** For a family of four, the average expense for utilities (i.e., water, gas, electricity, sewer, and telephone) is $229 per month.
$2,740	**Child Care:** Child-care expenses for working parents cost families living in poverty about $114 per month per child.
$2,481	**Health Care:** Even if an employer contributes part of the costs of health insurance, a family of four at the poverty line pays an average of $207 per month for medical expenses (doctor visits, prescription and nonprescription medicines).
0	**Miscellaneous Expenses:** School supplies, toiletries, shoes, clothes, holiday and birthday gifts, education, life insurance, furniture, recreation, entertainment, and cleaning supplies.
$23,055	Total basic expenses
–$21,027	Poverty line for a family of four
–$2,028	Deficit

Source: The Catholic Campaign for Human Development (www.povertyusa.org). Poverty-line figures are from the U.S. Census Bureau, 2008 Current Population Survey Annual Social and Economic Supplement. Budget estimates are from the 2008 Consumer Expenditures Survey, Bureau of Labor Statistics, and the 2007 Expenditures on Children by Families, U.S. Department of Agriculture.

---

borhood. Of all of the members of the Hallway Hangers, the one named Shorty had the biggest problem with alcohol and drugs. He could be extremely violent, especially when he was drunk or stoned, and he had been known to pull a knife over small disagreements when he was experiencing a fit of rage. The boys in this group tended to blame their poverty on blacks, who were perceived as stealing jobs and other resources from them.

The Brothers, a group of 8 to 12 boys, were predominantly black. The group included Craig, who lived with both parents and four brothers and sisters, and who was considered the group's most likely leader. Super was another member of the Brothers.

He was an athlete but he got into trouble because he had a fiery temper, apparently inherited from his father. Juan, originally from the Dominican Republic, had just finished high school. He had not been a particularly good student and he was unemployed. He remained hopeful about his prospects, however, and seemed satisfied with much of what he had. Although all of the Brothers were from very poor families, they were more optimistic about the future on the whole.

Ain't No Makin' It tells about the lives of these high school students and shows how the two groups ultimately became two very different types of adults eight years after the initial study. The Hallway Hangers clique had dissolved and most of the members were living in poverty with relatively little hope for improving their situation. MacLeod had predicted that with their positive attitude and willingness to work, the Brothers would be able to secure jobs. Although they fared better than the Hallway Hangers, almost all were working in low-skilled, service-sector jobs (e.g., busboys and baggage handlers).

Of course, the story is more complicated than this – race, aspirations, family support, personalities, and countless other factors shaped the trajectories of the boys in early adulthood. *Ain't No Makin' It* skillfully explores many of the factors that make it difficult to predict and explain how aspirations translate into outcomes.

(*Source:* Summarized from Jay MacLeod, 1995. *Ain't No Makin' It: Aspirations and Attainment in a Low-Income Neighborhood.* Boulder, CO: Westview Press.)

Key Concepts

Achievement	Positive approach
Ascription	Power
Cultural capital	Prestige
Economic stratification	Residential segregation
Elite	Resource access
Ethnicity	Social class
Family structure	Social differentiation
Financial wealth	Social mobility
Income	Social stratification
Income distribution	Socioeconomic status (SES)
Inequality	Structured inequality
Inequality of condition	Underclass
Inequality of opportunity	Upper class
Middle class	Wealth
Normative approach	Wealth distribution
Poor class	Working class

Questions for Thought

1. Is inequality acceptable as long as incomes continue to rise? Consider the relationship between income and inequality in Figure 1.5. Is this acceptable?
2. What would it take to eliminate all inequality? Is this possible? Is it desirable?

3. Consider the concept of structured inequality. Is it deliberate? For example, does the upper class perpetuate inequality to protect its advantaged position? Or does structured inequality occur naturally?

4. Which factors might explain why some children who grow up in poverty have high aspirations about the future, whereas others have little hope that they will succeed?

5. To what extent is success the result of individual effort and achievement versus inherited status and environmental influences?

Exercises

1. *Identify yourself in the distribution.*
   Consider your total household income (if you are an unemployed college student, consider your parents' total household income). Do you guess that this places you in the top, middle, or bottom of the income distribution? Use the Internet and other resources to determine where your family is positioned. Were you correct? (Hint: Internet resources are listed at the end of every chapter.)

2. *Compare income and wealth distributions.*
   Use the Internet and other available resources to identify the following:
   a. The percentage of household income earned by the top 5 and top 10 percent in a recent year.
   b. The percentage of household wealth owned by the top 5 and top 10 percent in a recent year.
   Which resource is more unequally distributed? Speculate about why you found this difference.

Multimedia Resources

Print

Domhoff, G. William. 2002. *Who Rules America? Power and Politics* (4th edition). New York: McGraw Hill.

Ehrenreich, Barbara. 2001. *Nickel and Dimed: On (Not) Getting by in America.* New York: Metropolitan Books.

Lardner, James, and David Smith. 2006. *Inequality Matters: The Growing Economic Divide in America and Its Poisonous Consequences.* New York: The New Press.

Oliver, Melvin O., and Thomas M. Shapiro. 1995. *Black Wealth/White Wealth.* New York: Routledge.

Stanley, Thomas J., and William D. Danko. 1996. *The Millionaire Next Door: The Surprising Secrets of America's Wealthy.* Atlanta, GA: Longstreet Press.

Internet

- www.inequality.org. A site devoted to disseminating information about the degree and causes of inequality in the United States.
- www.parade.com/news/what-people-earn/. *Parade Magazine*'s interactive companion to its annual issue on salaries, "What People Earn." Illustrations highlight critical differences among occupations in wages and salaries.

- www.pbs.org/peoplelikeus/. A companion to the PBS documentary, *People Like Us*, about class in America. It contains information about the documentary, video clips, and other resources.
- www.povertyusa.org. A site sponsored by the Catholic Campaign for Human Development that provides information and instructional tools related to poverty.

Films

Antz. 1998. Directed by Dan Aykroyd. An animated movie starring Woody Allen, Sharon Stone, and Gene Hackman. The movie is about a worker ant who struggles to reconcile his own desires and dreams with the communal work ethic of his colony. The film is a light-hearted introduction to social class.

People Like Us. 2001. A companion to the Web site (see Internet listings), this film illustrates the realities of growing up in a particular social class.

How Much Is Enough? 1992. This film looks at global inequality, highlighting issues such as overpopulation, consumption differences, and environmental problems that accompany dramatic differences in well-being across countries.

Works Cited

Blank, Rebecca. 1994. "The Widening Wage Distribution and Its Policy Implications." In *Aspects of Distribution of Wealth and Income*, edited by D. B. Papadimitriou (pp. 185–93). New York: St. Martin's Press.

Blau, Peter, and Otis D. Duncan. 1967. *The American Occupational Structure*. New York: Wiley & Sons.

Danziger, Sheldon H., and Peter Gottschalk. 1993. *Uneven Tides: Rising Inequality in America*. New York: Russell Sage Foundation.

Domhoff, G. William. 2002. *Who Rules America? Power and Politics* (4th edition). New York: McGraw Hill.

Downey, Douglas B. 1995. "When Bigger Is Not Better: Family Size, Parental Resources, and Children's Educational Performance." *American Sociological Review* 60: 746–61.

Duncan, Otis Dudley. 1961. "A Socioeconomic Index for All Occupations." In *Occupations and Social Status*, edited by J. Reiss (pp. 109–38). New York: The Free Press.

Forbes Magazine, November 2010. "The World's Billionaires." Available at www.forbes.com/billionaires.

Lampman, Robert J. 1962. *The Share of Top Wealth-Holders in National Wealth, 1922–56*. Princeton, NJ: Princeton University Press.

MacLeod, Jay. 1995. *Ain't No Makin' It: Aspirations and Attainment in a Low-Income Neighborhood*. Boulder, CO: Westview Press.

Massey, Douglas, and Nancy Denton. 1993. *American Apartheid: Segregation and the Making of the Underclass*. Cambridge, MA: Harvard University.

Oliver, Melvin L., and Thomas M. Shapiro. 1995. *Black Wealth/White Wealth: A New Perspective on Racial Inequality*. New York: Routledge.

Organisation for Economic Cooperation and Development. 2008. Available at OECD.org.

Survey of Consumer Finances. 2007. Available at federalreserve.gov.

United Nations Development Programme (UNDP). 2004. *Cultural Liberty in Today's Diverse World*. Washington, DC: United Nations Development Programme.

United States Census Bureau. 2008. Available at www.census.gov.

Williamson, Jeffrey G., and Peter H. Lindert. 1980. *American Inequality: A Macroeconomic History.* New York: Academic Press.

Zhou, Xueguang. 2005. "The Institutional Logic of Occupational Prestige Ranking: Reconceptualization and Reanalyses." *American Journal of Sociology* 110: 90–140.

2 Explaining Stratification
Theories and Ideas

We raised important questions in Chapter 1 regarding stratification and inequality, but we offered little explanation for those patterns. The objective of this chapter is to examine the major theoretical traditions in the study of inequality and to begin to apply these ideas to understand modern stratification.

As you read Chapter 1 and considered trends in inequality, you probably developed your own explanations for the patterns. Your explanations were based on facts learned through formal education and training, but they also probably were based on informal observations, experiences, opinions, and intuition. This is similar to what social scientists do when they provide theoretical explanations for social phenomenon such as inequality. However, social scientists organize their ideas and observations more formally within *paradigms*, or scientific points of view. In the *Structure of Scientific Revolutions*, Thomas Kuhn (1970) defined *paradigms* as the fundamental points of view that distinguish a science. Some well-known paradigms in the natural sciences include Einstein's theory of relativity, Newtonian mechanics, and Darwin's evolution.

It is appealing to think about the history of science as gradual transitions from one paradigm to another that occur as understanding of the world improves and scientific ideas build on one another. Kuhn pointed out, however, that it is more common for a paradigm to become ingrained and for scientists to resist significant deviations from the well-accepted paradigm. Only when there is considerable evidence demonstrating that the current way of thinking is flawed does a new paradigm displace an old one. In the natural sciences, the change from one paradigm to another is typically a change from false thinking to true thinking. As a result, when the new paradigm becomes accepted, the old one is no longer considered useful. It is this revolutionary change that Kuhn referenced in the title of his book. The shift from *geocentricism* (i.e., the theory that the earth is the center of the universe) to *heliocentricism* (i.e., the theory that the sun is the center of the universe) is a classic example of a paradigm shift.

There are also social-science paradigms, or points of view, that explain social behavior (Babbie 2003). In Chapter 1, we discussed stating hypotheses to describe a relationship between pairs of variables. The paradigm on which one draws influences the nature of the hypotheses that one states. As in the natural sciences, different paradigms were dominant in the social sciences at different times in history. However, when a new social-science paradigm becomes popular, the alternatives rarely are discredited completely. Rather, the new way simply becomes the more common way to approach social behavior. It is typical for social scientists to draw on multiple paradigms when they try to explain a single problem and to use data and statistical analyses to adjudicate multiple ways of thinking. An advantage of drawing on multiple paradigms is that each may highlight parts of social life that others ignore, and the alternative ways of thinking may shed new light on complex social questions that a single approach cannot.

The remainder of this chapter presents dominant paradigms that are used to understand inequality. As you read about these ideas, be aware of the strengths and weaknesses of each and consider how each might address the most interesting aspects of inequality. However, avoid trying to decide which is right and which is wrong; this type of thinking prevents you from understanding the important benefits of each approach.

Inequality through History

As Gerhard Lenski (1966) pointed out in *Power and Privilege: A Theory of Social Stratification*, to understand explanations of inequality throughout history, it is necessary to consider how inequality has changed over time. For most of human history (i.e., from approximately 100,000 B.C. to 8,000 B.C.), humans lived in *hunting and gathering societies*. In these early societies, people depended on hunting, fishing, and the collection of wild plants for subsistence. Although there were differences among hunting and gathering societies, all tended to be relatively geographically mobile, were seldom able to store food for any significant length of time, and rarely domesticated animals. In hunting and gathering societies, men and women performed different tasks but there was no real division of labor into occupations or jobs because everyone participated in food production. In addition, families did not own land and did not accumulate considerable material wealth to pass on to their heirs; there was a relatively high degree of equality in those societies.

It was only about ten thousand years ago that humans slowly began to live in semi-permanent communities that resemble the towns and cities we live in today. When people learned to cultivate edible plants and domesticate animals, they were able to stop migrating in search of food. *Simple horticultural societies*, the most basic stationary societies, were not very different from hunting and gathering societies. They were slightly larger, more productive, and more unequal than hunting and gathering societies. In addition, the first evidence of a division of labor appeared in simple horticultural societies as people developed specializations related to the production of food. It also became possible to transmit belongings – and, thus, wealth – across generations, leading to the first evidence of social inequality. Yet, under comparable conditions, hunting and gathering societies and simple horticultural societies were similar (Lenski 1966, chap. 6).

The best historical and archeological evidence suggests that *complex horticultural societies* (also called *advanced horticultural societies*) first appeared around 4,000 B.C. In these societies, the cultivation of plants and domestication of animals became more entrenched and specialized, and large-scale agriculture ultimately became common. People established permanent residences in rural areas, small communities, and large cities. Related to changes in the production of food and the emergence of permanent communities, specialization in occupations developed. It was no longer necessary or efficient for everyone to be engaged full time in gathering food, and a clear division of labor emerged: Some specialized in agricultural occupations; others began to specialize in a range of other occupations including economic, political, and religious positions. Landownership made it possible to accumulate wealth and to transfer wealth across generations. Compared to previous societies, complex horticultural societies enjoyed considerable economic surplus. However, a distinction between landowners and laborers followed from the increasingly detailed division of labor and became the basis for extremely high levels of inequality. There were dramatic differences between the governing class and the governed, between the small urban population and the rural masses, and between the literate minority and the illiterate majority (Lenski 1966, chap. 7).

Technological innovation was relatively rare in most of the history of agrarian societies, but the rate of technological change increased rapidly in the later agrarian era. By the late eighteenth century, the Industrial Revolution was clearly under way, and nations were beginning to rely more on machine-based production for income and less on agrarian activity. The Industrial Revolution also marked the start of the *modern capitalist society* (also called the *industrial society*). This type of society is marked by the political dominance of powerful nation-states, widespread private ownership, and a heavy reliance on advanced technology. Food production is no longer the focus of most people's work in most industrial societies; rather, less than 10 percent of the population typically is involved (Sanderson and Alderson 2004). Since the Industrial Revolution, the world's population has expanded dramatically despite the fact that women give birth to significantly fewer children, the importance of the family as a unit of production has diminished, the power of government has increased dramatically, public education has largely eliminated illiteracy, and the division of labor has become extremely complex (Sanderson and Alderson 2004; Lenski 1966).

There also have been important changes in the nature of social stratification since the Industrial Revolution (Lenski 1966). In many industrial societies, a distinct political elite is evident, and politicians and economic elites have close ties that affect both politics and business (Domhoff 2002; Dye 1995). There is tremendous variation in wealth and income ownership both across and within industrial societies and, as discussed in Chapter 1, both income and wealth tend to be concentrated in a small number of countries and a small number of families within those countries (Keister 2000; Morris and Western 1999; Wolff 1995). As discussed in the remainder of this book, industrial societies also tend to be characterized by considerable occupational, educational, racial/ethnic, and gender inequality.

Sources of Stratification

Two of the most fundamental theoretical questions about social stratification are: Why is there inequality? Is inequality necessary? These questions have occupied thinking about society for hundreds of years, and modern theorists continue to try to answer them. Theoretical answers to these questions fall into two broad groups: (1) those that view stratification as necessary or functional for society, and (2) those that view stratification as unnecessary or dysfunctional. *Functionalist theories* (also called *structural-functional theories*) approach inequality as a necessary and normal part of society. These theories have their roots in early thinking that assumes deep, innate differences among people and that social structure reflects a hierarchy of talent among individuals. Classical thinkers (including Plato) were proponents of this way of thinking, which assumes that societies are largely orderly and that more talented individuals occupy more desirable social positions. Early sociologists including William Graham Sumner (1840–1910) also assumed that ability is innate in individuals, and he proposed that competitions such as education sort people by ability into corresponding social positions. Modern functionalist thinking originates from French sociologist Émile Durkheim and was developed in the 1930s and 1940s. Durkheim argued that society operates like a biological organism and that all social positions are necessary for the healthy functioning of a society, just as all human organs are necessary for the healthy functioning of a body. He proposed that order is maintained by a general consensus of values.

In contrast, theories that consider stratification to be dysfunctional are usually called *conflict theories* because they assume that force and oppression – neither functional necessity nor large-scale agreement – lead to inequality. Conflict theory is usually associated with the thinking of Karl Marx and typically starts with the idea that dominant classes, or elites, impose their will on lower classes to maintain order. Elites have access to social, economic, and political resources, which they use to maintain their privileged positions. The middle and poor classes follow the rules imposed by the elite because they have no choice; they have relatively little power and few resources, leaving few alternatives other than working within the current system.

Sociological approaches to stratification tend to fall into one of these broad categories even though society is seldom either completely ordered or disordered. In the next two sections, we investigate the basic tenets of functional and conflict theories before turning to theoretical answers to other questions about inequality.

Functionalism: Davis and Moore's Theory of Stratification

One of the most influential modern functionalist theories is the Davis and Moore theory of stratification. Kingsley Davis and Wilbert Moore outlined their theory in the 1945 article, "Some Principles of Stratification" ([1945] 2001). The starting point for their way of thinking is that society resembles a biological organism similar to the human body. The body has many organs that must work together for the whole to operate properly. If any bodily organ is unhealthy or missing, it becomes difficult or impossible for a person to function. If the heart stops, the body also stops; if a kidney or a lung is lost, a person can still function but not as effectively as with both organs. Similarly, according to Davis and Moore, every society has many positions that must be filled for it to work correctly. Some people must produce food; others must make machines, furniture, vehicles, and other products; still others must fill professional, managerial, and political positions. If any position is left unfilled or is filled by someone without proper skills and training, the society will not function correctly.

To explain inequality, then, functional theorists address two questions: (1) How does society place people in the right positions? (2) Once people are in those positions, how does society ensure that they are motivated to do their job? Davis and Moore began by proposing that some social positions are more important than others. Just as some organs are more essential to the body, some social positions are more essential to the functioning of society. More important positions require more specialized training or skills, and only a small number of people have the talent that can be turned into the skills needed to fill these positions. Furthermore, when people go to school or otherwise undergo training to develop the skills necessary to fill the most important positions, they must sacrifice valuable time and other resources. To convince the most talented people to go through the training necessary to fill the most important positions and to ensure that the most qualified people continue to do the important jobs, the positions need to be desirable. That is, they need to provide higher levels of pay, benefits, prestige, and other resources. The crucial result is that those who fill the most important positions receive the greatest rewards and have access to the most resources.

Social inequality, then, is inevitable and necessary. All societies are stratified, and inequality reflects the relative importance of social positions and the talents of those who fill the positions. Davis and Moore state that "a society must have, first, some kind of rewards that it can use as inducements, and, second, some way of distributing these rewards differentially according to positions. The rewards and their distribution become a part of the social order, and thus give rise to stratification" (1945: 243). Consider doctors, for example: Most people agree that doctors are important and that we need talented and skilled people to become doctors. It takes years and a lot of money to learn the skills necessary to become a doctor, but the resulting financial rewards and esteem make the time and initial investment worthwhile. According to Davis and Moore's theory, society stays in balance and functions most effectively when positions are rewarded adequately. Of course, although this type of system serves the needs of society, it does not necessarily follow that it is the best system for every individual.

Functionalism: Talcott Parsons and the Structure of Social Action

Talcott Parsons' theory of social action is another functionalist theory that explains social inequality. Compared to Davis and Moore's theory, Parsons' functionalist approach is a much broader statement about how a society works. In fact, it is considered one of the most influential general theories of social organization in modern sociology. Parsons developed his ideas in several major works, including two books titled *The Structure* of *Social Action* (1937) and *The Social System* (1951). He revised his ideas many times during his life, ultimately admitting that many of his early ideas were overly broad and difficult to test with empirical data. Nonetheless, Parsons' ideas were tremendously influential in thinking about social stratification throughout the 1960s and 1970s.

Similar to Davis and Moore, Parsons considered society to be an organism and emphasized the importance of the components working together for the entity to operate properly. However, according to Parsons, status is central to understanding social inequality. Parsons proposed that every society has a dominant value system that is a result of the historical and environmental circumstances unique to that society. In every society, people evaluate others according to how well they adhere to dominant social values, and everyone is ranked accordingly. Different societies may consider different social values important, but the underlying process is the same regardless of the values. People desire status, but differences in compliance with social values mean that everyone ends up with a different level of status. The system then sorts the highest-status people into the most important positions. Practically, Parsons came to the same conclusion as Davis and Moore: The best people fill the most important positions and are awarded accordingly. However, Parsons proposed that status – rather than talent and skills – determined who should have the most vital positions.

Conflict: Stratification as a Problem

The functionalist approach can seem appealing – at least, at first. It is straightforward and seems consistent with many of the realities of stratification. It requires considerable sacrifice and financial investment to become a doctor, a lawyer, or another professional that commands a high salary. Moreover, people tend to agree that these positions are important. Perhaps these are legitimate reasons for certain professions to be well compensated. Yet, if we look closer, there are difficulties with the functionalist approach; critics have raised several concerns about the perspective. The primary critics are conflict theorists who disagree with the assumption that inequality is necessary and normal. They point to power differentials among people and positions, and they argue that unequal power allows the dominant classes to impose their will on others. One of the most direct criticisms was levied by Melvin Tumin (1953) and directed at Davis and Moore, but the arguments against functionalism apply to Parsons' ideas as well. The critiques can be grouped into the following five broad categories.

First, critics ask how a society decides which positions are most functionally important. To revisit the biological analogy, if all positions are important for the entity to survive, why would one position be more important than another? Even if we agree that some positions are more important than others, it is not always obvious which positions are most important and why. We usually think of doctors as very important and janitors as relatively unimportant because it takes years of training to become a doctor, whereas most people can perform the job of a janitor. However, an example from Ohio State University (OSU) suggested that janitors might be more important than we first imagined (Dixon and Roscigno 2003). In the spring of 2000, the Communications Workers of America (CWA) went on strike against OSU. This union included all university custodians as well as other service, skilled-trade, and maintenance workers. OSU is one of the largest universities in the country, with more than fifty thousand students and thousands of faculty, staff, and other employees. Classes and other activities continued, and a tremendous amount of trash and dirt was generated by that large community. As expected, after three weeks, the campus really missed its custodians.

Of course, we would also quickly miss doctors if they were to go on strike: Imagine hospitals, doctors' offices, and clinics all shutting down. However, the custodians' strike highlights the criticism that it is not only years of training or job specialization that determine the importance of a position. Similarly, consider the compensation that professional athletes and other performers receive. Do these high salaries suggest that these are society's most important positions? What about teachers? They receive relatively low salaries, yet we generally consider them critical to the functioning of a society. Conflict theorists propose, instead, that people in powerful positions use their resources to ensure that their own positions remain powerful. A common criticism is that the American Medical Association unnecessarily limits admission to medical schools, thereby artificially raising demand for doctors and keeping their salaries high.

Second, critics question the assumption that only a limited number of people have the skills to be trained to fill the most important positions. Functionalists propose that people have different abilities, and anyone who has the ability to finish the schooling or training will be able to move into an important position. In contrast, conflict theorists argue that rigid and well-established class differences prevent many highly talented people from receiving the training they need to move into the best positions. The functionalist argument assumes a relatively high degree of equality of opportunity, and conflict theorists point out that the assumption is unrealistic. Consider two hypothetical teenagers, one growing up in a poor urban neighborhood and the other in an affluent suburb. Regardless of their innate talent, the suburban teenager will have better access to resources (e.g., good guidance counselors) and training (e.g., SAT-preparation courses) that will ensure admission to a good college and entry into a more promising occupational trajectory. Critics charge that the functionalists' assumption of equality of opportunity is an ideal but that, in reality, we limit ourselves as a society by preventing talented people from consideration for the most vital positions. According to Tumin: "Social stratification systems function to limit the possibility of discovery of the full range of talent available in a society" (p. 393).

Third, and related to the second point, critics also question the functionalist assumption of free movement of labor among jobs. That is, the functionalist approach assumes that people are relatively free to pursue the jobs they want and to change jobs when they find better opportunities elsewhere. Conflict theorists disagree on this point: They argue that power differences allow certain positions to maintain their privilege and prevent free movement of labor. Moreover, conflict theorists suggest that if labor were free to move at will, people would gravitate toward high-paying jobs. Before long, salaries in those jobs would decline because there would be a surplus of workers willing to take the positions. Of course, not everyone has the talent or training to fill the highest-paid jobs, but conflict theorists argue that enough people would be willing and able to take these positions to result in downward pressure on salaries. Likewise, people would gravitate away from low-paying jobs, thereby creating labor shortages. An increased need for people to fill those jobs would push wages up. Ultimately, this movement should lead to relatively equal salaries across positions. In reality, there has been increasing *inequality* in salaries, and conflict theorists use this as evidence that there is more to filling important positions than the most talented people taking them.

Fourth, critics address the functionalist assumption that talented people make sacrifices to acquire the training necessary to fill important positions. They argue that in most cases, people who grow up in privileged families are those trained for rewarding positions, and their parents typically pay the bills for their training. Moreover, conflict theorists argue that the parents are able to pay for the training because of their privilege, rather than the children receiving the training because they are particularly talented. Tumin noted that "the parents' ability to pay for the training of their children is part of the differential reward they, the parents, receive for their privileged positions in the society. And to charge this sum up against sacrifices made by the youth is falsely to perpetrate a bill or a debt already paid by the society to the parents" (p. 390). Again, the conflict argument rests on power differences. In this instance, the point is that privileged parents have greater power because they have access to more resources, and they use that power to perpetuate their advantage by placing their children in equally powerful positions.

Fifth, critics raise a number of objections that can be grouped together as questions about how much inequality is necessary. These critiques address the functionalist assumption that inequality is inevitable and normal. Critics ask whether any inequality is necessary. If they grant that some inequality may be unavoidable, they then ask whether it is necessary to have as much inequality as we have in modern economies. A related criticism is that there is little reason for all of the benefits of some jobs to be significantly higher than they are in others. That is, they question whether it is necessary for high-reward positions to have high salaries, high benefits, high prestige, and desirable working conditions. In addition, conflict theorists propose that inequality is far from functional, and they point to all the problems it can cause. For example, they argue that inequality leads to anger, hostility, suspicion, and distrust among the poor. They also point to evidence that inequality may lead to more crime, lower esteem among much of society, reduced feelings of significant membership in society for the lower classes, and reduced motivation for those who do not have easy access to the rewards enjoyed by the upper classes.

Lenski: Integrating Functionalist and Conflict Ideas

An alternative to either a strict functionalist or a strict conflict perspective in understanding the sources of stratification is to consider how the two sets of ideas work together. Gerhard Lenski's (1966) theory of social stratification was an important effort to integrate ideas from both approaches. Lenski started with two assumptions. First, he assumed that self-interest or the interest of one's group (e.g., family, friends, and community) motivates most of human behavior. Second, he assumed that what people want and need is generally scarce; that is, there is not enough of everything to go around.

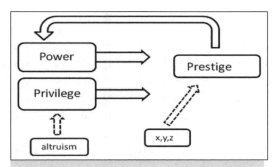

Figure 2.1 Lenski's theory of social stratification.

Together, basic principles are likely to lead to conflict. However, Lenski also proposed that most self-interested needs and desires can be met only by establishing cooperative relationships. As a result, self-interest ultimately induces people to cooperate. Lenski called this the *first law of distribution*: People "share the product of their labors to the extent required to insure the survival and continued productivity of those others whose actions are necessary or beneficial to themselves" (1966: 44). This proposal acknowledges the functionalist belief that people are basically cooperative, and it addresses how basic goods and services are distributed.

Lenski's first law of distribution is concerned with meeting basic needs, but it does not address the issue of surplus. That is, the first law does not account for what happens when a society produces more than it needs for survival. In modern industrial economies, there is nearly always surplus – although not everyone enjoys equally in that surplus. The key to understanding how surplus is distributed, according to Lenski, is power – or the ability that some people and groups have to carry out their will even when others oppose it.[1] Lenski's *second law of distribution* is that "power will determine the distribution of nearly all of the surplus possessed by a society" (1966: 44). That is, people with the most power will be the most influential in deciding how the surplus is divided. This law acknowledges the conflict notion that some people are in a better position in society to impose their will on others and that those people enjoy more rewards. From this second law, Lenski deduced that privilege is largely a function of power and – to a much lesser degree – altruism. Figure 2.1 illustrates the relationship among power, privilege, and altruism in Lenski's theory. It also includes prestige, a third element of distributive systems that Lenski also addressed. He argued that prestige is defined as the ownership and control of surplus and, as indicated in Figure 2.1, a result of having both power and privilege. Other factors (labeled *x, y,* and *z* in the figure) contribute to prestige, but power and privilege are the primary influences. Of course, prestige creates more power, thereby creating a loop that accounts for increasing concentrations of power, privilege, and prestige in the same families over time.

---

[1] This is actually Weber's definition of power, which Lenski acknowledged (1966: 44).

The Structure of Stratification

Theories about social stratification also attempt to explain the nature (or structure) of stratification. Most of the earliest theories described stratification as class-based. *Class-based theories* assume distinct groups, or social classes, and explain why each class has (or lacks) certain resources and advantages. *Social class* refers to groups of people with similar education, income, wealth, occupation, and prestige. People in the same social class also often have similar tastes and mannerisms, and they may share a general ideology as well. Lower, middle, and upper classes are the basic classes, but it is possible to identify more detailed class groupings. Later theorists began to perceive society as a more continuous progression from rich to poor. These *gradational theories* assume that society is a continuum along which people can be arrayed rather than focusing on distinct classes. Gradational theories usually focus on *socioeconomic status* (*SES*), a single measure of well-being that generally incorporates income, wealth, occupation, and education. The remainder of this chapter outlines class-based theories of stratification; subsequent chapters discuss gradational theories in describing current research and modern trends in inequality.

Marxist

Karl Marx (1818–1883) was one of the most influential theorists in the social sciences, including the study of social stratification and inequality. He was born in Trier, Germany, to a relatively prosperous family; his father was a lawyer and politician. Marx studied law at the Universities of Bonn and Berlin, and received a Ph.D. in philosophy from the University of Jena in 1841. He was unable to find a job as an academic and worked intermittently as a part-time newspaper correspondent. He spent most of the remainder of his life in London living in abject poverty. His family was seldom able to afford food, shelter, and clothing; one of his sons died because the family could not afford a doctor. Living in poverty provided Marx firsthand experience with the trials that lower classes face, and the struggles he and his family had certainly shaped his attitude toward capitalism. While in London, however, Marx wrote most of his influential works including *Capital*, a three-volume book that critiques standard economic thinking, describes much of his perspective on capitalism, and addresses the role of labor in the capitalist system. His lifelong friend and collaborator, Friedrich Engels, was an affluent capitalist who funded much of his work. Marx's other more well-known works include the *Grundrisse* (which was not published until 1941 and is thought to be among the most lucid statements of Marx's theoretical ideas) and *The Communist Manifesto* (written with Engels for the Communist International, an organization Marx helped found).

It is impossible to summarize all of Marx's ideas; indeed, there are numerous volumes discussing his work, and many scholars have spent their entire career attempting to better understand it. To a large extent, scholars are still trying to completely understand the works that Marx left behind and, because some have been published only recently (including the *Grundrisse*), it is no wonder that the depth of Marx's ideas is still emerging. Yet, because they are so central to the way scholars understand the structure of stratification, it is crucial to articulate the basic ideas underlying his perspective and, at least briefly, to consider the more modern theoretical perspectives that his ideas generated. Although the following description of his ideas may seem relatively simple, it is a simplification of a set of highly complex ideas that Marx articulated over many years in numerous related writings.

Primacy of the Economic Foundation

The notion of *historical materialism* is central to Marx's ideas, and it is a good place to start in understanding his thinking about social stratification. Historical materialism is an approach to societies by first understanding how the people in them make the basic products they need to survive. Although Marx never used the phrase "historical materialism," he felt strongly that to explain the structure of a society, it is essential to first identify how it produces basic necessities such as food. Before they can think about anything else, people need to eat, drink, clothe themselves, and find shelter and other necessities. In *German Ideology*, Marx stated that "Life involves before everything else eating and drinking, a habitation, clothing, and many other things. The first historical act is thus the production of the means to satisfy these needs, the production of material life itself" (Marx and Engels 2001).[2] The system by which people produce material necessities is called the *mode of production*. Throughout history, the dominant mode of production has changed, which has led to changes in people's ideologies and their relationships to one another. The economic base, or *substructure*, forms the foundation. Every other part of society – including government, family, religion, education, and dominant ideologies – is important but usually secondary. These other layers comprise the *superstructure*.

The structure of agrarian (or complex horticultural) societies provides a useful illustration of Marx's thinking. In these societies, people primarily survive on agricultural products. Their occupations are related mostly to farming, producing the goods needed for farming, and processing or distributing agricultural products. All other institutions develop in response to the central emphasis on agriculture. The main focus of political activity is farming, family life centers on farming, religious values reflect the importance of agriculture, and the educational system develops to meet the needs of agriculture. More specifically, it might be that large families are common because farming is labor-intensive and having more children helps to increase agricultural output. Similarly, religious customs and ceremonies may include showing gratitude for the bounty of the land and religious holidays may focus on key events in the agricultural cycle (e.g., planting and harvesting crops). Likewise, educational practices may include teaching skills that are useful in agricultural occupations. To some extent, the superstructure is determined by the substructure. However, Marx was clear that "life is not determined by consciousness, but consciousness by life" (Marx and Engels 2001). In other words, daily activities shape our philosophies, institutions, and culture, but they are not completely determined. The degree to which the substructure determines the superstructure fueled

---

[2] Marx and Engels first co-authored the *German Ideology* in 1845–1846, and it was first published (in German) in 1932.

intense debate among academics, but the bottom line is that there is room for choice and change.

Inequality and Control of the Means of Production

Our original question was: What determines the structure of stratification? To answer this question, Marx points to differences in how people are related to the mode of production. Specifically, Marx's response draws on two concepts: the means of production and the relations of production. The *means of production* are the physical inputs used to create economic output, including land, tools, factories, machines, natural resources, and (more recently) office space and equipment. The *relations of production* are the social ties that follow from the dominant means of production and influence how goods are produced. In a capitalist economy, the relations can be divided into three groups: (1) relations among workers, which vary depending on whether workers spend their day in isolated settings, in small groups, or as part of a large mass-production team; (2) authority relations between workers and their bosses; and (3) relations that develop around the ownership and distribution of goods (Giddens 1973).

Society is divided into two basic groups: (1) those that own the means of production, and (2) those that do not. The owners (i.e., the *bourgeoisie* or *capitalist class*) thrive from the profits of their land, tools, machinery, and factories. The others (i.e., the *proletariat* or *working class*) do not own the means of production and have no choice but to sell their labor to survive. Owners tend to control most of society's wealth even though the workers produce the goods that create that wealth. These divisions are clear in both agricultural and industrial societies. In agricultural societies, landowners are the bourgeoisie and serfs are the proletariat. The serfs generally work for the landowners and keep a percentage of what they produce to feed their families. Inequality is extremely high and mobility between classes is rare. Similarly, in industrial societies, there are those who own the means of production (e.g., factories and offices) and those who work for the owners. In these societies, inequality may be slightly lower than in agrarian societies, but inequality can become extreme as the bourgeoisie amass large amounts of wealth and the workers continue to own little.

Although inequality is extreme in nearly all societies, the classes are highly dependent on one another. Capitalists need the workers to continue selling their labor and producing the goods and services that generate profits. Likewise, workers depend on capitalists for employment; without the owners, the working class would have no income and could not purchase basic necessities. Yet, it is clear that capitalists have a tremendous advantage because they enjoy the bulk of the rewards that the society produces, and workers are exploited easily because of their lack of control. Workers produce more value than what they are paid for – in fact, they produce enough to support themselves and the capitalists. This excess value is called the *surplus value of labor*, which is what allows capitalists to continue getting rich despite doing little manual labor. This relationship can lead to exploitation of workers because (1) capitalists want to rely on workers as little as necessary, and (2) capitalists want to pay workers as little as possible to maximize their own profit. Capitalists reduce dependence on workers by using machines and creating narrow, segmented jobs that can be performed by anyone with few or no skills or training. Workers ultimately become completely interchangeable and can be replaced easily. Marx also argued that because all people are driven to create, workers become increasingly alienated because there is nothing creative about their job and they cannot keep what they produce.

Class Conflict

The result of this level of inequality and exploitation should be that workers rise up and overthrow the capitalist class. After all, workers should see the advantages that owners have, and they should recognize that their labor makes it possible for the owners to enjoy them. Moreover, workers significantly outnumber capitalists, and most economies would stop functioning if workers refused to do their job. The possibility of class struggle was definitely an important part of Marx's thinking. In fact, *The Communist Manifesto* (co-authored with Engels and originally published in 1848) was an action plan for a proletarian revolution to overthrow capitalism and create a classless society. The first section of the book lays the foundation for the action plan by noting that the

> history of all hitherto existing society is the history of class struggles. Freeman and slave, patrician and plebeian, lord and serf, guild-master and journeyman, in a word, oppressor and oppressed, stood in constant opposition to one another, carried on an uninterrupted, now hidden, now open fight that each time ended either in a revolutionary constitution of society at large, or in the common ruin of the contending classes (Marx and Engels [1848] 1888).

Marx's historical materialism is evident in this passage but so too is his notion of the inevitability of class conflict.

However, there are unequal owner–worker relations in most modern societies, yet there are few examples of successful large-scale worker uprisings. At least three obstacles described by Marx and modern Marxists explain the absence of this type of uprising. First, workers have no choice but to accept and follow society's basic rules, which are developed and enforced by capitalists. For example, workers may prefer to work fewer hours in a week but owners require 40 hours. Workers can choose to work 40 hours and receive a paycheck or not work and no paycheck. The second option (i.e., not work) is unrealistic if workers want to have food, shelter, and clothing. Workers also have little say in the pay that they receive. They produce enough to create a profit for the owner, but the owner decides wage levels. Again, workers have little choice but to accept the wages offered. These conditions also make it difficult for workers to save enough money to become owners themselves. Marx concluded that any substantial change to the class structure requires dramatic, revolutionary change that would allow more equal ownership of the means of production.

Second, capitalists also control government; that is, members of the capitalist class are often state representatives as well as business owners, and they can shape regulations to protect their own interests. If capitalists are not government officials, they typically have strong ties to officials who protect their interests. In this sense, the capitalist class is also a *ruling class*.

Third, the capitalist (or ruling) class influences the dominant values or ideologies in a society and, therefore, affects even the most basic thoughts that workers have about equity. Capitalists influence the educational system, religious organizations, and media, and they shape the messages that are communicated to their members.

If the message that people are socialized to accept in schools, churches, and daily life is one of acceptance of the status quo, workers will be less likely to consider challenging social inequality. In other words, workers suffer from *false consciousness*, or a misguided acceptance of a system that is unfair because they are not aware of the true forces influencing their own values. Engels wrote that "Ideology is a process accomplished by the so-called thinker consciously, indeed, but with a false consciousness. The real motives impelling him remain unknown to him; otherwise, it would not be an ideological process at all" (Engels [1893] 1968: 177). In other words, workers are not aware of their true class interests because they are not aware of the influence that capitalists have on their thinking.

Social Change

Social and economic changes are clearly central to Marxist theory. Marx started with a notion of historical change propelling inequality, and his ideas naturally led to conclusions about how society would be organized in the future. The primary change that Marx envisioned for the postcapitalist world was one in which equity would replace class division and worker exploitation would no longer occur. Prior to capitalism, Europe was dominated by feudal states in which noble landowners comprised the ruling class. Capitalism replaced feudalism when peasants became free to sell their labor and when industrial technology made it possible to employ the lower classes in factories rather than on farms. Similarly, Marx felt that capitalism eventually would be replaced by a better system. Capitalist economies are capable of incredible growth when owners reinvest profits in infrastructure and innovative technologies. Marx reasoned that capitalism also is vulnerable to cyclical crises because owners are inclined to invest more in technology than in labor. Because labor creates profits, profits would decline despite continued economic growth, thereby causing a recession or depression and the possible collapse of certain sectors of the economy. Yet, a crisis of this type would lead to even lower wages, which would fuel investment in additional technologies and pave the way for expansion into new industries and further growth.

This cycle of growth and crisis would intensify over time, causing increasing discontent among workers, and ultimately leading them to overthrow the ruling class. Once workers became aware of their true class interests, they would unite to become a powerful force. The revolution Marx envisioned was violent and enormous but well organized. He imagined a new system in which ownership of the means of production was more equitable and not prone to crisis than those that he experienced under capitalism. However, his vision for the subsequent systems was rather vague. The immediate result of the revolution would be a temporary system of uncertain duration, which he referred to as socialist. A *socialist system* is characterized by a collective ownership of the means of production and the elimination of markets, capital, and labor used as a commodity. Marx used the term *dictatorship of the proletariat* to describe the nature of the state that would emerge. This term acknowledges that there still would be a government or a state, but it elevates the proletariat to the ruling class and suggests that former workers would be the ultimate authority.

Socialism would erode social classes and pave the way for the emergence of the final postcapitalist system: the *communist system*. Like a socialist system, a communist system is characterized by collective ownership of the means of production; however, a communist system is classless and stateless. Communism is a utopian ideal in which there is no inequality, exploitation, or feelings of alienation. Although Marx's utopia is appealing in thought, we know now that it did not become a reality. Class struggle never became as intense as Marx imagined, and workers found ways to share in the profits of companies for which they work. Labor unions allow workers to unite and demand higher wages and better benefits; innovative plans such as profit sharing also allow workers to receive directly a percentage of corporate profits in some organizations. Class divisions also never became as distinct as Marx envisioned; rather, class has become more complex as occupational specialization increases. Moreover, because stock ownership is increasingly common, it is not always clear who is an owner and who is a worker. Finally, Marx imagined that class would be an essential component of a person's identity, which has not happened either. Many people identify more with their racial group, for instance, than their social class, which makes it difficult for classes to recognize their common interests.

Lasting Contributions

Although many of Marx's predictions about future social and economic structures did not come true, his ideas have been extraordinarily influential and remain fundamental to our understanding of inequality. First, Marx proposed that social class is fundamental to understanding social relations, conflict, and change. As noted previously, not every person in every society identifies primarily (or even strongly) with social class, but Marx's argument that class differences are the key to understanding much of what we know about how society functions is undeniably important.

Second, Marx's notion that government is linked fundamentally to the economy in ways that reproduce the class system among generations is both tremendously important and influential in thinking about class, inequality, and other aspects of social interaction. His insight about the significant overlap between socioeconomic class and political power influenced scholarship in sociology, economics, political science, and other disciplines.

Third, Marx observed that class ideology is not random; rather, many of our perspectives are learned and, therefore, reinforce class divisions. We are all born into a social class, and those we interact with – including close family members, extended family, friends, and acquaintances – are likely to be in the same class. We continually learn lessons about values and how to approach the world because others teach us directly or we observe their actions and thinking. Most lessons are from subtle clues that we observe in daily interactions and conversations, but the influence of these lessons can be powerful. Over time, class ideologies become both distinctive and highly influential. Marx proposed that people ultimately accept the ideas that they learn and do not question the social order. This allows the wealthy and powerful class to maintain its privilege with little or no objection from other classes. It is difficult to determine whether each element of this approach is true empirically. However, it has intuitive appeal and the ideas have fueled the debate about them for decades.

A testament to the importance of Marx's ideas is the continued influence his thinking has on modern research. Modern scholars recognize that Marx did not foresee the exact nature of modern capitalism and – even among those who find his ideas appealing – there is agreement that many of his writings were ambiguous and contradictory. Even decades later, it is difficult for researchers to determine unequivocally what Marx meant in some of his most important writings, which makes it difficult to apply his ideas to contemporary issues. Along with other difficulties of Marx's thinking, he did not anticipate that the modern class system would become as complex as it is. In addition, Marx did not predict the changing roles that owners and workers have in modern economies (Grimes 1991).

However, there are researchers who continue to draw on Marx's ideas to understand modern class divisions. One scholar who usefully adapted Marx's ideas to understand the nature of class today is Erik Olin Wright. He accepts the basic Marxist notion that class should be defined by relation to the means of production, but he develops a more elaborate class scheme that better reflects modern class divisions. Wright's model emphasizes control of three important economic resources: the means of production (e.g., factories, office buildings, and banks), financial capital, and labor. From that basis, Wright identifies four classes based on their relation to these resources. The capitalist class, or bourgeoisie, controls all three resources. It owns the major means of production, controls significant financial capital, and has authority over workers. The manager class includes managers of large companies who oversee corporate operations but do not own the company. They neither own the means of production nor control financial capital. Moreover, managers sell their labor to the capitalists, those who own the companies. Yet, managers have authority over other workers in the company, which gives them control of one of the three significant resources (i.e., labor). The working class is similar to Marx's original idea: It has no control of significant economic resources and therefore has no choice but to sell its labor to the capitalists.

Finally, Wright proposes that the petty bourgeoisie (i.e., self-employed small-business owners) comprises a fourth relevant class in modern capitalist economies. Because it has some control of small means of production and financial capital, it forms a clearly distinct class. Yet, the petty bourgeoisie employs few (if any) workers, resulting in little authority over labor resources (Wright 1978). Wright also acknowledged contradictory class positions; that is, there are people who do not fall neatly into one of the categories. Professionals such as doctors and lawyers have little control of the means of production, but they can influence their own work and may have employees that they control (e.g., nurses and secretaries). In a later work, Wright elaborated his earlier ideas to include additional class categories (Wright 1985; 1997). In all of this work, however, Wright is committed to the notion that class is central to understanding stratification and should be defined in terms of people's relation to the means of production.

Weberian

Max Weber (1864–1920) is considered another influential sociological theorist and even has been credited as the founder of modern sociology. Weber was born into an upper-middle-class family in Erfurt, Germany, the oldest of seven children of Max Weber Sr., a lawyer and politician, and Helen Fallenstein. The younger Weber enrolled in the University of Heidelberg as a law student, intending to follow his father's career path. Although he completed the requirements to become a lawyer, he also developed a keen interest in economics, history, and theology while at the university. He eventually passed the *Referendar* (i.e., the German equivalent of the American bar examination) but then continued his studies and earned a doctorate in law in 1889.

Weber's scholarly interests initially were in social policy and agricultural economics, and his first academic position was as a professor of economics. He was a prolific writer and a skillful empirical researcher, and he made major contributions to research in agricultural economics. However, he resigned his faculty position in 1903 after suffering bouts of depression following his father's 1897 death. Unlike Marx, who lived outside the academic system, Weber continued to live the life of a scholar and retained his connections to academic organizations. He published some of his more influential works when he was an associate editor at the Archives for Social Science and Social Welfare, and he was instrumental in helping establish sociology as a distinct academic discipline later in his career. Weber died in 1920 in Munich, Germany, but his wife, Marianne Weber, continued to publish some of his papers. Still, Weber's works are less voluminous than Marx's; however, as with Marx, it is useful to consider more broadly Weber's ideas even though some do not directly address the issues of stratification.

Conflict

Although Weber and Marx were not contemporaries, Weber's work clearly built on Marx's ideas. Weber did not disagree with Marx; rather, he added to the theoretical foundation that Marx had established. Both Weber and Marx saw conflict in human relationships as the key to understanding the structure of society; that is, both were conflict theorists. However, Marx was more of an optimist than Weber: Marx believed that conflict, inequality, and exploitation eventually could be eliminated and that a utopian social order would take their place. Weber had the advantage of living significantly later and recognizing that many of Marx's predictions had not been realized. He was more fearful of the potential for society to become increasingly unequal and unpleasant for those in the working and lower classes. Another important difference is that Weber was an advocate of value-free social science. That is, he argued that social scientists should try to understand society (i.e., be positive) rather than advocate a particular political agenda (i.e., be normative). As a result, Weber did not articulate a vision for an ideal society; instead, he developed ideas to better describe the world he experienced.

Weber's thinking starts with the idea that conflict is a critical component of social organization, but he did not identify dominant individuals or groups that act together to create an efficiently functioning society. He also did not perceive of people as predetermined, helpless actors who could not change their own destiny. Rather, he viewed people as acting deliberately in their individual interests. This does not mean that he considered people selfish or that they maximized personal gain at all cost; however, he recognized that humans are conscious, reflective beings who act intentionally within a well-defined structure. Unlike Marx, Weber also took a multidimensional approach to understanding social structure; that is, he did not focus on conflict between owners (i.e., bourgeoisie) and workers. Instead, he identified a wide range of conflicting interests – economic, social, and political – and explored how conflicts in each arena shape social structure. In Weber's thinking, a person's position in the stratification order is determined by three factors: class, status, and party (or power).

Class, Status, and Party

Class. In Weber's work, *class* refers to the *economic order*, or access to material resources. Similar to Marx, Weber recognized that control of property is a crucial determinant of stratification. However, whereas Marx believed that property alone determines class, Weber suggested that other factors were involved. Weber proposed that people in the same class have common factors influencing their life chances, and he acknowledged that income and wealth are important factors in determining class position. Weber proposed that "We may speak of 'class' when (1) a number of people have in common a specific causal component of their life chances, insofar as (2) this component is represented exclusively by economic interests in the possession of goods and opportunities for income, and (3) is represented under the conditions of commodity labor or labor markets" (Gerth and Mills 1946).

However, Weber had the advantage of writing significantly later than Marx, and he observed that class distinctions were becoming more complex and changing in ways that Marx did not imagine. Weber saw that technological changes led to a redefinition of some occupations that concerned Marx and the emergence of new occupations that Marx had not anticipated. Therefore, Weber elaborated Marx's view of class, incorporating more detailed class distinctions (particularly of the middle class) and giving occupation a more central position in the definition of class. For example, Weber observed that both a professor and a janitor work in a university and neither owns land. However, the two occupy different class positions. As this example suggests, it is not just landownership that improves one's life chances. Other resources, such as skills or specialized knowledge, also can increase income and wealth. Therefore, Weber proposed that people with similar occupations, incomes, and wealth are in the same class.

Status. Yet, stratification is more complex than access to economic resources, and Weber's ideas about inequality and the structure of society incorporate other dimensions in which people are unequal. For example, Weber's notion of *status* denotes a person's position in the *social order*. Weber observed that people tend to evaluate one another based on a set of shared ideals, and those who live up to or exceed those ideals have high status. That is, status is the honor, prestige, or respect that certain people possess because of their lifestyle. Whereas class comes from people's relations to production, status comes from their consumption, culture, social interests, and other elements of their lifestyle. High-status people tend to drive expensive automobiles, live in exclusive neighborhoods, wear fashionable clothes, join elite country clubs, attend theatrical events, and send their children to private schools. Those with lower status, of course, do the opposite: Their vehicles are modest, their neighborhood and home are not exceptional or pretentious, their children likely attend public schools, and other elements of their lifestyle follow similar patterns. Clearly, status is a more subjective measure of standing than class, but it is nonetheless an important determinant of a person's social position. Perhaps more interesting – as Weber was aware – people who live in the same society tend to share an understanding of which behaviors and lifestyles constitute high status.

Weber emphasized that although status and class are distinct, they are certainly related: People who have access to economic resources usually have high status as well. It is rare that a rich person (i.e., a person who has high income or high wealth) does not also live a lifestyle that involves high-status consumption. Imagine those who spend their time yachting: They are likely to be business owners, professionals, and others with high income and wealth. This is partly because yachting (or skiing at Telluride, summering in the Hamptons, or living in an exclusive neighborhood) is expensive, and generally only those with sufficient economic resources can afford to consume this way. However, consumption choices also partly reflect family background and the choices that people learn to make as children. Working-class and poor families may never consider spending the summer in the Hamptons – even if they suddenly were able to afford such a luxury – because they have never known anyone to do so.

Considering both class and status highlights the complexities involved in deciding how people are stratified. Imagine two people: One is a nurse, the other is an assembly-line worker in an automobile factory. The two are likely to have similar incomes and they may even consume similarly: they might live in similar neighborhoods, drive the same type of vehicles, send their children to the same schools, and vacation in the same places. If we consider only economic resources, we would probably place them in the same class. However, if we also think about status, we might rank the nurse higher than the factory worker. The nurse likely has a college degree, whereas the factory worker probably has a high school diploma (or less education). Moreover, nursing is simply a higher-prestige occupation than working on an assembly line. Both occupations are necessary and the assembly-line worker may earn more than the nurse. Yet, most people rank nursing as a higher-prestige occupation than factory work; therefore, nurses tend to have higher status.

Status also can be used to draw boundaries around similar groups; in fact, status groups tend to have a group quality more than classes. Weber used the term *status community* to refer to a group of people with similar social interests, culture, consumption patterns, and lifestyles. People with similar status tend to interact with one another. They usually live and work with people who have similar lifestyles and consumption patterns. They tend to marry people of similar status and send their children to schools with others of similar status, reinforcing status communities across generations. In the extreme, some groups may use status to draw a boundary around their status community and restrict interactions across it. Consumption and lifestyle patterns are clear signals of a person's social position, and it is easy to avoid interaction with those of a different status if it seems desirable to do so. It is easy to imagine high-status parents discouraging their children from marrying out of the family's status community. The result, of course, is that these actions reinforce status and reproduce status communities across generations.

Party (or political power). The third component of Weber's scheme is *party* or *political power*; that is, a person's position in the *political order* matters. *Party* or *power* refers to a person's position relative to established bureaucratic organizations whose goal it is to influence a type of collective action. For example, a position in a formal political organization or another political party, a labor union, a professional association, an ethnic group, a business group, or a related organization confers a degree of power. Today, the purpose of many groups is to influence government officials, and the opinions of people with a position in an influential group are more likely to be listened to by relevant government officials. Like status, Weber's party concept is fairly abstract and refers to control of intangible resources. Yet, political influence is certainly desirable and can be a significant determinant of the structure of stratification. Many politicians and others with influence over politicians are average in class and status, but their political influence affords them an important social position that class and status do not tap.

Weber pointed out that the influence that these groups has varies over time and across space because there are differences in who makes important decisions. He also emphasized that "The structure of parties differs in a basic way according to the kind of social action which they struggle to influence.... [T]hey differ according to whether or not the community is stratified by class or status. Above all else, they vary according to the structure of domination" (Gerth and Mills 1946). In modern Western societies, influencing political decision makers gives a person power, and parties (and related groups) are designed to affect political decision makers. However, in a nation under a military dictatorship, it is more useful to have connections to military leaders or those close to them. Regardless of the type of system, the underlying idea that political power also matters is significant.

Unlike Marx, Weber did not develop a general historical theory of stratification. Weber emphasized that every society has divisions based on all three dimensions – class, status, and party – but he also recognized that certain divisions were more important at different points in history. Weber stressed that people who are high in one dimension are also likely to be high in other dimensions. There is no question that privileged people tend to be privileged in multiple dimensions. However, there are examples in which people are high in one dimension and not in others (e.g., the nurse and the factory worker), and the ability of Weber's thinking to incorporate these examples is part of what makes it complex and nuanced in its ability to describe and explain social structure. Weber also differed from Marx in his approach to understanding why people do not always act in their apparent class interest. Marx (and Engels) referred to this as *false consciousness* or a mistaken acceptance of an unfair system that results from not understanding the factors that influence behavior. Weber cautioned that we should avoid assuming that people suffer from false consciousness. Instead, he proposed that when people act in ways inconsistent with their class position, it is likely that the behavior is consistent with their status or party position, or both.

Bureaucracy and Authority

Power is central to understanding inequality, and it was a major part of both Marx's and Weber's theories of stratification. Yet, the two differ in their thinking about the sources of power. Weber defined power as the "chance of a man or a number of men to realize their own will in a social action even against the resistance of others who are participating in the action" (Gerth and Mills 1946). That is, power is the ability to carry out one's desires even when others are in opposition, and both people and groups can be powerful. This highlights a critical difference between Weber and Marx: In Weber's thinking, power is not identical to control of economic resources, and people may want power for various reasons. Weber pointed out that the "emergence of economic power may be the consequence of power existing on other grounds. Man does not strive for power only to enrich himself economically. Power, including economic power, may be valued for its own sake. Very frequently, the striving for power is conditioned by the social honor it entails" (Gerth and Mills 1946). People and groups can have power for numerous reasons, including control of economic resources but also social and political positions (i.e., status and party). Likewise, people recognize that power has many advantages, and they desire it for reasons beyond the economic benefits that it entails.

Weber also differed from Marx in his emphasis on the role of formal organizations in creating and maintaining power. In particular, he focused on the role of bureaucracies in shaping social life. A *bureaucracy* is a unique type of organization that separates work into specialized units acting together to perform tasks quickly and efficiently. A bureaucracy also uses legal rules to coordinate and control administrative functions that might otherwise be decided by those filling positions in the organization. *Bureaucracy* is a term commonly used today to refer to organizations such as corporations, governments, militaries, schools, and churches.

In modern societies, people take bureaucracy for granted because it is so pervasive, and they often lament the growth and problems associated with it. However, at the turn of the twentieth century, bureaucracies were much less common. Weber recognized that bureaucracy was one of the most efficient and successful organizational forms. He pointed out the need for bureaucratic solutions to problems of social organization, and he argued that bureaucratic organizations are precise, competent, prompt, stable, and unambiguous. He even proposed that bureaucracy eventually would become the only form of organization. However, Weber recognized the potentially high social costs associated with relying on bureaucracy. Much of his work on bureaucracy sought to describe why these organizations function as they do to better describe, in part, how bureaucracies shape power relations. In this work, he highlighted the following six characteristics of modern bureaucratic systems.

Bureaucracies are specialized. Administrative rules specify who is responsible for which jobs. Regular activities are assigned and people work until they complete their job. They have an assigned job and they do not perform other jobs. Firefighters do not teach schoolchildren, nurses do not arrest people, and policemen do not extinguish fires. Even more specifically, jobs are clearly assigned within a bureaucracy: One firefighter drives the truck and operates a water pump at a fire; another is an inspector whose job it is to prevent fires. In all bureaucracies, these roles continue regardless of the person filling the position.

A bureaucracy has a hierarchy of offices. There is a well-defined, hierarchical system of subordination and superordination. This structure makes it possible for people lower in the hierarchy to appeal decisions upward if they believe a mistake was made at one level.

Every bureaucracy has written rules, regulations, and files that create the organizational memory. That is, the rules, regulations, and files enable the collective, enduring memory about how tasks should be performed and how they have been performed in the organization in the past.

Bureaucracies are characterized by technical competence. Every position in the organization requires specialized training. Moreover, the competence, training, and skills necessary for each position are written in an organization's records and used to appoint people to positions. This feature of bureaucracy relates meritocracy to the structure of bureaucracy.

Bureaucracies are impersonal and they require the full working capacity of employees. Official activities require that people complete their job regardless of how long it takes; people work to finish their responsibilities, not to spend a certain number of hours on the job.

Bureaucracies rely heavily on written communication and rules. Daily operations in a bureaucracy are based on a comprehensive, stable, and established set of rules and procedures for accomplishing tasks. Each person's duties are clearly defined and are learned through specialized training. An important result of the reliance on rules is that office holders cannot make decisions based on their own preferences. Rather, guidelines are clearly established for most functions. Of course, the reliance on rules is one reason that bureaucracies frustrate the people who work in them as well as those who interact with them in other capacities: People in the bureaucracy are seldom able to act independently of the written rules, even when a particular case suggests they should.

Bureaucracies also confer authority on some people who are part of them, and Weber argued that the hierarchical nature confers power on certain individuals. He identified three types of authority that may result. *Traditional authority* results from custom and well-established practices. This type of authority is possible because most people accept social customs and acquiesce to those with authority. An example of this authority is the rule of monarchs. *Rational-legal authority* is an outcome of formal, written rules. As noted previously, bureaucracies rely on written rules, and those who implement or enforce them derive a certain authority from their position. Judges, police officers, teachers, traffic guards, and even customer-service representatives have authority in certain domains because they enforce established rules. Modern societies rely on rational-legal authority for stability and continuity, and most people accept the authority of those enforcing the rules and laws; if they did not, it would be difficult to maintain social order.

Charismatic authority derives from a person's own allure, magnetism, inspiration, or perceived divine connection. More than the other two types, charismatic authority is related to personality traits of an individual with authority. If a leader claims authority from God or another supreme being, that person has charismatic authority. Similarly, if others grant a person authority because of his or her personal charm, that person has charismatic authority. Charismatic authority can become the stimulus for revolutions and social movements because people are willing to follow the edicts of the charismatic leader regardless of the person's other authority. Modern leaders with charismatic authority include minister Billy Graham, U.S. presidents Ronald Reagan and Bill Clinton, New York mayor Rudolph Giuliani, business tycoon Donald Trump, and basketball coaches Mike Krzyzewski and Bobby Knight. Charismatic authority seldom endures, although it is likely to last longer when it is combined with other forms of authority or relevant leadership, business, coaching, or related job skills. In almost all cases, charismatic authority ultimately defers to other forms of authority.

Lasting Contributions

Like Marx, Weber's work has had a lasting and profound effect on our understanding of social stratification and class relations. Marx's proposal that stratification derives exclusively from relations to the means of production was useful, but Weber's multidimensional approach provided a foundation for social scientists to understand more clearly some of the more complex realities of inequality. For example, racial, ethnic, and gender stratification are among the most pervasive forms of inequality in the United States and cannot be explained only by access to the means of production. Weber's notions of class, status, and party have informed thinking about social stratification across the social sciences, and his work on the nature and implications of bureaucracy and authority made an explicit connection between organizations and inequality.

It is tempting to think of Marx and Weber as entirely distinct from one another, but sociologists writing after Weber have shown that the two sets of ideas can be integrated informatively. Ralf Dahrendorf is an important example. He usually is considered a Weberian, but his ideas actually draw on both Marx and Weber. He agreed with Marx that society is most usefully perceived as divided into two different classes, that one is dominant and the other is subordinate, and that they are in conflict with one another (Dahrendorf 1959). However, Dahrendorf disagreed with the Marxian idea that ownership of the means of production is the reason for class differences and conflict. He suggested that the focus on production relations was outdated by the 1950s, when it was clear that modern economies would be characterized by a separation between capitalist owners and managers who control operations. Instead, he drew on ideas from Weber to propose that authority differences – or differences in legitimate power – create and maintain class differences.

Dahrendorf pointed out that large, impersonal organizations dominate everyday life in modern societies. From the time we are born, organizations – including hospitals; schools; business, government, and religious organizations; and media groups – dictate much of what we do in life. Nearly all organizations are hierarchical structures in which a few people have authority over the majority. Most people have no choice but to follow the rules that the organizations establish and to obey the commands of those in charge. Dahrendorf claims that class "signifies conflict groups that are generated by the differential distribution of authority in imperatively coordinated associations" (1959: 204). Dahrendorf used the term *imperatively coordinated associations* to mean organizations characterized by authority relations that exist in every society and, as the quote suggests, he argued that different levels of authority in imperatively coordinated associations are the root of class conflict. Class conflict emerges because the classes differ in their interests related to maintaining the authority relations. Specifically, people develop interests in maintaining authority (those who are superordinate, or who have authority) or undermining authority (those who are subordinate, or who have little authority) as a result of their position in an organization. As these details suggest, Dahrendorf made a significant effort to synthesize ideas from Marx and Weber as well as a useful independent statement about class divisions.

Summary

(1) Paradigms are the fundamental points of view that distinguish a science, and paradigm shifts guide progress in the social sciences much like they do in the natural sciences. In the natural sciences, paradigm shifts are usually dramatic and complete, as in the shift from thinking that the earth is the center of the universe to thinking that the sun is the center. In contrast, in the social sciences, a paradigm rarely is replaced completely. More often, when a new social-science paradigm emerges, it becomes a more common way of thinking and some may continue to draw on prior paradigms.

(2) It is helpful to understand the history of social stratification to appreciate theories that explain the sources and structure of inequality. The first humans lived in hunting and gathering societies, in which there was no real division of labor by occupation and equality was high. When people stopped migrating in search of food, simple horticultural societies developed. As jobs became more specialized and people acquired property, inequality began to increase. In complex horticultural societies, agricultural production and occupations became more specialized. These societies enjoyed considerable surplus, but the growing distinction between landowners and laborers led to extreme levels of inequality. In modern capitalist (or industrial) societies, reliance on advanced technology has increased, and only a small percentage of the population is involved in agricultural production. In modern societies, there is extremely high inequality by income, wealth, occupation, education, race/ethnicity, and gender.

(3) Functionalist theorists start with the idea that inequality is natural and essential in any society. Similar to most functionalist theorists, Davis and Moore proposed

that societies are like biological organisms: They need each part to work together for the whole to operate. Some positions or jobs are more functionally important to society, and only a small number of people have the skills or talents necessary to fill them. The most important positions provide the highest pay and most attractive benefits that lead to inequality. Talcott Parsons, another functionalist theorist, also started with the idea that society is similar to a biological organism, but he proposed that differences in compliance with social values lead to status differences, which – rather than skills or talents – determine who fills the most important roles.

(4) Conflict theorists disagree with the assumption that inequality is normal and necessary; instead, they assume that inequality is a problem. Conflict theorists propose that it is not always apparent which positions are most important; suggest that rigid class differences prevent many talented people from receiving the training necessary to be competitive for the best positions; argue that the notion of labor mobility is a myth; and point out that people who grow up in a privileged family have better access to the training required to fill society's most desirable positions. Moreover, conflict theorists question how much inequality is necessary: Even if some inequality is unavoidable, the high levels of inequality common in modern societies are extreme. Lenski combined elements from both functional and conflict theories when he argued that what people need and want is scarce, and those with the most power are best able to decide how surplus is distributed. Lenski deduced that privilege is largely a function of power and, to a lesser degree, altruism.

(5) Theories of stratification also explain the structure of stratification. Marxist theories propose that a person's relation to the means of production determines his or her social position. Society is divided into owners, or bourgeoisie, and others, or proletariat. Owners control the majority of society's wealth and survive on the profits generated by the factories and other capital they own. Workers own little and they sell their labor to survive which results in extreme inequality and exploitation of workers. Marx envisioned a future socialist system in which a dictatorship of the proletariat would replace the current system, allowing former workers to become the ultimate authority.

(6) Weber agreed with Marx that conflict is a critical component of social organization, but he took a multidimensional approach to understanding the structure of stratification. He proposed that class (economic order), status (social order), and party (political order) contribute to a person's position. He also agreed that power is central to understanding stratification, but he proposed that power results from many sources including control of economic resources, status, and political influence. Weber identified six characteristics of modern bureaucracies that affect power, and he identified three types of authority that result from bureaucratic hierarchies.

Box 2.1 Golden Arches: Alienation or Opportunity?

Contemporary workers in most developed countries are protected from many of the dangers and difficulties that motivated Marx – and, to a lesser extent, Weber – to write about the need for changes to their conditions. Regulations regarding child labor, work hours, breaks, minimum wages, and safety standards have made dramatic improvements in conditions. Yet, some contemporary jobs still may be alienating and otherwise undesirable for workers. Fast-food restaurants often are criticized for this, and McDonald's is a major example because it is the largest fast-food restaurant in the world. In 2005, McDonald's had more than $20 billion in revenues and 450,000 workers. McDonald's restaurants are located in 118 countries and territories throughout the world, and they serve nearly 50 million customers every day. Approximately one in eight U.S. workers has been employed by McDonald's at some time in their life. McDonald's is the largest purchaser of beef, pork, potatoes, and apples in the United States (Schlosser 2002).

In addition to facing criticism for contributing to obesity problems and environmental degradation (because of some packaging it uses), McDonald's faces frequent criticism for creating substandard working conditions. Critics argue that McDonald's focuses on increasing profits at the cost of the health and social conditions of its workers. Work in most fast-food restaurants is highly standardized to guarantee uniformity of products across locations. A significant downside of standardization is that working at a fast-food restaurant is not fulfilling and workers are completely interchangeable. Every step in the process of producing and serving the food is dictated from above, making the individual worker totally dispensable. Critics also argue that pay and benefits are not adequate for most workers, opportunities for advancement are nearly nonexistent, and attempts to unionize are squelched by higher-ups. The result is that entry-level workers, as well as more advanced workers, are exploited and alienated unnecessarily from their work (Schlosser 2002). For workers in developing countries who are not protected by laws governing safety and work conditions, exploitation can be particularly severe.

Proponents of the fast-food chain point out that McDonald's offers temporary employment for thousands of low-skilled workers who otherwise might not have a job. They note that although the work may not offer superb training or advancement opportunities, McDonald's provides reliable wages, clean working conditions, and flexible entry-level jobs. Moreover, proponents argue that McDonald's is not intended to be a permanent job for most workers. Jobs in the fast-food industry provide steady income for entry-level workers who are likely to move to another job before long. For some workers (e.g., disabled and elderly workers), these jobs require limited skills. Proponents also point out that McDonald's provides training for many franchisees and other employees (primarily at its facility known as Hamburger University in Oak Brook, Illinois). McDonald's has demonstrated that it is willing to change its business practices. For example, when it was criticized for using environmentally damaging polystyrene packaging, it replaced the containers and dramatically reduced the amount of waste produced. Outside the United States, McDonald's is credited with providing opportunities for people who otherwise would not have a job. There also is evidence that McDonald's improves service standards when it opens in another country; for example, customers in some areas of East Asia became accustomed to the quality of the facilities and began to demand clean restrooms, elevated health standards, and better service from other restaurants (Watson 1998).

Box 2.2 Enron

It is not always obvious when owners take advantage of workers or that their intentions are as malicious as Marx suggested. The counterargument to Marx is that owners take risks in starting companies, and the profits generated are the rewards for those risks. However, events that unfolded at Enron Corporation in the early 2000s suggest that owners sometimes profit excessively and their intentions are malicious.

Box 2.2 (*continued*)

Enron Corporation was formed in 1985 when Kenneth Lay coordinated the merger of Houston Natural Gas and Internorth. Lay became CEO of the new company that was headquartered in Houston, Texas, and employed more than 21,000 people. With revenues of $101 billion in 2000, the company was one of the world's largest electricity, natural gas, paper and pulp, and communications corporations. Enron was listed by *Fortune Magazine* as one of America's Most Innovative Companies each year between 1996 and 2001, and it was included as one of *Fortune's* "100 Best Companies to Work for in America" in 2000. In 2001, it became clear that Enron's positive financial situation was upheld by systematic and institutionalized accounting fraud. Investigations ultimately revealed that an enormous proportion of the company's assets and profits were exaggerated or fabricated. Enron filed for bankruptcy in 2001, and four thousand employees lost their job.

In the years following Enron's bankruptcy, investigators demonstrated that the company and its executives had been involved in a host of illegal practices for many years. There was clear evidence of insider trading by executives, and auditors found convincing proof that they were transferring company funds directly into their own bank accounts. Executives eventually were charged with bank fraud, making false statements to auditors and banks, securities fraud, wire fraud, and money laundering as well. Enron had created offshore entities that allowed it to avoid paying taxes and further inflate profits. Each quarter, the company was forced to perform creative accounting deception to appear profitable when Enron actually was losing money.

In August 2000, Enron's stock prices hit their highest value, and executives who knew of the company's hidden fraud began to sell their stocks. They made millions of dollars but continued to tell investors and employees that the company would rebound. Kenneth Lay and his wife sold more than $70 million in Enron stock, even as he issued statements encouraging investors and employees to continue to buy shares. Thousands of Enron employees and investors lost their life savings, their children's college funds, and their pensions. Because neither stocks nor the company's pension plan (i.e., a 401(k) plan) were insured, those who lost money had little recourse. Court documents later revealed that Enron executives not only deliberately orchestrated the company's fraudulent practices; they also cavalierly acknowledged that the company's profits and their own earnings were at the expense of employees' savings and retirement.

Kenneth Lay was found guilty of all charges brought against him by federal prosecutors. However, he died suddenly on July 5, 2006, before the sentencing phase of his trial. As a result, his estate may not be responsible for any forfeiture of assets that the court mandated.

Stratification Classics 2. The Modern Office: The Dynamics of Bureaucracy

You do not have to watch the TV sitcom *The Office* very long to know that office dynamics have changed dramatically since Peter Blau (1955) wrote *The Dynamics of Bureaucracy*, a detailed look at office interactions and politics in the 1950s. Not only did the book suggest how office politics have changed in recent decades, it also provides good evidence about how power is distributed in office settings even today.

Blau described interpersonal interactions in two departments of a federal agency (i.e., a *bureaucracy*, in Weber's term). Whereas Weber proposed that power in a bureaucracy is largely a result of a person's position in the structure, Blau proposed that complex interpersonal relations also are critical in determining how much power a person has. According to Blau, power reflects a person's ability to overcome opposition. People are dependent on others who control the resources they need. Blau showed that agents in the offices that he studied controlled many resources that others needed, not all of which were material resources. For example, when one person had specialized knowledge about a subject and another person needed the information and skills, the person with the special knowledge had a great deal of power regardless of his or her position in the organization. According to Blau, "rewards that are exchanged can be either intrinsic (love, affection, respect) or extrinsic (money, physical labor). The parties cannot always reward each other equally; when there is inequality in the exchange, a difference of power will emerge within an association (p. 59)."

Imagine the interaction between a secretary and a boss. Normally, the boss would be more powerful than the secretary because the boss has a higher position in the organization. Now imagine that the boss is relatively new to the job and needs to know how to do something in the organization, such as get money to take an important trip. The secretary might know exactly who to contact to organize the trip. Of course, the secretary must be willing to make the contact, and the boss will be wise to be kind to the secretary until the task is complete. In this case, the secretary has power as a result of specialized knowledge. We can generalize this idea and realize that the secretary may have power all of the time (not just in this task) as a result of other specialized knowledge. A savvy boss realizes this and is careful to maintain a good relationship with secretaries and others with similar knowledge.

Blau's description of the federal agency recounts in detail the interactions that produce this type of power and the resulting interactions. As a result of the informal power structure, many of the relations play out very differently than might be expected given the formal structure of the organization. Of course, access to nontangible resources such as specialized knowledge cannot always overcome the structural impediments that contribute to power imbalances and social stratification. Yet, it is important to be aware that power can come from access to many different resources, some of which are not tangible.

(*Source:* Excerpted from Peter Blau, 1955. *The Dynamics of Bureaucracy.* Chicago: University of Chicago Press.)

Key Concepts

Advanced horticultural society
Bourgeoisie
Bureaucracy
Capitalist class
Charismatic authority
Class-based theories
Communist
Complex horticultural society
Conflict theories
Dictatorship of the proletariat
Functionalist theories

Gradational theories
Historical materialism
Hunting and gathering society
Imperatively coordinated associations
Industrial society
Means of production
Mode of production
Modern capitalist society
Paradigm
Party (political power)
Proletariat

Rational-legal authority	Status community
Relations of production	Substructure
Ruling class	Superstructure
Simple horticultural societies	Surplus value of labor
Social class	Theory
Socialist	Traditional authority
Socioeconomic status (SES)	Working class
Status	

Questions for Thought

1. Recall the recent trends in wealth inequality outlined in Chapter 1. How would a functionalist explain why there is wealth inequality? What are the advantages and disadvantages of this approach to explaining inequality?
2. Membership in labor unions has declined in recent years. Does this suggest that Marx was incorrect in predicting increasing unity among workers? If so, where did he go wrong? If not, how would he explain this important change in union membership?
3. What did Weber mean by class, status, and party? How well do these concepts explain the structure of modern stratification? Give specific examples of the modern patterns that Weber's conception explains and neglects.
4. Inequality varies enormously across countries (i.e., some countries are very wealthy whereas others are extremely poor). Which theory defined in this chapter best explains this pattern? Is cross-country inequality acceptable? Is it inevitable?
5. The United States restricts immigration from other countries. Is this good for workers (consider both U.S. workers and immigrant workers)? Use the theories discussed in this chapter to support your answer.

Exercises

1. *Masses of information about stratification: The poster.*
   Stephen Rose and Dennis Livingston (2005) summarized a tremendous amount of information about inequality in a poster titled "Social Stratification in the United States." Identify the different dimensions of stratification included on the poster. Who are the most affluent in each dimension? Who are the most disadvantaged in each dimension? Use the theories discussed in this chapter to identify the factors that account for a person's position.
2. *Explaining the test-score gap.*
   Black and Hispanic students routinely score lower on standardized tests than white students. Use the theories introduced in this chapter to explain this difference.

Multimedia Resources

Print

Babbie, Earl. 2003. *The Practice of Social Research* (10th edition). New York: Wadsworth Publishing.

Calhoun, Craig, Joseph Gerteis, James Moody, Steven Pfaff, Kathryn E. Schmidt, and Indermohan Virk. 2007a. *Classical Sociological Theory*. New York: Blackwell.

_____. 2007b. *Contemporary Sociological Theory*. New York: Blackwell.

Kuhn, Thomas. 1970. *The Structure of Scientific Revolutions*. Chicago: University of Chicago Press.

Popper, Karl R. 1935/1959. *The Logic of Scientific Discovery*. New York: Basic Books.

Schlosser, Eric. 2002. *Fast Food Nation: The Dark Side of the All-American Meal*. New York: Houghton Mifflin.

Watson, James L. 1998. *Golden Arches East*. Palo Alto, CA: Stanford University Press.

Internet

(1) www.asatheory.org: Homepage of the American Sociological Association's section on social theory. Contains detailed links to theory-related Internet resources.

(2) www.marx.org: Internet site operated by a nonprofit volunteer organization dedicated to educating people about Marxism. The site contains detailed information about Karl Marx, later Marxists, and modern Marxian theory.

(3) www.marxists.org/archive/marx: Online access to most of Marx and Engel's writings.

(4) www.faculty.rsu.edu/~felwell/Theorists/Weber/Whome.htm: An online resource for information on Max Weber.

(5) www.hewett.norfolk.sch.uk/curric/soc/PARSONS/Parsons.htm: Information and resources related to Talcott Parsons.

Films

A History of Social Classes. 1999. This film explores whether Marx's notion of two classes is appropriate for understanding stratification today. It examines how different societies were divided into classes and traces the history of stratification.

Matewan. 1987. An independent film that illustrates class conflict between a union and a coal company in West Virginia during the 1920s. The film highlights the process by which class bridges can develop even across race and ethnic boundaries when conditions are right.

Norma Rae. 1979. A classic film about a single mother who works in a Southern textile mill under extremely poor working conditions. Norma Rae takes a lead role in unionizing her factory, a difficult and dangerous process in the 1970s.

Works Cited

Babbie, Earl. 2003. *The Practice of Social Research* (10th edition). New York: Wadsworth Publishing.

Blau, Peter M. 1955. *The Dynamics of Bureaucracy*. Chicago: University of Chicago Press.

Dahrendorf, Ralf. 1959. *Class and Class Conflict in Industrial Society*. Stanford, CA: Stanford University Press.

Davis, Kingsley, and Wilbert Moore. [1945] 2001. "Some Principles of Stratification." In *Social Stratification*, edited by D. B. Grusky. Boulder, CO: Westview Press.

Dixon, Marc, and Vincent J. Roscigno. 2003. "Status, Networks, and Social Movement Participation: The Case of Striking Workers." *American Journal of Sociology* 108: 1292–327.

Domhoff, G. William. 2002. *Who Rules America? Power and Politics* (4th edition). New York: McGraw Hill.

Dye, Thomas R. 1995. *Who's Running America? The Clinton Years.* Englewood Cliffs, NJ: Prentice-Hall.

Engels, Friedrich. [1893] 1968. "Letter to Franz Mehring." In *Marx and Engels Correspondence.* London: International Publishers.

Gerth, Hans, and C. Wright Mills. 1946. *From Max Weber.* New York: Oxford University Press.

Giddens, Anthony. 1973. *The Class Structure of the Advanced Societies.* New York: Harper & Row.

Grimes, Michael D. 1991. *Class in Twentieth-Century American Sociology: An Analysis of Theories and Measurement Strategies.* New York: Praeger.

Keister, Lisa A. 2000. *Wealth in America: Trends in Wealth Inequality.* New York: Cambridge University Press.

Kuhn, Thomas S. 1970. *The Structure of Scientific Revolutions.* Chicago: University of Chicago Press.

Lenski, Gerhard E. 1966. *Power and Privilege: A Theory of Social Stratification.* New York: McGraw-Hill.

Marx, Karl, and Frederick Engels. 2001. *The German Ideology Part One, with Selections from Parts Two and Three, together with Marx's Introduction to a Critique of Political Economy.* New York: International Publishers.

Marx, Karl, and Friedrich Engels. [1848] 1888. *Manifesto of the Communist Party.* Chicago: C.H. Kerr & Company.

Morris, Martina, and Bruce Western. 1999. "Inequality in Earnings at the Close of the Twentieth Century." *Annual Review of Sociology* 25: 623–57.

Parsons, Talcott. 1937. *The Structure of Social Action.* New York: The Free Press.

_____. *The Social System.* Glencoe, IL: The Free Press.

Rose, Stephen J., and Dennis Livingston. 2005. *Social Stratification in the United States: The New American Profile Poster, Revised and Updated Edition.* New York: The New Press.

Sanderson, Stephen, and Arthur Alderson. 2004. *World Societies: The Evolution of Human Social Life.* Boston, MA: Allyn and Bacon.

Schlosser, Eric. 2002. *Fast Food Nation: The Dark Side of the All-American Meal.* New York: Houghton Mifflin.

Tumin, Melvin M. 1953. "Some Principles of Stratification: A Critical Analysis." *American Sociological Review* 18: 387–94.

Watson, James L. 1998. *Golden Arches East.* Palo Alto, CA: Stanford University Press.

Wolff, Edward N. 1995. *Top Heavy: A Study of the Increasing Inequality of Wealth in America*. New York: Twentieth Century Fund.

Wright, Erik Olin. 1978. *Class, Crisis and the State*. New York: Schocken Books.

_____. 1985. *Classes*. London: Verso.

_____. 1997. *Class Counts: Comparative Studies in Class Analysis*. New York: Cambridge University Press.

3 Understanding Social Stratification

Methods of Evaluation

The study of social stratification and inequality relies heavily on the analysis of data to adjudicate competing claims. This chapter presents useful skills for designing, conducting, and evaluating social-science research, including research on inequality that is useful when reading subsequent chapters and evaluating evidence related to inequality outside of this course. The first part of the chapter outlines the steps involved in research design, including what makes an effective question for the social sciences and how to plan a study to answer those questions. The second part introduces statistical methods for describing quantitative (or numerical) data, using them to make generalizations and drawing on them to support arguments and hypotheses. In this part of the chapter, students learn sampling basics as well as measures of central tendency, variation, and skew. They also learn about *social inference*, which is the process of making inferences from the data to larger groups or populations. These skills enable students to design and conduct their own research, but they also are useful in evaluating conclusions made in published research papers and books. This chapter and its exercises focus on evaluating evidence related to social stratification and inequality, but the skills are general and useful beyond the study of stratification.

It may seem unusual to include information on research design and statistics in a book about social stratification and inequality. However, the techniques covered herein are fundamental to making informed judgments about the tremendous volume of quantitative evidence related to inequality. Increasingly, published research and even discussions in the popular press use statistical evidence to support inequality-related arguments. In the past, studies of inequality did not rely on quantitative data and statistical analyses; however, these are becoming less common because high-quality data are readily available and statistical techniques are better able to analyze data. To be a competent consumer of this evidence, it is helpful to understand the basic techniques used to collect and analyze the data. In fact, with the basic skills introduced in this chapter, students will be able to make educated assessments of all of the information discussed in the remainder of this textbook, as well as most of the information encountered elsewhere (e.g., the media).

The methods described in this chapter are useful for evaluating the evidence included in this book as well as evidence that may be encountered in supplementary readings assigned by the instructor, in other courses, and in the media. The skills identified here enable students to evaluate research and draw their own conclusions about patterns of stratification and inequality. This chapter is not a substitute for courses in research design or statistics; rather, it provides basic skills for students to feel comfortable evaluating the evidence presented in the book and other basic statistics. The information also can be used as a refresher for students who previously studied research design and statistics. At the same time, it is not necessary to be apprehensive about learning the skills needed to evaluate statistical evidence; only simple arithmetic is required to understand the material.

Research Design

Scientific research is designed to isolate and identify what we know about the world. There are many ways to know facts, and we constantly use the skills that we have learned since we were young to make decisions about what is real and what is not. Science is a formal way of knowing things. Scientific research, including social-scientific research, implies a precise, systematic set of steps that make it easier to identify facts.

Research design is the systematic planning and execution of scientific research. It involves identifying a clear question, specifying the population to be studied, formulating hypotheses, collecting evidence to evaluate the hypotheses, processing and evaluating the evidence, and disseminating the results. Understanding stages of the research process is fundamental in evaluating published research and conducting one's own research. If any step in the process is not followed correctly, the validity of the research may be questionable and the findings may not be reliable. Following are the nine basic steps in research design.

1. *Identify a question.* Sociologists conducting scientific research start with a problem that needs a solution or a question that needs an answer. The goal is to establish a causal relationship between two concepts or ideas. The orientation typically is positive rather than normative (i.e., establishing *what is*, not what *should be*). Similar to the physical realities that physical scientists (e.g., physicists and chemists) can uncover, there also are social realities and regularities that social scientists can uncover. The first step in identifying a question is to decide on a general area of interest. If students are doing the research, the area of interest might be related to something they read or to the research a professor is conducting, or it might be something that they observed and found interesting. The question should have theoretical or practical importance, and it typically includes both a clear outcome of interest and a central factor that might affect the outcome.

For example, one area of interest that attracts interest in stratification research is why some people complete more years of education than others. An important factor that affects education is a person's childhood family traits. A possible question that incorporates an interest in family processes and educational outcomes is as follows: How does childhood family structure affect education? This question has a clear outcome of interest (i.e., education) and a central factor that may affect that outcome (i.e., childhood family structure). This question also is important because education affects other outcomes such as income and wealth; that is, completing school affects a person's well-being throughout life. The question must be clearly stated because it guides the remainder of the research process. It also is important to identify which question is being asked when evaluating published research. It should be stated in the first part of the book or paper, and the author should provide a compelling explanation for its importance. If the question is not immediately apparent, it is not necessarily because there is no clear question; the book or paper may have to be read more closely. Be careful to identify the question before evaluating the rest of the work.

2. *Specify the unit of analysis.* The *unit of analysis* is the population on which the study is focused. The entire group is the focus of the research question. Social-science research typically focuses on individuals as the unit of analysis, but there is almost no limit to what or who can be the subject. When individuals are the unit of analysis, the true population of interest is all individuals of a given type. In the question identified in Step 1, the individual is the unit of analysis because individuals attain education. More precisely, the unit of analysis is all individuals in the United States, assuming that the United States is the focus area of the research. Other units of analysis that are often the focus of social-stratification research include groups and organizations. Groups are families, friendship groups, married couples, work groups, neighborhoods, cities, states, and regions. Similarly, organizations are corporations or firms, nonprofit organizations, and churches. It is useful to create an image of a group by aggregating traits of its members. For example, when educational levels of all people in the population are available, it is possible to create the average level and use this measure to understand the group. A population that has an average of 8 years of education likely behaves differently than a population that has an average of more than 16 years (e.g., more than college, on average). Remember, though, that if the question focuses on the individual, then the individual is the unit of analysis, even if aggregate measures are available.

Understanding the unit of analysis helps to recognize and avoid the *ecological fallacy. Ecological* refers to the group and the *fallacy* is assuming that something we know or learn about a group informs us about the individuals in the group. For example, in a now-classic illustration, Robinson (1950) showed that in states with a relatively high percentage of foreign-born people, a high percentage of the population is literate in American English. The ecological fallacy suggests that foreign-born people are more likely to speak American English than those who are native-born. This is false: As expected, those who are native-born are more likely to speak American English. The fallacy arises because foreign-born tend to live in states where higher proportions of native-born are literate.

3. *Specify key concepts.* The third step in the research process is identifying the key concepts examined by the study. *Concepts* are relatively abstract ideas we can name that tend to have shared meaning across populations. *Conceptualization* is the process of identifying and naming a concept. Think about when the term *conceptualize* is used. Perhaps it was when trying to decide which terms to use to express an idea for a class paper or other project. The objective is similar: to provide a general name for the

main pieces of a question to ensure that others understand it. In stratification research, family financial well-being is a common concept that conveys information about the welfare and security of a family. In our example, both childhood family structure and education are concepts. Other concepts common in research on inequality include *social class*, *occupation*, and *fertility*, which are general terms that convey meaning but are not precise enough to be measured. The next step in the research process moves us closer to measuring our idea.

4. *Specify variables.* To measure concepts and test ideas that relate concepts to one another, it is necessary to operationalize the concepts with specific variables. *Variables* are clearly defined indicators of concepts. Whereas concepts are abstract and general, variables are precise, concrete, and measurable; that is, it should be possible to imagine a way to quantify a variable. *Operationalization* is the identification of variables that correspond to concepts. In research on stratification, family financial well-being is commonly operationalized as income or wealth. In our example, education could be operationalized as the number of years of education completed or with a series of variables indicating education completed (e.g., less than high school, high school, some college, college, or more than college). Family structure might be operationalized as number of siblings, total number of people in the household, or single- versus two-parent household.

5. *State hypotheses.* Remember that to answer questions, social-science research typically intends to establish a causal relationship between two concepts. The research question (see Step 1) identifies two concepts that might be related, and the variables (see Step 4) operationalize the concepts. *Hypotheses* are statements that establish a logical connection between variables. Recall the example question: How does childhood family structure affect education? We said that family structure might be operationalized as number of siblings and education as years of schooling completed (i.e., number of siblings and years of schooling are variables). A simple hypothesis is: As the number of siblings increases, years of education completed decreases.

More commonly, researchers make rather complex arguments that involve a set of related hypotheses, which should be logically connected and articulate the connection between variables in more depth than a single hypothesis. For example, researchers who study the relationship between number of siblings and years of education argue that the following set of hypotheses is more precise:

1. As the number of siblings increases, parental resources that can be used for education decrease.
2. As parental resources that can be used for education decrease, educational attainment for each child decreases (Downey 1995).

This set of hypotheses introduces a third concept (i.e., family financial well-being) that is operationalized as parents' resources that can be used for education. Intuitively, this set of hypotheses implies that in larger families, parents have more expenses and less money remaining for their children's educational pursuits. As family size increases, then, parents have less money available to pay for private schools, books and computers, dance and music lessons, trips to the museum and theater productions, and other activities that have been shown to improve their children's ability to succeed in school.

As a result, children from larger families (on average) do more poorly in school and do not complete as many years of education. When hypotheses are clearly identified, evaluating the research is more straightforward. However, remember that hypotheses are not always stated clearly, even in published research. If arguments are not clearly identified as hypotheses, they may be clearly stated in the text. In this case, the reader can identify the hypotheses, evaluate whether they are logical, and then make a reasonable argument.

6. *Select a sample.* To evaluate whether the hypotheses are plausible, it is necessary to select a sample to study. Step 2 of the research process states the importance of knowing the unit of analysis – or population – that is the subject of the question. The *sample* is a subset of that population that can be studied easily. The example question introduced in Step 1 focuses on educational attainment, and the relevant population for that question is all individuals in the United States. Of course, it would be time-consuming and expensive to interview everyone in the United States about their education (which is why the government conducts a census only every 10 years!). It would take years and cost millions of dollars if researchers had to contact everybody in the country, spend time interviewing them, and electronically record all of their answers. Even if they sent questionnaires to everyone, it would cost millions of dollars to print and mail them. Fortunately, there are techniques that make it possible to select a sample of the population and to study only that sample without jeopardizing the accuracy of the results.

A sample typically includes about one thousand to three thousand individuals or households. Although this is expensive, the time and cost saved by sampling are enormous. Moreover, because researchers identified precise and accurate methods of selecting and using samples, it is possible to conduct research on a sample that ensures that the findings are accurate – not only for the sample but also for the entire population. To represent the population adequately, a sample must be sufficiently large. It is possible to draw conclusions about a population from a small sample, but it is ordinarily desirable to have a larger sample, which is more likely to include unusual but important cases.

Modern sampling methods are quite advanced and researchers can select from numerous techniques for identifying their sample. The nature of the research question, characteristics of the population, and type of available information all affect selection of the sampling method. A *simple random sample* is one of the most basic methods because it is straightforward and highly accurate. It involves identifying as accurately as possible all members of the population, then selecting a sample of the desired size by randomly choosing people from the population. This method makes certain that every member of the population has an equal chance of being included in the sample. *Random* does not mean that the researcher arbitrarily selects the members of the sample; in this context, it means without bias toward any member of the population.

Many alternative methods of sampling are commonly used to address unique data situations or unusual questions. A *stratified sample* is drawn by dividing the population into groups and sampling from each, which is useful for making sure certain small groups (e.g., racial minorities and the very wealthy) are included in the sample. A *cluster sample* involves dividing the population into groups and exhaustively sampling a small number of them. For example, if we want to study something about neighborhoods, we would randomly select a small number of neighborhoods and interview everyone who lives there (imagine doing something similar for towns, companies, or schools).

A *convenience sample* is probably the easiest sampling method, but it also can be the most problematic for making generalizations. Convenience sampling is any sample selected because it is readily available. For example, we want to study student performance in high school, so we interview everyone who is in detention on a given day. It might be easy to conduct the interviews because our subjects are all in one place, and they might be willing to talk with us because they would otherwise be in detention. However, if we draw conclusions about how students are performing in class, we are likely to decide that they are not performing well. Of course, our sample is probably biased, meaning that it does not represent all students in the school. As a result, our conclusions about the population are not going to be accurate. This is a blatant example of why convenience sampling is risky; however, we must beware of more subtle uses of the method. It is more important to be cautious of the conclusions drawn from information about convenience samples: This sampling method is not universally problematic, but it is more prone to bias than other methods.

Although additional discussion of these methods is beyond the scope of this book, the importance of choosing an appropriate method to select the sample cannot be overemphasized. Studying a poorly selected sample yields untrustworthy results because it is unlikely to represent the population. If a study uses an appropriate sampling method, the results generated for the sample also are true for the population. If the study does not use an appropriate sampling method, there is no way to tell what the results mean. These techniques work equally well regardless of the unit of analysis. It is possible to select samples of individuals, large firms, churches, or any other interesting population.

7. *Choose an appropriate research method* for evaluating the hypotheses and answering the question. Once the researcher has a sample, the next step is to identify a method for collecting information about members of the sample. Although there are many methods for conducting research, one method is usually most appropriate for a given study. Psychological studies often are best conducted using laboratory experiments. *Survey research* tends to be appropriate for answering questions that lend themselves to self-reports in questionnaires. *Field research* is appropriate when in-depth interviews are necessary, usually because the question involves how or why a relationship exists. Researchers often rely on *secondary data* (i.e., data that other researchers collected and made available for public use). For example, it is increasingly possible to draw on secondary datasets with information from interviews with large numbers of people. Another advantage is that many of these public datasets also followed members of the sample for many years and reinterviewed them yearly or on another regular schedule. Collecting data of this type is extremely time-consuming and expensive. The public availability of secondary datasets allows researchers to ask questions that they would be unlikely to have answered if they were forced to collect new data. Other secondary datasets are available to study populations such as firms, churches, cities, and countries. The Internet has made large public datasets and other data sources more readily available for the first time in history. A drawback of using secondary data, however, is that the dataset may not always contain the information

needed to answer a given question because it was collected or compiled for an unrelated purpose.

8. *Carry out statistical analyses to answer the question.* After collecting or otherwise obtaining appropriate data, a researcher conducts statistical analyses. *Statistical analysis* is a critical stage in the research process, and basic statistics is discussed later in this chapter. There are thousands of statistics books available, and these will inevitably be more thorough than the discussion in this chapter. Yet, because understanding the statistical analyses on which the majority of research on inequality and stratification are based is crucial, it is worth devoting a bit of time to introduce basic concepts.

9. *Write and disseminate the results.* The final stage in the research process is writing about and disseminating the results to relevant audiences. Writing about the results involves (1) presenting them graphically in tables, figures, and other illustrations; and (2) describing them in text. Tables, figures, and textual descriptions enable the interpretation of the findings, demonstrate whether they provide support for the hypotheses and how they relate to previous research, and what the broader implications of the study are. Researchers usually disseminate their findings by publishing articles, books, chapters in books, and other types of reports. The *scientific review process*, in which other scholars evaluate research before it is published, is designed to ensure that the researcher followed each stage of the research process and that the findings are accurate. Because the review process is usually intense, it tends to be highly accurate. Unfortunately, it is not a perfect process and imperfect research findings may be published. Therefore, it is important to approach even published research with a critical eye.

What Is Statistics?

Statistics may seem like a small part of the research process when considering all of the steps that are involved, but conducting statistical analyses is a critical step and deserves particular attention. *Statistics* is a set of techniques for collecting, organizing, and interpreting numerical information or data, as well as the numbers produced using these techniques. We encounter data everyday when we hear about government statistics on unemployment, inflation, poverty, and so on. Similarly, researchers frequently use data and statistical analyses to make arguments about many of the issues we study in this book. To understand and evaluate this evidence, it is important to have at least a basic understanding of statistical methods used to create it. Specifically, statistical analysis enables the evaluation of evidence related to a question and determination of whether it supports related hypotheses. The following basic terms used in statistics are helpful in exploring data and interpreting other researchers' data analysis.

Variables are clearly defined indicators of concepts, and two types are encountered in statistical analysis. A *dependent variable* is a variable that the research is trying to explain. In the previous example, years of education comprise the dependent variable because we want to understand which factors affect how much education a person has. An *independent variable* is a variable that does the explaining. That is, an independent variable affects the dependent variable. In the example, the number of siblings is an independent variable. Another way to think about this is that the independent variable is the cause and the dependent variable is the effect. The term *dependent* suggests that the dependent variable relies on another variable for its value. Both dependent and independent variables can be measured in multiple ways. *Continuous variables* can assume any value (e.g., income can be measured precisely and assume almost any value), whereas *discrete variables* can assume only certain values, usually whole numbers (e.g., number of siblings is discrete because there cannot be half a sibling).

There are two types of statistics. *Descriptive statistics* are measures and techniques that illustrate or describe data but do not generalize the description to a larger group (i.e., the population). Descriptive statistics can be used to study either a population or a sample. *Inferential statistics* are measures and techniques that allow researchers to make general claims about the population from information about a sample. The remainder of this chapter describes both types of statistics.

Descriptive Statistics

The primary goal of descriptive statistics is to summarize data to convey information more efficiently. Imagine that we have data about family size (i.e., number of siblings) for a sample of 100 people. We could make a long list that includes an identification number for each person along with the number of siblings they reported. The list of 100 pairs would span several pages and, although it probably contains interesting information, it would be difficult to comprehend. For example, we might review closely the list and decide that the smallest value is zero and the largest value is 12. We also might be able to decide that small numbers such as 2 and 3 seem to occur more often than large numbers like 12. However, it would be difficult to simply look at the numbers and make other meaningful conclusions about patterns. It would be difficult, for instance, to know whether it is more common to have four siblings or five, or to decide which value occurs most frequently. Descriptive statistics allow the information contained in those types of lists to be condensed to reduce the amount of information needed.

Distributions

The first step in calculating descriptive statistics is organizing the data in a way that allows us to interpret them. *Distribution* is a general term for the placement of values for a single variable. If we sorted the 100 people by how many siblings they have, we would have a distribution of values that starts at zero and goes to 12. A *frequency distribution* is a more specific term for the placement of values with indicators for the number of times that value occurs in the data. Table 3.1 is a frequency distribution for an actual sample of 100 people from the National Longitudinal Survey dataset (NLS 1979). The first column in the table lists all reported numbers of siblings for this sample. In the second column, the label "frequency" refers to the number of people in the sample who have the corresponding number of siblings. In the third column, the "percentage" refers to the percentage of those who have the corresponding number of siblings. Because there are 100 people in the sample, the number of people with each sibling size is equivalent to the percentage of people at that level. This simple table already reduces our data in a way that allows us to observe patterns. It is clear that

Table 3.1 Frequency Distribution: Number of Siblings

Siblings (#)	Frequency	Percentage
0	13	13
1	13	13
2	21	21
3	20	20
4	12	12
5	8	8
6	5	5
7	3	3
8	1	1
9	1	1
10	1	1
11	1	1
12	1	1
Total	100	100

smaller numbers are definitely more common and that more people in this group have four siblings than five: twelve people report having four siblings, whereas only eight people have five siblings.

Frequency distributions most often are represented graphically with *frequency tables* and *histograms*. A frequency table includes all possible values of a variable and the number of times (i.e., frequency) that each value appears in the data. Table 3.1 is an example of a frequency table, which usually includes additional information such as the percentage of times a certain value occurs, as in the third column of the table. Table 3.2 is another example of a frequency table. It summarizes data for the same sample of 100 people; however, in this table, it is the highest level of education completed. The first column is the number of years of education, the second column is the frequency (or

Table 3.2 Frequency Distribution: Education

Education (years)	Frequency	Percentage
8	1	1
9	1	1
10	1	1
11	2	2
12	8	8
13	13	13
14	21	21
15	11	11
16	14	14
17	8	8
18	11	11
19	4	4
20	5	5
Total	100	100

number of people who reported that education level), and the third column is the percentage of people who reported that education level. Notice that some education levels are particularly common, as expected in the United States. For example, relatively few people have less than 12 years of education, and a moderate number of people continue schooling after completing college. There are patterns in the data and the table begins to make them clear.

A histogram is an alternative way to represent information in a dataset. It is a graph that includes the possible values on the *x*-axis (or horizontal axis) and the number of occurrences of that value on the *y*-axis (or vertical axis). The shape of the histogram varies with the size of the sample, the choice of values included on the axes, and other choices that a researcher makes in deciding how to construct the graph. However, histograms are extremely useful for summarizing large amounts of data and for representing patterns in the data. Figure 3.1 is a histogram of the data in Table 3.1. The figure makes it easy to see that "2" and "3" are the most common responses, and that frequency declines at higher values. Figure 3.2 is a histogram of the data in Table 3.2. Again, patterns become apparent when the data are displayed in a histogram. It is immediately clear, for instance, that the most common response is 14 (i.e., two years of college). The figure also shows that most people in the sample at least graduated from high school, and the majority completed some college. Although some people may not know that these figures are called histograms, they are used commonly in newspapers, magazines, and textbooks; in fact, Chapter 1 uses histograms to convey information about levels of inequality.

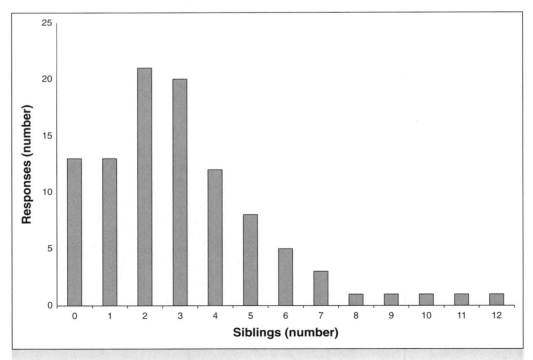

Figure 3.1 Histogram: Number of siblings.

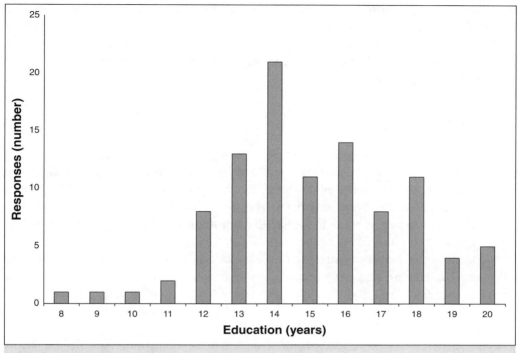

Figure 3.2 Histogram: Education.

Percentages, Proportions, and Percentiles

Three commonly known descriptive statistics are *percentages*, *proportions*, and *percentiles*. Percentages range from zero to 100, and they indicate the share of the whole. If 13 of the 100 people have no siblings, we know that 13 percent of the sample is an only child. Most students are familiar with the concept of percentage, which already has been used in this book. However, there is a subtle difference between percentages and proportions that is worth noting because it can affect how data are interpreted. Although proportions convey the same general meaning as percentages, they range from zero to 1. Proportions are calculated by dividing the percentage by 100. The 13 percent of the sample who are an only child would be written as 0.13 in proportional terms.

The percentile is the point on a distribution that has a given percent of the whole equal to or below it. If a value is in the 80th percentile of a distribution, 80 percent of the other values are equal to or below that value. The higher the percentile value, the higher the score is in the distribution. This additional terminology may seem complicated, but it is useful in describing the distribution as opposed to simply identifying the position of one value. Three specific percentiles used frequently in research on stratification are the *decile*, *quartile*, and *quintile*. Deciles are the values that divide a distribution into 10 equally sized groups. The bottom decile refers to the bottom 10 percent of scores; the top decile refers to the top 10 percent of scores. Quartiles and quintiles are the values that divide a distribution into four and five equal groups, respectively. In each case, the logic is the same: A lower decile, quartile, or quintile value indicates a lower position in the distribution. These measures are particularly useful for characterizing the shape of the distributions of income and wealth. Because we know that a small percentage of the population owns most of the wealth, for example, we expect that the value of wealth identifying the top decile is fairly large.

Central Tendency

Whereas frequency distributions summarize the range of values of a particular variable, measures of *central tendency* provide a single value that identifies the midpoint of the distribution. Central tendency measures are extremely useful in summarizing information about a distribution because they convey a significant amount with a single value. The three measures of central tendency used most often and particularly useful in studying inequality are *mode, median,* and *mean.*

The mode is the more straightforward measure of central tendency and is the easiest to calculate. It is the most frequently occurring value in a distribution. Consider the following values for number of siblings:

$$0, 1, 1, 2, 2, 2, 3, 3, 4, 7, 9.$$

The values range from 0 through 9, but 2 occurs most often (three times); this means that the mode is 2.

Occasionally, a dataset is *bimodal,* indicating two modes. The following values for number of siblings are bimodal:

$$0, 1, 1, 2, 2, 2, 3, 3, 3, 7, 9.$$

Both 2 and 3 occur three times and both are considered modes. In rarer circumstances, there are three modes and the distribution is called *trimodal.* In both bimodal and trimodal distributions, each mode should be reported.

The median is another measure of central tendency. To calculate the median, all values are arrayed from low to high. The median is the central value. Consider the following list of reported numbers of siblings:

$$0, 1, 1, 2, 2, 2, 3, 3, 3, 7, 9.$$

This list of values is presorted from low to high. The number that falls in the physical center of the list is the median; in this case, the median is 2. If there is an even number of responses, the median is the sum of the two central numbers divided by 2 (i.e., it is the mean of the two central numbers).

The mean is the final measure of central tendency that we discuss. It is the sum of all values divided by the number of values reported. Consider the following values for numbers of siblings:

$$0, 1, 1, 2, 2, 2, 3, 3, 3, 7, 9;$$

$$\text{The mean} = (0 + 1 + 1 + 2 + 2 + 2 + 3 + 3 + 3 + 7 + 9) \div 11$$
$$= (33) \div 11$$
$$= 3$$

How do the three measures of central tendency compare? Of the three, the mode is the most intuitive and easiest to calculate. However, the mode should never be used as the only measure of central tendency because it can change drastically among samples, even when the samples are from the same population. The mean is the most common measure of central tendency. It contains information about every response, is widely understood, and has properties that make it useful for developing other statistical measures. However, the mean is not appropriate when a distribution is biased or skewed toward high or low values. When several responses fall at either very high or very low values of a variable, the mean is biased toward those values, making it an inaccurate measure of central tendency. In such cases, the median is a more accurate measure of the center of the distribution. The following section describes and illustrates skewed distributions.

Variation

Measures of *variation* also are powerful tools for describing data. Whereas measures of central tendency locate the center of a distribution, measures of variation are statistics that describe how the data are spread or dispersed around the center. Intuitively, measures of variation indicate how similar or different values of a variable are. If how much variation there is in a distribution is known, then how different a given score is from the typical score also is known. The most common measures of variation are the *range*, *variance*, and *standard deviation*.

The range is the most straightforward measure of variation and the easiest to calculate. It is the difference between the highest and lowest values of a variable. We often want to know the high and low values as well as the difference. For example, for the list of numbers 2, 3, 4:

$$\text{The range} = 4 - 2$$
$$= 2$$

The variance is the average squared distance of each value of a variable from the mean of that variable. That is, the variance is the typical difference from the center of the distribution. If a distribution has a small variance, most of the scores are similar to the mean. The mean and variance for the numbers 2, 3, 4 are calculated as follows:

1. $\text{mean} = (2 + 3 + 4) \div 3$
   $= 9 \div 3$
   $= 3$

2. $\text{variance} = [(2 - 3)^2 + (3 - 3)^2 + (4 - 3)^2] \div 3$
   $= [(-1)^2 + (0)^2 + (1)^2] \div 3$
   $= (1 + 0 + 1) \div 3$
   $= 0.67$

The standard deviation is the most common measure of variation and is closely related to the variance. It is simply the square root of the variance. For the numbers 2, 3, 4:

$$\text{variance} = 0.67,$$
$$\text{standard deviation} = \sqrt{0.67}$$
$$= 0.82$$

The variance and standard deviation convey the same information. Each statistic is an estimate of the average distance from the center of the distribution. However, because the standard deviation has mathematical properties that make it useful in more advanced statistics, it is used more often than the variance, even in simple practical situations. In fact, it is relatively rare to see the variance reported, whereas the standard deviation appears frequently in scientific articles, research reports, and even the popular press. The variance must be defined to understand the standard deviation.

Skew

Skew refers to the symmetry of a distribution. Figure 3.3 includes illustrations of distributions with no skew, positive skew, and negative skew. If a distribution of a variable is perfectly symmetrical, it has *no skew* and the tails are perfectly even. The normal distribution – or *bell curve* – is an example of a distribution with no skew. The normal distribution has useful statistical properties that are discussed herein; it also is useful because many variables in social-science research are normally distributed or very close to it. For example, the distributions of heights of people and test scores typically have no skew.

Other variables have some degree of skew, either positive or negative. A distribution is skewed if one tail is longer than the other. In a distribution with a *positive skew*, the right tail is relatively long, which indicates that there are fewer frequencies at the high end of the horizontal axis. Distributions with a positive skew are fairly common in social-science research. In fact, positive skew is particularly important in studying stratification because some of the distributions that are central to understanding inequality are highly skewed. The distribution of income, for example, has a positive skew. Most people earn $35,000 to $40,000 per year, but a small number of people earn much higher incomes. In the United States, the distribution of household wealth is even more

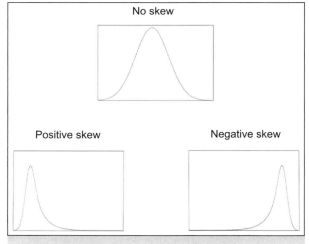

Figure 3.3 Skewed distributions.

skewed than the distribution of income. Most people have relatively low savings, and a very small percentage of the population is extremely wealthy. Similarly, the distribution of number of siblings (see Figure 3.1) has a positive skew. Most people have a small number of siblings, and it is rare to have very large families.

In a distribution with a *negative skew*, the left tail is relatively long, which indicates fewer frequencies at the low end of the horizontal axis. Negative skew is rare compared to positive skew in social-science research, but there are variables with a negative skew. Imagine an exam on which most students performed well but a few did poorly. The distribution of exam scores for this group is negatively skewed. The distribution of education (see Figure 3.3) has a slight negative skew because most people finish high school, and higher education is not unusual.

Recall from the previous discussion that the mean can be a misleading measure of central tendency when a variable has a skewed distribution. Imagine using the mean to describe the center of income distribution in the United States. Because the mean is the sum of all values divided by the number of people, the small number with large incomes increases the sum and, therefore, the mean is higher than it would be without those people. The higher mean is not a problem, but it can provide a misleading estimate of the center of the distribution. The median is not biased in this way because the very large income values are factored in only once in identifying the median as for every other value in the distribution. Mean income might be as high as $80,000 in a skewed distribution, even when median income is only about $35,000. The high mean suggests that the sample is more affluent than the rather moderate median and any conclusions drawn or policy recommendations made about the distribution may be misinformed about the reality of the distribution. If the mean and median are very different from one another, it is likely to be a skewed distribution, and it is better to rely on the median to reflect the central tendency. For this reason, average income and wealth are usually reported in the news and popular press with a median rather than a mean.

Scatterplots

So far, we only consider statistics that describe a single variable. However, it often is helpful to describe two variables at the same time, particularly how two variables are related. A *scatterplot* is a useful tool for depicting the relationship between two variables. It is a plot of the scores on one variable against the scores on another variable. Imagine that we have two pieces of information about ten people: their age and the number of years of education completed. The data may look like that shown in Table 3.3. The first column lists the age of the person and the second column lists the number of years of education that the *same person* completed. For example, the first person is 14 years old and completed 8 years of schooling.

If we plot age against education for this group, the scatterplot looks like Figure 3.4. Each dot represents one person, and it is placed at the intersection between the person's age and education. The resulting figure shows graphically that as people age, they tend to have more education. However, we limited the age of the people in this example; that is, there are no very young people and no one older than 29. If we include additional

Table 3.3 Age and Education

Age (years)	Education (years)
14	8
16	10
18	12
19	12
21	11
21	12
23	16
25	18

older people, we would probably see a tapering off in education because people typically complete their education when they are fairly young.

Scatterplots are useful for identifying *outliers* – that is, observations that are abnormally high or low on a specific dimension. If Figure 3.4 included a 15-year-old with 20 years of education, we logically would suspect that the data are wrong. After all, a 15-year-old has not been alive long enough to have completed that much education. However, some outliers are legitimate. The 15-year-old with 20 years of schooling simply may be a child prodigy: Because the child is only 15 years old, there is no logical way he or she could have had 20 years of education; instead, he or she may have skipped educational years. In research on stratification, we are likely to see cases that appear to be

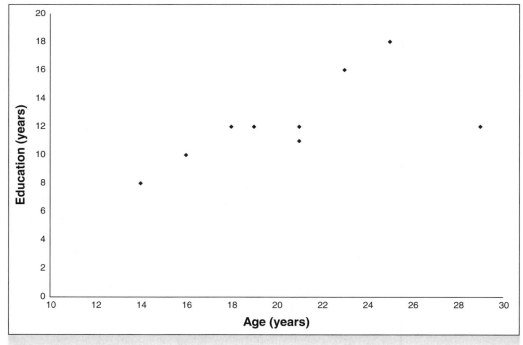

Figure 3.4 Scatterplot.

outliers. Recall the very wealthy people mentioned in Chapter 1. Bill Gates has such an enormous amount of wealth that if we plotted him on a scatterplot with more ordinary people, he would appear as an outlier.

Outliers are important because they can affect the conclusions drawn from data. If we calculate mean wealth with Bill Gates included, the mean is much higher than if we omit him. As in the case of a skewed distribution, using the median rather than the mean to measure central tendency is one solution. Yet, most researchers also approach cases that are particularly extreme with suspicion. After all, it is possible that there is an error in the data because either (1) the information available to the data collector was wrong (e.g., the information was reported incorrectly); or (2) there is a mistake in the recording of the data. If it is possible to verify the information, it is ideal to do so; if that is not possible and the case is particularly extreme, a researcher might discard the case as an error. Alternatively, it is possible to note that there are apparent outliers and then explore whether omitting the extreme cases changes the conclusions drawn from the data. Using the median instead of the mean and reporting statistics with and without the outlier included clarifies how much the outlier affects the conclusions drawn from the data. There is no universal decision rule for addressing outliers, but it is important to be aware that they are relatively common and can affect statistical results.

Gini Coefficient

An important statistical measure used frequently in the study of inequality is the *Gini coefficient*. It is a measure of dispersion that indicates total inequality, usually in a single geographic location (e.g., a country). The Gini varies from 0 to 1 and is usually expressed as a proportion; larger numbers indicate greater inequality. The Gini most commonly is calculated for income, but it also can be calculated for wealth and other variables. The Gini coefficient is interpreted as the total amount of income (or wealth, e.g.) that must change hands to have total equality. For example, a Gini coefficient of 0.90 for income indicates that 90 percent must be redistributed for perfect equality.

Correlations

Statistics has terminology for describing the relationship between two variables such as those shown in Figure 3.4. If two variables are related, the relationship is either direct or indirect. A *direct relationship* means that as one variable increases, the other increases. A direct relationship also is called a *positive relationship*. For example, the relationship between age and education graphed in Figure 3.4 is a positive relationship. Similarly, we know that education and income tend to be directly related: People with more education tend to have higher incomes. There also tends to be a positive relationship between parents' wealth and the wealth of their children. Parents with high wealth can transfer money to their children, pay for higher-performing schools, and leave an inheritance. As a result, their children also tend to have high wealth.

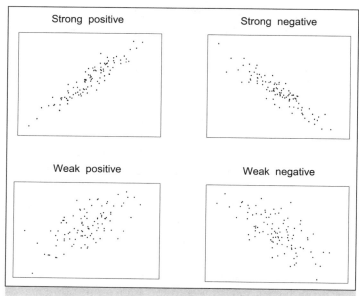

Figure 3.5 Correlations.

An *indirect relationship* means that as one variable increases, the other decreases. It follows logically that an indirect relationship also is referred to as a *negative relationship*. There is generally a negative relationship between number of class days missed and exam scores: The more a student misses class, the lower is the exam score. Similarly, the relationship between number of siblings and education is an indirect relationship. We hypothesized previously that people from larger families complete less education when they are adults. That is, as the number of siblings increases, the number of years of education completed decreases.

The *correlation* is a statistic that describes how closely two variables are related. There are many measures of correlation, but the most common is the *Pearson Product Moment Correlation* (or *Pearson's correlation*). *Correlation* most often refers to Pearson's correlation, a single number ranging from −1 to +1 that indicates the strength of a relationship. The correlation contains two pieces of information about the relationship: direction and strength. Figure 3.5 depicts the four possible combinations of these traits.

1. *Direction* refers to whether the correlation is greater than or less than zero.
   a. Positive (greater than zero): A *positive correlation* means that the variables have a direct relationship. For example, education and income tend to have a positive correlation.
   b. Negative (less than zero): A *negative correlation* means that the variables have an indirect relationship. For example, number of siblings and years of education completed tend to have a negative correlation.
   c. Zero: A *zero correlation* means that there is no relationship between two variables. For example, astrological sign and income tend to have a zero correlation.

d. One: A *correlation of one* indicates that there is a perfect relationship between two variables. Few variables used in social-science research are perfectly correlated because of the variation among people. For example, a positive correlation between class attendance and test scores is expected, but some students who always attend class may do poorly on tests. An example of a pair of variables that are close to perfect is a man's waist size and the size of his pants.

2. *Strength* refers to whether the correlation is large or small. The larger the size of the correlation, the stronger is the relationship between the two variables. Values closer to one are strong correlations and indicate a strong relationship, whereas values closer to zero are weak and indicate a weak relationship. For example, income and wealth (i.e., savings) tend to have a strong positive correlation: People with high incomes tend to have more wealth. In contrast, the number of siblings and children a person has tends to have a weak correlation: People from large families tend to have more children; however, the correlation is relatively weak.

Inferential Statistics

So far, we discuss only descriptive statistics – that is, statistics used to describe a population or a sample. However, statistics also can be used to make inferences – or draw conclusions – about a population when there is only information about a sample. *Inferential statistics* are the techniques that make this possible. Although the field of inferential statistics is vast, we cover only the three topics that are most useful in evaluating research: *normal distributions*, *probabilities*, and *hypothesis testing*.

Normal Distribution

Normal distribution is a useful tool for making inferences about a population. Frequently, making valid statistical inferences assumes that characteristics in the population are normally distributed. Recall that the normal distribution is a distribution that has no skew; it is perfectly symmetrical, such as the distribution shown in Figure 3.3. What makes a normal distribution useful is that the mean is in the very center and the other cases are spread evenly around the mean, forming a bell curve. As a result, without knowing much else, it is possible to know what percentage of cases is at any point in the distribution and to decide how common or rare a particular case is. For example, with relatively little information, researchers can decide how much confidence they should have in making assumptions about how common or unusual a particular case is.

More precisely, if a variable is normally distributed, approximately 68 percent of the population is plus-or-minus one standard deviation of the mean. Furthermore, approximately 95 percent of the population is in the area of plus-or-minus two standard deviations of the mean. Figure 3.6 is a normal distribution with the mean marked. It also shows the areas accounted for by 68 and 95 percent of the population. The following two examples illustrate how this works:

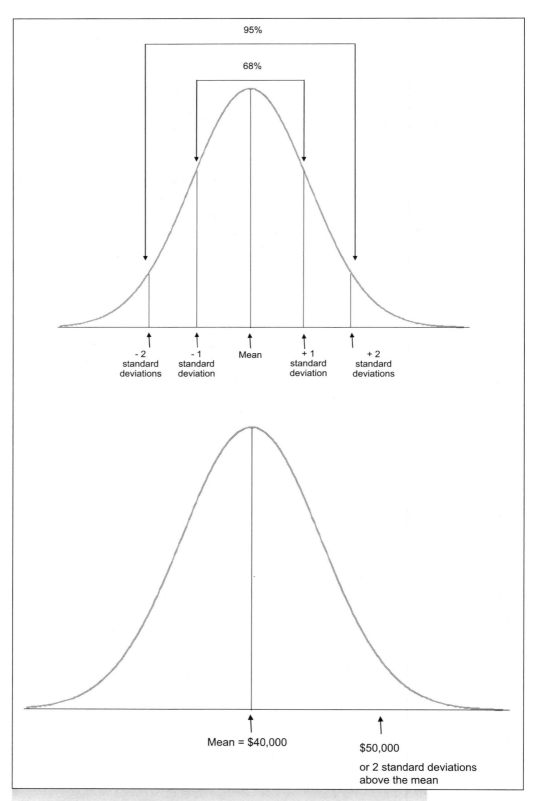

Figure 3.6 Normal distribution.

1. *Test scores.* Imagine that test scores are normally distributed with a mean of 300 points and a standard deviation of 50 points.
   a. From this basic information about the distribution, we know important details; for example, if a student from this population has a score of 150, she would be 3 standard deviations below the mean: $(300 - 150) \div 50 = 3$.
   b. We also know that a student with a score that is one standard deviation above the mean would have 350 points; a student with a score that is two standard deviations above the mean would have 400 points; and a student with a score that is one standard deviation below the mean would have 250 points.
   c. Finally, we know that 68 percent of students have between 250 and 350 points; 95 percent of students have between 200 and 400 points; and, conversely, only 5 percent have fewer than 200 or more than 400 points.
2. *Income.* Imagine that household income is normally distributed, with a mean of $40,000 and a standard deviation of $5,000.
   a. If a family from this population reports that it has $120,000 in income, it would be 16 standard deviations above the mean: $(\$120,000 - \$40,000) \div \$5,000 = 16$. That family would be in the far part of the right tail of the distribution, and we can conclude that it is fairly unusual.
   b. We also know that a household with income one standard deviation above the mean would have $45,000 in income; a household with $50,000 is two standard deviations above the mean; and a household with $35,000 is one standard deviation below the mean.
   c. Finally, we know that 68 percent of this population has between $35,000 and $45,000 in income; 95 percent has between $20,000 and $50,000; and only 5 percent has less than $20,000 or more than $50,000.

This is a hypothetical example in which income is normally distributed. In reality, the distribution of income is highly skewed in the United States: More people have limited incomes and very few have high incomes. When we address skewed distributions, remember that it is not possible to draw the same conclusions as with a normal distribution.

Understanding the unique traits of the normal distribution is important because many of the variables we study in social sciences, including stratification research, are normally distributed. If we know the mean and standard deviation for an interesting variable that is normally distributed, we can understand much about the cases for which we have data. We also can determine how confident we should be in making generalizations about the population from a particular sample or assuming that our hypotheses are correct. The unique traits of the normal distribution also make it possible to select samples that accurately represent populations that social scientists want to study, and they facilitate testing hypotheses about those populations. Before we describe those benefits in more detail, a brief discussion about the meaning of probability is helpful.

Probability

Probability is the subfield of statistics that focuses on how probable or likely an event is. The common use of the term *probability* – as in how probable or likely is it that it will rain today – is generally familiar. This use of the term may be associated with related terms such as *chance* and *odds*: What is the chance of rain today? What are the odds of rain today? These common uses are not far from their more technical use in probability theory and statistics. Although the terms *probability*, *chance*, and *odds* have precise definitions, they are related and often used interchangeably.

The probability that an event will occur is the number of outcomes of that event divided by the total number of possible events. More precisely, the probability that event (E) will occur is defined as follows:

$$\frac{\text{the number of times E occurs}}{\text{the total number of possible events}}$$

Probabilities are usually expressed as percentages, where 0 percent is completely unlikely and 100 percent is certain. In our common example of the probability of rain, we expect to read in the newspaper that there is an 80 percent chance of rain if showers are likely. Alternatively, probabilities might be expressed as proportions on a scale of 0 to 1, where 0 is completely unlikely and 1 is certain. Common examples are as follows:

1. *Tossing a coin.* The probability of heads or tails, when tossing a coin, is $1/2 = 0.50$, or 50 percent.
2. *Playing cards.* The probability of drawing a heart from a well-shuffled deck of 52 playing cards is $13/52 = 1/4 = 0.25$, or 25 percent.
3. *Selecting balls from a jar.* The probability of selecting a white ball from a jar that has two white balls, five red balls, and three green balls is $2/10 = 1/5 = 0.20$, or 20 percent.

Using Probabilities: Sampling

Probabilities are an important part of statistics because they make it possible to state precisely how likely certain events are. For example, consider the samples that social scientists select, which make it possible to conduct their research studies without information on the entire population. However, how can we know that the sample represents the population? The sampling methods discussed in the previous section use the unique traits of the normal distribution and probability theory to draw samples within one or two standard deviations of the mean for the population. The important point is that if researchers do not use accepted sampling theory, they might select a sample that represents members of the population in the tails of the distribution rather than in the center.

Recall the example of test scores from the previous section: Scores were normally distributed with a mean of 300 points and a standard deviation of 50 points. If we had a sample from this population with a mean test score of 600, we know that the sample is, on average, six standard deviations above the mean: $(600 - 300) \div 50 = 6$. We also know that only 5 percent of the population has a score that high; therefore, our sample is unusual. If we draw conclusions about the population from this sample, they are likely to be incorrect.

This may seem overly cautious, but nonrepresentative samples are common in both social-science research and the popular press. Unfortunately, it is also common for both authors and readers to draw conclusions about a population from these nonrepresentative samples. Imagine a newspaper article that selects two impoverished households – that is, those that are clearly in the left tail of the income distribution – and draws conclusions about the population of people in the city from this sample. We must be cautious about those conclusions because we know that the sample is unusual. There are important uses of in-depth research on segments of a population. In particular, a close look at two households often can make general statistics about the population more accessible and accurate. Detailed stories also help understand why certain patterns are true (e.g., why some households are impoverished). An effective way to use detailed information of this type is in conjunction with statistics on the population to ensure that the case is understood in context. For our purposes, it is important to recall these ideas when evaluating published research or drawing conclusions from our own statistical estimates.

Using Probabilities: Hypothesis Testing

Probabilities also are useful in evaluating hypotheses given statistical evidence. Recall the following two hypotheses regarding the relationship between number of siblings and years of education:

1. As the number of siblings increases, parental resources that can be used for education decrease.
2. As parental resources that can be used for education decrease, educational attainment for each child decreases.

If we have a sample that represents the population, we expect the statistical evidence to show that: (1) the mean resources available for education in larger families is lower than those available for the entire sample; and (2) the mean number of years of education completed in larger families is lower than the mean number completed for the entire sample. Probability theory makes it possible to evaluate whether these differences actually appear in the statistical evidence and, as a result, whether our hypotheses are likely to be true. For our purposes, it is important to notice whether published research evaluates the claims made using this approach.

Summary

(1) Research design is the systematic planning and execution of scientific research. The nine steps in research design are as follows: identify a question, specify the unit of analysis, specify key concepts, specify variables, state hypotheses, select a sample, choose an appropriate research method, conduct statistical analyses, and write and disseminate results.
(2) Statistics is a set of techniques for collecting, organizing, and interpreting numerical information or data. Statistical analysis allows us to evaluate evidence related to a

question and to determine whether the evidence supports related hypotheses. There are two basic types of statistics: descriptive and inferential.

(3) Descriptive statistics are measures and techniques that illustrate or describe data from a sample or a population but do not try to generalize the description to a larger group.

- Measures of central tendency are descriptive statistics that identify the middle of a distribution. The mode, median, and mean are three common measures of central tendency.
- Measures of variation are descriptive statistics that indicate how much spread a distribution has. The range, variance, and standard deviation are three important measures of variation.
- Skew refers to the symmetry of a distribution. Distributions can be described as having no skew, positive skew, or negative skew.
- Correlation is a descriptive statistic that measures the relationship between two variables, which can have a positive correlation, a negative correlation, a zero correlation, or a correlation of one (i.e., a perfect correlation). The larger the value of the correlation, the stronger is the relationship between the two variables.

(4) Inferential statistics are used to draw conclusions about a population using information from a sample. The normal distribution – or bell curve – is an important tool in inferential statistics. If a variable is normally distributed, 68 percent of cases fall within one standard deviation of the mean and 95 percent fall within two standard deviations.

(5) Probability is a subfield of statistics that addresses the likelihood of events. The probability of an event is the number of outcomes of that event divided by the total number of possible events.

(6) Probabilities make it possible to select representative samples of populations and draw conclusions about the population from the sample with a known amount of confidence. Probabilities also contribute to understanding how rare cases are, allowing researchers to understand them in the context of their position in a distribution. Probabilities also are useful in evaluating hypotheses given statistical evidence.

Box 3.1 Poor Samples Lead to Bad Conclusions: Predicting Election Results

Selecting a representative sample is important in all social-science research. Yet, the consequences of choosing an inadequate sample are more immediately noticeable in some areas. Political polls, for example, often use samples to predict election results. Rather than interview all voters – a process that would take longer than the official counting of votes – polling organizations interview samples of voters to make quick predictions. As expected, the accuracy of these predictions relies heavily on the sample quality. If the sample is poorly chosen, the prediction can be wrong. In extreme cases, announcing a winner before voting is completed can affect the outcome of the election because it might discourage people from voting when they might otherwise have done so.

Until recently, the most famous example of a mistaken electoral prediction was the 1948 presidential election between Harry Truman and Thomas E. Dewey. The Gallup Organization (i.e., a well-known polling organization) used a quota sample to predict the winner. That is, it attempted to interview a specified number of people from selected gender, race, income, and

Box 3.1 (*continued*)

other categories. This sampling method was common in political polling at the time; the idea was that it would accurately capture patterns in a range of demographic groups. As long as people had the specified traits, they were entered into the sample. In the 1948 election, Gallup predicted that Dewey had won, and large newspapers announced him as the winner. The *Chicago Daily Tribune*, for instance, ran the famous headline: "Dewey Defeats Truman." The problem was that the quota sampling method allowed people to self-select into the sample (i.e., respondents with certain traits were allowed to enter themselves in the poll). For various reasons, Dewey supporters were more likely to enter the sample. When all of the votes were counted, Truman was the actual winner. Quota sampling has since been replaced by simple random sampling, and the Gallup Poll has accurately predicted most elections since the early 1950s.

Another example of an election-prediction blunder occurred in the 2000 presidential election between George W. Bush and Al Gore. In that election, the result was extremely close and was decided by a few hundred votes in Florida. That year, several major television networks and news organizations, including ABC, CBS, and NBC, formed a consortium called the Voter News Service (VNS) to select the sample and predict the election as quickly as possible. The VNS used exit polls (i.e., polls of people who had just voted) and followed through on its mandate to make a quick prediction. Among other problems, there was a degree of self-selection into the sample that compromised the sample quality.

Unfortunately, the VNS reacted too quickly. First, it called Florida a win for Al Gore before some polls closed in the state's panhandle. Then the VNS called the election for George Bush. Eventually, it admitted it was too close to call. The final decision took nearly a month, and George Bush was declared the winner by a few thousand votes. However, critics argued that the incorrect prediction of the winner affected voter turnout and, therefore, the result of the election. One estimate predicted that as many as fifteen thousand did not vote because they thought the election had been decided.

The Bush–Gore election was one of the closest in U.S. history, and the mistaken prediction of the winner was only one of many errors that plagued the voting. Today's political polls are actually quite accurate and it is usually only in extremely close cases that there are problems. Yet, the mistaken predictions highlight what can happen when a sample is not representative of the population. We will never know how much they changed history.

Box 3.2 The Census: Population or Sample?

Should the U.S. census – that is, the decennial counting of all Americans – be conducted using a population or a sample? What may sound like an innocent statistical question has become the focus of heated public attention and has used considerable time in all three branches of the government surprisingly often.

At issue is whether a statistical sample of the type used in social-science research would produce more effective estimates of population size and attributes. The current strategy is for the Census Bureau to attempt to collect demographic information on every person in the country using at least a basic mail questionnaire (some people also complete a longer, more detailed survey). Many people never return their census forms, and sending census workers on multiple visits to unresponsive households is expensive. Moreover, it is accepted that the current method misses many people, including minorities, poor residents of inner cities, homeless people, and some immigrant groups. The alternative method involves selecting a sample and estimating population size and traits based on that information. The Census Bureau successfully uses samples in other surveys, but it is mandated by the Census Act of 1976 to use an entire population for the official decennial census.

The controversy arises because population estimates from the census are used to determine the size and shape of congressional districts. Democrats typically favor sampling because the people who are missed using the current method often vote Democrat; Republicans typically oppose sampling and note that the Constitution requires a census (or population survey). It is likely that

(*continued*)

Box 3.2 (*continued*)

the Republican position also is motivated by a fear that the party will lose congressional seats if the census determines that there are, indeed, more inner-city poor residents.

The issue erupted prior to the most recent census in 2000, and a federal court ruled that sampling was not allowed in that round. That census proceeded using the traditional method of attempting to contact every person in the country, but it also collected sample data. The Supreme Court determined that any changes in congressional seats that were scheduled for after the 2000 census must use the population data. Critics are already charging that the 2000 population data were flawed as they have been in the past, and they are preparing to revisit the issue in the 2010 census. The conclusion of this story certainly has not been written yet, and the 2010 census is likely to be an important stage for deciding the nature of that conclusion.

Key Concepts

Bimodal
Cluster sample
Concept
Conceptualization
Continuous variable
Convenience sample
Correlation
Data
Decile
Dependent variable
Descriptive statistics
Direct relationship
Discrete variable
Distribution
Ecological fallacy
Frequency distribution
Frequency table
Histogram
Hypothesis
Independent variable
Inferential statistics
Mean
Median
Mode
Negative correlation
Negative relationship
Negative skew

Operationalization
Outlier
Percentage
Percentile
Positive correlation
Positive relationship
Positive skew
Probability
Proportion
Quartile
Quintile
Range
Research design
Sample
Scatterplot
Scientific research
Scientific review
Secondary data
Simple random sample
Skew
Standard deviation
Statistics
Trimodal
Unit of analysis
Variable
Variance

Questions for Thought

1. Select any published article (or summary of one) that outlines a study related to stratification. Identify whether the authors followed the nine research-design steps. If not, which steps were omitted and how did this affect the findings? If so, were the findings believable?

2. What are the advantages and disadvantages of conducting research using secondary datasets collected by other researchers?
3. How could statistics be used to misrepresent facts or otherwise be misleading? Identify some strategies for detecting misleading statistical information.
4. Under what conditions might the prediction of an election by a polling organization affect the outcome of the election?
5. Should the census be conducted on the entire population or on a sample? List the pros and cons.

Exercises

1. *Sampling*
   Why do we sample? What are two advantages of sampling? What are some dangers of improper sampling?
2. *Concepts and Variables*
   What is the difference between a concept and a variable? How would you operationalize each of the following concepts?
   a. Alienation
   b. Poverty
   c. Modernization
3. *Skew*
   What are negatively and positively skewed distributions? Give real-life examples of each. Why is it important to know how skewed a distribution is?
4. *Descriptive Statistics*
   Calculate the mode, median, mean, range, variance, and standard deviation for the following and explain each measure in your own words.

   Percentage of People Living Below the Poverty Line, 2005

State	Percentage
Alabama	13
California	13
Louisiana	19
New Hampshire	7
Ohio	12
Washington, DC	18

   Source: 2004 American Communities Study, U.S. Department of the Census.

5. *Descriptive Statistics*
   Create a scatterplot for the following variables. Would you expect there to be a correlation between the variables? Would the correlation be positive or negative? Weak or strong?

Mother's Education	Daughter's Education
1	7
3	4
5	13
7	16
9	10
11	22
13	19
13	19

6. *Distributions*

A sociologist interested in philanthropy is studying how the wealthy contribute to charitable organizations. She finds that the mean contribution is $250, with a standard deviation of $50. What are the upper and lower bounds that define where 95 percent of the population falls in this distribution? If the sociologist finds a person who contributed $500, would she decide that this person is rare? Why?

Multimedia Resources

Print

Babbie, Earl. 2005. *The Basics of Social Research*. Belmont, CA: Thomson/Wadsworth.

Babbie, Earl, F. Halley, and J. Zaino. 2003. *Adventures in Social Research: Data Analysis Using SPSS*. Thousand Oaks; CA: Pine Forge Press.

Cohen, Bernard P. 1988. *Developing Sociological Knowledge: Theory and Method*. Belmont, CA: Wadsworth Publishing Company.

Frost, Peter J., and Ralph E. Stablein. 1992. *Doing Exemplary Research*. Newbury Park, CA: Sage Publications.

King, Gary, Robert O. Keohane, and Sidney Verba. 1994. *Designing Social Inquiry*. Princeton, NJ: Princeton University Press.

Stinchcombe, Arthur L. 2005. *The Logic of Social Research*. Chicago, IL: The University of Chicago Press.

Wallace, Walter. 1971. *The Logic of Science in Sociology*. Chicago: Aldine.

Most libraries have a large selection of the many statistics books available that provide varying levels of technical detail. Popular examples are as follows:

Elifson, Kirk W., Richard P. Runyon, and Audrey Haber. 1983. *Fundamentals of Social Statistics*. Boston, MA: Addison-Wesley.

Knoke, David, and George W. Bohrnstedt. 1991. *Basic Social Statistics*. Itasca, IL: Peacock.

Moore, David S., and George P. McCabe. 2004. *Introduction to the Practice of Statistics*. New York: W. H. Freeman and Company.

For an accessible and lighthearted approach to statistics, see:

Kranzler, Gerald, and Janet Moursund. 1998. *Statistics for the Terrified* (2nd edition). New York: Prentice Hall.

Internet

(1) Statistics Glossary available at www.cas.lancs.ac.uk/glossary_v1.1: A comprehensive glossary of statistical terms.

(2) Rice Virtual Lab in Statistics available at www.ruf.rice.edu/~lane/rvls.html: Includes a textbook, interactive demonstrations, case studies, and an analysis lab.

(3) Institute for Social Research (ISR) available at www.isr.umich.edu: Renowned statistics and survey research organization; Web site includes many links to statistics-related resources.

(4) Inter-university Consortium for Political and Social Research (ICPSR) available at www.icpsr. umich.edu: Stores data, helps researchers identify datasets, offers courses in statistical techniques.

(5) Datasets that include information on inequality are increasingly available and accessible online. Common datasets used by stratification researchers include the following:

- NLS available at www.bls.gov/nls/: Includes detailed demographic, educational, life transition, financial, employment, and other information about large samples that are interviewed biannually. Includes several different samples (i.e., cohorts) interviewed on different time schedules since the 1950s and 1960s.
- Panel Study of Income Dynamics (PSID) available at psidonline.isr.umich.edu/: Like the NLS, it includes detailed demographic, educational, life transition, financial, and other information for a large sample interviewed repeatedly since the 1960s.
- Survey of Consumer Finances (SCF) available at www.federalreserve.gov: Contains excellent data on wealth ownership and individual/household demographic information.
- Survey of Income and Program Participation (SIPP) available at www.sipp.census.gov/sipp. Contains data on household demographics and participation in government assistance programs; excellent information on historically poor and minority groups.
- U.S. Census available at www.census.gov. Contains data collected by the U.S. Census Bureau on topics such as housing, poverty, and health insurance.
- www.censusscope.org: Tool for analyzing census data.

(6) Most real-world statistical analysis is performed on computers because today's large datasets make manual calculations impractical. Widely used statistical software packages include the following:

- Minitab (Minitab, Inc., University Park, PA) available at www.minitab.com.
- SAS (SAS Institute, Inc., Cary, NC) available at www.sas.com.
- SPSS (SPSS, Inc., Chicago, IL) available at www.spss.com.
- SYSTAT (SYSTAT, Inc., Evanston, IL) available at www.systat.com.

Recommended Films

Against All Odds: Inside Statistics. 1989. This film series includes 26 separate films on unique topics in statistics. Topics of particular interest include What is statistics? (Program 1), Picturing Distributions (Program 2), Describing Distributions (Program 3), Normal Distributions (Program 4), Normal Calculations (Program 5), Describing Relationships (Program 8), Correlation (Program 9), What is probability? (Program 14), and Samples and Surveys (Program 15). *The Standard Deviants: Statistics.* Cerebellum Corporation. 1998. This is a three-part film series that intuitively conveys statistical ideas using dynamic animations, graphics, and illustrations. Part 1 (2005) covers basic topics such as central tendency, variance, and the difference between samples and populations. Part 2 (1998) is slightly more advanced and covers distributions, probability, and related topics. Part 3 (1998) is the most advanced segment, addressing hypothesis testing and other issues related to statistical inference.

Works Cited

Downey, Douglas B. 1995. "When Bigger Is Not Better: Family Size, Parental Resources, and Children's Educational Performance." *American Sociological Review* 60: 746–61.

NLS. 1979. "National Longitudinal Survey": U.S. Department of Labor, Bureau of Labor Statistics.

Robinson, William S. 1950. "Ecological Correlations and the Behavior of Individuals." *American Sociological Review* 15: 351–7.

4 Class and the Structure of Inequality

The notion of social class is fundamental to understanding the structure of inequality and stratification. Debates are ongoing about how to define and measure social class, which social classes exist in the United States, and how much class consciousness Americans have. There also are debates about whether social class or other personal traits – such as race, ethnicity, and gender – matter more for determining well-being. Despite these debates, however, there is widespread agreement that social class is extremely important. This chapter explores the most consequential dimensions of social class and addresses why social class might matter. The chapter begins by defining *social class* and exploring various meanings of *class*. Economic and cultural (or lifestyle) dimensions of class and how they differ are discussed next. Methods for identifying social classes and differences in estimates of the size of social classes that emerge are described. The process by which class and class characteristics are transmitted across generations is explored, and the chapter concludes with a discussion of the meaning and importance of *class consciousness*.

What Is a Social Class?

Most people have a sense of what social class is, and many of us occasionally mention class in everyday conversations. We understand that class is the basis on which societies are divided. We think about upper, middle, lower, and perhaps professional classes, and we have a sense of who falls into which group. We also have a sense of where we fit in the class structure. When researchers ask Americans which class they belong to, nearly everyone has an answer. Despite this general agreement about the basic concept of class, however, there is little consensus about the details regarding how classes are divided. That is, there is not complete agreement about questions such as whether groups like professionals comprise a unique class and whether we need fine gradations such as upper-upper class and lower-middle class (rather than simply upper class and middle class). There also is little agreement about whether people have an accurate sense of what class they belong to, whether class membership means anything to most people, and whether social class is an important determinant of other outcomes. For example, there is significant disagreement about whether the social class to which we are born determines outcomes such as adult income and education or other factors such as race/ethnicity and gender matter more. Sociologists and other social scientists disagree about the specifics of the definition of social class, how to measure class, and where to draw class boundaries.

Given all of these complications, we may wonder why anyone would think about stratification in terms of class. Why not just rely on continuous scales from high to low (e.g., high income to low income, or high wealth to low wealth) to discuss inequality? The first reason is that the continuous-scale approach suggests that it is possible to array people clearly across a wide range of values on relevant characteristics such as income, wealth, education, and occupation. In reality, that is unlikely because people tend to group together. There are a limited number of occupations, and people in those occupations generally have roughly the same education, income, and pattern of wealth ownership. We can try to circumvent this issue by identifying detailed occupational differences such as types of lawyers, ministers in different religious traditions, or teachers in private versus public schools. Yet, the patterns still emerge: Even when we use detailed occupational markers, people are generally similar in other status dimensions. As a result, clear groups are likely to emerge even in the most carefully executed ranking system.

The second reason to pursue the idea of groups is that the groups – or classes – can be meaningful to the people who are members of them. Naturally, the relevance of class identity varies across people, over time, and from place to place. We discuss this in more detail later in the chapter, but for now it is useful to be aware that class can be an important part of a person's identity. This suggests that people have a conception of class groups and, therefore, that the groups are real. To fully understand the definition and measurement of *class* and why debates arise regarding its meaning and implications, it is helpful to consider two dimensions: economic and cultural. We address those dimensions before considering how many classes there are, class consciousness, and implications of social class.

American Class Structure: Economic Dimensions

A common way to identify class position is to use economic traits. Recall from Chapter 1 that one way to define *social class* is as a group of people with common levels of relative wealth, income, occupation, and education. Social classes typically are relatively large groups of people who are similar to one another on these measures and distinct from others. Using economic characteristics to identify class is a relatively *objective method* of categorizing people. Sociologists often refer collectively to objective indicators of social class as *socioeconomic status* (*SES*). The process of grouping people based on these traits can be complicated because the measures are interrelated but not perfectly correlated, which leads to difficulty when deciding where one group ends and the other begins. For example, people with high incomes usually have high wealth because greater income makes it easier to save money.

Disagreements arise when identifying social classes because the relationships among these variables are not perfect. Imagine a retiree who has very low income because she is no longer working but high wealth because she saved money during her working years. We usually think of income and wealth as being positively related (i.e., if one is high, the other is high); however, that is not the case for this retiree. Similarly, a person who inherited a fortune may not need to work. This person might have relatively low income (e.g., in the form of dividends and interest) but high wealth. In contrast, imagine a surgeon who has high income but does not save money because he reasons that he will always be able to earn enough to support himself. His income is high but his wealth is low. Adding education and occupational prestige to the mix further complicates the scenario. Many high-prestige occupations pay high salaries (e.g., doctors, lawyers, and corporate presidents have high occupational prestige and typically high salaries); yet, some occupations have high prestige but generally low salaries – for example, clergy members, firefighters, nurses, and teachers. Likewise, education generally is associated with higher income, but it is possible to identify occupations that require high levels of education but do not pay particularly high salaries (e.g., teachers and college professors).

Although there are cases in which income, wealth, education, and occupational prestige are not highly correlated, they tend to be highly consistent for most people. This overlap makes it possible to identify a relatively unique and stable set of social classes, and various efforts in recent decades have produced fairly similar estimates of American class structure. An early effort to identify how many social classes exist in America – which is still relevant today – was made by W. Lloyd Warner. He and his students conducted a series of studies starting in the 1930s in communities in New England, the South, and the Midwest using interviews to identify social classes. Warner referred to one of the communities as Yankee City, a seaport near Boston that was once a center of commerce and whose residents' ancestors had lived there for 300 years. He noted that the interviews in Yankee City and other similar towns "were filled with references to 'the big people with money' and 'the little people who are poor'" (Warner and Lunt 1941: 26). He also pointed out that community members "assigned people to high status by referring to them as bankers, large property owners, people of high salary, and professional men, or placed people in a low status by calling them laborers, ditch diggers, and low-wage earners. Other similar economic terms were used, all to designate superior and inferior positions" (Warner and Lunt 1941: 26).

In the decades since Warner first conducted his community studies, other researchers confirmed that people rely heavily on economic measures to make determinations about social class. Many years after the Yankee City study became well known, Richard Coleman and Lee Rainwater, two of Warner's former students, replicated the community studies in larger cities and found that similar economic measures determine class divisions in those contexts as well (Coleman and Rainwater 1978). Some details of the class structure they outlined in a book titled *Social Standing in America: New Dimensions of Class* differed from Warner's, but Coleman and Rainwater agreed with the earlier work that the level of occupational prestige, education, and income provided the basis for class divisions in America. Their book also included interesting findings about how the determinants of class are related to one another (Coleman and Rainwater 1978; Wright 1980). For example, the authors showed that up to nearly four times per capita household income (i.e., about $14,000 in 1971), income and income status are roughly linear, which means that as household income increases, so does the status associated with that income. If income increases by 10 percent, status increases by 10 percent; if income doubles, status doubles. However, at income levels above four times per capita household income (i.e., for the richest households in the population), the relationship is much weaker. In the relatively rich households, if income increases by a dollar, the status associated with that income increases only by the square root of income. Thus, people at the top of the income distribution do not gain as much as people lower in the distribution when income increases.

Another significant finding reported by Coleman and Rainwater is that income is the most important component of overall status (Coleman and Rainwater 1978; Wright 1980). They found that if income doubles, overall status increases by nearly 50 percent, even if occupational and education status stay the same. In contrast, if occupational status were to double, overall status would increase by only 22 percent. If education status doubled, overall status would increase by only 7 percent. This does not imply that income is the central *cause* of overall status because, for example, education determines both occupational status and income status; therefore, it is a much stronger cause of total status. However, the finding suggests that income was the decisive factor used by the people in Coleman and Rainwater's study to assess status. Other scholars criticized Coleman and Rainwater for issues such as a lack of theoretical precision and how they gathered and analyzed their data (Wright 1980). However – and perhaps most important – the model that Coleman and Rainwater developed still is used widely today to describe American class structure (Gilbert 2003; Thompson and Hickey 2005). Moreover, as discussed in the next section, the class boundaries that Coleman and Rainwater identified are also useful for describing subjective features of social class in contemporary America.

American Class Structure: Cultural Dimensions

In addition to economic traits, there is an equally important cultural, or behavioral, component to social class. *Cultural elements* are the behaviors, lifestyles, attitudes, beliefs, and preferences common among members of the same social class. These characteristics can be used to provide a more *subjective definition* of social classes that is comparable – but perhaps not identical – to the definition that emerges when economic indicators are used. Although the cultural component is real, it is more difficult to measure than economic traits and, therefore, contributes to disagreements about where to draw class boundaries. The cultural dimension of class reflects the physical and social environments shared by members of the same class and may contribute to creating consistent approaches to and views of the world. The contrast between people from extremely different classes illustrates the differences that environment can make on lifestyle. For example, a person from a very poor class may face financial uncertainty, lack job autonomy, and live in an unpleasant or unsafe environment.

These conditions can contribute to a negative worldview and a pessimistic approach to the future. In contrast, a person from a wealthy or upper class context is likely to experience life very differently. Financial security, an occupation that provides power and autonomy, and the ability to buy enjoyable things and live in a comfortable environment contribute to a more positive approach to life and a more optimistic worldview.

What types of behaviors and preferences are included in subjective definitions of social class? Examples include speech patterns, leisure activities, home-decorating styles, and preferences in music, clothing, food, beverages, vehicles, and other consumer products that vary in predictable ways with social class. Imagine, for example, that we are asked to identify the behaviors and preferences associated with the upper class. We might think about the types of homes that wealthy people own, the schools and universities they attend, the vacation locales they frequent, the sports they participate in, and the jobs they are likely to hold. We also might imagine the foods and beverages that wealthy people eat and drink and the automobiles they drive. Similarly, we could identify behaviors and preferences more often associated with the middle, working, and poor classes. If we had information only on cultural or behavioral indicators, we could arrange people in distinct groups similar to the way we did with economic indicators. Moreover, the groups we identified would be similar to those that emerge when we rely exclusively on economic indicators. Naturally, there is variation in any population, and not all upper-class people drive the same type of vehicle, live in the same neighborhood, or prefer the same style of clothing; however, general patterns often are sufficient to identify fairly distinct groups. These patterns suggest that there is more to social class than simply statistical differences in economic measures.

Class-specific behaviors and preferences are sometimes referred to as *cultural capital* (Bourdieu 1986; Lamont and Lareau 1988). The term often is used to imply knowledge of or comfort with "high-brow" or upper-class behaviors, activities, and tastes. Yet, it also is used to refer to the unique cultural repertoire of the middle, working, and poor classes. Cultural capital includes both formal knowledge (i.e., knowledge gained in schools and universities) and informal knowledge (e.g., knowledge gained through less-structured interactions). It can include formal credentials, such as holding a particular advanced degree, as well as status markers that are not the result of formal training. Lamont and Lareau used familiarity with wine as an example (Lamont and Lareau 1988: 156). They noted that high-status cultural capital includes having a certain attitude toward wine (i.e., knowing a good wine is important), knowing how to drink and evaluate wine, having the confidence to have slightly unique preferences in wine (e.g., liking one that is not popular), being able to tastefully yet conspicuously consume wine, and perhaps owning good wine in a wine cellar. Cultural capital is distinct from *financial capital*, which refers to economic resources. Like financial capital, however, cultural capital can be used to identify a person as understanding the behaviors and traits necessary to be considered part of a particular group. Cultural capital can be traded and leveraged much like economic resources, making it an important component of class membership. Moreover, like financial capital, cultural capital can be used to exclude outsiders from sharing in desirable outcomes (Lamont and Lareau 1988).

Economic and cultural indicators of class (e.g., financial and cultural capital) are distinct concepts, but they are related in important ways. For example, it is more expensive to play polo (which requires a horse, riding lessons, and other expensive equipment) than to play basketball (which can be played with a ball and a hoop). Similarly, it is expensive to sail the Caribbean, live in an exclusive neighborhood, have dinner at the Four Seasons Hotel in New York City, attend the ballet, and drive a Bentley. It is less expensive to go tent-camping for vacation, live in a modest neighborhood, eat casseroles at home, and drive an affordable car such as a Ford Escort. In other words, engaging in many of the behaviors associated with the upper class can be financially demanding. As a result, behaviors, preferences, and consumption patterns often correspond to a person's level of income and wealth. Weber referred to this correspondence when he defined *status groups*. Weber's notion of class refers to material resources, whereas his notion of status indicates a person's position in the social order and is defined by consumption, social interests, and other aspects of lifestyle (see Chapter 2). Weber emphasized that class and status are distinct concepts but they are related for the reasons discussed in this chapter.

The relationship between financial capital and cultural capital is not always precise, but it becomes apparent when a person changes social class – particularly if the change is a result of an adjustment in financial capital. Imagine a person who gains financial capital relatively quickly because she started a successful business or won the lottery. That is, the person suddenly has much higher wealth or income than in the recent past. Her financial resources may quickly move her up to a relatively high social class, but her cultural capital may not increase as rapidly. The person may be able to afford to live or vacation with other wealthy people, but the newly rich person may not have the same cultural capital as the others. Although cultural capital can change when a person changes social class, it often does not change as quickly as financial capital because the norms that generate cultural capital are deeply ingrained from early in life. As a result, the typical correspondence between financial and cultural capital is weaker. The distinction between "old money" and the "newly rich" – a difference that can be used derogatorily to imply cultural inferiority – reflects this discontinuity.

American Class Structure: Identifying Classes

Clearly, numerous economic and cultural factors contribute to class composition, but how do we decide how many classes exist? Moreover, what determines where the boundaries fall between classes? One conclusion that students may be drawing correctly at this point is that identifying class boundaries is not a precise science. It is possible to make factual claims about many of the components of class such as average income and wealth ownership, and it is also possible to identify where people fall relative to those averages. We can attach a numerical value to the prestige associated with an occupation. However, synthesizing this information and using it with information about lifestyle to generalize about class boundaries is ultimately a subjective process that reflects the unique perspectives of the person making the judgments. Early social scientists agreed that devising a simple method to identify class structures would be useful for understanding much of human social behavior. Since the early days of American sociology, social class has been measured in various ways. Although the approaches and details vary, the underlying class structure that emerges has consistent traits. In this section, we review dominant methods of identifying social class and discuss important contributions to articulating detailed class structures.

Methods of Identifying Class

Methods of identifying the number and size of social classes can be divided into three general categories: *objective*, *subjective*, and *reputational* approaches. Objective methods of identifying classes use measures such as income, wealth, education, and occupation either alone or together to identify groups of people who constitute social classes. Objective approaches attempt to use information that is personal but that is not influenced by personal opinion or evaluation to identify class boundaries. An early attempt to use objective information to identify class was a residential approach. Researchers from an ecological school, many of whom were from the University of Chicago, used information about the places where people lived in a city to identify class groupings (Frazier 1932; Zorbach 1929). This approach assumed that people lived near others of the same social class; it was limited by the fact that class and geography do not always correspond perfectly. Another early example of a method that used objective information to identify class was occupational prestige ranking. These methods used a person's evaluation of the prestige associated with an occupation to identify occupational status and associated groupings of occupations to create class boundaries (Duncan 1961).

Contemporary objective methods are more likely to use socioeconomic data to identify class groups. For example, a researcher might use survey data on status measures to identify a ranking of people and then look for logical boundaries or groupings that suggest class limits. Contemporary objective measures of class identification have the advantage of not being biased by people's misconceptions of their position in a social or economic ranking system. It also is relatively easy to objectively identify social classes using information available in numerous surveys. These methods do not require any special information beyond basic demographics, which tend to be repeated in most social and economic surveys. A major disadvantage of objective methods to identify class is that they seldom include cultural or lifestyle elements. As discussed previously, there are important differences across social classes in behaviors and other elements of lifestyle that are difficult to measure. It is possible to include indicators that tend to vary, such as consumption patterns (e.g., amount of money spent on certain foods and products), time spent engaged in certain activities (e.g., vacations at five-star resorts versus less-expensive vacations), and class-specific factual knowledge (e.g., knowledge of wine and food pairings) in an objective measure of class. However, this information is more difficult to find in surveys, is generally less reliable than other objective measures (e.g., income and education), and does not necessarily correspond precisely with class.

Subjective methods of identifying classes allow individuals to identify their own social class. For example, a survey that asks "Do you consider yourself part of the upper class, the middle class, the working class, or the poor class?" is an example of a subjective method for identifying social class. Such a survey assumes that respondents understand the meaning of class and the particular classes identified in the question, and that they have a conception of their own position in the class structure. Indeed, when surveys include questions of this type, the majority of respondents are able to answer the question, suggesting that they have at least a basic concept of class and their own position.[1] Subjective measures also assume that there is utility in allowing people to self-identify with a social class rather than assigning them to a group based exclusively on their income, wealth, education, and occupation regardless of their identity. The advantage of subjective measures of class identification is the inclusion of information about individuals beyond numerical data, including information about lifestyle that can be used alone or in conjunction with objective measures. This is important, for example, for people who may have changed position in an objective ranking of social status (e.g., moved from beyond low income in childhood to higher income in adulthood) but who continue to identify with a prior social class (e.g., still consider themselves to be part of the working class). Unfortunately, it is more difficult to obtain data on subjective class ranking; standard social and economic surveys rarely contain this information because it is time-consuming and resource-intensive to collect. Moreover, even when surveys do contain subjective class evaluations, a person's self-evaluation may vary over time depending on mood, length of the survey, or framing of the question.

Reputational methods of identifying classes use yet another strategy to identify the number and size of social classes. They rely on other people to identify people's social class. Typically, selected informants make judgments about the social-class membership of other people in the community. These methods have been used most often to identify members of the upper classes who may be missed or under-represented in social and economic surveys because of their small numbers. Warner is credited with developing this approach in his Yankee City studies discussed previously (Warner 1963). In those studies, Warner and his collaborators used extensive observation of and participation in the community in conjunction with direct questioning to identify the status that people assigned to their peers. A contemporary example of a reputational approach to class identification was a study conducted in Columbus, Ohio that identified a small number of elites based on objective measures and then asked those early respondents to identify other elites, who would later become part of the same survey (Keister and Cornwell 2009). Similar to subjective methods, reputational methods have the benefit of including information about individuals other than numeric data. Another advantage of reputational methods is inclusion of information about the social standing of a person or a family. However, collecting reputational class data is time-consuming and subject to variation resulting from factors external to the survey (e.g., a respondent's mood).

How Many Class Groups?

Similar to variation in the methods used to identify social class, there is variation in the number and nature of classes identified. Warner and Lunt developed one of the first models of social class (Warner 1949; Warner and Lunt 1941). It was the result of detailed

---

[1] The General Social Survey is an example of an annual, nationally representative survey of Americans that asks respondents to identify their position in the class structure.

ethnographic research that Warner oversaw (described previously) and incorporates ob-jective class measures (e.g., wealth and inheritance, amount of income and income sources, education, and home value) and subjective class measures (e.g., social skills). Warner proposed six distinct classes in the United States, as follows:

Upper-upper class: This class is composed of old-money families, an elite that has sufficient wealth to live in the most prestigious neighborhoods. Wealth for this class has been in the family for at least a generation but probably longer. Families with connections to European nobility are included. Generational continuity ensured proper social training and indoctrination into society.

Lower-upper class: This class is composed of new-money families and also can be con-sidered elite; however, because they were not born into the upper-upper class, they are considered a separate, lower group. This group includes entrepreneurs, celebri-ties, athletes, and some professionals with exceptional wealth.

Upper-middle class: This class is composed of professionals, business people, politi-cians, and others with high levels of education, relatively high incomes, and some wealth. Members of the upper-middle class typically have advanced degrees, in-cluding MBAs, PhDs, MDs, and JDs. Education and social skills are important but family lineage does not matter. Doctors, dentists, bankers, corporate executives, college and university professors, pharmacists, and high-level civil servants are included here.

Lower-middle class: This class includes lower-paid white-collar workers such as own-ers of small businesses, schoolteachers, administrative assistants, engineers, ac-countants, nurses, sales representatives, clergy, and technicians. This group does not include manual laborers; rather, it refers to the class slightly above manual laborers.

Upper-lower class: This class includes members of the working class; that is, manual laborers and blue-collar workers. Warner referred to these people as respectable members of society who held jobs, kept their houses clean, and stayed out of trou-ble.

Lower-lower class: This class is the truly poor and includes homeless people, those who are permanently unemployed, and the working poor. Families who depend on pub-lic assistance are included here.

Warner and his colleagues proposed that the boundaries between these classes were clear and the groups were well established. They identified behaviors and lifestyle traits typical of members of these classes, and they discussed the social clubs that class mem-bers were likely to join. As this description of class structure suggests, the classes became obvious to the researchers after they spent considerable time in the community listening to residents and attempting to map local social structure and rankings. However, most people in the community could not have described the class structure as well, nor could they have accurately placed themselves in the structure. In this way, the people studied by Warner and his colleagues were much like Americans today.

Another early attempt to identify the number of social classes was in Davis, Gardner, and Gardner's (1941) *Deep South: A Social-Anthropological Study of Caste and Class.*

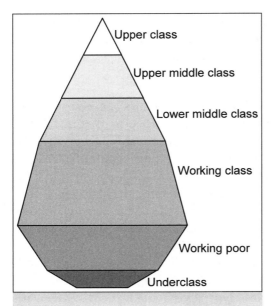

Upper class

Upper middle class

Lower middle class

Working class

Working poor

Underclass

Figure 4.1 The American class structure.

Warner's colleagues started with the hypothesis that class structure looked different depending on one's position in it. That is, people at the top are likely to describe a different map of social structure than those at the bottom. Their research confirmed this expectation and identified variation in perspectives on the nature of class given one's position. Figure 4.1 shows how each class depicts the class structure. As suggested by the figure, there are similarities across class in their sense of the social structure and the number of classes in the community. However, the groups identified different numbers of classes and routinely provided greater detail at levels close to their own and less detail at levels farther away. Moreover, although there were significant differences in the labels that people used to describe the classes, they agreed on the placement of particular families. In other words, upper-upper-class members and lower-lower-class members may have labeled the upper classes differently, but they agreed on the placement of families within those classes. Finally, there were important differences in the reasons that people gave for their placement of families within the social structure. Upper-class people, for example, were more likely to use time (e.g., "old money" versus "new money") as a basis for distinguishing among families. In contrast, middle-class people relied more on moral issues (i.e., where people "should be") in describing social position. Lower-class people articulated a ranking based more clearly on wealth than other respondents.

Coleman and Rainwater, Warner's students, developed their own map of the social classes based on their research in Boston and Kansas City (Coleman and Rainwater 1978). Table 4.1 summarizes the detailed class structure that they produced from their research. As suggested in the table, the basic classes that comprise this schema are similar to those used by Warner and his colleagues but with important differences. Coleman and Rainwater used

Table 4.1. Social Perspective and Social Class.

Upper-Upper Class/Lower-Upper Class

"Old Aristocracy"	UU	"Old Aristocracy"	
"Aristocracy, but not old"	LU	"Aristocracy, but not old"	
"Nice, respectable people"	UM	"Nice, respectable people"	
"Good people, but 'nobody'"	LM	"Good people, but 'nobody'"	
"Po' whites"	UL	"Po' whites"	
	LL		

Upper-Middle Class/Lower-Middle Class

"Old Families" "Society"	UU	"Old aristocracy" (older)	"Broken-down aristocracy" (younger)
"Society" but Not "old families"	LU		
"People who should be upper class"	UM	"Nice, respectable people"	
"People who don't have much money"	LM	"Good people, but 'nobody'"	
"No 'count lot"	UL	"Po' whites"	
	LL		

Upper-Middle Class/Lower-Middle Class

"Society" or	UU	"Society" or
the "folks with money"	LU	the "folks with money"
"People who are up because they have a little money"	UM	"Way-high-ups," but not "society"
"Poor but honest folk"	LM	"Snobs trying to push up"
"Shiftless people"	UL	"People just as good as anybody"
	LL	

Source: Davis, Gardner, and Gardner (1941). Reprinted with permission.

both subjective and objective information about families (e.g., income, wealth, education, and occupation) to identify the following seven predominant groups:

1. *Upper Americans*

   Upper-upper: These people typically have inherited their wealth and have high incomes and advanced or professional degrees. Their education is likely from Ivy League or other elite universities. These generally are the old-money families who may serve as board chairmen or in another capacity as owners of large corporations.

   Lower-upper: These are top professionals and senior executives in large corporations. They also have high wealth and income but they are likely to have earned and accumulated rather than inherited these resources. They are likely to have graduated from good colleges and to have advanced or professional degrees.

Upper-middle: These people are middle-level professionals and managers with college degrees and moderate to high income and wealth.

2. *Middle Americans*

Middle class: These people are lower-level managers, owners of small businesses, and other lower-status professionals such as teachers, sales clerks, pharmacists, and technicians. They are likely to have high school diplomas and may have some college; their incomes are at the median.

Working class: These are blue-collar workers such as craftsmen and lower-paid sales and clerical workers. They generally have high school diplomas and moderate to low incomes.

3. *Lower Americans*

Upper-lower: These are semi-poor people, unskilled laborers, and service workers. They may have high school diplomas but may have left high school before graduation. Their incomes are below average.

Lower-lower: This is the truly poor class of people who are likely to be unemployed and/or dependent on government-transfer payments. They may have some high school but could have less education. Their income is low.

Coleman and Rainwater provided precise estimates of family income for each group and specified the percentage of the population that falls into each category. For instance, they estimated that about 2 percent of the population falls into the upper-upper or the lower-upper class, 19 percent in the upper-middle class, 13 percent in the upper-lower or lower-lower class, and the remainder in the middle class. Although these percentages are likely to be different today, the distribution is similar (i.e., there are still few people in the upper classes and a larger proportion in the middle- and lower-class groups). As shown, the details vary between the Warner and the Coleman–Rainwater models, but the general structure identified was similar – even though decades had elapsed between the studies.

What does the class structure look like today? As in earlier eras, it is still difficult to state unequivocally how many classes exist, where the boundaries should be drawn, and who falls where in the distribution. Yet, there is still considerable agreement that the basic structure of social classes has not changed markedly since the Warner and Coleman–Rainwater studies. For instance, contemporary efforts to identify nationally the class structure suggest that the upper class (or capitalists) account for about 1 percent of the population, the upper-middle class is 14 percent, the middle and working classes comprise about 60 percent of the population, and the working poor and underclass account for the remaining 25 percent (Gilbert 2003). For the remainder of this book, we refer to the contemporary depiction of the class structure illustrated in Figure 4.1, which is based on the model that Gilbert and his colleagues proposed (Gilbert 2003). Although there is no single, accurate class schema, this map reflects much of what contemporary social scientists accept about the nature of social class. The figure obscures many important details about the various classes. We revisit the nature and meaning of class differences in Chapter 4 (upper class), Chapter 5 (middle class), and Chapter 6 (working class).

Transmission of Class

A remarkable characteristic of the various efforts to map the nature of social class in different historical periods is the amount of similarity that researchers identify in the basic class structure – that is, the class structure is rigid. When we review the Warner and Coleman–Rainwater approaches, for instance, we note that there is considerable similarity even though these social maps are based on studies that occurred decades apart. Likewise, when we review contemporary research on class structure, we observe that the same classes emerge. Of course, there are differences in the details proposed – recall the variation on class structure that Wright proposed using a contemporary Marxist approach (see Chapter 2). By and large, however, there is little variation in the structure of the classes. Moreover, many argue that members of the same families occupy similar positions in the structure over time. Early research suggested that children do not stray far from their parents in terms of occupation and income (Blau and Duncan 1967). Contemporary evidence suggests that there is considerable similarity across generations in occupation, income, education, wealth, and even consumption (i.e., what people buy) (Keister 2005; Mulligan 1997). That is, if we want to know how one will fare on any of these dimensions, we do not have to look much farther than one's parents. We discuss whether there is change in Chapter 8; for now, it is sufficient to note the persistence of class structure over time.

The general term for this process is the *intergenerational transmission of class* – that is, the process by which parents and other adults affect the social class that children ultimately will join. The term *social reproduction* refers to the process by which social class is re-created from generation to generation through conscious and unintentional practices, behaviors, and social connections. Both the objective (i.e., financial, work-related, and educational) and subjective (i.e., lifestyle and behavioral) characteristics that are markers for social class in any generation were conditioned by the same traits in prior generations. Distinct behaviors and preferences result from common social and physical conditions that people of different classes experience throughout their life. Family, neighborhood, school, and work environments all contribute to the conveyance of class-specific information. The process by which this occurs attracts considerable research attention across the social sciences. Although we are beginning to understand how parents and other adults pass along class traits, there are many parts of the process only vaguely understood. An important remaining debate is the degree to which social reproduction occurs consciously versus through behaviors and processes of which neither parents nor children are aware.

Which factors account for similarity in class structure over time? Some argue that upper-class parents deliberately use their power and financial resources to cultivate behaviors and attitudes in their children to ensure that they also will enjoy privileged positions and to consciously re-create social class across generations. An early study proposed that upper-class children learn to perceive themselves not just as individuals but also as an important link in "the development of a historical family" (Caven 1969). Even if this same sense of history is replicated in the middle and lower classes, the upper classes have the resources to ensure at least a degree of financial similarity across generations. Those who perceive upper-class parents as re-creating social class suggest that elite parents, particularly mothers, deliberately cultivate proper attitudes, behaviors, and social connections in their children in an effort to perpetuate class. Upper-class women are "the mistresses of the social institutions that keep this collection of rich families in intermarrying social class. In other words, they are the gatekeepers and caretakers of upper-class societal institutions" (Domhoff 1970: 39–41). The re-creation of social class also involves fathers, of course, as in the exercise of self-control that Cookson and Persell (1985) argued is involved in social reproduction:

> When we think of power and the exercise of social control, we are apt to think of a higher person or group imposing themselves on a lower person or group. We are less apt to think of how those in power must exercise social control over themselves and their children. Sacrifices must be made, and upper-class fathers, in particular, have been willing to sacrifice their sons and their lives for the sake of their class.

They proposed that the upper class willingly undergoes a lifetime of personal denial and regulation to ensure the perpetuation of social class from generation to generation. They argued that the loss of self experienced by the upper classes is compensated for by an acquisition of character. Specifically, self-denial leads to a character that has strong self-discipline and is fair at least to those of equal social stature (Cookson and Persell 1985: 25).

Others who argue that the upper classes deliberately re-create social class point to the role of philanthropy and other "good deeds" in this process. According to this argument, the upper class – particularly upper-class women – engage in philanthropy not only to benefit the needy but also to benefit themselves and their families in current and future generations (Kendall 2002; Ostrower 1995). Gifts of time and money ensure that a family enjoys current social prestige and that their children and grandchildren also will be assured a place among the elite. Ostrower interviewed wealthy philanthropists in the New York City area about the motivations of the donors and the implications of their contributions. Although she emphasized that motivation varies dramatically across individuals and families, she also argued that making a substantial financial contribution involves more than simply writing a check. Improving and maintaining a family's social position is a common motive that can contribute to social reproduction. In addition, many wealthy donors are motivated by preserving the organizations that contribute to the current class structure. Supporting elite schools and colleges, for instance, that impart similar values may ensure that wealthy families maintain their upper-class status in future generations. Ostrower pointed out that

> although donors themselves may be influenced by concerns about the fate of their own individual fortune, name, and favorite causes when making bequests, the class consequences of their decisions should also be emphasized. Philanthropic bequests represent a potential vehicle for passing wealth on to support institutions and values central to the elite, thereby preserving these for future generations (1995: 101).

Similarly, Kendall (2002) proposed that upper-class women use their social power not only to benefit others but also to legitimize and maintain elements of the class structure.

Yet, social reproduction also is likely to occur through less deliberate processes. Upper-class socialization generally involves exposure to behaviors, lifestyles, and social connections that are not accessible to lower classes. Elite private education, domestic employees, travel on private jets to exotic locales, and other experiences that require significant financial capital simply are not part of the experience of those born to any other than the very upper classes. Exposure to these experiences unconsciously transmits information to children that contributes to the perpetuation of class across generations.

Occupation is one of the most important class characteristics that influence the intergenerational transmission of class. Parents with high-prestige occupations are likely to have children with high-prestige occupations (Blau and Duncan 1967; Duncan and Hodge 1963; Kohn 1959a). High-prestige occupations usually are associated with other benefits such as financial security, including high salaries and valuable benefits, political influence, and social status. A high-prestige occupation usually also implies a degree of authority over others in the workplace, task autonomy, job stability, and opportunities for advancement and career development. Authority and autonomy in the workplace affect both the experience of work and a person's ability to affect future employment. Opportunities for advancement and career development provide those in the upper and upper-middle classes with structured opportunities to progress further in their fields and to improve their financial security. At the other end of the spectrum, those in the lower classes generally have little financial security, no political influence, low social status, minimal authority, and few opportunities for advancement.

Although the advantages and disadvantages of occupation for a single generation are clear, there also are intergenerational implications of variation in occupational benefits. Sociologists proposed the *learning-generalization hypothesis* to describe how lessons learned in part of life (e.g., work) affect behaviors and outcomes in other realms (Kohn and Schooler 1983). A large body of research on this hypothesis shows that experiences related to work and career can affect a person's perspectives and values well beyond the workplace. Indeed, work and occupation can influence more generally and even dominate a person's social values and orientations, self-concept, and intellectual functioning. Through its effect on values and orientations, occupation and job experiences affect how parents interact with their children, thereby shaping their experiences, their values and orientations, and – ultimately – their social class. Kohn, a pioneer in this research that started in the 1950s, focused on the role of self-direction in the workplace in shaping a person's broader social values and, ultimately, the transmission of social class. Throughout multiple decades, Kohn and his colleagues showed that occupational traits and the experience of work are influential in shaping a range of outcomes such as parental values (Kohn 1959a), parental exercise of authority (Kohn 1959b), parent–child relationships (Kohn 1963), the allocation of parental responsibilities (Kohn and Carroll 1960), psychological functioning (Kohn and Schooler 1973), and a range of other important outcomes in the United States and other countries (Kohn and Schooler 1983; Kohn and Slomczynski 2001; Kohn, Slomczynski, Janicka, et al. 1997).

Childrearing practices also vary by class, transmitting class-specific behaviors in less deliberate ways. Lareau showed that middle- and upper-class parents are more likely to engage in the process of *concerted cultivation*, which refers to efforts to foster children's talents through organized leisure activities and reasoning (Lareau 2002, 2003). Middle- and upper-class parents are likely to reason with their children and to ensure that they participate in a variety of organized activities, such as piano lessons, sports practice, and classes to improve their academic performance. Lareau's research showed that concerted cultivation leads children to question and develop a sense of entitlement that affects their behavior in school, college, and work. In contrast, children from lower classes generally have more unstructured leisure time characterized by child-initiated play with friends rather than organized, adult-lead activities. Lower-class parents also tend to engage their children in discussion less often and to resort to reasoning less frequently. This parenting style is called the *accomplishment of natural growth*; it conveys different information to children and is less likely to lead to a sense of entitlement.

Although much of social reproduction takes place in families, experiences outside the family contribute to the process as well. Schools, for example, have an important role in re-creating social class from generation to generation. Upper-class families have access to an elite education starting with early education and continuing through university and graduate school. This elite education can ensure access to a position at the top of the stratification system. In elite boarding schools, preparatory schools, and universities, students learn class-appropriate behaviors and develop useful social connections that virtually ensure they will continue in the upper class (Cookson 1997; Cookson and Persell 1985). This implies that it matters *where* one goes to school, not just how much education is received (Persell and Cookson 1985). Elite boarding schools, for example, provide comprehensive training that dramatically increases the likelihood of entry into the elite worlds of business, government, and the arts.

> By isolating students from the natural environment, the family community, the schools are also able to intervene in the adolescent growth process, and a result of which the schools hope will be intellectual and psychic transformation of their students. By stripping away the students' private selves, they are more easily able to socialize them (Cookson and Persell 1985: 20).

Through a complex process of training, advocacy, and the use of social connections, elite boarding schools prepare students for a level of success that is not available – at least, not readily – to members of other social classes. Students who attend elite boarding schools, for instance, are more likely to be accepted at and to attend Ivy League universities, ultimately landing jobs in prestigious companies and other organizations (Cookson and Persell 1985).

What happens in the working class to perpetuate class structure? In a classic study of the relationship between education and adult employment, Willis argued that working-class young people are trained to do working-class jobs (Willis 1981). Willis started his study by asking why it is that middle-class young people are *allowed* to get middle-class jobs. He asks why others let them take these jobs, and he also asks why working-class young people let themselves take working-class jobs. He is unwilling to admit that they simply have no other choice. Willis acknowledged that there now are societies – and there have been historically – in which people's occupations are determined by powers other than the individual. However, the society he studied (i.e., Great Britain in the 1970s), similar to contemporary American society, applied no obvious physical coercion that would limit a person's self-direction. Part of the answer is that working-class children attend schools where they learn skills necessary for working-class jobs. Unlike the children of upper-class families, there is no concerted effort in working-class schools to ensure entry into an elite occupation and lifestyle. Yet, Willis argued, it is not simply that the educational system fails the working class but also that students in working-class schools deliberately withdraw, recognizing the inevitability of no other option than to take a working-class job. Neither is the solution a simple difference in aspirations or motivation. In a similar and more recent study of two groups of students in an American school, MacLeod argued that despite their different aspirations, both groups of teenagers that he studied ultimately found themselves in low-paying factory or service jobs (MacLeod 1995). MacLeod concluded that the students he studied "illustrate how rigid and durable the class structure is. Aspiration, application, and intelligence often fail to cut through the foundations of structural inequality" (1995: 241).

Class Consciousness

Recall from Chapter 2 that class consciousness was central to Marx's ideas about class conflict and historical materialism. Throughout our discussion of class in this chapter, we reference a person's recognition of class and class structure. However, we have not yet asked specifically: Do Americans have class consciousness? *Class consciousness* is a general term that refers to a person's perception of class and his or her own position in the class structure. Class consciousness is composed of at least four subconcepts that range from basic acknowledgment of the existence of classes to action based on strong feelings of membership in a class group. Although these terms are similar to the concepts that Marx and other early social scientists used, they assume different meanings in contemporary society.

Class awareness is the most basic level of class consciousness; it implies only a cursory recognition of the existence of social classes and presumes no ability to place oneself in that structure. *Class identification* suggests a greater degree of self-recognition; it implies both an awareness of the presence of social classes and an ability to place oneself in the class structure. *Class solidarity* refers to an even stronger concept of class consciousness: A person who feels class solidarity shares interests, values, and desires with other members of the class group. Class solidarity also tends to imply awareness of other classes as *out-groups*. Finally, *class action* refers to the strongest degree of class consciousness that leads to behaviors or actions taken on behalf of the class group.

One reason that people question whether Americans have class consciousness is the predominance of the ideology of individualism in the United States. Some argue that the denial of the existence of classes reduces feelings of guilt about the extent to which American society is unequal. Denying the existence of social classes also reduces attention that otherwise might be focused on the advantages of inherited wealth and privileges associated with inheritance. Some propose that media coverage about the difficulties that celebrities face (e.g., pregnancies, divorces, and family problems) reduces class awareness by implying that even those who are rich experience the same troubles as those in the lower classes (Rothman 2005). Despite these challenges, however, there is evidence that most Americans are aware of social class and their own position in the class structure. Social scientists have studied class divisions since at least the 1930s (Centers 1949; Davis, Gardner, and Gardner 1941; Parsons 1937; Warner and Lunt 1941). Since then, they consistently have found evidence of class awareness, identification, and a degree of solidarity (Collom 2003; Davis, Gardner, and Gardner 1941; Warner and Lunt 1941). Only a small percentage – typically less than 2 or 3 percent – claim that America is classless (Zeller 2000).

Although class awareness and even class identification may be common in the United States, class action is not. One reason is that labor unions and political parties – two organizations that might encourage class action – focus more on issues that attract interest from across classes rather than a single class. The role of labor unions in particular has declined in recent decades. Despite employer resistance to labor-union movements, membership was strong in the early part of the twentieth century, particularly during and following the Great Depression. However, membership began to decline in the 1970s; currently, only about 15 percent of the workforce is in a labor union. Union membership in Western European countries, in contrast, ranges from about 30 percent in Germany to almost 90 percent in Sweden. One common reason given for the low interest in union membership in the United States is that labor unions suffer from a "free-rider" problem. That is, high union-negotiated wages are available to all workers regardless of their individual union status, and union membership involves costs, including membership dues, as well as nonfinancial costs, including the stigma attached to membership. As a result, many workers join unions only if they perceive a benefit that they otherwise would not receive (Booth and Bryan 2004).

Labor unions and political parties are not the only challenges to class consciousness and class action in the United States. Marriage across class lines, for example, is common, which implies that a single family may have members of multiple classes. In addition, because women often earn lower wages than men, a couple that originated in the same social class may be placed in different classes on certain objective measures. These family differences alone can dramatically reduce class identification and class action. In addition, America's history of relative prosperity has been credited with reducing class identification. Although Americans have experienced poverty, there has never been a period of widespread and dramatic deprivation that would lead to the type of class action that Marx referenced in his theoretical writings. Again, an ethos of individualism leads Americans to believe that individual talent and motivation – rather than class – are the most important determinants of success and upward mobility. This ethos is caused and strengthened by a history of immigration from around the world. Social mobility is discussed in more depth in Chapter 8, but it is important to point out that there is movement among the income and wealth distributions during and between generations. This social mobility further contributes to minimum levels of class identification and class action in the United States. If social mobility were less common, or if it were perceived to be less common, class identification would likely be stronger.

Summary

(1) There is general agreement that classes exist, but there is little consensus about the details of class groupings.

(2) A common way to identify class groups is to use economic and other objective traits such as wealth, income, occupation, and education. The relationship among these traits is not perfect, which leads to disagreement in the grouping of social classes. However, there generally is a high degree of consistency in judgments of people's social class based on these traits.

(3) Another common way to identify class groups is to use subjective characteristics (e.g., cultural and lifestyle traits) to identify social classes. Speech patterns, leisure activities, styles of home, music preferences, clothing, food choices, and other elements of lifestyle are fairly common among members of the same class. Cultural capital and financial capital typically are correlated within class.

(4) Determining the boundaries among classes is difficult, and the methods used to make these distinctions vary. Yet, the underlying class structure that emerges from different strategies has consistent traits. Researchers use either objective (e.g., based on income, wealth, education, and occupation), subjective (e.g., allowing people to identify their own social class), or reputational (e.g., allowing people to identify others' social class) strategies to identify class groupings.

(5) Warner and Lunt developed one of the first models of social class. Warner's students refined and updated this strategy in recent decades. Based on these models, current American society can be divided into the following classes: upper class, upper-middle class, lower-middle class, working class, working poor, and underclass.

(6) Historically, class structure has been rather rigid due in part to the intergenerational transmission of class, or social reproduction. Some argue that the upper class deliberately uses its power and financial resources to replicate the class structure across generations, ensuring that their children will enjoy the same privileges they enjoy. Others argue that less deliberate processes such as exposure to certain behaviors, lifestyles, and social connections account for social reproduction. For instance, there is evidence that parents' occupations and the influence of their occupation on children's socialization contributes to social reproduction.

(7) Childrearing practices also may contribute to the transmission of class across generations. Middle- and upper-class parents are more likely to use concerted cultivation in interactions with their children, whereas poor parents are likely to use a parenting style known as the accomplishment of natural growth. Variation in childrearing may have an important role in re-creating class from generation to generation.

Box 4.1 Debutante Balls and Social Reproduction

The debutante presentation is one avenue through which upper-class cultural traditions and social norms are reproduced across generations. Debutante presentations are the formal introduction of elite young women into society. The term *debutante* is derived from the French *debuter*, which means "to lead" or "to enter society." The debutante presentation originally signaled that a young woman had reached marriageable age and could begin participating in social functions as an adult. Today's debutante presentations can be traced to the European tradition in which landed elites presented their daughters to the monarch at court for her to find a husband who was of a similar social class. The contemporary debut can involve months of parties and dances that allow young women and their escorts to create friendships, make potential marriage connections, and announce their social positions. Whereas the debutante presentation originally was strictly a Caucasian custom, similar functions are now sponsored by predominantly African American, Latino, and other ethnic organizations.

Although the formal debutante presentation attracts the most attention, a lengthy selection and socialization process precedes it. Early social scientists described the debut as a "way of living" that "begins almost with the birth of the child" (Bossard and Boll 1948: 250). Today, a lengthy selection process and many accompanying rituals continue to determine which young women can participate in the presentation (Kendall 2002). Elite organizations that sponsor the debutante balls have complex rules and procedures to identify qualified candidates, usually based on their father's social position, and to determine which debutantes will be selected as royalty (e.g., the Queen or some other high-status position). Although selection procedures vary, the social standing and connections of a girl's family typically are central to the process.

Those who are selected to participate represent their family in the elaborate rituals surrounding the presentation. The debutantes typically wear floor-length designer gowns to the main ball and often perform a well-rehearsed and often dramatic bow to signal their passage (Kendall 2002). Conspicuous consumption marks many of the activities as debutantes make the circuit, hosting their own elaborate celebrations and attending the parties sponsored by other young women both domestically and abroad. Lavish parties, expensive clothing, gifts, and other outward signs of status demonstrate class position and ensure that only a small proportion of the wealthy are able to participate. The accompanying ritual also creates emotional bonds and attachment, both of which contribute to social reproduction.

There also is a significant connection between the debutante presentation and philanthropy. As Kendall (2002) pointed out, the relationship dates to the early twentieth century. Prior to that time, increasingly elaborate debutante parties were the norm and involved – as they do today – expensive parties, teas, dinners, and balls. Criticism of the excess surrounding the debut led a group of debutantes to organize and volunteer together to demonstrate their ability to do good works. Kendall states that the social service and philanthropic components of the debutante process continue today. It is common for the sponsoring organization to require debutantes to volunteer or make large donations. Kendall argues that this is an important part of how privileged women ensure the reproduction of social class.

Box 4.2 Can You Buy Your Way into an Elite College? The Price of Admission

Is it possible to buy your way into an elite college? Do Brown, Duke, Harvard, Notre Dame, Princeton, and other prestigious universities sell spots in their student bodies to the children of upper-class families? If so, how does this happen and does it matter?

In *The Price of Admission*, Daniel Golden (2007) argues that it happens routinely. He offers a glimpse into the process and claims that it matters for the students, the universities, and the qualified students who are not admitted.

Box 4.1 (*continued*)

It is now common for affluent parents to hire private tutors to coach their children in their classwork, improve their performance on standardized exams such the SAT, help them prepare admissions materials for college, and ensure that they excel in their athletic pursuits. Much of the motivation for this paid assistance is the increased odds that their children will win spots in the most prestigious colleges and universities. In recent years, the pressure has started earlier and earlier. Paid counselors help toddlers "ace" kindergarten and preschool admissions interviews in many cities, preschools offer early admission for two- and four-year-olds, and even competition for entry into the best play groups has increased. Golden offers a journalistic account of how performance in these areas may be irrelevant for admission to the most sought-after colleges. Rather, he argues, wealthy parents simply must commit to making a major donation and their children may be offered admission regardless of merit.

Golden provides numerous examples in which the sons and daughters of wealthy, famous parents are given preference in admissions. Some are the children of alumni, which is unlikely to surprise most people. However, many who receive preferential treatment are from families that are wealthy enough to contribute to a university's endowment, pay for a building, or otherwise donate. He points to examples in which the children of famous people, faculty, and other parents of note are admitted without appropriate qualifications. He singles out universities that have strategically sought to increase their endowments by seeking to admit the children of wealthy parents, who ultimately will contribute financially. He includes examples of the special privileges that varsity athletes enjoy at many elite colleges.

If these students had test scores, grades, and other qualifications that made them competitive, it would be more difficult to argue that there is a problem with this practice. However, Golden claims that many of these children are not qualified for admission. The implication is that qualified applicants who are not upper class are denied admission in favor of their upper-class peers. If this is true, it is likely to contribute to the intergenerational persistence of social class by denying the advantages of an elite college education to the children of middle- and lower-class parents.

Of course, Golden's book has received criticism. He uses anecdotal evidence rather than systematic data collection and analysis. As a result, it is difficult to ascertain how widespread this practice is and to know how many students are denied admission if this practice occurs. Moreover, it is possible to argue that the universities and their students benefit from the gifts. A university with a large endowment can provide unique experiences, superb courses, and other advantages to a large number of students.

What do you think? Does this happen at your university? If so, does it matter?

Source: Daniel Golden. 2007. *The Price of Admission: How America's Ruling Class Buys its Way into Elite Colleges and Who Gets Left Outside the Gates.* New York: Three Rivers Press.

Key Concepts

Accomplishment of natural growth	Learning-generalization hypothesis
Class action	Objective class definition
Class awareness	Objective method (of identifying classes)
Class consciousness	Reputational method (of identifying classes)
Class identification	Social class
Class solidarity	Social reproduction
Concerted cultivation	Socioeconomic status (SES)
Cultural capital	Status
Financial capital	Subjective class definition
Intergenerational transmission of class	Subjective method (of identifying classes)

Questions for Thought

1. Historically, has social class structure changed much over time? Why or why not?
2. Explain the difference between concerted cultivation and the accomplishment of natural growth. How might these patterns make it difficult for people to change social class over time?
3. Black and Hispanic students routinely score lower than white students on standardized tests. Are there class-related issues that might explain this difference? If so, explain how class might matter. If not, explain why not.
4. In addition to debutante balls, which rituals and traditions might reinforce social class structure over time? How?
5. Is class consciousness stronger among the lower, middle, or upper classes? Why? Design a research study to test your ideas.
6. Daniel Golden argues that it is possible to buy a position in an elite college (see Box 4.2). If he is correct, does it matter? Defend your position.

Exercises

1. *Identifying American Social Classes*
   Use what you have learned so far to identify the social classes that apparently operate in the United States. Is the list you created different from the lists discussed in this chapter? If so, how? Design a study to test whether your list of classes is empirically accurate.
2. *Race, Ethnicity, and Class*
   African American and Latino representation in the upper class has grown in recent decades. Which characteristics of African American and Latino upper classes do you hypothesize are different from the Caucasian upper class? Why? Are these patterns likely to vary regionally? Use the Internet and written sources to test your ideas.
3. *University Endowments and Inequality*
   Use the Internet to identify the size of endowments of some well-known colleges and universities. How much variation can you find in endowment size? What difference does this make for the students attending those colleges and universities? Does this have implications for stratification and inequality?

Multimedia Resources

Print

Duncan, Greg J., Timothy M. Smeeding, and Willard Rogers. 1992. "The Incredible Shrinking Middle Class." *American Demographics* 14: 34–8.

Florida, Richard. 2002. *The Rise of the Creative Class: And How It's Transforming Work, Leisure, Community and Everyday Life.* New York: Basic Books.

Johnson, Jennifer. 2002. *Getting by on the Minimum: The Lives of Working-Class Women.* New York: Routledge.

Kiyosaki, Robert T., and Sharon L. Lechter. 2000. *Rich Dad, Poor Dad: What the Rich Teach their Kids about Money that the Poor and Middle Class Do Not.* New York: Warner Books.

Ostrander, Susan. 1984. *Women of the Upper Class.* Philadelphia: Temple University Press.

Pattillo-McCoy, Mary. 1999. *Black Picket Fences: Privilege and Peril among the Black Middle Class.* Chicago: University of Chicago Press.

Sullivan, Teresa A., Elizabeth Warren, and Jay Lawrence Westbrook. 2000. *The Fragile Middle Class: Americans in Debt.* New Haven, CT: Yale University Press.

Wright, Erik Olin. 1997. *Class Counts: Comparative Studies in Class Analysis.* New York: Cambridge University Press.

_____. 2005. "Approaches to Class Analysis." New York: Cambridge University Press.

Internet

(1) www.nytimes.com/pages/national/class/: *New York Times* special section on social class. "Class Matters" reports on the year that a team of reporters spent exploring how social class affects people.

(2) www.uoregon.edu/~vburris/whorules: Homepage of Val Burris, University of Oregon sociologist and expert on class power. The Web site contains extensive resources related to power structure.

(3) www.bartleby.com/95/18.html: Emily Post's 1922 description of how a young woman is presented to society.

(4) www.socialcapitalgateway.org: Social-capital gateway; extensive resources related to social capital.

Films

Rich Kids: The Fertitta Family. 2003. This film depicts the lives of the four children of Tilman Fertitta, CEO of Landry's, a billion-dollar amusement park and restaurant corporation based in Houston. This documentary highlights both the hard work involved in entrepreneurship and the privilege that heirs to empires of this type enjoy.

The One Percent. 2008. This film examines the lives and economic impact of the upper-upper class. It discusses the unique lives of families such as the Whitneys, Vanderbilts, Forbeses, Gateses, and Buffets and addresses how they react to market shifts and economic booms and busts.

Untold Wealth: The Rise of the Super Rich. 2008. A CNBC film that documents the rise of record numbers of billionaires and multimillionaires in the United States. Some of today's fortunes are so large that this is called the "New Gilded Age." This film explores the lives of the extraordinarily wealthy members of the upper class.

Works Cited

Blau, Peter, and Otis D. Duncan. 1967. *The American Occupational Structure.* New York: Wiley.

Booth, Alison L., and Mark L. Bryan. 2004. "The Union Membership Wage-Premium Puzzle: Is There a Free-Rider Problem?" *Industrial and Labor Relations Review* 57: 402–21.

Bossard, James H. S., and Eleanor S. Boll. 1948. "The Rite of Passage: A Contemporary Study." *Social Forces*, March, 247–54.

Bourdieu, Pierre. 1986. "The Forms of Capital." In *Handbook of Theory and Research for the Sociology of Education*, edited by J. G. Richardson (pp. 241–58). Westport, CT: Greenwood Press.

Caven, Ruth. 1969. *The American Family.* New York: Crowell.

Centers, Richard. 1949. *The Psychology of Social Classes*. Princeton, NJ: Princeton University Press.

Coleman, Richard P., and Lee Rainwater. 1978. *Social Standing in America: New Dimensions of Class*. New York: Basic Books.

Collom, E. 2003. "Two Classes and One Vision? Managers' and Workers Attitudes toward Workplace Democracy." *Work and Occupations* 30: 62–77.

Cookson, Peter W. 1997. *Lessons from Privilege: The American Prep School Tradition*. Cambridge: Harvard University Press.

Cookson, Peter W., and Caroline Hodges Persell. 1985. *Preparing for Power: America's Elite Boarding Schools*. New York: Basic Books.

Davis, Allison, Burleigh B. Gardner, and Mary R. Gardner. 1941. *Deep South: A Social-Anthropological Study of Caste and Class*. Chicago: University of Chicago Press.

Domhoff, G. William. 1970. *The Higher Circles*. New York: Random House.

Duncan, Otis Dudley. 1961. "A Socioeconomic Index for All Occupations." In *Occupations and Social Status*, edited by J. Reiss (pp. 109–38). New York: The Free Press.

Duncan, Otis Dudley, and Robert W. Hodge. 1963. "Education and Occupational Mobility: A Regression Analysis." *American Journal of Sociology* 68: 629–49.

Frazier, Edward Franklin. 1932. *The Negro Family in Chicago*. Chicago: University of Chicago Press.

Gilbert, Dennis. 2003. *The American Class Structure in an Age of Growing Inequality* (6th edition). Belmont, CA: Thomson/Wadsworth.

Golden, Daniel. 2007. *The Price of Admission: How America's Ruling Class Buys its Way into Elite Colleges – and Who Gets Left Outside the Gates*. New York: Three Rivers Press.

Keister, Lisa A. 2005. *Getting Rich: America's New Rich and How They Got That Way*. Cambridge: Cambridge University Press.

Keister, Lisa A., and Benjamin Cornwell. 2009. "The Origin of Influence Hierarchies: The Role of Visible and Obscure Status Characteristics in the Emergence of Elite Social Hierarchies." *Sociological Analysis* 2: 5–27.

Kendall, Diana. 2002. *The Power of Good Deeds: Privileged Women and the Social Reproduction*. Boston: Rowman and Littlefield.

Kohn, Melvin L. 1959a. "Social Class and Parental Values." *The American Journal of Sociology* 64: 337–51.

———.1959b. "Social Class and the Exercise of Parental Authority." *American Sociological Review* 24: 352–66.

———.1963. "Social Class and Parent–Child Relationships: An Interpretation." *The American Journal of Sociology* 68: 471–80.

Kohn, Melvin L., and Eleanor E. Carroll. 1960. "Social Class and the Allocation of Parental Responsibilities." *Sociometry* 23: 372–92.

Kohn, Melvin L., and Carmi Schooler. 1973. "Occupational Experience and Psychological Functioning: An Assessment of Reciprocal Effects." *American Sociological Review* 38: 97–118.

———. 1983. *Work and Personality: An Inquiry into the Impact of Social Stratification*. Norwood, NJ: Ablex Publishing Corporation.

Kohn, Melvin L., and Kazimierz M. Slomczynski. 2001. "Social Structure and Self-Direction: A Comparative Analysis of the United States and Poland." In *Self in Society*, edited by A. Branaman (pp. 111–28). Malden, MA: Blackwell.

Kohn, Melvin L., Kazimierz M. Slomczynski, Krystyna Janicka, Valeri Khmelko, Bogdan W. Mach, Vladimir Paniotto, Wojciech Zaborowski, Roberto Gutierrez, and Cory Heyman. 1997. "Social Structure and Personality under Conditions of Radical Social Change: A Comparative Analysis of Poland and Ukraine." *American Sociological Review* 62: 614–38.

Lamont, Michele, and Annette Lareau. 1988. "Cultural Capital: Allusions, Gaps and Glissandoes in Recent Theoretical Developments." *Sociological Theory* 6: 154–68.

Lareau, Annette. 2002. "Invisible Inequality: Social Class and Childrearing in Black Families and White Families." *American Sociological Review* 67: 747–76.

_____. 2003. *Unequal Childhoods: Class, Race, and Family Life.* Berkeley: University of California Press.

MacLeod, Jay. 1995. *Ain't No Makin' It: Aspirations and Attainment in a Low-Income Neighborhood.* Boulder, CO: Westview Press.

Mulligan, Casey B. 1997. *Parental Priorities and Economic Inequality.* Chicago: University of Chicago Press.

Ostrower, Francie. 1995. *Why the Wealthy Give: The Culture of Elite Philanthropy.* Princeton, NJ: Princeton University Press.

Parsons, Talcott. 1937. *The Structure of Social Action.* New York: The Free Press.

Persell, Caroline Hodges, and Peter W. Cookson Jr. 1985. "Chartering and Bartering: Elite Education and Social Reproduction." *Social Problems* 33: 114–29.

Rothman, Robert A. 2005. *Inequality and Stratification: Race, Class, and Gender.* New York: Prentice Hall.

Thompson, William E., and Joseph V. Hickey. 2005. *Society in Focus: An Introduction to Sociology* (5th edition). Boston, MA: Allyn and Bacon.

Warner, W. Lloyd. 1949. *Social Class in America: A Manual of Procedure for the Measurement of Social Status.* New York: Harper.

_____. 1963. *Yankee City.* New Haven, CT: Yale University Press.

Warner, W. Lloyd, and Paul S. Lunt. 1941. *The Social Life of a Modern Community.* New Haven, CT: Yale University Press.

Willis, Paul E. 1981. *Learning to Labor: How Working-Class Kids Get Working-Class Jobs.* New York: Columbia University Press.

Wright, Erik Olin. 1980. "Social Standing in America: New Dimensions of Class, A Review." *American Journal of Sociology* 85: 1434–9.

Zeller, Tom. 2000. "Calculating One Kind of Middle Class." *The New York Times*, p 5WK.

Zorbach, Harvey W. 1929. *The Gold Coast and the Slum: A Sociological Study of Chicago's Near North Side.* Chicago: University of Chicago Press.

II | Applications

5 The Upper Class and the Elite

Although the majority of the U.S. population falls into the middle class, it is often the people at the ends of the distribution who attract the most attention. This chapter discusses the top end of the hierarchy: the upper class. Of the approximately 106 million households in the United States, only about 430,000 have a net worth of $10 million or more, about 17,000 have a net worth between $50 million and $99 million, and only about 7,000 have a net worth of more than $100 million (Havens 2004). Those at the very top (i.e., the 7,000 richest families) account for only about 0.01 percent of the population; however, they own approximately $2 trillion of the country's $43 trillion in household wealth and earned $40 billion of the total $7 trillion in household income (Havens 2004; Schervish 2005).

In this discussion of the upper class, we include all families with high wealth and high income. We include those with a legacy of upper-class status (i.e., "the old rich") and those who recently joined the upper class (i.e., "the new rich"). We discuss how researchers identify who is in the upper class and their assets, debts, jobs and occupations, consumption patterns, and resulting lifestyles. Because the rich make significant philanthropic contributions, we also address charitable giving and volunteering among the upper class. There is a long tradition of social theory that attempts to explain how wealth and power are related and that identifies a group typically called the *power elite*. We discuss the main theories in the literature and explore their relevance for the distribution of power today. We then explore the role of women and under-represented groups in the elite. We conclude with a discussion of how business cycles and inequality are related.

Identifying the Upper Class

As discussed in Chapter 1, there are more millionaires and billionaires now than ever before and, in Chapter 3, we conclude that there is indeed an upper class. Yet, the wealthy often are overlooked in systematic studies of stratification and inequality because there are still relatively few of them. One method traditionally used to identify and study the wealthy is a public roster, such as the Forbes 400. The creation of public rosters dates to Samuel Ward McAllister's registry of upper-class families in New York society in 1892. McAllister was born in 1827 in Savannah, Georgia, to wealthy parents. He married a millionaire's daughter and became the arbiter of New York City and Newport, Rhode Island, societies. Caroline and William Astor, one of the wealthiest American couples at the time, headed his list. Mr. Astor had little interest in his place in society, but Mrs. Astor was concerned about defining "Society." Together, Mrs. Astor and Mr. McAllister created one of the first lists of the top 400 wealthiest Americans. The list actually included about 300 names – that is, the number of people who could fit into Mrs. Astor's ballroom. Since McAllister's efforts to create a list of the wealthiest Americans, many other rosters that identify and describe the wealthy have been compiled. The *New York Tribune* (1892), the *World Almanac* (1902), *America's 60 Families* (Lundberg 1939[1937]), *The Rich and the Super-Rich* (Lundberg 1968), and the Marquis's *Who's Who* are examples of efforts to identify wealthy individuals and families.

A recent and unique roster is *The Wealthy 100*, an effort to identify the 100 wealthiest Americans ever (Klepper and Gunther 1996). The compilers estimated wealth at the time of death whenever possible and included only those individuals who died after the 1776 founding of the United States. They used multiple estimates of wealth as often as possible, but they omitted people who lost their fortune after making it. The list, as well as the book written about it, is intriguing because it includes the names of the wealthiest individuals, estimates of their estate relative to gross national product (GNP) at the time of their death, and descriptions of the origins of each person's fortune. Although the authors of this list do not draw causal relationships among behaviors, historical circumstances, and origins of the estates they discuss, patterns undeniably emerge from the stories they tell. Table 5.1 lists the top 30 people from this list; Table 5.2 summarizes the source of wealth for all those included.

One of the most recognizable public rosters today is the Forbes 400. In 1982, *Forbes Magazine* began to compile an annual list of the 400 wealthiest Americans; today, the list is updated regularly at its Web site, www.Forbes.com. The Forbes 400 is derived from public records and includes estimates of the size of the members' estates. It is important to remember that the Forbes's numbers actually are estimates: The very wealthy seldom divulge details about their wealth, and they are unlikely to share such private information with a magazine. Although it is estimating wealth, the Forbes team does a fairly reliable job identifying who is at the top of the distribution, a group that is otherwise hidden. Recall from Chapter 1 the lists of the wealthiest Americans and the wealthiest people in the world (see Box 1.1); the lists are from the Forbes 400. Notice that there are two predominant sources of wealth in the recent Forbes list: technology and retail (people with the last name of Walton are heirs of Sam Walton, founder of Wal Mart); industries that accounted for early fortunes are noticeably absent.

It also is interesting that among the top 10 Forbes members – and, indeed, throughout the Forbes 400 – there is a remarkable amount of self-made wealth. That raises the question of change in the upper class. How much movement into and out of

Table 5.1 The 100 Wealthiest Americans Ever

	Wealth Source	Estimated Wealth (2006 dollars)
1. John D. Rockefeller (1839–1937)	Oil	$192 billion
2. Cornelius Vanderbilt (1795–1877)	Shipping	$143 billion
3. John Jacob Astor (1763–1848)	Fur/Land	$116 billion
4. Stephen Girard (1750–1831)	Banking	$83 billion
5. Bill Gates (1955–)	Microsoft	$82 billion
6. Andrew Carnegie (1835–1919)	Steel	$75 billion
7. Alexander Turney Stewart (1803–1876)	Retail	$70 billion
8. Frederick Weyerhaeuser (1835–1914)	Lumber	$68 billion
9. Jay Gould (1836–1892)	Finance	$67 billion
10. Stephen Van Rensselaer (1765–1839)	Inheritance	$64 billion
11. Marshall Field (1835–1906)	Retail/Land	$61 billion
12. Henry Ford (1863–1947)	Automobiles	$54 billion
13. Sam Moore Walton (1918–1992)	Retail	$53 billion
14. Andrew W. Mellon (1855–1937)	Banking	$48 billion
15. Richard B. Mellon (1858–1933)	Banking	$48 billion
16. Warren E. Buffet (1930–)	Investing	$46 billion
17. James G. Fair (1831–1894)	Mining	$45 billion
18. William Weightman (1813–1904)	Chemicals	$44 billion
19. Moses Taylor (1806–1882)	Banking	$44 billion
20. Russell Sage (1816–1906)	Finance	$43 billion
21. John I. Blair (1802–1899)	Railroads	$43 billion
22. Edward Henry Harriman (1848–1909)	Railroads	$39 billion
23. Henry Huddleston Rogers (1840–1909)	Oil	$39 billion
24. John Pierpont Morgan (1837–1913)	Finance	$38 billion
25. Col. Oliver H. Payne (1839–1917)	Oil/Finance	$37 billion
26. Henry C. Frick (1849–1919)	Steel	$36 billion
27. George Pullman (1831–1897)	Industry	$34 billion
28. Collis Potter Huntington (1821–1900)	Railroads	$33 billion
29. Peter A. B. Widener (1835–1915)	Railroads	$32 billion
30. James C. Flood (1826–1889)	Mining	$31 billion

Data source: Klepper and Gunter (1996).

the upper-upper class is there? One way to gauge movement is to look at change in membership in the Forbes 400. Notable people have been in the Forbes 400 for years (e.g., Bill Gates, Warren Buffett, and Larry Ellison), but there is significant change in the full list even over short periods. Kennickel (2003) reveals that of the 400 people in the Forbes list in 2001, 230 were not listed in 1989. He points out that this is a relatively long period but notes that if there were little mobility, such movement would

Table 5.2 The 100 Wealthiest Americans Ever: The Source of Their Wealth

Primary Source of Wealth	Percentage of People in Top 100
Transportation, long distance (railroads, shipping)	18
Banking/finance	14
Natural resources (fur, land, lumber, mining)	12
Retail	10
Industry, heavy (automobiles, steel)	9
Oil	8
Agriculture/food/beverages (beer, cereals, tobacco)	7
Industry, light (chemicals, medical, textiles)	7
Publishing/communications	5
Technology (computers)	4
Transportation, local	4
Inheritance	2

Data source: Klepper and Gunter (1996, 2007).

be less pronounced. Kennickel also looks at changes between 1998 and 2001, which is obviously a much shorter period. He shows that nearly 25 percent of those on the list in 1998 were replaced by 2001. It is possible that this change reflects mortality and the inheritance of great fortunes. Yet, Kennickel's evidence suggests that merely 20 percent of the 1989 list that had disappeared by 2001 can be explained in this way. Kennickel's evidence suggests that the greatest persistence in the Forbes lists occurred in the top 100, where 45 of those who were listed in 1989 were still on the list of the top 100 in 2001. In contrast, of those in the lowest 100 in 1989, only 29 were still on the list in 2001.

Old Money versus New Money

Tension between old and new wealth has existed since perhaps money itself. The *old rich* are those from families that historically have been in the upper class. The American upper class developed during the last part of the nineteenth and beginning of the twentieth centuries during what is now called the Gilded Age. Some families were already wealthy, including the Astors, who created their fortune in the fur trade. However, during the Gilded Age, the ranks of the elite began to grow as entrepreneurs including the Carnegies, Fords, Fricks, Rockefellers, and Vanderbilts amassed large fortunes in industry. These fortunes established certain families as elite and created old-money legacies as they passed their wealth down through the generations. New York emerged as the center of social life for the upper class, and membership on lists such as the Social Register became a mark that a family had "made it." Lifestyle traits that continue to characterize the upper class today began to develop during this time as well. Upper-class families filled the ranks of exclusive clubs and associations, conducted business at private country clubs, and sent their children to exclusive boarding schools and Ivy League universities. The resulting social connections formed the foundation of elite social networks that began to define the upper-upper class.

The *new rich*, in contrast, refers to individuals and families who recently came into money. Conflicts between the two groups date to ancient Greece, when the landed gentry battled with traders who began to amass fortunes by importing and exporting goods. Similar conflicts occurred during America's Gilded Age as the new elite challenged the European aristocracy, which comprised the first American elite. The expansion of the new rich in recent decades has been so extreme that this period has been referred to as the New Gilded Age (Bartels 2008; Frank 2007; Remnick 2001). The source of a considerable amount of today's new wealth is the information and technology industry. As discussed previously, an increasing number of the extremely wealthy built their fortune in the computer-software and related fields. Bill Gates, founder of Microsoft, and Larry Ellison, founder of Oracle, are well-known examples. Both are college dropouts who made their fortune in computer technology and they have been among the wealthiest Americans since the 1990s.

Frank's (2007) bestselling book, *Richistan: A Journey through the American Wealth Boom and the Lives of the New Rich*, documents countless examples of new wealth and provides entertaining but insightful details of the lives that the rich lead. His description of the International Red Cross Ball – a Palm Beach, Florida fundraiser and long-standing tradition among the elite – highlights the ongoing struggle between new rich and old rich that continues today. The elaborate ball is an extravaganza of conspicuous consumption attended by "tanned trophy wives in skintight Scassi and Isaac Mizrahi gowns," "nipped-and-tucked socialites with hair the shape of cotton candy and jewels the size of strawberries," and "real-estate honchos, software magnates, buyout artists, and money managers." Frank explains that the position of Red Cross chair was considered the most prestigious social honor in Palm Beach, a winter magnet locale for prominent families from large Northeastern and Midwestern cities. The lucky woman – and it nearly always was a woman – who chaired the ball typically worked her way up as leader of lower-ranked social functions to this pinnacle. In 2003, Simon Fireman, a member of the new rich who made his fortune selling inflatable pool toys, made the Red Cross's largest donation ever of $1 million. He quickly took the position of chair, ousting the socialite who had "earned" her position the traditional way. Frank refers to the ensuing clash of new- and old-money cultures as barbarians entering the ballroom. "Palm Beach society was outraged. They accused Fireman of being a showy arriviste trying to buy his way into society" (Frank 2007). Although these colorful descriptions are extreme, they highlight an important social fact: The old and new rich are distinct groups that do not always see eye to eye.

Middle-Class Millionaires

The expansion of wealth has been so extreme in recent decades that some researchers and observers now talk about *middle-class millionaires*. This and related terms first appeared in books such as Stanley and Danko's (1996) *The Millionaire Next Door*, which observed that there are increasing numbers of millionaires in the United States, and that more millionaires look like ordinary Americans in terms of their job, education, and lifestyle. An important point that Stanley and Danko made is that wealth expansion (and a generally expanding stock market) combined with changing job opportunities (e.g., jobs in technology) make it possible for people to save and invest money from earnings and thereby become wealthy. In other words, the upper class includes the new rich and perhaps a large number of them. In a more recent work that takes a similar approach, Prince and Schiff (2008) identify middle-class millionaires as those with a net worth between $1 million and $10 million. They conducted interviews with 200 people who were in this category and provided a glimpse into work habits, personal and family characteristics, and lifestyle traits. The picture that emerges is a hard-working person who faced and overcame work and personal challenges. For instance, the average person in their sample works more than 70 hours per week, is more likely than the average worker to say they are always available for work, and is more likely to continue on a particular business strategy despite an earlier failure.

Terms such as *middle-class millionaires* suggest that anyone can be rich with the right amount of hard work, perseverance, and determination. Research on large samples that originate in the social sciences suggests that it is possible for people to become rich regardless of their starting point in life, that education and entrepreneurship can contribute to that process, and that, indeed, more people become rich over time than would be expected by pure chance. Yet, contrary to "rags-to-riches" stories, there also is convincing evidence that people face serious constraints to becoming rich, particularly if they begin their life at the bottom of the wealth and income distributions (Keister 2000; 2005b). Simply having the will or resolve to be rich is not enough. Education is an important part of the path that takes people from poor to rich, and the poor are unlikely to have access to the same type of education as those raised in the upper class (Keister 2005a; Morgan, Grusky, and Fields 2006; Svallfors 2005). Consider, for example, those who are raised in extreme poverty and who attend inner-city schools, where discipline and violence might garner more attention than class content (Kozol 1991); it takes more than determination to overcome obstacles of this magnitude. We discuss the importance of education in Chapter 7 and revisit the issue of mobility (i.e., movement from one class to another) in Chapter 8.

Wealth of the Rich

How rich are the rich? Table 5.3 compares the wealth and income of the wealthy to the rest of the distribution. The table divides families into five groups based on net worth; the first group consists of those with less than $25,000 in net worth in 2004. The table shows that the median net worth for these families is about $2,000, and their mean net worth is less than zero! In other words, some families at the bottom of the wealth distribution have more debt than assets, and a simple average of the wealth of these families is negative. For those in the middle of the distribution, mean and median net worth are not that different from one another. The highlighted row includes values for the wealthiest families – that is, the top 10 percent of the distribution. For the wealthy, the mean naturally is much higher than in the other groups; it is large because some families have extremely high wealth, pulling the mean up much higher than the median. Even if we

Table 5.3 How Rich Are the Rich?

Net Worth Percentile	Net Worth (Thousands of $)		Income (Thousands of $)		Families
	Median	Mean	Median	Mean	Who save (%)
Less than 25	1.2	−2.2	23.4	29.1	40.5
25–49.9	54.3	58.1	41.1	46.5	52.8
50–74.9	220.3	227.7	56.7	66.6	59.1
75–89.9	573.8	588.6	82.3	93.0	68.9
90–100	1,892.5	3,985.9	157.9	347.6	80.4

Data source: Survey of Consumer Finances, 2007.

refer to only median net worth, Table 5.3 indicates that a median family in the top 10 percent (i.e., in the 90 to 100 percentiles) has $1,430,000 in net worth. This same median family earns $144,000 per year, compared to only $21,000 at the bottom of the distribution. This means that the median wealthy family (i.e., top 10 percent) earns nearly 7 times more income and has more than 700 times net worth than the median poor family (i.e., bottom 25 percent).

There also are important differences between the wealthy and other families in saving behavior. As Table 5.3 indicates, 35 percent of families at the bottom of the wealth distribution save (i.e., they regularly put money into saving). A higher percentage of families at the middle of the distribution save and, not surprisingly, the highest percentage of savers is at the top of the distribution. A full 76 percent of families in the top 10 percent of wealth owners save money. Perhaps more interesting, however, is that so few wealthy families save. A family with very low income might not save because there simply is not enough money to contribute to a savings account or other investments. However, nearly a quarter (i.e., 24 percent) of wealthy families does not save money from their current income. There are many reasons that rich families might not save. First, they may feel as if they already have enough wealth. The primary reason that families save, according to the same Survey of Consumer Finances data used to create the table, is retirement.[1] If a family already has enough savings and investments to pay for retirement, they may not feel they need to contribute more to personal savings. Another major reason that people save is to pay for their children's education; similarly, if a family is wealthy, they already may have sufficient savings for education and may not need additional savings.

We also may wonder where the wealthy keep their savings. Using the same groups as in Table 5.3, Table 5.4 shows the median value of three types of investments for families across the wealth distribution. Table 5.4 shows that the median value of a family's total checking and savings accounts for those at the bottom of the wealth distribution is about $1,300. In contrast, the top 10 percent has more than $150,000 in checking and savings (i.e., more than 100 times as much). Retirement accounts – private accounts re-

---

[1] Of those who save, 35 percent reported that retirement is the most important reason; 11.6 percent reported that education is the most important reason.

Table 5.4 Financial Assets of the Rich, Current Account Value (thousands of dollars)

Net Worth Percentile	Checking & Savings Accounts		Retirement Accounts		Stocks	
	Mean	Median	Mean	Median	Mean	Median
Less than 25	1.9	.7	7.2	3.0	3.5	1.1
25–49.9	5.2	2.0	21.4	15.0	8.7	3.0
50–74.9	13.2	6.0	64.8	50.0	22.9	6.0
75–89.9	31.9	15.5	158.5	120.0	53.4	20.0
90–100	147.0	46.5	548.9	318.0	683.5	125.0

Data source: Survey of Consumer Finances, 2007.

served for retirement spending to which people and perhaps their employer contribute – are growing in popularity. Yet, the value of retirement-account assets owned by the wealthy still far exceeds that of other families. The median family in the top 10 percent owns nearly $430,000 in retirement assets, whereas the median family at the bottom of the distribution owns $5,000.

The difference between the bottom and the top is even more extreme when we consider riskier assets, such as stocks. We refer to stocks as risky because – unlike checking and savings accounts – stock assets rarely are insured by government agencies. Checking and savings accounts are typically insured (up to a certain value), but they earn relatively low interest (if any). Stock values also can make significant swings with little warning, as during the 2008–2009 financial crisis. The risk associated with stock ownership is that these assets become less valuable over time. Of course, risky assets also have the potential to increase in value, sometimes significantly. The value of stocks over several decades, for instance, has been positive, and stocks can grow rapidly in value. The median family at the bottom of the distribution has about $4,000 in stocks, whereas the median wealthy family has nearly $470,000 in stock assets (i.e., 117 times that of families at the bottom). Naturally, for those who have more assets, it is easier to invest in risky assets. An important outcome of the ownership of assets that can grow significantly in value – such as stocks – is that ownership creates more ownership at a faster rate than with other assets (i.e., "the rich get richer").

Wealthy people also are more likely to own real estate and business assets, and their holdings of these assets far outpace those of other families. Tangible assets such as a home, other real estate, a business, vehicles (e.g., automobiles, planes, and boats) are called *real assets*. They contrast with *financial assets* such as stocks, bonds, and checking accounts, which cannot be touched but have value nonetheless. Table 5.5 shows that the median family at the top of the wealth distribution owns a primary home valued at $450,000. The first column refers to the *primary residence* – that is, the family's main home. In contrast, the median family at the bottom of the distribution owns a home valued at $65,000. Differences in asset ownership are even more striking when we compare ownership of other homes (e.g., vacation homes) and business assets. The median value of other homes is $325,000 for those at the top of the distribution, whereas the median for the bottom is zero; in other words, the typical

Table 5.5 Other Assets of the Rich, Current Market Value (thousands of dollars)

Net Worth Percentile	Home, Primary		Home, Others		Business Equity	
	Mean	Median	Mean	Median	Mean	Median
Less than 25	111.3	85.2	16.6	12.0	3.9	.5
25–49.9	124.6	100.0	55.8	30.0	23.2	11.5
50–74.9	219.4	200.0	130.0	60.0	71.2	50.0
75–89.9	353.7	315.0	176.3	146.0	182.7	100.0
90–100	824.4	561.8	720.8	400.0	2,487.5	610.0

Data source: Survey of Consumer Finances, 2007.

family at the bottom of the distribution does not own a second home. Indeed, the value of homes other than the primary residence is quite low across the distribution except at the very top. Business-asset ownership is similar in comparison. Table 5.5 compares families on ownership of *business equity*, or the value of business assets less business debt. Those at the top of the distribution have business equity of $527,000, whereas ownership of business assets is very low at most other points.

Debts of the Rich

At first thought, we might imagine that the rich have no debt. After all, if we are rich, we should not need to borrow money from others. *Debt* – or liabilities – refers to money owed to another party and includes home debt, credit-card debt, student loans, and vehicle loans. In reality, the rich are like most Americans and have considerable debt. In fact, the average rich family is likely to have more overall debt than the average family in other social classes. The rich have *mortgage debt*, or debt on the home. A mortgage has a unique name because it is a unique type of liability, involving the transfer of interest in a property to a lender – usually a bank – for a loan of money. Table 5.6 shows that families in the top 10 percent of wealth owners have median mortgage debt of $67,000 on their primary residence, more than any other net-worth group. In addition to a mortgage on the primary home, the wealthy

Table 5.6 Debts of the Rich, Current Value (thousands of dollars)

Net Worth Percentile	Home Mortgage		Other Mortgages		Credit Card Balances		Ratio of Debt Payments to Family Income
	Mean	Median	Mean	Median	Mean	Median	
Less than 25	129.0	107.0	*	*	5.7	1.5	15.0
25–49.9	105.9	84.2	67.8	74.0	6.6	2.8	22.4
50–74.9	130.4	104.0	157.1	72.0	7.8	3.6	20.3
75–89.9	160.5	128.0	119.3	94.0	8.2	4.0	17.0
90–100	285.6	180.0	267.4	160.0	12.4	5.0	8.0

Data source: Survey of Consumer Finances, 2007 (*indicates 10 or fewer observations).

tend to have significant debt in other mortgages. Table 5.6 indicates that the median family in the top 10 percent of wealth owners has $66,000 in other mortgages, nearly identical to the debt they have on the primary home because they typically own additional real estate.

Why do the rich have mortgages? Why do they not simply buy their homes with other savings? There are at least three reasons. First, many families in the top 10 percent may be considered wealthy, but they may not have enough savings to buy a home without a mortgage. Because the average house costs more than $100,000, it is a considerable investment. When we consider ownership of properties other than the primary residence (e.g., vacation houses), the cost of housing for the wealthy increases even more. Moreover, the wealthy are likely to buy homes that are more expensive than the average home, making a mortgage even more necessary. Second, even if a family could afford to buy a home without a mortgage, it might prefer to put some savings in other investments (e.g., stocks and bonds). As mentioned previously, the potential returns to financial assets are high, which makes it appealing to own these types of assets, if possible. Third, there are tax advantages to having a mortgage. Because the government encourages homeownership, interest paid on a mortgage can be deducted on tax returns. Wealthy families who want to reduce their taxes may decide to have a mortgage, even if they otherwise could afford to pay for a home.

Although the wealthy have debt, most are still financially secure. Although they have mortgage debt, their other assets often can exceed the value of their mortgage debt. In addition, the wealthy are less likely to be victims of predatory lending practices, such as aggressive mortgage brokers who encourage debt that a family cannot afford (Karger 2005). Another indicator of the relative financial security of the wealthy is consumer credit, such as credit-card debt; the wealthy have more than other families but only by a small margin. Table 5.6 shows that most families have total credit-card balances of $1,000 to $1,500, whereas those in the top 10 percent of wealth owners have $2,200. The wealthy also are less likely to carry balances on their credit cards from month to month, a practice that incurs high interest payments and can lead to bankruptcy (Sullivan, Warren, and Westbrook 1989). Perhaps more important, the ratio of total debt to total income is relatively low for a median wealthy family. This ratio identifies the resources available for a family to pay off debt if necessary; a lower number suggests a greater ability to pay off the debts. Table 5.6 demonstrates that this ratio ranges from 13 percent for those at the bottom of the wealth distribution up to about 20 percent for the middle class. By contrast, the wealthiest families have a debt-to-income ratio of just 8.5 percent, suggesting that they are much more able than other families to pay off their liabilities, if necessary.

Income and Jobs

So far, we are discussing the upper class in terms of net worth, but we know by now that income also is an important indicator of wealth. We would be partially correct to expect that income and wealth are perfectly correlated; they are correlated but the relationship is not perfect. Many people with a high income have high wealth, but there are many high-income earners who have little savings. Recall from Chapter 1 that income is the

Table 5.7 Household Income, Current Value (thousands of dollars)

	Median	Mean
All Families	43.7	84.3
Income percentile		
Less than 20	12.3	12.3
20–39.9	28.8	28.3
40–59.9	47.3	47.3
60–79.9	75.1	76.6
80–89.9	114.0	116.0
90–100	206.9	397.7
Net worth percentile		
Less than 25	23.4	29.1
25–49.9	41.1	46.5
50–74.9	56.7	66.6
75–89.9	82.3	93.0
90–100	157.9	347.6

Data source: Survey of Consumer Finances, 2007.

flow of money into a household (e.g., from a job or a government program), whereas wealth or net worth is the value of what people own (e.g., homes, stocks, and bonds). As mentioned in Chapter 3, upper-class families tend to have both high income and high wealth, but this is not always the case. Table 5.7 compares the wealth and income of those at various points in the distributions. The table shows that the average income (both mean and median) for those at the bottom of the income distribution is about $11,000 per year. At the top of the distribution, the median annual household income is more than $180,000 and the mean is more than $320,000. The major difference between these two averages reflects the small number of people who earn exceptionally high incomes (i.e., their values increase the mean). Perhaps more interesting, the second part of Table 5.7 lists the median and mean income by net-worth percentile. The median income for those at the bottom of the wealth distribution is about $20,000 per year; the mean is $26,000.

Although earnings can vary considerably for the same job in different regions or even in different industries, some positions are consistently associated with high pay: Doctors, lawyers, engineers, and business executives earn among the highest salaries. Indeed, 2008 data from the U.S. Census shows that 9 of the top 25 highest paid occupations are in medicine, including surgeons, anesthesiologists, obstetricians and gynecologists, oral surgeons, internists, orthodontists, psychiatrists, and pediatricians. Chief executive officers (CEOs), lawyers, engineers, airline pilots, and computer-information-system managers also have among the highest median incomes. These estimates are interesting but they have flaws. For instance, they can overlook self-employed people. They also may include basic wages and salaries as well as bonuses, commissions, and overtime yet can miss or under-report compensation such as stock options, which are easily omitted from reports of income and for which it is difficult to assess value. However, if the other income sources are included, it is likely that these occupations still would rank extremely high.

A controversial subject related to high incomes is the extraordinarily high incomes earned by some CEOs. On one side of the argument, labor activists such as the American Federation of Labor and Congress of Industrial Organizations (AFL-CIO) argue that it is wrong for CEOs to earn millions of dollars a year when some company workers may not earn enough for basic necessities. The Corporate Library estimates that CEOs of Standard and Poor's 500 companies averaged more than $14 million of income in 2008. On the other side of the argument are those who contend that companies need good leadership to remain competitive. As a result, a market for the best leaders (i.e., CEOs) developed, and the relatively few sought-after people in this market can command exceptionally high salaries. Frank and Cook (1995) compared CEOs to other high-income earners (e.g., professional athletes and movie stars) and explained their salaries as a result of "winner-takes-all" markets. In these fields, rewards are concentrated in a relatively small number of people. The key to understanding these markets, according to Frank and Cook, is that the top people are just slightly better than the competition. For example, there are probably hundreds of talented actors and actresses who will never be as famous or as rich as Julia Roberts. Likewise, there are likely many people who successfully could lead a large company but they will never be considered for a position as CEO of Proctor and Gamble. The certainty of hiring the person with the proven track record ultimately means that the rewards are "stuck" at the top.

Consumption and Luxury Fever

Americans spend money, and the rich spend more money than most. Consumption has increased dramatically since World War II; consumer goods now account for about two-thirds of the $11 trillion that changes hands in the United States each year. Spending on shoes, jewelry, and watches alone accounts for $100 billion, whereas spending on higher education accounts for only $99 billion (DeGraaf, DeGraaf, and Kraaykamp 2000). In 1986, there were more high schools than shopping malls in the United States but, by 2000, there were more than twice as many shopping malls as high schools (i.e., 46,438 versus 22,180) (DeGraaf, DeGraaf, and Kraaykamp 2000). In her book, *The Overspent American*, Juliet Schor (1998) showed that the definition of a necessity also has changed considerably in recent decades. Since the early 1970s, increasing percentages of Americans believe that basic cable service, a second automobile, automobile air conditioning, and other similar consumer items are necessities. Even at the beginning of 2009 – during what has been called the worst recession since the Great Depression – consumers were still spending record amounts on expensive cell phones, videogame consoles, laptop computers, children's toys, shoes, dining out, and movie tickets (*Forbes Magazine* 2009b). In a companion article, *Forbes Magazine* identified several luxury items (which purportedly will last a lifetime) that the savvy spender cannot be without. Included on the list were $590 Dior pumps (for women), a $1,395 Burberry trench coat, $325 Gucci sunglasses, a $3,170 Valextra handbag, a $9,000 Chanel suit (for women), a $4,600 Brioni suit (for men), and, of course, a $6,000 Rolex watch (*Forbes Magazine* 2009a).

Among the advantages of wealth, consumption is one of the more visible. Thorstein Veblen coined the term *conspicuous consumption* in his early sociology of what he called "the leisure class" (Veblen 1989). Robert Frank (2007) coined a more contemporary synonym for conspicuous consumption that captures current habits; he called it *luxury fever*. These terms refer to the demonstration of wealth and social position through the purchase of extraordinary goods and services measured by either quantity or price. Veblen proposed that the wealthy engage in conspicuous consumption to identify themselves as part of the elite. From billion-dollar houses, to million-dollar handbags, to space tourism and lavish vehicles (e.g., automobiles, planes, and yachts), examples of conspicuous consumption are everywhere today. The market for expensive homes, luxury-home amenities, and luxury vehicles (including planes and yachts) has grown rapidly. The average American home is about 2,000 square feet, but the number of homes larger than 5,000 square feet grew nearly five times (up to 30,000 square feet) between 1995 and 2005 (Frank 2007). Bill Gates's house (see Chapter 1) is super large, but it is not the only example of an extreme house. Billionaire financier Ira Rennert owns a 66,000-square-foot house on Long Island; hedge-fund manager Steven Cohen's 30,000-square-foot house has an indoor basketball court, an Olympic size swimming pool, and a 6,700-square-foot ice rink with its own zamboni (Frank 2007).

The reasons for the "ratcheting up" of spending are understood only vaguely, although there is evidence that a simple desire to "keep up with the Joneses" accounts for a large amount of conspicuous consumption (Frank 1999; Schor 1998). Another potential explanation is a need for distinction: People want to be unique, or distinct, and extreme spending can create that distinction (Bourdieu 1987). One thing is clear: Consumption does not increase happiness. DeGraaf and his co-authors (2000) referred to excess spending as a disease – that is, *affluenza* – and they argued that a range of problems such as loneliness, rising debt and bankruptcy, and even environmental degradation result from this disease. Psychologists have shown that extrinsic rewards – such as wealth, fame, and appearance – are much less important for happiness and personal satisfaction than intrinsic rewards – such as giving and receiving love (Kasser 2002; Kasser and Kanner 2003; Kasser and Ryan 1993). In fact, those who are overly focused on extrinsic rewards are likely to suffer negative consequences, such as depression and low self-esteem (Kasser and Ryan 1993). Of course, conspicuous consumption is not a perfect indicator of fixation on extrinsic rewards, but the two are positively correlated.

Philanthropy

The rich do more with their money than consumption. Indeed, wealthy families have a long history of charitable giving in the United States. They currently donate billions of dollars to charity and other worthy causes each year, and their giving has increased in recent decades. Recent estimates suggest that the top 0.01 percent of households contribute about $14 billion (i.e., 7.0 percent) of the total $201 billion in charitable contributions made each year (Havens 2004; Schervish 2005). If we expand our definition of wealthy, it becomes clear that the wealthy make the majority of all charitable donations each year. Households earning more than $200,000 gave more than 40 percent of all charitable contributions in 2003, up from 25 percent in 1991. Those households with a net worth greater than $1 million gave nearly 47 percent of all charitable contributions, up from 30 percent in 1991 (Schervish 2005). Schervish also uses data on *estates*, or wealth that remains after a person dies, to provide further evidence that charitable giving has increased. He shows that the value of all estates grew considerably between 1992 and 2004, from $84 billion to $121 billion (in 2004 dollars). In that time, the allocation of funds to charity from estates increased from $9 billion to $15 billion. The amount of funds left to heirs grew during that time but more slowly than bequests to charity, suggesting that charitable contributions became more important than gifts to heirs (Schervish 2005). In addition to gifts of money, elites make sizable gifts of time by volunteering. Research shows that more than half of U.S. adults volunteer, but elites tend to contribute more than people in other socioeconomic statuses (Bradley 2007; Daniels 1988).

The reasons that the wealthy give – both money and time – vary tremendously across people and families, and they are complex even within a single family. A common explanation is that their position entails an obligation to attempt to improve the well-being of those who are less fortunate. This sense of responsibility generally is referred to as *noblesse oblige*, which refers to an altruistic motivation to improve the lives of others or, at least, to comply with the social norm that suggests the wealthy should give. Others propose that charitable contributions and volunteering among the wealthy are motivated by a sense of obligation to family traditions and an attempt to reify its position in society. Ostrander argued that upper-class mothers consciously instill in their children a sense of obligation to the community by volunteering and fundraising and involving them in these activities from a young age (Ostrander 1984). According to Kendall, a desire to reproduce privilege is a more central motivator. She stated, "Elite women use their social power to enforce class and racial boundaries and to protect and enhance privilege, either intentionally or unintentionally" (Kendall 2002: 167). Similarly, Odendahl suggested that upper-class families are motivated by self-interest and that as elites become more embedded in the "culture of philanthropy," they learn new skills, make important contacts, and are socialized regarding the proper use of their wealth and position. At the extreme, some young upper-class adults struggle with understanding their position and the meaning of their wealth until they find ways to use it to help society (Odendahl 1990).

Wealth and Power: Elite Theories

There is no question that power and wealth often are related. We discuss the role of politics and political power in creating and maintaining stratification in more depth in Chapter 9. This section describes the relationship between the upper class and power. To begin, we think about who we consider powerful: leaders of universities, mayors of cities, presidents of countries, justices of the Supreme Court, heads of companies, editors of newspapers and magazines, leaders of religious organizations, and others in similar positions. Although these people may be members of the upper class, there is no financial requirement (e.g., wealth or income) associated with any of these positions. Power comes from having a significant voice and an ability to make decisions in central economic, political, and social organizations. Wealth and power are not the same; however, because the wealthy often hold these positions, it often is difficult to disentangle class and wealth from power. Sociologists and political scientists have explored the relationship between wealth and power for decades. The resulting work is known as *elite research* – that is, research that asks who is powerful and why. We now explore some of the major ideas in the field.

The Power Elite

C. Wright Mills's book, *The Power Elite*, is among the early sociological works that explored the structure of power in the United States. Mills challenged the common wisdom of the 1950s, which suggested that the American power structure was a loose coalition of leaders of various interest groups that lacked cohesion and a common set of objectives (Mills 1956). He pointed out that there is a cadre of people whose positions enable them to live outside the ordinary environment in which most people spend their life. Mills described the power elite as those who had "the most of what there is to have" and who are powerful or "able to realize their will even when others resist it" (1956: 9). Perhaps most important, he argued that the power elite are members of the "political, economic, and military circles which as an intricate set of overlapping cliques share decision having at least national significance" (1956: 18). Mills also argued that wealth and power are nearly always shared because of their influence in large corporations, politics, and the military.

The Ruling Class

Other scholars concluded more definitively than Mills that there is a single unified elite. William Domhoff is among the most influential and his research has had a significant effect on our understanding of the relationship between wealth and power (Domhoff 1967; 1970; 1978; 1983; 1990; 2002). In a book titled *Who Rules America?*, Domhoff (1967) contended that members of the upper class disproportionately continue to hold the top leadership roles in America. Furthermore, membership in the upper economic class is the primary route to power within business, government, and cultural sectors. "Those corporate owners who have the interest and ability to take part in general governance join with top-level executives in the corporate community and the policy-formation network to form the *power elite*, which is the leadership group for the corporate rich as a whole." Domhoff suggested that power is rooted in "a wide range of well-organized interest groups that are often based on economic interests, but can form around other interests as well. These interest groups join together in different coalitions depending on the specific issues" (Domhoff 1967: 2).

Domhoff concluded that the upper class is a ruling class: There is a clear relationship among the wealthy, those who control important business organizations, and those who make political decisions. This ruling or governing class is a cohesive group that is a product of the same private schools and universities, socializes together, works together in business organizations, and influences political decision making. Domhoff acknowledged that measuring power is difficult. He noted that "to say that power is the ability to produce intended and foreseen effects on others, and that no one form of power is more basic, does not mean it is a simple matter to study the power of a group or social class. A formal definition does not explain how power manifests itself or how it is to be measured" (1967: 18). Thus, he developed what he called *indicators of power* that assume that power is best understood through its effects. The indicators of power that Domhoff studied include who benefits (i.e., who owns what most people want), who governs (i.e., who occupies important government and institutional positions), who wins (i.e., whose initiatives and policies are used), and who "shines" (i.e., who has a reputation as being powerful).

Domhoff provided empirical evidence to support his claims that there is a unified group of elites who enjoy most of these privileges. He showed that members of the upper class own disproportionate amounts of stock, that large stockholding families continue to manage and direct large corporations, that members of the upper class are over-represented on the boards of large companies, and that middle-class managers who become professional managers in large corporations often are assimilated into the upper class both socially and economically (1967: 71–2). Furthermore, Domhoff argued that his data showed a high degree of both class unity and class consciousness: "The corporate rich are drawn together by bonds of social cohesion as well as their common economic interests. This social cohesion is based in the two types of relationships found in a membership network: common membership in specific social institutions and friendships based on social interactions within those institutions" (1967: 72). He also concluded that the elite share an attitude of fully deserving their privilege, an attitude that is useful in managing employees who often share this perspective.

Institutional Wealth

Thomas Dye is a political scientist who made an important contribution to understanding the relationship between wealth and power (Dye 1990). Dye's variation on the power-elite model is similar to those proposed by Mills and Domhoff, but he came to important conclusions that differ from the other power-elite models. Dye proposed an oligarchic model of national policy making. He argued that the power elite are those who lead the organizations that control "roughly half of the nation's resources in industry, finance, insurance, mass media, foundations, education, law, and civic and cultural affairs" (Dye 2002, #5070: 207). He agreed with Mills and Domhoff that there is a small group of corporate leaders who have disproportionate economic power and it is socially cohesive and very powerful. They influence political decision making by funding the initial research, study, and planning that underlie public policy. Dye differs from Mills and Domhoff in that he did not argue for a close relationship between wealth and power. It is possible to identify many wealthy people who have little power (e.g., billionaires, wealthy widows, and those who have inherited great fortunes but do not control organizations). He also downplayed the importance of social clubs and other social organizations in creating and maintaining the elite. Dye acknowledged that these clubs and organizations exist, but he argued that their members are primarily business leaders who have little political influence.

The Justified Elite

Not all observers of the elite are critical of the concentration of power that it implies. E. Digby Baltzell, for example, agreed with Domhoff and Mills that there is a strong link between those who have great wealth and those who are powerful. However, Baltzell argued that this relationship is both warranted and socially beneficial (Baltzell 1958, #2921; Baltzell 1964, #2352). Baltzell distinguished three groups at the top of the social hierarchy. The very top, or the elite, includes those who lead and make decisions in critical business, political, media, and educational organizations. The second group, the upper class, is a socially cohesive group that comes from old-money families and lives privileged lives. The third group, the establishment, consists of those who are both elites and members of the upper class. The establishment is a ruling class similar to Domhoff's conception. Baltzell argued that there are advantages of having the same families – those who inherited both their wealth and power – fill leadership roles across generations. Social continuity and stability are chief among the benefits. He also recognized, however, that the establishment needs new members to prevent it from becoming complacent and neglecting leadership duties. It must remain willing to accept new members from among those who become elites based on their abilities.

Strategic Elites

Alternatively, there are those who concluded that there are multiple, interacting elites. For instance, Suzanne Keller, who coined the term *strategic elites*, claimed that there are multiple, fragmented elites in modern society rather than a single upper class. In *Beyond the Ruling Class*, Keller (1963) argued that strategic elites, not the upper class, are the most powerful members of American society. Strategic elites are those in society that are responsible for maintaining an institution, its roles, and its norms. The strategic elite preside over sectors of society including key economic, political, and cultural organizations. They are not a single ruling class but rather a collection of nonintegrated groups with power in separate arenas. Keller's underlying orientation is akin to functionalism (see Chapter 2); she proposed that the elite are responsible for the realization of important social goals and the continuity of social order. According to Keller, there are four factors that explain the existence of a strategic elite: population growth, occupational specialization (i.e., division of labor), growth of formal organizations and related bureaucracy, and expansion of moral diversity (1963: 65). Whereas a pluralist approach is appealing given the diversity of arenas requiring leadership in contemporary society, there clearly is extensive interaction among elite groups. That is, even if there are multiple elites, they do not exist in complete isolation and some people may simultaneously fill multiple elite positions.

These approaches represent only a small sample of the perspectives taken on the relationship between wealth and power. Other approaches include those who argue that there are psychological distinctions that unify the elite. For example, Lerner and his colleagues argued that "class rules exist because the cultural, political, ethical, and intellectual elites articulate a worldview that everyone, ruling and ruled, comes to uphold" (Lerner, Nagai, and Rothman 1996: 2). Others attempted to combine ideas from various approaches. Higley and Moore (1981), for instance, argued that there is a need for an integrated elite model that incorporates aspects of various perspectives. They contended that "there is an inclusive network of formal and informal communication, friendship, and influence-wielding among the top position holders in all major elite groups" (1981: 584). In addition, they proposed that no single elite group is predominant in this network; rather, "interaction among all elite groups is frequent and is markedly centralized in and between a relatively small number of persons from all major groups" (1981: 584). Yet, Higley and Moore asserted that the political–governmental elite are targets of interaction among the elites and that these elites are switching points in the interaction (1981: 584).

How accurately do these early theories explain current patterns? Contemporary theorists agree that although patterns have changed since Mills's time, there is still a remarkable concentration of wealth and power in the hands of a small percentage of the population. Mills (1956) acknowledged that at the time he was writing, Americans were living in a "materialist boom, a nationalist celebration, and a political vacuum." When he and his contemporaries made their comments on the status of the elite, local elites had largely been replaced by a national elite that crossed the boundaries of the three arenas (Wolfe 2000). At the same time, ignorance and apathy among the masses meant that this convergence of power went unchecked. Although many of the companies that Mills pointed to as powerful still exist and top executives are still among the very wealthy, there have been remarkable changes in industry since the 1950s that he could not have anticipated (Wolfe 2000). Mergers and acquisitions have changed the structure of industry; foreign competition and globalization make CEOs more accountable than they otherwise might be; the emergence of high-tech industry changed the shape of organizations and their environments; and economic shocks such as the financial crisis that began in 2007 highlight the fragility in even some core industries, such as financial services and automobile production. Even where corporate greed and power are extremely obvious – as in the collapse of Enron Corporation in 2001 – the nature of the greed has changed.[2] Similarly, important military and political changes suggest that some of the observations of early theorists are still relevant despite changes in the details (Wolfe 2000).

Race, Nationality, and Religion in the Elite

Race, nationality, and religion are important determinants of many status indicators, including membership in the elite. In earlier decades, elite "inner circles" in the United States were dominated by white males and Protestants (Domhoff 1970, 2002; Useem 1979, 1980, 1984). Although it is difficult to identify and study the elite, some argue that Protestant

---

[2] Enron's collapse was largely a result of financial deals with limited partnerships that it controlled, and many of its debts and losses were not reported in its financial statements.

groups continued to be over-represented in the elite through the 1990s (Pyle 1996). Using data from the *Who's Who* in 1950, 1970, and 1992, Pyle asked whether there have been changes in the elite representation of whites, Protestants (particularly Episcopalians, main-line Presbyterians, and United Church of Christ/Congregationalists), males, and graduates of Ivy League and other elite universities. Pyle found increasing numbers of Catholics, Jews, women, and African Americans in the elite, but he concluded that despite these changes, there is significant persistence in the representation of groups with histories of privilege in the upper echelons of society.

Consistent with Domhoff's argument that new entrants into the upper class often assimilate quickly to the dominant group's perspectives, others argue that new elites assimilate regardless of race, ethnicity, and gender. Richard Alba concluded that

> ethnicity is related to the attainment of an elite position and to the possibility of that attainment within different sectors. But once such a position is attained, ethnicity has little, if any, relation to such indicators as service on federal advisory commissions, membership in exclusive social clubs, and reputation for influence. And in the few cases where a relationship exists, as is true of corporate board memberships, it is not strong and is explained for the most part by the different sectoral concentrations of groups (Alba and Moore 1982).

Similarly, Zweigenhaft found that newcomers to the upper class find ways to demonstrate their loyalty to traditional elite values and attitudes, regardless of race, ethnicity, or gender (Zweigenhaft and Domhoff 1982, 1998).

Upper-Class Women

Women have an important role in the upper class, but the nature of that role and the costs and benefits are hotly contested. On one hand, women continue to be under-represented on their own merits in the upper class. There are equally large numbers of men and women in the upper class, but the argument is that fewer women are able to move into the upper class based on their own accomplishments as opposed to their ancestry. Likewise, there are relatively few women in the power elite. Women clearly have gained admission to elite political and economic positions that were dominated by males in prior generations; business, academics, law, and other paths have allowed women to move into positions that were unheard of even a couple of decades ago (Zweigenhaft and Domhoff 1998). Yet, women continue to be under-represented among the decision makers in the largest business, political, and military organizations (Zweigenhaft and Domhoff 1998). In a recent report, Catalyst (an organization that conducts research related to women in business) reported that an analysis of the Fortune 500 showed that women gained little ground in moving into business-leadership positions (Catalyst 2008). Only 15 percent of board directors of these firms were women (3 percent were women of color), few companies had more than a single female board member, women held only 6 percent of top-earner positions in the Fortune 500, and more than one woman of color serving on a board was extremely rare.

On the other hand, women who are upper class can enjoy a type of social power from their position that is unique to their class and gender. Recall from our previous discussion that upper-class women have an important role in philanthropy and social organizations. Kendall (2002) defined power as access to and control of scarce resources, and she acknowledged that if we think of power strictly as control of traditional business and political resources, then women clearly are less powerful. However, she argued that upper-class women have a unique type of social power derived from their control of social resources. Drawing on her research on upper-class women and their philanthropic, volunteering, and other public social activities, she argued that their power is "based on a combination of the economic power that they hold either individually or jointly with other members of their families and the social power that they derive from influential social connections and prestigious organizational affiliations" (Kendall 2002). Others came to similar conclusions in research on upper-class women and philanthropy among the elite (Ostrander 1984; Ostrower 1995). Yet, these researchers cautioned that focusing exclusively on upper-class women as wives, mothers, club members, and community volunteers places too high a value on civic participation and underestimates the social costs of having relatively few women in economic- and political-power positions (Ostrander 1984; Ostrower 1995).

For women who hold positions of power in traditionally male-dominated arenas, the experience of power can be significantly different from the male experience. For instance, there is evidence that women experience pressure to assimilate in ways that men do not. Zweigenhaft pointed out that a woman cannot pass as a man in the same way that a Jewish man could pass as a Gentile (Zweigenhaft and Domhoff 1998). Women who make it into the corporate elite are expected to be competitive and tough – but not too competitive and not too tough (Jamieson 1995). Women executives are expected to be feminine and attractive but not too feminine and certainly not weak or overly emotional (Jamieson 1995). Zweigenhaft also speculated that women find themselves in power positions for different reasons than men. He argued that "men who run America's corporations have women in higher management and on their boards not only to present a corporate image of diversity, and not only to deflect criticism from their wives, daughters, and granddaughters, but to provide a valuable buffer between the men who control the corporation and the corporation's labor force" (Zweigenhaft 1998: 57). In addition, female elites organize their private life differently than male elites. They are less likely to be married, and having children becomes more difficult as well (Neale 2000). Indeed, female elites are likely to forego traditional female family roles and, in turn, adopt roles similar to those of unmarried men, which makes it possible for them to succeed in historically male-dominated positions of influence (Neale 2000).

Business Cycles and Inequality

Fluctuations in economic activity often have important implications for the wealthy and for patterns of inequality. As discussed previously, wealthy families tend to keep significant portions of their savings in stocks and bonds, which can make their net worth vulnerable to changes in the values of those assets. *Business cycles*, which are fluctuations in economic activity over long periods, include expansion (i.e., growth or booms) followed by downturns (i.e., contractions, economic recessions, and economic crises) that merge into the next expansion. The wealth of the very rich tends to grow and contract with the economy. Indeed, there is evidence that the wealth of the very rich follows a long-term pattern similar to the long-term trend of the stock market. During an economic expansion, or a period of relative economic growth, those who own large amounts of stock and bonds (as the wealthy do) tend to see their personal assets grow as the value of stocks increases. Likewise, during economic contractions, the wealth of the very rich tends to decline as the value of their stocks is reduced. This pattern is particularly pronounced during a *recession*, which is an economic contraction usually involving a significant decline in business and other economic activity lasting more than a few months and resulting in declines in income, asset values, production, retail sales, and employment. During a recession, the value of stocks usually drops significantly along with the wealth of stock owners. An *economic crisis* is an even more extreme downturn during which economic sectors suffer extreme losses in value and output. During an economic crisis, the wealth of the rich tends to drop even more dramatically. Investment strategies can protect against this type of vulnerability, but even the most protected assets are vulnerable to extreme crises.

Business cycles also affect inequality – that is, the distribution of well-being across households – but the effect on inequality can be complicated. Economic expansions and contractions characterize much of history. Although the effect of each on inequality has been unique, common patterns characterize most of these cycles. Well-known (and somewhat extreme) examples of economic booms and busts include the Tulip Mania of the 1630s in Holland, the California Gold Rush of the 1840s, the Roaring Twenties in the United States followed by the 1929 Stock Market Crash, the Dot-Com Bubble of the late 1990s, and the Subprime Mortgage Crisis of 2006 (Gramlich 2008; Shiller 2008). During an economic expansion, employment levels rise, salaries and wages increase, and wealth levels grow. It is difficult to ascertain who benefits and who loses the most, and the benefits of such an expansion extend across the income and wealth distributions. However, the statistical evidence suggests that those with high incomes and high wealth benefit disproportionately during times of economic growth.

During an expansion, the salaries and wealth of those at the top of the hierarchy grow faster than for those at the middle and lower levels of the distribution (Keister 2005a; Kennickell 2003). The middle class and poor may see growth in their income; however, because they have little wealth, they typically do not enjoy growth in their assets. As a result, both income and wealth inequality tend to grow during an expansion. In contrast, during an economic contraction, the salaries of top earners typically are more stable because those with a professional occupation tend to have relatively high job security and compensation. Those at the middle and lower levels of the distribution are more likely to suffer job loss or a pay cut. As a result, income inequality may stagnate or even worsen. Wealth inequality, however, can improve during an economic contraction. Given that middle class and poor families usually have limited savings, their wealth positions do not change significantly with an economic decline. However, the wealth of the rich usually drops (see the beginning of this section), thereby reducing inequality.

Summary

(1) The wealthiest families in the United States account for approximately 0.01 percent of the population, but they own a disproportionate share of the country's wealth and earn a disproportionate share of income.

(2) Identifying who is in the upper class is difficult because there are relatively few people in this group. One strategy for studying the wealthy is the public roster, or a listing of members of the upper class (e.g., the popular Forbes 400).

(3) The American upper class that began to develop during the last part of the nineteenth and early part of the twentieth centuries was known as the Gilded Age. Today's old rich typically can trace their roots to ancestors whose wealth was established during the Gilded Age, whereas today's new rich made their fortune more recently. Middle-class millionaires are families who made their fortune very recently and who are wealthy – but not wealthy enough to be at the top of the distribution.

(4) America's wealthiest families own assets and earn income that is dramatically higher than those in the middle and bottom of the distributions of wealth and income. Wealthy families also save more from current income. Then the wealthy invest in financial assets (e.g., retirement account and stocks) and real assets (e.g., real estate and businesses).

(5) Like other people, the very rich also have debts, including mortgage debt and consumer debt (e.g., credit-card debt). Although the rich have debt, they tend to be more secure financially than other families. For example, the ratio of total debt to total income for wealthy families is much lower than for other families.

(6) Conspicuous consumption and "luxury fever" are particularly evident among the upper class. Commentators offer various explanations for conspicuous consumption, including a need to demonstrate membership in the elite, keeping up with the Joneses, a desire for distinction, and "affluenza."

(7) The wealthy also give billions of dollars each year to charitable causes. Reasons for philanthropy include noblesse oblige, obligation to family traditions, efforts to reify a family's social position, and perhaps self-interest.

(8) The power elite is a subset of the upper class that has both wealth and power. Explanations of the nature and implications of the elite have attracted research attention since the early days of social science. Contributors to elite research vary in their arguments; the important ideas include the notion of a power elite that lives outside the ordinary existence that most people experience, a single ruling class that has money and leads important organizations, a socially cohesive class that funds initial research underlying public policy, a justified elite, and a strategic elite.

(9) Whereas traditionally under-represented groups are becoming more common in the upper class and the power elite, some groups still are not represented proportionally to their position in the population. African Americans, Hispanics, non-Protestants, and women tend to remain under-represented.

(10) Business cycles affect the wealth of the upper class and they also contribute to changes in levels of inequality over time. Income and wealth levels as well as inequality respond to economic changes (e.g., booms and busts) in complex but significant ways.

Box 5.1 Summer in the Hamptons

Where does America's elite go for summer vacation? The Hamptons is a traditional destination that continues to hold wide appeal to the upper class. Residents of Manhattan, in particular, have a long history of spending part of their summer – or the entire summer, in some cases – on the eastern end of Long Island. The Jersey Shore, the Berkshires, the Catskills, Vermont, and Maine all vie for a piece of the business, but the Hamptons have an allure for the wealthy that other destinations cannot rival. The area's attractions include everything that the upper class could want: upscale restaurants and clubs, high-end boutiques, fabulous resorts, even more fabulous homes, tennis and racquet sports, sailing, polo tournaments, spas, museums, wine tasting, and, of course, beaches.[1]

Real-estate prices reflect the appeal of the Hamptons and suggest that demand for a "piece of the action" remains high even during difficult economic times. Ron Baron, of Baron Funds, demonstrated the resilience of demand for the Hamptons when he paid $103 million for a 40-acre lot in East Hampton (without a house). Another home sold in 2007 for $29.5 million, about a million dollars higher than the asking price. Indeed, in 2007, one realtor who specializes in high-end residential real estate on the Hamptons sold more than 10 homes for more than $15 million each – recall that 2007 was the start of one of the most serious recessions in U.S. history (Lee 2007). The Web site Forbes.com features related stories including tours of beach cottages and mansions in the Hamptons (available at http://video.forbes.com/fvn/lifestyle/jal_mansion051807).

Whereas the summer visitors arrive at the Hamptons seeking a break from their daily routine, the increased population pressure and related demands are anything but a break for the area's permanent residents. The owner of East Hampton Business Services called it a "culture clash" and said that in the summer, she "has 18 people double-parked, some with their motors running, and standing in front of (her) punching their BlackBerrys. A lot of the urgency, let's face it, is artificial" (Kaufman 2008). Demand for restaurants, bars, spa services, pet-care services, retail goods, and entertainment increases dramatically during the summer months, adding to the pressure felt by year-round residents, most of whom are not upper class. Local shop owners report that they may not like the people who visit for the summer but most of the area's income is earned during the summer. As one business owner noted, "We endure summer because we have to" (Kaufman 2008).

---

[1] *Born Rich*, one of this chapter's recommended films, includes a segment on what life is like for wealthy families who spend their summers there.

Box 5.2 Living Extremely Well Has Its Costs

What exactly does it cost to keep up with the lifestyle of the ultra rich? Each year, Forbes compiles the Cost of Living Extremely Well Index (CLWI), a list of the prices associated with many luxury items.

Coat: natural Russian sable at Bloomingdale's	$225,000
Silk dress: Bill Blass classic	$1,975
Loafers: Gucci	$445
Shirts: 1 dozen cotton, bespoke, Turnbull & Asser, London	$3,900
Shoes: men's black-calf wingtip, custom-made, John Lobb, London	$4,566
School: preparatory, Groton, 1-year tuition, room, board	$42,040
University: Harvard, 1-year, tuition, room, board	$45,620
Catered dinner: for 40, Ridgewell's, Bethesda, Maryland	$9,795
Opera: two tickets, eight performances, Metropolitan Opera, Saturday, parterre box	$5,760

(continued)

Box 5.2 (*continued*)

Caviar: Imperial Special Reserve Persicus, 1 kilo, Petrossian	$9,800
Champagne: Dom Perignon, case, Sherry-Lehmann, New York	$1,679
Filet mignon: 7 pounds, Lobel's, New York	$231
Dinner: La Tour D'Argent, Paris, estimated per person (includes wine and tip)	$436
Piano: Steinway & Sonds, concert grand, Model D, ebonized	$107,100
Flowers in season: arrangements for 6 rooms, changed weekly, monthly cost, New York	$8,175
Sheets: set of linen lace Figna, Pratesi, queen size	$3,940
Silverware: Lenox, Williamsburg Shell pattern, 5-piece place setting for 12	$6,960
Hotel: 2-bedroom suite, Four Seasons, New York	$3,650
Face-lift: American Academy of Facial Plastic & Reconstructive Surgery	$17,000
Hospital: VIP, 1 day, concierge, security, gourmet meals, Washington, DC	$1,395
Psychiatrist: 45 minutes, standard fee, Upper East Side, New York	$300
Lawyer: average hourly fee for estate planning by partner, established NY firm	$795
Spa: basic weekly unit, The Golden Door, California	$7,750
Perfume: 1 ounce, Joy, by Jean Patou	$400
Sauna: 8x10x7 feet, 8-person, Nordic spruce/abachi, Finnleo, Sauna and Steam	$14,945
Motor yacht: Hatteras 80 MY (with 1,550-hp Caterpillar C-32 engines)	$5,118,000
Sailing yacht: Nautor's Swan 70	$4,771,550
Shotguns: pair of James Purdey & Sons (12-gauge side-by-side)	$196,854
Thoroughbred: yearling, average price, Fasig-Tipton Saratoga summer sale	$289,310
Swimming pool: Olympic (50 meters) Mission Pools, Escondido, California	$1,312,500
Tennis court: clay, Putnam, Tennis and Recreation, Harwinton, Connecticut	$55,000
Helicopter: Sikorsky S-76C++ VIP options	$11,775,000
Automobile: Rolls-Royce Phantom	$340,000

Additional categories, the most current data, and graphs showing how the CLWI compares to the Consumer Price Index (CPI) are available at www.Forbes.com.

Key Concepts

Affluenza	Luxury fever
Business cycle	Middle-class millionaires
Business equity	Mortgage debt
Conspicuous consumption	New rich
Debt	Noblesse oblige
Economic crisis	Old rich
Elite research	Primary residence
Estate	Real assets
Financial assets	Recession
Liability	Strategic elites

Questions for Thought

1. There are important differences in the types of assets owned by the upper, middle, and lower classes. Use the information in this chapter to list some of those differences. Which factors account for these variations in asset ownership?
2. The chapter mentions that the government gives tax incentives for mortgages because it wants to encourage homeownership (not only by the wealthy). Why does the government want to encourage homeownership?
3. Not all wealthy families save money. This chapter lists two reasons why that might be true. Can you think of other explanations?
4. In "winner-takes-all" markets, a small number of people earn most of the rewards (Frank and Cook 1995) (see the discussion of income for more details). Do you expect that markets of this type will continue to reward a small number of people? Consider the growth of companies such as Google and Facebook that have innovative business plans and corporate structures.
5. Which is more important: equality of condition or equality of opportunity? Design a set of government policies that would lead to the ideal balance between the two.
6. Identify an early social theorist who studied elites (e.g., a contemporary of C. Wright Mills). Outline the theorist's arguments. How well do those arguments apply to the nature of stratification and inequality today?
7. Identify an example of an economic boom or bust (examples are included in the last section of this chapter). Learn more about the history of the event and identify how it affected inequality.
8. When wealthy families arrive in the Hamptons for summer vacation (see Box 5.1), there is some culture clash between year-round residents (who are more likely to be middle class than upper class) and summer residents. Can you think of examples of clashes between the upper class and others? What role does this type of interaction have in creating and maintaining class consciousness?

Exercises

1. In the classroom, distribute pennies so that every student has two. Students pair up; one student flips, the other calls heads or tails. The winner keeps the penny. Repeat the pairings and observe the distribution of pennies after many iterations. Why do some people end up with so many pennies whereas others have none? Discuss the role of luck, skill, and rules of the game.
2. Use the Internet to identify recent salaries of some of the highest paid CEOs. Create a list of pros and cons for the size of these salaries. What is your opinion about CEO salaries?
3. The nation of Bhutan recently decided to track national happiness in much the same way that other nations track economic indicators (e.g., production and expenditures). Use the Internet to learn more about Bhutan's plan. Is this a worthwhile effort? Should other nations adopt the same strategy? Why or why not?

Multimedia Resources

Print

Aldrich, Nelson W., Jr. 1988. *Old Money: The Mythology of America's Upper Class*. New York: A. A. Knopf.

Auchincloss, Louis. 1989. *The Vanderbilt Era: Profiles of a Gilded Age*. New York: Charles Scribner's Sons.

Bogle, John C. 2009. *Enough: True Measures of Money, Business, and Life.* New York: John Wiley & Sons.

Brooks, David. 2000. *Bobos in Paradise: The New Upper Class and How They Got There.* New York: Simon and Schuster.

Cowles, Virginia. 1979. *The Astors: The Story of a Transatlantic Family.* London: Weidenfeld and Nicolson.

Daniels, Arlene Kaplan. 1988. *Invisible Careers: Women Civic Leaders from the Volunteer World.* Chicago: University of Chicago Press.

Domhoff, G. William. 1970. *The Higher Circles.* New York: Random House.

Galbraith, John Kenneth. 1958. *The Affluent Society.* Boston: Houghton Mifflin Company.

Kanter, Rosabeth Moss. 1977. *Men and Women of the Corporation.* New York: Basic Books, Inc., Publishers.

Schor, Juliet B. 2004. *Born to Buy.* New York: Charles Scribner's Sons.

Sorokin, Pitirim. 1925. "American Millionaires and Multi-Millionaires." *Social Forces* 4: 627–40.

Swiss, Deborah. 1996. *Women Breaking Through: Overcoming 10 Obstacles at Work.* Princeton, NJ: Peterson's/Pacesetter Books.

Thomas, Dana. 2007. *Deluxe: How Luxury Lost its Luster.* New York: Penguin Books.

Internet

(1) Forbes.com/lists/: *Forbes Magazine* lists of the richest Americans and richest people in the world. It is an nteresting source of information on the upper class and power elite.

(2) Socialregisteronline.com: The official Web site of the Social Register Association. Membership in this organization, according to the Web site, is "drawn from the country's most prominent families, and many of those currently listed are direct decedents of the original members."

(3) www.aflcio.org/corporateamerica/Eye on Corporate America: The AFL-CIO homepage is devoted to corporate behavior, CEO compensation, and related issues. It contains detailed information about CEO compensation and provides resources for comparing one's own finances to those of the wealthy.

Films

Born Rich. 2003. An HBO documentary about the lives of children who are born into extreme wealth. Among other portraits, the film provides a glimpse into life of the heir to the Johnson and Johnson fortune, whose 21st-birthday gift was inheriting more money than most people can spend in a lifetime.

History's Mysteries: Secret Societies. 2006. An episode of the History Channel's *History's Mysteries* that investigates secret societies including the Skulls and Bones, the Bilderbergs, and the Tri-Lateral Organization. The documentary explores who joins these societies and the purposes served by them.

The Richest Man in the World. 1988. A biography of Aristotle Onassis, who was born a middle-class Greek and became one of the richest people in the world. It provides a glimpse into the life of a very upwardly mobile and extremely wealthy man.

Enron: The Smartest Guys in the Room. 2005. This film, based on the book by *Fortune* reporters Bethany McLean and Peter Elkind, details the collapse of Enron Corporation in 2001. It highlights the nature and consequences of corporate greed in contemporary business.

Works Cited

Alba, Richard D., and Gwen Moore. 1982. "Ethnicity in the American Elite." *American Sociological Review* 47: 373–83.

Baltzell, E. Digby. 1958. *Philadelphia Gentlemen: The Making of a National Upper Class.* Chicago: Quadrangle.

———. 1964. *The Protestant Establishment: Aristocracy and Caste in America.* New York: Random House.

Bartels, Larry M. 2008. *Unequal Democracy: The Political Economy of the New Gilded Age.* Princeton, NJ: Princeton University Press.

Bourdieu, Pierre. 1987. *Distinction: A Social Critique of the Judgment of Taste.* Cambridge, MA: Harvard University Press.

Bradley, Sara. 2007. "Volunteerism among Elites of River City." *Working paper.*

Catalyst. 2008. *Catalyst 2008 Census of the Fortune 500.* New York: available at Catalyst.org.

Daniels, Arlene Kaplan. 1988. *Invisible Careers: Women Civic Leaders from the Volunteer World.* Chicago: University of Chicago Press.

DeGraaf, Nan Dirk, Paul M. DeGraaf, and Gerbert Kraaykamp. 2000. "Parental Cultural Capital and Educational Attainment in the Netherlands: A Refinement of the Cultural Capital Perspective." *Sociology of Education* 73: 92–111.

Domhoff, G. William. 1967. *Who Rules America?* Englewood Cliffs, NJ: Prentice-Hall.

———. 1970. *The Higher Circles.* New York: Random House.

———. 1978. *Who Really Rules? New Haven and Community Power Reexamined.* New Brunswick, NJ: Transaction Books.

———. 1983. *Who Rules America Now?* Englewood Cliffs, NJ: Prentice-Hall.

———. 1990. *The Power Elite and the State: How Policy Is Made in America.* New York: Aldine de Gruyter.

———. 2002. *Who Rules America? Power and Politics* (4th edition). New York: McGraw Hill.

Dye, Thomas R. 1990. *Who's Running America: The Bush Era.* Englewood Cliffs, NJ: Prentice Hall.

———. 2002. *Who's Running America: The Bush Restoration.* Englewood Cliffs, NJ: Prentice Hall.

Forbes Magazine. 2009a. "10 Lasts-A-Lifetime Luxury Buys." Available at www.forbes.com/2009/01/13/luxury-shopping-classic-forbeslife-cx_jp_0113style_slide_12.html?thisSpeed=15000.

———. 2009b. "In Depth: 10 Things We're Still Buying." Available at www.forbes.com/2009/01/20/consumer-spending-essentials-forbeslife-cx_ls_0120spending_slide_11.html?thisSpeed=15000.

Frank, Robert. 2007. *Richistan: A Journey through the American Wealth Boom and the Lives of the New Rich.* New York: Three Rivers Press.

———. 1999. *Luxury Fever: Why Money Fails to Satisfy in an Era of Excess.* New York: The Free Press.

Frank, Robert H., and Philip J. Cook. 1995. *The Winner-Take-All Society.* New York: Simon and Schuster.

Gramlich, Edward M. 2008. *Subprime Mortgages: America's Latest Boom and Bust.* Washington, DC: Urban Institute Press.

Havens, John J. 2004. *Estimation of Distribution of Charitable Bequests by Level of Estate.* Chestnut Hill, MA: Center on Wealth and Philanthropy, Boston College.

Higley, John, and Gwen Moore. 1981. "Elite Integration in the United States and Australia." *The American Political Science Review* 75: 581–97.

Jamieson, Kathleen. 1995. *Beyond the Double Bind: Women and Leadership.* Oxford: Oxford University Press.

Karger, Howard. 2005. *Shortchanged: Life and Debt in the Fringe Economy.* San Francisco: Berrett-Koehler Publishers.

Kasser, Tim. 2002. *The High Price of Materialism.* Cambridge, MA: MIT Press.

Kasser, Tim, and Allen D. Kanner. 2003. "Psychology and Consumer Culture: The Struggle for a Good Life in a Materialistic World." Washington, DC: American Psychological Association.

Kasser, Tim, and Richard Ryan. 1993. "A Dark Side of the American Dream." *Journal of Personality and Social Psychology* 65: 410–22.

Kaufman, Joanne. 2008. "Hamptons Prep Work." In *The New York Times*, April 25. Available at NYTimes.com.

Keister, Lisa A. 2000. *Wealth in America.* New York: Cambridge University Press.

_____. 2005a. *Getting Rich: A Study of Wealth Mobility in America.* Cambridge: Cambridge University Press.

_____. 2005b. *Getting Rich: America's New Rich and How They Got That Way.* Cambridge: Cambridge University Press.

Keller, Suzanne. 1963. *Beyond the Ruling Class: Strategic Elites in Modern Society.* New York: Random House.

Kendall, Diana. 2002. *The Power of Good Deeds: Privileged Women and the Social Reproduction.* Boston: Rowman and Littlefield.

Kennickell, Arthur B. 2003. *A Rolling Tide: Changes in the Distribution of Wealth in the U.S., 1989–2001.* Washington, DC: Federal Reserve Board.

Klepper, Michael, and Robert Gunther. 1996. *The Wealth 100: A Ranking of the Richest Americans, Past and Present.* Secaucus, NJ: Citadel Press.

Kozol, J. 1991. *Savage Inequalities: Children in America's Schools.* New York: Crown Publishers.

Lee, Jennifer. 2007. "The Hamptons: Elite Summer Playground." Available at *Forbes.com*. May 26.

Lerner, Robert, Althea K. Nagai, and Stanley Rothman. 1996. *American Elites.* New Haven, CT: Yale University Press.

Lundberg, Ferdinand. 1939[1937]. *America's 60 Families.* New York: Halcyon House.

_____. 1968. *The Rich and the Super-Rich: A Study in the Power of Money Today.* New York: Lyle Stuart, Inc.

Mills, C. Wright. 1956. *The Power Elite.* New York: Oxford University Press.

Morgan, Stephen L., David B. Grusky, and Gary S. Fields. 2006. *Mobility and Inequality: Frontiers of Research from Sociology and Economics.* Stanford, CA: Stanford University Press.

Neale, Jenny. 2000. "Family Characteristics." In *Gendering Elites*, edited by M. Vianello and G. Moore (pp. 157–68). Great Britain: MacMillan Press LTD.

Odendahl, Teresa. 1990. *Charity Begins at Home: Generosity and Self-Interest Among the Philanthropic Elite.* New York: Basic Books.

Ostrander, Susan. 1984. *Women of the Upper Class.* Philadelphia: Temple University Press.

Ostrower, Francie. 1995. *Why the Wealthy Give: The Culture of Elite Philanthropy.* Princeton, NJ: Princeton University Press.

Prince, Russ Alan, and Lewis Schiff. 2008. *The Middle-Class Millionaire: The Rise of the New Rich and How They are Changing America.* New York: Broadway Books.

Pyle, Ralph E. 1996. *Persistence and Change in the Protestant Establishment.* New York: Praeger.

Remnick, David. 2001. *The New Gilded Age: The New Yorker Looks at the Culture of Affluence.* New York: Modern Library.

Schervish, Paul G. 2005. "Today's Wealth Holder and Tomorrow's Giving: The New Dynamics of Wealth and Philanthropy." *Journal of Gift Planning* 9:15–37.

Schor, Juliet. 1998. *The Overspent American: Why We Want What We Don't Need.* New York: Basic Books.

Shiller, Robert J. 2008. *The Subprime Solution: How Today's Global Financial Crisis Happened and What You Can Do about It.* Princeton, NJ: Princeton University Press.

Stanley, Thomas J., and William D. Danko. 1996. *The Millionaire Next Door: The Surprising Secrets of America's Wealthy.* Atlanta, GA: Longstreet Press.

Sullivan, Teresa A., Elizabeth Warren, and Jay Lawrence Westbrook. 1989. *As We Forgive our Debtors: Bankruptcy and Consumer Credit in America.* New York: Oxford University Press.

Survey of Consumer Finances. 2007. Available at federalreserve.gov.

Svallfors, Stefan. 2005. *Analyzing Inequality: Life Chances and Social Mobility in Comparative Perspective.* Stanford, CA: Stanford University Press.

Useem, Michael. 1979. "The Social Organization of the American Business Elite." *American Sociological Review* 44: 553–71.

———. 1980. "Corporations and the Corporate Elite." *Annual Review of Sociology* 6: 41–77.

———. 1984. *The Inner Circle.* New York: Oxford University Press.

Veblen, Thorstein. 1989. *The Theory of the Leisure Class.* New York: MacMillan.

Wolfe, Alan. 2000. *Afterward to the Power Elite* (new edition). Oxford: Oxford University Press.

Zweigenhaft, Richard L., and G. William Domhoff. 1982. *Jews in the Protestant Establishment.* New York: Praeger Publishers.

———. 1998. *Diversity in the Power Elite: Have Women and Minorities Reached the Top?* New Haven, CT: Yale University Press.

6 The Middle Class and Workers

When asked, 9 of 10 Americans respond that they are middle-class or upper middle-class (Taylor et al. 2008). However, ask them to clarify what it means to be middle class and they often reply it is because some people have more and some people have less than they do. Being middle class, then, is a default category that says little about what class membership holds.

What it means to be middle class has long interested sociologists. Finding a precise definition is an ongoing process in the social sciences; it has been situated between rich and poor, prompting some to call it a "rhetorical device whose characteristics are created mainly to illuminate groups above and below" (Stearns 1979: 378). Others have found a particular ideology, grouping of occupations, and lifestyles associated with the middle class. However, it remains an illusive stratum as social scientists cannot agree on the form, membership, or numbers associated with the class. Today, the middle class consists of about three-quarters of the American population who earn between $30,000 and $150,000 annually (U.S. Census Bureau 2009). This group is not cohesive; indeed, it consists of different classes of people grouped into one category that is neither rich nor poor.

Theories of the Middle Class

There are two major theoretical interpretations of the middle class: the conflict and functionalist perspectives. The discussion of middle-class theories begins by examining the conflict position that set the foundation of class analysis within sociology. First, we look at a historical analysis of class by Karl Marx (1818–1883), followed by his successor, Max Weber (1864–1920). Then, we turn to the functionalist perspectives of Otis Duncan (1921–2004) and Donald Treiman (1940–). Both perspectives are used today and drive scientific ideas and research regarding a middle class.

Conflict Perspective

As discussed in Chapter 2, a strong proponent of conflict theory was Karl Marx, who provided an empirical analysis of class as a study of conflict among social groups across time. Marx argued that social class is economically determined. Consequently, all material matter (i.e., knowledge, thoughts, and ideology) is determined by economic relations, which he termed *materialism*. Prior to Marx, a popularly held belief was that the ultimate nature of reality was in thoughts and ideas, termed *idealism*. The principle of idealism is illustrated by the familiar quote of the philosopher Descartes: "I think, therefore I am."

Marx argued that social class is structured by *dialectic materialism* – that ideology, knowledge, thoughts, culture, and all material things are a result of the economic relations of a society – also called the *means of production*. The means of production are distinct from the mode of production because they do not include human input; rather, they account for material tools or physical inputs (as described in Chapter 2). As the relations of production shift across time, so too does material matter, including social classes. The changes between social epochs, according to Marx, result from the inherent conflict among groups, known in philosophy as *dialectics*. Dialectics asserts that the seeds of one social epoch exist within the previous epoch and are created by the conflict among groups. This process, then, is what drives social change.

As a dialectic materialist, Marx perceived the entire history of the human species as a series of class struggles and revolutions. Chapter 2 explores the latter stages of social progress; however, Marx's theory was informed by a historical perspective that includes early man. His *theory of social progress* begins with *primitive communism*. According to the theory, early man did not create more than what was consumed; consequently, groups could not monopolize resources. In these early societies, no surplus existed; therefore, stratification was not based economically. When surplus was created, social classes formed around the groups who struggled with one another for control. Subsequently, *slavery* followed as groups grew more powerful. Through man's relations to production, Marx claimed, slavery was revolutionized into *feudalism*, during which a small aristocracy – families of nobility and clergy – controlled arable land and the means of production. A complex form of social stratification arose from the divisions of labor from which the middle class was created. Within this social configuration, groups formed trade unions and professional associations that created privilege for some people despite their lower-class standing as compared to the noble class.

The inherent conflict between aristocracy and *vassals* (i.e., those who tended the land) found within feudalism sowed the seeds for *capitalism*, which is the privatized control of the means of production. Marx held that two social classes exist in capitalism: the *bourgeois* and the *proletariat* – that is, the owners and the workers. Although he considered small business owners and property owners who collected rents to be *petit bourgeois* (i.e., little owners), in the final analysis, he perceived class conflict like a centrifuge that hurls everyone into one of two camps – the petit bourgeois landed in the proletariat camp.

The struggle between owners and workers within a capitalistic society was of great interest to Marx. With unyielding power, owners of the means of production exacted labor from workers of all ages; in return, they gave nothing but wages that often were docked when work was missed because of illness or injury. No labor laws existed at the time; consequently, workers had no legal rights and no security against harsh labor practices. The conflict between owners and workers, according to Marx, would result in a revolution in which the workers would overthrow the owners and gain control of the means of production.

Marx's perspective on revolution and power relations was impacted greatly by the French Revolution, which ended fewer than 20 years before he was born. During the French Revolution, the means of production were taken from noble French families and the Catholic Church on a bloody scale never before witnessed. After decades of upheaval, the nation developed into modern France, embraced the Enlightenment (i.e., a philosophical school of reason), citizenship, and inalienable rights – ideas that would later influence the modernization of America.

The social-progress theory of Marx did not end with capitalism. Indeed, the unequal power relations between owners and workers comprise the driving force for the revolution for *socialism* – in which the means of production are held publicly instead of privately. From socialism, Marx predicted a return to *communism*, in which the means of production would not be owned but rather shared by all people as during primitive communism. Although some contemporary nation-states claimed communism as a political format, they have not achieved the form envisioned by Marx.

Critiques of Marxian theory highlight three major flaws. The first is relative to a class consciousness that Marx assumed would bring on the proletariat revolution and move capitalism dialectically into socialism, a system in which rules are made by the proletariat. Indeed, a large-scale social revolution of workers has not occurred in America (see Chapter 2). In fact, the proletariat generally shows little sign of class consciousness.

The second flaw in Marx's work is that of joint-stock ownership. In a modern corporation, ownership occurs across nation-states with board members and managers from various geographical locations. In his later years, Marx acknowledged the complete separation of the bourgeois from the means of production. He foresaw the power and control of the capitalist class reaching into a global economy and that the owners would continue to exploit natural assets, even when they were not linked to those assets (like colonists in the past). However, he did not consider the ensuing rise of the managerial class. In modern capitalism, there are additional strata that include managers who do not own a corporation but earn well above what an average worker earns and have a voice in how the corporation is run.

The third flaw is the rise of *trade unions*. A *union* is an organization of workers with the power to bargain collectively with owners on behalf of workers' rights and privileges. *Collective bargaining* means that there is negotiation between labor and management and, therefore, less likelihood for the type of revolution that Marx predicted.

In America, unions helped to organize labor over various issues (e.g., wages, benefits, and working conditions) and introduced many of the privileges taken for granted today. In the 1930s, labor unions faced violent attempts at "union-busting." By the 1940s, nearly a third of all U.S. workers were union members; in 1955, at the height of union membership, 35 percent of all U.S. workers were under union protection (U.S. Bureau

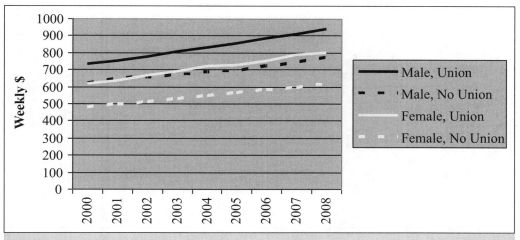

Figure 6.1 Average weekly earnings per week by union membership between 2000 and 2008 by gender.
Data source: Union affiliation data from the Current Population Survey, U.S. Department of Labor, U.S. Bureau of Labor Statistics (2009).

of Labor Statistics 2009b). Unions obtained the 40-hour/5-day work week, maternity leave, occupational health and safety, pay increases, and worker's compensation, to name but a few benefits. Moreover, union members earn more per week compared to non-union members. Distinct earning gaps exist between union and non-union members by sex and race/ethnicity. Figure 6.1 compares male and female average weekly earnings per week by union membership between 2000 and 2008. The figure shows that union membership increases the earnings for both genders; for women, membership increases earnings close to parity with non-union males.

Comparing the average weekly earnings for union and non-union workers by race/ethnicity reveals divergent patterns. Again, union members earn more than non-union members, but the earnings gap varies among ethnicities.

Asian workers, represented in Figure 6.2, have a smaller earnings gap compared with other ethnicities. Black union members earn $148 more than non-union members per week (Figure 6.3). White union workers, represented in Figure 6.4, earn $195 a week more than non-union members. Hispanic union workers earn $212 per week more than non-union members (Figure 6.5).

Despite the better working conditions provided by union membership, membership began a steep decline in the 1980s. Some suggest that the decline was due to federal policies that ended the strike of air traffic controllers in 1981, thereby sending a strong message to labor unions that strikes will not be tolerated. With no strike power available, unions lost bargaining power and, consequently, membership. Others point to power relations within unions as a reason for the decline. Many workers believed unions were not in their best interest and many businesses – particularly in the service sector – have non-union shops. Since 2006, union membership has been growing (see Figure 6.6); today, about 12 percent of workers are protected by unions.

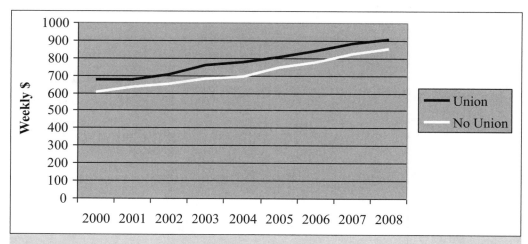

Figure 6.2 Asian average weekly earnings per week by union membership between 2000 and 2008.
Data source: Union affiliation data from the Current Population Survey, U.S. Department of Labor, U.S. Bureau of Labor Statistics (2009).

Marx assumed that revolutions would overturn capitalism; although that has not happened, they have occurred in recent history. However, the majority resulted in a divestment of imperial control and decolonization – and not necessarily in consciousness of the workers to overturn and control a nation. Examples include the African nations of Algeria, Cameroon, Gabon, Mauritania, Rwanda, Sudan, Somalia, and Tunisia.

More recently, in 2011, a series of revolutions began in Tunisia when a young man who could not find a job committed suicide after police confiscated the fruit he sold illegally without a permit. The nation erupted in protest and the workers demanded the

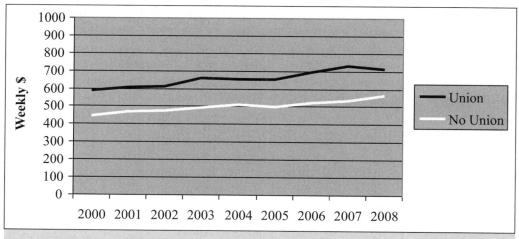

Figure 6.3 African American average weekly earnings per week by union membership between 2000 and 2008.
Data source: Union affiliation data from the Current Population Survey, U.S. Department of Labor, U.S. Bureau of Labor Statistics (2009).

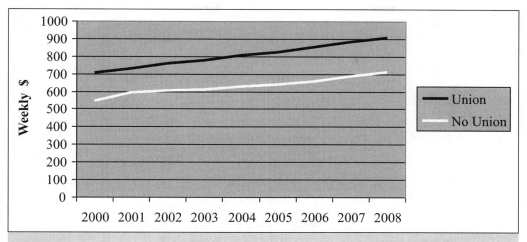

Figure 6.4 Caucasian average weekly earnings per week by union membership between 2000 and 2008.
Data source: Union affiliation data from the Current Population Survey, U.S. Department of Labor, U.S. Bureau of Labor Statistics (2009).

ouster of President Ben Ali. Soon after, uprisings spread to Yemen, Jordan, and Egypt. With the assistance of social-networking Web sites, workers and students began a general strike and took possession of Tahrir Square in the Egyptian capital city of Cairo. The people insisted that President Mubarak step down and allow a democratic process to determine the new leader of Egypt. As consciousness galvanized in the Arab world and people demanded change, some nations in the region staged protests with little effect on the powers that be. In summary, revolutions can affect the status quo; however, power has yet to be restored to the people, as Marx predicted.

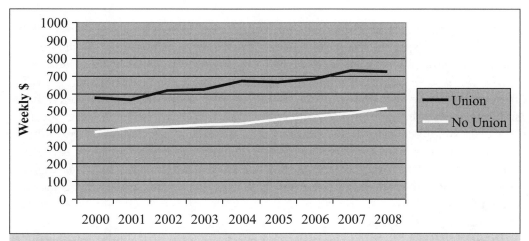

Figure 6.5 Hispanic average weekly earnings per week by union membership between 2000 and 2008.
Data source: Union affiliation data from the Current Population Survey, U.S. Department of Labor, U.S. Bureau of Labor Statistics (2009).

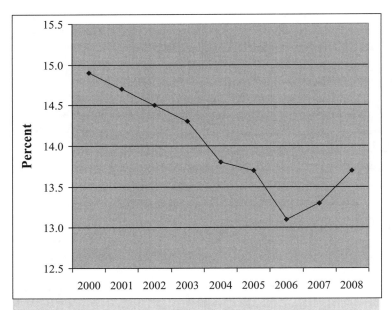

Figure 6.6 Percentage of U.S. workforce represented by a union.
Data source: Current Population Survey, U.S. Department of Labor,
U.S. Bureau of Labor Statistics (2009).

Max Weber was another conflict theorist who articulated the structure and divisions of social class. He rethought Marxian theory and reconciled much of Marx's work. Most importantly, Weber defined *class* as more than only the relations to production; he added the acquisition of goods and the patterns of principles associated with their consumption to class analysis. Market position is another dimension to modern classifications of social class. In a word, Weber considered *lifestyle* to be the best indicator of class and status.

Economic resources are important; however, Weber argued for three distinct forms of power relations: class, status, and party (i.e., voluntary membership). By adding the concept of *status*, Weber addressed the lack of class consciousness of the middle class. *Status groups* comprise a collective of people who have a similar social standing. They share a culture (i.e., behaviors, ideology, and material belongings) and an individual is simultaneously a member of many status groups. We all have different status positions that exist simultaneously: On holiday, we are Americans; at school, we are students; at home, we are mothers, fathers, sons, and daughters; and with each status position comes a different set of expectations, allegiances, and potential actions. Additionally, Weber observed that status groups often form parties that are groups of people who come together to effect social action on their own behalf (i.e., political parties, unions, and voluntary associations).

To Weber, class had more to do with the process of allocation – that is, how resources are divided and secured among society. These resources included Marxian concepts of economy, politics, and culture. However, Weber added to the list of resources three more types of capital: social, honorific, and civil. Honor determines the status of specific positions, which varies across societies, thereby explaining the rise of the management class that Marx's theory cannot explain. In short, conflict theory assumes that the middle class consists of workers. The stratification of workers depends on economy, politics, status, affiliations, and lifestyle within society.

Functionalist Perspective

The functionalist perspective views class divisions as a function of naturally distributed positions on an occupational hierarchy. Studies of occupational hierarchies show great consistency and durability in job categorizations (Blau and Duncan 1967; Hauser and Warren 1997). In other words, most industrial societies hold in high esteem doctors, scientists, and engineers and less so manual workers and laborers (Treiman 1970). Think of all the jobs available in any given industrialized society and rank them according to occupational status, where status equates to earnings, power, prestige, and social standing. The middle-class, then, is any area on a *continuum of occupations* that is situated between the lowest and highest groups. Many social scientists over time have developed an occupational status scale or prestige scale. Today, many agencies and social scientists use an updated version of the *Duncan Socioeconomic Index* that was developed by sociologist Otis Duncan (1921–2004) (Blau and Duncan 1967; Ganzeboom and Treiman 1996).

Functionalist theory (see Chapter 2) assumes that an occupation is linked to prestige by the amount of expertise associated with it. Because doctors need more knowledge than street sweepers, it is argued, they have higher levels of prestige and income. Moreover, a credential is needed by professionals. To earn a degree, individuals must take time – which could be spent in earning income – to attend school. This suggests that there must be a mechanism to encourage people to delay entry into the workforce. High prestige and earnings entice individuals to take on the necessary tasks needed to be employed within the well-educated and skilled workforce. Similarly, a musician and an athlete may earn more than a physician because society values their skills and awards them more status. Society determines which occupations are needed, and the ability of an individual determines who fills each position.

By conceptualizing social class as linear, in which status is placed on a continuum of the stratification structure, functionalists define the middle class as any group of people with similar levels of prestige and status. A doctor and a lawyer have similar prestige levels; indeed, they often have similar lifestyles. People are grouped not by discrete social classes but rather by percentiles associated with the prestige scale. Many middle-class studies use the phrase, "the average American," which corresponds to the middle 64 percent.

In summary, the middle class consists of workers. Whereas some sociologists believe divisions within workers are due to ability, others believe divisions occur from power relations. Both perspectives agree that members of the middle class generally share an *ideology* and are able to *mobilize* to create social and societal change and to retain power through group membership (e.g., labor unions). Some in the middle class hold occupational positions with little power, some have a marginal amount, and others have substantial power. To differentiate the subgroups within the middle class, social scientists use terms such as *white-* and *blue-collar workers*, *manual* and *nonmanual workers*, and *middle class* and *working class* (Glenn and Alston 1968).

Origins of the U.S. Middle Class

C. Wright Mills (1916–1962), a leading sociologist in the 1950s, reflected on the origins of the American middle class. He classified members of the middle class by their occupation. Owners and operators of independent retail and productive enterprises were categorized as the "older middle class." The "new middle class" was composed of white-collar workers, those in managerial positions, retail clerks, and office workers (Mills 1951). According to Mills, a shift in the U.S. economy corresponded to a rise in the new middle class over the old. In the early 1800s, Mills estimated that four of five workers were self-employed; by 1870, this was reduced to one of three (Ryan 1983). With this rise of the new middle class came less social connection to others of the same class; sociologists term this *class solidarity*. The old middle class shared in trade unions or professional associations, whereas the new middle class has no such connections (Burris 1986).

During the 1800s, Americans experienced a shift in social life – what Ferdinand Tönnies (1855–1936) called *gemeinschaft* to *gesellschaft*, which in German is *community* to *society*. Rural living eroded as cities grew, changing how people associated with one another. During this shift, Americans evolved into a middle-class society through the emergence of five prominent characteristics of lifestyle: work, consumption, residential location, formal and informal voluntary associations, and family organization and strategy (Blumin 1989).

The most influential factor that contributed to the rise of the middle class in antebellum America was the change within the occupational structure. Prior to the Industrial Revolution, the average American family lived near the production of crops, trading posts, or in homes with cottage-manufacturing such as mills. They often hired workers, used indentured servants, and acquired slaves to work in the fields or in industries that supported the production and distribution of goods. In large cities such as New York, Boston, and Philadelphia, the emergence of factories made redundant smaller cottage industries, often found in family homes. In New York, for example, cotton goods created a production industry that included mills, in which a full spectrum of labor was needed. In addition to skilled mill workers, owners needed wood-choppers, cart-pullers, and others to maintain production. The structuring of industry into manual workers and nonmanual workers separated two groups. The physical separation widened the social space between the working and middle classes. Although the workers labored in proximity to one another – an office being close to a factory, for example – they lived in different social spaces defined by their activities outside of work. Some of these differences were found in their leisure activities, the stores where they shopped, and the voluntary organizations that they joined. Memberships and associations with churches, lodges, fire companies, and reform societies bifurcated workers and created separate social spaces.

Perhaps the most predominant difference between workers and the middle class is found in a family's domestic life (Vinovskis 1991). A large family was the norm before the Industrial Revolution. Children were seen as the "flesh and blood" of the family and a natural extension of its labor. More hands to assist meant the family could accomplish more tasks in less time. Some believed a large family was evidence that Providence had intervened and that marrying young was a way to live up to the Divine design. In 1900, there were 1.75 million workers between the ages of 11 and 15 (Fisk 2003). Labor laws did not exist and children were perceived as small-bodied people who did not need special protections (Zelizer 1994). On the contrary, children were considered labor that was owned by the family. In one study of the middle class in Utica, New York, between 1790 and 1865, a reward for $5 was posted for the "arrest and delivery" of a farmer's runaway son. The ad read, "Left my employment, my son Patrick" (Zelizer 1994: 26). Children as young as four were particularly valued because of their small size, which made them better able to run between moving machine parts. Sociologist Lewis Hine (1874–1940) spent his professional life photographing child workers. His photographs of child laborers galvanized the labor movement and encouraged lawmakers to enact child-labor laws. It was not until 1941 that children were perceived as a special class of people who require legal protection from exploitation.

Great changes in the American workforce had occurred in the nineteenth century. In 1900, the number of workers older than age 10 was 24 million. By 1999, it was 139 million (and the minimum age of workers was 16). Not only were more people needed in the occupational structure, the structure itself also had changed dramatically. At the beginning of the twentieth century, about 38 percent of jobs were on farms; at the end of the century, it was less than 3 percent. During the same period, goods-producing jobs (e.g., mining and manufacturing) decreased from 31 to 19 percent and service-industry jobs increased from 31 to 78 percent (Fisk 2003).

An important aspect within the changing workforce is the division of labor by gender. During the 1900s, women entered the workforce in droves. The changing roles of women during this period are discussed in detail in Chapter 10. In the 1800s, women were much less likely to work outside the home. This fact solidified a particularly important characteristic of the middle-class family, which is termed the *culture of domesticity*.

The culture of domesticity, often shortened to the cult of domesticity, was a value system in place in white upper- and middle-class homes in the United States during the nineteenth century that emphasized women's embodiment of virtue. According to this system of ideals, women were to uphold the four cardinal virtues: piety, purity, submission, and domesticity (Welter 1966). Women were to be more spiritual and pure than men, accept their subjugation to men – father, brothers, husband, clergy, and God – and accept their true social sphere as the child bearer and homemaker. In this ideological system, value was placed on the home, which became more than a place to merely exist; rather, a man's home was a testament to his status in society and his wife was the barometer of family virtue.

The cult of domesticity set forth an ideal in which women – virtuous women, that is – do not labor outside the home. Although many of us today acknowledge the work required to rear a child, women generally were considered too pure to work outside the home. Therefore, a man was valued by his ability to provide a secure home, one that did not require his wife to leave. The home, then, became the center of the family and its trappings the proof of success. This cultural disposition heralded consumption patterns very different from those of the working class. This is a strong indicator of the ideology of the middle class that, in some respects, continues today.

The Industrial Revolution caused cities to grow and small cottage industries to decline. Machines took over many tasks previously done by workers. Farms and factories no longer needed a large workforce for production. As a result, work became more specialized and families became smaller.

Family organization and strategy also shifted dramatically during this period. The Industrial Revolution shifted the economy and changed the structure and dynamics of the American family. An integral characteristic of the middle class is the notion of opportunity for upward mobility. In the United States, a commonly held belief is that children will fare better than their parents. This was indeed the case throughout the twentieth century. As industrialization grew, so too did opportunities for advancement. Although the importance of education became more distinct, a laborer still could maintain a home and care for his family even with only one person – generally, his wife – working in the home. As industrialization declined, so too did this often-idealized state of the family. Today, about two-thirds of all U.S. women and more than half of all married women work outside the home (U.S. Bureau of Labor Statistics 2009a).

Traditional middle-class families, consisting of a heterosexual couple and their children, allowed for a certain lifestyle that included a safety net for unforeseen crises. With the wife staying home while her husband went to work, families had a built-in mechanism to care for the sick and the aging, assistance with spells of unemployment of the husband, and a skilled and able-bodied adult available to provide security against many crises.

When middle-class families shifted away from the culture of domesticity and women entered the workforce, the second paycheck most often was used to maintain a standard of living, not saved or invested. Today, when a child or grandparent needs care, families turn to others for help, often at great economic loss. When one adult loses a job, there is a great reduction in household income, which causes many to not only change their lifestyle but also to file for bankruptcy. When women entered the workforce, a safety net for the family was removed.

The Middle Classes

Those in "middle-class" occupations typically fill important societal roles such as managing the work of others and acting as technical specialists. What defines middle class is constantly in flux, however. Today, we think of the middle class as white-collar workers, business people, and managers. In the 1960s and 1970s, we included those occupations as middle class, but we also included well-paid blue-collar workers in the definition. Occupational categories help to identify the middle class; however, different occupational groups overlap in time and are not fully distinct entities (Archer and Blau 1993).

Similar to the differences among classes, there are differences among groups of people within the middle class. Professional and managerial occupations are defined increasingly as middle-class occupations. Depending on our definition of middle class, exactly who is included varies. Nevertheless, differentiation in the middle class has become more commonplace. Today, we may think of *upper-middle class, lower-middle class*, and *working class* as distinct groups.

Individuals who comprise the upper-middle class share distinct characteristics. They are, on average, the 15 percent of Americans who are well-educated professionals earning more than $75,000 but less than $150,000 per year (U.S. Census Bureau 2009). In addition to high earnings, this group has high levels of autonomy at work. Typical jobs associated with the upper-middle class are white-collar, managerial positions – that is, doctors, lawyers, upper management of corporations, and so on. Work is rarely separated from other spheres of life. This group tends to partner within the same social class and often chooses a mate from the pool of candidates met at school and through club memberships.

The lower-middle class consists of 30 percent of Americans who work as semiprofessionals (e.g., teachers and craftsmen), who have some college education, and, on average, earn between $35,000 and $74,500 per year. Most of these Americans have white-collar jobs with some autonomy.

About 40 percent of Americans are in the working class (Beeghley 2005). Typically, they are blue-collar workers with a high school education who earn between $16,000 and $34,500 per year. They have little autonomy at work because their tasks are highly routinized. There is little economic security for the working class, and their lifestyle often depends on the number of earners in the home.

Military

One group of middle-class workers often ignored in scholarly literature is members of the military. Statistics generated by federal and state agencies generally exclude military personnel because they do not fall within the private or public occupational sectors. Nearly 1.5 million people serve in the armed forces and more than three-quarters of a million are reservists (U.S. Department of Defense 2009b). This means that more than 1 percent of American workers are members of the military.

Military members earn income based on their rank and number of years of service. Whereas five-star and ranked officers' earnings and status place them in the upper class, the majority of military personnel are middle class. Salaries for members of the armed forces range between $16,794 at the lowest rank (i.e., E-1) with less than 5 years service to $102,157 for the highest rank (i.e., W-5) with 38 and more years of service, not including officers (U.S. Department of Defense 2009a).

In addition to salaries, service members receive benefits for a range of circumstances; for example, hazardous conditions and specialized medical training constitute additional pay. Moreover, the G.I. Bill (enacted in 1944) guaranteed monetary assistance to all armed-forces members for college or vocational training, student-loan repayment, and various loans designed to help soldiers transition into civil society after serving the nation.

The middle class consists of a large and diverse group of American workers. The rise in the middle class was a result of the economic restructuring of the Industrial Revolution. As the occupational hierarchy shifts across time, those of the middle class are at most risk of needing to adapt to the changes. As America's manufacturing base increased, so did the middle class and its benefits, such as home ownership, pensions, and leisure activities. Today, however, as a result of globalization and a reduction in manufacturing, the American occupational hierarchy has shifted toward information-technology and service-sector jobs.

Middle-Class Ideology

The values and ideals of the middle class are perceived as the dominant American values, often called "the American Dream." This is easily observed in mass media: TV families generally have two parents, live in a comfortable home furnished with state-of-the-art appliances and decor, wear the latest fashionable clothing, drive new and up-scale vehicles, and rarely experience the type of anxiety that actual families do. The ease of living portrayed on TV is taken for granted as the "average" experience in America. Often, other groups are held to these fabricated middle-class standards despite the fact that they are not realistic.

How the middle class became America's point of reference is the subject of an in-teresting study on symbols. By analyzing syndicated comic strips between 1925 and 1975, sociologists showed how the middle class emerged as the prominent image in America (Kasen 1979). In 1925, the number of upper-class characters was 27; by 1975, this number had decreased to 12. In 1925, the number of upper- and lower-middle-class characters was 9 and 37, respectively; by 1975, the numbers had increased to 13 and 58. A gradual shift in cartoon characters of interest to the average reader corresponds to the rise of middle-class identification. Images in the media do not accurately describe living people; they do, however, help sociologists to articulate American ideology.

From a multitude of studies defining the middle-class ideology, sociologists enumer-ated values of primary importance to the majority of Americans. These values include activity and work, achievement and success, moral orientation, humanitarianism, ef-ficiency and practicality, science and secular rationality, material comfort, progress, equality, freedom, democracy, external conformity, nationalism and patriotism, individ-ual personality, and racism and related group superiority (Mills 1956; Williams 1967). Many of these values contradict one another. How can a person value equality and democracy yet also embrace group superiority? The answer is found in a different value: individualism. Some people believe in equality for themselves – they should not be treated differently – but do not afford similar treatment to others. This type of contra-diction in ideology has led some scholars to add elitism, self-absorption, and selfishness to middle-class values, which emerge from a fear of falling from middle-class status and ending up in poverty (Ehrenreich 1989).

This fear of many members of the middle class is not farfetched. Findings of a poll by the Pew Research Center and Gallup Organization reveal that more than three-quarters (i.e., 78 percent) of the middle class report that it is more difficult for middle-class people to maintain their standard of living compared to five years ago. Twenty-five percent of surveyed Americans believe that they have made no progress in life, and 31 percent feel as though they have fallen backwards. These findings are at the lowest levels of middle-class self-assessments in nearly 50 years of polling (Taylor et al. 2008).

Middle-Class Squeeze

Structural and ideological changes in the last 40 years have led to a decline in the middle class. In part, the *"shrinking" of the middle class*, often called the *middle-class squeeze*, is caused by the bifurcation of wage and wealth structures in the United States. The middle class is "squeezed" when wages keep up with inflation only for the upper class. Lifestyles are difficult to maintain when wages do not increase and jobs decrease. Many middle-class families became upwardly mobile in the past three decades (see Chapter 5); however, a substantial number also moved down the stratification ladder in the same period. A drop in the number of middle-class families is an important explanation of the growth of inequality in the United States.

Indeed, the middle class is shrinking. The gap between upper and lower classes has been widening; by the early 1990s, paychecks of full-time male workers had 10 percent less purchasing power than 20 years earlier (Farley 1996). Figure 6.7 compares the purchasing power of the dollar across five decades and reveals a dramatic reduction.

In 1950, the dollar was worth more than seven times what it is worth today. Increases at the upper end of the wealth and income distributions occurred when real earnings for low-income households stagnated. The late 1980s saw a reduction in upward mobility of lower-income households and increased downward mobility of many at the lower range of the middle-income distribution. In addition, the 1986 Federal Tax Reform reduced the number of middle-class households. In the 1980s, prime-age adults in the middle-income category had a greater probability of slipping into the lower class than rising into a higher class (Duncan, Smeeding, and Rodgers 1993).

Some sociologists argue that the middle class is shrinking and others claim that it is not – that change in occupations is simply that: change. What has had a more dire effect on middle-class workers is the economic recession and high rates of unemployment. The amount of change that the middle class faces depends on theoretical perspective.

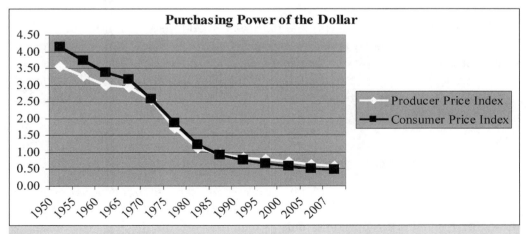

Figure 6.7 Purchasing power of the dollar, 1950–2008.
Data source: Bureau of Labor Statistics, Consumer Price Index Detailed Report, monthly; and Producer Price Indexes, monthly and annual.

Table 6.1 The Percentage of Unemployed Within Group by Age and Race

Major Worker Groups	% Unemployed Within Group
Adult men	10.3
Adult women	7.8
Teenagers	25.9
By Race/Ethnicity	
Asian	7.4
White	9.0
Hispanic (any race)	12.7
Black	15.4

Data source: U.S. Bureau of Labor Statistics, Selected Employment Indicators (2009).

Whereas conflict theorists show a growth in low-wage jobs and a decrease in worker benefits, functionalists point to the growth of a global middle class.

Recession and the Middle Class

In December 2007, America began the longest economic turndown since the Great Depression. In 2008, employers cut approximately 2 million jobs across all industry sectors. Between May and July of 2009, nearly 250,000 jobs were lost, many in the major industry sectors. Between May and October of 2009, on average, 331,000 jobs were lost each month, which was down from the 645,000 lost jobs per month between November 2008 and April 2009. Unemployment reached more than 10 percent nationally; for some regions, the rate was as high as 15 percent (U.S. Bureau of Labor Statistics 2009a).

When the unemployment rate is disaggregated, a distinct pattern emerges that explains how inequality occurs in America. Rates of unemployment are sensitive to gender, race/ethnicity, and age, as shown in Table 6.1.

The recession has affected men more than women and the young more than adults. Moreover, unemployment is patterned by race/ethnicity. A black worker is more than twice as likely to be unemployed compared to an Asian worker. As discussed in the study of race/ethnicity in Chapter 11, racial patterns of inequality are quite durable despite efforts to reduce them. The economic crisis has further damaged the shrinking middle class, particularly the black middle class.

Consumption and Debt

One reason why the middle class is doing less well compared to past generations is debt due to consumption. Recall from Chapter 5 that just over half, about 60 percent, of those in the middle class put aside some income to save for retirement. The remaining income is used to provide the material goods that constitute a family's lifestyle. Table 6.2 shows the expenditure categories of the CPI – that is, where the middle class spends its income.

Table 6.2 Consumer Price Index Expenditures by Category

Expenditure Category	CPI
Housing	41.31
Transportation	17.07
Food and Beverage	16.94
Recreation	5.45
Medical Care	5.36
Apparel	3.98
Communication	3.69
Other Goods and Services	3.67
Education	2.53
All Items	100

Data source: U.S. Bureau of Labor Statistics Table 1 (2005–2006 Weights). Relative importance of components in the Consumer Price Indexes: U.S. City Average, December (2008).

Whereas some suggest that the high amount of debt owed by the middle class today is due to over-consumption or "luxury fever" (Frank 2001) (see Chapter 5), scholars are quick to point out that it is far less than in previous decades (Warren and Tyagi 2005). Less than 20 percent of the CPI is allocated to transportation today: Compared to the 1970s, families keep their automobiles longer, 7 years compared to 5.5 years, and a family of four spends 20 percent less than their parents did per vehicle. Nearing the cost of transportation is food and beverage, just under 17 percent of the CPI. Between 2008 and 2009, the price of food increased about 5 percent and, coupled with the recession (U.S. Department of Agriculture 2009), middle-class families changed their habits – they eat at home more often and pack more lunches for school and work. Compared to the previous generation, families today spend 22 percent less on food.

Housing is the most notable commodity of the middle class and accounts for 40 percent of the CPI (including mortgage, rent, and furnishings). The majority of middle-class families owns their home and spends approximately 69 percent more on their mortgage, 44 percent less on appliances, and 30 percent less on furniture than their parents. In America, owning a home is more than merely shelter – it dictates which school children may attend, as well as the amount of crime and risk a family may experience.

In 2007, a combination of banking practices and a housing "bubble" that greatly inflated home prices burst. Many middle-class Americans purchased and refinanced a home at higher rates than the current value of the home. This prompted the largest foreclosure crisis since the Great Depression: In January 2007, the national foreclosure rate was 0.128 percent; by September 2009, it had jumped to 0.260 (RealtyTrac 2009).

In the discussion of the elite class in Chapter 5, we learned that conspicuous consumption of the leisure class included large homes and that this fact was echoed in the purchases made by the middle class – what Frank (2001) termed *luxury fever*. Yet, current census data report a decrease in the average home size after a four-decade-long trend in home-size increases. In the most recent data report of new builds, the average home size of 2,521 square feet in 2007 has decreased to 2,392 square feet in 2011 (U.S. Census 2011).

Other factors negatively impact the middle class. In recent years, out-of-pocket health-care costs, credit-card debt, and educational loans have become more burdensome. In one generation's time, out-of-pocket health-care costs have increased about 90 percent (Warren and Tyagi 2005). Credit-card default rates are higher than ever before: The average family carries $9,797 in credit-card debt (Sherman 2009). As consumers accrue large amounts of debt, credit-card issuers add to it by increasing and changing credit terms. The Federal Reserve Bank and other agencies have called these practices "unfair and deceptive," according to a Pew Charitable Trusts Executive Report (Pew Research Center 2009). In a recent study, Pew (2009) surveyed card issuers and found that

> 100 percent of cards allowed the issuer to apply payments in a manner which, according to the Federal Reserve, is likely to cause substantial monetary injury to consumers; 93 percent of cards allowed the issuer to raise any interest rate at any time by changing the account agreement; 87 percent of cards allowed the issuer to impose automatic penalty interest rate increases on all balances, even if the account is not 30 days or more past due. The median allowable penalty interest rate was 27.99 percent per year; 72 percent of cards included offers of low promotional rates which issuers could revoke after a single late payment.

In response, President Obama signed a consumer protection bill entitled the Credit Card Accountability, Responsibility, and Disclosure Act of 2009. The aim of this bill is to make the process of using credit more transparent, thereby allowing for better decision making by consumers. How well this bills works in assisting consumers has yet to be evaluated. (Chapter 14 discusses efforts to decrease inequality by enacting policy.) In addition to credit-card debt, lower-income families are more likely to use fringe banking, check-cashing centers, and pawnshops to assist with debt (Caskey 1994). These alternatives to banks charge high interest rates, thereby further exacerbating household financial troubles.

Financial debt from college costs also disproportionately affects the middle class. Given that part of the middle-class ideology is upward mobility and educational in-vestment, children's education – particularly college education – is perceived as not only important but necessary. Unfortunately, a college education is increasingly more costly than in the past. State universities were designed to provide affordable educa-tion for an equitable distribution despite the economic status of a family. Yet, they have been the hardest hit by the economic recession and they look to tuitions to reverse the losses. In 2009, for example, University of California Regents increased college tuition by 32 percent. Students now pay more than three times what they did a decade ago. In California, the Master Plan organized state universities and colleges into three tiers. The top tier includes the University of California (UC) schools (e.g., UCLA) and provides the top-ranked 12.5 percent of California students with a superb undergraduate and graduate educational experience. The second tier serves the top third and includes the California State University (CSU) schools (e.g., CSULB). The remaining two-thirds of California students are expected to attend community colleges throughout the state. With the increase in tuition, many qualified students will be turned away from the top two tiers. The CSU system expected to turn away 45,000 qualified students in 2010. Other states also increased college tuition in 2011 – for example New York raised state-school tuitions by 7 percent.

Few students can afford to attend school without some form of financial support. According to data from the National Center for Education Statistics (2009), in 2007–2008, more than 60 percent of students earning a Bachelor's degree accrued student-loan debt – the median amount was $19,999. However, 25 percent of loan-seeking students borrowed $30,562 and 10 percent borrowed $44,668 or more. Comparing the same data from the 2003–2004 school year, there is a 4 percent increase in students borrowing more than $40,000 to earn a Bachelor's degree. Parents also take out loans to help fund their children's college education. The 14 percent of parents who secured a PLUS loan (a federal loan for families with college students) owed a cumulative $23,298 at the end of the four years. This amount does not consider private loans borrowed by the family.

Graduate students accrue even more debt than undergraduates. Students typically borrow between $30,000 and $120,000 during graduate school. The median debt for a Master's degree is $25,000, a doctorate is $52,000, and a professional degree is $80,000. At the upper range of debt (i.e., the 90th percentile), cumulative debt is significantly higher: $59,869 for a Master's degree, $123,650 for a doctoral degree, and $159,750 for a professional degree (National Center for Educational Statistics 2009).

Bankruptcy is another factor that has diminished the middle class. Reasons for bankruptcy include employment problems (e.g., layoffs, "skidding" to a lower-paying job, and part-time work), the overuse of credit cards, unpayable medical bills, loss of income from illness or accident, and the financial burden on single-adult households that results from divorce (Sullivan, Warren, and Westbrook 1989; 2000).

In 2004, an American family filed for bankruptcy every 15 seconds; today, that number is higher. Between 2006 and 2009, the number of bankruptcy filings more than tripled (Figure 6.8), and more than 90 percent of bankruptcies are filed by middle-class families.

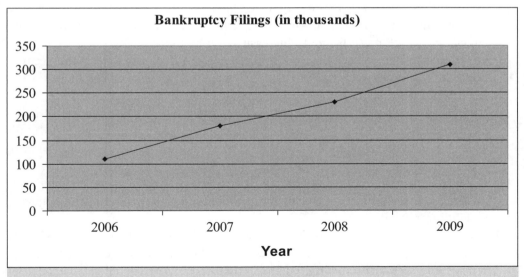

Figure 6.8 Number of bankruptcy filings, 2006–2009.
Data source: Bureau of Labor Statistics, Consumer Price Index Detailed Report (2009).

Between 1980 and 2000, the number of females declaring bankruptcy rose 662 percent (Warren and Tyagi 2004). Investigating this fact, scholars found the best predictor of bankruptcy for any household is having a child in the home: Married couples with children are more than twice as likely to file for bankruptcy compared to those with no children; single women with children are more than six times as likely to file as those with no children. Households with children are more than 75 percent as likely to be late in paying a bill as those with no children. In all, one of every seven families with children declares bankruptcy; for perspective, in any given year, more people will file for bankruptcy than suffer from a heart attack or cancer, graduate from college, or file for divorce.

Although filing for bankruptcy is meant to provide families a fresh start, research shows that those who file accumulate less wealth, pay higher credit rates, and have more difficulty obtaining credit even years after they file (Han and Li 2009). As a result, growing bankruptcy rates negatively impact the middle class in the long term.

Summary

(1) The middle class is often treated as a default category that distinguishes a group of workers who are not poor but who also are not rich.

(2) The middle class galvanized during the Industrial Revolution as agrarian societies evolved into industrial societies, from *gemeinschaft* to *gesellschaft* (i.e., from community to society).

(3) Conflict theorists view the middle class as a product of class conflict that results from a dialectic relationship between workers and the means of production.

(4) Marx envisioned a proletariat revolution that would free workers from exploitation by owners of the means of production, but he did not foresee government policies restricting and prohibiting general strikes or trade unions.

(5) Trade unions work on behalf of organized labor. Workers who are union members are paid more than non-union members. The rate of union membership has declined since 1945 but it began to increase again in 2007.

(6) Functionalist theorists see the middle class as a group of workers on the occupational hierarchy between the rich and the poor. Today, social scientists use scales (e.g., the Duncan Status Index) to measure socioeconomic status.

(7) Middle-class whites adopted the culture of domesticity, which resulted in the subordination of women and a focus on the home as a barometer of social success. To this day, many middle-class families structure work so that the woman may stay home to care for domestic duties while the man goes to work.

(8) The middle class has a distinct lifestyle. They embrace the American Dream, home-ownership, a secure job, a vehicle, and a family with the opportunity for upward mobility from work.

(9) Many middle-class Americans share values that include activity and work, achievement and success, moral orientation, humanitarianism, efficiency and practicality, science and secular rationality, material comfort, progress, equality, freedom, democracy, external conformity, nationalism and patriotism, individual personality, and racism and related group superiority.

(10) Many middle-class families take on debt from home loans, college tuition, and credit cards. Often, this debt cannot be repaid, causing families to file for bankruptcy. Whereas some critics argue that Americans spend too much, others show that they actually spend less than previous generations.

Box 6.1 Middle-Class Children: Works in Progress or No Time Left to Be a Child?

How families rear children differs by social class. Sociologist Annette Lareau uses ethnographic research to demonstrate how the production logics differ between middle- and working-class families. In her research, she followed African American and white families from two schools: One school was predominantly middle class, the other was working class.

She found no differences between black and white families; instead, the differences were between social classes. Working-class families structure their childrearing practices around a belief of *natural growth* so that students are separate from adults in the home, allowed "to be kids" with little adult direction in activities, and much like their parents' attitudes toward work – that is, after a student is home from school, school is no longer a consideration. These families instill values in their children that manifest as distrust of authority.

Middle-class families, conversely, engage in a production logic of childrearing that Lareau calls *concerted cultivation*. Parents organize their children's time around activities that they believe will provide them with the most benefit in life. They perceive their children as works in progress and invest in them accordingly.

These different child-production logics, in turn, affect children's own perception and their surrounding environment. For instance, when the two groups are followed to a medical appointment, the differences in interactions with the doctor are evident. The working-class child does not speak with the doctor, neither the parent nor the child makes eye contact with the doctor, and there are no probing questions from the family. Instead, they are intimidated and fearful that a wrong answer could jeopardize the family because a doctor has the authority to remove a child from the home.

The middle-class family, by contrast, began preparing for the doctor's visit the day before, with the mother telling the child that the visit is his opportunity to ask the doctor questions about his body and that he should think about any concerns he has. Once in the office, the child spoke for himself and even joked with the doctor, showing an ease in communication with superiors. The child perceived himself as an equal and not as a subordinate to the doctor.

These production logics inform sociologists about how stratification processes work in the family. Due to these different sets of values, students perform differently in school. Working-class children see school as the site of education and, once away from school, education is over; whereas middle-class students look at education much like their parents' work, as ongoing and continuous. Additionally, language is used differently between these classes. Students from working-class families do not use much language. The parents give direct orders that the children are expected to obey. This differs in middle-class families, where communication between a child and parent is encouraged. Parents negotiate and teach their children to verbally express themselves, often at the expense of the parents' will. Middle-class children argue and negotiate with their parents.

Lareau makes no claims as to which production logic is best – it is not the purpose of science to make ethical claims. However, she suggests that children who are reared under the concerted-cultivation method are not allowed to structure their own time and she wonders if this may have long-term effects not anticipated by parents.

Source: Lareau, Annette. 2003. *Unequal Childhoods: Class, Race, and Family Life*. Berkeley: University of California Press.

Box 6.2 Better Red Than Dead: A Critical Look at Communism
and Wealth Accumulation

The 1930s were rife with political upheaval in America. Unionism was on the rise and many corporations fought to decrease labor's influence in the workforce. One weapon used to decrease union memberships and control was called the *red scare*. Casting the labor movement as a move toward communism deterred many Americans from full participation in the movement. By presenting the labor–owner contest as freedom versus communism, business was able to situate labor demands as a move to lessen freedom.

In the 1950s, there was increased concern that communism was infiltrating America. This was the era of the Cold War, when relations between Russia and the United States and China and the United States were strained. At the time, Joseph McCarthy, a Republican Senator from Wisconsin (1947–1957), gave a face to the anticommunist movement. The result was a sweeping away of individuals with leftist ideologies and opinions. For instance, colleges across America were purged of left-wing faculty (Schrecker 1986).

In addition to McCarthy, The House Committee on Un-American Activities (HUAC) (1935–1978) was charged with ensuring the American people that no threats of communism would develop on U.S. soil. One way the HUAC kept communism at bay was through the development of blacklists. Once a name appeared on a blacklist, that person could obtain no work. In 1947, forty-three members of the Hollywood community were subpoenaed to testify before the HUAC. The witnesses included Ronald Reagan, Walt Disney, Gary Cooper, Jack Warner, and many others who were both in front of and behind the camera. During preliminary hearings that were closed to the public, a small group within the Hollywood community accused other members of being communists. Of the 43 members, 19 were considered unfriendly witnesses. These men (they were all men) included a mix of screenwriters, directors, writer-directors, a writer-producer, and a playwright. The men held openly radical political beliefs; indeed, some were members of the Communist Party of America. However, so were many other members of the Hollywood community who were not put before the HUAC (Dick 1988). Members of the Screen Actors Guild (SAG) and other occupational associations were considered potentially dangerous. The HUAC considered SAG to be communist-infested.

As defined by Marx, communism includes a more equitable distribution of wealth. Rarely does someone ask the critical question: Was inequality decreased through communism? Sociologist Gerhardt Lenski (1952–)(1994) answers this question by providing a detailed empirical analysis of state socialist nations (what were once considered communist states) and shows that significant levels of inequality existed although their explicit goals were set to be equalizing power among the workers. He shows that in Bulgaria, other parts of Eastern Europe, and Bolivia, political rulers who touted a communistic line of "power to the people" actually were guilty of mass material accumulation. The "peoples' rulers" had appropriated wealth at the expense of their nation, often depositing these profits in Swiss bank accounts for personal use. Additionally, Lenski reveals that property such as mansions that were once owned by the bourgeois was taken for the personal use of the new leaders. Lenski provides evidence that even with these improprieties, levels of inequality between the richest and poorest people in state socialist nations do not come close to the inequality in industrialized nations such as the United States, England, and Japan.

Key Concepts

American Dream

Bourgeois

C. Wright Mills – new middle class

Class solidarity

Continuum of occupations

Culture of domesticity

Dialectics – dialectic materialism

Duncan Socioeconomic Index

Gemeinschaft and *Gesellschaft*

G.I. Bill

Idealism

Ideology

Lifestyle   *Petit bourgeois*
Lower-middle class   Proletariat
Materialism   Status groups
Means of production   Theory of social progress
Middle class   Trade unions
Middle-class squeeze   Upper-middle class
Mobilize   Working class

Questions for Thought

1. Although members of the middle class represent a wide range of education and income levels, they also have many common characteristics. What are some of these characteristics?
2. The proportion of the middle class composed of self-employed individuals (e.g., shop and restaurant owners) is currently increasing (Wright 1997). What are some causes of this increase?
3. How does the American Dream affect different ethnic groups of middle-class Americans? Why and in what ways?
4. The ways in which parents rear children differ by social class. What other rituals differ by social class? What causes these differences?

Exercises

1. *Characteristics of Middle-Class Communities*
   Think about an area in or near your hometown that you consider a "middle-class neighborhood." List some of the characteristics of this neighborhood that lead you to believe it is middle class. Is this list representative of the population that comprises the U.S. middle class? Why or why not?
2. *Identifying Media Images of the Middle Class*
   List all of the families you have watched on TV programs. Describe their family structure, occupations, income level, social-club memberships, and lifestyle. Are there similarities among these idealized families? Do they differ from your experiences and those of your classmates? If so, how?
3. *Middle-Class Membership*
   Design a survey to test with which social class the majority of people in your community identify. Which criteria do they use to establish social classes? Do these criteria differ from those used by social scientists? If so, how?

Multimedia Resources

Print

Arnowitz, Stanley. 1974. *False Promises: The Shaping of America's Working Class Consciousness.* New York: McGraw-Hill.

Bearman, Peter S., and Glenn Deane. 1992. "The Structure of Opportunity: Middle-Class Mobility in England, 1548–1689." *American Journal of Sociology*, 98: 30–66.

Bledstein, Burton J., and Robert D. Johnston. 2001. *The Middling Sorts: Explorations in the History of the American Middle Class.* New York: Routledge.

Mills, C. Wright. 1956. *White Collar: The American Middle Classes.* New York: Oxford University Press.

Mischel, Lawrence, Jared Bernstein, and Sylvia Allegretto. 2005. *The State of Working America, 2004/2005.* Washington D.C.: Economic Policy Institute.

Sullivan, Tereasa A., Elizabeth Warren, and Jay Westbrook. 2000. *The Fragile Middle Class: Americans in Debt.* New Haven, CT: Yale University Press.

Internet

www.as.ysu.edu/~cwcs/: Center for Working Class Studies at Youngstown State University. This site contains facts and figures about working-class people and information about policies affecting and programs geared toward the working class.

www.pbs.org/peoplelikeus/about/index.html: This film has supplemental and background information, including stories about what it is like to grow up in various classes in America, to accompany the PBS film, *People Like Us.*

www.pbs.org/now/resources/politics.html: A source for information on government agencies, think tanks, and the like.

www.cnn.com/SPECIALS/2009/map.economy/index.html: Interactive map of home foreclosures between 2007 and 2009.

www.pbs.org/now/thisweek/index_020604.html. A brief discussion of Elizabeth Warren's research on the economy where she finds Americans are not necessarily over-spending.

Now with Bill Moyers – Guest: Elizabeth Warren

Bill Moyers goes in-depth with Harvard law professor Elizabeth Warren, who reveals some surprising facts about the plight of America's two-income families.

www.onpointradio.org/shows/2005/06/20050610_a_main.asp

"The Vanishing Middle Class"

Aired: Friday, June 10, 2005 7–8PM A debate on the issue of whether there is a vanishing middle class and what this means to American democracy, culture, and civil society.

www.historyplace.com/unitedstates/childlabor/: A provocative look at the practice of child labor, the site focuses on Mill Children in America.

Films

Home Economics: A Documentary of Suburbia. 1996. This film illustrates the American Dream and solidly middle-class achievement of homeownership. This film also explores how elements of middle-class life are not always as realistic as they are depicted in some forms of media.

Middletown: Continuity or Change? 1999. This documentary focuses on the changing attitudes and beliefs of the residents of Middletown and the American middle class in general.

People Like Us. 2001. This film clearly illustrates the material and ideological effects of growing up in a specific social class.

Works Cited

Archer, Melanie, and Judith R. Blau. 1993. "Class Formation in Nineteenth-Century America: The Case of the Middle Class." *Annual Review of Sociology* 19: 17–41.

Beeghley, Leonard. 2005. *The Structure of Social Stratification in the United States*. Boston: Pearson/Allyn and Bacon.

Blau, Peter, and Otis D. Duncan. 1967. *The American Occupational Structure*. New York: John Wiley and Sons.

Blumin, Stuart M. 1989. *The Emergence of the Middle Class: Social Experience in the American City, 1760–1900*. Cambridge, MA: Cambridge University Press.

Burris, Val. 1986. "The Discovery of the New Middle Class." *Theory and Society* 15: 317–49.

Caskey, Richard. 1994. *Fringe Banking: Check-Cashing Outlets, Pawnshops, and the Poor*. New York: Russell Sage Foundation.

Dick, Bernard F. 1988. *Radical Innocence: A Critical Study of the Hollywood Ten*. Lexington: University Press of Kentucky.

Duncan, Greg J., Timothy M. Smeeding, and Willard Rodgers. 1993. "W(h)ither the Middle Class? A Dynamic View." In *Poverty and Prosperity in the USA in the Late Twentieth Century*, edited by D. B. Papadimitriou and E. N. Wolff (pp. 240–71). New York: St. Martin's Press.

Ehrenreich, Barbara. 1989. *Fear of Falling: The Inner Life of the Middle Class*. New York: Pantheon.

Farley, Reynolds. 1996. *The New American Reality: Who We Are, How We Got Here, Where We Are Going*. New York: Russell Sage Foundation.

Fisk, Donald M. 2003. "American Labor in the 20th Century." U.S. Department of Labor, Bureau of Labor Statistics, Washington, DC.

Frank, Robert H. 2001. *Luxury Fever*. New York: The Free Press.

Ganzeboom, Harry B. G., and Donald J. Treiman. 1996. "Internationally Comparable Measures of Occupational Status for the 1988 International Standard Classification of Occupants." *Social Science Research* 25: 201–39.

Glenn, Norval D., and Jon P. Alston. 1968. "Cultural Distances Among Occupational Categories." *American Sociological Review* 33: 365–82.

Han, Song, and Geng Li. 2009. "Household Borrowing after Personal Bankruptcy." Federal Reserve Bank, Washington, DC.

Hauser, Robert M., and John Robert Warren. 1997. "Socioeconomic Indexes for Occupations: A Review, Update, and Critique." *Sociological Methodology* 27: 177–298.

Kasen, Jill H. 1979. "Exploring Collective Symbols: America as a Middle-Class Society." *Pacific Sociological Review* 22: 348–81.

Lenski, Gerhard. 1994. "New Light on Old Issues: The Relevance of 'Really Existing Socialist Societies' for Stratification Theory." In *Social Stratification: Class, Race, and Gender in Sociological Perspective*, Edited by David Grusky (Pp. 55–61).

Mills, C. Wright. 1951. *White Collar: The American Middle Classes*. New York: Oxford University Press.

_____. 1956. *The Power Elite*. New York: Oxford University Press.

National Center for Education Statistics. 2009. "National Postsecondary Student Aid Study (NPSAS)." U.S. Department of Education, Institute of Education Sciences, Washington, DC.

Pew Research Center. 2009. "Safe Credit Cards Standards: Policy Recommendations for Protecting Credit Cardholders and Promoting a Functional Marketplace." Washington, DC: Pew Charitable Trusts.

Realty Trac. 2009. "Foreclosure Activity by Month." Irvine, CA.

Ryan, Mary P. 1983. *Cradle of the Middle Class: The Family in Oneida County, New York, 1790–1865*. New York: Cambridge University Press.

Schrecker, Ellen W. 1986. *No Ivory Tower: McCarthyism and the Universities*. New York: Oxford University Press.

Sherman, Lauren. 2009. "Worst Cities for Credit Card Debt." In *Forbes*, retrieved June 1, 2009. Available at www.forbes.com/2009/05/20/american-consumers-overspending-lifestyle-real-estate-credit-card-debt.html.

Stearns, Peter N. 1979. "The Middle Class: Toward a Precise Definition." *Comparative Studies in Society and History* 21: 377–96.

Sullivan, Teresa A., Elizabeth Warren, and Jay Lawrence Westbrook. 1989. *As We Forgive our Debtors: Bankruptcy and Consumer Credit in America*. New York: Oxford University Press.

_____. 2000. *The Fragile Middle Class: Americans in Debt*. New Haven, CT: Yale University Press.

Taylor, Paul, Rich Morin, D'Vera Cohn, Richard Fry, Rakesh Kochhar, and April Clark. 2008. "Inside the Middle Class: Bad Times Hit the Good Life." Washington, DC: Pew Research Center.

Treiman, Donald J. 1970. "Industrialization and Social Stratification." *Sociological Inquiry, Special Issue: Stratification Theory and Research* 40: 207–34.

U.S. Bureau of Labor Statistics. 2009a. "Labor Force Statistics from the Current Population Survey." U.S. Department of Labor, Washington, DC.

_____.2009b. "Union Affiliation of Employed Wage and Salary Workers." U.S. Bureau of Labor Statistics, Washington, DC.

U.S. Census Bureau. 2009. "Table HINC-06. Income Distribution to $250,000 or More for Households: 2008." U.S. Census Bureau, Washington, DC.

_____. 2011. "Characteristics of New Single Family Houses Completed." U.S. Census Bureau, Washington, DC.

U.S. Department of Agriculture. 2009. "Food CPI and Expenditures: Analysis and Forecasts of the CPI for Food." U.S. Department of Agriculture, Washington, DC.

U.S. Department of Defense. 2009a. "2009 Military Pay Tables." U.S. Department of Defense, Washington, DC.

_____. 2009b. "Active Duty Military Personnel by Rank/Grade." U.S. Department of Defense, Washington, DC.

Vinovskis, Maris A. 1991. "Stalking the Elusive Middle Class in Nineteenth-Century America: A Review Article." *Comparative Studies in Society and History* 33: 582–7.

Warren, Elizabeth, and Amelia W. Tyagi. 2004. *The Two-Income Trap: Why Middle-Class Mothers and Fathers are Going Broke*. New York: Basic Books.

Warren, Elizabeth, and Amelia Warren Tyagi. 2005. "What's Hurting the Middle Class: The Myth of Overspending Obscures the Real Problem." In *Boston Review*, September/October. Boston, MA. (http://bostonreview.net/BR30.5/warrentyagi.html)

Welter, Barbara. 1966. "The Cult of True Womanhood: 1820–1860." *American Quarterly* 18 (2): 151–174.

Williams, Robin M., Jr. 1967. "Individual and Group Values." *Annals of the American Academy of Political and Social Science* 371: 20–37.

Wright, Erik Olin. 1997. Class Counts: Comparative Studies in Class Analysis. NY:Cambridge University Press.

Zelizer, Viviana A. Rotman. 1994. *Pricing the Priceless Child: The Changing Social Value of Children*. Princeton, NJ: Princeton University Press.

7 The Working Poor and the Underclass

What does it mean to be poor? Or, more precisely, what material things comprise "What is enough?" This is the central question to scholars who study poverty. The number of people living in poverty varies by the agency that collects the data and the percentage of poor used by governmental agencies is only a general estimate. This chapter considers the definition of poverty and how this construction affects who is considered poor and eligible to receive assistance. We then turn to the determinants of poverty and sociological theories that seek to explain who are the poor and predict how many people will fall below the poverty line in any given period. We conclude with the consequences associated with poverty as well as broad national policies and their effectiveness at reducing poverty.

What Is Poverty?

Poverty is a dearth of resources such as money or material possessions that are needed for survival. In modern society, it is defined as the lack of both income and wealth. The official poverty measure reveals that about 14.3 percent of the nation or 1 in 7 people is experiencing poverty, the highest rate since 1994 (U.S. Census Bureau 2010). The aggregate poverty rate varies by region with the Northeast having the lowest rate of 12.2 percent and the South with the highest rate of 15.7 (U.S. Census 2010).

Poverty is often a difficult concept to construct and measure because it encompasses morals, ethics, politics, demographics, and epistemology. For example, consider this seemingly simple question: "What does it mean to be poor?" We might answer, "Being poor is a condition of life in which one does not have enough to survive." What, then, is enough to survive? The answer to this question is complex and hinges on the economy as much as on one's belief system. For some, *enough* is earning an income that can sustain a family; home; health care; at least two automobiles; and expenses like college tuition, vacations, and hobbies – yet still have enough to save for a comfortable retirement. Others think *enough* is having a safe place to sleep at night, clean water, and one meal a day. The definition of poverty is a social construction by social scientists, governments, and the general public (Iceland 2003). The discussion of poverty begins by examining the measures used to describe the poor.

Poverty rates are used by various agencies for different reasons. Because of this fact, scientists constructed different poverty measurements, the six most common of which are *absolute, relative, official, subjective measures, hardship indicators*, and *social exclusion*. Poverty can be measured by an absolute measure such as the poverty rate, as it relates to other individuals and their social classes, or by considering the subjective, daily experiences of the poor. Each measure is discussed in detail.

Absolute poverty is the inability to sustain oneself – it is also called *extreme poverty*. The United Nations (UN) calculates the absolute-poverty threshold as one dollar a day. The threshold is calculated as the amount a person needs to purchase the total amount of goods that an adult consumes each year for survival. This is considered a *needs-based measure*, meaning that it is based on the minimum amount needed for survival. The requirements for survival typically include food, water, sanitation facilities, and shelter. The UN also includes education, communication, and access to health services as indicators of absolute poverty.

The strength of the absolute poverty measure is that it can be used in cross-national comparisons because the resources should be similar across time and space. It has limited usefulness due to great variation in economic conditions among countries. The question, "What is enough?," as discussed previously, is complex. How can we compare people in New York City, where the poverty rate is just over 12 percent, to those in Haiti, the poorest nation in the Western Hemisphere? In Haiti, 80 percent of the population lives below the poverty line. Clearly, when a person is in Mid-town Manhattan, water, food, and a lean-to shelter are not enough for survival, whereas in Haiti, many live with less.

Relative poverty compares people on a distribution of resources and then defines the poor as those who fall below the average-income threshold for the economy. In other words, people who have less than comparable to others are considered poor. Agencies often use this poverty measure to calculate need based on the local context. The average income in New York City in 2007 was $47,581. Using the official poverty threshold, an individual must earn less than $10,000 a year to be considered poor. However, most agencies understand that needs are relative to social standards. Using relative poverty measures, agencies and government officials can set poverty standards relative to the median income (e.g., 50 percent of the median annual income), in which case, earning less than $23,790 would constitute poverty.

Needs-based constructions consider the poverty rate as dynamic – it has a different meaning to people in various parts of the nation. Consider how much a person needs to exist in San Francisco compared to cities with lower living standards. The minimum wage is $8 an hour; however, a person needs to earn at least $31.88 an hour to live in San Francisco (Wardrip, Pelletiere, and Crowley 2009).

Official poverty, sometimes referred to as *federal poverty*, is computed by the U.S. Census Bureau and is a measure of relative poverty. There are two different versions of the official poverty rate: *thresholds* and *guidelines*. Thresholds are computed by the U.S. Census Bureau; the U.S. Department of Health and Human Services then uses the numbers to compute poverty guidelines for agencies, programs, and other outreach needs. In 2009, for instance, the poverty thresholds for an individual and a family of four were $10,830 and $22,050, respectively. These data, in turn, are used to calculate the official poverty rate.

The U.S. poverty rate is approximately 13.8 percent (U.S. Census Bureau 2010b). This means that 13.8 percent of all Americans live on less than $10,999 a year. Figure 7.1 shows the number of people living in poverty and the poverty rate between 1959 and 2009. This graphic representation shows that beginning in 2000, the poverty rate has been steadily increasing. Indeed, the effect of the 2008 recession shows a dramatic increase in the rate and number of people living in poverty.

The official poverty rate tells only part of the story because poverty rates vary greatly by region. Between 2007 and 2008, poverty rates in the South (14.3 percent) and the Northeast (11.6 percent) did not change significantly; however, in the West, poverty increased 1.5 percent (13.5 percent) as in the Midwest, with an increase of 1.3 percent (12.4 percent). This trend continued through 2009 when the South (15.7 percent), Midwest (13.3 percent) and the West (14.8) experienced statistically significant increases. Disaggregating the population by state, the poverty rate ranges from 7.4 percent in New Hampshire to 20.6 percent in Mississippi (Table 7.1). The numbers are estimates, not counts, and due to the lag time in data collection, official poverty rates are soon outdated.

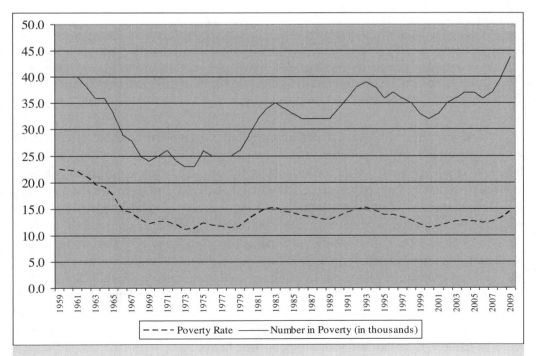

Figure 7.1 Number in poverty and poverty rate: 1959 to 2007.
Data source: U.S. Census Bureau, Current Population Survey, 1959 to 2009 (2010).

Table 7.1 Poverty Rate by State 2010

State	%	State	%
Alabama	15.4	Montana	13.2
Alaska	9.9	Nebraska	10.2
Arizona	19.6	Nevada	11.9
Arkansas	17.7	New Hampshire	7.4
California	15.0	New Jersey	9.3
Colorado	11.7	New Mexico	19.3
Connecticut	8.2	New York	15.0
Delaware	10.9	North Carolina	15.4
District of Columbia	17.2	North Dakota	11.4
Florida	13.9	Ohio	13.5
Georgia	16.9	Oklahoma	13.3
Hawaii	11.2	Oregon	12.0
Idaho	13.0	Pennsylvania	11.0
Illinois	12.8	Rhode Island	12.9
Indiana	15.2	South Carolina	13.9
Iowa	10.1	South Dakota	13.6
Kansas	13.2	Tennessee	15.8
Kentucky	17.0	Texas	16.6
Louisiana	16.2	Utah	8.6
Maine	11.7	Vermont	9.2
Maryland	9.1	Virginia	10.5
Massachusetts	11.1	Washington	11.0
Michigan	13.5	West Virginia	15.5
Minnesota	10.5	Wisconsin	10.3
Mississippi	20.6	Wyoming	9.7
Missouri	14.4		

Data source: U.S. Census Bureau, Current Population Survey, 2007 to 2010 Annual Social and Economic Supplements. (2010b).

Agencies use these thresholds to generate eligibility for programs meant to serve those with low or no income. The amount a person or family needs to survive a year in a specific location demands a needs-based construction of the poverty measure. This is considered a subjective measure of poverty because program eligibility is contingent on local context. Factors included in this poverty construction are the cost of local housing, employer-subsidized health care, child care, and transportation. Each factor contributes directly to the economic well-being of a family but is not included in the official poverty threshold.

The most comprehensive measure of poverty used in eligibility determination considers *hardship indicators*. Life circumstances are used to describe more fully the deprivation experienced to determine the extent of poverty. In addition to limited or no income or wealth, some agencies also consider whether a person paid a utility bill late or could not pay it at all, pawned or sold a possession, went without meals, sought assistance from an agency, or could not afford to heat their home.

The poverty measures generated by the U.S. Census Bureau are estimates. It does not count the poor; rather, it uses statistical methods to estimate the rate and thresholds based on social and economic indicators. Counts of the poor occur only at points of service. That is, only those who provide services to the poor know how many exist within their jurisdiction.

The final measure of poverty important to our discussion casts poverty as a sociopolitical situation that excludes the poor from full participation in society. *Social inclusion* is a political term used to describe social-structural determinants of poverty with an eye toward enacting social change. For instance, social inclusionists show that coming from an area of social exclusion greatly affects life chances. Those who are from the inner city are more likely to be poor – they are less likely to graduate from high school, less likely to accumulate wealth, more likely to have children outside of marriage, and more likely to have a shorter life compared with those from the suburbs. It is not an individual that causes these circumstances but rather the environment. Topics associated with social inclusion include unemployment, low income, poor housing, crime, poor health, and family breakdown. Researchers and stakeholders alike have used the concept of social inclusion to explain cycles of poverty that can be intergenerational and regional.

How Much Poverty Exists?

According to the U.S. Census Bureau, about 39.1 million people in the United States lived in poverty in 2008, an increase of 1.1 million people from 2007 (Bishaw and Renwick 2009). Just under half (i.e., 40 percent) of all Americans will fall into poverty at least one time in 10 years (Zweig 2004), with more than half of adults (58.5 percent) between the ages of 25 and 75 spending at least one year below the poverty line. In 2008, the family poverty rate was 10.3 percent, up from 9.8 percent in 2007. Moreover, the poverty rate of children younger than 18 increased by 1 percent, from 18 to 19 percent, between 2007 and 2008 (U.S. Census Bureau 2009).

Poverty is distributed unevenly across regions. Stratification scholars point to neighborhoods as areas that create poverty, due in part to discrimination in housing markets, employment opportunities, and levels of social exclusion. For example, consider the inner city; during the 1950s, the center of social life moved from the urban centers to the suburbs. Housing and racial discrimination left inner cities with a disproportionate number of poor people of color. This was followed by a disinvestment of the city by businesses, leaving few jobs. By the 1980s, the inner cities had higher concentrations of poverty than rural areas across America. Today, they have little economic base and high rates of violence. Spatial-mismatch theory explains how those in the inner city are separated from resources that moved to the suburbs. The high cost of commuting, lack of information regarding jobs, and unwillingness of employers to hire people from the inner city (Kirschenman and Neckerman 1991) all contribute to reproducing poverty.

Not only do poverty rates disproportionately affect people by age and region, they also vary by race. Whites have a lower poverty rate (8.6 percent) compared with Asians (11.8 percent), blacks (24.7 percent), and Hispanics (23.2 percent) (U.S. Census Bureau 2009). Whites account for just under half (43 percent) of the poor in America. Race also patterns the number of children living in poverty. According to the U.S. Census Bureau (2007), compared with white children, the poverty rate was higher for black and

Hispanic children. In 2007, 10 percent of white children, 35 percent of black children, and 29 percent of Hispanic children lived in poverty.

Women are more likely to suffer from cycles of poverty. Persistent gender inequalities in the family, including a woman's role as caretaker, contribute to inequalities in wealth and power (Grusky and Kanbur 2006). According to the U.S. House of Representatives in 1992 (reported in National Coalition for the Homeless 1999), the number of poor people increased 41 percent between 1979 and 1990; families and children under the age of 18 accounted for more than half of that increase. Today, 39 percent of people living in poverty are children, leading some to call this the *feminization of poverty*. The poverty rate is almost twice as high for children compared with other groups, and 33 percent of all female-headed families live in poverty (down from 47 percent in the early 1990s) (Lichter and Crowley 2002). In contrast, married couples have a 5.5 percent poverty rate (U.S. Census Bureau 2009). Figure 7.2 compares the number

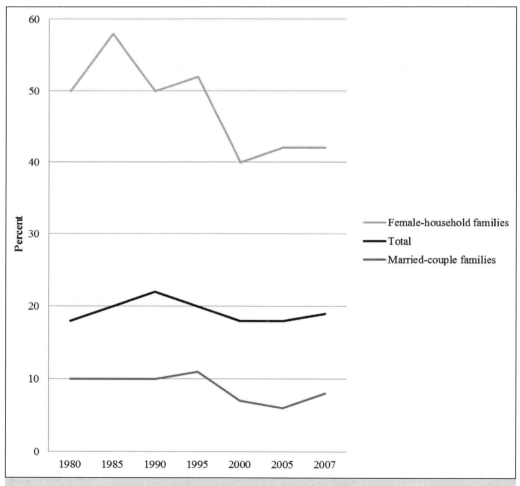

Figure 7.2 Poverty rates by female household and married couples: 1980–2007.
Data source: U.S. Census Bureau, Current Population Survey, Annual Social and Economic Supplements (2007).

of children in poverty by family structure across time. The number of families living in poverty for those with two parents is much lower than those living in poverty with female heads of households.

Why Does Poverty Exist?

The explanations for poverty have been varied and numerous. Often, we think of poverty as individually determined. Poor individuals may vary in their skills, work ethic, and abilities or they may hold unique value systems that establish class positioning. Social scientists, however, use structural models to explain the existence and maintenance of poverty. Research focusing on differences in life chances, access to resources, and societal changes is particularly helpful in understanding why some groups have higher rates of poverty than others.

Chapter 2 discusses how sociological theories generally fall into one of three schools of thought. Indeed, sociologists also study poverty from these three major theoretical perspectives: functionalist, conflict, and symbolic interaction. To review, the first two perspectives – functionalist and conflict – are considered macroperspectives, meaning that they are interested in questions about society as a whole. The third perspective, symbolic interaction, takes a microperspective and is interested in the processes involved in "doing poverty": What are the meanings associated with being poor? Each perspective makes different theoretical assumptions. Functionalism considers individual determinants (Lewis 1959: 98), conflict theory considers structural determinants (Sorenson 1996), and symbolic interactionists assume poverty is a construction with different meanings across time and groups (Shannon 1998). Each perspective helps us to better understand what causes poverty.

Functionalists have shown that poverty is an important feature of stratification found in most societies (Davis and Moore 1945). This perspective assumes that a person's economic well-being is an indicator of ability that can be represented as a normal distribution curve. Those who are less fit fall into the lower quintile and the more able rise to the top of the distribution. Moreover, functionalists show that this fact actually can serve society. For example, one latent function of poverty regards social control: People who see the poor are encouraged to behave in such a way as to avoid poverty. In many cases, this means taking on additional jobs, staying in school longer, or waiting to have children to avoid the trappings of poverty. People work, jobs are filled, and tasks are completed; therefore, society functions.

The conflict perspective views poverty as a byproduct of class struggle (Marx [1867]1977). In capitalist societies, the profiting by the few is achieved at the sacrifice of the many. If we consider wealth as finite – that there is only so much in a pie – the ownership of most of the pie by the few leaves many with little or no pie at all. From this perspective, capitalism requires a group of people to be poor in exchange for dominant-class ownership. Using the most recent data available, we see that between 1962 and 2004, the amount of wealth owned by the bottom 80 percent of the wealth distribution fell from 19.1 to 15.3 percent. That decrease of nearly 4 percent was redistributed to the top 5 percent in the wealth distribution (Mishel, Bernstein, and Shierholz 2009). According to the old adage, "As the rich get richer, the poor get poorer."

Other structural factors that explain how poverty is created include the deinstitution-alization of mentally ill people, invention of crack cocaine, rising joblessness among men, declining marriage rates, cuts in welfare benefits, and destruction of Skid Row (Jencks 1994).

Culture of Poverty

A popular misconception regarding poverty is that certain types of people are poor. Characteristics associated with being poor include slothfulness, uncleanliness, and de-valuing education (Gans 1995). The prevailing theory from this perspective is termed the *culture of poverty* (Lewis 1959) and it uses the term *underclass* to denote the poor. Proponents of the culture of poverty assume that poverty is experienced across genera-tions wherein families create a subculture that does not embrace middle-class values. The theory was the primary force of government policies for the poor in the 1960s, such as the War on Poverty.

Recently, sociologists distinguished four rankings within the underclass: an impov-erished underclass, a jobless underclass, an educational underclass, and an underclass that violates idle-class values (Jencks 1994). An impoverished underclass focuses on wealth as the key component in poverty. By this standard, a person maintains poverty by owning little income and wealth. A jobless underclass denotes those who can-not obtain the means to survive due to a lack of jobs. Such a situation is observed in the Midwest, in cities such as Detroit and Flint, Michigan, where the automobile and steel industries eroded as did the jobs. In Michigan, in the decade between 1999 and 2009, the state lost more than 700,000 jobs. Figure 7.3 shows the increase in the unemployment rate from about 4 percent in 2000 to more than 15 percent in 2009, which corresponds to a loss of one in five jobs in Michigan. People who worked in the

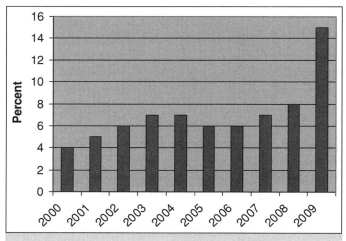

Figure 7.3. Michigan unemployment rate: 2000–2009.
Data source: Michigan Department of Energy, Labor, and Economic Growth, U.S. Bureau of Labor Statistics (2010).

manufacturing industry often are unable to find new employment and subsequently fall into poverty.

Another ranking within the underclass, the educational underclass, remains impoverished due to a lack of education. Shown in the example of Michigan, as jobs within the manufacturing industry disappeared, new opportunities arose in information-oriented industries, such as computer technologies in Silicon Valley, California. People lacking education generally are not qualified for technological positions and are more likely to be impoverished. The final ranking, the poor as violators of the idle-class culture, understands poverty as a condition that reproduces through behaviors that do not align with the dominant culture. One example is the rise in gang activities in many areas across America. By relying on illegal avenues to sustain their daily existence, gang members often end up incarcerated. While they are in prison, they cannot support a family. Both the inmate and the family members are more likely to be poor due in part to the gang culture.

The culture-of-poverty theory takes the position that social class is socially reproduced through the actions of individuals. Although it acknowledges structural forces such as jobs and educational access, it assumes that an individual has autonomy in the decision-making process. The decisions of poor people generally reinforce their poverty status. A significant shortcoming of the culture-of-poverty theory is that it cannot explain how a majority of people cycle in and out of poverty.

Cycle of Poverty

Contrary to the culture-of-poverty theory, poverty is not confined to certain types of people or found only in families that do not embrace middle-class values. Instead, the *cycle-of-poverty theory* views the lack of material goods as a condition that many people experience, most often for short periods. For example, between 2001 and 2003, almost one-third of Americans had at least one instance of poverty lasting two or more months. Nearly one-third of those in the lowest income quintile in 2001 were in a higher quintile in 2003, and a third of those in the highest income quintile in 2001 were in a lower quintile in 2003 (DeNavas, Proctor, and Smith 2008). Clearly, wealth is not static and, therefore, poverty is a dynamic condition that is affected by many factors, including education, job availability, the economy, cost of living, and personal decisions.

Proponents of the cycle-of-poverty theory voice concern over the term *underclass* because it blames victims for creating their circumstances despite well-documented structural factors known to create and maintain poverty. Indeed, the culture-of-poverty theory suggests that the poor shun common values and therefore are undeserving of societal resources (Gans 1995). The ideology of an *undeserving poor* maintains inequality because those with power and resources can ignore the plight of the many by rationalizing that the poor are there by their own making.

Some sociologists have found a more nuanced understanding of poverty by balancing both the structural and individual perspectives. For instance, William Julius Wilson (1935–), a leading scholar on race and poverty, developed a spatial-mismatch theory that explains how structure and culture work to disadvantage some people. As described previously, structural forces work to create ghettos with high concentrations of blacks and Hispanics, joblessness, and reduced access to education, whereas the cultural dynamics in the inner city constrain personal choices, such as erosion of the family. Wilson explained that inner-city women found that men could not be breadwinners due to lack of jobs and were instead economic liabilities. Coupled with the growing acceptance of single parenthood, this encouraged women to have children but not to marry (Wilson 1997).

The majority of scholarship on poverty takes a macroperspective but some microanalyses deserve consideration. Symbolic interactionists often are concerned with the processes of labeling. They ask: "Who decides which factors make one poor?" As discussed herein, what constitutes being poor is contingent on many socially constructed factors. The very definition of *poverty* is mutable and therefore problematic. Consider the official poverty rate. Many believe that government estimates under-report the actual condition of the poor in the United States. The author of *The Threshold*, Mollie Orshansky (1915–2006), created a poverty threshold to measure income inadequacy, saying "if it is not possible to state unequivocally 'how much is enough,' it should be possible to assert with confidence how much, on an average, is too little (Orshansky 1965)." She knew the poverty rate would be a conservative estimate. However, she did not foresee the implications of setting a conservative threshold for poverty measures. By underestimating the number of poor, policies and outreach programs can never effectively combat poverty.

In summary, there are both individual and structural reasons for poverty. Sociologists are careful not to blame the victim but have shown that individuals often reproduce social class by their own actions. When no jobs exist, how then can a person make ends meet? Conversely, if someone lacks education and adheres to a subculture at odds with the mainstream, how can that person survive? Structural constraints as well as cultural dispositions contribute to poverty.

Working Poor

It is a common misconception that people who are poor do not work, but a growing phenomenon in America is the *working poor*. This group has gainful employment but their wages are so low that they are ranked in the bottom percentile of the income and wealth distributions.

In America, the working poor constitute about 25 percent of all workers, 18 years and older. The percentage of working poor varies by state – the lowest is in Maryland (0.9) and the highest is in Hawaii (35.6). Although the wages of the working poor are most often above the federal minimum wage, workers still do not have the purchasing power to ensure a life outside of the poverty threshold. In Hawaii, for example, earning the state average of $12.40 per hour combined with the cost of living reduces the purchasing power so that working a 40-hour week still places a worker in the lowest income percentile. Both percentages of working poor and the wage threshold are reported by state in Table 7.2.

Contrary to the culture-of-poverty theory, the reason why there are so many low-wage workers is due to the current structure of the U.S. job market. As the United States

Table 7.2 Percentage of Workers in Low-Wage Jobs and Hourly Low-Wage by State

State	Percentage of workers ages 18 and older in low-wage jobs	State hourly low-wage (National low wage adjusted for state cost of living)
United States	25	$10.19
Maryland	15	$9.93
Minnesota	18	$9.68
Wisconsin	18	$9.70
Virginia	19	$9.72
Georgia	19	$9.34
Wyoming	20	$9.77
South Dakota	21	$9.37
Michigan	21	$9.68
Florida	21	$9.61
Colorado	21	$10.30
Missouri	22	$9.47
North Carolina	22	$9.37
Indiana	22	$9.81
Iowa	23	$9.52
Alaska	23	$11.35
Nebraska	23	$9.56
Tennessee	23	$9.45
Kansas	23	$9.51
North Dakota	23	$9.49
Washington	23	$10.61
Ohio	23	$9.99
Connecticut	24	$11.43
West Virginia	24	$9.25
Vermont	24	$10.56
Alabama	24	$9.45
Kentucky	24	$9.34
New Hampshire	24	$11.06
Idaho	24	$9.69
South Carolina	25	$9.41
Louisiana	25	$9.46
Nevada	25	$10.27
Delaware	25	$10.50
New Mexico	25	$9.96
Oregon	26	$10.08
Montana	26	$9.72
Texas	26	$9.26
Oklahoma	26	$9.40
Utah	26	$10.22
Mississippi	27	$9.21
Arizona	27	$10.23
New Jersey	27	$11.59
Arkansas	27	$9.27
California	27	$10.40

(*continued*)

Table 7.2 (*Continued*)

State	Percentage of workers ages 18 and older in low-wage jobs	State hourly low-wage (National low wage adjusted for state cost of living)
Illinois	28	$10.22
Massachusetts	28	$11.64
Maine	28	$10.69
Pennsylvania	29	$10.67
New York	31	$11.54
Rhode Island	31	$11.28
Hawaii	36	$12.40
District of Columbia	18	$10.62

Data source: Population reference Bureau analysis of 2007 Basic Monthly Current Population Survey, Working Poor Families Project (2009).

shifted from a manufacturing base to the service sector, workers' wages were greatly reduced. In 2008, 23 percent of all jobs paid below the poverty threshold.[1]

Another reason that the working poor cannot cycle out of poverty is the cost-of-living-to-wage ratio. The cost of living includes housing, food, cost of employment, and health care. About 80 percent of families earning less than the poverty threshold spend more than a third of its income on housing. The median wage needed to afford a two-bedroom apartment is more than twice the minimum wage (Alston 1998). The U.S. Department of Agriculture reports that the food CPI increased 5.5 percent between 2007 and 2008 – the highest annual increase since 1990 (U.S. Department of Agriculture 2009). In 2008, the average American commuted to work about 25.2 minutes a day (U.S. Census Bureau 2010c), when gasoline prices increased to a record high of more than $4.50 per gallon. Being sick also contributes to poverty. In 2005–2007, just less than half of all families earning less than the poverty threshold had no health insurance. These examples are only some of the many structural conditions that constrain workers.

Many sociologists study the working poor from a symbolic interactionist perspective. One method most often used is *participant observation*, defined as living as or among low-wage workers. Sociologist Barbara Ehrenreich studied the working poor by taking minimum-wage employment in various cities across America. Moving from Florida to Maine to Minnesota, she waitressed, cleaned homes, was an aide at a nursing home, and worked retail at Wal-Mart, trying to understand how millions of Americans live on minimum wage. In her book, *Nickel and Dimed: On (Not) Getting by in America*, she discovers the difficulties – physical and mental – associated with trying to survive. Indeed, she realizes that one job is not enough and, to live indoors, one needs to have at least two low-paying jobs. What becomes all too clear in her journalistic experiment

---

[1] This statistic varies greatly among states. The range of jobs paying below the poverty threshold is from 8 percent in Alaska to 41 percent in North Carolina.

is that there is a great divide between the working poor and those that the poor serve. The privilege afforded to members of the middle-class is exposed when Ehrenreich, who holds a Ph.D. in biology, cannot complete the most banal tasks required of her. Despite her educational advantage, the service workers she befriends outperform her. She cannot solve the dilemma of living on low wages, yet millions of Americans do. Although 40 percent of families living below the poverty threshold have at least one parent without a high school diploma or GED, they find ways to survive that eluded Ehrenreich. She found that her cultural disposition of being a white middle-class female disadvantaged her while trying to "do poverty."

Another study of the working poor points to the powerlessness associated with low-wage positions (Shipler 2004). In one instance, a garment worker in 1999 was earning $6.80 an hour, only 80 cents more than when she was hired in 1970. When a pediatrician called a landlord to explain that unsafe housing conditions were causing health problems in his patient, he received no response – that is, until he added lawyers to the mix. Shipler argues that the poor are at high risk of losing resources (i.e., jobs and housing) and therefore do not "have the luxury of rage."

It is not true that the poor are lazy. In fact, as we have seen, the poor work very hard, often at more than one job. The cost of living and low wages constrain some workers to remain impoverished despite their attempts to pull themselves up. Moreover, these workers are voiceless to change their poor conditions because they have few options and opportunities to better their circumstances.

Social Isolation

One of the biggest obstacles to cycling out of poverty is *social capital*, which is defined as "the aggregate of the actual or potential resources which are linked to possession of a durable network of more or less institutionalized relationships of mutual acquaintance or recognition" (Bourdieu 1985: 248). The network serves as a path to resources. We have all heard the phrase, "It is not only what you know but also who you know." This phrase underscores the power of social capital.

People hold information that can benefit others. Case in point: You are looking for a job but reading the help-wanted ads in the newspaper or searching online provides only a limited scope of available positions. Now consider the number of jobs that the placement office posts at your school; it probably has many more connections to agencies in your community than you do. What if you are a member of a fraternity or hold other social memberships, such as a Mason or a religious congregation? Your opportunity for finding a job increases exponentially by adding more connections to your network. You do not necessarily need to know the person who is offering the position, but knowing someone who knows about the position is a form of capital. This is what is known as the "strength of weak ties" (Granovetter 1974). These social networks can help locate potential jobs as well as provide assistance in obtaining a position through recommendations. Jobs are only one example of the capital that is acquired through social networks.

The poor have less social capital than the nonpoor and they suffer from *social isolation*. Comparing African Americans in high- and low-poverty areas revealed that those in poor neighborhoods not only had fewer social ties than those in nonpoor neighborhoods, they also had less social worth – meaning that the networks of the poor had fewer social resources to offer one another (Wacquant and Wilson 1989). A similar situation is found in rural areas. Living in a high-poverty neighborhood reduces network size. Moreover, living in a poor neighborhood is particularly detrimental to the likelihood of having an employed or college-educated discussion partner (Tigges, Ziebarth, and Farnham 1998). In the United States, housing is determined by socioeconomic status – that is, those of similar social classes group together. Those who are poor are concentrated in neighborhoods that contribute to their poverty status through the isolation of social networks.

Poverty is a condition that strikes approximately one-third of all Americans at one time or another. For many, the job market creates low-paying wages that constrain many to live below the poverty threshold. The structure of job markets, discrimination in housing and job placement, and disinvestments by businesses in the inner city all contribute to increases and concentrations of poverty in specific neighborhoods. Additionally, personal choices contribute to a lack of wealth, including teenage pregnancies, females as single-parent heads of household, and membership in subcultures whose values are incongruent to those of the dominant social class.

We examined what poverty is, how many are impoverished, and theories to understand why poverty exists; we now turn to what it means to be poor. The discussion begins by looking at the daily life of poor people.

Homelessness

Living in poverty has important implications for the daily lives of the people who experience it. One outcome of poverty is homelessness. One of the most ignored groups by policy makers and social scientists is the homeless. Homeless men, women, and children are among the poorest people in the United States, and their ranks are growing.

The U.S. definition of *homelessness* comes from the Stewart B. McKinney Act (1994), which is part of the Homeless Assistance Act (1987). The Act defines a homeless person as an individual who lacks a fixed, regular, and adequate night-time residence or a person who resides in a shelter, welfare hotel, transitional program, or place not ordinarily used as regular sleeping accommodations (e.g., streets, automobiles, movie theaters, and abandoned buildings). This does not include those who are imprisoned or who stay with relatives or friends. The official definition considers what is known as the *visible homeless*.

Counting the homeless is a challenge. The available data are estimates because data collection is difficult. The population is elusive, typically migrant, and moves irregularly – hourly, daily, and seasonally. Homelessness is a condition that can be seasonal, occurring in bouts, short or long, singularly or repetitively, or as a chronic condition. Double counts during the census taking also are problematic.

As a group with social stigma, the homeless often try to stay out of sight of officials. In the United States, social scientists and homeless-service agencies have developed methodologies to estimate the number of homeless by going out and physically counting people – known as a *point-in-time street count*. A large staff of trained individuals is assigned to areas within a county; over three or more nights, they meet the homeless on the streets and in shelters. During these meetings, interviewers ask a series of questions designed to provide much-needed information to better serve the homeless in the following fiscal year.

Every year since 2007, the Los Angeles Homeless Service Authority (LAHSA) (2009) has undertaken a survey of the nation's largest homeless population and provides data that corresponds with the national survey conducted by the U.S. Conference of Mayors (2001). Both surveys show that more than three-quarters (85 percent) of the homeless population does not reside in shelters. The majority of homeless individuals are male (59 percent), with 24 percent female, 2 percent transgendered, and 15 percent children under the age of 18, for which gender is not recorded.

A commonly held belief is that homeless people typically are single; however, of the total count in Los Angeles, about 24 percent of homeless individuals are in a family. Some surveys report that families comprise 20 to 43 percent of the homeless population (Fleming, Burns, and Haydamack 2004). Many homeless families survive by living on the streets. About 80 percent of homeless families are unsheltered and about 20 percent live in emergency shelters, transitional housing, or hotels using vouchers. The majority of homeless people are unemployed but 7 percent have either a full- or a part-time job.

The racial composition of the homeless varies by location but the surveys generally show that just over 50 percent are African American, 19 to 35 percent are Caucasian, 12 to 24 percent are Hispanic, 2 percent are Native American, and 1 percent are Asian; 4 percent identify as multiethnic. When we examine race/ethnicity in Chapter 11, we discuss why people of color, particularly African Americans, have such high rates of poverty.

Not including the many children living on the streets, the median age of the homeless population is 45; more than half (58 percent) fall between the ages of 41 and 60. Veterans comprise approximately 12 to 20 percent of the homeless; studies have shown that they are twice as likely to become homeless compared with nonveterans (Wolch et al. 2007).

Being homeless is linked to higher rates of disease and illness. Homeless people have higher rates of mortality and greater risks associated with exposure. Approximately 25 percent of the homeless population is physically disabled. Decreases in mental-health access exacerbate the health risks of the homeless. Approximately 20 percent of homeless people suffer from a mental illness, although most mentally ill people rarely become homeless (National Center for Homelessness 2002).

Homeless people also are at high risk of contracting and subsequently spreading HIV/AIDS with

> many homeless adolescents find[ing] that exchanging sex for food, clothing, and shelter is their only chance of survival on the streets. In turn, homeless youth are at a greater risk of contracting AIDS or HIV-related illnesses. HIV prevalence studies anonymously performed in four cities found a median HIV-positive rate of 2.3 percent for homeless persons under age 25 (National Coalition for the Homeless 1999).

The homeless also face an increased risk of substance abuse (National Coalition for the Homeless 1999). In addition, 20 percent are victims of domestic violence, 27 percent lived in foster care as a child, and 33 to 66 percent abuse drugs and/or alcohol (Wolch et al. 2007).

As with the general attitudes regarding the poor, many people believe that homelessness is due to personal choices such as drug and alcohol abuse. Although many homeless people abuse alcohol and drugs, no study to date has established causality – it is not known whether drug and alcohol abuse came before or after homelessness. Homeless people experience higher rates of violence; 22 percent claim to have left their last place of residence because of domestic violence. The U.S. Conference of Mayors (1999; 2000; 2001) identified domestic violence as a primary cause of homelessness.

From this demographic information, we can see that many homeless people faced obstacles in their life that placed them at a higher risk for social exclusion. Coming from foster care, living as a soldier in a land with no war, or being in a physically abusive situation all contribute to the probability of becoming homeless. Poverty reduces social capital and when employment is difficult to find – or nonexistent, as is the case in many urban areas – individuals and families have little choice but to live on the streets.

Consequences of Poverty

Given the number of people who live under the poverty line, what are the consequences of poverty? In short, poverty constrains the resources in a person's life. Individuals who live in poverty are limited in their access to resources such as health care, education, employment, and housing.

Impoverished individuals often are in worse health than those in the upper classes and they are much more limited in their access to quality health care. The homeless population suffers higher rates of multimorbidity compared to the nonhomeless population. Long-term homelessness increases the likelihood of reporting arthritis, heart disease, tuberculosis, depression, and anxiety disorder. Although there are no gender differences in chronic-disease rates of the homeless, females are more likely to report a psychiatric problem (Holohan 1997).

Childhood poverty is a strong determinant of failing school, low achievement scores, and nonmarital childbearing. Each factor contributes to a higher probability of living in poverty (Duncan et al. 1998). In other words, living in poverty re-creates poverty – a concept that sociologists term *social reproduction* (see Chapters 2 and 6). With the reproduction of poverty comes a host of ill effects for children. Children living in poverty have increased neonatal and postneonatal mortality rates; greater risk of injuries resulting from accidents, physical abuse, or neglect; higher risk for asthma; and lower developmental scores in a range of tests at multiple ages (Aber et al. 1997).

The outcomes of poverty are not only individualistic; in fact, being associated with a poor neighborhood also decreases a person's occupational opportunities. One study looked at an employer in Chicago who was hiring for an entry-level position. One candidate was an African American man who had grown up in a poor neighborhood. The employer asked where he received his education and when told he attended a school in the inner city, the employer prejudged the candidate as incompetent. Moreover, the employer made a decision regarding the potential productivity of the candidate by his ethnicity and neighborhood. In the end, the employer remarked that he could not trust anyone from the inner city and would give the job to the candidate that probably needed it least – a white, married female from the suburbs who wanted extra money for the household (Kirschenman and Neckerman 1991). The poor are unemployed and underemployed at much higher rates than other groups.

Social Welfare Programs

Several *social welfare programs* have been designed and implemented in an attempt to eradicate poverty. Americans generally agree that poverty negatively affects the nation but they differ greatly on how to eradicate conditions that lead to becoming poor.

Two poverty policies in the United States that were met with resistance and controversy were Franklin D. Roosevelt's New Deal in the 1930s and Lyndon B. Johnson's War on Poverty in the 1960s. The New Deal prescribed structural treatments to reduce poverty through the Social Security Act of 1935. At the time, the unemployment rate was about 25 percent (higher in some urban areas) and property values were rapidly shrinking as mortgages were foreclosed. As unemployment increased, so did the number of homeless and helpless. To combat this downward trend, federally funded initiatives and work programs were fostered across the nation, as was the establishment of national parks. Two major initiatives of the New Deal, Medicare and Social Security, targeted those in society who are most at risk of poverty: the ill and the elderly. Both programs remain an integral part of American social services despite the controversial nature of social welfare in the United States.

The War on Poverty was enacted when the unemployment rate was approximately 19 percent. One successful program still in place is Head Start, which is a federally funded program that focuses on early childhood – it provides food and education for the poor. Although the efficacy of the program has been challenged, scholars are confident that children who have been through the Head Start program are more likely to graduate than those who did not participate in the program (Currie and Thomas 1995). The Head Start program feeds millions of children who would otherwise go to school hungry. Both policies aimed to increase jobs and assist Americans through opportunities, and both were criticized for being too expensive, lacking in coherency, and expanding government (Russell 2003).

The Aid to Families with Dependent Children (AFDC), established by the Social Security Act of 1935, was the largest federal program serving the poor children of America. It allocated funds to states that, in turn, would provide assistance to needy children who had been deprived parental support through absence, disability, unemployment, or death. The AFDC allowed states to determine need by setting their own poverty thresholds. In 1996, the AFDC was replaced by Temporary Assistance for Needy Families (TANF) when Congress passed the Personal Responsibility and Work Occupation and Reconciliation Act. This federal act replaced many social-welfare programs such as the AFDC, the Job Opportunities and Basic Skills Training (JOBS) program, and the Emergency Assistance (EA) program. TANF, unlike AFDC, limits the amount of time a family may receive federal funds, increases work-participation rate requirements of the states, and allows states to broadly design welfare programs. Moreover, TANF funds may be used by a state in any way that aligns with TANF's four goals: "to provide assistance to needy families so that children can be cared for at home; to end the dependence of needy parents on government benefits by promoting job preparation, work and marriage; to prevent and reduce the incidence of out-of-wedlock pregnancies; and to encourage the formation and maintenance of two-parent families" (U.S. Department of Health and Human Services 2004).

Scholarly response to the change in the U.S. welfare system was met with criticism. Proponents of TANF argue that it has been effective in reducing poverty, as witnessed by the declining welfare rolls (i.e., the number of people seeking assistance from welfare services). Others are less convinced; the decline could mean that homeless populations are not being served, rather than the numbers or proportions are declining (Lichter and Crowley 2002).

Today, new welfare policies are used in an attempt to stop further development of an underclass. Reforms have met with criticism and mixed results. Within his first year of being elected, President Obama signed into law the American Recovery and Reinvestment Act of 2009, which included the Homelessness Prevention and Rapid Re-Housing Program (HPRP). This program aims to reduce chronic homelessness across America. Philip Mangano was appointed by George W. Bush as the "homelessness czar" and he continues to serve under President Obama. In 2000, Mangano designed a 10-year plan to eradicate chronic homelessness; although homelessness still exists, there has been a 12 percent decline.

Attitudes Surrounding Poverty

Why do Americans resist social-welfare programs? First, we must understand that compared to other industrialized nations, the United States provides little welfare support to its citizens. The United States is the only industrialized nation with no universal health care, education is provided only through secondary school, and existing welfare programs are designed to be temporary and allocated at the state level.

A popular view of poverty – at least, in the United States – is that it is an individually driven phenomenon. According to this argument, those in poverty are poor because they do not work or do not work hard enough to achieve a higher social-class status; they are the undeserving poor. Many believe that the undeserving poor misuse benefits, as represented in the caricature of a "welfare mother." They believe that women have children to receive money from welfare – although scientific analysis has shown that this is not true. Being a recipient of welfare does not increase the likelihood of being a single parent (Blau, Kahn, and Waldfogel 2004); a better predictor of single parenthood is lack of education (McLaughlin and Luker 2006).

Scholars have discovered that cultural attitudes dictate how individuals think about welfare. For example, for those who value individualism and consider that those on welfare misuse public funds, welfare is perceived as providing too much. These people believe that the minimum income they need is far less than what the government provides through welfare assistance. This group generally feels that the poverty rates are dubious, that there is less poverty than reported, and that therefore welfare should not provide assistance to the undeserving (Hallöröd 2004).

Others point to the gap between the competing ideologies of individualism and concern for public good as the fundamental difference in attitude regarding welfare. Chapter 6 explores the middle class and finds that a primary characteristic of the American culture is individualism. The idea that each person deserves what he or she earns is termed *meritocracy*. Some voice concern that by giving away resources, people lose their incentive and learn to rely on assistance; above all, they believe that welfare is not fair.

In other nations, the dominant ideology seeks to protect individualism rather than serve to protect the nation or community as a whole. These nations, including Sweden and the Netherlands, are termed *welfare states*. Social services are plentiful and distributed among all people, not only the poor. For instance, welfare states provide universal health care; transportation to and from health centers; assistance with job placement; free education (at all levels); and assistance with home care of infants, the sick, and the elderly. Although welfare states have higher tax burdens, they also have lower levels of social inequality.

All industrialized nations use a system of taxation to reallocate funds to those who are in need; however, some nations are more effective at reducing levels of poverty. For example, the rate of children living in poverty is one measure that nations target for reduction. The effect of U.S. tax policies and transfers on the number of children living in poverty, in 2006, was compared to 15 other industrialized nations (Allegretto 2006). Without the redistribution of public money, the average number of children living in poverty in the sample is 21.1 percent. After the redistribution of taxes, the number is greatly reduced in all nations except the United States. In the other nations in the sample, the number of children living in poverty was cut in half after tax redistribution; the reduction in the United States was only 4.7 percent. America is a country of great wealth and great poverty, which leads many to question how best to reduce poverty but not reduce the ability to accumulate wealth.

Welfare states have the lowest levels of poverty compared with other political forms. Industrialized nations with the lowest rate of poverty include Finland, 5.4 percent; Norway, 6.4 percent; and Sweden, 6.5 percent. The United States has the highest rate of poverty of all industrialized nations: 17 percent (Mishel, Bernstein, and Shierholz 2009).

Some suggest that an alternative to welfare in the United States is privately funded outreach. Indeed, Americans are known throughout the world for having a charitable spirit as well as more private charities than other nations: more than a million and adding more than 50,000 a year. During the national crises of 9/11 and Hurricane Katrina, for example, thousands of charitable organizations across the country mobilized to aid in the rescue and relief of victims. However, there are serious concerns regarding private organizations and charity, as noted in a 2006 article in *The New York Times* (Storm 2006). A major concern is that an organization's primary function is to survive. Charities receive tax-free donations that are not regulated and may be used however the organization pleases. In the aftermath of Hurricane Katrina, one charity collected money on behalf of Louisiana residents – but, instead, they sent toys to children in

China. Another organization in Texas used funds to distribute literature on alternatives to Darwinism; another charity provided leather jackets for sadomasochists in New Orleans. Clearly, exclusion and graft are major concerns regarding privately funded charities and welfare.

America is one of the richest nations in the world. Comparing 17 industrial nations including the United States, America ranked first in annual income per capita and eighth in productivity. Despite the massive amounts of wealth, it also has the dubious honor of ranking first in total poverty as well as first in child poverty (Mishel, Bernstein, and Shierholz 2009). Efforts to reduce poverty have been considered, debated and applied since the 1930s but have been ineffective in their goals. America is a nation with the richest people and the poorest people, living side by side.

Conclusion

Poverty is a fluid condition that is relative to the standard of living in a community. Social scientists have multiple definitions of poverty to estimate the number of impoverished at various levels – national, state, county, city, and community. How many people live in poverty depends on which definition of poverty is used. Currently, the number is growing due to structural factors such as the reduction in jobs, high cost of housing, and increasing cost of food.

The determinants of poverty are explained through three separate sociological perspectives. Symbolic interactionists look at how people "do poverty," which shows that the very definition of poverty is not fixed and, therefore, the poor are a diverse group that is contingent on structural conditions such as the economy and the labor and housing markets. Moreover, the labels associated with poverty affect how society views the poor. The functionalist perspective views poverty as serving a purpose in society. Because abilities and skills are on a continuum, those who have lower skills and fewer abilities than other members in society by necessity have less access to social resources. Poverty, then, serves to motivate individuals to work hard to avoid being impoverished. The conflict perspective views poverty in America as an outcrop of capitalism. The wealth that is accumulated by a very few has been redirected away from the majority of people who live below the elite – this redistribution of wealth maintains the upper class at the expense of the underclass.

Supporters of the cycle-of-poverty theory show that poverty comes in spells and that a significant proportion of Americans at least once in their life will experience poverty; the majority of those also will exit poverty. However, some families experience intergenerational poverty that leads to the suggestion of a culture of poverty. Families living in poverty often cannot access societal resources such as a "good" education, a job, or housing, which leaves them ill equipped to cycle out. Instead, some families socially reproduce poverty.

The number of working poor is increasing. Due to the minimum wage and growth in the service sector, coupled with a decline in the manufacturing sector, American workers often earn very little and do not have pensions, health care, and other social services. The result is social isolation – a condition in which people have limited or no access to societal resources.

Homelessness is an extreme indicator of poverty. Many governmental policies aim to reduce or eradicate poverty. Although there has been a measurable reduction in homelessness according to some street counts, the homeless population often is invisible to a census; therefore, the numbers of homeless individuals and families are imprecise. Most of the information about homelessness comes from points of service; therefore, when funding of services is low, it appears that there are fewer homeless.

The conditions of poverty include higher rates of poor health. The poor have more illness than the nonpoor because they cannot access health care and maintenance. Common myths about the poor are that women have babies to receive more money from the government and that those who are on welfare are lazy and deceptive. Although there is likely to be some graft in the system of social-service allocation, the majority of recipients are indeed needy. The most recent changes in welfare policies disallow individuals to collect assistance for more than five years, regardless of the conditions that created the episode of poverty. Social services aimed at reducing poverty often have been met with resistance by Americans who feel as though giving to the "undeserving" undermines the American value of working hard for success.

Other industrialized nations use public monies to reduce the number of impoverished. Using taxes instead of relying on market factors to pull people out of poverty, these nations have reduced the number of poor and children in poverty by approximately half. Welfare states (e.g., Sweden) have greatly reduced their levels of poverty; however, Americans generally resist the idea of more welfare because many believe that need is caused by individual rather than structural factors.

Summary

(1) The very concept of poverty is highly political. How we measure poverty, what constitutes "enough," and efforts to reduce poverty are all complex issues tethered to political and theoretical perspectives.

(2) Income and wealth are distributed unevenly in America, which causes some to suggest that poverty is a necessary condition and others to view poverty as the byproduct of capitalism and individualistic ideology. Regardless of perspective, poverty in the United States is growing despite efforts to reduce it.

(3) Economic relations in the United States shifted from a manufacturing base to one of information and service, which created a significant number of unemployed and underemployed. Moreover, the concentrations of poverty in certain neighborhoods contribute to an underclass through reproduced social isolation and a lack of social capital and education.

(4) Policies aimed at reducing poverty have had mixed outcomes. The New Deal and the War on Poverty were highly controversial, yet they reduced poverty by affecting structural and cultural barriers such as joblessness and education. A recent effort by both the Bush and Obama administrations has resulted in a reduction in homelessness by about 12 percent.

(5) A debate rages about how best to decrease poverty. Politics and ideology drive divisions in treatments and today, as in the past, concerns arise over the expense, coherency, and growth of government.

(6) Less public discourse is spent on the effect that poverty has on families, communities, states, and the nation as a whole. Although poverty may be a necessary evil, the numbers of those living in poverty is dynamic and contingent on socioeconomic factors.

Box 7.1 A Night at the Shelter: The Lived Experience of Homelessness

Theresa is a 21-year-old female. She has three children and recently left her husband of four years due to his physical and emotional abuse against her. Her mother passed away from cancer two years ago and she never knew her father. She met her former husband while in high school but dropped out when she became pregnant. After her divorce, Theresa found it difficult to locate reasonably priced housing. She works as a domestic helper and earns about $8 an hour. She does not have health-care coverage and, as a result of a violent episode with her former husband, she has recurring headaches and her vision is impaired. Some days she could not work and subsequently lost her job. Soon after, she was evicted from her apartment because she could not pay the $850 rent. Theresa walks the streets of Los Angeles, the city that has the most homeless people in America. She pushes a shopping cart that she stole from a local grocery store before the new shopping carts with wheels that lock if taken off the store's property were implemented; the store had been losing too many carts.

The children hold onto the cart as she pushes it through downtown Los Angeles. The two toddlers, ages four and three, are quiet when Theresa speaks with me. The infant is in the cart buried under blankets and clothes – this is everything the family owns. Because she has children, many of the homeless shelters cannot house her. The fact that she has a baby causes problems because infants are building their immune systems; the exposure to an open environment can cause serious harm, including death.

Theresa has found assistance at a shelter. A representative from the Department of Health and Human Services secured her a hotel room for two weeks. She can bring her children and work on finding employment for two weeks, at which point she will have to find different housing. However, the hotel is in the San Fernando Valley, about 15 miles away. A caseworker gives her a token to use on the trains. Public transportation in Los Angeles is improving; a new system of trains now connects many parts of the city and crosses counties. It takes Theresa more than an hour to push her cart and walk with her children through the city to board the train. She takes her cart with her on the train because it is filled with all she has.

That same night, the Winter Shelter Program (WSP) started, which aims to provide temporary housing during the cold months and to curtail fatalities caused by exposure. The program consists of at least 10 shelters in Los Angeles. The homeless people begin to line up at one shelter, called *Starting Over*, about 2 hours before it is officially open. When it opens, a man uses a bullhorn to give directions on how to navigate the intake process. I ask a man in line how this form of communication affects him. He says that although it feels like he is being herded like an animal, he is too thankful for the housing to say anything negative against the program. Inside the massive warehouse are more than 150 beds, which are fold-up cots with a thin mattress. There is barely enough room to walk between the cots. Women are separated from men, even married couples, and housed in a smaller room in the back of the shelter. The few toilets and showers quickly become steeped in the odors of chronically homeless people.

There is a small table at the front of the large room with a tube of toothpaste and a roll-on deodorant stick. To use these items, the clients may not remove them; instead, they must use the toothpaste and deodorant at the table – in front of the others. I watch as both men and women approach the table. A social courtesy emerges – most people look away when someone is at the table.

Box 7.1 *(contined)*

Theresa was fortunate that night; she did not have to return to the WSP. Despite her long trek to a part of the city with which she was unfamiliar, she at least was able to keep her family together and could sleep safely, knowing she would not be robbed, raped, or harassed.

Does your city have a WSP? If so, how many people does it serve? What happens to the homeless people when the program closes in the spring?

Source: Interviews and observations during the WSP data collection by Darby E. Southgate. 2003. Fictitious identifiers are used to protect the clients, shelters, and agencies that provide service.

Box 7.2 *Ain't No Makin' It*: How Poverty Reproduces Itself

How is social inequality reproduced through differences in attitudes, behaviors, family, peers, education, and other social structures and socializing influences encountered by young people? What reproduces upper- and middle-class social position? To answer these questions, sociologist Jay MacLeod ([1995]2008) studied two groups of male high school students.

Focusing on two distinct groups, the Hallway Hangers and the Brothers, within a single public-housing project, *Ain't No Makin' It* illustrates how social-structural constraints reproduce inequality across generations. Among the starkest differences between the two groups are their views on values, aspirations, and life expectations.

The Hallway Hangers, a mostly white group, believe in loyalty, toughness, and mental quickness. They often engage in unmotivated and illegal behaviors such as hanging out, drinking, smoking, and fighting. In contrast, the Brothers, a mostly black group, value hard work, getting ahead, future success, and delayed gratification. They rarely engage in illegal or illicit behavior and act in a way that is consistent with typical values of upward mobility. The two groups differ in their aspirations (i.e., what they wish to happen) and their expectations (i.e., their views toward future goals). Characteristically, the Hallway Hangers believe that they will not obtain a middle-class lifestyle and are fatalistic; the Brothers have contrary views.

MacLeod diffused the traditional understanding of race and class; that is, the stereotype of black teenagers being defeatist and doomed to the underclass is challenged by the behavior of the Brothers. Conversely, the white teenagers are more defeatist and fit some of the worst stereotypes of the poor. Ultimately, despite differences in attitudes and behaviors, MacLeod found that the Brothers do no better than the Hallway Hangers in obtaining employment, income, wealth, and other hallmarks of a middle-class lifestyle (see Chapter 6). Rather, he found that the social-stratification system is reproduced from generation to generation through structural constraints placed on the poorest individuals in the United States. Additionally, the cultural behaviors associated with poverty block opportunity – combined with problems in the educational system and other social structures.

Source: MacLeod, Jay. [1995]2008. *Ain't No Makin' It: Aspirations and Attainment in a Low-Income Neighborhood.* Boulder, CO: Westview Press.

Key Concepts

Absolute poverty

Aid to Families with Dependent Children (AFDC)

Culture of poverty

Cycle of poverty

Feminization of poverty

Hardship indicators

Head Start Program

Homeless Assistance Act

Homelessness

Homelessness Prevention and Rapid Re-Housing Program (HPRP)

Medicare

Minimum wage

Needs-based

New Deal

Official poverty

Point-in-time street count

Poverty

Relative poverty

Social exclusion

Social isolation

Social reproduction

Social Security

Social welfare programs

Spatial-mismatch theory

Stewart B. McKinney Act

Subjective measures

Temporary Assistance for Needy Families (TANF)

Theories of poverty

Underclass

Undeserving poor

War on Poverty

Welfare states

Working poor

Questions for Thought

1. Compare the various measures of poverty. Which is the most useful and why? Which is the least useful and why?
2. Why are women more at risk of being poor compared to men?
3. What is the difference between the culture-of-poverty and social-reproduction theories?
4. What is the wage that constitutes a working-poor job in your state? How many people in your state are considered working poor? Should there be an increase in the minimum wage? Why or why not?
5. Do social-welfare policies work? Discuss the pros and cons of recent welfare policies.

Exercises

1. Compute the cost of living in your area. Include the costs of housing, food, utilities, transportation, and child care. Divide the approximate number in dollars per month by 160 (i.e., the number of working hours in a month). Compare the jobs available to the wage needed to survive.
2. Contact a local homeless shelter and ask about the intake process. How easy or difficult is it to obtain and locate services?
3. Compare the U.S. Census Bureau data with local rates on poverty from the U.S. Department of Health and Human Services. How well do the federal rates describe the poor? Are there more or less impoverished people?
4. Offer to tutor homeless children; many cities and homeless-service agencies are in dire need of assistance. After you tutor a child, debrief the class about what you learned. How did your experience compare with your expectation?

Multimedia Resources

Print

"Counting the Poor: Do the Poor Count?" Available at www.brettonwoodsproject.org/article.shtml?cmd[126]= i-126–241b14a5be9a5b47cd5a88778ac79532.

Classic Reading

Grusky, David B., and Ravi Kanbur. 2006. *Poverty and Inequality*. Stanford, CA: Stanford University Press.

Lichter, Daniel T., and Martha L. Crowley. 2002. "Poverty in America: Beyond Welfare Reform." *Population Bulletin* 57: 36.

MacLeod, Jay. [1995]2008. *Ain't No Makin' It: Aspirations and Attainment in a Low-Income Neighborhood*. Boulder, CO: Westview Press.

Massey, Douglas S. 1990. "American Apartheid: Segregation and the Making of the Underclass." *The American Journal of Sociology* 96: 329–57.

Massey, Douglas S., Andrew B. Gross, and Mitchell L. Eggers. 1991. "Segregation, the Concentration of Poverty, and the Life Chances of Individuals." *Social Science Research* 20: 397–420.

Mayer, Susan E., and Christopher Jencks. 1989. "Poverty and the Distribution of Material Hardship." *Journal of Human Resources* 24: 88–114.

McLanahan, Sara S., and Erin Kelly. 1999. "The Feminization of Poverty." In *Handbook of the Sociology of Gender*, edited by J. Chafetz (pp. 127-145). New York: Plenum Press.

Morgan, Stephen L., David B. Grusky, and Gary S. Fields. 2006. *Mobility and Inequality: Frontiers of Research from Sociology and Economics*. Stanford, CA: Stanford University Press.

Rank, Mark Robert. 2004. *One Nation, Underprivileged: Why American Poverty Affects Us All*. New York: Oxford University Press.

Russell, Judith. 2003. *Economics, Bureaucracy, and Race: How Keynesians Misguided the War on Poverty*. New York: Columbia University Press.

Smeeding, Timothy M. 2008. "Poverty, Work, and Policy: The United States in Comparative Perspective." In *Social Stratification: Class, Race, and Gender in Sociological Perspective*, edited by D. B. Grusky (pp. 327–39). Boulder, CO: Westview Press.

Wilson, William Julius. 1997. *When Work Disappears: The World of the New Urban Poor*: New York: Vintage Books.

Wilson, William Julius, and Kathryn M. Neckerman. 1986. "Poverty and Family Structure: The Widening Gap between Evidence and Public Policy Issues." In *Fighting Poverty: What Works and What Doesn't*, edited by S. H. Danziger and D. H. Weinberg (pp. 232–59). Cambridge, MA: Harvard University Press.

Internet

Poverty Maps

"Chronic Under-nutrition among Children: An Indicator of Poverty." Available at www.povertymap.net/mapsgraphics/graphics/undernutrition_en.cfm.

"Global Distribution of Poverty": Available at sedac.ciesin.org/povmap/.

"State of the World's Children": Available at www.unicef.org/sowc99/index.html.

Films

Feature Films

The Soloist. (Directed by Joe Wright, 2009) The story is of Nathaniel Ayers, a homeless violinist, who caught the attention of an *LA Times* newspaper reporter.

The Pursuit of Happyness. (Directed by Gabriele Muccino, 2007) Based on a true story, this film follows the struggles of a father and his young son as they battle homelessness and unemployment. In the end, the father finds not only a profession but also fortune.

Slums of Beverly Hills. (Directed by Tamara Jenkins, 1998) This comedy is a semi-autobiographical look at a poor and dysfunctional family that moves among apartments in Beverly Hills to keep the children in a good school district.

Documentaries

Skid Row. (Directed by Ross Clarke, 2008) Pras Michel of the Fugees goes undercover among the homeless of downtown Los Angeles, presenting an intimate view of life on the streets.

The End of Poverty. Available at www.theendofpoverty.com/. Martin Sheen narrates this evaluation of poverty from a conflict perspective. He argues that poverty is the byproduct of colonization and domination. In summary, the film shows how poor countries are exploited by rich ones.

Faces of Poverty. Available at elfenworks.org/project_facesofpovertyfilm.html.

Dark Days. (Directed by Marc Singer, 2000) Documentary about a community of homeless people living in a train tunnel beneath Manhattan.

Homeless in America: Without a Home. (Film for the Humanities and Sciences, 2006) The documentary explores the lives of several homeless teens and dispels many of the myths regarding the homeless.

It Was a Wonderful Life. (Directed by Michèle Ohayon, 1993) The documentary follows six women who had secure lives, are educated, and who are now living out of their car or in a cheap motel.

Jupiter's Wife. (Directed by Michel Negroponte, 1996) Maggie is a woman living in Central Park who claims to be the daughter of Robert Ryan and married to the Roman god Jupiter. This is an emotional and poignant look at mental illness and homelessness.

Life in a Basket. (Directed by David Hogan, 2005) Homeless people discuss life on the street in this documentary that focuses primarily on their respective shopping carts.

Waging a Living. (Directed by Roger Weisberg, 2006) This documentary profiles four of America's working poor as they struggle to get out from beneath the poverty line. It underscores injustices inherent in the American economic system.

30 Days Minimum Wage. (Directed by Morgan Valentine Spurlock 2005). This documentary follows Spurlock and his girlfriend as they move to America's heartland, Columbus, Ohio, to work for $5.15 an hour for one month.

Works Cited

Aber, J. Lawrence, Neil G. Bennett, Dalton C. Conely, and Jiali Li. 1997. "The Effects of Poverty on Child Health and Development." *Annual Review of Public Health* 18: 463–83.

Allegretto, Sylvia A. 2006. "U.S. Government Does Relatively Little to Lessen Child Poverty Rates." Economic Policy Institute, Washington, DC.

Alston, Philip. 1998. "Hardship in the Midst of Plenty" In *The Progress of Nations* (pp. 30–35). UNICEF, Washington, DC.

Bishaw, Alemayahu, and Trudi J. Renwick. 2009. "Poverty: 2007 and 2008 American Community Surveys." U.S. Census Bureau, Housing and Household Economic Statistics Division, Washington, DC.

Blau, Francine D., Lawrence M. Kahn, and Jane Waldfogel. 2004. "The Impact of Welfare Benefits on Single Motherhood and Headship of Young Women: Evidence from the Census." *Journal of Human Resources* 39: 382.

Bourdieu, Pierre. 1985. "The Forms of Capital." In *Handbook of Theory and Research for the Sociology of Education*, edited by J. G. Richardson (pp. 241–58). Westport, CT: Greenwood Press.

Currie, Janet, and Duncan Thomas. 1995. "Does Head Start Make a Difference?" *The American Economic Review* 85: 341–64.

Davis, Kingsley, and Wilbert Moore. 1945. "Some Principles of Stratification." *American Sociological Review* 10: 242–9.

DeNavas, Carmen, Nernadette D. Proctor, and Jessica C. Smith. 2008. "Income, Poverty, and Health Insurance Coverage in the United States: 2007." U.S. Department of Commerce, Economics, and Statistics Administration, U.S. Census Bureau, Washington, DC.

Duncan, Greg J., W. Jean Yeung, Jeanne Brooks-Gunn, and Judith R. Smith. 1998. "How Much Does Childhood Poverty Affect the Life Chances of Children?" *American Sociological Review* 63: 406–23.

Ehrenreich, Barbara. 2001. *Nickel and Dimed: On (Not) Getting by in America*. NY: Metropolitan Books.

Fleming, Dan, Patrick Burns, and Brent Haydamack. 2004. "Homeless in LA." Economic Roundtable, Los Angeles, CA.

Gans, Herbert. 1995. *The War Against the Poor: The Underclass and Antipoverty Policy*. Lanham, MD: Rowman & Littlefield Publishing Group.

Granovetter, Mark. 1974. *Getting a Job*. Cambridge: Harvard University Press.

Grusky, David B., and Ravi Kanbur. 2006. *Poverty and Inequality*. Stanford, CA: Stanford University Press.

Halleröd, Björn. 2004. "What I Need and What the Poor Deserve: Analyzing the Gap between the Minimum Income Needed for Oneself and the View of an Adequate Norm for Social Assistance." *Social Forces* 83: 35–60.

Holohan, T. 1997. "Health Status, Health Service Utilisation, and Barriers to Health Service Utilisation among the Adult Homeless Population of Dublin." Dublin, Ireland: Eastern Health Board.

Iceland, John. 2003. *Poverty in America: A Handbook*: Berkeley: University of California Press.

Jencks, Christopher. 1994. *The Homeless*. Cambridge: Harvard University Press.

Kirschenman, Joleen, and Kathryn M. Neckerman. 1991. "'We'd Love to Hire Them but...': The Meaning of Race for Employers." *Social Problems* 38: 433–47.

Lichter, Daniel T., and Martha L. Crowley. 2002. "Poverty in America: Beyond Welfare Reform." *Population Bulletin* 57: 36.

Los Angeles Homeless Service Authority. 2009. "2009 Greater Los Angeles Homeless Count Report." Los Angeles, CA.

Lewis, Oscar. 1959. *Five Families*. New York: A Mentor Books.

_____. 1998. "The Culture of Poverty." *Society* 35(2): 7–9.

MacLeod, Jay. [1995]2008. *Ain't No Makin' It: Aspirations and Attainment in a Low-Income Neighborhood*. Boulder, CO: Westview Press.

Marx, Karl. [1867]1977. *Capital: A Critique of Political Economy*. New York: Vintage Books.

McLaughlin, Christine C., and Kristin Luker. 2006. "Young Single Mothers and Welfare Reform in the U.S." In *When Children Become Parents: Welfare State Responses to Teenage Pregnancy*, edited by A. D. C. Nativel (pp. 21–44). Bristol, UK: The Policy Press.

Mishel, Lawrence, Jarod Bernstein, and Heidi Shierholz. 2009. *The State of Working America 2008/2009*, edited by A. E. P. Institute. New York: Sage.

National Center for Homelessness. 2002. Washington, DC.

National Coalition for the Homeless. 1999. "Homeless Youth." Washington, DC.

Orshansky, Mollie. 1965. Social Security Bulletin. January 1965. Office of Retirement and Disability Policy, Social Security Administration, Washington, DC.

Russell, Judith. 2003. *Economics, Bureaucracy, and Race: How Keynesians Misguided the War on Poverty*. New York: Columbia University Press.

Shannon, Patrick. 1998. *Reading Poverty*. Westport, CT: Heinemann.

Shipler, David K. 2004. *The Working Poor: Invisible in America*: New York: Alfred A. Knopf, Inc.

Sorenson, Aage B. 1996. "The Structural Basis of Social Inequality. " *The American Journal of Sociology* 101: 1333–65.

Storm, Stephanie. 2006. "Many Charities Founded After Hurricane Are Faltering." New York: *The New York Times*. March 13, 2006. http:// www.nytimes.com/2006/03/13/national/nationalspecial/13charities.html

Tigges, Leann M., Ann Ziebarth, and Jennifer Farnham. 1998. "Social Relationships in Locality and Livelihood: The Embeddedness of Rural Economic Restructuring." *Journal of Rural Studies* 14: 203–19.

U.S. Census Bureau. 2009. "Income, Poverty and Health Insurance Coverage in the United States: 2008." U.S. Census Bureau, Department of Commerce, Washington, DC.

_____. 2010. "Income, Poverty, Health Insurance Coverage in the United States: 2009." U.S. Census Bureau, Department of Commerce, Washington, DC.

_____. 2010b. "Current Population Survey, 2007 to 2010 Annual Social and Economic Supplements." U.S. Census Bureau, Department of Commerce, Washington, DC.

_____. 2010c . "2005-2009 American Community Survey." U.S. Census Bureau, Department of Commerce, Washington, DC.

U.S. Conference of Mayors, 2001. "A Status Report on Hunger and Homelessness." In U.S. Conference of Mayors, 1999; 2000; 2001, "Hunger and Homelessness Up Sharply in Major U.S. Cities," Washington, DC.

U.S. Department of Agriculture. 2009. "Food CPI and Expenditures: Analysis and Forecasts of the CPI for Food." U.S. Department of Agriculture, Washington, DC.

U.S. Department of Health and Human Services. 2004. "Aid to Families with Dependent Children (AFDC) and Temporary Assistance for Needy Families (TANF)." The Office of Human Services Policy, Washington, DC.

Wacquant, Loic J. D., and William J. Wilson. 1989. "The Cost of Racial and Class Exclusion in the Inner City." *Annals of the American Academy of Political and Social Science* 501: 8–25.

Wardrip, Keith E., Danilo Pelletiere, and Sheila Crowley. 2009. "Out of Reach: 2009." National Low Income Housing Coalition, Washington, DC.

Wilson, William Julius. 1997. *When Work Disappears: The World of the New Urban Poor*. New York: Vintage Books.

Wolch, Jennifer, Michael Dear, Gary Blasi, Dan Flaming, Paul Tepper, and Paul Koegel. 2007. "Ending Homelessness in Los Angeles." Inter-University Consortium Against Homelessness, Los Angeles, CA.

Zweig, Michael. 2004. *What's Class Got to Do With It?: American Society in the Twenty-First Century*. NY: ILR Press.

8 Social Mobility

Most Americans have thought about the chance that they will change social positions during their life. Trying to improve social status – that is, to move up the status hierarchy over time – is usually considered a desirable objective and a positive individual trait. It is common for young people to imagine that they can achieve more in their life than their parents, and many elements of the way we socialize children encourages or assumes that social mobility is a real possibility. Whereas we have begun to take for granted that social mobility is at least possible, the potential for change of this type is relatively recent. Throughout most of history and in most societies, people grew up to occupy the same social positions as their parents: Peasants remained peasants, elites remained elites, and those in the middle remained in the middle. People even had surnames to indicate their social position (e.g., Bishop, Carpenter, Miller, and Wainwright). Today, we accept that through education, occupational change, entrepreneurship, and other processes, at least some people will not follow the same patterns as their parents. However, determining who is socially mobile and why is not a simple task.

In this chapter, we explore patterns of social mobility and ask which factors affect a person's chances of mobility. Pitirim Sorokin, one of the first scholars to produce a comprehensive treatment of social mobility, wrote that mobility is "any transition of an individual or social object or value – anything that has been created or modified by human activity – from one social position to another" (Sorokin 1959/2001: 133). That is, *social mobility* is change in social status over time, for either an individual or an entire group. Mobility can be measured across generations (i.e., a change in status compared to a person's parents) or within a generation (i.e., a change in status in a person's own life). It refers to movement up and down various social hierarchies, including income, wealth, education, and occupation. *Social mobility* refers to both upward and downward mobility; that is, some people achieve more than their parents, others achieve less.

In this chapter, we discuss what social mobility is and how it is measured. We explore how much mobility there is and ask why some people are unable to change positions. Although we might assume that individual effort has a role in mobility, the effort is contingent on restrictions and rules imposed by the society in which an individual operates. We identify and discuss the nature and consequences of different systems of stratification to understand the interplay between an individual and the system. We address the role of education in facilitating and impeding mobility as well as issues specific to ethnicity, gender, and religion. Although there is only limited scholarly research on the subject, we also ask whether there is significant downward mobility, how downward mobility changes over time, and what this reverse mobility means for a society. Finally, we explore theoretical approaches to understanding mobility.

Social Mobility: Meaning and Measurement

Research on social mobility identifies the degree to which people and groups are mobile and it specifies the sources and constraints on that mobility. Researchers dating back to Sorokin (1927) and his contemporaries start by articulating and measuring several dimensions of mobility. Underlying these questions are evaluations of the degree to which *ascribed traits* (i.e., inherited from parents such as their social class) versus *achieved traits* (i.e., acquired during the life cycle such as education) affect mobility.

Direction

Direction is one dimension along which mobility varies. *Vertical mobility* – or upward and downward mobility – is straightforward: *Upward mobility* refers to an improvement in status; *downward mobility* is a decline in status. When we think about mobility, upward mobility is the idea that usually comes to mind: for example, images of an entrepreneur who becomes part of the new rich or a professional athlete who moves up the social ladder (see Chapter 4). Yet, there are examples of individuals and entire groups who have experienced downward mobility. For example, during an economic slowdown (e.g., the Great Depression or, more recently, less severe recessions), increased job losses can lead to downward mobility for entire groups or in certain geographic regions. Downward mobility subsequently is discussed in more detail.

Horizontal or *lateral mobility* refers to movement that is neither better nor worse but rather sideways or at the same level. Examples of horizontal mobility include changing from one occupation to another of similar status and changing jobs to a new organization but in the same occupation. For instance, a professor who decides to leave a university and become a professional consultant has a different job but similar social status. Likewise, an attorney who changes law firms changes organizations but not status. Similarly, geographic mobility, or moving to a new neighborhood or town, can involve lateral mobility. Often, a lateral change in status on one dimension (e.g., occupation) involves a lateral change in status on other dimensions as well (e.g., income and wealth).

Generation. Mobility also can be measured in terms of generation. *Intergenerational mobility* refers to movement between generations. Sociologists measure this type of mobility by comparing a person's ranked positions (e.g., occupation, wealth, income, and education) to that of their parents or grandparents. A man whose father was a laborer but who becomes a doctor is considered upwardly mobile. Sociologists argue that intergenerational mobility is particularly important because individuals tend to gauge their own success relative to that of their parents, usually their same-sex parent (Blau and Duncan 1967; Easterlin, MacDonald, and Macunovich 1990; Keister and Deeb-Sossa 2000). *Intragenerational mobility* is mobility within a single generation (i.e., within a person's own lifetime). This type of mobility also is referred to as *career* or *occupational mobility* because it often is used to measure a change between a first job and a current job. For instance, a woman who begins her career working as a cleaner in an office building and eventually owns that building is clearly upwardly mobile.

Structure. Patterns of mobility also are classified based on their sources. *Structural mobility* results from changes in the structure of a society. For instance, when demand to perform a certain job increases and more people are needed to fill the positions, the resulting mobility is structural. For example, during times of economic growth, opportunities for people to surpass their parents' standard of living are relatively plentiful because job and career opportunities are growing. Indeed, it has been the case throughout most of American history that economic growth allowed the majority of people to do better than their parents. *Circulation* or *exchange mobility* – either upward or downward – results from the innate skills and ambitions of individuals rather than changes in the occupational structure. Americans assume a certain degree of opportunity, or exchange mobility, but not all societies take this potential for granted. Moreover, it is not always easy to determine how much structural or exchange mobility there is. Research evidence suggests that, in recent years, circulation mobility in the United States has increased, signaling a decline in the strength of the relationship between social origins and adult status. However, the evidence also suggests that in the last 25 years, structural mobility has declined (Cookson 1997; Grusky and DiPrete 1990). Yet, economic fluctuations and changing generational patterns make it difficult to ascertain how much mobility there is.

Absolute versus relative. *Absolute mobility* refers to changes in position that result because living standards are changing in absolute terms. We are better off than our parents, our children will be better off than us, and their children will be better off than them. Structural changes such as industrialization or advancements in technology can lead to absolute mobility. Indeed, mobility studies suggest that in most industrial societies, absolute mobility has increased in the last century as a result first of industrialization and then of advancements in technology that increase demand for skilled, nonmanual occupations.

Relative mobility refers to the degree to which a person moves up or down in the various hierarchies (e.g., wealth, income, occupation, and education) compared to other people in the same generation. Because relative mobility is measured in comparison to others, it is a zero-sum phenomenon: If one person moves up, another must move down.

Absolute and relative mobility can be controversial subjects because people disagree strongly about which is more important. Moreover, although there is support for increases in absolute mobility, research has different conclusions about changes in relative mobility. Some argue that relative mobility remains largely unaltered despite changes in absolute mobility; others conclude that the association between an individual's class of origin and eventual destination has remained remarkably stable over time despite economic expansion (Featherman [1978]2001; Grusky and Hauser [1984]2001). Part of the difficulty in drawing clear conclusions reflects the multiple dimensions on which mobility can be measured.

Mobility Patterns through History

Because social mobility is measured in many ways, it is difficult to reach a consensus on how much mobility there is. Furthermore, many cultural items – including movies, books, and newspaper articles – emphasize social mobility through "rags-to-riches" tales and, in the process, portray upward mobility as more common than it actually is. Historically, information on income, assets, education, and jobs has been limited; therefore, our understanding of general trends in mobility throughout history is particularly limited. Yet, there is useful evidence that suggests basic patterns. For instance, Pessen (1974) reviewed the best available historic data from large cities and attempted to piece together a picture of how much mobility people could anticipate in their life. He divided the rich into three classes, given their parents' standing: rich/eminent, middling, or poor/humble. Table 8.1 summarizes his results for New York, Philadelphia, and Boston. As expected, the majority – more than 90 percent – of those classified as rich were born to rich parents; fewer than 10 percent were born to either middle-class or poor parents. In a similar study of career mobility, Kaelble (1985) showed that there was little career mobility in the United States between 1820 and 1910. Table 8.2 summarizes Kaelble's findings for six cities, omitting information for cities or years that was not available. Whereas both studies suggest that our understanding of mobility in early eras of U.S. history is limited, the data also suggest that available evidence indicates mobility was limited prior to 1900.

Intergenerational Correlations

More recently, researchers have used survey data and modern statistical methods to provide more reliable estimates of mobility. Two methods for determining levels of mobility

Table 8.1 Historical Mobility Rates in the United States, 1828–1848

City	Rich Parents	Middle-Class Parents	Poor Parents
Boston	94%	4%	2%
New York	95%	3%	2%
Philadelphia	92%	6%	2%

Data source: Pessen, Edward. 1990. *Riches, Class, and Power: America before the Civil War.* Piscataway, NJ: Transaction Publishers.

Table 8.2 American Career Mobility, 1820–1910

	Philadelphia	Boston	Poughkeepsie, NY	Waltham, MA	Warren, IN	Seattle, WA
Proportion of Mobile Individuals						
1820–30	14	–	–	–	–	–
1830–40	19	11	–	–	–	–
1840–50	15	10	–	–	–	–
1850–60	20	16	22	17	–	–
1860–70	–	–	24	22	–	–
1870–80	–	–	23	17	–	–
1880–90	–	21	–	–	–	28
1890–00	–	–	–	–	22	–
1900–10	–	–	–	–	–	9

Data source: Kaelble (1985).

are particularly common: intergenerational correlations and transition studies. *Intergenerational correlations* are correlations between quantitative indicators of parents' and children's status indicators (Bowles and Gintis 2001; Mulligan 1997). These correlations represent the amount of variation in one generation's well-being that is associated with the same measure in the previous generation. In an early effort to estimate intergeneration correlations in status, Blau and Duncan (1967), for example, estimated the intergenerational correlation for income or earnings among American men as about 0.15 and concluded that parental advantages disappear rather quickly in the United States. However, critics charge that errors in reporting parents' income and high levels of error in incomes for both generations made the correlation coefficients artificially low.

In recent years, a sizeable literature has begun to explore intergenerational persistence of a number of adult outcomes including education, earnings, wages, and even consumption using better data and more reliable measures (Mulligan 1997). These estimates suggest that there is persistence across generations in a number of status measures. Table 8.3 summarizes the findings from this literature. As shown, there is considerable variation in studies of intergenerational persistence; however, on average, there appears

Table 8.3 Intergenerational Correlation

	Persistence (Mean)	Number of Estimates	Range
Family wealth (log)	0.50	9	0.28–0.76
Education	0.29	8	0.14–0.45
Earnings or wages (log)	0.34	16	0.11–0.59
Family income (log)	0.43	10	0.14–0.65
Consumption (log)	0.68	2	0.59–0.77

Data source: Mulligan (1997). The table reports the average correlation (i.e., mean persistence) and range for the various estimates across a number of different estimates.

to be considerably less mobility than early studies suggested. Average estimates for persistence in education and individual earnings or wages are approximately comparable, whereas persistence in family income is even greater. Mulligan's are the only estimates of persistence in consumption, and they suggest that the intergenerational correlation of parental and offspring consumption is even higher than correlations for other status measures.

Whereas research on persistence in education, earnings, and wages is now relatively common, studies of intergenerational persistence of wealth ownership are still rare. Table 8.3 shows that with the exception of consumption, wealth is the most persistent status measure in this group. This is not surprising given that wealth can be passed directly from parents to children in the form of inheritance. However, other research reveals relatively low levels of wealth mobility. Menchik (1979), for example, obtained the probate records of 1,050 parents who died in Connecticut in the 1930s and 1940s and who left a net estate of $40,000 or more in current dollars. He then located the probate records of their children who died in Connecticut by 1976. He found that the correlation between their estates was 0.76. Similarly, Harbury and Hitchens (1979) studied wealth mobility in England by collecting information on fathers who died in 1902 and then also tracking as many of their sons as possible until they died. Their study estimated the intergenerational correlation of wealth to be 0.46. Kearl and Pope (1986) found somewhat less intergenerational persistence in their study of Utah Mormons between 1850 and 1870. Looking at sons only, this study found a correlation in wealth ownership of 0.27. As Mulligan (1997: 208–9) pointed out, all three are unusual samples. Both Menchik (1979) and Kearl and Pope (1986) included only fathers and sons who died in the same state. Harbury and Hitchens (1979) and Menchik (1979) included only very wealthy families, and Harbury and Hitchens (1979) limited their research to Great Britain.

Transition Studies

Transition matrices also can be used to study upward and downward mobility. The *transition matrix*, or *mobility table*, arrays individuals within groups (e.g., occupations, quintiles, and regions) in a start year and shows the proportion of who moved to another or stayed in the same group in a finish year. Table 8.4 is a mobility table that uses 1966 and 1981 as the start and finish years, respectively. The table is divided into *quintiles*, or fifths, of the wealth distribution. The cell labeled 62.33 means that 62.33 percent of those who started in the bottom quintile in 1966 were still in the bottom quintile in 1981. Similarly, the cell labeled 60.79 (i.e., bottom right of the table) means that 60.79 percent of those who started in the top quintile of the wealth distribution finished in the top quintile. Indeed, all of the cells along the diagonal (e.g., 62.33, 37.42, 34.51, and so on) are people who started and ended in the same quintile. Those in the off-diagonal cells are people who moved from one place to another in the distribution. For example, the cell labeled 1.80 indicates that 1.80 percent of the sample started in the bottom quintile and moved up to the top quintile. In other words, those people started very poor and became very rich. There also are people who moved down; for example, the cell labeled 1.74 indicates that 1.74 percent of the sample started at

Table 8.4 Intragenerational Mobility, 1966–1981 (percentage)

Early Adulthood Quintile	Later Adulthood Quintile				
	Quintile 1	Quintile 2	Quintile 3	Quintile 4	Quintile 5
Quintile 1	62.3	25.8	7.6	4.4	1.8
Quintile 2	23.8	37.4	23.1	13.8	2.0
Quintile 3	9.1	23.0	34.5	22.8	10.1
Quintile 4	3.0	7.1	25.8	37.5	25.3
Quintile 5	1.7	6.7	8.9	21.5	60.8

Data source: "National Longitudinal Survey of Mature Men (1966)." Later adult quintiles based on 1981 net assets. Early adulthood quintiles based on 1966 net assets. Cells indicate the percentage of people in adult quintiles who originated in each early adulthood quintile.

the top of the distribution and moved to the bottom during the period covered by the table.

Studies that use a single number to indicate intergenerational transmission – such as the intergenerational correlation coefficient described previously – provide information about mobility but they neglect the details and variation that underlie the single correlation. Individual paths vary, household paths vary, and the processes that lead to outcomes can be unique. Transition matrices provide more detail about who moves and where. For this reason, transition tables also are more easily exploited in an effort to understand factors that lead to mobility. Intuitively, this approach is attractive because mobility implies movement between categorical groups, and the transition matrix captures those changes. Of course, there also are drawbacks to the transition-matrix approach. Creating a transition matrix requires specialized data that are difficult to collect. It also is difficult to determine from a transition matrix the degree of immobility in a sample or whether movement upward or downward was between adjacent or more separated cells. Yet, transition tables deserve special attention because sociologists have a history of categorically studying mobility and have used transition matrices extensively to understand occupational (Biblarz, Raftery, and Bucur 1997; Blau and Duncan 1967), income (Breiger 1990; Singer and Spilerman 1979), career (Abbott and Hrycak 1990; Stovel, Savage, and Bearman 1996), and even geographic mobility (Quillian 1999).

Historical estimates suggest that mobility changed in important ways in the past century. Steckel (1990; Steckel and Krishman 1992) used a national sample from 1850–1860 census records to estimate patterns of mobility in the nineteenth century. He compared them with estimates of modern mobility patterns to answer questions about change over long periods. He found that in the modern data (i.e., 1960s and 1970s), more than 58 percent of households at the top 10 percent of the wealth distribution in the first period (i.e., the 1960–1970 data) remained in that position in the second period. He also found that those who left the top of the distribution typically moved only a short distance. Fewer than 10 percent of those who moved out of the top decile fell to a position at the lower half of the distribution, and fewer than 2 percent fell into the very bottom. By contrast, nineteenth-century households were less likely to remain in the top wealth group; that is, they were more mobile than similar households in the 1960s and 1970s. Those who moved from the upper portions of the distribution in the nineteenth century moved farther than their modern counterparts. Steckel (1990) also found that nineteenth-century households at the lower end of the wealth distribution were less mobile than those in the modern sample.

Wealth mobility continued to vary across the wealth distribution into the 1980s. Table 8.4 uses data from the 1960s and 1980s (the same men are included in both years) and shows that more than 62 percent of those in the top quintile in 1966 remained there in 1981. Likewise, more than 60 percent of those in the bottom quintile in the first period were still there in the second period. Few moved into the extremes of the distri-bution: Less than 2 percent moved between the lowest and highest quintiles in either direction. Yet, there is considerable overall movement. Indeed, more than 60 percent of those who started in one of the three middle quintiles experienced some movement, and nearly 40 percent of those who began in the bottom or top quintile moved. Jianakoplos and Menchik (1997) reported similar findings in their analysis of these data. They also reported that mobility among blacks in this sample is significantly less than for whites and that these general trends hold for different definitions of wealth (i.e., augmented wealth, which in addition to the wealth value used here, includes the capitalized value of future expected pension and Social Security income).

To investigate even more recent mobility patterns, it is useful to review a different dataset that followed respondents until 2000. The estimates in Table 8.5 show wealth-mobility patterns between 1985 (when the survey respondents were in their twenties) and 2000 (when they were in their late thirties and forties). The table shows that 36.76 percent of those who started in the top quintile in the younger sample ended in the top quintile, whereas approximately 12 percent of those who started in the top quintile actually finished in the bottom quintile. There was considerably more movement out of the bottom of the distribution, where a full 70 percent of those who started in the bottom quintile in 1985 had moved up by 2000. Similarly, more than 70 percent of those who started in the middle quintiles left those positions by 2000.

Although both of the mobility tables provide important information about social mo-bility during the life of the respondents (i.e., intragenerational mobility), none of the

Table 8.5 Intragenerational Mobility, Net Worth: 1985–2004 (percentage)

Early Adulthood Quintile	Later Adulthood Quintile				
	Quintile 1	Quintile 2	Quintile 3	Quintile 4	Quintile 5
Quintile 1	37.7	24.6	16.3	10.9	10.5
Quintile 2	26.1	26.2	20.6	16.0	11.2
Quintile 3	16.5	22.1	23.5	21.2	16.7
Quintile 4	9.4	17.2	23.8	25.9	23.8
Quintile 5	6.0	9.5	17.8	27.7	39.0

Data source: "National Longitudinal Survey of Youth, 1979." Later adult quintiles based on 2004 net worth. Early adulthood quintiles based on 1985 net worth. Cells indicate the percentage of people in later adulthood quintiles who originated in each early adulthood quintile.

Table 8.6 Intragenerational Mobility, Total Family Income: 1985–2006 (percentage)

Early Adulthood Quintile	Later Adulthood Quintile				
	Quintile 1	Quintile 2	Quintile 3	Quintile 4	Quintile 5
Quintile 1	37.9	21.5	15.3	14.1	11.2
Quintile 2	21.5	29.0	20.0	17.7	11.7
Quintile 3	15.4	20.6	22.8	22.6	18.6
Quintile 4	10.7	20.2	19.6	25.2	24.3
Quintile 5	8.5	12.3	16.9	22.6	39.7

Data source: "National Longitudinal Survey of Youth, 1979." Later adult quintiles based on 2006 total family income. Early adulthood quintiles based on 1985 total family income. Cells indicate the percentage of people in later adulthood quintiles who originated in each early adulthood quintile.

estimates address mobility between generations (i.e., intergenerational mobility). Table 8.6 represents intergenerational-mobility patterns for the same sample as Table 8.5. The information in Table 8.6 shows that between childhood and adulthood, more than half of the respondents who started in the top quintile remained there. Similarly, 45 percent of those who started in the bottom quintile were still there in 2000. Yet, more than half of respondents who started in the bottom quintile moved up during their life, and nearly half of those who were in the top quintile as adults had moved up from lower ranks.

One of the most difficult questions to answer about mobility is whether a mobility table indicates considerable or only limited mobility. Two people reading the same table easily can come to different conclusions. The question becomes even more difficult when we look at multiple samples of people and multiple measures of mobility (e.g., wealth, income, and occupation). The tables in this chapter are all wealth-mobility tables and we find generally that there is more mobility in income and occupation; however, it is not the case for all people at all times. A way to summarize the amount of mobility in a given period is a synopsis table such as Table 8.7. Those estimates summarize the findings from Tables 8.4, 8.5, and 8.6 by isolating the amount of mobility that occurs out of each quintile. The tables illustrate that between 37.7 and 62.3 percent of people starting in the top quintile left that quintile by the subsequent period represented in the respective table. Mobility out of each quintile was greatest for the 1985–2000 sample, which

Table 8.7 Changes in Mobility over Time: Percentage Whose Position Changed in Mobility Tables

	1966–1981 (Table 8.4)	1985–2004 Net Worth (Table 8.5)	1985–2006 Income (Table 8.6)
Quintile 1	37.7	62.3	62.1
Quintile 2	62.6	73.8	71.0
Quintile 3	65.5	76.5	77.2
Quintile 4	62.5	74.1	74.8
Quintile 5	39.2	61.0	60.3

Note: Cells indicate the percentage of people who were in a different quintile in the end year (i.e., 1981, 2004, or 2006) than in the start year (i.e., 1966 or 1985).

is likely because this group was in a life stage that typically includes significant change. Again, if we used income or occupation as our measures of mobility, we likely would find more mobility than shown here, but it is important to recall particular characteristics of the sample and the period.

Systems of Stratification

Understanding why some people are mobile and others are not requires a discussion of the role of the stratification system. Some systems offer tremendous opportunities for advancement; others restrict opportunities and virtually prevent social mobility. Sociologists use several terms to categorize stratification systems. The two general types are *open* and *closed systems.*

Open stratification systems. An open stratification system is one that facilitates and even encourages social mobility. In an open system, individual merit, achievement, motivation, and talent have a central role in determining who has high or low status. People can move up or down the hierarchy depending on their effort and accomplishments. Family background, race, ethnicity, gender, and religion are less important determinants of position in these systems.

Closed stratification systems. In contrast, a closed stratification system is one in which mobility is rare and formal laws and social norms aim to prevent it. People are given a social status at birth and there is little they can do to change that status throughout their life. Family characteristics determine status in a closed system, and it is extremely rare for individual effort, determination, or merit to affect a person's status. This means that those who are born into low-status positions are unlikely to move up despite their achievements, and it also means that people born into high-status positions are unlikely to move down the hierarchy despite their failures.

The open stratification system is relatively common in modern, industrialized nations. At the very least, modern societies hold the open stratification system as the ideal and implement social policies that encourage mobility. The closed stratification system is more common in traditional societies, in which social norms often indicate that inequality is normal and perhaps necessary. Of course, all societies – regardless of whether they are more open or closed – have varying degrees of fluidity. Within the general category of open and closed stratification systems, there are several more specific systems.

Class systems. A class system is among the most open stratification systems, with which people in modern societies are most familiar. In a class system, people are not formally prevented from moving up or down and they are not guaranteed to retain their position. Even those at the extremes – low and high – of the distribution have the potential to change position. Class systems first developed in eighteenth-century Europe during the Industrial Revolution. Rapid industrialization required more workers than prior systems, and this demand for human labor required that the social system become more permeable. Since industrialization, class systems have become the norm in modern and modernizing societies, and laws and norms have emerged that encourage mobility.

Estate systems. Prior to the advent of the class system, many societies were feudal and had estate systems of stratification. Feudalism was common in Europe in the Middle

Ages but also has been the norm in some areas of Asia and Latin America, particularly in agrarian societies. In feudal Europe, a small percentage of the population – that is, the nobility who were known as lords – controlled the majority of resources, whereas at the bottom of the hierarchy, a large peasantry known as serfs was dependent on wealthy landowners for survival. Serfs worked for landowners in exchange for protection and a small portion of what they produced. Marriage occurred within class in these societies, and it was extremely rare for people to move either up or down in the hierarchy. The norms and laws that made feudalism possible were endorsed by the powerful lords and the equally powerful Catholic Church, which held the perspective that inequality was ordained by God.

Caste systems. In a caste system, social position is fixed strictly by hereditary social group. That is, a person inherits caste position and remains there for life. *Caste* usually refers to a social group or position that is firmly set and nearly impossible to escape. The well-known Indian caste system has survived for centuries and is composed of four primary groups: the Brahmins (i.e., priests, intellectuals, and scholars), the Kshatriyas (i.e., nobility, warriors, and princes), the Vaishyas (i.e., merchants and business people), and the Shudras (i.e., farmers, workers, service providers, and other ordinary people). Those not included in a caste are referred to as *untouchables*. The Indian caste system is relatively enduring in part because of the pervasiveness of belief in reincarnation. One's moral responsibility in this system is to accept one's caste position and work to improve that position in the next life. Although the Indian caste system is perhaps the most recognized in the West, the system has existed in other societies as well. South African *apartheid*, an elaborate and rigid stratification system enforced by laws and norms prior to the 1980s, has been referred to as a caste system. Similarly, the system of white control that existed in the United States following slavery, called *Jim Crow*, had elements of a caste system.

Slavery. The most extreme form of a closed stratification system involves slavery. There is evidence of slavery throughout history and in all regions; indeed, slavery still occurs today in many parts of the world. *Slavery* is forced labor in which slaves are captured, held unwillingly, and sold as property. The use of slaves was common in the early history of the United States, beginning with a system in which blacks were essentially indentured servants similar to those in Europe and that evolved into a more extreme system involving harsh cruelty. Slavery in Brazil was even more pervasive and enduring than in the United States, although Brazilian slaves had more rights than American slaves. Today, trafficking in humans is a form of slavery with many traits of early slavery systems. For instance, the capture, sale, and forced labor – usually of women and children in the sex industry and sweatshops – comprise a form of slavery that affects people in many parts of the world.

Theories of Mobility

Explaining how and why people move among the rungs of the social ladder has also attracted the attention of social scientists who have developed several theories of social mobility.

Individual Influences

Theories that identify the determinants of social mobility generally take either an individual or a structural approach. Those taking an individual approach focus on how characteristics of individuals and their families affect social mobility. The characteristics that receive the most attention are individual effort, talent, determination and perseverance, education, gender, and race/ethnicity. A common ideology in America that takes an individual approach suggests that anyone can get ahead with the right amount of effort and hard work. Even those at the bottom of the distribution can move ahead if they invest time and energy. More systematic research that focuses on individual traits addresses issues such as the role of education in facilitating social mobility. Indeed, some argue that education is the most important factor affecting mobility prospects. Achieving higher education provides job and occupational opportunities, income, wealth, and numerous related benefits (education is addressed in detail in Chapter 9). A person's gender, race, and ethnicity also can affect mobility prospects (see Chapters 10 and 11). Recently, the role that social networks have in mobility has attracted more attention. Having or creating networks can provide many benefits that ultimately lead to mobility. Of course, luck also is important in mobility but it receives little formal attention in social research. One aspect of luck that attracts attention includes family traits, particularly those of the family into which a person is born. For example, being born into a family that values education or has social networks that can provide mobility opportunities increases mobility possibilities, whereas being born into a family without those traits offers no mobility advantages.

A well-researched theory of social mobility that takes an individual approach is the *status attainment model*. This model proposes that the degree to which people do well in life – their *attainment* – is influenced by traits that they inherit from their family as well as from individual achievement. Status attainment research views mobility as movement along a status hierarchy, in which individuals are ranked according to income, wealth, and occupational prestige (Duncan 1961). Blau and Duncan first proposed the status attainment approach in their classic work, *The American Occupational Structure* (1967). Their original work asked two important questions: (1) To what extent is adult status influenced by social origins (i.e., by ascribed characteristics)?; and (2) How does status attainment, either ascribed or achieved, at one point in a person's life affect attainment later in life? They used *path models* to answer these questions, which are time-ordered models based on empirical data that attribute cause to various factors, such as – in the case of status attainment – ascribed and achieved characteristics. Blau and Duncan originally concluded that both characteristics predict adult attainment but only ascribed characteristics have a more mediating and enabling than predictive role. Their early analyses had flaws, and the work subsequently was criticized for issues such as including only men, data quality, and lack of empirical support for the hypotheses.

Although Blau and Duncan's early work was far from perfect, the ideas they introduced launched a new way of thinking and answering questions about mobility. Many theorists have since modified and refined their model, producing a large body of contemporary literature that articulates details about how status attainment occurs. One particularly well-researched approach is known as the *Wisconsin model*, or the social psychological model of educational and occupational attainment (Sewell 1992). Researchers in this tradition introduced additional family and background characteristics (e.g., parent's attainment, grandparents' attainment, and family religion), contextual traits (e.g., neighborhood and geography), individual traits (e.g., first job as a predictor of subsequent jobs), peer influences, and even social-psychological variables (e.g., aspirations and motivations) into their models. Status attainment models usually conclude that achieved characteristics are stronger predictors of attainment (particularly educational and occupational attainment) than ascribed characteristics (Krymkowski 1991; Rijken 1999; Sewell, Haller, and Portes 1969).

Structural Influences

In contrast, theories that take a structural approach emphasize the role that factors such as changes in economic conditions, distribution of demographic traits in the population, and technological innovations have in facilitating or impeding mobility. This group of theories begins with the assumption that individual effort, talent, and determination all operate within social structures, and most mobility results from structural change rather than individual behaviors and processes. This approach finds fault with the common American assumption that individual desire and hard work are all that is required to get ahead. Hard work and perseverance are important, but this approach suggests that even considerable hard work is not enough to create mobility if the structural conditions are not favorable. Imagine, for example, trying to establish a career during the Great Depression. The prevailing economic conditions at the time were so dire, it was nearly impossible to advance in any field; indeed, many struggled simply to survive during the Depression years. It is conditions of this type that are the focus of structural approaches to understanding mobility.

Economic conditions comprise an important structural trait that affects mobility, but there are other factors as important. For example, the cohort or generation into which a person is born can facilitate or impede mobility. If a person is born into a relatively "crowded" generation, it can be difficult to be accepted at a good college and to find a job for the simple reason that there are more people competing for those positions (Easterlin 1980). *Generational crowding* refers to the increased competition and related issues that those in large birth cohorts experience. Baby boomers – born in the years after World War II – have found that generational crowding affected their educational, occupational, income, and even marriage prospects (Easterlin, MacDonald, and Macunovich 1990; Keister and Deeb-Sossa 2001). Although there is still only limited evidence to support such claims, observers are beginning to speculate that the children of baby boomers also are going to face negative effects of generational crowding. In addition, characteristics of the nation in which a person is born affect mobility prospects. Imagine, for instance, being born in a country that prevents girls from going to school. In that context, it is nearly impossible for a female to achieve as much education or other measures of status as her male counterparts. At a more local level, there is growing evidence that the neighborhood into which a person is born also can pose structural constraints on mobility. Consider how the neighborhood we lived in as a child affected where we are today. The schools and related opportunities in our neighborhood probably had an important effect on our current position, and research has shown that the effect has the potential to follow us through life (Browning and Cagney, forthcoming).

Mobility Example: Roman Catholics

To understand how individual and structural factors work together to generate social mobility, it is useful to consider a group whose social position has changed considerably in recent years. Prior to the 1970s, white Roman Catholics in the United States were predominantly members of the lower and working classes.[1] Many were recent immigrants or had parents that emigrated from Europe in the recent past. Catholic education, income, occupational prestige, and wealth were all relatively low. Catholic fertility rates also were relatively high, exceeding both the general population and many other religious groups. The increases were disproportionately high during the post–World War II baby boom (Lehrer 1996; Westoff and Jones 1979). Since the 1970s, however, the social position of Catholics has increased considerably, making this group a major example of upward mobility (Keister 2007).

Before thinking more about the specific Catholic case, it is useful to consider why religion might affect mobility. Indeed, religion has a strong effect on many of the indicators used to measure social status and mobility, including income, education, occupation, and wealth. Adult social status is a function of behaviors and strategies learned early in life that influence fertility, the timing of marriage, educational aspirations and attainment, job-related outcomes, and attitudes toward saving. Religion affects many of these behaviors and processes, including fertility, marriage, and divorce (Alwin 1986; Lehrer 1996); education; female employment rates; and earnings (Darnell and Sherkat 1997; Lehrer 1999). Religion also affects saving behavior and wealth ownership. Children learn how to save from their families and other acquaintances, and religion can influence the financial lessons they learn. Religion shapes values and priorities and contributes to the set of competencies from which actions such as saving behavior is constructed (Keister 2003). Nearly all churches and related religious organizations offer some guidance for living, often including specific advice for which jobs are desirable, budgeting and other uses of income, how much debt is acceptable, and saving and investing. Together, these processes create a powerful influence of childhood religion on adult social status.

How did religion affect mobility for white Catholics? At least three factors made upward mobility possible. First, marriage and divorce are an important part of the story. Researchers have shown that religion affects marriage in several ways, including the likelihood of getting married at all (Hammond, Cole, and Beck 1993; Mosher, Williams, and Johnson 1992), the choice of a spouse (Lehrer 1998; Sherkat 2004), marital stability (Lehrer and Chiswick 1993), and the likelihood of divorce (Call and Heaton 1997; Filsinger and Wilson 1984). Catholics have particularly high marriage rates, high rates

---

[1] In the remainder of this section, we refer to white Roman Catholics in the United States simply as Catholics. The patterns described may not hold for nonwhite Catholics and Catholics from other countries.

of marital stability, low rates of divorce, and high rates of homogamy (Lehrer 1998; Sherkat 2004). Marriage increases wealth because two individuals combine their assets when they create a single household. It also creates common goals (e.g., homeownership and retirement objectives) that encourage couples to save. *Religious homogamy* refers to marriage to someone of the same religion (*homogamy* is marriage to someone with similar characteristics). Religious homogamy increases the likelihood that a couple has similar values, priorities, and competences regarding education, finances, and other issues that promote stable marriage and financial well-being. When those values favor saving as they do for Catholics (see the following discussion), agreement can increase saving and wealth. Homogamy also reduces the likelihood of divorce for Catholics, contributing to even greater wealth (Curtis and Ellison 2002; Lehrer 1998; Sherkat 2004). Divorce tends to reduce wealth because assets are divided, couples maintain two households, and there may be direct costs such as associated legal fees. High marriage rates, marital stability, and religious homogamy contributed to upward mobility for Catholics.

Children are a second factor that contributed to Catholic mobility. High fertility rates in prior generations meant that Catholics once had relatively large families (Alwin 1986; Sherkat and Ellison 1999). However, fertility rates declined rapidly for Catholics following the post–World War II baby boom, resulting in significant decreases in family size (Lehrer 1996; Westoff and Jones 1979). Like other groups, Catholics also began to marry and have children later or not at all (Lehrer 1996; Sherkat and Ellison 1999). Most Catholic adults are now two or three generations from immigration, and distance from the immigrant experience is at least part of the reason for fertility changes. Changes in fertility and family size, in turn, made upward social mobility more likely for Catholics. Remaining childless facilitates upward mobility by keeping expenses low, thereby making it easier to save money. Postponing children also increases social-mobility prospects because it facilitates educational attainment, career development, occupational advancement, and initial saving and investing that can contribute to lifelong asset appreciation (Keister 2005).

Education is a third determinant of mobility; Catholics have been highly upwardly mobile on nearly all educational measures in recent decades. Religion affects orientation toward education and educational attainment (Darnell and Sherkat 1997; Lehrer 1999). As a result, religion can affect both school quality and years completed. Both men and women raised in Catholic families have achieved relatively high levels of education in recent years even though they tend to have parents who achieved relatively modest educations. Again, distance from the immigrant experience may be part of the explanation for Catholic educational achievement. Regardless of the causes for this change, improved educational attainment has contributed to overall upward trends in social standing for Catholics. Education improves occupational outcomes, including prestige and income. Highly educated people also tend to experience greater career stability and benefits (e.g., the opportunity to save before taxes in special retirement accounts).

Many Catholics attended Catholic schools, which are associated with higher test scores (Bryk, Lee, and Hollan 1993; Hoffer, Greeley, and Coleman 1985), higher probabilities of completing high school and attending college (Evans and Schwab 1995; Neal 1997), increased rates of college graduation (Neal 1997), and higher adult salaries and wages (Neal 1997). The success of Catholic-school students may result from stricter discipline, increased social capital produced by dense parental networks, and governance structures that allow for more parental choice and consensus than is possible in public schools. Although not all people raised in Catholic families attended Catholic schools, the majority of those who were Catholic and of elementary-school age in the 1970s did. Indeed, 60 percent of American Catholics surveyed in 1999 had attended Catholic school as a child for at least a short period, and 36 percent had attended seven or more years (D'Antonio, Davidson, Hoge, and Meyer 2001). Ultimately, these patterns worked together with changes in marriage and fertility rates to produce upward wealth mobility for Catholics.

Fourth, religion can influence mobility directly by shaping the values that people use to make occupation and financial decisions. Religious beliefs attribute value to the act of working, to working for certain organizations, and to working in some occupations. Religious beliefs also attribute value to money, saving, charitable giving, and other behaviors that directly involve money. The values associated with work and financial behaviors vary dramatically by religious belief, but there is little question that money is meaningful, that values and finances are intimately connected, and that Americans recognize the connection.

There is evidence that Catholics have unique values related to work and money, and these values may have been yet another important factor contributing to upward mobility. Compared to other religious groups, Catholics tend to have an instrumental attitude toward work. Tropman's research showed that Catholics approach work as an activity that produces a result rather than something pleasurable in itself (Tropman 1995; 2002); work is a way to earn money to buy necessities. Catholics also have a strong orientation toward family, and their motivation to work is extrinsic. Whereas white non-Hispanic Catholics largely have assimilated, Tropman (2002) found that the strong family-focus characteristic of recent immigrants persists. Although an instrumental attitude toward work may reduce the incentive to work, the added effect of a strong family orientation has led Catholics to work relatively hard. Egalitarian gender roles suggest that there also are likely to be two earners in Catholic households with two adults, which is another predictor of mobility.

Similarly, Catholics have an instrumental attitude toward money. As with work, there is evidence that Catholics perceive money as a means to acquire necessities (Keister 2007). Money is necessary to meet needs, but it is only a tool rather than something with intrinsic value (DeBerri and Hug 2003; Thibodeau, O'Donnell, and O'Connor 1997). Catholics tend to save to care for their families (Tropman 2002); that is, whereas an instrumental view of money may reduce saving, a strong extrinsic motivation, in contrast, will lead Catholics to save and invest in ways that ensure their family is secure – which ultimately contributes to upward mobility. Chapter 11 discusses in more detail how religion and other elements of family culture affect social stratification; however, the recent Catholic experience provides an illustration of the processes described herein.

Downward Mobility

When discussing social mobility, we often assume *upward* mobility. Of course, it is also possible to move down a social hierarchy. Indeed, if we define the hierarchy in terms of a person's position relative to others, every time one person moves up, another must move down. Perhaps it is our collective fascination with the rich and wealth accumulation that leads us to focus on upward mobility, but there is a notable lack of attention given to a relatively common experience. Despite this relative neglect, however, there is no doubt that the experience of downward mobility can provide insight into how and why mobility happens.

One researcher who recognized the importance of downward mobility is Katherine Newman (1988/1999), whose book, *Falling from Grace*, reports on her in-depth interviews with those who moved down in the social hierarchy. Newman's objective was to understand how people internalized and experienced the process of downward mobility. She interviewed 150 people from four groups: mostly male, former white-collar managers who had lost their job; former air traffic controllers who were fired by the government; blue-collar workers who became unemployed when their Singer plant closed in New Jersey; and divorced women who were once middle class. Newman concluded that downward mobility was more troubling for the executives and professionals that she interviewed than for the lower white- or blue-collar workers. She speculates that those who already were relatively low in the social hierarchy were more accustomed to the experience of downward mobility and job loss, either personally or by watching friends and family members confront it. Therefore, blue-collar workers were better able to accept and cope with the process when they experienced job loss and downward mobility. White-collar workers had less experience with job loss and downward mobility. They had little social support and were more likely to blame themselves – and to be blamed by others – for causing their job loss. Divorced women were similar to white-collar workers. Because they had learned that marital stability and happiness are a wife's responsibility, they saw divorce as a personal failure.

Sorokin ([1959]2001) noted that as with upward mobility, downward mobility can take two forms: (1) the dropping of an individual from a higher to a lower social position; and (2) the reduction in status that an entire group can experience. "The first case of 'sinking' reminds one of an individual falling from a ship; the second of the sinking of the ship itself with all on board, or of the ship as a wreck breaking itself into pieces" (Sorokin [1959]2001: 134). Newman's interviews included examples of both types of downward mobility. The women who lost their social position through divorce exemplify individuals who experience a decrease in social standing. In contrast, both former managers and blue-collar workers from the Singer plant lost their job and experienced downward mobility during the mid-1980s, when hard economic times led many companies to lay off workers. The opening vignette in Newman's book recounts the story of an executive in the computer industry who lost his job when companies fired thousands of workers in the mid-1980s.

A pair of notable examples from recent U.S. history underscores the seeming ease with which even those with great fortunes can find themselves moving down the social hierarchy. The first example is the Vanderbilt family, which was extremely prominent during the 1800s. Cornelius "Commodore" Vanderbilt established the family's fortune in the railroad and shipping industries in the nineteenth century. When he died, he had accumulated more than $100 million in assets – or approximately $160 billion in today's dollars – making him one of the ten wealthiest American's in U.S. history

(Forbes 2010). Commodore Vanderbilt provided the initial $1 million endowment that established Vanderbilt University in Nashville, Tennessee, and his family dominated the social scene in the Northeast during the Gilded Age. However, this domination of society did not last long. When 120 of the Commodore's descendents had a family reunion at Vanderbilt University in 1973, there was not a millionaire among them (Vanderbilt II 1989).

Excess consumption and lavish living were a significant part of the downward mobility of both the Vanderbilts and the Hartfords. Commodore Vanderbilt always lived in a modest home, but his descendents built Fifth Avenue mansions in New York City, summer cottages in Rhode Island, the Biltmore Mansion in the mountains of North Carolina, and many other exclusive homes and mansions. Commodore's grandson William and his wife Alva attended and hosted balls that cost millions of dollars in their lavish Fifth Avenue mansion. Another grandson, Cornelius II, and his wife Alice entered into a luxury-spending competition with William and Alva: "When Willie's (Alva's husband's) carriage was seen traveling up Fifth Avenue with two footmen on the box, Cornelius and Alice assigned two footmen to their carriage. When the Willie Vanderbilts stationed a watchman in front of their home, Cornelius and Alice stationed two of the biggest servants they could hire..." (Vanderbilt II, 1989: 182). Alice and Alva also competed on the size and lavishness of their New York mansions and summer "cottages." Both families adored the family's Newport, Rhode Island, mansion known as The Breakers, but Alva wanted more. She had her husband build her a marble house that far surpassed The Breakers in lavishness. When the original Breakers burned down, however, Alice insisted that the mansion be rebuilt with even greater lavishness. Two years later, the new Breakers was complete; The result was a four-story mansion with 70 rooms, 30 bathrooms with hot and cold fresh and salt water, 33 rooms for servants, a 2-story formal dining room, a library, an arcade, music and billiards rooms, and countless other luxuries (Vanderbilt II, 1989 #10308).

Another family that experienced downward mobility is the Hartfords. George Huntington Hartford founded the Great Atlantic and Pacific Tea Company (A&P) in 1859 in Elmira, New York. When he died in 1917, his estate was worth more than $125 million dollars, making him one of the richest men in U.S. history. Mr. Hartford's business still exists (A&P is a successful corporation now headquartered in Montvale, New Jersey), but his family fortune essentially was squandered (Gubernick 1991). Hartford's grandson Huntington Hartford II was born in New York in 1911 to Edward and Henrietta Hartford. His father died when he was only 12 years old, and his mother's obsession with social status and spending led some observers to suggest that she was the ultimate source of the family's downward mobility. Henrietta spent lavishly on her home in Rhode Island, other real estate, automobiles and chauffeurs, yachts, and other extravagant purchases. Huntington's own accomplishments did not extend much beyond spending habits similar to his mother's. He was an average student despite attending St. Paul's (i.e., an elite boarding school) and Harvard, performed poorly, ultimately was fired from an entry-level statistics clerk at A&P, which is now run by his uncles, and invested in failed business ventures. Hartford also continued to spend lavishly, much like his mother; Two of his most visible and financially harmful purchases were Hog Island in The Bahamas and the Gallery of Modern Art in Manhattan. Both purchases were intended to be business deals, but both were financial disasters that ultimately contributed to his bankruptcy in the late 1960s.

Neither example provides decisive information about the causes of downward mobility. Yet, they contribute ideas about which factors contribute to the process. Future research could provide more systematic analysis of the process of downward mobility and might consider the complex interaction among personal characteristics, family traits, and contextual influences that lead families to move down the social hierarchy.

Summary

(1) Social mobility refers to changes in social status over time for individuals or entire groups. Researchers attempt to identify the degree to which people are mobile and the factors that contribute to mobility.

(2) Much mobility research attempts to identify the relative importance of ascribed versus achieved characteristics in producing social mobility.

(3) Mobility varies along several dimensions, and its direction indicates whether it is upward, downward, or horizontal/lateral. *Generation* refers to whether mobility is intergenerational or intragenerational (also referred to as career or occupational mobility).

(4) It is important to distinguish structural mobility from circulation (or exchange) mobility. Structural mobility results from changes in social structure; circulation mobility results from individual attributes.

(5) Absolute mobility also is different from relative mobility. It occurs when living standards change in absolute terms and nearly all people experience some type of movement. Relative mobility indicates change that an individual experiences relative to others in the hierarchy.

(6) Historically, interpretations of the degree to which people have been mobile vary widely, and researchers use several empirical measures to attempt to summarize mobility patterns. Common approaches include intergenerational correlations and transition studies or mobility tables.

(7) Intergenerational correlations indicate a significant persistence in status across generations, particularly in wealth ownership. Similarly, mobility tables suggest that few people change status over time. Yet, both also suggest that more people than expected experience social mobility by chance.

(8) Stratification systems are categorized as open or closed. Within these two general categories, there are class, estate, caste, and slavery systems. The structure of the stratification system can affect the degree to which people are mobile independent of individual attributes.

(9) Theoretical approaches to understanding mobility are either individual or structural. The status attainment approach, an individual-oriented model of mobility, proposes that attainment is influenced by both inherited traits and individual achievement. Others argue that structural influences, such as generational crowding and economic conditions, are more critical determinants of mobility prospects.

(10) Recent generations of white Catholics in the United States comprise an example of an upwardly mobile group. Demographic factors such as fertility, marriage patterns, and education affected their mobility. Similarly, unique Catholic attitudes toward work and money contributed to increased income and wealth that, in turn, increased mobility.

(11) Downward mobility is generally neglected but it is a common and important social process. Like upward mobility, downward mobility can occur to an individual or an entire group.

Box 8.1 Oprah Winfrey

Oprah Winfrey is modern example of a person who was upwardly mobile despite a troubled background. Oprah was born in 1954 in Kosciusko, Mississippi, a small farming community in the central part of the state. It was a difficult time and place to be an African American female, and Oprah's family situation added to the challenges she faced. Her parents were unmarried, and she lived in extreme poverty with her mother and grandmother. She was sexually abused as a child by her mother's friends and relatives and was eventually sent to live with her father, who was a barber in Tennessee.

Oprah started working in radio and television in the early 1970s while attending Tennessee State University, and she worked in Tennessee and Baltimore after graduating. She landed a job hosting a faltering Chicago television chat show in 1976 and quickly turned it into a huge success, outdoing even established shows such as the *Phil Donahue Show*. She introduced the *Oprah Winfrey Show* in 1986 and grossed $125 million in the first season, from which she received $30 million. She launched Harpo Productions ("Oprah" spelled backward) shortly afterward, thereby gaining control of her television show and the millions of dollars generated in royalties. Oprah also gained fame for her role in Steven Spielberg's motion picture *The Color Purple*, for her notorious book club, for founding Oxygen Media (i.e., cable and Internet programs for women), and for establishing the highly successful *O: The Oprah Magazine*. When Oprah recorded the final episode of her wildly-popular television show in 2011, she received a royal sendoff from celebrities from around the world.

Oprah is one of few African American women in the Forbes list of the 400 Richest Americans. As of 2010 her net worth exceeded $2.4 billion and was growing despite the recent recession. In 2005, *Business Week* called her the greatest black philanthropist in history, pointing to the more than $50 million in funds she has raised for causes such as educating African girls and aiding victims of Hurricane Katrina.

To learn more about Oprah Winfrey, read any of the numerous biographies written about her, including the following:

Helen S. Garsen. 2004. *Oprah Winfrey: A Biography*. New York: Greenwood.
Katherine Krohn. 2008. *Oprah Winfrey: Global Media Leader*. New York: Lifeline.

Box 8.2 Henry, Not Horatio

Horatio Alger stories (i.e., about people who defied the odds and experienced upward social mobility) are popular because we all want to hope that circumstances can get better, particularly if we face hardships. Stories about people who have beaten the odds also are more common than those about people who worked hard to get ahead but never quite made it. After all, the people who tried and failed simply are not as memorable as people like Oprah Winfrey (see Box 8.1), who worked hard and succeeded. One problem with Horatio Alger stories is that they suggest that getting ahead is easier than it really is. Henry is a real person who has worked hard; his story illustrates how difficult it can be to succeed when the circumstances do not cooperate, regardless of how much determination, drive, and motivation a person has.

Box 8.2 (*continued*)

Henry was born in a small town in Wyoming in 1948. His father worked in a factory and his mother worked part-time in a local shop to help make ends meet. Although his parents were never wildly successful financially, they always had enough money to provide necessities for Henry and his two sisters. Henry was an above-average student throughout school, and he graduated near the top of his class. He always was determined to be a success. He saw how hard his parents struggled at times, which motivated him even more. Because college was too expensive, Henry decided to join the army after high school to save money and attend a university later.

While in the army, Henry met Michelle; they married and had three children. Henry had been trained as an electrician and he continued to work as an electrician when he left the army and the family moved back to Wyoming. He still planned to go to college, but he decided to wait until the children were a little older and Michelle could go back to work. In the meantime, Henry started a couple of different businesses while continuing his job, hoping that entrepreneurship would pay off for him. Neither business survived, however: Slow economic times ended the first and his business partner pulled out of the second, taking his share of the startup funds. About the same time that the second business failed, one of Henry's children was diagnosed with a nonlife-threatening disease that nonetheless required extra attention during the day and kept her out of school. Michelle was unable to go back to work because she needed to care for the sick child.

As the years passed, Henry's dream of going to college faded, but his determination did not. He started various other small businesses and, although none succeeded, he eventually opened his own electrician business. Even now as Henry approaches retirement age, his will to do something spectacular has not faded. As of this writing, Henry has not yet struck it rich but he does earn enough to provide for his family. His children are grown and married, and one of his sons-in-law works for Henry's business. Henry's sister has lived with him and Michelle since her husband died several years ago, and Henry's income also supports his grown daughter who has never been able to work full-time because of her disability. When you ask Henry, he says that he has indeed been a success, but it is unlikely that we will ever hear about Henry. His is certainly not a Horatio Alger story.

Henry is a real person who told his story to Lisa Keister as part of a research study. We changed his name and other identifying features; otherwise, his story is a real experience of trying to get ahead.

Key Concepts

Absolute mobility

Achieved traits

Ascribed traits

Attainment

Career mobility

Caste

Caste system

Circulation mobility

Class system

Closed stratification system

Downward mobility

Estate system

Exchange mobility

Generational crowding

Homogamy

Horizontal mobility

Intergenerational correlation

Intergenerational mobility

Intragenerational mobility

Lateral mobility

Mobility table

Occupational mobility

Open stratification system

Path models

Relative mobility

Religious homogamy

Slavery

Social mobility

Status attainment model

Structural mobility

Transition matrix

Upward mobility

Vertical mobility

Questions for Thought

1. Explain the difference between absolute and relative mobility. Which is more important? Defend your answer.
2. Recall the difference between intergenerational and intragenerational mobility. Use the tables in this chapter and others you can find online to decide which is more common. Why do you think you see the patterns that you observe?
3. Are modern societies really open stratification systems? Why or why not? Design a research study that allows you to test your answer.
4. Speculate about the reasons that downward mobility attracts less attention from researchers than upward mobility. What unique lessons can patterns of downward mobility contribute to our understanding of mobility? Is downward mobility a real social problem? Why or why not?

Exercises

1. Create a transition matrix (i.e., mobility table) that describes your ideal society. Would there be more or less mobility than we have seen historically? How much? Do not be overly concerned about making the rows and columns work out mathematically, but do capture the key elements of your ideal society. Be ready to defend your choices!
2. Go to www.pbs.org/peoplelikeus/games/index.html and take the "Identify This" quiz. Based on your results, how well would you be able to fit into another class? How easy do you think it is for the average U.S. citizen to transition between classes? What does this tell us about mobility in the United States?
3. Use the Internet and other external sources to learn more about caste systems of stratification. Explore the Indian caste system in more detail. Also, gather more information on South African apartheid, U.S. Jim Crow, and other systems considered to be caste systems. What traits are common to each system? Can you imagine a set of social policies that would dismantle a caste system?
4. Read the news release by the Economic Policy Institute entitled "Pulling Apart: A State by State Analysis of Income Trends" (www.epi.org/content.cfm/studies_pulling_apart_2006), which addresses how the gap between the wealthiest families and poor and middle-income families significantly increased in the past 20 years. Do you agree with the arguments? What does this tell us about mobility in the United States?

Multimedia Resources

Print

Blau, Peter, and Otis D. Duncan. 1967. *The American Occupational Structure.* New York: John Wiley and Sons.

Bowles, Samuel, and Herbert Gintis. 2001. "The Inheritance of Economic Status: Education, Class, and Genetics." Pp 119–42 In *International Encyclopedia of the Social and Behavioral Sciences,* edited by N. Smelser and P. Baltes. Oxford: Elsevier Press.

Breiger, Ronald L. 1990. *Social Mobility and Social Structure.* New York: Cambridge University Press.

Keister, Lisa. *Getting Rich.* New York: Cambridge University Press.

Lipset, Seymour Martin, and Reinhard Bendix. 1963. *Social Mobility in Industrial Society*. Berkeley, CA: University of California Press.

MacLeod, Jay. 1987. *Ain't No Makin' It*. Bolder, CO: Westview Press.

Morgan, Stephen L., David B. Grusky, and Gary S. Fields. 2006. *Mobility and Inequality*. Stanford, CA: Stanford University Press.

Newman, Katherine S. 1988. *Falling from Grace*. Los Angeles: University of California Press.

Sorokin, Pitirim A. 1927. *Social Mobility*. New York: Harper & Brothers.

Internet

(1) Arasite.org/socmoby1.htm: Homepage for the Oxford Studies on Social Mobility, which summarizes the results of this study on social mobility.

(2) Povertycenter.cwru.edu/urban_poverty/dev/pdf/9802mov_.PDF: Information on the characteristics that aid individuals in moving from welfare to work.

Films

Caught in the Crossfire. 1993. The primary focus of this film is violence in a New York City housing project. However, it also examines the aspirations of children living in the projects and the challenges they face in fulfilling them.

Maid in Manhattan. 2002. This romantic comedy about a single mother from the boroughs of New York City who works as a maid in an upscale Manhattan hotel is a fairly direct depiction of class differences in the United States. Although the story is not subtle, it raises questions about whether mobility is possible and what it means to cross social-class boundaries.

Pride and Prejudice. 2005. A film version of Jane Austen's novel about social class and mobility in nineteenth-century England raises questions about how class and mobility vary across national boundaries and over time.

Spellbound. 2002. This documentary follows eight grade-school students from cities, suburbs, and small towns as they prepare for and compete in the annual Scripps Howard grade-school spelling bee. The varied class backgrounds and ambitions of the competitors and their parents illustrate some of the realities that make social mobility challenging.

Social Class in America. 1957. This film follows three male babies from different social classes. One succeeds his father as president of the family's company, another middle-class worker leaves his hometown and becomes an art director in New York, and a third takes a working-class job (i.e., mechanic) in a small town. The obvious story of class division and mobility illustrates how class boundaries and the mobility process have changed since the 1950s.

Roger and Me. 1989. A documentary about how downsizing at General Motors affected the residents of Flint, Michigan.

Works Cited

Abbott, Andrew, and Alexandra Hrycak. 1990. "Measuring Resemblance in Sequence Data: An Optimal Matching Analysis of Musicians' Careers." *American Journal of Sociology* 96: 144–85.

Alwin, Duane. 1986. "Religion and Parental Childbearing Orientations: Evidence for a Catholic–Protestant Convergence." *American Journal of Sociology* 92: 412–20.

Biblarz, Timothy J., Adrian E. Raftery, and Alexander Bucur. 1997. "Family Structure and Mobility." *Social Forces* 75: 1319–41.

Blau, Peter, and Otis D. Duncan. 1967. *The American Occupational Structure.* New York: John Wiley and Sons.

Bowles, Samuel, and Herbert Gintis. 2001. "The Inheritance of Economic Status: Education, Class, and Genetics." Pp 119–42. In *International Encyclopedia of the Social and Behavioral Sciences,* edited by N. Smelser and P. Baltes. Oxford: Elsevier Press.

Breiger, Ronald L. 1990. *Social Mobility and Social Structure.* New York: Cambridge University Press.

Browning, Christopher R., and Kathleen A. Cagney. Forthcoming. "Moving Beyond Poverty: Neighborhood Structure, Social Processes and Health." *Journal of Health and Social Behavior.*

Bryk, Anthony S., Valerie E. Lee, and Peter B. Hollan. 1993. *Catholic Schools and the Common Good.* Cambridge: Harvard University Press.

Call, Vaughn R. A., and Tim B. Heaton. 1997. "Religious Influence on Marital Stability." *Journal for the Scientific Study of Religion* 36: 382–92.

Cookson, Peter W. 1997. *Lessons from Privilege: The American Prep School Tradition.* Cambridge: Harvard University Press.

Curtis, Kristen Taylor, and Christopher G. Ellison. 2002. "Religious Heterogamy and Marital Conflict: Findings from the National Survey of Families and Households." *Journal of Family Issues* 23: 551–76.

D'Antonio, William V., James D. Davidson, Dean R. Hoge, and Katherine Meyer. 2001. *American Catholics: Gender, Generation, and Commitment.* Walnut Creek, CA: Altamira Press.

Darnell, Alfred, and Darren E. Sherkat. 1997. "The Impact of Protestant Fundamentalism on Educational Attainment." *American Sociological Review* 62: 306–15.

DeBerri, Edward P., and James E. Hug. 2003. *Catholic Social Teaching: Our Best Kept Secret* (4th edition). Maryknoll, NY: Orbis Books.

Duncan, Otis Dudley. 1961. "A Socioeconomic Index for All Occupations." In *Occupations and Social Status,* edited by J. Reiss (pp. 109–38). New York: The Free Press.

Easterlin, Richard A. 1980. *Birth and Fortune: The Impact of Numbers on Personal Welfare.* New York: Basic Books.

Easterlin, Richard A., Christine MacDonald, and Diane J. Macunovich. 1990. "How Have American Baby Boomers Fared? Earnings and Economic Well-Being of Young Adults, 1964–1987." *Population Economics* 3: 278–90.

Evans, William N., and Robert M. Schwab. 1995. "Finishing High School and Starting College: Do Catholic Schools Make a Difference?" *The Quarterly Journal of Economics* 110: 941–74.

Featherman, David L., and Robert M. Hauser. [1978]2001. "Modern Analysis of Class Mobility." Pp 129–60 In *Social Stratification,* edited by D. B. Grusky. Boulder, CO: Westview Press.

Filsinger, Erik E., and Margaret R. Wilson. 1984. "Religiosity, Socioeconomic Rewards, and Family Development: Predictors of Marital Adjustment." *Journal of Marriage and the Family* 46: 663–70.

Forbes Magazine. "The World's Billionaires." *www.forbes.com/billionaires/*

Grusky, David B., and Thomas A. DiPrete. 1990. "Structure and Trend in the Process of Stratification for American Men and Women." *American Journal of Sociology* 96: 108–43.

Grusky, David, and Robert M. Hauser. [1984]2001. "Comparative Social Mobility Revisited: Models of Convergence and Divergence in 16 Countries." Pp 161- 180 In *Social Stratification,* edited by D. B. Grusky. Boulder, CO: Westview Press.

Gubernick, Lisa R. 1991. *Squandered Fortunes: The Life and Times of Huntington Hartford.* New York: G.P. Putnam's Sons.

Hammond, Judith A., Bettie S. Cole, and Scott H. Beck. 1993. "Religious Heritage and Teenage Marriage." *Review of Religious Research* 35: 118–33.

Harbury, Colin D., and David M. W. N. Hitchens. 1979. *Inheritance and Wealth Inequality in Britain*. London: George Allen & Unwin.

Hoffer, Thomas, Andrew M. Greeley, and James S. Coleman. 1985. "Achievement Growth in Public and Catholic Schools." *Sociology of Education* 58: 74–97.

Jianakoplos, Nancy A., and Paul L. Menchik. 1997. "Wealth Mobility." *Review of Economics and Statistics* 79: 18–31.

Kaelble, Hartmut. 1985. *Social Mobility in the 19th and 20th Centuries: Europe and America in Comparative Perspective*. Dover, NH: Berg.

Kearl, James R., and Clayne L. Pope. 1986. "Unobserved Family and Individual Contributions to the Distributions of Income and Wealth." *Journal of Labor Economics* 4: S48–79.

Keister, L. 2003. "Religion and Wealth: The Role of Religious Affiliation and Early Adult Asset Accumulation." *Social Forces* 82: 173–205.

Keister, L. A. 2005. "Getting Rich: A Study of Wealth Mobility in America." Cambridge: Cambridge University Press.

Keister, Lisa A. 2007. "Upward Wealth Mobility: Exploring the Roman Catholic Advantage." *Social Forces* 85: 1195–226.

Keister, L. A. and N. Deeb-Sossa. 2001. "Are Baby Boomers Richer Than Their Parents? Intergenerational Patterns of Wealth Ownership in the United States." *Journal of Marriage and Family* 63: 569–79.

Krymkowski, Daniel H. 1991. "The Process of Status Attainment among Men in Poland, the U.S., and West Germany." *American Sociological Review* 56: 46–59.

Lehrer, Evelyn L. 1996. "Religion as a Determinant of Fertility." *Journal of Population Economics* 9: 173–96.

———. 1998. "Religious Intermarriage in the United States: Determinants and Trends." *Social Science Research* 27: 245–63.

———. 1999. "Religion as a Determinant of Educational Attainment: An Economic Perspective." *Social Science Research* 28: 358–79.

Lehrer, Evelyn L., and Carmel U. Chiswick. 1993. "Religion as a Determinant of Marital Stability." *Demography* 30: 385–404.

Menchik, Paul L. 1979. "Intergenerational Transmission of Inequality: An Empirical Study of Wealth Mobility." *Economica* 46: 349–62.

Mosher, William D., Linda B. Williams, and David P. Johnson. 1992. "Religion and Fertility in the United States: New Patterns." *Demography* 29: 199–214.

Mulligan, Casey B. 1997. *Parental Priorities and Economic Inequality*. Chicago: University of Chicago Press.

National Longitudinal Survey of Mature Men, 1966. www.bls.gov/nls/.

National Longitudinal Survey of Youth, 1979. www.bls.gov/nls/.

Neal, Derek. 1997. "The Effect of Catholic Secondary Schooling on Educational Achievement." *Journal of Labor Economics* 15: 98–123.

Newman, Katherine. [1988]1999. *Falling from Grace: Downward Mobility in the Age of Affluence*. Berkeley: University of California Press.

Pessen, Edward. 1974. *Riches, Class, and Power*. New York: D. C. Heath and Company.

Quillian, Lincoln. 1999. "Migration Patterns and the Growth of High-Poverty Neighborhoods, 1970–1990." *American Journal of Sociology* 105: 1–37.

Rijken, Susanne. 1999. "The Effect of Social Origin on Status Attainment in First Job." In *Educational Expansion and Status Attainment: A Cross-National and Over-Time Comparison*, edited by S. Rijken (pp. 79–110). Utrecht: Netherlands Organization for Scientific Research.

Sewell, William H., Jr. 1992. "A Theory of Structure: Duality, Agency, and Transformation." *American Journal of Sociology* 98: 1–29.

Sewell, William H., Archibald Haller, and Alejandro Portes. 1969. "The Educational and Early Occupational Status Attainment Process." *American Sociological Review* 34: 82–92.

Sherkat, Darren E. 2004. "Religious Intermarriage in the United States: Trends, Patterns, and Predictors." *Social Science Research* 33: 606–25.

Sherkat, Darren E., and Christopher G. Ellison. 1999. "Recent Developments and Current Controversies in the Sociology of Religion." *Annual Review of Sociology* 25: 363–94.

Singer, Burton, and Seymour Spilerman. 1979. "Clustering on the Main Diagonal in Mobility Matrices." *Sociological Methodology* 10: 172–208.

Sorokin, Pitirim A. 1927. *Social Mobility*. New York: Harper & Brothers.

_____. 1959. *Social and Cultural Mobility*. Glencoe, IL: The Free Press.

Sorokin, Pitirim. [1959]2001. "Social and Cultural Mobility." Pp 56-71 In *Social Stratification*, edited by D. Grusky. Boulder, CO: Westview Press.

Steckel, Richard H. 1990. "Poverty and Prosperity: A Longitudinal Study of Wealth Accumulation, 1850–1860." *Review of Economics and Statistics* 72: 275–85.

Steckel, Richard H., and Jayanthi Krishman. 1992. "Wealth Mobility in America: A View from the National Longitudinal Survey." *National Bureau of Economic Research*, Working Paper Series, Working Paper No. 4137, Cambridge, MA.

Stovel, Katherine, Michael Savage, and Peter Bearman. 1996. "Ascription into Achievement: Models of Career Systems at Lloyds Bank, 1890–1970." *American Journal of Sociology* 102: 358–99.

Thibodeau, Richard, Edward J. O'Donnell, and John C. O'Connor. 1997. *The Essential Catholic Handbook: A Summary of Beliefs, Practices, and Prayers*. Liguori, MI: Liguori Publications.

Tropman, John E. 1995. *The Catholic Ethic in American Society: An Exploration of Values*. San Francisco, CA: Jossey-Bass.

_____. 2002. *The Catholic Ethic and the Spirit of Community*. Washington, DC: Georgetown University Press.

Vanderbilt II, Arthur T. 1989. *Fortune's Children: The Fall of the House of Vanderbilt*. New York: William Morrow.

Westoff, Charles F., and Elise F. Jones. 1979. "The End of 'Catholic' Fertility." *Demography* 16: 209–17.

9 Education and Inequality

A Sociology of Education

Education is arguably the most important institution in modern society. Although societies always have transmitted knowledge from one generation to another, education today functions as a moderator of stratification and inequality (Buchmann and Hannum 2001; Shavit and Blossfield 1993). As we can imagine, the lives of the 15 percent of students who drop out of school before earning a high school diploma are very different compared to those of the 10 percent who earn a graduate or professional degree (U.S. Census Bureau 2010). As discussed herein, education helps determine what some researchers consider personal characteristics, such as social status (Shavit and Blossfield 1993), occupation (Buchmann and Brakewood 2000; Shavit and Mueller 1997), and family size (Astone and Upchurch 1994). Moreover, these same factors also predict educational achievement (Blake 1989; Bourdieu and Passeron 1977) and the attainment levels of one's children (Astone and McLanahan 1991; deGraaf 1988; Pong 1997; Powell and Steelman 1993). Education systems can be both formal and informal; however, this chapter focuses primarily on the former.

We may ask, "Why do sociologists study education; isn't that the job of educationalists?" Yes and no. Whereas educationalists generate knowledge about teaching and learning as well as organization and policy, sociologists focus primarily on the structures and processes of education systems around the world. In general, sociologists look at education and, specifically, schools as institutions (Trent, Braddock, and Henderson 1985) that create social membership (Anderson 1982), workplaces (Dreeben 1973), and organizations (Bell 1980; Bidwell 1974; Campbell 1975). Of particular interest is how education affects a person's life course considering class, race, and gender.

This chapter introduces the sociological concept of education systems, provides a brief history of education types and membership, and describes sociological theories that explain the function of education and how education and inequality are related.

We then turn to the relationship between stratification and education and education policy. Two fundamental questions organize this chapter and guide the sociology of education discipline: How does education affect stratification, and how does stratification affect education?

Systems of Education

There are many forms of education: A parent educates a child, a cleric educates a community, and even some TV shows educate children. However, sociologists of education are primarily concerned with formal institutions and how they generate knowledge around which forces bring people together to organize and create membership and set goals for education.

Before we discuss how social relations affect education, it is necessary to review the levels of education. Five major categories are used to describe the various levels of formal institutions of education: early childhood, primary school, secondary school, postsecondary school, and higher education. Each category is explained and includes a description of current membership.

Early childhood describes an array of educational practices prior to kindergarten; this often includes child care. For example, in 2005, on average, 57 percent of children ages 3 to 5 were enrolled in early-childhood programs. However, when we disaggregate this number, enrollments vary greatly by race/ethnicity: 66 percent African American, 59 percent white, and 43 percent Hispanic children are enrolled in early-childhood programs (National Center for Education Statistics 2006a). Recent studies focus on early-childhood education because of the impact these early days have on the trajectory of a young person's life course. As discussed in the status attainment model, children come to school with various abilities that set them on a track ultimately leading to open or closed opportunities later in life. Particular attention is given to children at risk because attending a high-quality early-childhood program has been shown to have a positive effect on cognition, language, and social skills (National Research Council and Institute of Medicine 2000). Unfortunately, these skills often fade during primary school, but they reappear later in secondary school, where children at risk who participated in early-childhood development programs are more likely to graduate from high school compared to their counterparts who did not participate (Campbell et al. 2007). This early learning-center based education is associated with parents' level of education. As the parents' education increases, so also does the likelihood of their children attending an early education program (National Center for Education Statistics 2006a). As shown in Figure 9.1, whites and Asians are advantaged in early education, which leads some to view early-childhood programs (e.g., Head Start) as a possible way to decrease inequality.

Primary school, more commonly known as elementary school, includes kindergarten through about fifth grade and is mandatory in most nations. Primary education is of great interest to sociologists because it is during this time that children integrate with society through socialization and allocation (Parsons 1959), acquire human capital (i.e., skills) (Becker 1964, 1993; Coleman 1988; Schultz 1961), and begin moral development (Durkheim 1956).

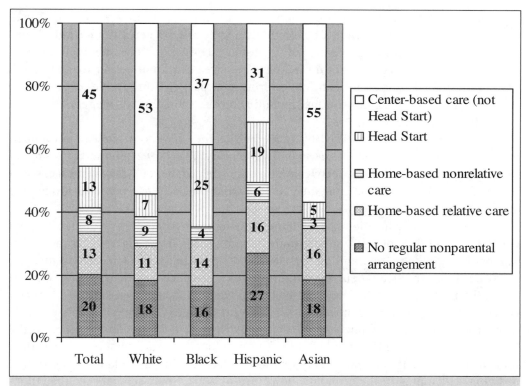

Figure 9.1 Percentages of 4-year-olds in child-care arrangements by race/ethnicity, 2005–2006. *Data source*: NCES (2006a).

Throughout developed nations, education is compulsory and begins at approximately age 5 or 6 continuing to age 16 to 17; the ending age is slightly lower for developing nations (UNESCO 2011). Although in America, most states require students to attend school until 10th grade (i.e., about age 16), it is not always the case. According to the 2010 U.S. Census, about 7 percent of Americans leave school prior to the ninth grade.

Secondary school follows primary school and takes various forms around the world. In the United States, secondary school includes middle and high school. Whereas about 30 percent of students graduate from high school, 9 percent of adolescents attend high school but drop out before graduating. *Attrition* (i.e., dropping out) during secondary school follows well-established patterns of stratification. Those most susceptible to leaving before completion are poor, rural and urban, and children of color (National Center for Education Statistics 2008). In 2006, 9.3 percent of students between the ages of 16 and 24 were not enrolled in school and did not have a diploma or GED. Of this group, 5.8 percent were white, 10.7 percent were black, and 22.1 percent were Hispanic.

Leaving school before earning a diploma has a detrimental effect on income, wealth accumulation, and health. In industrialized nations such as the United States, education and occupation are strongly correlated. Those who fail at school most often hold jobs at the lower end of the occupational hierarchy (e.g., day laborers and roustabouts) (Needleman 2009).

Postsecondary school consists of college and university. Slightly more than 7 percent of Americans have earned an associate's degree and 17 percent a bachelor's degree; that is, one in four Americans holds a college degree. However, about 19 percent of Americans attend college but do not earn a degree (National Center for Education Statistics 2008). This is significant considering that participation in higher education is known to increase opportunities, including occupation, higher wages, and good health (Ross and Wu 1995).

College enrollment is stratified by race. Despite the increase in college enrollment by people of color throughout the twentieth century, Figure 9.2 reports the scores in the persistent enrollment gap between Hispanics and whites and between blacks and whites from 1996 to 2006. Compared to the white population, these two groups are disadvantaged.

A recent trend in education has been the growing membership in two- and four-year colleges. In 2000, about 15 million students attended college; eight years later, that number had grown to 18.3 million. By 2016, college attendance is expected to increase to 20.4 million. In 2008, about 7.2 million students attended public four-year colleges, 6.5 million attended public two-year colleges, 4.3 million attended private four-year colleges, and 0.3 million attended private two-year colleges. Despite an increase in college enrollments, demographers and the National Center for Education Statistics (NCES) (Aud, et al. 2011) recently observed a shift in enrollment toward two-year rather than four-year schools. This is most likely due to the decrease in the middle-class standard of living, articulated in the economic downturn of 2008. Some scholars see the reduction of four-year-college enrollment as a barometer of a nation's economic health. Traditionally, parents would rather impose family budgets to maintain educational investments for their children's future; however, during a recession, middle-class families cannot afford the educational investment.

College enrollment is affected not only by race and the economy but also by gender. More females attend college than males (10.6 million and 7.7 million, respectively, in

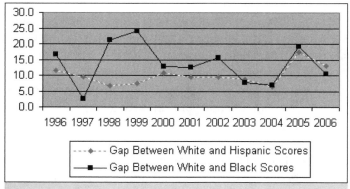

Figure 9.2 College enrollment gaps by ethnicity.
Data source: U.S. Department of Commerce, Census Bureau, Current Population Survey (CPS), October Supplement, 1972–2006, Table 24–1.

2008) and females are more likely to graduate with a degree compared to their male counterparts. Gender also affects the choice of majors: Many fields, such as education and English, are "feminized," which means that women are highly concentrated within them. This negatively affects women in the long term because feminized occupations result in lower wages. Moreover, later cohorts of males are less interested in these fields due to "too many females," which in turn suppresses wages (England and Li 2006). Why women choose fields that are feminized can be explained by *socialization theory*. Scholars have shown that family, peers, and school characteristics interact with gender and race/ethnicity, resulting in fewer women and people of color choosing science and engineering majors (Huang, Taddese, and Walter 2000).

Higher education is used to describe graduate school or other professional degrees such as those from medical and law schools. Fewer than 10 percent of Americans graduate with an advanced degree; in 2002, about 45,000 doctoral degrees were earned. According to the U.S. Census, those with a professional or doctoral degree, on average, earned $82,320 in 2006 compared to those with less than a high school diploma, who earned $20,873 (Bernstein 2008).

The gendered pattern of stratification discussed herein is found in higher education as well. Between 1971 and 2002, the proportion of women who earned a doctoral degree increased from 14 to 41 percent (England, Allison, Li, Mark, Thompson, Budig, and Sun 2007). The increase in doctoral degrees in the 30-year period was the net result of more females entering higher education, whereas the rates of males earning doctoral degrees remained consistent in this period. The feminization of majors also holds true in higher education: Women are more likely to engage in language-oriented majors and males are more likely to major in math-oriented fields.

Dropping Out

Given the importance of education, why do more than a third of college students quit school before obtaining a degree? Table 9.1 lists the top reasons that students give for dropping out of college in 1996. A more recent analysis of data from the NCES shows nearly half (i.e., 42 percent) of college dropouts do so due to financial reasons (Campbell

Table 9.1 Top Reasons for Leaving Postsecondary School without a Diploma

Reasons for Leaving	%
Job/financial demands	10.6
Family demands	4.5
Moved to another city/state	4.4
Completed desired classes	3.0
Not satisfied	2.5
Other or unknown reason	9.8
Total percentage who left	34.8

Data source: U.S. Department of Education, National Center for Education Statistics, 1996/2001 Beginning Postsecondary Students Longitudinal Study (BPS:96/01). Table B09.

2003). From these two datapoints, we can infer that the number of dropouts for financial reasons increased between 1996 and 2003.

The cost of attending college differs by the type of college. For example, it is more than twice as expensive to enroll in a private college compared to a public university. In 2006, the average annual cost of tuition, room, and board for a private college was estimated at $28,384, whereas the cost for a public college or university is estimated at $11,034 (NCES 2008). The tuition at private schools is prohibitive for most families and therefore serves as a gatekeeper to social mobility.

The process by which students are placed at institutions of higher education contributes to inequality. Students who attend elite boarding schools are more likely to attend elite colleges and universities, and those from lower socioeconomic classes are more likely to attend schools with lower selectivity (Hearn 1991). This affects a person's social-network membership during school, as well as other outcomes including occupational opportunity (Domhoff 2002).

Brief History of Education in the United States

During the colonization of America, schools were established in communities and shaped by their founding interests, which were often religious in nature. These early schools were exclusive and only open to those who shared the belief system of the sponsoring organization. This resulted in inequality for those who were not members; that is, Native Americans and secular people were denied access to education (Spring 1994).

In 1784, a movement for a Department of Education began in the state of New York. A collective of public and private schools joined with museums and libraries to establish the first accrediting agency in the United States. To *accredit* is to recognize officially that a preestablished standard has been met. Schools are institutions of accreditation. Even today, schools must pass a rigorous series of assessments to provide legitimized education. A year later, in 1785, the *Land Ordinance* was passed, which allowed the U.S. government to collect revenue on the sale of newly acquired Western territories; *Section 16* of the Land Ordinance allowed for the maintenance of public schools. This effort to educate the masses is perceived as one reason that the United States gained world-renowned prosperity and that by 1800 had the most literate society in the world. Schools were publicly maintained; however, attendance was not free. By the mid-nineteenth century, nearly 90 percent of white males were literate (Sokoloff and Engerman 2000); however, this was not the case for women or people of color.

Whether or not government should supply mass education, government-sponsored education for all was and still is debated vigorously in America. One well-known proponent of public schooling, Thomas Jefferson, lobbied for an education system sponsored and designed by the government, available to all regardless of social class, and free from religious interest and input. By the early 1800s, *common schools* were founded across America. They comprised a series of public primary schools that provided education to all individuals regardless of socioeconomic status or religious affiliation. By 1870, every U.S. child was provided a free primary education.

Private and Public Schooling

Some groups were opposed to public schooling, including the Catholic Church, which had created its own private system of schooling. In 1925, the U.S. Supreme Court rule in *Pierce vs. Society of Sisters* supported the Church by allowing students to attend private school and not compelling them to attend a common school.

Primary education now is viewed as a civil right guaranteed by both national policy and the UN. However, primary education still takes two forms: public and private. Comparing public to private schools is a topic that interests sociologists because each carries an implicit meaning to members of society that affects social stratification and inequality.

There are about 35,000 private and 97,000 public schools in the United States (NCES 2009). Public and private schools are found in all educational categories. In the fall of 2008, 49.8 million students attended public elementary and secondary schools in the United States and 6.2 million students attended private schools. That is, only 11 percent of the 56 million U.S. students attended private school.

Public schools are government-sponsored and do not require fees or tuition. Funding is a controversial issue in American education and is discussed in more detail later in this chapter. Generally, to attend public school, students are matched to a school by residency. Funds are collected from the government through local taxes, bonds, levies, and lotteries and then distributed to schools. On average, it cost $10,441 to educate a student in public school in 2007-08 (NCES 2011).

Most private schools, conversely, require tuition and are not required to accept students based on residency. The annual cost of tuition in private schools in 2006 varied greatly. Parochial (i.e., religious) school tuition was about $5,839 and nonsectarian tuition was about $13,419 (NCES 2007). Because private schools do not generally accept public funds, they are not required to disclose information like public schools, which limits a close comparison.

The high cost of tuition is only one aspect of private school that can contribute to inequality; another issue is membership. Private boarding schools are highly selective. In addition to limiting access, they confer status rights to students, which in turn results in the social reproduction of privilege (Persell and Cookson 1985). These schools hold membership within tight social networks and can lobby elite colleges and universities on behalf of their students. An example is found in the top boarding schools that have coordinated a ranking system that differs from that of nonelite schools. In the elite schools, no student is ranked as bottom of the class – instead, elite-school advisors argue that their students carry a more rigorous curriculum compared to nonelite students and cannot be compared using the conventional ranking system. The lowest-performing students at these elite boarding schools are placed in a nonranking category or given a percentile ranking, grouping them with others in their class regardless of actual placement. Private schools are well suited to assist their students in various ways that public schools cannot.

Clearly, the high cost of tuition at a nonsectarian private school prohibits most families from accessing an elite education. Between 1989 and 2005, private-school enrollments in Grades K–12 decreased from 11 to 9 percent in the United States. In addition to the general decrease, the distribution of students in private schools shifted during this period. Catholic schools, which maintain the largest private enrollment, decreased from 55 to 44 percent, whereas conservative Christian schools increased from 11 to 16 percent.

Race/ethnicity factors also contribute to the distribution of students in private schools. Comparing private to public school enrollment by race/ethnicity reveals that whites comprise the majority of the student body in private schools – that is, 75 percent private compared to 58 percent public schools. Blacks and Hispanics are disadvantaged in private school: blacks account for 10 percent of private and 16 percent of public-school students; even fewer Hispanics (9 percent) attend private and public schools (20 percent) (NCES 2006a).

Do Private Schools Provide a Higher Standard of Education?

The general consensus is that private schools provide a better education than public schools (Coleman et al. 1982). A consistent finding is that Catholic-school students show higher achievement than non-Catholic-school students (Hoffer et al. 1985). Some researchers thought that perhaps a self-selection mechanism sorted higher-performing students into Catholic schools (Cain and Goldberger 1983). A second theory is that students gain *social capital* via the Catholic community, which translates into higher achievement (Coleman 1987). This perspective assumes that a more educationally supportive social network surrounds Catholic schools compared to public schools. Sociologists term this an *open network*, in which students are exposed to many more adults than only their parents or teachers (Coleman 1988). Within this experienced community, more opportunity exists to handle situations for which public schools are less equipped. However, sociologists have found that when non-Catholics are removed from the sample, there is no benefit from a Catholic education. Indeed, the only benefit is found at the school level; Catholic-school students tend to skip school less and do more homework compared to non-Catholic-school students (Sander 1996). When schools control for these behaviors, there is no discernable difference between public and Catholic schools (Coleman et al. 1982).

According to both sociologists of education and the NCES, private schools are not significantly better than public schools (Braun, Jenkins, and Grigg 2006; Sander 1999). By looking solely at the raw reading score, for example, we might assume that the 14-point advantage of private-school fourth-graders translates into "private schools are better at educating students." However, when scientific controls are introduced for individual characteristics (e.g., socioeconomic status, race/ethnicity, English-language learners, and disability status) and school characteristics (e.g., school size, location, and student-body composition), there is no significant difference in educational outcomes between private and public schools. The NCES report also separately reviewed Catholic, Lutheran, and conservative Christian schools and came to the same conclusion: These schools do no more to educate students than public schools. Today, despite the evidence, the debate continues about the merits of public and private school.

The attitudes and expectations surrounding public and private schools contribute to inequality. The average person assumes that private schools are better in educating students but the science does not support this. Instead, evidence reveals that schools function to stratify students by race/ethnicity, disability status, home language, and socioeconomic status. Returning to the central questions posed at the beginning of this chapter, education affects stratification by ranking some students above others. This has lifelong consequences because private-school graduates often have more opportunities garnered from social networks and school influence.

Some families choose not to send their children to school at all and instead home-school them. A recent trend in the United States is an increase in home-schooling; about 1.1 million, or 2.2 percent of all students in Grades K-12, were home-schooled in 2002, up from about 1.7 percent in 1999. Again, well-established patterns of stratification can be seen in those who home-school; 77 percent of home-schooled children are white. Whereas the majority of home-schooled children (i.e., 82 percent) attended no school, 18 percent attended school part time – often as many as 25 hours per week. Family structure greatly impacts home-schooling. Of the home-schooled children, 82 percent were from two-parent households and 54 percent lived in two-parent households in which one parent worked. Parents report various reasons to home-school; in 2003, the most frequently cited were an undesirable school environment (85 percent), religious instruction (72 percent), and dissatisfaction with academic instruction (68 percent) (NCES 2006a).

Despite the various forms of education, most children receive education from kindergarten through 12th grade. To understand the role of education in modern society, we first must understand the theories that explain the importance of education and its relationship to inequality.

Theories of Stratification and Education

What does it mean that 25 percent of Americans have a bachelor's degree? Or that more than 80 percent of all nations provide and require a primary education? Why do certain groups outperform other groups? Stratification of and in education is explained by three theoretical perspectives: functionalist, conflict, and social interaction.

Sociologists conceptualize education as a link between where one begins in life and where one ends. Although mobility occurs, most families remain in the social class of previous generations. The most reliable way to reach upward mobility or at least rise to the top of one's opportunity structure is through education (Blau and Duncan 1967).

Perhaps the most important structural-functionalist study of education was conducted by the sociologists Blau and Duncan (1967), who studied the relationship between social location and destination. They measured the effect that particular influences have on social destination. They found the status of a person's father – specifically, what he does for a living, how much he earns, and his educational achievement – greatly impacts where the child ends up in life. However, the strongest predictor of upward social mobility is an individual's education level. Subsequent studies showed that both parents directly and indirectly affect a child's status through the child's aspirations (Sewell and Hauser 1980). Additionally, mothers more directly affect daughters' aspirations and fathers more directly affect sons' aspirations, and these effects differ by race and ethnicity (Reeder and Rand 1984). Functionalists have shown that in modern society, education determines the ranking that a person has in society. This finding contributed to the *status attainment model* that is prominent in sociology even today.

Social attainment theory suggests that a person's social status dictates many of their life experiences. To understand how this concept explains stratification, we examine the relationship between education and occupation. Sociologists ranked occupational structures by prestige and found that they are similar across societies (Featherman and Hauser [1978]2001). In other words, people in most societies believe a doctor holds a more important position in society compared to other occupations and therefore is rewarded more highly. High-prestige occupations require specialized knowledge and individuals who wish to pursue these positions must excel in both educational achievement (i.e., gains made through personal merit) and attainment (i.e., years of schooling and/or educational degrees). Compare this to low-skilled occupations that require little or no education but suffer from low prestige.

We turn to income for a closer analysis of how education and occupation are related. As shown in Figure 9.3, education is positively associated with income; that is, as education increases, so does income.

The functional approach assumes that education is motivated by a natural distribution of abilities. In the spirit of Darwinism – which is based on the functionalist theory of sociologist Herbert Spencer – the fittest students survive, whereas those who are less

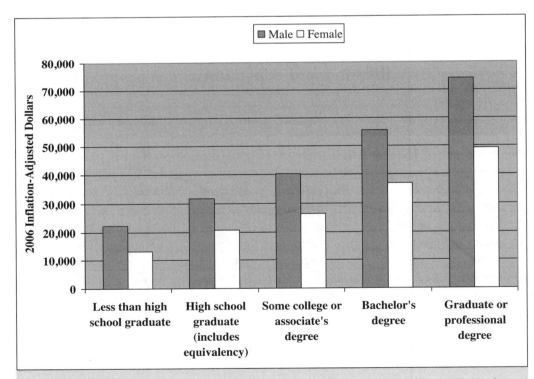

Figure 9.3 Median earnings in 2005–2006 (in 2006 inflation-adjusted dollars) by educational attainment for the population 25 years and older.
Data source: U.S. Census Bureau, American Community Survey (2006).

fit either adapt or fail to exist. In the realm of education, this means that struggling students must work harder and that failing students earn lower grades or drop out of school. These actions further inequality by limiting the ability of failing students to compete for placement in the occupational hierarchy. Indeed, educational sociologists suggest that students who do not pass secondary school in fact are failing a modern right of passage: Without education, a person is not fully an adult with full rights and privileges (Stevenson and Baker 1992).

An important functionalist study, conducted by Ralph Turner (1960), compared the British class system to the United States on *meritocracy* – that is, the ideal that everyone has equal opportunity to work hard for success. He noted a difference between the British and American education systems in that the United States experienced an *open system* of education, whereas in the United Kingdom, it was *closed*. At the time, in the 1960s, the United Kingdom was under what Turner called *sponsored mobility*. A person could gain entrance to an elite school only if he or she was sponsored by a former member. No matter how intelligent, determined, or tenacious a student was, there would be no admittance without a formal nod from a legacy. Turner believed that this was due to the history of Great Britain, which has a strict closed class system. In contrast, the United States exhibited *contest mobility*, in which members of society from various social classes coexist in classrooms and those who show the most ability are promoted. To Turner, it was as if education was a contest in America: Everyone began at the same starting line, and whoever finished first was deemed the winner and duly rewarded. This construction of education – that it is a contest in which the fittest excel and the weak are weaned out – persists today.

At the heart of functionalist theory is the concept of *biological determinism*. This theory claims that individual characteristics (e.g., ability, cognition, and effort) are due to biological forces. Some people, for example, are born intelligent, work hard, and hold high aspirations. This theory often is extended to groups, as discussed in the next section and in Chapter 11 on race and ethnicity. To functionalists, stratification in education is natural and regulates members of society. When students must compete with one another for limited space in prestigious colleges and positions in the occupational hierarchy, they are more likely to work harder than if no competition existed. The brightest students find their way to elite schools followed by prestigious occupations as doctors, lawyers, and CEOs. Their success can be traced from school to home and – to some theorists – back to their genetic composition.

Conflict theorists disagree with their functionalist colleagues (Collins 1971). Whereas functionalists believe that inequality is a natural process based on variations in ability, conflict theorists view inequality as a derivative of competition between groups for scarce resources. Conflict theory claims that every struggle between groups found in the society-at-large also are found in the classroom. The most prominent struggles are between groups of differing social classes, gender, and race/ethnicity.

When evaluating functionalism, conflict theorists ask, "Is there indeed an explicit start and finish in American education?" We must remember that Turner was writing in the 1950s, when postwar America was very different than it is today. In some regions, Jim Crow laws were still in existence, as was segregation. In fact, many colleges were segregated by not only race but also by gender. Conflict theorists argue that all students do not begin in the same place; that is, there is no fair start to the "contest." We explore this idea later when achievement gaps are discussed. Another of Turner's assumptions that conflict theorists critique is that there is no sponsored mobility in the United States. More recent studies of private clubs and elitism in schools show that sponsorship matters in education (Kingston and Lewis 1990; Useem and Karabel 1986). The best predictors of a student's success are socioeconomic status, race/ethnicity, and gender – not innate or achieved merit.

The most prominent conflict theory in stratification of education is *social reproduction*. Conflict studies consistently show that dominant members of society re-create stratified structures (e.g., education) to maintain the status quo. Inequality is transmitted across generations, directly affecting the opportunities of children of the rich and the poor. Parents with many resources and opportunities advantage their children by placing them in elite schools and providing private tutors and formal classes outside of school, whereas poor families lack the resources to advantage their children.

Indeed, the strongest predictor of educational attainment is parental levels of attainment. Therefore, IQ tests and other achievement scores account for only a small portion of inequality, and schooling reproduces rather than diminishes inequality (Bowles and Gintis 2003).

Another characteristic of schooling social reproduction to which theorists point is the curriculum. What society considers important is tied to values of dominant members of society. For example, in the United States, most students learn about history from a Eurocentric position. Although it is important to acknowledge great civilizations (e.g., the Greek and Roman empires) through the European schools of thought (e.g., Rationalism and the Enlightenment), there is no even treatment of the great civilizations of Asia, Africa, India, and Central America, among others. In fact, it was not until 1980 that an American history book was written from a conflict perspective, in which Zinn's (1980) claims were centered on conflict theory – that governments are not neutral but rather share the economic interests of the powerful. These interests, according to the conflict perspective, also set the rules and curriculum of schools.

The phrase *hidden curriculum* is used by conflict theorists to describe the covert function of education. Although a consensus exists that the purpose of education is to impart knowledge to young members of society, there is no consensus about what is considered important. The pedagogic discourse – that is, the ways in which students are taught – is scrutinized as a method of social control (Bernstein 2003). For example, consider the structure and composition of a typical classroom. Some suggest that the mere structure inculcates students to domination (Bourdieu and Passeron 1977). Students are required to adhere to punctuality, respond appropriately to directives, and accept lessons without question. These behaviors – conflict theorists are quick to point out – create a docile workforce that is easy to manipulate and at ease with powerlessness. Students who do not fit in with the curriculum (e.g., Native Americans) find school to be culturally insensitive and irrelevant and they often drop out in response (Coladarci 1983), thus making them appear "unfit."

The third theoretical perspective used to understand inequality in education is that of social interactionists. This group of sociologists argues that the macro forces that affect student performance result from the negotiated actions of individuals. According to interactionists, microprocesses are the mechanisms that create and maintain social reality and, therefore, inequality.

A particular interactionist theory receiving recent attention from scholars is *code theory* (Bernstein 2003), which claims that language reflects and shapes assumptions of particular groups. The theory assumes that individuals learn in a social context. That is, meaning is not static but rather varies by those who engage it. To learn how this theory helps to understand inequality, we look more closely at language, codes, and education.

Sociology has a rich history of examining language, codes, and meaning (Bourdieu 1991; Garfinkle 1967; Saussure [1964]1990; Wells 1999). Saussure (1964) argued that language as a cultural symbol is the impetus of social action. Words are used to organize meaning, yet they function simultaneously as both signifier and signified. Every individual, he argued, is born into a culture using a language that preexists current social configurations and that this language determines cognition.

Bernstein added that language signifies one's social identity and social class. His work compared working-class with middle-class groups and showed that two forms of codes exist: *restricted* and *elaborated*. Restricted codes are short and used by insiders who understand the meaning and assumptions to be made; elaborated codes need to be explained for outsiders to understand. Moreover, he argued that restricted codes are used by the working class due to their living conditions and socialization process, compared with the middle class, which uses both restricted and elaborated codes. Each socialization process happens during the education process. Inequality, therefore, is activated at the school level through inconsistent use of language.

Sociological theories assist in exploring the social relations of education. All three schools of thought have merit and provide rich evidence that maintains a conversation among scientists. In the following section, we examine how these theories explain variations in education outcomes.

Measures of Education

There are two general measurements used to compare students, schools, and institutions in education studies: *attainment* and *achievement*. Although these measures are far from perfect, they allow scientists to study education within and across nations and time.

At the beginning of this chapter, we discuss in detail the state of education attainment currently found in the United States. Despite the many Americans who do not graduate from primary or secondary school, on average, 86 percent of those 25 and older have completed high school, and 29 percent have at least a bachelor's degree.

Attainment is determined by many factors. The national context is the first consideration. Some nations are well equipped to fund public schools, whereas others cannot or will not. For example, although the United States provides primary and secondary education at no cost, postsecondary education is not free of charge; students must provide their own tuition, housing, books, lab fees, and materials.

Achievement

The second measurement used to study education is achievement. Education achievement describes a host of indicators including IQ, periodic assessments based on state standards (e.g., CAHSEE – California High School Exit Examination and STAR – Standardized Testing and Reporting), and other high-stakes tests such as high school exit examinations, SAT, (Scholastic Assessment Test), GRE (Graduate Record Examination), and even surveys that compare students (e.g., ECLS (Early Childhood Longitudinal Survey), NELS (National Education Longitudinal Survey), PISA (Programme for International Student Assessment, and TIMMS (Trends in International Mathematics and Science Survey). Assessments are used by educators throughout the world to measure student cognition, ability, retention, application, and even attitudes regarding education. Results of the assessments are used to rank students according to demonstrated ability. Assessments are highly controversial because some claim that they are culturally sensitive and therefore do not measure cognitive ability but rather test-taking ability. An outcome of this fact is a rise in formal learning centers in Northern America (Aurini and Davies 2004). Because families are faced with competition to place students in prestigious colleges, they turn to outside help to bolster SAT scores. Although test makers argue that students cannot study for these high-stakes tests, the learning centers claim that their graduates score higher compared to other students.

Sociologists have learned that standardized assessment ranking is determined primarily by socioeconomic, gender, and race/ethnicity statuses. Despite the generally held belief that intelligence is a biological and individual attribute, we now explore how social status affects stratification within education. Specifically, we begin by examining achievement gaps.

Achievement Gaps

Educational gaps are persistent phenomena that keep Americans focused on inequality. Gaps occur when two or more groups are compared on any given measure. For example, durable gaps exist in the academic achievement based on socioeconomic status, race/ethnicity, and gender. Two familiar theoretical perspectives explain these differences: *biological determinism* and *social reproduction.*

In 1966, sociologist James Coleman was asked to investigate educational opportunity in the United States. He and his colleagues gathered data from more than 150,000 students across the nation. The document they generated, commonly referred to as the Coleman Report (Coleman et al. 1966), showed that family effects are stronger than school effects in maintaining inequality. Four decades later, achievement gaps still exist along social-class lines. Socioeconomic status has been shown repeatedly to directly affect education.

In addition to socioeconomic status, ethnicity is linked to achievement. It is commonly assumed that increased access to education results in greater equality of educational outcomes and overall social equality. However, this is not necessarily the case. The landmark decision of *Brown vs. Board of Education* (1954) challenged the previous U.S. Supreme Court ruling, *Plessy vs. Ferguson* (1896), which upheld racial segregation and found that "separate but equal" was not equal. A new epoch began and public access to education was opened to all. However, this ruling and the subsequent actions of minority students were met with great resistance. Violent uprisings reflected daily in newspapers across the nation forced the U.S. Government to intercede on behalf of black children, and the National Guard accompanied students to school.

As schools across the United States were desegregated, more blacks had access to education. Blacks, who had been denied access and, in fact, were often punished for learning to read, were now sitting in classrooms next to white students, albeit with much resistance by many whites. Although the opening of access to education indeed helped many blacks to earn advanced degrees and placement in prestigious occupations, an achievement gap between whites and blacks still exists.

In the 50 years since desegregation, much research has been devoted to the learning gaps between ethnicities. Figure 9.4 plots the white–black and white–Hispanic reading-scale score gaps for fourth- and eighth-graders between 1992 and 2007. Despite efforts to decrease the gaps (the figure reveals a gradual decrease), the gap remains more than 20 points.

Many believe the reason that minority students perform at a lower level than whites is due to the lack of *aspirations*, that some groups do not value education. This is contrary to scientific evidence. Nonwhites, on average, have higher educational

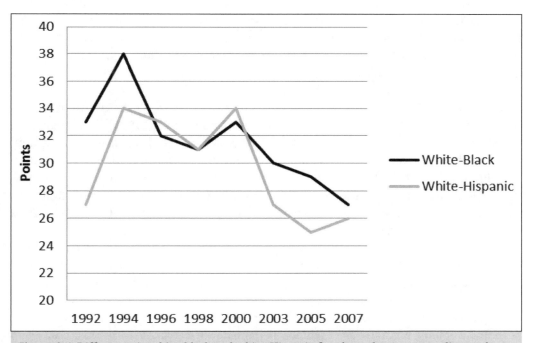

Figure 9.4 Differences in white–black and white–Hispanic fourth-grade average reading-scale scores, 1992–2007.
Data source: U.S. Department of Education, National Center for Education Statistics, National Assessment of Educational Progress (NAEP), selected years, 1992–2007 Reading Assessments, NAEP Data Explorer.

aspirations than whites (Qian and Blair 1999). Moreover, the acquisition of social and human capital impacts the formulation of expectations and aspirations regarding education. For African American and Hispanic students whose parents are engaged in school activities (or social capital), expectations and aspirations increase. Asians are more likely to have increased expectations and aspirations when English is their native language.

As scientific measures advance, sociologists are better able to measure advantage in school. One advancement in measuring students at the beginning and the end of the school year uncovered the *summer learning gap* discovered by Barbara Heyns (1978). Using data that tested children at both the end and the beginning of the school year, sociologists were able to measure student learning within the school year as well as during the summer. It was found consistently that the higher-socioeconomic-status students continued to learn during the summer months away from school and that low-socioeconomic-status students fell farther behind and often experienced a decrease in substantive learning. Again, these findings highlight the importance of family differences or, more specifically, the relationship between spatial location and educational achievement.

A highly controversial book that attempts to answer why the gaps occur is Herrnstein and Murray's (1994) *The Bell Curve*. The authors argued that intelligence (measured as IQ) varies between races. In contrast to status attainment theory, these authors proposed *biological determinism* – that is, some groups are biologically more fit than others. The theory claims that innate intelligence propels students to do well in school, thereby sending them on a trajectory of occupational attainment that leads to better lifestyles than those with no education. They showed that a persistent gap remains between blacks and whites and that this gap can be attributed to differences in IQ. Additionally, they show that IQ is negatively correlated with poverty, out-of-wedlock childbearing, and unemployment.

Sociologists were quick to refute the biological determinist theory. Instead, they provided a wealth of research showing that structural racial differences contribute to the persistent gap, and that the gap is closing (Jencks and Phillips 1998). In this body of literature, two major reasons are given that account for reproduction in stratification: funding of schools and social location as a determinant of educational opportunity (Roscigno 1998, 1999). Public schools are faced with many more expenses than private schools and they often have less discretion in terms of how to spend the funds. Although social location has long been known as a source of inequality to sociologists, the achievement-gap debate invigorated the field of study.

Although the black/white test-score gap was given national attention, modest attention has been afforded other race/ethnicity gaps. Hispanic and Native American students generally under-perform when compared to whites. However, on average, Asians have higher achievement than whites. Instead of applying biological theory, researchers argue that this variation is due to cultural differences between Asians and whites (Kao and Thompson 2003). One common belief is termed *effort/ability*. Most Caucasian Americans believe intelligence comes in the form of capacity. Consider, for example, a typical attitude of students: "I am good at writing but bad at math." This statement assumes that cognition is like a bucket – a large-capacity bucket exists for writing but a small-capacity bucket for math. This attitude has been linked to Protestantism and early

American education, in which cognition was thought to be predestined by God – one was either born with or without it. We compare this to Buddhist values that link ability to effort: "The more I apply myself in any subject, the better I will become."

In response to the Asian advantage, some sociologists ask why minority groups have such performance dissimilarities. One ecological theory seeks to explain race/ethnicity gaps by classifying minority students in terms of migration status (Ogbu 2003). One group that Ogbu terms *voluntary immigrants* chose to come to America. With hopes of achieving the American Dream, these groups leave their homeland to better themselves in the new land and therefore are optimistic about their future. The majority of Asians exemplify voluntary immigrants. The second group, *involuntary immigrants*, is forced to migrate – for example, Africans during slavery. They were torn from their homeland and, according to Ogbu, are pessimistic about their future. Because of these divergent paths of migration, Ogbu theorized that nonwhites have various performance levels when compared with whites. The oppositional culture theory gained interest because it explains why groups start out in different places; however, it fails to explain how the differences among ethnicities endure. It also explains less about Native Americans, who were not immigrants at all.

A third theoretical perspective from social psychology is used to explain how learning gaps endure. Social psychologists view psychological forces as having social foundations. Many use social interaction theory to explain how individuals create their social self in a series of externalizations and internalizations.

Box 9.1 American Classrooms as Influence

Many teachers across America start the day with a ritual intended to promote good citizenship, nationalism, and pride. From kindergarten through secondary school, students, teachers, and administrators face the American flag and recite the *Pledge of Allegiance*. The version known today follows:

"I pledge allegiance to the flag of the United States of America and to the republic for which it stands: one nation under God, indivisible, with liberty and justice for all."

Despite criticism that the word *God* in the pledge is in violation of the separation of church and state, this ritual has endured since the beginning of America. Or has it? The majority of Americans do not know the origin of the pledge, its author, who introduced it to the education system, or how it has evolved over time.

The *Pledge of Allegiance* was written in 1892 by Francis Bellamy, a Baptist minister. It originally appeared in a popular boys' magazine called *The Youth's Companion* on September 8 to celebrate the 400th anniversary of Columbus Day – when Columbus "discovered" America. Today, many find this idea offensive because America was populated by various Native American tribes; they prefer to say that Columbus *introduced* Europe to the Americas, rather than saying *discover*. Daniel S. Ford, a member of the Boston elite at that time and editor of *The Youth's Companion*, wanted a revival of patriotism in a time when "single-heartedness in national feeling was at a low ebb" (Bellamy 1953). Bellamy wrote that the times were filled with an increase in the pursuit of the dollar – industries, monopolies, and concerns about stocks caught the attention of people, yet labor and industry were at opposing ends of a struggle. In 1890, President Harrison pleaded in speeches across the nation to bring back reverence for "the little red schoolhouse" before industrialization. In response, James B. Upham, a nephew of Ford and marketer of *The Youth's Companion*, planned an event that he called the "National Public-School Celebration of Columbus Day." Its purpose was to shift the American culture back to one that embraced nationalism. To gain momentum, Ford and Upham enlisted Bellamy to write a piece for inclusion in the commemorative issue of the magazine. According to Bellamy, Ford remarked, "James is very much interested in a patriotic propaganda to get the public

(continued)

Box 9.1 (*continued*)

school children to raise flags over their schools. It's a good thing. It would be contrary to our policy to push it very much in our editorials, but James sees how it can be done through his promotion work. Perhaps you would enjoy helping him in it" (Bellamy 1953). With that request, the original *Pledge of Allegiance*, reprinted here, appeared and President Harrison proclaimed that students should recite the pledge on Columbus Day in 1892:

I pledge allegiance to my flag and the republic for which it stands: one nation indivisible with liberty and justice for all.

Students were to stand and face the flag with their right arm outstretched, called the "Bellamy salute" (Leepson and DeMille 2006), which was similar to the Nazi salute in World War II. In 1942, when Congress recognized the pledge as the official national pledge, the stance was changed to placing one's hand over the heart.

The original pledge is quite different from the pledge we know today. The additions occurred between 1923 and 1954. Some people suggest that adding "flag of the United States of America" was in response to the large number of immigrants. The words *under God* were added in 1954 as a result of lobbying efforts from various religious groups (e.g., Sons of the American Revolution and the Knights of Columbus) between 1948 and 1953. The *Pledge of Allegiance* serves as a testament to nationalism, but it also provides insight to how a few may influence so many.

Social psychologists looked at achievement gaps through this constructionist lens and found something interesting: Groups that have more status in society tend to do better on exams than subordinate members. However, this changed when the examiner prefaced the test with a statement that achievement gaps typically exist but the exam about to be undertaken was created without that bias (Spencer, Steele, and Quinn 1999). After this disclaimer, females scored as high and, in some cases, even higher than their male counterparts on college mathematics tests. Subordinates somehow censored themselves in response to feelings of subordination. Although the initial study was small and included only a few college students from one campus, the findings are being used to redevelop the scientific understanding of achievement gaps today.

This phenomenon, called *stereotype threat*, is complex and well known although it was not applied to large groups of people until more recently with the interest in achievement gaps. Box 9.2 examines how stereotype threat affects academic achievement. The fact that groups can suffer from stereotype threat does not mean that structural discriminatory forces also are not at play. Other possible sociological explanations of achievement gaps include the gender and ethnicity of instructors and proctors at high-stakes examinations. For example, blacks were found to perform better on tests when their interviewer also was black; however, race did not affect the scores of white respondents (Huang 2009). Teacher expectation also has been shown to affect student achievement; that is, they have different expectations according to their own race and the race of their students (Roscigno and Ainsworth-Darnell 1999). When a teacher has high expectations, students do better than if an instructor has low expectations.

Achievement gaps also occur between the genders. In general, boys outperform girls in mathematics and girls outperform boys in language skills. Again, a popular view is that a biological difference exists between the genders that causes the differences. Sociologists compiled studies that show that this is not the case but rather that socialization processes differ by gender, directly affecting academic achievement. For example,

---

Box 9.2 Stereotype Threat

The first recorded study of stereotype threat occurred in the 1960s when a primary-school teacher in Iowa was at a loss for how to teach acceptance and understanding after the assassination of Martin Luther King, Jr. Her story is the subject of a PBS film aptly named *A Class Divided*. After the assassination, teacher Jane Elliott found some of the questions posed by the media to be racist: one particular question haunted her. A journalist had asked Mrs. Coretta Scott King, "Who will lead your people now?" The teacher wondered why no one had asked Jackie Kennedy the same question when John F. Kennedy was assassinated. Why had no one thought to ask Mrs. Kennedy who would now lead the white people after her husband's death? Indeed, the question was packed with racism. First, it assumed that all African Americans think alike, that they move as one body. Second, it assumed that all blacks were in support of Martin Luther King, Jr. Mrs. Elliott decided to teach her students a new way to look at race relations and devised an exercise that is still being used today.

To deliver a lesson of acceptance and understanding, Mrs. Elliott knew she must do something unconventional. Lecturing to students about acceptance would not change their core beliefs about differences among ethnicities. In 1960s Iowa, there was little ethnic diversity; most of her students and their parents did not have interactions with people other than Caucasians. Mrs. Elliott stratified her class, which consisted entirely of white students, by eye color: the blue/green-eyed and the brown-eyed students. Prior to her study, she had been assessing students on how quickly they could go through a series of vocabulary words, documenting in a daily log the number of correct items and the students' completion times. On the first day, the brown-eyed students were considered "privileged." She presented the blue/green-eyed students with collars to be worn around their neck.

Any issue that arose with the collared group (e.g., one boy forgot his eyeglasses) was blamed on eye color. All of the individual problems with the collared children were reduced to their eye color. Within 5 minutes, a division began to occur between the students; in one instance, a brown-eyed boy hit a blue/green-eyed boy because of his subordinate status.

Not only did they act differently toward one another, they also performed differently on the vocabulary test. Each day, the subordinate group did more poorly than previously. The teacher sent the tests to an educational testing agency at Stanford University and was told that the students' *cognition* changed during this short study. In summary, on days that they were collared, the students' aptitude was reduced. The reduction in aptitude certainly cannot be blamed on eye color because, the following day, she reversed the experiment – the brown-eyed children had to wear the collars. Again, in a short time, she convinced her students that being brown-eyed was tantamount to being subordinate in status. This experiment showed clearly that status can define aptitude and that people are sensitive to general norms and stereotypes. Mrs. Elliott asked her students whether we can judge someone by their eye color or another physical characteristic, such as skin color. In resounding unison, the class replied, "No, Mrs. Elliott." She then asked them what they wanted to do with the collars; some of the suggestions were to burn them or throw them away. When she asked if they should get rid of them, the children screamed, again in unison, "Yes, Mrs. Elliott." As they removed the collars, one child focused on tearing it apart so that no other child would ever have to feel that way again.

---

although the gender gap is decreasing, boys' math-reasoning scores in the first two years of school are higher than girls' scores. Sociologists found this was due in part to boys' gains in math-reasoning achievement being more sensitive to environmental factors outside the home. Boys were socialized differently than girls within communities, and this treatment caused higher scores on math reasoning (Entwisle, Alexander, and Olson 1994). Another study concluded that boys' low performance was due in part to poor classroom behavior and that activities outside of school should be considered when discussing learning gaps (Downey and Pribesh 2004).

Another gender issue that affects education is the number of women in power positions at schools. As discussed at the beginning of this chapter, schools employ more than 115,000 principals. While children are growing, their environment greatly affects their expectations. If they see women as teachers but not as principals, then the scope of women's abilities is limited. This is another example of what sociologists mean when they speak of the hidden curriculum. The process of getting an education maintains current patterns of stratification and inequality. In this case, gender inequality is reinforced by limiting women to the role of teacher and not principal.

Figure 9.5 shows the distribution of principals by gender in both elementary and secondary schools and compares three sets of years: 1993–1994, 1999–2000, and 2003–2004. This graphic representation shows that private schools remained relatively stable during the decade: about 68 and 34 percent of elementary and secondary principals, respectively, are female. In the same decade, public schools greatly increased in female principals but still lag behind private schools.

Female public primary-school principals decreased to fewer than half by 2004. Despite the differences between public and private schools, there is an important similarity for the study of inequality; that is, the percentage of female principals greatly decreases as students move from primary to secondary schools in both public and private schools. In private schools, the decrease is about 50 percent; in public schools, it is more than 50 percent.

The distribution of power is of primary concern to sociologists. If we look more closely at American principals, a disturbing pattern of inequality emerges, which extends to higher education. According to the NCES (2006a), about 16 percent of U.S. faculty in colleges and universities were minorities in 2005. (This is based on a total faculty count excluding people whose race/ethnicity was unknown but including nonresident aliens who were not identified by race/ethnicity.) Of these faculty members, 6 percent is black, 6 percent is Asian/Pacific Islander, 4 percent is Hispanic, and a half-percent is American Indian/Alaska Native. Nearly 45 percent of college faculty are white males, whereas 36 percent are white females. Less than 20 percent of executive, managerial, and administrative staffs were minorities in 2005, compared to about 32 percent of the nonprofessional staff. The percentage of minority staff at public four-year colleges and universities was similar to private four-year colleges and universities (23 and 21 percent, respectively).

Family Effects

Family affects education in many ways. As the primary institution of socialization, the family directly impacts children by establishing a family culture. Within this culture, children learn how to set goals, create habits of mind, formulate preferences, and are socialized to perform in society. Sociologists have long been interested in the relationship between the family and educational outcomes. We discussed in detail the effects that socioeconomic status, race/ethnicity, and gender have on attainment and achievement. Now, we discuss how the family structure influences education.

Family structure, which is the composition of members within the family and in the home, affects academic performance. A persistent finding of family structure relative

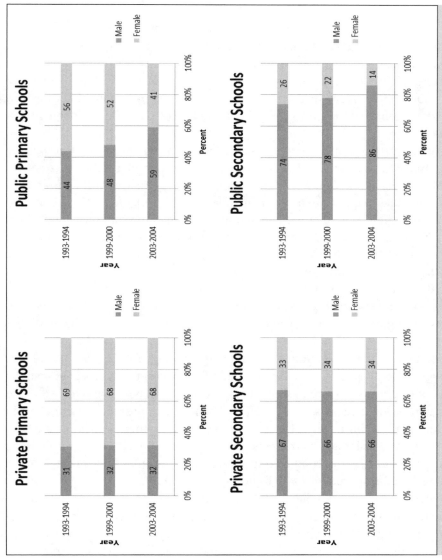

Figure 9.5. Percentage distributions of male and female primary- and secondary-school principals, by school level and school type: School years 1993–1994, 1999–2000, and 2003–2004.
Data source: U.S. Department of Education, National Center for Education Statistics, Schools and Staffing Survey, "Public School Principal Data File" and "Private School Principal Data File," 1993–1994, 1999–2000, and 2003–2004, and "Charter School Principal Data File," 1999–2000.

to educational outcomes is that an increase in household members corresponds to a decrease in academic performance (Downey 1995). Moreover, the number of parents in the home has been shown to affect academic performance. Single-parent homes tend to have children with lower performance, whereas adoptive parents have children with higher performance than natural parents (Astone and McLanahan 1991).

Funding

Achievement gaps are important not only in terms of a student's life, they also are used to generate government policy and move nations in various ways. Educational policies do more than regulate education; they create the educational structure of nations and control processes according to decisions made by those with political influence. We review and evaluate the efficacy of those educational policies in Chapter 14. However, many sociologists point to funding as the primary source of educational inequality in America today.

The majority of Western industrialized nations centrally fund education, through the national government, so that all schools face similar costs and budgets. Many countries also pay for higher education. Centrally funded schools are premised on the idea that a better-educated populace equates to a better-prepared nation – one that is best suited to compete with innovation and advancing economic markets. For example, the Netherlands, which is a socialized nation, offers a college education with no tuition. It is one of the top-scoring nations in mathematics and is one of two countries (i.e., the Netherlands and Sweden) that have no significant inequality between social location and social destination (Shavit and Blossfeld 1993).

America does not have a centralized education system. Not only do states have the right to create curriculum standards, they also are responsible for providing educational funding.

Much of the inequality in education is attributed to funding. The United States relies on a complicated system of taxation to fund public schools. Property taxes comprise the majority of school funds, which are then supplemented by local bonds and levies. These supplemental efforts to increase school funding often do not pass because taxpayers vote down additional tax burdens and may distrust administrators' decisions in school districts. The state and federal governments also provide support to school districts; however, this funding often is encumbered to target specific populations and programs (e.g., Title I, Special Education, and Early Childhood Education).

In the United States, funding by local, state, and federal agencies has been shown to exacerbate inequality because local taxes are tethered to property taxes, which are determined by home values. Those who live in poor neighborhoods have fewer resources, and residential segregation causes schools to maintain existing patterns of inequality (Roscigno 1995). Racial segregation ended when the U.S. Supreme Court voted in favor of desegregation in the 1954 *Brown vs. Board of Education* ruling; however, due to structural discrimination, some forms of segregation continue to exist. Of particular importance is the effect of racial segregation in housing on education systems. Desegregation policy in the classroom has not succeeded in decreasing inequality in communities. Although desegregation opened opportunities for people of color, residential concentration maintains levels of inequality. In fact, some sociologists have termed this *resegregation* (Orfield and Eaton 1996; Orfield and Yun 1999) and show that the *Brown vs. Board of Education* ruling actually was reversed through residential segregation.

High concentrations of people who live in poverty have a different schooling experience than those who live in more affluent areas. A study undertaken by sociologist Jonathan Kozol (1936–) titled *Savage Inequalities* (1991) investigated the educational experiences of children in six urban areas across America, highlighting differences such as per-pupil expenditures. In Camden, New Jersey, schools spent $3,000 on each student, which compared to $15,000 per student in the more affluent neighborhood of Great Neck, Long Island. He found that urban schools are overcrowded and understaffed and have inadequate textbooks and educational materials, and that in many areas, industrial pollutants are found on school playgrounds. In one disturbing scenario, a child rode his bicycle across the playground and the friction of the tires caused the toxic-filled ground to spark under him. School funding has been shown to be a major reason for such poor conditions.

Due to funding differentials – particularly residential segregation – education systems were found to be unconstitutional across America. Since 1971, a series of lawsuits target states on the grounds that they do not provide "adequate" levels of funding (Augenblick, Myers, and Anderson 1997). Indeed, since 1980, 45 of 50 state Supreme Courts heard complaints regarding unconstitutionality in education, with the majority finding that inadequate funding exists (West and Peterson 2006). Although a more equitable distribution of education is important, critics have shown that states do so at the expense of other publicly funded projects, such as welfare, health, hospitals, and general services (Baicker and Gordon 2006).

Summary

(1)   Education systems refer to the interconnectedness among students, families, communities, schools, districts, counties, states, and nations.

(2)   Membership in educational levels reflects social status. Those with the highest levels of education have high levels of social status; those with low levels of education have low status. On average, the majority of Americans graduate from secondary school and many go on to college or a university.

(3)   American education has a history of conflicting ideas regarding who should be educated and how it should be funded. By the 1800s, there was common primary education – that is, education for all regardless of religious affiliation or economic status. By the mid-1900s, mandatory education extended to secondary school.

(4)   Differences in opinion still exist about the merits of public and private education. Despite evidence that learning is similar in both, private schools provide different types of social and cultural capital compared to conventional public schools.

(5)   Scientists use attainment and achievement as measures of education. Both measures reflect well-established patterns of stratification by class, race/ethnicity, and gender. There is an Asian and white advantage in education whereas black and Hispanic youth are disadvantaged. Although boys outperform girls in math, they generally exhibit poor in-class behavior; thus, girls are better students.

(6) The socialization of students greatly impacts their educational choices. Stereotype threat hampers achievement, and the feminization of college majors tracks students into gendered roles in the labor market.

(7) Achievement gaps persist although many are decreasing. The gaps highlight differences between school and nonschool time, particularly the home environment.

(8) The family is an important institution that affects education, not only by instilling aspirations and expectations but also by its structure.

(9) Policies aimed at increasing equality have made modest gains. The integration of the 1950s in the long term has been replaced by resegregation due to housing policy. However, more people of color attend institutions of higher education now than in the past. Community-based school funding contributes to inequality as states battle unconstitutional education systems in the hope of obtaining adequate funding.

(10) Inequality seems to be inherent in social systems such as education. Many efforts have been made to increase equality; however, only two nations have achieved parity between socioeconomic status and educational performance (i.e., the Netherlands and Sweden).

Key Concepts

Accredit

Achievement gaps

Affirmative Action

Aspirations

Attainment/achievement

Biological determinism

Code theory: restricted and elaborated

Common schools

Contest mobility

Early childhood

Education policies

Family structure

Funding

Hidden curriculum

Higher education

Home-schooling

Land Ordinance, Section 16

Meritocracy

Pierce vs. Society of Sisters

Postsecondary

Primary

Private/public

Secondary

Social capital

Social reproduction

Socialization theory

Special Education

Sponsored mobility

Status attainment theory

Stereotype threat

Summer learning gap

Systems of education

Title IX

Questions for Thought

1. How well do performance indicators accurately describe the intelligence of a child? What are the risks and benefits of using indicators such as standardized test scores and class ranking?

2. What should be the overarching goal of the U.S. education system? In your discussion, compare creating a "whole person" to "obtaining a job." Which is more important and for whom?

3. In some nations, there is a tight link between institutions of higher learning and occupational placement. How tight is the link between these two institutions in America? Refer to contest mobility and sponsored mobility in your answer.
4. How would public funding of higher education in America affect the nation? What are the potential pros and cons?
5. Compare school choice (public or private) to educational equality. Are the two mutually exclusive by definition?

Exercises

1. Before distributing the syllabus on the first day of school, assign each copy a letter grade between A and F and write the letter on the back of page 1. On the first day of class, after reading the syllabus and engaging in other administrative tasks, ask the students to turn to the back of page 1 and note the grade. Tell them that this is the grade they will earn in the class. Ask their opinion of this method of achievement assessment. *Teaching moment*: Use this opportunity to open a discussion about meritocracy, social location and achievement, and expectations and aspirations. Draw on this conversation during the course to cement ideas.
2. *Replicate the collar experiment of Jane Elliot in* A Class Divided *(1968).* In this infamous study, Mrs. Elliot collared students with blue and green eyes, explaining that blue- and green-eyed people were socially lower than brown-eyed people. During class, use eye color as the rationale for all behaviors. All bad behaviors are found to be by blue- and green-eyed students and all good behaviors are by brown-eyed students. The next day, switch the power relationship – blue- and green-eyed students are now superior. On both days, administer an examination. Compare each student's score on the two days. Ask the students how they felt and treated one another during this experiment.
3. Using your state's Department of Education Web site, compare the scores of students by race, class, and gender. Choose schools that reflect neighborhoods that differ greatly. What did you find? Are your findings in line with sociological theories of education and stratification?

Multimedia Resources

Print

Bourdieu, Pierre. 1973. "Cultural Reproduction and Social Reproduction." In *Knowledge, Education, and Cultural Change*, edited by R. Brown (pp. 71–112). London: Collier-McMillan.

Bourdieu, Pierre, and Jean-Claude Passeron. 1977. *Reproduction of Education, Society and Culture*. London: Sage.

Bowles, Samuel, and Herbert Gintis. 1976. *Schooling in Capitalist America: Education Reform and the Contradictions of Economic Life*. New York: Basic Books.

Coleman, James S., E. Q. Campbell, C. F. Hobson, J. McPartland, A. M. Mood, F. D. Weinfeld, and R. L. York. 1966. *Equality of Educational Opportunity*. Washington, DC: U.S. Department of Health, Education, and Welfare.

Coleman, James S., and Hoffer, Thomas. 1987. *Public and Private High Schools*. New York: Basic Books.

Collins, Randall. 1979. *The Credential Society: An Historic Sociology of Education and Stratification*. New York: Academic Press.

Downey, Douglas B., Paul T. von Hipple, and Beckett Broh. 2004. "Are Schools the Great Equalizer?" *American Sociological Review* 69(5): 613–35.

Heyns, Barbara. 1978. *Summer Learning and the Effects of Schooling.* New York: Academic Press.

Jencks, C., and Phillips, M. 1998. *The Black–White Test Score Gap.* Washington, DC: Brookings Institution Press.

Lareau, Annette. 2000. *Home Advantage: Social Class and Parental Intervention in Elementary Education.* Lanham, MD: Rowman & Littlefield.

MacLeod, Jay. 2008. *Ain't No Makin' It: Aspirations and Attainment in a Low-Income Neighborhood.* Boulder, CO: Westview Press.

Mickelson, R. A. 1989. "Why Does Jane Read and Write So Well? The Anomaly of Women's Achievement." *Sociology of Education* 62: 47–63.

Shavit, Yossi, and Walter Mueller. 1997. *From School to Work: Comparative Educational Qualifications and Occupational Destinations.* Oxford: Clarendon Press.

Internet

http://nces.ed.gov/fastfacts/: U.S. Department of Education, National Center for Education Statistics, provides educational data from multiple levels of education: federal, state, county, school district, and school.

http://nces.ed.gov/fastfacts/display.asp?id=171: U.S. Department of Education, National Center for Education Statistics, provides SAT mean scores by race/ethnicity 1990/1991–2008/2009.

http://nces.ed.gov/fastfacts/display.asp?id=147: Average reading-scale score by age, sex, and race/ethnicity; selected years, 1971 to 2004.

http://nces.ed.gov/nationsreportcard/states/: U.S. Department of Education, National Center for Education Statistics, provides educational data across the nation for ease of comparison.

State Profiles

http://nces.ed.gov/programs/stateprofiles/: Allows researchers to investigate state-level assessments and obtain information on elementary and secondary education characteristics and finance, postsecondary education, public libraries, assessments, and selected demographics.

http://nces.ed.gov/edfin/search/search_intro.asp: U.S. Department of Education, National Center for Education Statistics, provides Public School District Finance Peer Search allowing a comparison of district finances to similar school districts.

Films

Feature Films

Following is a list of inspirational films about caring teachers and their impact on the lives of their students:

Stand and Deliver (Director John G. Avildsen, 1988)
Lean on Me (Director Ramón Menéndez, 1988)
Dead Poets Society (Director Peter Weir, 1989)
Mr. Holland's Opus (Director Stephen Hereck, 1996)
Freedom Writers (Director Richard LaGravenese, 2007)

Documentaries

A Class Divided (Director William Peters, 1985)

www.pbs.org/wgbh/pages/frontline/shows/divided/: This documentary explores the effect of domination on educational outcomes. Although the film generally explores race relations, one aspect of Jane Elliot's experiment is that students who are dominated score lower than they do on the day that they are dominators. The scores of her students are sent to Stanford University and she is told that it is impossible that these scores could be from the same children – the scores show different aptitude. This helped articulate what scientists today term *stereotype threat*.

LaLee's Kin: The Legacy of Cotton (Directors Deborah Dickson, Susan Frömke, and Albert Maysles, 2001)

This film documents the real-life events of a family living in poverty in the Delta of Mississippi. It focuses on the structural forces of illiteracy and the inability to provide for children due to broken families, incarceration, and early death of the family's men, and the lack of resources such as water and a safe living environment. The film is centered on the need of the local school to bring up its standardized scores to avoid being sanctioned by the federal and state governments.

Works Cited

Anderson, Carolyn S. 1982. "The Search for School Climate: A Review of the Research." *Review of Educational Research* 52: 368.

Astone, Nan Marie, and Sara S. McLanahan. 1991. "Family Structure, Parental Practices and High School Completion." *American Sociological Review* 56: 309–20.

Astone, Nan Marie, and Dawn M. Upchurch. 1994. "Forming a Family, Leaving School Early, and Earning a GED: A Racial and Cohort Comparison." *Journal of Marriage and the Family* 56: 759–71.

Aud, S., Hussar, W., Kena, G., Bianco, K., Frohlich, L., Kemp, J., Tahan, K. (2011). *The Condition of Education 2011* (NCES 2011-033). U.S. Department of Education, National Center for Education Statistics. Washington, DC: U.S. Government Printing Office.

Augenblick, John G., John L. Myers, and Amy B. Anderson. 1997. "Equity and Adequacy in School Funding." *The Future of Children* 7(3): 63–78.

Aurini, Janice, and Scott Davies. 2004. "The Transformation of Private Tutoring: Education in a Franchise Form." *Canadian Journal of Sociology*.

Baicker, Katherine, and Nora Gordon. 2006. "The Effect of State Education Finance Reform on Total Local Resources." *Journal of Public Economics* 90: 1519–35.

Becker, Gary S. 1964. *Human Capital: A Theoretical and Empirical Analysis, with Special Reference to Education.* New York: Columbia University Press.

Becker, Gary Stanley. 1993. *Human Capital: A Theoretical and Empirical Analysis, with Special Reference to Education.* Chicago: The University of Chicago Press.

Bell, Lee Ann. 1980. "The School as an Organization: A Reappraisal." *British Journal of Sociology of Education* 1: 183–9.

Bellamy, Francis. 1953. "The Story of the Pledge of Allegiance to the Flag." *University of Rochester Library Bulletin.*

Bernstein, Basil B. 2003. *Class, Codes, and Control.* New York: Routledge.

Bernstein, Robert. 2008. "One-Third of Young Women Have Bachelor's Degrees." Washington, DC: U.S. Census Bureau.

Bidwell, Charles E. 1974. *The School as a Formal Organization*. Ann Arbor: University of Michigan Press.

Blake, Judith. 1989. *Family Size and Achievement*. Los Angeles: University of California Press.

Blau, Peter, and Otis D. Duncan. 1967. *The American Occupational Structure*. New York: John Wiley and Sons.

Bourdieu, Pierre. 1991. *Language and Symbolic Power* (G. Raymond and M. Adamson, Translators). London: Polity Press.

Bourdieu, Pierre, and Jean-Claude Passeron. 1977. *Reproduction of Education, Society and Culture*. London: Sage.

Bowles, Samuel and Herbert Gintis. 2003. "Schooling in Capitalist America Twenty-Five Years Later." *Sociological Forum* 18: 343–8.

Braun, Henry, Frank Jenkins, and Wendy Grigg. 2006. "Comparing Private Schools and Public Schools Using Hierarchical Linear Modeling. NCES 2006-461." Washington, DC: National Center for Education Statistics. p. 66.

Buchmann, Claudia, and Dan Brakewood. 2000. "Labor Structures and School Enrollments in Developing Societies: Thailand and Kenya Compared." *Comparative Education Review* 44: 175–204.

Buchmann, Claudia, and Emily Hannum. 2001. "Education and Stratification in Developing Countries: A Review of Theories and Research." *Annual Review of Sociology* 27: 77–102.

Cain, Glen G., and Arthur S. Goldberger. 1983. "Public and Private Schools Revisited." *Sociology of Education* 56: 208–18.

Campbell, F. A., E. P. Pungello, S. Miller-Johnson, M. Burchinal, and C. T. Ramey. 2007. "The Development of Cognitive and Academic Abilities: Growth Curves from an Early Childhood Educational Experiment." *Developmental Psychology* 37: 231–42.

Campbell, Ronald F. 1975. *The Organization and Control of American Schools*: C.E. Merrill Publishing Company.

Campbell, Susan. 2003. "Short-Term Enrollment in Postsecondary Education: Student Background and Institutional Differences in Reasons for Early Departure, 1996–98." Washington, DC: U.S. Department of Education, National Center for Education Statistics.

Coladarci, Theodore. 1983. "High-School Dropouts among Native Americans." *Journal of American Indian Education* 23: 15–22.

Coleman, James S. 1987. "Families and Schools." *Educational Researcher* 16: 32–8.

———. 1988. "Social Capital in the Creation of Human Capital." *The American Journal of Sociology* 94: S95–S120.

Coleman, James S., E. Q. Campbell, C. F. Hobson, J. McPartland, A. M. Mood, F. D. Weinfeld, and R. L. York. 1966. "Equality of Educational Opportunity." Washington, DC: U.S. Department of Health, Education, and Welfare.

Coleman, James, Thomas Hoffer, and Sally Kilgore. 1982. "Cognitive Outcomes in Public and Private Schools." *Sociology of Education* 55: 65–76.

Collins, Randall. 1971. "Functional and Conflict Theories of Educational Stratification." *American Sociological Review* 36: 1002–19.

deGraaf, Paul M. 1988. "Parents' Financial and Cultural Resources, Grades, and Transition to Secondary School in the Federal Republic of Germany." *European Sociological Review* 4: 209–21.

Domhoff, G. William. 2002. *Who Rules America? Power and Politics* (4th edition). New York: McGraw Hill.

Downey, Douglas B. 1995. "When Bigger Is Not Better: Family Size, Parental Resources, and Children's Educational Performance." *American Sociological Review* 60: 746–61.

Downey, D. B., and Shana Pribesh. 2004. "When Race Matters: Teachers' Evaluations of Students' Classroom Behavior." *Sociology of Education* 77: 267–82.

Dreeben, Robert. 1973. "The School as a Workplace." *Second Handbook of Research on Teaching: A Project of the American Educational Research Association.* Chicago: Rand McNally: 450–473.

Durkheim, E. 1956. *Moral Education: A Study in the Theory and Application of the Sociology of Education.* Glencoe, IL: The Free Press.

England, Paula, Paul Allison, Su Li, Noah Mark, Jennifer Thompson, Michelle J. Budig, and Han Sun. 2007. "Why Are Some Academic Fields Tipping Toward Female? The Sex Composition of U.S. Fields of Doctoral Degree Receipt, 1971–2002." *Sociology of Education* 80: 23.

England, Paula, and Su Li. 2006. "Desegregation Stalled: The Changing Gender Composition of College Majors, 1971–2002." *Gender & Society* 20: 657.

Entwisle, Doris R., Karl L. Alexander, and Linda Steffel Olson. 1994. "The Gender Gap in Math: Its Possible Origins in Neighborhood Effects." *American Sociological Review* 59: 822–38.

Featherman, David L., and Robert M. Hauser. [1978]2001. "A Refined Model of Occupational Mobility, pp. 265-275." In *Social Stratification*, edited by D. B. Grusky. Boulder, CO: Westview Press.

Garfinkle, Howard. 1967. *Studies in Ethnomethodology.* Englewood Cliffs, NJ: Prentice-Hall.

Hearn, James C. 1991. "Academic and Nonacademic Influences on the College Destinations of 1980 High School Graduates." *Sociology of Education* 64: 158–71.

Herrnstein, Richard J., and Charles Murray. 1994. *The Bell Curve: Intelligence and Class Structure in American Life.* New York: The Free Press.

Heyns, Barbara. 1978. *Summer Learning and the Effects of Schooling.* New York: Academic Press.

Hoffer, Thomas, Andrew M. Greeley, and James S. Coleman. 1985. "Achievement Growth in Public and Catholic Schools." *Sociology of Education* 58:74–97.

Huang, Gary, Nebiyu Taddese, and Elizabeth Walter. 2000. "Entry and Persistence of Women and Minorities in College Science and Engineering Education." *Education Statistics Quarterly* 2: 59–60.

Huang, Min-Hsiung. 2009. "Race of the Interviewer and the Black–White Test Score Gap." *Social Science Research* 38: 29–38.

Jencks, Christopher, and Meredith Phillips. 1998. *The Black–White Test Score Gap.* Washington, DC: Brookings Institution Press.

Kao, Grace, and Jennifer S. Thompson. 2003. "Racial and Ethnic Stratification in Educational Achievement and Attainment." *Annual Review of Sociology* 29: 417–42.

Kingston, Paul W., and Lionel S. Lewis. 1990. *(The) High-Status Track.* New York: State University of New York Press.

Kozol, J. 1991. *Savage Inequalities: Children in America's Schools.* New York: Crown Publishers.

Leepson, Marc, and Nelson DeMille. 2006. *Flag: An American Biography.* New York: Macmillan.

National Center for Education Statistics (NCES). 2006a. "The Condition of Education." Washington, DC: U.S. Department of Education.

_____. 2008. "The Condition of Education 2008 (NCES 2008-031)." Washington, DC: U.S. Department of Education.

_____. 2009. "Fast Facts." Washington, DC: U.S. Department of Education.

_____. 2011. U.S. Department of Education, National Center for Education Statistics. (2011). *Digest of Education Statistics, 2010* (NCES 2011-015), Table 190.

National Research Council and Institute of Medicine. 2000. "From Neurons to Neighborhoods: The Science of Early Child Development." Washington, DC: Board on Children, Youth, and Families, Commission on Behavioral and Social Sciences and Education.

Needleman, Sarah E. 2009. "Doing the Math to Find the Good Jobs." In *The Wall Street Journal.* January 6, 2009., page D2 New York.

Ogbu, John. 2003. *Black American Students in an Affluent Suburb: A Study of Academic Disengagement*. Mahwah, NJ: Laurence Erlbaum Associates.

Orfield, Gary, and Susan E. Eaton. 1996. *Dismantling Desegregation: The Quiet Reversal of Brown v. Board of Education*. New York: The New Press.

Orfield, Gary, and John T. Yun. 1999. *Resegregation in American Schools: The Civil Rights Project*. Cambridge: Harvard University Press.

Parsons, Talcott. 1959. "The School Class as a Social System: Some of its Functions in American Society." *Harvard Educational Review* 29: 297–318.

Persell, Caroline Hodges, and Peter W. Cookson Jr. 1985. "Chartering and Bartering: Elite Education and Social Reproduction." *Social Problems* 33: 114–29.

Pong, Suet-Ling. 1997. "Sibship Size and Educational Attainment in Peninsular Malaysia: Do Policies Matter?" *Sociological Perspectives* 40: 227–42.

Powell, Brian, and Lala Carr Steelman. 1993. "The Educational Benefits of Being Spaced Out: Sibship Density and Educational Progress." *American Sociological Review* 58: 367–81.

Qian, Zhenchao, and Sampson Lee Blair. 1999. "Racial/Ethnic Differences in Educational Aspirations of High School Seniors." *Sociological Perspectives* 42: 605–25.

Reeder, Amy L., and D. Conger Rand. 1984. "Differential Mother and Father Influences on the Educational Attainment of Black and White Women." *The Sociological Quarterly* 25: 239–50.

Roscigno, Vincent J. 1995. "The Social Embeddedness of Racial Economic Inequality: The Black–White Gap and the Impact of Racial and Local Political-Economic Contexts." *Research in Social Stratification and Mobility* 14: 135–65.

——. 1998. "Race and the Reproduction of Educational Disadvantage." *Social Forces* 76: 1033–60.

——. 1999. "The Black–White Achievement Gap, Family–School Links, and the Importance of Place." *Sociological Inquiry* 69: 159–86.

Roscigno, V. J., and J. W. Ainsworth-Darnell. 1999. "Race, Cultural Capital, and Educational Resources: Persistent Inequalities and Achievement Returns." *Sociology of Education* 72: 158–78.

Ross, Catherine E., and Chia-ling Wu. 1995. "The Links Between Education and Health." *American Sociological Review* 60: 719–45.

Sander, William. 1996. "Catholic Grade Schools and Academic Achievement." *The Journal of Human Resources* 31: 540–8.

——. 1999. "Private Schools and Public School Achievement." *The Journal of Human Resources* 34: 697–709.

Saussure, Ferdinand. [1964]1990. "Signs and Language." In *Culture and Society: Contemporary Debates pp55–63*, edited by J. C. A. Seidman. New York: Cambridge University Press.

Schultz, Theodor W. 1961. "Investment in Human Capital." *The American Economic Review* 51(1): 1–17.

Sewell, William H., and Robert M. Hauser. 1980. "The Wisconsin Longitudinal Study of Social and Psychological Factors in Aspirations and Achievements." *Research in Sociology of Education and Socialization* 1: 59–99.

Shavit, Yossi, and Hans Peter Blossfield. 1993. *Persistent Inequality: Changing Educational Attainment in Thirteen Countries*. Boulder, CO: Westview Press.

Shavit, Yossi, and Walter Mueller. 1997. *From School to Work: Comparative Educational Qualifications and Occupational Destinations*. Oxford: Clarendon Press.

Sokoloff, Kenneth L., and Stanley L. Engerman. 2000. "History Lessons: Institutions, Factors Endowments, and Paths of Development in the New World." *The Journal of Economic Perspectives* 14(3): 217–32.

Spencer, Steven J., Claude M. Steele, and Diane M. Quinn. 1999. "Stereotype Threat and Women's Math Performance." *Journal of Experimental Psychology* 35: 4–28.

Spring, Joel. 1994. *The American School 1642–1993*. New York: McGraw Hill, Inc.

Stevenson, David Lee, and David P. Baker. 1992. "Shadow Education and Allocation in Formal Schooling: Transition to University in Japan." *The American Journal of Sociology* 6: 1639–57.

Trent, William T., II, Jomills Henry Braddock, and Ronald D. Henderson. 1985. "Sociology of Education: A Focus on Education as an Institution." In *Review of Research in Education* vol. 12, edited by E. W. Gordon (pp. 295–336). Washington, DC: American Educational Research Association.

Turner, Ralph H. 1960. Sponsored and Contest Mobility and the School System. *American Sociological Review* 25(6): 855–67.

UNESCO. 2011. Universal Primary Education. UIS Fact Sheet, May 2011, No. 8. Montreal, Quebec: United Nations Educational, Scientific and Cultural Organization.

U.S. Census Bureau. 2010. "2005–2009 American Community Survey." Washington, DC: U.S. Census Bureau.

Useem, Michael, and Jerome Karabel. 1986. "Pathways to Top Corporate Management." *American Sociological Review* 51: 184–200.

Wells, C. Gordon. 1999. *Dialogic Inquiry: Towards a Sociocultural Practice and Theory of Education.* New York: Cambridge University Press.

West, Martin R., and Paul E. Peterson. 2006. *School Money Trials: The Legal Pursuit of Educational Adequacy.* Washington, DC: Brookings Institution Press.

Zinn, Howard. 1980. *A People's History of the United States: 1492–Present.* New York: Harper & Row.

10 Women and Their Changing Positions

Is There a Difference between Sex and Gender?

Before we discuss the sociology of sex stratification, we first must address the definitions of *sex* and *gender*. Some might ask, "Are the two not the same? There are two sexes and men are masculine and women are feminine, right?" This common perception fails to acknowledge the complexities associated with both sex and gender.

The birth of a child is most often a glorious occasion. Modern technology provides the opportunity to know the sex of the child before it is born, allowing family members to adorn the world of the newborn child in pink or blue. We take for granted that children are born either a boy or a girl, that there are only two possible sex categories. It seems simple: According to modern biology, a child is born with two *sex chromosomes*. If the chromosomes are XX, the child is female; if they are XY, the child is male – but what about babies that are born with a different chromosomal composition?

There are many deviations from a simple two-sex schema (Butler 1990). For instance, some children are born with XY chromosomes but lack the SRY gene, causing *Swyer syndrome*, a condition in which a female has XY chromosomes with internal and dysfunctional gonads. In other instances, some children are born with multiple sex organs and others are born with none. *Intersexual* individuals – that is, those who cannot be classified as male or female – generally live normal lives despite the difficulty of classification. One form of intersexuality that has received much attention is *ambiguous genitalia*.

Every year, thousands of children are born with ambiguous genitalia; that is, their sexual organs are not easily identifiable or do not meet the acceptable social standards decided by the medical profession. According to the American Medical Association (AMA), "Phallus size <1.5 cm at term is considered inadequate for development of a functional penis (ability to have intercourse and to urinate standing up)" (Phornphutkul,

Fausto-Sterling, and Gruppuso 2000). In these cases, the AMA advises sex-reassignment surgery, as in the case of David Reimer (see Box 10.1). The definition of a functioning penis – that is, the ability to have intercourse and to stand when urinating – demonstrates that even sex may be socially constructed.

Clearly, there are more than two simple sexual categories. One biologist suggested the addition of three sexual categories in addition to *him* and *her*: *herm* (i.e., testes and ovaries), *merm* (i.e., testes and some female genitalia), and *ferm* (i.e., ovaries and some male genitalia but no testes) to distinguish other forms of sexuality that do not fit neatly into the common male and female categories (Fausto-Sterling 2004). Many people were outraged at the suggestion, claiming that this type of classification would do more harm than good to the intersexual community. Regardless of the classification schema, sexuality is complex despite the fact that many assume it is as simple as male or female.

The view on the sexes has changed in time. Prior to the 1700s, there was only one sex. People believed that female sex organs were actually a male's organs turned inside. Today, this idea that a woman's vulva is actually the internalization of a penis and scrotum is considered ludicrous. By the eighteenth century, the medical profession had developed precise knowledge of the biology of reproduction (Lorber 1993), yet clear divisions between men and women endured despite new scientific knowledge regarding their similarity.

Contemporary biologists have demonstrated that there are no differences in the biological composition of the brain (Fausto-Sterling 1992). The sexes are similar in all ways other than reproduction. Indeed, sociologists have shown that the reasoning behind the two-sex classification is heterosexuality (Butler 1990; Kimmel 2004); that is, any deviation from the male or female categorization threatens the institution of heterosexuality. If biological difference occurs only in sexual reproduction, why is there so much emphasis on separating women from men? To answer this, sociologists turn to the concept of gender.

Gender results from any social relationship separating people, behaviors, and objects into differential statuses. Why are little boys dressed in blue and girls in pink? Why would parents need to identify the sex of a child of a nonfamily member? The sex of the child needs to be determined by strangers because society has differential actions toward males and females. These disparate behaviors include cooing and speaking in a high voice around girls and being brasher and speaking in a lower voice around boys; when carrying babies, boys face outward and girls inward. Later in life, these differential behaviors emerge as lower pay for women and more hours of housework and childcare compared to men.

Whereas sex is biologically based, gender is socially constructed: We "do gender" (West and Zimmerman 1987). Attached to sex is the concept of gender – boys are expected to be *masculine* and girls *feminine*. As we learned, however, sex has more than two categories, as does gender (Lorber 1995). Scholars who focus on women of color argue that gender relations subordinate all women and men of color (Collins 1989, 2000; Hooks 1984). Those who study masculinity argue that domination occurs by men who are outwardly heterosexual, economically successful, and racially superior (Connell 1987). In other words, gender relations separate people by status and confer dominance and subordination through the gendering process.

Sociologists who study gender have shown that it is a "process of social construction, a system of social stratification, and an institution that structures every aspect of our lives because of its embeddedness in the family, the workplace, and the state, as well as in sexuality, language, and culture" (Lorber 1995: 5; 2004). Gender is both a structure and a process (Bielby 1991). Gender is a social construction in that we "do gender" daily: For example, we dress ourselves (and our children) in "sex-appropriate" clothing and jewelry, wear gendered hair styles, divide household labor by men's and women's tasks (e.g., men take out the trash and mow the lawn, women care for children and clean the home). Gender is a system of stratification because gender relations rank groups, thus conferring power on some but not others. Gender also is an institution that structures our daily life (Martin 2003). A woman is expected to be maternal and compassionate and therefore is more likely to become a teacher, nurse, or caretaker compared to a male, not necessarily because of a biological condition but rather social expectations.

Upholding gendered roles and stereotypes, societies create and maintain the processes, stratification, and institutionalization of gender. The remainder of the chapter explores these differences and focuses on the changing roles of women and their subsequent status in the United States.

Gender Roles and Stereotypes

Often, sociologists see beyond the obvious. Peter Berger (1929–) wrote: "[T]he fascination of sociology lies in the fact that its perspective makes us see in a new light the very world in which we have lived all our lives" (1969: 10). Gender studies certainly help us to see in a new light the world in which we live.

Gender roles are social expectations that are attached to the sexes. In most societies, men and women have separate roles. As noted previously, these roles prescribe the behaviors, occupations, and legal rights of individuals. In studying gender, scholars have observed groups that do not fit comfortably into a two-gender classification system to better understand how gender works in America. We now discuss the social construction of gender – that is, gender from the perspective of symbolic interactionists.

The *third gender*, as some refer to it, is a classification that fails to be captured by male/female role expectations. As discussed previously, intersexual individuals are not clearly identifiable as either male or female nor are individuals who do not fit neatly into gender roles, such as women who do not wear makeup and act feminine or men who do not necessarily act masculine. To better understand how gender is constructed, sociologist Harold Garfinkel (1917–) studied intersexed individuals. He found that many "passed" (i.e., went unnoticed by others) by adopting gender roles. One study included the observation of Agnes, a man who was transitioning to a woman. Although her appearance was that of a woman and she studied the most minute details of "doing femininity," Agnes lacked certain traits that women were socialized to since birth. She learned from her fiancé how to be a woman through his comments of other women. Agnes learned not to display herself to other men, not to insist on having her own way, and not to offer her opinions and demand equality with men (Garfinkel 1967).

Despite a person's sexual status, doing gender steers individuals into one of two camps: male or female. In some cases, individuals are mistaken for attempting to "bend gender." For example, scholars show that a woman who does not "do femininity" (i.e., regularly wear a dress or skirt and makeup) may be considered a male or a lesbian, regardless of her sexual orientation (Lorber 2004). When women fail to signal femininity by adopting gender roles, observers place them in the default sexual category, which is male.

Gender roles are so engrained within our social interactions that we often take them for granted. In the late 1970s, sociologist Erving Goffman (1922–1982) published a book entitled *Gender Advertisements* (Goffman 1979). In it, he explored the arrangement and use of male and female images in twentieth-century advertising. His work significantly contributed to our understanding of the way that images are used to communicate social information. Goffman also illuminated the manner in which media images have been incorporated into our social expectations. He described gender advertisements as "both shadow and substance: they show what we wish or pretend to be" (1979: 15). This becomes relevant in that we use these images to assign gender value to objects and concepts.

A central theoretical concept used by sociologists is *hegemony*, which is the political creation and maintenance of dominance by one group over another within a social structure that makes the power relationship seem natural. Gendered roles are clearly visible in advertising: Men are in control, showing independence and strength, whereas women are beautiful companions – emotional, weak, and in need of protection. Chapter 12 discusses hegemony and the ways in which the mass media portray images that maintain inequality.

Hegemonic masculine identity exists through effective media-image saturation. Men are supposed to be masculine, which corresponds to other activities including "smoking, drug and alcohol abuse, fighting, sexual conquests, dominance and crime" (Majors and Billson 1992: 34). Women are not expected to smoke, drink, fight, have casual sex, commit crimes, or dominate. Indeed, as we learned in the discussion of the culture of domesticity (see Chapter 6), women are held to a different standard than men. A man who has many sexual escapades is considered a "stud" or a "player"; women, conversely, are called a "slut." We now explore the gender roles of women through the institutions of religion, family, work, and the state.

Women's Subordination

Sociological theories have long worked on locating the origins of gender stratification. Talcott Parsons (1902–1979) thought of gender roles in terms of internalized shared norms. Huber (2004: 260) wrote: "[S]eparate sex roles were good for society because sexual competition makes for marital stability." However, no concrete evidence was presented as to *why* these norms emerged.

Other more recent sociological explanations have been criticized for their lack of precision in explaining *why* stratification structures and processes subordinate women (Huber 2004). Feminist scholars tend to describe the process of gender inequality but do not explain gender stratification because they ignore structure in their perspective.

Moreover, as a backlash to defining women only in relation to men, feminists often ignore reproductive forces that greatly affect women and work. Yet, reproduction is an important aspect for most women and certainly contributes to the way society is organized and labor is divided.

Sociologist Friedrich Engels (1820–1895) located male domination and women's subordination in the economic relations of society. In his *Patriarchal Family* (1999[1884]), Engels argued from a Marxian theoretical stance that the family is a material product relative to the means of production. Because surplus was an intergenerational asset (e.g., land, farming tools, and property), the legitimization of ownership became important. If, for example, a lord owned a large estate with land, animals, workers, and tools, and he was near death, who would he entrust with his estate? Women could not own property but male children could. This, however, was before DNA testing; therefore, the lord's rightful heir was difficult (at best) to identify without some type of contractual agreement among the lord, his heir, and the state. To legitimize an heir, Engels argued, contractual marriage appeared. Thus, marriage and the system of property inheritance formed the modern family, with the wife as a form of property owned by the husband for the purpose of conferring legitimacy to male heirs. Dominant groups – the aristocracy, lords, and clergy – benefited from female subordination. When no male heir was present, the Church took ownership of the estate. From a conflict perspective, women's subordination is not natural but rather is socially constructed from the need to control property.

Women's subordination was – and, in some respects, is still – considered natural by many. Some cite religious doctrines and others cite science to justify the separation of men and women and male domination. Despite the view that women are "great mysteries" who give birth to humankind, throughout the world, religions assert that women are unclean, evil, and dangerous. In Greek mythology, Pandora opened the forbidden box and let loose on mankind horrific plagues and untold misery. The Judeo-Christian creation myths center on Eve, the female created from Adam's rib to be his helpmate. Long forgotten and relegated to legend is the original Hebrew myth of Lilith, the alleged first wife of Adam. She refused to subjugate herself to Adam, was banished from Eden, and replaced by Eve. Even Eve, the new and improved wife, was not perfect – indeed, she was temped by evil and betrayed God and all humanity by eating the forbidden fruit. Although we must be careful not to accept religious texts as science, the point of the ancient myth is that women are *naturally* subordinate to men, dangerous, and should be controlled. Early feminist Elizabeth Cady Stanton asked, "Has Christianity benefited woman?" In her answer, she wrote:

> In the fifth century the church fully developed the doctrine of original sin, making women its weak and guilty author. To St. Augustine, whose early life was licentious and degraded, we are indebted for this idea, which was infused into canon law, and was the basis on all the persecutions women endured for centuries, in the drift of Christian opinion from the extremes of polygamy to celibacy, from the virtues of chivalry to the cruelties of witchcraft, when the church taught its devotees to shun woman as a temptation and defilement. It was this persecution, this crushing out of the feminine element in humanity, more than all other influences combined, that plunged the world into the dark ages, shadowing the slowly rolling centuries till now with woman's agonies and death, paralyzing literature,

science, commerce, education, changing the features of art, the sentiments of poetry, the ethics of philosophy, from the tender, the loving, the beautiful, the grand, to the stern, the dark, the terrible (Stanton and Spalding 1885: 395).

The *natural subordination* of women is not found in all religions. Wiccans worship a female divinity, the Goddess. In Ancient Egypt, women were Pharos and High Priestesses able to rule a nation, negotiate with other nation-states, own property, and hold powers not afforded them in more modern times. The Germanic tribes also placed women in positions of high status; although the tribes were of a warrior culture and sent men to fight, they consulted their women on all matters. The men were proud to be monogamous and chaste and did not subordinate women (Stanton and Spalding 1885).

In America, many still accept the traditional value of *male domination* – that is, the natural superiority of man over woman. It began with the original American colonizers, the Puritans, who firmly believed in male domination – so much so that in the seventeenth century, women who sought political power were branded as witches, culminating in the infamous 1692 Salem Witch Trials (Rosenthal and Adams 2009). Women often were portrayed as dangerous and unclean, resulting in particular religious laws prohibiting them from many activities (e.g., reading and studying). Men were prohibited from interacting with women at particular times (e.g., during menstruation), and sexual intercourse with a wife during the years she was breastfeeding was not allowed, a doctrine that was upheld by the Catholic Church for centuries (Salmon 1994).

In addition to religious foundations of gender inequality, women have been considered by scholars and scientists as naturally inferior to men. Using Darwinian logic, scientists reasoned that women are less fit than men because the menstrual cycle causes derangement and hysteria. Also, it was believed that women were unable to learn – too much study would cause irreversible damage to their reproductive system (Fausto-Sterling 1992). In fact, women who lobbied for the right to vote were considered social pariahs and often were removed from the home so as not to taint the family's virtue; in some cases, they were lobotomized!

The first region that allowed women the right to vote was the Isle of Man in the United Kingdom, in 1880; the first nation was New Zealand, in 1893. In the United States, New Jersey women had the right to vote between 1776 and 1820. It was removed with the extension of the vote to former slaves under the Fourteenth and Fifteenth Amendments. When abolitionists realized that the Fourteenth Amendment would not be sufficient to end slavery in the South, the Fifteenth Amendment was introduced. When it was ratified in 1869, women were again excluded (Paxton and Hughes 2007).

Wyoming was the first state that allowed women to vote. Some suggest this was due to the need for more women in the pioneer state, which was heavily populated by men. Congress was intent on blocking Wyoming's statehood if it continued to allow women to vote, but the state legislature wrote: "We'll stay out a thousand years rather than come in without our women" (Paxton and Hughes 2007: 39).

Many women advocated for political power throughout American history, including America's first feminist, Lucretia Mott (1793–1880), a Quaker and abolitionist; Susan B. Anthony (1820–1906), who introduced America to the suffrage movement; Elizabeth Cady Stanton (1815–1902), who wrote in 1848 the Declaration of Sentiments, which was presented at the Seneca Falls Convention in New York and organized the American Suffrage Movement; Sojourner Truth, who gave her "Ain't I a Woman?" speech in 1851 at a woman's convention, which articulated the plight of black women as subordinates of whites; and Carrie Chapman Catt (1859–1947), who was president of the National American Woman Suffrage Association when the nation adopted the Nineteenth Amendment to the U.S. Constitution in 1920, granting women the vote. The final ratification by the states was not easily accomplished. The final two states to vote in favor of the Nineteenth Amendment – North Carolina and Mississippi – did not do so until 1971 and 1984, respectively.

The limitations placed on women in the name of religion, science, and the state have had far-reaching implications for inequality. Generations of men were educated, employed, and created laws while women were restricted to the home. Since 1920, women have made considerable progress in all three arenas – education, employment, and government – but they still lag behind men in equality.

Gender Inequality and the Education Process

Historically, women were less likely to be educated than men; however, the gender gap in education is closing globally. Today, 28.7 percent of women compared to 30.4 percent of men have a college degree (U.S. Department of Labor 2009). A multitude of studies focuses on the impact of gender in educational attainment and cognitive ability. A strikingly consistent finding is that girls outperform boys in most subjects in most grades. Women generally perform better in school and today have higher rates of college completion compared to men (Buchmann and DiPrete 2006). However, there is still gender segregation in the types of majors that men and women choose in college and in their subsequent occupational fields (Bobbitt-Zeher 2007). Men tend to gravitate or are steered toward math and science and women toward the humanities and language. Although women perform better in school, they receive fewer academic returns when they enter the workforce (Mickelson 1989). In total, this can have a tremendous impact on gender stratification in adulthood, such as occupational steering.

Differential treatment of students based on sex occurs throughout the educational experience. From the first day in school, children are lined up by their sex – girls to one side, boys to the other. In some schools, children are segregated by sex. Teachers treat boys and girls differently in class. In one study of high school mathematics classes, researchers found that teachers call on boys more than girls; have more interactions with boys than girls; give 70 percent of positive feedback to boys and 30 percent to girls; and physically touch boys, such as placing a hand on a shoulder for encouragement, whereas girls are not physically encouraged. Boys are lauded as having previous experience in visualizing three-dimensional problems in shop class, whereas girls were not provided any linking of previous knowledge to a current problem. These findings were the same regardless of the sex of the teacher (Becker 1981).

As discussed in Chapter 9, education is tightly tethered to a person's life chances. In industrialized nations such as the United States, this occurs through the link between education and occupation. The experiences that people have in school directly affect their placement in the occupational hierarchy. Women's educational experiences maintain inequality by steering them away from high-paying occupations in math and science.

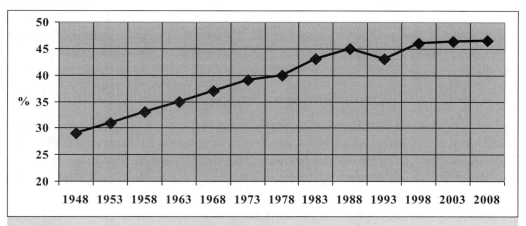

Figure 10.1 Percentage of women in workforce 1948–2008.
Data source: U.S. Bureau of Labor Statistics, Employment and Earnings, January 2009, Table 39.

Women and Work

Women's participation in the labor market greatly increased during the twentieth century. Today, about 60 percent of women work full time, compared to only 19 percent in 1900 (U.S. Census Bureau 2009). Figure 10.1 shows that the percentage of women in the workforce has increased significantly since the end of World War II.

Women comprise 46.5 percent of the total workforce today, compared to less than 30 percent in 1948 (U.S. Department of Labor 2009). Despite great gains made by women entering the workforce, inequality still exists through inequality of wages.

The *gender gap* in earnings is one way that gender inequality is maintained. Figure 10.2 shows the steady decrease of the ratio between male and female annual earnings since 1955.

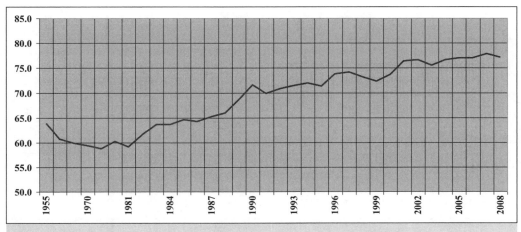

Figure 10.2 Median annual earnings, female to male ratio, 1955–2008.
Data source: U.S. Bureau of Labor Statistics, Gender Wage Ratio, 1955–2009, Full-Time Workers (2009).

In 1955, the average female worker earned 63.9 cents for every dollar a male worker earned; today, that ratio has increased to about 81 cents for every dollar. Couple this fact with the 2 percent reduction in women's annual earnings in 2008 (men lost 1 percent) and the average full-time female worker earned $34,745 – three-quarters of the average male who earned $46,367 (U.S. Bureau of Labor Statistics 2009b). This form of *wage discrimination* existed throughout the twentieth century (Goldin 1994).

Figure 10.3 shows that the gender gap is sensitive to age. Young females are near parity with young males, those under 24 years of age; however, when workers become 25 years old, they generally enter an enduring occupation that they will stay with over time, and the gap becomes quite pronounced.

Why does the gender gap persist? Women and men generally do not fill similar occupational roles and men's occupations earn more than women's. Indeed, there is stability in the occupational hierarchy in terms of the division of jobs by sex, which often is termed *sex segregation*. In the 1980s, the odds of a woman entering a male-dominated occupation as she enters the workforce were one in three. Similarly, the odds of a woman changing into a male-dominated job – even if her previous job was in a male-dominated, female-dominated, or integrated job – also was one in three (Jacobs 1989). By the 1990s, improvements for women had stalled. The small improvement in earnings was due to an increase of jobs in the labor market, many of which were filled by women. However, women still lagged behind men in labor-market earnings and ranked positions. For example, in 2007 and 2008, women accounted for only 15 percent of all corporate directorships and officer positions in Fortune 500 companies (Cohen, Huffman, and Knauer 2009).

Another reason for the gap (discussed in Chapter 6) is the change in the occupational structure in America from farming to manufacturing to service. Women are more likely to be employed in service-sector jobs that are generally low-paying, and they are more likely to be employed in jobs in which there is a high concentration of females (i.e., 70 percent or more). In fact, men and women who work in professions with a

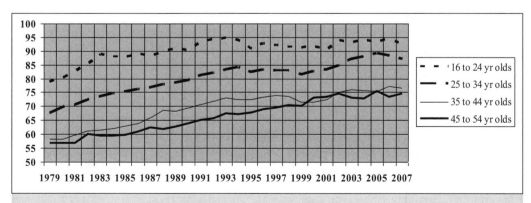

Figure 10.3 Women's weekly earnings as a percentage of men's by age 1979–2007.
Data source: U.S. Bureau of Labor Statistics, women's earnings as a percentage of men's, 1979–2007, Current Population Survey (2008).

disproportionate number of women earn less than men and women in male-dominated occupations; this is called the *feminization of labor.*

Consider the following occupations: caregiver, teacher, high school principal, college professor, nurse, and medical doctor. If we are asked to place each job in one of two columns titled male and female, which jobs would we consider to be female occupations? Like most Americans, we would probably answer caregiver, teacher, and nurse, whereas high school principal, college professor, and medical doctor would be considered male occupations. An example of the disparity between males and females is found in college professors. For every one female professor who reaches the highest ranking, there are four male professors (Thornton 2009). Recalling from Chapter 6 the discussion about the middle class and women's roles, women are considered domestic whereas men are not. General role expectations demand that women be "touchy-feely," compassionate, loving, responsible for others at their own expense, and – in a word – nurturing.

Scholars generally provide two competing theories to explain sex segregation and the gender gap in earnings: (1) the *specialized human capital thesis*, and (2) the *devaluation thesis* (Tam 1997). The first thesis argues that women are concentrated in jobs that require less training than jobs with a high concentration of men. The reasoning behind this may be self-selection (i.e., personal choice), discrimination, or both. This line of research focuses on earnings by occupation, industry, and firms. The second thesis assumes that there is a general devaluation of women's labor that leads to low wages for all workers in occupations with a high concentration of women (England, Hermsen, and Cotter 2000).

We may wonder why women choose occupations with lower pay relative to other occupations with higher pay. Given their educational advantage, it seems counterintuitive for women to accept jobs that pay less. Part of the reason is indeed biological. Most societies consider childrearing to be women's work. Most women have babies, often meaning that they are absent from the workforce for at least a few months. However, is this absence enough to warrant the wage gap? In other words, how much impact does bearing a child have on a woman's workforce participation? First, we must know how many women have babies and how many children the average mother has.

Since the invention of the birth control pill, women are having fewer babies. As one sociologist wrote: "In the 1800s, the Industrial Revolution made brains more important than brawn and, in the 1900s, medical technology enabled our species to separate procreation and recreation" (Huber 2004: 265). The birth control pill and other contraceptives allowed women the freedom to choose if and when to procreate, which in turn has had a major impact on their daily life.

Prior to contraceptives, women were tethered to the biological duties of childrearing. A woman having control over her own body and reproductive decisions is a strong measure of equality. In 1830, the average American mother had 7.8 children. Her life was filled with sustaining children, breastfeeding as often as every 15 minutes (Huber 2008). In connection with the rise in democracy and liberty rhetoric, colonial women began what scholars term the *fertility transition*. Despite women's limited political power, there was a move toward liberation through fertility control. By 1850, the average American woman had 6.5 children; for women in regions where there was talk of democracy and a republic, the number was much lower – in the Mid-Atlantic and New England regions, for example, the average number of children was 5.5 and 4.4, respectively (Klepp 2009).

The reduction of fertility in America was met with resistance. The Comstock Law of 1873 made it illegal to send anything deemed obscene, lewd, and/or lascivious through the mail; birth-control devices of the time were included on the list. In 1918, Margaret Sanger was charged with distributing contraceptive information. The charges eventually were repealed on the grounds that the promotion of birth-control methods and devices could prevent and cure disease. Sanger devoted her life to women's rights and "birth control," a phrase that she coined. In 1936, a federal court decided in her favor that no agency could come between a doctor and a patient, thereby allowing the shipment of prophylactics that she had procured from Japan to be delivered to doctors in America. The next year, 1937, the AMA endorsed contraception as a medical service and included the topic as a vital component of medical education. Sanger started the American Birth Control League, which in 1942 was renamed the Planned Parenthood Federation of America (Margaret Sanger Papers 2009).

The fertility transition continues today. A recent census survey revealed that the average American female has 1.9 children compared to 2.9 children 30 years ago. Moreover, 1 in 5 women age 40 to 44 have no children, an increase from 1 in 10 in 1970 (Dye 2008). Women have fewer children and some have no children, as a result of either infertility or personal choice. Clearly, childrearing obligations should have less importance on earnings today compared to the past.

Returning to the central question of why women are paid less than men, we now explore the second theory: the devaluation of women's work. Occupations with high concentrations of women include teaching, counseling, providing health services, and supervising children – in summary, women are concentrated in caregiving occupations, sometimes referred to as *pink ghettos*. Comparing similar groups in terms of level of education and years of experience, occupational and industry characteristics, and personal characteristics, sociologists have found that, indeed, occupations with high concentrations of women pay less. Even men who work in these fields are paid less than comparable men in other nonfeminized occupations. Because there are more women in these occupations, the gender gap is attenuated in aggregate statistics – that is, when we review American occupational earnings, women are paid significantly less due to the feminization of occupations. Occupations that require nurturing skills pay less than similar occupations without a nurturing requirement (Kilbourne, Farkas, Beron, Weir, and England 1994).

Moreover, women occupy jobs in various levels of the occupational hierarchy – low, medium, and high – although few women have broken through the highest echelons of occupations. Regardless in which occupational strata women work, they are paid less than men; indeed, there seems to be a devaluation of women's work (Guillen et al. 2004). This led some scholars to look at issues of *comparable worth* – that is, the revaluing of women's work considering gendered roles treated as equally important within occupational categories. In other words, women's work (particularly teachers, nurses, and other caregivers) should be considered more valuable and paid more to be comparable to similar male-dominated jobs.

During the second half of the twentieth century, women's participation in the work-force grew by about 20 percent. They entered occupations previously held by men, yet they failed to rise in rank in many of these professions. When women (or other power minorities) do not rise in rank despite qualifications, they are said to experience a *glass ceiling*. It is as if they reach a certain status that they cannot advance past. In addition to limited advancements, some workers experience what is termed a *sticky floor* – that is, certain groups, particularly women, never rise in rank because they are passed over for any type of advancement. In other words, discrimination has a part in how women are subordinated.

Women have made great gains in the workforce despite sex segregation, wage dis-crimination, and the earnings gap. In the past century, women entered many domains previously unavailable to them. Table 10.1 lists the top 10 occupations with the highest weekly earnings among women who were full-time wage and salary workers in 2008.

If sex segregation is stable, how did women transform the workforce in such poignant ways? Sociologists who study job markets have shown that a process of queuing ex-ists to place certain workers in occupations previously unavailable to them. *Job queues* consist of three structural properties: ordering of their elements, shape, and intensity of rankers' preferences (Reskin and Roos 1990). Queues consist of ordered elements – oc-cupations, jobs, and groups of workers. If one group of workers is favored over another group by an employer, then the first group dominates the market and the second group is unable to secure positions within it. If, for instance, a hospital prefers male physi-cians, then female physicians are disadvantaged. The shape of the queue is determined by the number of occupations and jobs within the market. If an industry grows and the preferred group cannot fill the additional positions, others are hired to fill the newly created positions. Perhaps the hospital grew in size and added additional wings. During the hiring process, it exhausted the available qualified male physicians, allowing female physicians the opportunity to work. Queues also are affected by the intensity of rankers' preferences. If, for example, a highly qualified male doctor does not wish to practice in an isolated rural area, the job becomes available to others, allowing a different group

Table 10.1 Top Ten Highest Earning Occupations for Women

	Weekly Average
Pharmacists	$1,647
Chief executive officers	$1,603
Lawyers	$1,509
Computer software engineers	$1,351
Computer and information systems managers	$1,260
Physicians and surgeons	$1,230
Management analysts	$1,139
Human resource managers	$1,137
Speech-language pathologists	$1,124
Computer scientists and systems analysts	$1,082

Data source: U.S. Department of Labor, Bureau of Labor Statistics, Employment and Earnings, 2008 Annual Averages.

the opportunity for employment – albeit in a less desirable location. Through this queuing process, women have entered previously male-dominated professions.

Gender Inequality in the Family and Household

Gender inequality is often reinforced through familial roles and household duties. In the home, it has a significant impact not only on the economic circumstances of women but also on the likelihood of divorce, stress, and general mental health of all family members (Bianchi and Milkie 2010) . For instance, mothers who experience high stressors at work are more likely to withdraw from interacting with their preschoolers in the home. That is, a mother will talk less and exhibit less affection after a bad day at work (Repetti and Wood 1997).

Additionally, income inequality in a dual-income household (i.e., in which both the man and the woman earn an income) is an indicator of how gendered the household division of labor is. A woman who contributes to a household an equal income as a man is more likely to be treated equally than if she earns less. Few households exist in which women out-earn men (Raley, Mattingly, and Bianchi 2006).

Marriage is a major stratifying process in and of itself. Often, the combination of economic resources has important consequences for "defeminizing" poverty. However, these marriages can carry with them the reification of traditional gender roles. From an economic perspective, however, gender inequality also is exacerbated by the likelihood that certain women will marry. For instance, African American women are less likely to marry compared to white women (Teachman, Tedrow, and Crowder 2000); women in poverty with children are less likely to marry compared to women not in poverty (Qian, Lichter, and Mellott 2005).

Traditionally minded individuals suggest that women who work outside the home actually weaken the family unit. However, scholars have shown that there are no cognitive or social-ill effects for children whose mothers work during the first three years of a child's life (Huston and Rosenkrantz Aronson 2005) and that working women do not weaken happy marriages but rather allow women the freedom to leave unhappy ones (Schoen et al. 2002). Moreover, divorce negatively affects women and reinforces inequality – that is, a divorced woman generally loses about 20 percent of her standard of living, whereas a man increases his by about 10 percent (Peterson 1996). Today, families strategize ways to balance two careers and a family (Schneider and Waite 2005); part of the decision-making process includes how to manage time.

Women have less free time and generally spend more of it caring for children and in domestic tasks (Mattingly and Bianchi 2003). On an average day in 2008, 83 percent of women and 64 percent of men spent some time doing household activities, such as housework, cooking, cleaning, and lawn care. On days when individuals engaged in household activities, women spent an average of 2.6 hours whereas men spent only 2.0 hours. On an average day, 20 percent of men and 50 percent of women do housework; 38 percent of men clean up or prepare meals compared to 65 percent of women (U.S. Bureau of Labor Statistics 2009a). How parents divide the time they spend with children contributes to gender inequality in the home. Comparing the 1960s to the late 1990s, researchers show that men are spending more time with children engaged in both routine childcare and "fun time," but they still lag behind women (Sayer, Bianchi, and Robinson 2004). Free time within the family is experienced differently by women and men.

Violence against Women

Violence against women is perhaps the most brutal form of male domination. The majority of violence against women is perpetrated by a loved one, family member, boyfriend, or husband. According to current statistics from the U.S. Department of Justice (2006), there were 36 percent more rapes by nonstrangers than by strangers and 10 percent more violent crimes (Klaus and Maston 2007). In 2006, of the total cases in which the relationship between victim and perpetrator was known, 1,073 women were murdered by a family member, 1,268 by an acquaintance, and 253 by a stranger (Federal Bureau of Investigation 2008). To fully understand the impact of these numbers, on every day in 2006, an average of three women died at the hands of a loved one.

Sociologists argue that there are two types of domestic violence: (1) *common couple violence*, which is occasional outbursts of violence from either a husband or a wife; and (2) *patriarchal terrorism*, which is systematic male violence (Johnson 1995). The latter is considered more harmful to society because it reinforces gender inequality by entrenching subordination of women through force.

The U.S. Department of Justice identifies four forms of violence against women: domestic violence, sexual assault, stalking, and dating violence. Domestic violence can include physical, sexual, emotional, economic, or psychological abuse. Although these abuses happen between any configuration of male/female relationships, women have disproportionately higher rates of abuse than men.

According to the U.S. Department of Justice, Office on Violence Against Women (OVW), "*domestic violence* can be defined as a pattern of abusive behavior in any relationship that is used by one partner to gain or maintain power and control over another intimate partner" (U.S. Department of Justice 2009). Domestic violence can be physical, sexual, emotional, economic, or psychological action or the threat of action that influences another person. This includes any behavior that intimidates, manipulates, humiliates, isolates, frightens, terrorizes, coerces, threatens, blames, hurts, injures, or wounds someone.

"*Sexual assault* can be defined as any type of sexual contact or behavior that occurs without the explicit consent of the recipient of the unwanted sexual activity. Falling under the definition of sexual assault is sexual activity such as forced sexual intercourse, sodomy, child molestation, incest, fondling, and attempted rape" (OVW 2009). There are multiple collectors of crime statistics. In reviewing the different data, scholars estimate that about 18 percent of women (i.e., nearly one in five) and 3 percent of men have experienced rape in their lifetime. Due to the stigma associated with rape, as well as the insinuation that rape was instigated by the victim, about 87 percent of rapes are not reported. According to the FBI's Uniform Crime Reporting Program, *forcible rape* is defined as "the carnal knowledge of a female forcibly and against her will." *Carnal knowledge* is defined as "the act of a man having sexual bodily connections with a woman; sexual intercourse." Carnal knowledge applies only to penetration of the vagina by the penis, no matter how slight the penetration. Assaults and attempts to commit rape by force or threat of force are included in the data; however, oral and anal penetration is not (Kilpatrick, McCauley, and Mattern 2009). Given the under-reporting of rape and the narrow definition of forcible rape, the number of women having experienced some form of sexual assault is probably much higher and quite possibly one in three.

"*Stalking* can be defined as a pattern of repeated and unwanted attention, harassment, contact, or any other course of conduct directed at a specific person that would cause a reasonable person to feel fear" (OVW 2009). The U.S. Department of Justice affirms that a stalking incident has occurred when two or more of the following acts are committed on two or more occasions: making unwanted phone calls; sending unsolicited or unwanted letters or e-mails; following or spying on the victim; showing up at a place where the stalker had no reason to be; waiting at places for the victim; leaving unwanted items, presents, or flowers; and posting information or spreading rumors about the victim on the Internet, in a public place, or by word of mouth.

In a typical year, the U.S. Department of Justice estimates that 3.4 million people 18 or older were victims of stalking; females experienced 20 stalking victimizations per 1,000 females 18 or older compared to the rate of stalking victimizations for males (i.e., approximately 7 per 1,000 males 18 or older). One in seven victims reported that they moved as a result of the stalking and approximately 60 percent do not report victimization to the police (U.S. Department of Justice 2008).

"*Dating violence* is defined as violence committed by a person who is or has been in a social relationship of a romantic or intimate nature with the victim; and where the existence of such a relationship shall be determined based on a consideration of the following factors: the length of the relationship; the type of relationship; the frequency of interaction between the persons involved in the relationship" (OVW 2009).

Using data from the National Longitudinal Study of Adolescent Health, researchers show that in 2008, 1 in 10 teens reported being the victim of violence at the hands of a romantic partner in the previous year. More than 2 in 10 reported verbal or psychological abuse from their romantic partner. Boys and girls are equally abusive to one another but severe cases of violence disproportionately affect girls (Mulford and Giordano 2008).

Human trafficking is yet another form of male domination that maintains female subordination through violence. It is defined as the migration from one region to another of people who hope to find gainful employment but instead are forced into low- or no-paying positions when they arrive. These individuals have no way to escape their plight and, in a sense, are slaves to those who coordinated their relocation. At any given time, scholars estimate the number of victims of human trafficking to be 2.4 million (International Labor Office 2008). The estimated annual profit generated from human trafficking is $32 billion (USD).

Sex trafficking is a form of human trafficking that is found in all nations of the world, but it is most publicized as occurring in poor nations where the sex industry is tolerated. Women, girls, and boys are moved to regions where they are sold for slaves, prostituted, or both. The victims are taken in various ways: stolen from homes, sold by family members, kidnapped off the street, or lured into unsavory relationships that end in sexual exploitation for profit. Sex slaves are tortured in innumerable ways – through physical and psychological violence and, on average, they are raped between 10 and 20 times a day as they are exploited by traffickers and forced to serve customers in brothels and private homes around the globe. In 2006, there were 1.2 million sex slaves in the world, 10,000 of whom are in North America; one woman or child is trafficked for sexual exploitation every 60 seconds (Kara 2006).

Although women made tremendous gains throughout the twentieth century in education, the workforce, family relationships, division of time, and political representation, they still lag behind men. More women graduate from college but they see fewer returns from education once they enter the workforce. Women are paid less and typically fall into occupations with a majority of women, which in turn depresses the wage of the industry due to the devaluing of women's work. Of the women who have children, their work continues in the home. Women accomplish the majority of work in the home and spend less free time pursuing their own interests. Women face more violence by family members; are victims of domestic violence, rape, stalking, and date violence at much higher rates than men; and are more likely to be exploited by sex traffickers and forced into modern-day slavery. The political representation of women grew through the century but is still less than 20 percent. Some argue that until women's voices share parity with men's, these issues will endure, regardless of their advancements.

Conclusion

As the feminist adage says, "We've come a long way, baby!" Indeed, women in the twentieth century made tremendous gains in reducing inequality. As the economy shifted, so did the roles of women; no longer mandated to domestic tasks within the home, women made exceptional progress in many social spheres, including the home, workforce, culture, and political process.

The progress of women has been met with resistance from both men and women. Even today, some believe that women should return to traditional values, which are defined as domestic and family focused. Whereas some agree that women have a vital role in the family, more women are now head of the family than ever before. Today's women do not have to rely on men for survival, and many choose a life without marriage and children. When feminist Gloria Steinem was asked why she was not married, her reply was, "I do not breed well in captivity." Indeed, a growing segment of women have chosen to forgo having children. In tandem with the rights of women to choose not to marry are gay rights – that is, the right to love another same-sex adult without intervention from others. This battle for equality is still being fought.

Today, the majority of women work and more women than men earn college degrees. Despite the many successes of women in America, there is still inequality. Women are held to a standard of beauty that no man is expected to attain. Women are paid less and expected to perform more household and childrearing tasks compared to men. Moreover, women are more likely to be murdered or raped by a family member or to suffer from violence at the hands of a loved one.

Summary

(1) Sex is biological and gender is cultural.

(2) Although we consider sex biological, in many cases, the sex of a child is reassigned due to social expectations and policies adopted by members of the medical profession.

(3) Sexuality is complex and simplified by assuming that there are only two categories: male and female.

(4) Cultural norms dictate which gender roles are prescribed to which sex. Stereotypes limit the opportunities of individuals by constraining their actions to "gender-appropriate" categories.

(5) Individuals may be masculine and feminine, what some call a "third gender."

(6) Hegemonic masculinity results in inequality appearing natural, which maintains male domination.

(7) The stratification process of gender places men above women in the workforce, causing women to earn less than men. Occupations with a high concentration of female workers suppress wages for all, men and women alike.

(8) Women's work is generally devalued in society and they are less likely to receive promotions compared to men.

(9) Violence against women maintains male domination through domestic violence, sexual assault, stalking, and dating violence.

Box 10.1 "A Rose by Any Other Name Doth Smell as Sweet" – or Does It?

Canadian-born David Reimer was one of twin brothers but, during a routine circumcision, his phallus was accidentally removed by an electrocautery needle due to a technical mishap. Following the recommendations made by doctors and supported by the research of Dr. John Money from Johns Hopkins, America's leading research university, David was reassigned as a girl. The twins were studied in depth by Money, who was featured in *Time Magazine* as answering the nature-versus-nurture question. From his results with David, it seems that nurture won. David underwent surgery for a synthetic vagina, was given estrogen supplements, and reared as a girl. During his transition, he had great difficulty adapting to a "girl's life." He did not like dolls or wearing skirts or dresses and fought for his brother's toy cars and guns. Dr. Money studied the twins for several years – claiming perfect success in reassigning sex. David was not told of his reassignment until age 14, at the request of a psychiatrist who was treating David for his behavioral issues (Ritsko 2001).

    As an adult, David elected once again to surgically become a man. Throughout his life, he was used by scientists as an example of the appropriateness of sex reassignment of intersexuals and those who had suffered genital mutilation. Later, other scientists used him as a primary example of why sex reassignment should not be a legitimate medical procedure. Ultimately, David committed suicide after a tumultuous life filled with many highs and lows (Colapinto 2004).

Box 10.2 Gender Classics: Working Parents and the Household Division of Labor

Arlie Hochschild's classic book, *The Second Shift: Working Parents and the Revolution at Home* (1989), illustrates the difficulties of juggling work demands, household tasks, and family maintenance. Hochschild spent 10 years observing and talking to married, two-job couples with young children to find out how this complex balancing act of demands is accomplished. What she found is that women do the majority of the balancing. Compared to their husbands, women

Box 10.2 (*continued*)

work an extra month of 24-hour days per year. Hochschild claimed that this unequal distribution of work leads to marriage and familial strain and the questioning of self-identity.

Hochschild showed how men and women use gender strategies, course of action based on cultural messages from the media, social norms and rituals, stories, and family values to allocate housework and childcare. Gender strategies aid in the construction of "maleness" and "femaleness." According to Hochschild, the combination of personal and social gender strategies inform how housework and childcare are allocated. Because women often are seen as responsible for the housework and childcare, most working mothers take on those duties. This causes most women to have two shifts: in the workplace and at home.

Based on her observations and interviews, Hochschild found that less than 20 percent of the men in her sample do as much housework and childcare as their wives. Another 20 percent of men did some housework or childcare; however, 60 percent did very little domestic work. In contrast, one-third of the women were content with their husband's domestic contributions, one-third were attempting to convince their husband to increase his contributions, and one-third had given up on demanding that their husband do more at home.

Hochschild was somewhat optimistic about future gendered divisions of labor. She claimed that as women increasingly enter and obtain status in the workplace, they will have more leverage and resources to renegotiate gender strategies and division of labor at home. Additionally, as more couples become dual-earner parents, workplaces will have to recognize the strain that two jobs can put on families thereby becoming more accommodating by offering flexible hours, childcare, and parental leave.

Source: Excerpted from Arlie Russel Hochschild (1989). *The Second Shift: Working Parents and the Revolution at Home.* New York: Penguin Books.

Key Concepts

Common couple violence	Male domination
Comparable worth	Masculine/feminine
Dating violence	Natural subordination
Devaluation thesis	Patriarchal terrorism
Domestic violence	Pink ghettos
Feminization of labor	Sex
Fertility transition	Sex chromosomes
Gender	Sex segregation
Gender gap	Sexual assault
Gender roles	Social construction of gender
Glass ceiling	Specialized human capital
Hegemonic masculine identity	Stalking
Hegemony	Stereotypes
Herm, merm, ferm	Sticky floor
Intersexual	Third gender
Job queues	Wage discrimination

Questions for Thought

1. According to statistics from the U.S. Department of Education (2010), "57% of all new Bachelor's degrees and 61% of Master's degrees are awarded to women. Is the increasing number of educational and employment opportunities for women creating a reverse gender gap? Why or why not?

2. When comparable-worth and equal-pay policies are not enforced, women earn less than men. Does this mean that men are making more money under unequal conditions? If not, where does this money go?

3. How does religion today affect the choices that women make about reproduction? The topic of abortion is controversial, yet it is still practiced by many Americans despite the controversy. How does the separation of church and state reconcile with a woman's right to have control over her own body? Or does it?

Exercises

1. *Holidays and family power relations.*
   Think back to a family holiday celebration that included a large meal. Who made decisions about where the meal took place, what was served, and who was invited? Identify the sex of those who prepared the meal, set out the festive decorations, served the meal, and cleaned up. What do the answers reveal about the gendered division of labor in the household?

2. *Occupational hierarchy and women's work.*
   Review a ranked list of occupational-prestige scores for well-known jobs in the United States, particularly the stereotypically female "pink-collar" occupations. Where are these occupations in the ranking? Why? Do you think the prestige of these rankings has increased, decreased, or remained constant in the past 50 years?

3. *Gender advertisements today.*
   Are women and men portrayed similarly in the media? Break up into small groups and collect a sample of 30 advertisements from magazines, newspapers, online or other source. Ten advertisements within the sample should depict a man alone, 10 a woman alone and 10 of a man and woman together. Are there similarities or differences in the ways men and women are depicted? When shown together, is one taller, stronger, and more focused than the other sex? Is one looking away while the other is looking ahead? Discuss what this means in terms of power distribution and sex.

Multimedia Resources

Print

Bernhardt, Annett, Martina Morris, and Mark S. Handcock. 1995. "Women's Gains or Men's Losses? A Closer Look at the Shrinking Gender Gap in Earnings." *American Journal of Sociology*, 101: 302–28.

Budig, Michelle J., and Paula England. 2001. "The Wage Penalty for Motherhood." *American Sociological Review*, 66: 204–25.

Charles, Maria, and Karen Bradely. 2002. "Equal but Separate? A Cross-National Study of Sex Segregation in Higher Education." *American Sociological Review* 67: 573–99.

Charles, Maria, and David B. Grusky. 2004. *Occupational Ghettos: The Worldwide Segregation of Women and Men*. Stanford, CA: Stanford University Press.

Ehrenreich, Barbara, and Arlie Russel Hochschild. 2002. *Global Women: Nannies, Maids, and Sex Workers in the New Economy*. New York: Henry Holt and Company, LLC.

Hochschild, Arlie Russel. 1989. *The Second Shift: Working Parents and the Revolution at Home*. New York: Penguin Books.

_____ . 1997. *The Time Bind: When Work Becomes Home and Home Becomes Work*. New York: Henry Holt and Company, LLC.

Jacobs, Jerry A. 1989. *Revolving Doors: Sex Segregation and Women's Careers*. Stanford, CA: Stanford University Press.

Lorber, Judith. 1993. "Believing Is Seeing: Biology as Ideology." *Gender and Society* 7: 568–81.

Owings, Alison. 2004. *Hey, Waitress!* Berkeley: University of California Press.

Paxton, Pamela Marie, and Melanie M. Hughes. 2007. *Women, Politics, and Power: A Global Perspective*. Newbury Park, CA: Pine Forge Press.

Rothenberg, Paula. 2004. *Invisible Privilege*. Lawrence: University Press of Kansas.

Internet

http://www.dol.gov/wb/: Homepage of U.S. Department of Labor, Women's Bureau. This site contains facts about working women and information on policies and programs directed toward working women.

http://www.unfpa.org/swp/swpmain.htm: The UN Population Fund's page on gender equality and women's health throughout the world. "The State of the World Population 2002: Lives Together, Worlds Apart – Men and Women in a Time of Change."

http://www.msnbc.msn.com/id/19031210/ns/health-pregnancy: Interactive Web site on fertility in the United States.

Recommended Films

Beyond Macho (1989). This documentary depicts changes in men's work patterns and family-related gender roles, especially the increased amount of male participation in housework and childcare.

Keep Her Under Control: Law's Patriarchy in India (1998). This documentary explores gender stratification through an in-depth look at what happens when a woman defies the patriarchal laws of her northern Indian village. This film also highlights the demands placed on Indian girls as they grow up.

Red Light (2009). Actress Lucy Liu coproduced and narrates the movie, which follows the stories of a number of girls over the course of four years as they are kidnapped and sold to brothels in Cambodia.

Seen Anything Good Lately (1997). This film documents the increasing focus on gays and lesbians in the media and other dominant social institutions. It also shows how gays and lesbians are still misrepresented in modern times.

Serving with Dignity (1997). This film depicts the difficulties endured by women working in the fast-food industry, such as sexual harassment, low wages, long working hours, and balancing time between work and home.

She's Nobody's Baby (1983). This film shows the changing status of women throughout twentieth-century America, focusing on how gender roles are often socially constructed to fit societal expectations.

Works Cited

Becker, Joanne R. 1981. "Differential Treatment of Females and Males in Mathematics Classes." *Journal for Research in Mathematics Education* 12: 40–53.

Berger, Peter L. 1969. *Invitation to Sociology*. New York: Penguin Books.

Bianchi, Suzanne M. and Melissa A. Milkie. 2010. "Work and Family Research in the First Decade of the 21st Century." *Journal of Marriage and Family* 72:705-725.

Bielby, William T. 1991. "The Structure and Process of Sex Segregation." In *New Approaches to Economic and Social Analyses of Discrimination* (pp. 97–112), edited by Richard R. Cornwall and Phanindra V. Wunnava Portsmouth, NH: Praeger Greenwood.

Bobbitt-Zeher, Donna. 2007. "The Gender Income Gap and the Role of Education." *Sociology of Education* 80: 1–22.

Buchmann, Claudia, and Thomas A. DiPrete. 2006. "The Growing Female Advantage in College Completion: The Role of Family Background and Academic Achievement." *American Sociological Review* 71: 515–41.

Butler, Judith. 1990. *Gender Trouble: Feminism and the Subversion of Identity.* New York and London: Routledge.

Cohen, Philip N., Matt L. Huffman, and Stefanie Knauer. 2009. "Stalled Progress? Gender Segregation and Wage Inequality Among Managers, 1980–2000." *Work and Occupations* 36: 318–42.

Colapinto, John. 2004. "Gender Gap: What Were the Real Reasons behind David Reimer's Suicide?" Retrieved September 25, 2009, from www.slate.com/id/2101678/.

Collins, Patricia Hill. 1989. "The Social Construction of Black Feminist Thought." *Signs* 14: 745–73.

_____. 2000. *Black Feminist Thought: Knowledge, Consciousness, and the Politics of Empowerment.* New York: Routledge.

Connell, Raewyn W. 1987. *Gender and Power: Society, the Person, and Sexual Politics.* Palo Alto, CA: Stanford University Press.

Dye, Jane Lawler. 2008. "Fertility of American Women: 2006." Washington, DC: U.S. Department of Commerce, Economics and Statistics Administration, U.S. Census Bureau.

Engels, Friedrich. 1999[1884]. "The Patriarchal Family." In *Social Theory*, edited by C. Lemert (pp. 66–9). Boulder, CO: Westview Press.

England, Paula, Joan M. Hermsen, and David A. Cotter. 2000. "The Devaluation of Women's Work: A Comment on Tam." *The American Journal of Sociology* 105: 1741–51.

Fausto-Sterling, A. 1992. *Myths of Gender: Biological Theories about Women and Men.* New York: Basic Books.

_____. 2004. "The Five Sexes: Why Male and Female Are Not Enough." In *The Social Construction of Difference and Inequality*, edited by T. E. Ore (pp. 107–14). New York: McGraw-Hill.

Federal Bureau of Investigation. 2008. "Supplementary Homicide Reports 1980–2006." Washington, DC: Federal Bureau of Investigation.

Garfinkel, Harold. 1967. "Passing and the Managed Achievement of Sex Status in an Intersexed Person." In *Studies in Ethnomethodology (pp. 116–85),* edited by Harold Garfinkle. Englewood Cliffs, NJ: Prentice Hall.

Goffman, Erving. 1979. *Gender Advertisements.* New York: Harper & Row.

Goldin, Claudia. 1994. "Understanding the Gender Gap: An Economic History of American Women." In *Equal Employment Opportunity: Labor Market Discrimination and Public Policy*, (pp. 17–27), edited by Paul Berstein. Edison, New Jersey: Aldine Transaction.

Guillen, Mauro F., Randall Collins, Paula England, and Marshall Meyer. 2004. "Economic Sociology: Developments in an Emerging Field." New York: Russell Sage Foundation.

Hooks, Bell. 1984. *Feminist Theory, from Margin to Center.* Boston: South End Press.

Huber, Joan N. 2004. "Lenski Effects on Sex Stratification Theory." *Sociological Theory* 22: 258–68.

_____. 2008. "Reproductive Biology, Technology, and Gender Inequality: An Autobiographical Essay." *Annual Review of Sociology* 34: 1–13.

Huston, Aletha C., and Stacey Rosenkrantz Aronson. 2005. "Mothers' Time with Infant and Time in Employment as Predictors of Mother–Child Relationships and Children's Early Development." *Child Development* 76: 467–82.

International Labor Office. 2008. "ILO Action Against Trafficking in Human Beings." Geneva: International Labor Office.

Jacobs, Jerry A. 1989. *Revolving Doors: Sex Segregation and Women's Careers*. Palo Alto, CA: Stanford University Press.

Johnson, Michael P. 1995. "Patriarchal Terrorism and Common Couple Violence: Two Forms of Violence Against Women." *Journal of Marriage and the Family* 57: 283–94.

Kara, Siddharth. 2006. *Sex Trafficking: Inside the Business of Modern Slavery*. New York: Columbia University Press.

Kilbourne, Barbara S., George Farkas, Kurt Beron, Dorothea Weir, and Paul England. 1994. "Returns to Skill, Compensating Differentials, and Gender Bias: Effects of Occupational Characteristics on the Wages of White Women and Men." *The American Journal of Sociology* 100: 689–719.

Kilpatrick, Dean, Jenna McCauley, and Grace Mattern. 2009. "Understanding National Rape Statistics." Enola, PA: National Sexual Violence Resource Center.

Kimmel, Michael S. 2004. "Masculinity as Homophobia: Fear, Shame, and Silence in the Construction of Gender Identity." In *The Social Construction of Difference and Inequality*, edited by T. E. Ore (213–219). New York: McGraw-Hill.

Klaus, Patsy, and Cathy Maston. 2007. "Table 63. Personal Crimes of Violence, 2006: Percent Distribution of Incidents, by Victim–Offender Relationship, Type of Crime and Place of Occurrence." Washington, DC: U.S. Department of Justice, Bureau of Justice Statistics.

Klepp, Susan E. 2009. *Revolutionary Conceptions: Women, Fertility, and Family Limitation in America, 1760–1820*. Chapel Hill: University of North Carolina Press.

Lorber, Judith. 1993. "Believing Is Seeing: Biology as Ideology." *Gender and Society* 7: 568–81.

_____. 1995. *Paradoxes of Gender*. London: Yale University Press.

_____. 2004. "Night to His Day: The Social Construction of Gender." In *The Social Construction of Difference and Inequality*, edited by T. E. Ore (pp. 99–107) New York: McGraw-Hill.

Majors, Richard, and Janet Mancini Billson. 1992. *Cool Pose: The Dilemmas of Black Manhood in America*. New York: Touchstone.

Margaret Sanger Papers. 2009. "Margaret Sanger Papers, 1761–1995: Biographical Note." Northampton, MA: Five College Archives and Manuscript Collection.

Martin, Patricia Y. 2003. "Gender as Social Institution." *Social Forces* 82: 1249–73.

Mattingly, Marybeth, and Suzanne M. Bianchi. 2003. "Gender Differences in the Quantity and Quality of Free Time: The U.S. Experience." *Social Forces* 81: 999–1030.

Mickelson, R. A. 1989. "Why Does Jane Read and Write So Well? The Anomaly of Women's Achievement." *Sociology of Education* 62: 47–63.

Mulford, Carrie, and Peggy C. Giordano. 2008. "Teen Dating Violence: A Closer Look at Adolescent Romantic Relationships." *National Institute of Justice* 261: 1–7.

Paxton, Pamela Marie, and Melanie M. Hughes. 2007. *Women, Politics, and Power: A Global Perspective*. Newbury Park, CA: Pine Forge Press.

Peterson, Richard R. 1996. "A Re-Evaluation of the Economic Consequences of Divorce." *American Sociological Review* 61: 528–36.

Phornphutkul, Chanika, A. Fausto-Sterling, and Anne Philip Gruppuso. 2000. "Gender Self-Reassignment in an XY Adolescent Female Born with Ambiguous Genitalia." *Pediatrics* 106: 135.

Qian, Zhenchao, Daniel T. Lichter, and Leanna M. Mellott. 2005. "Out-of-Wedlock Childbearing, Marital Prospects and Mate Selection." *Social Forces* 84: 473–91.

Raley, Sara B., Marybeth J. Mattingly, and Suzanne M. Bianchi. 2006. "How Dual Are Dual-Income Couples? Documenting Change from 1970 to 2001." *Journal of Marriage and Family* 68: 11–28.

Repetti, Rena L., and Jennifer Wood. 1997. "Effects of Daily Stress at Work on Mothers' Interactions with Preschoolers." *Journal of Family Psychology* 11: 90–108.

Reskin, Barbara F., and Patricia A. Roos. 1990. *Job Queues, Gender Queues: Explaining Women's Inroads into Male Occupations.* Philadelphia, PA: Temple University Press.

Ritsko, Alan. 2001. "Sex: Unknown." Produced by Andrew Cohen and Stephen Sweigart In *NOVA.* Original Airdate Oct. 30, 2001. A BBC/WGBH Boston Co-Production. Public Broadcasting Service.

Rosenthal, Bernard, and Gretchen A. Adams. 2009. *Records of the Salem Witch-Hunt.* New York: Cambridge University Press.

Salmon, Marylynn. 1994. "The Cultural Significance of Breastfeeding and Infant Care in Early Modern England and America." *Journal of Social History* 28: 247–69.

Sayer, Liana C., Suzanne M. Bianchi, and John P. Robinson. 2004. "Are Parents Investing Less in Children? Trends in Mothers' and Fathers' Time with Children." *American Journal of Sociology* 110: 1–43.

Schneider, Barbara L., and Linda J. Waite. 2005. *Being Together, Working Apart: Dual-Career Families and the Work-Life Balance.* New York: Cambridge University Press.

Schoen, Robert, Nan Marie Astone, Kendra Rothert, Nicola J. Standish, and Young J. Kim. 2002. "Women's Employment, Marital Happiness, and Divorce." *Social Forces* 81: 643–62.

Stanton, Elizabeth Cady, and J. L. Spalding. 1885. "Has Christianity Benefited Woman?" *The North American Review* 140: 389–410.

Tam, Tony. 1997. "Sex Segregation and Occupational Gender Inequality in the United States: Devaluation or Specialized Training?" *American Journal of Sociology* 102: 1652–92.

Teachman, Jay D., Lucky M. Tedrow, and Kyle D. Crowder. 2000. "The Changing Demography of America's Families." *Journal of Marriage and the Family* 62: 1234–46.

Thornton, Saranna. 2009. "On the Brink: The Annual Report of the Economic Status of the Profession, 2008–09." Washington, DC: American Association of University Professors.

U.S. Bureau of Labor Statistics. 2009a. "American Time Use Survey Summary – 2008 Results." Washington, DC: U.S. Department of Labor.

———. 2009b. "Highlights of Women's Earnings 2008." Washington, DC: U.S. Department of Labor.

U.S. Census Bureau. 2009. "Historical Statistics of the United States, Colonial Times to 1970." Washington, DC: U.S. Bureau of the Census.

U.S. Department of Education, National Center for Education Statistics. 2010. *Condition of Education 2010*, Table A-23-2 (NCES 2010-028).

U.S. Department of Justice. 2008. "Stalking Victimization in the United States Special Report." Washington, DC: Bureau of Justice Statistics, Office of Violence Against Women.

U.S. Department of Justice. 2009. "The Facts About the Office on Violence Against Women Focus Areas." Washington, DC: U.S. Department of Justice, Office on Violence Against Women.

U.S. Department of Labor. 2009. "Women in the Labor Force in 2008." Washington, DC: U.S. Department of Labor, Women's Bureau.

West, Candace, and Don H. Zimmerman. 1987. "Doing Gender." *Gender and Society* 1: 125–51.

11   Race and Ethnicity

Race: A Social Construction

To most people, *race* is essential – meaning that it is necessary, basic, and defining. We generally speak of race as based on physical characteristics, nationality, and religion. However, as discussed in this chapter, racial categories often are arbitrary in nature and do not precisely describe groups of people. Sociologists often refer to *ethnicity* rather than race when discussing a nexus of behaviors shared by a particular group of people.

Ethnic groups are those groups in society that are set off from others through unique cultural traits. When members of ethnic groups try to shed their ethnicity, we refer to this as *assimilation*. Ethnicity eventually fades as progressive generations assimilate to the dominant culture. Assimilation, however, requires that individuals not only shed their ethnicity but also that the dominant group accept them.

In popular usage, we speak of race as something based on physical features (e.g., skin color), nationality (e.g., Hispanic), or religion (e.g., Jewish), ranging up to its broadest usage encompassing all of humanity (i.e., the human race). Race refers to people who share similar physical or genetic characteristics. Racial categories are not distinguished by clearcut differences; rather, groups tend to overlap and blend into one another. Differences among individuals within the same race often are greater than differences among races. For example, think of people who are considered black but whose skin color is as light as those considered white and vice versa. This scheme of racial categories also excludes people who do not easily fit into one category. Where do East Indians – people with Caucasian features but dark skin – or groups like Indonesians, who have thoroughly mixed ancestry, fit? Moreover, what about people who are of multiple races? How can we classify multi-ethnicity and, when we do, what do the categories mean?

Our popular divisions are oversimplified and something that we constructed – they are not rooted in biological differences. This is seen easily when we examine how race works in the daily life of Americans. Despite the repeal of Jim Crow laws (discussed later in this chapter), racial classifications continue to affect daily life.

Race/ethnicity, defined as a class of people with shared characteristics, interests, or habits, is socially created and not rooted in true biological difference. Sociologists have a long history of viewing race through a critical lens (Lieberman 1968), and recent findings from biologists support what many social scientists have long believed: Race is a social construction. In 2003, biologists from around the world reported their findings from a 13-year study of human genes. This work resulted in *The Human Genome Project*, which reports that people are 99.9 percent genetically identical. Of the fraction-of-percent difference between *all* people of the world, only 3 to 10 percent is attributed to geographical ancestry (Feldman and Lewontin 2008); that is, about 0.01 to 0.03 percent of genetic variation can be attributed to ancestry – some ancestral attributions are *potentially* due to race. Furthermore, there is not one gene or trait associated with all people within one race that distinguishes them from another race.

If race is a socially constructed concept, how then can we explain racial differences in diseases and life outcomes? To answer this question, we first must understand how racial categorizations have been constructed, review the immigration patterns in America, and discuss racial policies.

Racial Differentiation

The concept of race is tethered securely to power and inequality. In the United States, *racial differentiation* has been used to maintain ethnic communities and create social cohesion. This is observed in the cultivation of cultures within cities across the United States, in places such as Chinatown, the barrio, and Little Italy. Differentiating by race also functions to legitimize one group's political domination over another group. For example, race is the foundation of slavery, Native American genocide, Japanese American internment, and deceptive medical practices in the Tuskegee syphilis study of African Americans. Racial differentiation creates a structure of stratification because one group is generally more powerful than another.

Race is one of the most misconceived and misunderstood ideas of the modern world. First, the term *race* is not applied consistently and therefore may mean different things to different people. In the United States, race includes multiple classifications of the same group. For example, during the European immigration waves of the early 1900s, many were not considered white (e.g., immigrants from Poland, Ireland, and Italy).

Racial stratification systems are found in most *heterogeneous* societies. That is, in most countries with different ethnic groups, a system of ranking by ethnicity exists. The status of a group is determined by the different paths by which people come to inhabit a region. Immigration patterns help us understand some of the origins of racial demarcations (Portes and Zhou 1993). As demographers, Portes and Zhou see immigration as the result of two forces – a push and a pull. People move from place to place because they are *pushed* (e.g., hostile environment, politics, and unhappy social relationships) or *pulled* (e.g., economic opportunities and family members who reside in the host country). In general, groups that are pulled fare better than groups that were pushed from their home nation. This classification has been extended to include *voluntary* and *involuntary migration* (Ogbu 2003), in which some groups choose and other groups are forced to move – as was the case for blacks who were taken from Africa as slaves. Those who are involuntarily in the host nation, it is argued, do not make the same gains as natives and voluntary immigrants.

Immigrant groups generally are studied using an *assimilation perspective*. From this viewpoint, those who come to a host country are expected to adapt and accept the new customs, language, and ways of life – in a word, the *culture* of the host nation. Some groups are better able to accomplish this than others. The idea that some groups are not "melt-able," in terms of the American "melting pot," is attributed to different resources that groups brought from their original starting point. Whereas earlier immigrants who maintained their ethnic identity were less likely to assimilate, enclaves of immigrants now are more able to preserve their ethnic identity and succeed in America by possessing three resources: knowledge of business practices, capital, and labor (Portes and Manning 2005).

In addition to assimilation, social stratification of race/ethnicity may be studied from a perspective of *pluralism*. Instead of assuming that there is a national culture that all will or will try to adopt (i.e., the melting pot), pluralism acknowledges *multiculturalism* – that is, many immigrant groups maintain their own and share in a common American culture. The rise of multicultural heritage seriously challenged previously accepted theories of race. Assumptions about race, identity, and group membership have been reexamined (Rockquemore, Brunsma, and Delgado 2009), supporting the sociological assumption that race indeed is a social and not necessarily biological construct (Skinner 2007). Growing interracial unions, Asian and Latino immigration, and the availability of a mixed-race demarcation on official documents all contribute to a paradigm shift on race relations (Bean and Lee 2009).

History of the American Racial Classification System

Although scientists agree that humans do not have subspecies, there is a long history of creating race in the United States. In the early colonial days, race was fluid whereas social class was distinct. In 1616, John Rolfe married Pocahontas, causing an uproar in England – not because of an interracial marriage but rather because a princess married a commoner (Higginbotham and Kopytoff 1989). In 1676, Bacon's Rebellion united indentured servants from Europe and black slaves against wealthy plantation owners. In 1705, the Virginia Slave Code was written to divide slaves by race; poor whites, who had been indentured servants, were promoted to overseers of slaves and blacks were made permanent slaves.

In 1775, a racial hierarchy was legitimated when a leading scientist, Johann Blumenbach, claimed that a skull was *Caucasian*, named after a region between Europe and the Russian Federation. Distinguishing regional differences among people, the pseudoscientific terms *Caucasian*, *Mongoloid*, and *Negroid* set the foundation for a system of racial hierarchies as scientists created "evidence" showing that whites were superior to other races (Haller 1971). One way that scientists proved white superiority was by examining skull shapes, finding white skulls to be the "most beautiful" with a large capacity for a big brain (Wiegman 1995). Although we find *phrenology* – that is, the study of brain size to determine behavioral attributes – to be unscientific, in the days it was seen as scientific and therefore valid and reliable.

Racial differentiation continued to affect the allocation of power in the newly created nation of America. The 1790 Naturalization Act restricted American citizenship to whites only and the first census that included racial categories was taken. The determinant of race was less biological but rather whether a person was free – a free man counted as one person, a slave was three-fifths of a person (women had no political power). In 1825, the federal government allotted land to the Osage Indians based on the degree of Indian blood.

During colonial days, immigrants from Europe classified "white" as a race to create social exclusion from Native Americans – "white" was used to signify officially that an individual was not American Indian (Allen 1997). This was an important consideration because those who were white could own land and had other civil rights, whereas Native Americans could not own land and had no rights while being pushed out of ever-encroaching colonial territories. This began the legacy of what sociologists term *white privilege.*

Throughout the centuries, American definitions of *race* have changed. Even those who were European were not always considered white. For example, during their early migration to the United States, Italians and Irish were considered nonwhite and were limited in which occupations they could seek and who they could marry (Feagin and Feagin 1989).

Today, racial classifications commonly are accepted as essential and most agree to the classification system put in place by the current U.S. Census. In 1977, the U.S. Census Bureau established four racial categories: American Indian or Alaskan Native, Asian or Pacific Islander, Black, and White. In addition, two ethnicity categories were established: Hispanic Origin and Not of Hispanic Origin. In 2000, the Census added another category – Some Other Race – and allowed individuals to select one or more races. Moreover, the category of Asian or Pacific Islander was expanded to include more specific information, and the categories of American Indian, Eskimo, and Aleut were combined into the category of American Indian, with the option to write in tribal affiliation (U.S. Census Bureau 2008b).

Racial classifications allow the separation of ethnic groups to be legitimized. Ethnic groups may suffer from (1) *discrimination* – defined as the act of treating people differently based on a predetermined ranking of personal criteria such as race, ethnicity, gender, religion, or sexual orientation by dominant groups; and (2) *racism* – the result of perceiving one group as superior over another, which in America traditionally has been whites over nonwhites (Twine 1998). The most extreme form of discrimination is *genocide* – the killing of one group by another. Moreover, simplifying people by a predetermined category creates *stereotypes* – that is, the preconceived notion that all members of a group share generalized commonalities. As discussed herein, ethnicity binds people by commonalities; however, sharing a culture does not make people monolithic. Just as no one gene is found in any one racial category, no one cultural element is found within any one ethnic group. People are diverse and race/ethnic categories attempt to reduce people to simplified, one-dimensional caricatures.

Given the controversy surrounding racial categorizations, social scientists have considered the value of using race/ethnicity in data collection. Despite the dangers of simplifying people and complex human behaviors by attributing particular actions or conditions to race/ethnicity, the amount of information lost would be more problematic. For instance, we know that Hispanics and blacks receive harsher penalties in federal courts than whites (Steffensmeier and Demuth 2000). If we did not collect race/ethnicity data, discrimination could not be measured.

Meaning of Race/Ethnic Categories

Before we examine how race/ethnicity contributes to stratification and inequality, we must discuss what each category means – that is, which group of people is described by each category. Race/ethnicity are not in any way essential and monolithic; however, it is generally held that there are five categories: Asian, black, Latino, Native American, and white (many subcategories exist within each category). Table 11.1 reports the percentages of each category in the United States in 2008 and 2003 and the percentage of change between the years.

The term *minority* has a particular meaning in stratification studies because it points to the group with the least amount of power, not necessarily the group with the fewest members. For example, women are a minority group despite having more numbers than men. The groups described herein are sorted by the number of people who identify within the group, from most to least. Although Hispanic is not a race, it is a collective of many Latin-speaking people and is considered a separate ethnicity by the U.S. Census Bureau.

Anglo-Core (Whites)

In America, whites are the majority. Being white usually means having origins in Europe, the Middle East, and North Africa. Some might not consider people from the Middle East or North African white, but Syrians, Iranians, Egyptians, and Moroccans identify as Caucasian. Often, those who are white do not consider race a component

Table 11.1 U.S. Race/Ethnicity by Percentage and Change between 2003 and 2008

	2008	2003	Change
White	75.0	76.2	−1.2
Hispanic or Latino of any race	15.4	13.9	1.6
Black or African American	12.4	12.1	0.3
Asian	4.5	4.3	0.2
American Indian and Alaska Native	0.8	0.8	0.0
Some other race	4.9	4.8	0.1

Data Source: U.S. Census Bureau Current Population Study (2008a).

of identity; rather, race is noted for those groups who are not white (Smedley and Smedley 2005).

The first ethnic group to enter a territory (or colonize it) is called the *core group/charter group*. This core group has "the most to say" about what happens in society and retains many privileges and prerogatives, including decision making about which other groups may enter the society. In the United States, the core group was British as a result of the Puritan migration and colonization of America. Thus, major American social institutions still reflect British culture. Successive waves of immigration included populations that were different from the core – primarily Eastern European and Catholic – and although these groups were first segregated and discriminated against, they were able to assimilate into the larger "white" population.

Hispanic/Latino

Being Hispanic refers to those with ancestry from Central and South America – also known as Latin America – whose ancestry is from Spain. The term *Hispanic/Latino* encompasses many races and is a pan-ethnic term describing Spanish-speaking Latin Americans. The U.S. Census Bureau allows a respondent to identify with a race and choose either Hispanic or non-Hispanic.

The Hispanic population is heterogeneous, within which there is tremendous variation in how well some groups are doing. Recency of immigration, social location, and history all have a role in determining distribution of scarce resources. Table 11.2 reports the distribution of Hispanics in the top 10 states, in descending order, and compares the change from 2000 to 2009 (U.S.Census 2011).

This ethnic group is the fastest-growing segment in the United States. Part of the Hispanic migration was instigated by the U.S. Government during World War II during a labor shortage. The Bracero Program was established in 1945 and, by 1967, it had brought to America more than 2 million Mexican guest workers. By the program

Table 11.2 Top 10 States with the Highest Distribution of Hispanics and the Change between 2009 and 2000

	2009	2000	Change
New Mexico	44.8	42.1	2.7
California	36.1	32.4	3.7
Texas	35.9	32.0	3.9
Arizona	29.8	25.3	4.5
Nevada	25.2	19.7	5.5
Florida	20.6	16.8	3.6
Colorado	19.7	17.1	2.6
New York	16.3	15.1	1.2
New Jersey	15.9	13.3	2.6
Illinois	14.6	12.3	2.3

Data Source: U.S. Census, 2005–2009 American Community Survey 5-Year Estimates (2011).

mandate, the workers were guaranteed a good wage and, for many, the standard of living was much higher than what they experienced in Mexico.

Black

In general, being black refers to people having origins in Africa. The term *black* has been applied by whites to describe other ethnicities, such as Indians, Native Americans, and Hispanics, although this is not acceptable today. The history of African Americans in the United States is rife with legally sanctioned inequality. Slavery and later Jim Crow laws kept the black population separated from white America. Laws forbade blacks from marrying whites, learning to read or teaching other blacks to read, voting, leaving the plantation without permission, and observing or revering African culture, including music and religion.

Today, the social space between many blacks and whites is found in *residential segregation*, which has been an important factor in isolating blacks, making true integration difficult and overcoming inequality nearly impossible. In addition to residential segregation between whites and blacks, there is polarization within the African American community: some families do well and others struggle to survive (Pattillo-McCoy 1999) – this has been termed "two black Americas" (Hwang, Fitzpatrick, and Helms 1998).

Asian

According to the U.S. Census (2000), there are 12 Asian categories: Asian Indian, Cambodian, Chinese, Filipino, Hmong, Japanese, Korean, Laotian, Pakistani, Thai, Vietnamese, and Other Asian. Much like the Hispanic population, the Asian population in the United States is heterogeneous, with minorities within minorities (Eisenberg and Spinner-Halev 2005). Because each group has a specific history and group dynamic, there is tremendous variation in the "success" of Asian immigrants in the United States. Recency of immigration and country of origin are influential in determining patterns of success for different groups.

Asian immigration to the United States began in the 1800s with the growth of the West Coast and the Gold Rush. This group of mostly Chinese immigrants was at first accepted; however, in the late 1800s, laws were passed to prohibit them from full citizenship. During World War II, Japanese Americans were forced into internment camps for national-security reasons. Some argued that this form of *racial profiling* – that is, prejudging the intentions of a group of people based on race – was unfair because other nationalities were not placed in camps (e.g., Germans and Italians). During the internment process, Japanese American families were separated and stripped of their wealth and property. Of the more than 120,000 interned, more than half were children. Throughout the centuries, Asians have migrated from various regions and have become a *model minority* – meaning that the group has superseded the dominant group. In general, Asians have more success than whites in education, wealth and income, and health.

American Indian

Being American Indian refers to people with origins in any of the original peoples of North and South America (including Central America) who maintain tribal affiliation or community attachment. The history of American Indians in the United States is similar to that of African Americans. Largely destroyed by European settlers and often perceived as subhuman, many lost their life as America developed. Those that remained were forced to live on reservations at the mercy of the Bureau of Indian Affairs (BIA). Once numbering more than 75 million, today the American Indian population is less than 1 percent of the total U.S. population, which constitutes genocide.

American Indians came from many diverse nations but were reduced to a small group of people with minority status. The population suffers from high rates of poverty, alcoholism, depression, school attrition (i.e., dropping out), homicide, and suicide (Fisher, Bacon, and Storck 1998). Furthermore, American Indians are sequestered on land that often is used by the military to dump hazardous materials, leaving the population at risk of exposure to the toxicity (Hooks and Smith 2004).

How many people within the established racial/ethnic groups exist in America today? In 2008, the U.S. Census Bureau estimated that 97.7 percent of the U.S. population identify with one race and 2.3 percent identify with two or more races (U.S. Census Bureau 2008a). Figure 11.1 compares the percentages by race in the United States between 2003

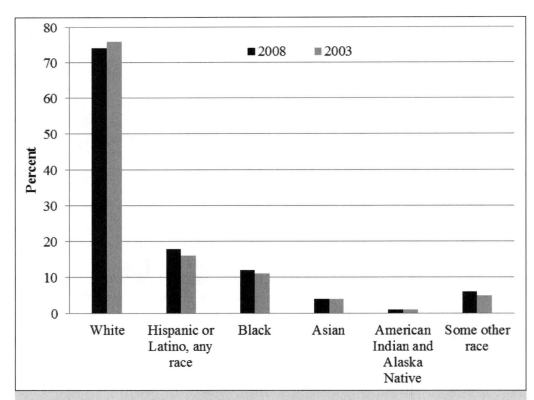

Figure 11.1 Percentage of U.S. population by race, 2008 and 2003.
Data Source: U.S. Census Bureau, Current Population Survey (2008).

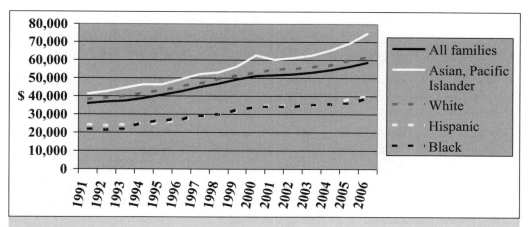

Figure 11.2 Family income by race/ethnicity in 2006.
Data Source: U.S. Census Bureau, Current Population Survey (2008).

and 2008. Whites remain the majority with three-quarters of the population identifying as white; however, this percentage decreased by 1.2 percent in the five years between 2003 and 2008. The reduction in white percentage is accounted for by the increases in ethnic minorities, particularly Hispanic, which increased by 1.6 percent in the same period.

The U.S. Census Bureau estimates that the Asian and Hispanic populations will triple by 2050, reducing the percentage of whites to about half (U.S. Census Bureau 2004). The estimates predict that the Hispanic (of any race) and Asian populations will increase to 24.1 and 8 percent, respectively.

The change in the racial composition of America is controversial. Some argue that the decrease in the white population will affect the American culture. Others point to the fact that America is a pluralist nation and that except for American Indians, we are all immigrants. The debate on the growing rates of nonwhites centers on the issue of power, particularly which group has the most and how they maintain their dominance (Blumer 1958). We now examine how power and race are related; the discussion begins by examining the racial hierarchy in America.

Race has an important part in the allocation of resources. For example, Figure 11.2 lists median income for families by race/ethnicity between 1991 and 2006. The distribution of income reflects the stratification hierarchy in America today.

Asians earn more than whites and whites and Asians earn more than blacks and Hispanics. As often happens in data collection, American Indians are not included in the figure; their number is too small for scientific estimates.

American Race/Ethnic Hierarchy

To understand the relationship between race and inequality, we first must understand the history of immigration in America. Not all immigrant groups entered the United States under the same circumstances, the result of which is a hierarchy of groups. The bottom tier of the hierarchy is the group for which race has had the greatest conse-quences and continues to shape aspects of social and economic life. The American race/ ethnic hierarchy is broadly divided into the following three comprehensive tiers:

1. The top tier is composed of European Americans, the majority of whom are Protes-tant, often referred to as "WASPs" (i.e., white Anglo-Saxon Protestants).
2. The intermediate tier is composed of European American Catholics and Jews and many Asian Americans. For these groups, race/ethnicity may continue to have a decreasing role in the access and allocation of valued resources.
3. The bottom tier is composed of other groups for whom race/ethnicity has the great-est consequences and for whom it continues to shape many basic aspects of social and economic life. This tier includes African Americans, most Latinos/Hispanics, Native Americans, and some Asian Americans.

A more important aspect of this hierarchy is that the gap between the bottom tier and the other two tiers is much greater than the gap between the first and second tiers. In terms of socioeconomic status, prestige, and access to political power, the division between the first two tiers is fading. However, differences between the third and other tiers remain firm.

Segregation and Discrimination

The history of race in America has been (and continues to be) plagued by segregation and discrimination. *Segregation* is the physical or social separation of groups based on a characteristic – race/ethnicity, gender, or class. The United States has a long history of laws pertaining to the segregation of nonwhites by whites. From the early colonial man-dates that segregated Native Americans and whites, to slavery and Jim Crow laws with the "one-drop-of-blood" rule, to *Plessey versus Fergusson* in which the U.S. Supreme Court ruled that separate but equal is equal, to the Civil Rights Act of 1965, America has a long history of racial segregation.

Often, laws designed to eradicate segregation were met with hostility and violence by the dominant group. An example of this is in the work of the Congress of Racial Equal-ity (CORE), which worked in the 1940s to educate blacks and raise the consciousness of America to accept equality as a fact for all, not an ideal for a few. During its efforts, untold numbers of CORE members went missing as they worked to educate people, primarily in the South. Similar ends befell young college students from the Student Non-Violent Coordinating Committee (SNCC), who desegregated lunch counters and registered black voters. Indeed, many people were killed fighting for equality and the enforcement of existing antidiscrimination laws.

Segregation has been the norm in the United States. In the early 1950s, a third-grader named Linda Brown from Topeka, Kansas, was forced to attend an all-black elementary school across town. On her daily walk to school, she had to walk through a train switch-yard, causing her and others to be at great physical risk – despite the fact that there was an elementary school (albeit an all-white school) about seven blocks from her home. Her parents and 13 other plaintiffs garnered support from the American Civil Liberties Union (ACLU) and won the right for black children to attend the closer school in the

1954 landmark case of *Brown versus Board of Education*. This ruling overturned *Plessy versus Fergusson* and began a series of integration actions. Despite the many efforts to reduce segregation, U.S. schools and neighborhoods still are often segregated today (Saporito and Sohoni 2006).

The civil-rights protests culminated in a series of three marches in Alabama that were broadcast around the world, changing race relations in America. On March 7, 1965, more than 600 protesters began to march from Selma to Montgomery. White state and local authorities met the protesters before they crossed the Edmund Pettus Bridge, beating them using billy clubs, teargas, and dogs to stop the march. The images of "Bloody Sunday" were broadcast via TV and print, and critics from around the world voiced disapproval of such inhumane treatment of citizens by authorities vested to protect and maintain peace and order. Two days later, Martin Luther King, Jr., joined in a symbolic march in which the protesters did not attempt to cross the bridge but rather mobilized resources such as the media and invited religious leaders of all faiths to join in the resistance. After acquiring court protection for the march, on Sunday, March 21, more than 3,000 people walked for 12 days from Selma to Montgomery, sleeping in fields along the way; by the time they reached the capitol in Montgomery, the number had grown to more than 25,000. Within months of Bloody Sunday, President Johnson signed the Civil Rights Act, which outlawed racial segregation in schools, employment, and public places.

Despite the Civil Rights Act, segregation survived in many social spheres; for example, between a man and a woman. *Miscegenation* – that is, marrying across races – was illegal in many states. In 1953, a black woman named Mildred Delores Jeter married a white man named Richard Perry Loving. The couple was arrested when authorities raided their home and found them in bed – which was in direct violation of the 1924 Racial Integrity Act that disallowed marriage between whites and blacks. When Mrs. Loving pointed to their marriage certificate on the wall, the authorities used the document as evidence that the couple indeed was married and involved in a criminal activity. They were charged with a felony and each sentenced to a year in prison. Instead of serving time, the couple was given a suspension for 25 years and forced to leave the state. In 1963, the ACLU filed a motion to repeal the charges. Despite its efforts, the repeal was not granted; instead, a series of lawsuits were filed on the grounds that antimiscegenation laws were unlawful because they violated the Fourteenth Amendment. In 1967, in *Loving versus Virginia*, the U.S. Supreme Court ruled that limiting marriage was unconstitutional and marriage was defined as a basic civil right (Pratt 1998). Antimiscegenation laws in the United States that prohibited people from marrying whites – primarily blacks, Asians, Native Americans, Indians, and Filipinos – were steadily repealed, state by state. The final antimiscegenation laws were repealed in 1998 in South Carolina and in 2000 in Alabama. In both states, the final vote included a marginal majority, 62 and 59 percent, respectively. Table 11.3 reports the percentage of households with partners of different races by state in 2000.

More recently, in October 2009, Keith Bardwell, a justice of the peace in Louisiana, denied an interracial couple a marriage certificate on the grounds that "he was concerned for the children who might be born of the relationship and that, in his experience, most interracial marriages don't last" (Simone 2009). Nevertheless, the couple was

Table 11.3 Percentage of Households with Partners of Different Races

Area	Married-Couple Households	Unmarried-Partner Households		
		Opposite-Sex Partners	Same-Sex Partners	
			Male Partners	Female Partners
United States	5.7	12.2	11.5	10
Alabama	2.8	6.7	4.5	4.6
Alaska	15.4	26	17.4	19.4
Arizona	8	15.7	12.2	13
Arkansas	3.6	8.4	6.1	6.5
California	12	21	19.8	17.3
Colorado	7.8	15	13.6	11.6
Connecticut	4.2	11.8	8.4	8.1
Delaware	4.1	10.5	9.8	7.1
Florida	5.2	10.4	8.6	8.4
Georgia	3.7	8.2	7.6	6.4
Hawaii	34.7	55.6	43.8	40.9
Idaho	5.3	11	8	8.1
Illinois	4.3	10	11	8.6
Indiana	2.9	8.2	5.8	6
Iowa	2.3	7.7	5.5	6.4
Kansas	5.4	14.5	8.4	9.2
Kentucky	2.3	7.3	4.6	5.6
Louisiana	3.3	7.2	6.5	5.2
Maine	2.3	4.9	4.2	4
Maryland	5.1	9.6	9.7	8.6
Massachusetts	4.1	10.3	9.9	8.1
Michigan	4.1	9.7	8.5	7.4
Minnesota	3.4	10.6	9.1	8
Mississippi	2.1	5.1	3.7	3.2
Missouri	3.5	8.8	7.3	7.5
Montana	5.3	11.2	8.8	8.4
Nebraska	3.4	11.2	5.7	8.3
Nevada	10.9	18.9	14.9	15.2
New Hampshire	2.6	5.2	5.3	4.2
New Jersey	5.1	12	11.2	8.8
New Mexico	10.8	18.6	15.8	16.4
New York	5.7	12.3	13.7	10.9
North Carolina	3.6	9.6	6.9	6.5
North Dakota	3.1	9.3	4.4	6.4
Ohio	2.9	8.5	6.9	6.7
Oklahoma	14.8	24.6	17.6	18.2
Oregon	7.4	14.1	12.4	11.7
Pennsylvania	2.4	7.5	7.1	5.6
Rhode Island	4.4	11.1	9	8
South Carolina	2.9	7.3	5.4	4.8
South Dakota	3.6	10.9	5.7	7.3

Table 11.3 (*continued*)

Area	Married-Couple Households	Unmarried-Partner Households		
		Opposite-Sex Partners	Same-Sex Partners	
			Male Partners	Female Partners
Tennessee	2.7	7.4	5.2	5.7
Texas	6.8	14.1	11.5	10.7
Utah	5.4	14.6	9.2	9.6
Vermont	2.6	4.7	4.7	4.5
Virginia	5.3	11.3	10.4	8.3
Washington	9.2	17.3	14.8	13.6
West Virginia	1.8	5.6	3.6	3.2
Wisconsin	2.9	8.7	7.2	6.8
Wyoming	5.3	10.8	7.5	7.6
District of Columbia	7.8	10.4	16	13.3

Data Source: U.S. Census Bureau, Census 2000, special tabulation from Summary File 1.

married by a different justice of the peace. Clearly, racism and segregation have not diminished despite federal protections.

Discrimination is defined as unfair actions resulting from prejudice due to the categorizing of people by a characteristic such as race/ethnicity, gender, or class. Social scientists acknowledge three forms of discrimination: pure, statistical, and institutionalized. *Pure discrimination* is the prejudiced actions against those who are considered inferior. This form of discrimination is evidenced in the actions of the White Power movement across the world. Particularly in America, there is a long history of White Power organizations, which believe in the biologically separate and superior nature of the white race. They do not tolerate other races and ethnicities and turn to violence to keep their race socially separated from others.

Statistical discrimination is a term often used in economics. It places the person holding power at the center of the relationship – for example, an employer. If two people of different races/ethnicities apply for the same position, the employer makes assumptions about each based on his or her own limited knowledge. Part of the decision-making process is risk aversion – that is, the employer wants to hire the most productive individual, although no productivity is available to be compared between candidates. Instead, the employer uses preconceived ideas to decide whom to hire. Most often, people in power choose the candidate who is most similar to themselves. The term *statistical* is used to denote a decision based on probabilities. Although no real comparison can be made, those in power tend to emulate themselves at the expense of others.

Institutionalized discrimination describes the biased indirect treatment of an individual in the process of laws, procedures, and policies (Feagin 1977). This measure shifts the source of discrimination from a bigoted individual to the social structure that is created and maintained by the dominant ethnicity. In the United States, institutionalized discrimination favors whites over others.

Race Theories

As in the case of gender inequality, there have been various attempts to explain race inequality, from biological to cultural to structural. In answering the question of why racial inequality exists, theories look to a range of determinants: biological theories look to the individual; cultural theories look to the behaviors of a group of people; and structural theories look to the superstructure in society, which is how people interact with the material form of society determined by power relations. Each group of theories helps scientists form and test hypotheses that, in turn, help build knowledge. There is no simple reason why racial inequality exists other than the answer that many factors contribute to its origination and maintenance.

Biological Theories

Biological theories argue that those who are at the bottom of the socioeconomic status hierarchy are there because they have low intelligence, which is genetically based. According to this logic, racial groups vary in intelligence because they have different genetic compositions. Because, it is asserted, a large portion of intelligence is genetically based, nothing can be done to improve their lot in life. Considering these biological theories, sociologists are eager to show that race is largely a political and cultural rather than biological construction. A distribution of abilities certainly exists, but race does not explain how the distribution is configured.

   The biological theories have been challenged seriously, yet they have a certain meaning and interpretation in society. Many believe that race is essential – that it is biologically real and defining - and some believe that one race is superior to others. *Racism* – that is, stereotypes and prejudices related to race – are grounded in biological theory. A subset of biological theory is the culture-of-poverty thesis (see Chapter 7). Rather than focusing on biological determinants, those who draw on this thesis draw on the behaviors and ideologies of the poor – many of whom are people of color.

Caste Analysis of Race Relations

In opposition to biological and cultural theories, sociologists often discuss racial inequality as a result of social structure. One structural theory uses *caste analysis*. Recall that a caste structure is an extreme form of status inequality in that relationships between groups involved are said to be fixed and supported by ideology and law. Membership in a particular caste is hereditary, mobility is virtually impossible, marriage outside of one's caste is prohibited, and occupation is strongly related to caste position. A 1944 study of white/black relations in the United States, undertaken by a Swedish economist who was considered unbiased, found that race relations between blacks and whites indeed comprised a caste system (Myrdal [1944]1962). Furthermore, the caste system is inconsistent with the characteristics of democracy. Americans share in the "American Creed," which fosters the values of equality, justice, liberty, and fair treatment for all. Caste systems are closed – that is, there is no mobility between groups – and in direct opposition to democratic values. The caste model continued to be used in recent times but a more complex system has developed. Caste analysis remains; however, class positions within each caste have become more elaborate and significant (Van den Berghe 1967). Indeed, caste analysis generally has been replaced by class-based theories.

Class-Based Explanations

Continuing the discussion of the caste model, some sociologists argue that the structural, cultural, and historical contexts in India, a definitive caste society, were different from those characterizing U.S. black/white relations. For instance, race relations and racism are relatively recent, do not typically involve narrow occupational restrictions, and are rooted in political-class conflict and capitalism. Rather than a caste argument, they view inequality in America as a product of *economic exploitation*. Racism as an ideology is not the tool of exploitation; rather, racism follows from and is used to justify economic exploitation (Cox 1948). These theories are also known as *domination theories*.

Various specific theories are included in the general category of domination theories, but all of them incorporate the historically crucial role of power and/or domination in shaping racial inequality. They neither anticipate the eventual and automatic assimilation of minorities nor emphasize the stability of the system or complicity of the minority group, as is often suggested in caste analysis. Three approaches are (1) Noel's theory of ethnic stratification, (2) imperialist/colonial explanations, and (3) normative race theory of racial inequality.

Domination Theory: Noel's Theory of Ethnic Stratification

According to sociologist Donald N. Noel, ethnic stratification is a system of stratification wherein a relatively fixed group membership (e.g., race, religion, or nationality) is used as a major criterion for assigning social positions with associated differential rewards (Noel 1968). For this system of ethnic stratification to develop, several conditions must be met. First, there must be prolonged *contact* between groups. Second, *ethnocentrism* – the belief that one's culture is the best – must be present, which fosters *in-group/out-group* ideologies. When a social situation is viewed as "us versus them," the out-group is always found to be lacking. Third, there must be *competition* – interaction between groups who are trying to attain the same scarce goal; the more intense the competition, the greater is the likelihood of stratification. Fourth, there must be *differential power*: One group must have the ability to impose its will on another. When the greater power of one group is established, the more powerful group develops measures to subordinate and regulate the other group and to stabilize the current distribution of differential rewards.

Internal Colonialism

This approach to understanding the domination of blacks by whites is based on analyses of the relationships between colonizing countries in the First World and those that have been colonized in the Third World. A noted difference between classic colonial and internal-colonial relationships is that the former generally involve groups from one country invading and dominating those of another country while, in the latter case, both groups are from and occupy the same country. However, it can be stated that the character of the relationship defines whether it is colonial, not the factor of geography. Blacks in the United States stand as colonial subjects relative to white society in three arenas: political, economic, and social (Carmichael and Hamilton 1967). Politically, although blacks are technically as free as whites, whites dominate the power structure, holding the most influential positions. Economically, blacks are more likely to be poor and unemployed and to pay exorbitant prices for shoddy goods. Socially, blacks are demeaned in daily contact with whites. Racial ideologies that argue for their basic inferiority and present negative stereotypes help to justify and maintain control over blacks.

The colonization complex consists of the following six basic characteristics: (1) the dominant-subordinate relationship begins with forced, involuntary entry; (2) the indigenous culture and social organization of the dominated group are altered, manipulated, or destroyed; (3) representatives of the dominant group control the subordinate group through legal and governmental institutions; (4) racism as an ideology is used to justify the oppression of the subordinate group; (5) the colonizers and colonized occupy different positions in the labor structure and perform different roles; and (6) colonized individuals can move up in class but cannot change their colonized position except through successful revolutionary movements that transform the structure of society (Blauner 1972).

A *normative race theory* asserts that the dominant race is the norm. This means that in a nation in which whites are the dominant race, any other racial category is anomalous. We can think of the dominant race, then, as the default category. As many have pointed out, it is rare that a person is challenged in ability due to being white. For example, during the 2008 presidential campaign, some asked if Barack Obama – who is considered black although he comes from a biracial family – was competent. Newspaper headlines questioned Obama's electability, qualifications, and whether he could expect the full support of other blacks. We never read the same of Joe Biden, for example, a white candidate; newspapers did not question whether he was "too white" to win. Moreover, pundits questioned how well Obama could capture the black vote – but how often do they ask whether a white candidate could capture the white vote? White is the norm and black is simplified as a monolithic group with no individual differentiation.

How does a normative race perspective affect society? By attributing one race with the status of "normal," all other races or groups of ethnicities are considered not normal; by default, they are abnormal. This has dire effects on the minority group, including a decrease in self-worth. In a series of experiments between 1947 and 2006, black girls were asked to select one of two dolls: one doll was white-skinned and the other was black-skinned. In the majority of cases, the girls chose the white doll because they were "prettier" (Clark and Clark 1950). Subsequent replications reproduced similar results with other ethnicities and found that children of a subordinate race tend to identify with the dominant race (Morland 1969). Despite a re-creation of the classic doll experiment by a TV station (although not scientific and perhaps suffering from bias selection) showing that the opposite is true (i.e., black girls chose black dolls), scholars found that even within the black community, "white" features (i.e., straight hair and light skin) are desirable (Keith and Herring 1991; Wade 2008).

Beauty standards are one way that a dominant class subordinates other classes. As discussed in Chapter 12, media images in particular help to create acceptable social arrangements. If – as was the case in the 1950s – the faces in the media are predominantly white, nonwhites are perceived as not belonging. This arrangement is accepted by both the dominant class and the subordinates, which maintains social-class configurations.

Future of Race/Ethnic Relations

What is the future of race/ethnic relations in America? Some scholars argue that the role of race is declining in American society (Wilson 1978). According to this perspective, the race theories outlined herein all contribute to how race and ethnicity are viewed and experienced in America throughout history. The role of race is declining when we view race relations as having progressed through three historical stages, the first being the plantation economy. Because blacks were purchased as slaves by white Southern landowners, they had no legal rights and, in fact, were property. This defined the relationship as *racial caste oppression*, and the spatial distance between whites and blacks was great.

The second stage of race relationships occurred in the New Deal era and the mass expansion of U.S. industry. Blacks left the South during the Great Northern Migration to take jobs in the growing manufacturing sector in Northern cities. According to *class-exploitation theory*, the introduction of blacks often pitted workers against one another, causing a *split-labor market* – in which owners created competition between two segments of workers for profit. Whites who had worked in the industrialized North were often replaced by blacks who were in need of work. The capitalists – industry owners – displaced the more expensive workers to cut production costs. The conditions of rural Southern blacks had been so poor that they were more likely to accept lower wages and work longer hours to obtain employment. This caused antagonism between blacks and whites as the spatial relationship between the two groups shifted and they now were much closer (Bonacich 1972). This prompted the owners to use the lower-paid labor to undercut the collective action of the higher-paid workers. In fact, white owners used black workers to strike-break and hedge against white workers' collective actions; subsequently, whites monopolized occupational markets and refused union entrance to blacks. While unions have traditionally been viewed as benefiting all workers, in the U.S. unions helped reinforce racial tension between groups of workers.

Some social scientists focus exclusively on the relationship between workers at that time. Racial *competition theory* views the root of racial antagonism as exclusively in the relationship between workers. They argue that threat is proportional to the rising numbers of ethnic or racial minorities, which causes white (or the dominant) middle class to fear that their own resources will be at stake if no action is taken to monopolize them.

Both theories, *class exploitation* and *competition theory*, argue for a similar process, that a higher rate of minorities activates an underlying fear that resources will be redistributed, with the loss being felt by the dominant groups as minorities make gains. The theories differ in who benefits from the antagonism.

Blacks were discriminated against, but during the second stage of race relations in the United States, they collectively gained power through the shift in industry: Demand for workers prompted more access to employment for minorities. Furthermore, from this development, the black middle class took shape. In tandem with the rise of the black middle class was the rise of the urban poor. Blacks had gained enough collective power to create parties aimed at decreasing racial inequalities, such as the National Association for the Advancement of Colored People (NAACP), and helped formulate the Pan-African movement. They changed the laws restricting equal access to education and helped African nations shed the oppressive hold of colonists and to become independent nations by revolting. However, the black middle class did not have enough power to stop the plight of the urban poor in the United States. The second stage is where racial oppression shifted into class oppression.

The third stage in the development of U.S. race relations is progressing from ethnic oppression to *class oppression* as caused by the "ghettoization" of urban centers. Where once great manufacturing industries provided opportunity for low- and no-skilled workers, the shift in the economy and in technology saw industry leave the United States and relocate abroad. Manufacturing is no longer the primary industry in the United States, and small businesses did not remain in center cities; instead, like the black (and white) middle class, they moved to the suburbs. This left cities with a growing number of jobless people (especially men), families with single-mother head of households, high levels of crime, and other social problems not experienced in the suburbs. This division of the middle class and the poor in the black community is class-based and cannot be attributed to race. There is a growing black middle class imbued with power.

Persistence of Racial Inequality

Other social scientists reject the theory that the role of race is declining in significance. Using the wages of black and white workers to measure equality between 1976 and 1985, sociologists found no decrease in the gap – whites still earned more than blacks (Cancio, Evans, and Maume, Jr. 1996). They attribute the 1980s decline to the weakening of *affirmative action*. In elite studies – that is, research devoted to understanding the elite class – there is ample evidence showing that the corporate community is a homogeneous group: white, male, and Protestant (Domhoff 2002). Furthermore, there are great disparities in black/white wealth accumulation (Oliver and Shapiro 1995; [1995]2006). When comparing blacks and whites and controlling for common characteristics such as occupational status and income, there is a gap of $42,000 between whites and blacks in terms of homeownership and assets. Blacks are less likely to obtain a mortgage; if they do, they pay higher interest rates than comparable whites. In addition, these differences cost the contemporary black community $83 billion. These costs result, in part, from higher interest rates, lower home values, higher levels of foreclosures and the number of subprime loans within the black community. If treated on par with whites, blacks on whole would own much more wealth than what is currently held.

Race still matters in poignant ways. Segregated neighborhoods add to the negative effect of being black (Massey and Denton 1988). Scientists rate areas according to the amount of dissimilarity in ethnicity/race. On a scale of zero, where there is no segregation, to 100, where there is complete segregation, 80 percent of America's largest cities score more than 50 percent. In other words, the majority of large cities are segregated. According to the 2000 Census, the top five cities in racial segregation (between black and white residents) were Detroit (84.72 percent); Gary, Indiana (84.14 percent); Milwaukee-Waukesha, Wisconsin (82.16 percent); New York City (81.82 percent); and Chicago (80.85 percent) (Quinn and Pawasarat 2003). In each city, people of differing ethnic groups are physically separated, despite the Civil Rights Act of 1968, which aimed to reduce segregation and discrimination. High levels of dissimilarity are known as *hyper-segregation* and *American Apartheid*.

Compounding the disadvantages brought about by residential segregation is the way that schools are funded through property tax in the United States. Neighborhoods with high levels of poverty – which blacks and Hispanics are more likely to occupy compared to whites – have lower levels of tax revenue; therefore, schools have fewer funds. Indeed, students who attend a segregated black school score lower in achievement whereas students who attend a segregated white school score higher (Roscigno 1998).

Racial inequality also is shown to exist in what is termed the *medicalization of race*. Using race as a biological concept – despite evidence showing that it is not reliable – requires the acceptance of two assumptions (both of which have been disproved): (1) genetic variation explains variation in disease, and (2) genetic variation explains racial variation in disease (Goodman 2000). Sociologists have long been aware that variations in disease can be accounted for by environment and behavior, which are social factors of health. Also, there is no evidence that diseases are racially determined, only that ethnicity may account for some variations in environment. However, some biologists and medical professionals are adamant that racial categorizations are useful in defining health risks in individuals (Risch et al. 2002).

The former president of the American Sociological Association, Troy Duster, conducted considerable research regarding how race is used in societies and found that racial classifications and the medicalization of race are divisive ideologies that serve particular groups. For instance, despite the minor level of genetics associated with ancestry, the National Institutes of Health (NIH) began research on pharmacogenetics in 2000 – exploiting the fraction of the 0.01 percent difference between people to benefit the pharmaceutical industry (Fullwiley 2007). Moreover, a note of caution is required when making race essential: Before the Civil Rights Era, this was the line of reasoning that perceived blacks as different and therefore "less than" whites.

Biologists have long argued that racial variations are due to environment and are not inherent differences in people. For instance, sickle cell anemia is a disease often thought to occur only in blacks. The NIH reports that sickle cell anemia affects millions of people worldwide and it is not racially determined – it is due to a recessive gene that provides immunity to malaria. Any group with ancestry in malaria-prone areas is at risk of contracting the disease. It is most common in groups whose ancestors are from Africa, South or Central America (especially Panama), the Caribbean Islands, Mediterranean countries (e.g., Turkey, Greece, and Italy), India, and Saudi Arabia. In the United States, approximately 1 in 500 African Americans and 1 in 36,000 Hispanics are born with sickle cell anemia (NIH 2009).

Access to health care is another resource that is distributed unequally across race/ethnic groups. Compared to people of color, whites are more likely to have health insurance. In 2008, the uninsured rate and number of uninsured for non-Hispanic whites increased from 10.4 percent and 20.5 million in 2007 to 10.8 percent and 21.3 million. For blacks in 2008, the rate and number were not statistically different from 2007, at 19.1 percent and 7.3 million. For Asians in 2008, the uninsured rate of 17.6 percent was not statistically different from 2007. The rate of uninsured Hispanics decreased to 30.7 percent in 2008, from 32.1 percent in 2007. The number of uninsured Hispanics was not statistically different in 2008, at 14.6 million. Based on a three-year average (i.e., 2006–2008), 31.7 percent of people who reported American Indian and Alaska Native as their race were without coverage. The uninsured three-year average rate for Native Hawaiians and Other Pacific Islanders was 18.5 percent (U.S. Census Bureau 2009).

Recall that persistent segregation and discrimination influence various arenas in life, including housing opportunities. Residential segregation is a form of discrimination that still persists today. In one study between 1999 and 2002, sociologists used different speech patterns to measure racial inequality in accessing rental housing in Philadelphia. Female and male auditors telephoned listings to ask about the availability of units using white middle-class English, black-accented English, and black English vernacular. Whites were more likely to be favored over blacks of the same gender when the auditor spoke black English vernacular. Housing access was lower in the suburbs compared with the central city (Fischer and Massey 2004).

Conclusion

Throughout the history of America, race has played an integral role in social relations. Today, race relations are complex because divisions among groups are less defined but linger in the practices of racism and segregation. Social policies attempt to address the conflict among ethnic groups but – although there have been successes such as the repeal of Jim Crow laws and the passing of the Civil Rights Act – there is still evidence that race has an important role in the unequal distribution of resources.

Although sociologists debate whether the role of race is declining in significance, they continue to reveal evidence that race is one ascriptive status that affects the allocation of resources. America has a long and tumultuous history of race relations due to the differential treatment of various ethnic groups by whites. Even today, all nonwhite ethnic groups (except for some Asians) are more likely to be in or live near families who are in poverty; have higher rates of crime in their neighborhoods; and are less likely to own a home, graduate from college, and obtain a good job. Despite evidence that race/ethnicity is not biological, it continues to affect the life chances of minority individuals.

Summary

(1) Race and ethnicity are dimensions of stratification that lead to differential life outcomes and therefore are important to study.

(2) Race and ethnicity are important factors in the distribution of valuable resources such as economic and political positions, income, housing, and wealth.

(3) Race is not essential, meaning that it is a social construction.

(4) Biologists recently found that people are more similar than they are different. Genetic research shows that all people are about 99.9 percent genetically similar and no group has one single genetic marker found in all group members. Humans have no subspecies.

(5) Sociologists prefer the term *ethnicity* to denote groups with a common heritage or shared cultural traits.

(6) Racial differentiation causes power differentials among groups. The amount of power found in a group is often the result of migration. Groups who have power in their country of nativity often have power in the host country.

(7) Power can be shared in a pluralist perspective, shown in the concept of multiculturalism, or is granted to the dominant group using an assimilation perspective, shown in the melting-pot metaphor.

(8) In the United States, race has been pivotal in the allocation of resources: Whites are privileged whereas people of color often are denied access.

(9) The racial categorization of groups has resulted in racism, discrimination, stereotypes, and even genocide. Five general ethnic categories are found in the United States: whites, Hispanics, blacks, Asians, and American Indians. American Indians now constitute less than 1 percent of the population. Today, whites are the majority and, although *Hispanic* is not a racial term, the number of people who identify as Hispanic and Asian are increasing; it is projected that by 2050, whites will become a minority.

(10) There is a race/ethnicity hierarchy in the United States that consists of three tiers. The first is white European Americans, many of whom are Protestants; the second is other European Americans and Asians; and the third is African Americans, Hispanics, Native Americans, and some Asians. The first and second tiers are least affected by race/ethnicity; however, groups in the third tier are most likely to suffer from the inability to access scarce societal resources.

(11) Segregation and discrimination are features of American society. From the early colonial days until recently, nonwhite groups have been separated from whites and denied access to education, housing, the right to protest, marriage, jobs, and many other resources.

(12) Many theories, ranging from biological to cultural to structural, are used to understand why race matters. Most sociologists refute biological theories and many consider cultural theories to blame the victim. Although personal choice has a decidedly important role in the outcome of a person's life chances, structural obstacles exist. Theories used to explain the power differential of race hierarchy include caste analysis, class-based and domination theories, internal colonization, and normative-race theory. Whereas some scholars argue that race/ethnicity is declining in significance, racial stratification still affects how resources are distributed unequally.

Box 11.1 Is the Significance of Race Actually Declining?

William Julius Wilson argued that race is declining in significance in America. To support his assertion, he used a historical analysis. From the point of view of slavery, we cannot argue with the assertion – indeed, race has less significance today compared with the 1800s. However, Wilson's final claim, that racial tensions have been replaced with class division, is arguable.

In Wilson's third stage (i.e., post-World War II), class divisions replaced racial divides. Indeed, a growing chasm existed between middle-class blacks and those concentrated in hyper-ghettos and living in poverty. Housing policies that favored whites in the development of the suburbs discriminated against people of color. As whites moved into suburbs, the black middle class also developed housing areas that separated them from blacks living in poverty. Even today, middle-class blacks are more likely than white families to live near a family in poverty (Oliver and Shapiro [1995]2006).

The current economic crisis has hurt more black than white families. Whites have higher employment rates than blacks and Hispanics (of any race); however, despite the fact that the white unemployment rate increased more than the black unemployment rate between 2007 and 2009, whites are still more likely to be employed. Hispanics are over-represented in occupations with high unemployment rates. Almost half of blacks and Hispanics (46 and 49 percent, respectively) report that they have trouble finding a good job or getting a raise compared to whites (32 percent). Twice as many blacks and Hispanics (43 and 46 percent, respectively) report having difficulty affording daily necessities such as buying food and paying for day care compared to whites (22 percent). One in four blacks (25 percent), one in five Hispanics (21 percent), and one in ten whites (10 percent) have lost health care due to the economic recession (Berndt and James 2009).

Race/ethnic inequality, although less than 300 years ago, still has an important part in the stratification of America. If we are to believe Wilson's claim that race has declined in significance, then certainly racial categories would be considered fluid and not essential. However, in 1982, Susie Guillory Phipps sued the Louisiana Bureau of Vital Records to have her racial classification changed from black to white. She was classified as black on her Louisiana birth certificate by a 1970 state law that declared anyone with at least 1/32 "negro blood" [sic] to be black. Notice that it does not matter if the other 31 parts are white – it only takes *one drop of black blood*. This was referred to as the "One-Drop Rule" and was an integral component of the Jim Crow laws. Poet Langston Hughes wrote a poem entitled *That One Powerful Drop* about the power of racial classification based on the rating of blood as "unpure" if not 100 percent white. Ms. Phipps's lawsuit was unsuccessful and she is still classified as black despite her identification as white.

How does race/ethnicity matter in your life? Do students sit together at lunch or are groups segregated by race/ethnicity? Do you find particular ethnic groups concentrated within subject areas, fraternities, and off-campus activities? What does this mean to you in terms of Wilson's hypothesis? More important, where do you think race/ethnicity relations are heading in your community?

Box 11.2 Housing, the Case of White Privilege and Government Support

Throughout America's history, the dominant classes set the tone for laws, policies, and regulations. Since colonization, this means that whites have written the rules that all people must follow. Since the 1930s, policies aimed at assisting average Americans have favored whites and often excluded people of color.

The elderly was one group disproportionately affected by the Great Depression. In response, the Social Security Act was passed in 1935. This safety net was aimed at workers who had no savings and often were left in dire straits when they retired. By paying into Social Security throughout the time spent in the workforce, the elderly were guaranteed at least a modest income at retirement. However, the Act excluded agricultural workers and domestic servants, occupations

Box 11.2 (*continued*)

staffed primarily by African Americans, Asians, and Hispanics. These occupations paid poorly, had no pensions, and demanded intense labor, placing workers at the highest risk for poverty after retirement. By excluding these occupations, the Social Security Act privileged whites while it exempted many people of color.

The government subsidized low-cost loans starting in the 1930s, which enabled average Americans to purchase homes, providing a safety net for families as well as the most significant component of the American Dream, one's own home. At this time, however, the government also introduced a national appraisal system that included race as one measure of risk. All-white communities were considered lower in risk than other communities and received low-cost loans from which whites benefited. Nonwhite neighborhoods were appraised as higher risk, resulting in higher interest rates and fewer loans written. Between 1934 and 1962, the government subsidized more than $120 billion in new housing, of which more than 98 percent went to white families.

Urban-renewal projects of the 1940s, run by the government, destroyed 90 percent of housing that was never to be replaced. More than two-thirds of the residents displaced by the projects were Hispanics and blacks. As housing in urban areas decreased, so did revenue from taxes, which had a negative impact on social services allocated by regional revenues. The result was "white flight." The economic housing boom of the 1950s created the suburbs. Whites could move to the newly created suburbs, where taxes provided good schools and social services, but people of color could not. Moreover, jobs and shopping centers also relocated to the suburbs, leaving urban areas blighted.

The Fair Housing Act of the 1960s attempted to amend the racial segregation found in housing. However, the Act had little impact until its amendment in 1988. There are still serious inequalities in housing in America. How does racial inequality affect where you live? Are there areas where only certain groups live? Are there racial differences comparing areas by homeownership and rental properties? What accounts for these differences?

Source: PBS, 2003. *Race: The Power of an Illusion*. California Newsreel. *Where Race Lives: Uncle Sam Lends a Hand*.

Key Concepts

Affirmative action	Medicalization of race
Assimilation perspective	Minority
Caste analysis	Miscegenation
Caucasian, Mongoloid, and Negroid	Model minority
Civil Rights Act of 1968	Multiculturalism
Class-exploitation theory	Noel's Theory of Ethnic Stratification
Class oppression	Normative Race Theory
Competition theory	Pluralism
Core group/charter group	Race
Differential power	Racial caste oppression
Discrimination, pure/statistical/	Racial differentiation
institutionalized	Racial profiling
Domination theories	Racism
Ethnicity	Residential segregation
Ethnocentrism	Segregation
Genocide	Split-labor market
Heterogeneous	Stereotypes
Hyper-segregation	Voluntary and involuntary migration
In-group/out-group	White privilege

Questions for Thought

1. Explain the difference between race and ethnicity. In your answer, discuss why race continues to be a significant characteristic in American ideology.
2. Review the three tiers of racial hierarchy. How can European whites be in both the first and second tier? What does this say about being white in America?
3. Discuss how the increase in the number of people who identify as Hispanic and Asian affects white privilege. In your answer, reflect on how white privilege was obtained.
4. Do you agree that race is declining in significance? Why or why not?

Exercises

1. Using a map of your city or town, draw borders around neighborhoods and then estimate their racial composition in percentages. Use the U.S. Census Fact Finder to check your estimates.
2. Make a list of 10 famous celebrities. Compare the lists with those of your classmates. Are there notable racial patterns to celebrity status? Are the people on the list easily identifiable in terms of race? Why or why not?
3. Locate the history of race laws in your state. When were the laws created? Were they dismantled? If so, why and by whom?

Multimedia Resources

Print

Bobo, Lawrence, and James R. Kluegel. 1993. "Opposition to Race-Targeting: Self-Interest, Stratification Ideology, or Racial Attitudes?" *American Sociological Review* 58: 443–64.

Calavita, Kitty. 1992. *Inside the State: The Bracero Program, Immigration, and the I.N.S. (After the Law)*. New York: Routledge.

Cancio, A. Silvia, T. David Evans, and David J. Maume, Jr. 1996. "Reconsidering the Declining Significance of Race: Racial Differences in Early Career Wages." *American Sociological Review* 61: 541–56.

Duster, Troy. 2003. *Backdoor to Eugenics*. New York: Routledge.

Haley, Alex. 1976. *Roots: The Saga of an American Family*. New York: Vanguard Press.

Ichioka, Yuji, and Eiichiro Azuma. 1999. *A Buried Past II: A Sequel to the Annotated Bibliography of the Japanese American Research Project Collection*. Los Angeles: University of California Los Angeles, Asian American Studies Center.

Keister, Lisa A. 2000. "Race and Wealth Inequality: The Impact of Racial Differences in Asset Ownership on the Distribution of Household Wealth." *Social Science Research* 29: 477–502.

Lareau, Annette. 2003. *Unequal Childhoods: Class, Race, and Family Life*. Berkeley: University of California Press.

Lieberman, Leonard. 1968. "The Debate over Race: A Study in the Sociology of Knowledge." *Phylon (1960)*: 127–41.

Murata, Kiyoaki. 1991. *An Enemy Among Friends*. Ann Arbor, MI: Kodansha International.

Oliver, Melvin L., and Thomas M. Shapiro. 1989. "Race and Wealth." *Review of Black Political Economy* 17: 5–25.

Robinson, Greg. 2001. *By Order of the President: FDR and the Internment of Japanese Americans*. New York: Harvard University Press.

Wilson, William J. 1978. *The Declining Significance of Race*. Chicago: University of Chicago Press.
———. 1997. *When Work Disappears: The World of the New Urban Poor*. New York:Vintage.
Zuberi, Tukufu. 2000. "Deracializing Social Statistics: Problems in the Quantification of Race." *Annals of the American Academy of Political and Social Science* 568: 172–85.

Internet

www.PBS.org/race. This site is interactive and surveys racial categorization of America.

http://www.cnn.com/SPECIALS/2009/black.in.america/: "Black in America I" and "Black in America II," by Soledad O'Brien.

http://www.cnn.com/SPECIALS/2007/hispanic.heritage/: "The Complicated Measure of Being Hispanic in America."

http://www.understandingrace.org/history/: "American Anthropological Association reviews race in America."

http://americanhistory.si.edu/ONTHEMOVE/themes/story_51_5.html: "America on the Move – Opportunity or Exploitation: The Bracero Program."

http://www.farmworkers.org/Welcome.html: The Farm Workers' Web site informative link to the Bracero Project.

http://www.calisphere.universityofcalifornia.edu/themed_collections/subtopic5c.html: Pictures of Braceros.

Films

Race to Execution by Rachel Lyon, Co-Producers Jim Lopes and Rachel Lyon. Available at www.racetoexecution.com/. *Race to Execution* examines the relationship between race and capital punishment in the United States. It combines scholarship with anecdotal evidence by following two Death Row inmates – one in Illinois and another in Alabama – through the criminal-justice system.

Children of the Camps. Available at www.children-of-the-camps.org/.

This documentary examines six Japanese American children who were interned during World War II.

The Adventures of Huckleberry Finn (1939/New York: Continuum, 1989). This interpretation of the classic novel evidences the representations of African Americans in America. Terms are used that today are considered inappropriate (e.g., Toms, Coons, Mulattoes, Mammies, and Bucks).

Amistad (1998, Directed by Steven Spielberg.) A full-length feature film of the slave revolt of 1839 on a ship bound for America from Africa.

Roots: The Saga of an American Family. The film version of Alex Haley's book tells of his search to find his family history that was stripped through the institution of slavery.

Eyes on the Prize. Available at www.pbs.org/wgbh/amex/eyesontheprize/. This film is a 14-hour documentary on America's Civil Rights Movement. It covers the majority of protests and actions taken by blacks but also includes the struggles of Hispanics and Asians.

Works Cited

Allen, Theodor W. 1997. *The Invention of the White Race*: Verso.
Bean, Frank D., and Jennifer Lee. 2009. "Plus ca Change…? Multiraciality and the Dynamics of Race Relations in the United States." *Journal of Social Issues* 65: 205–19.

Berndt, Julia, and Cara James. 2009. "Race, Ethnicity, & Health Care: The Effects of the Economic Recession on Communities of Color." Menlo Park, CA: The Henry J. Kaiser Family Foundation.

Blauner, Bob. 1972. *Racial Oppression in America*. New York: Harper.

Blumer, Herbert. 1958. "Race Prejudice as a Sense of Group Position." *The Pacific Sociological Review* 1: 3–7.

Bonacich, Edna. 1972. "A Theory of Ethnic Antagonism: The Split-Labor Market." *American Sociological Review* 37: 547–59.

Cancio, A. Sylvia, T. David Evans, and David J. Maume, Jr. 1996. "Reconsidering the Declining Significance of Race: Racial Differences in Early Career Wages." *American Sociological Review* 61: 541–56.

Carmichael, Stokely, and Charles Hamilton. 1967. *Black Power: The Politics of Liberation in America*. New York: Vintage.

Clark, Kennith B., and Mamie P. Clark. 1950. "Emotional Factors in Racial Identification and Preference in Negro Children." *The Journal of Negro Education* 19: 341–50.

Cox, Oliver C. 1948. "Caste, Class and Race." *Phylon (1940–1956)* 9: 171–2.

Domhoff, G. William. 2002. *Who Rules America? Power and Politics, Fourth Edition*. New York: McGraw Hill.

Eisenberg, Avigail, and Jeff Spinner-Halev. 2005. *Minorities within Minorities: Equality, Rights and Diversity*. New York: Cambridge University Press.

Feagin, Joe R. 1977. "Indirect Institutionalized Discrimination." *American Politics Quarterly* 5: 177–200.

Feagin, Joe R., and Clairece Booher Feagin. 1989. *Racial and Ethnic Relations*. Upper Saddle River, NJ: Prentice Hall.

Feldman, Marcus W., and Richard C. Lewontin. 2008. "Race, Ancestry, and Medicine." In *Revisiting Race in a Genomic Age* (Pp 89-101), edited by B. A. Koenig, S. S.-J. Lee, and S. Richardson. New Brunswick, NJ: Rutgers University Press.

Fischer, Mary J., and Douglas S. Massey 2004. "The Ecology of Racial Discrimination." *City & Community* 3: 221–41.

Fisher, Philip A., Jan G. Bacon, and Michael Storck. 1998. "Teacher, Parent, and Youth Report of Problem Behaviors Among Rural American Indian and Caucasian Adolescents." In *American Indian and Alaska Native Mental Health Research*, vol. 8. Denver, CO: The Journal of the National Center.

Fullwiley, Duana. 2007. "Race and Genetics: Attempts to Define the Relationship." *BioSocieties* 2: 221–37.

Goodman, Alan H. 2000. "Why Genes Don't Count (for Racial Differences in Health)." 90: 1699–702.

Haller, John S., Jr. 1971. *Outcasts from Evolution: Scientific Attitudes of Racial Inferiority, 1859–1900*. Carbondale: Southern Illinois University Press.

Higginbotham, A. Leon, and Barbara Kopytoff. 1989. "Racial Purity and Interracial Sex in the Law of Colonial and Antebellum Virginia." *Georgetown Law Journal* 77: 81–139.

Hooks, Gregory, and Chad L. Smith. 2004. "The Treadmill of Destruction: National Sacrifice Areas and Native Americans." *American Sociological Review* 69: 558–75.

Hwang, Sean-Shong, Kevin M. Fitzpatrick, and David Helms. 1998. "Class Differences in Racial Attitudes: A Divided Black America." *Sociological Perspectives* 41: 367–80.

Keith, Verna M., and Cedric Herring. 1991. "Skin Tone and Stratification in the Black Community." *The American Journal of Sociology* 97: 760–78.

Lieberman, Leonard. 1968. "The Debate over Race: A Study in the Sociology of Knowledge." *Phylon (1960)*: 127–41.

Massey, Douglas S., and Nancy A. Denton. 1988. "The Dimensions of Residential Segregation."
Social Forces 67: 281–315.

Morland, J. Kenneth. 1969. "Race Awareness Among American and Hong Kong Chinese Children."
The American Journal of Sociology 75: 360–74.

Myrdal, Gunnar. [1944]1962. "An American Dilemma: The Negro Problem and Modern
Democracy." *Race and Class* 4: 3–11.

National Institutes of Health. 2009. "Who Is At Risk for Sickle Cell Anemia?" Washington, DC:
U.S. Department of Health and Human Services.

Noel, Donald L. 1968. "A Theory of the Origin of Ethnic Stratification." *Social Problems* 16:
157–72.

Ogbu, John. 2003. *Black American Students in an Affluent Suburb: A Study of Academic Disengagement.* Mahwah, NJ: Laurence Erlbaum Associates.

Oliver, Melvin L., and Thomas M. Shapiro. 1995. *Black Wealth/White Wealth: A New Perspective
on Racial Inequality.* New York: Routledge.

_____. [1995]2006. *Black Wealth/ White Wealth: A New Perspective on Racial Inequality.* New
York: Routledge.

Pattillo-McCoy, Mary. 1999. *Black Picket Fences: Privilege and Peril among the Black Middle
Class.* Chicago: University of Chicago Press.

Portes, Alejandro, and Robert D. Manning. 2005. "The Immigrant Enclave: Theory and Empirical
Examples." *The Urban Sociology Reader* 38: 583–94.

Portes, Alejandro, and Min Zhou. 1993. "The New Second Generation: Segmented Assimilation and Its Variants." *Annals of the American Academy of Political and Social Science* 530:
74–96.

Pratt, Robert A. 1998. "Crossing the Color Line: A Historical Assessment and Personal Narrative of
Loving v. Virginia." *Howard Law Journal* 41: 229–501.

Quinn, Lois M., and John Pawasarat. 2003. "Racial Integration in Urban America: A Block-
Level Analysis of African American and White Housing Patterns." Milwaukee: University of
Wisconsin-Milwaukee.

Risch, Neil, Esteban Burchard, Elad Ziv, and Hua Tang. 2002. "Categorization of Humans in
Biomedical Research: Genes, Race and Disease." *Genome Biology* 3(7):1-12.

Rockquemore, Kerry Ann, David L. Brunsma, and Daniel J. Delgado. 2009. "Racing to Theory or
Retheorizing Race? Understanding the Struggle to Build a Multiracial Identity Theory." *Journal
of Social Issues* 65: 13–34.

Roscigno, Vincent J. 1998. "Race and the Reproduction of Educational Disadvantage." *Social
Forces* 76: 1033–60.

Saporito, Salvatore, and Deenesh Sohoni. 2006. "Coloring Outside the Lines: Racial Segregation
in Public Schools and Their Attendance Boundaries." *Sociology of Education* 79: 81–105.

Simone, Samira. 2009. "Governor Calls for Firing of Justice in Interracial Marriage Case." In *CNN
U.S.* Atlanta, GA.

Skinner, David. 2007. "Groundhog Day? The Strange Case of Sociology, Race and Science."
Sociology 41: 931.

Smedley, Audry, and Brian D. Smedley. 2005. "Race as Biology Is Fiction, Racism as a Social
Problem Is Real." *American Psychologist* 60: 16–26.

Steffensmeier, Darrell, and Stephen Demuth. 2000. "Ethnicity and Sentencing Outcomes in
U.S. Federal Courts: Who Is Punished More Harshly?" *American Sociological Review* 65:
705–29.

Twine, France W. 1998. *Racism in a Racial Democracy: The Maintenance of White-Supremacy.*
New Brunswick, NJ: Rutgers University Press.

U.S. Census Bureau. 2004. "Census Bureau Projects Tripling of Hispanic and Asian Populations in 50 Years; Non-Hispanic Whites May Drop to Half of Total Population." Washington, DC: U.S. Department of Commerce.

———. 2008a. "ACS Demographic and Housing Estimates: 2008." Washington, DC: U.S. Department of Commerce.

———. 2008b. "Racial and Ethnic Classifications Used in Census 2000 and Beyond." Washington, DC: U.S. Census Bureau.

———. 2009. "Income, Poverty and Health Insurance Coverage in the United States: 2008." Washington, DC: U.S. Department of Commerce.

———. 2011. "2005-2009 American Community Survey 5-Year Estimates." Washington, DC: U.S. Department of Commerce.

Van den Berghe, Pierre. 1967. *Race and Racism: A Comparative Perspective.* New York: John Wiley and Sons.

Wade, Peter. 1997. *Race and Ethnicity in Latin America.* London: Pluto Press.

Wade, T. Joel. 2008. "Skin-Color Biases: Attractiveness and Halo Effects in the Evaluation of African Americans." In *Racism in the 21st Century: An Empirical Analysis of Skin Color,* edited by Ronald E. Hall (Pp. 135-150). New York: Springer.

Wiegman, Robyn. 1995. *American Anatomies: Theorizing Race and Gender.* Durham, NC: Duke University Press.

Wilson, William J. 1978. *The Declining Significance of Race.* Chicago: University of Chicago Press.

12 Culture

So far, we know that groups of people are ranked according to various characteristics such as social class, gender, and race (see Chapters 4, 10, and 11, respectively) and that these distinctions often allow social scientists to predict the likelihood of particular events occurring in the groups. Groups share common behaviors, attitudes, and values as a result of a shared culture, although defining *culture* has proved problematic given the differing status memberships of individuals.

Culture consists of a nexus of complex social interactions, which are in relation to symbols, ideas, and material objects. Culture as a scientific discipline is often considered "squishy." That is, it is not as straightforward as income or wealth – constructs that are easily measured and validated through scientific scrutiny. Because of the lack of precision in measurement, culture as a sociological fact often has been underestimated. There are two reasons for this.

First, scientific subfields are socially constructed in academia (Wuthnow and Witten 1988) and are plagued with politics (including careerism); scientific fact "results from social processes of interpretation, demonstration, negotiation, and decision making rather than through correspondence with or reflection of 'nature'" (1988: 59). Fluid boundaries exist across disciplines but are sectioned off for area specialization; thus, they are made essential by those who pursue scientific endeavors. Culture as a field of study has suffered from these constructions because many different disciplines study culture in one form or another (Wolff 1999).

The second reason culture often is overlooked in sociological studies of stratification is that it is both a process and a product. This is problematic if our mission is to isolate and prove causality between distinct variables – which often is the goal of scientific inquiry. Furthering the complexity of culture is locating its origin – a paradox of "Which came first, the chicken or the egg?" Culture is produced and consumed, it is stratifying, and it aids in creating social boundaries simultaneously within a complex social system.

Recently, sociologists in areas of interest such as wealth, religion, education, gender and sex, markets, and politics have begun to disentangle the concept of culture, finding in the process a rich field within which to study the desired topic. Whereas culture is still controversial within many academic circles, to the public, it is often linked to political beliefs – that is, to power relations.

Culture is taken for granted because it is invisible and, like privilege, only noticed when it is challenged – when we face "culture shock." People generally assume that other people share a similar belief system, see the world similarly, and accept moralistic ideals of good and bad. When they do not, we are said to be in a *culture war*, a phrase that has been used since the 1800s to denote opposing beliefs among groups in a society. These differences often stem from political beliefs: the political left and the political right, the social conservative and the liberal, the religious and the secular. However, few scientists have used empirical methods to test whether it is indeed a culture that divides people or rather a contest for the allocation of power.

Culture consists of material matters, thoughts, habits, preferences, and ideology shared by a group of people. Cultural commonalities define *in-groups*, those who share in the culture, and *out-groups*, those who do not. A *dominant culture* is generally shared by members of a society and many *subcultures* exist within the dominant culture.

Subcultures may be organized around any number of ideas. Some groups share common interests but have little organization. Vegetarians, for example, typically do not lobby for any one political agenda; rather, they share a common behavior of not eating meat. Some vegetarians, however, have strong political intensions and organize accordingly (e.g., People for the Ethical Treatment of Animals [PETA]).

If a subculture is particularly posed against the dominant culture, it is known as a *counterculture*. The psychedelic movement of the 1960s is an example of a counterculture that grew in membership as well as notoriety. Headed by academics looking to expand their thoughts, work, and existence, the movement hit critical mass when Harvard professor Timothy Leary (1920–1996) told an audience to "tune in, turn on, and drop out" (Stevens 1998). The psychedelic subculture deeply affected the youth of America and galvanized much of the civil protest of the time, including resistance to the Vietnam War and the 1968 Democratic Convention in Chicago.

In addition to counterculture, some social scientists use the term *oppositional culture*. As discussed in Chapter 11, people of color generally have lower achievement scores compared to whites and Asians. Without testing for social structure or teachers' attitudes toward students, anthropologist John Ogbu interviewed black students in Shaker Heights, Ohio. He found that blacks had an oppositional culture to the dominant white educational process. Some black students would ridicule others who wanted to study and there was less academic support among the black students than Ogbu had expected (Ogbu 2003). Sociologists criticize this claim of oppositional culture for many reasons. First, Ogbu spoke only with blacks; any scientific study must include positive as well as negative cases, which means that he should have included more race/ethnicities and not spoken only to blacks. Second, many students ridicule one another for studying hard and focusing on academic endeavors; indeed, the term *geek* is synonymous with just that. Third, no tests were made to see whether the students actually held an oppositional culture – only interviews that cannot capture more precise structural measures such as teachers' attitudes toward black students, home environments, and social-background factors, all of which have been shown as important determinants of educational aspirations.

There are two forms of culture: *material* and *nonmaterial*. Nonmaterial culture consists of thoughts, preferences, habits, and distinctions of taste. Material culture may include items such as artwork, music, clothing, and food. Scientists often refer to material culture items as *cultural artifacts*.

To illustrate these concepts, consider a typical night in a recording studio in Los Angeles in 2002. It is 10:30 and the musicians and producers were hungry. They had been working on the current project for well over a week; they needed to add all the tracks for the upcoming CD before the night was through. Darby had no further obligations at the moment when Shorty B. asked if she would take one of the dancers along to pick up food from Roscoe's Chicken and Waffles in Hollywood. Of course; she loved Roscoe's despite the long drive out of the Valley to Hollywood. When they arrived at Roscoe's, there was a long queue waiting to be seated. The dancer accompanying Darby was wearing a jacket from the most recent Snoop Dog tour, which was given to her to wear for the night by Ludacris. As they approached, the host walked up to them and immediately ushered them in past the others in the queue. He asked if they would like to eat in the restaurant before heading back to the studio. They were immediately seated in a remote section of the restaurant. It was very small and tightly packed – even at the most remote table, they could be seen by the other patrons. Soon people began to whisper about the jacket – they recognized it. Some went over to the table to ask questions about the jacket, Darby, and the dancer. They quickly finished their dinner of chicken, waffles, collard greens, and cornbread and were given bags of food to go. As they left, people enthusiastically shouted, "Dog Pound" and "Woof."

To some, this behavior would be confusing. Why were the women seated before others who had been waiting in the queue? They were not celebrities. Why did people shout "Woof" at two young women, one a professional dancer in hip-hop videos? (The calls were definitely not derogatory.) Who eats chicken and waffles with cornbread and collard greens? To answer these questions, we must examine culture and its stratifying properties.

In this example at Roscoe's, the jacket worn by the dancer was a cultural artifact; that is, it conveyed information to other in-group members. In this instance, the jacket signified two successful celebrities: Snoop Dog and Ludacris. Had the two women eaten at a different restaurant, they probably would have gone unnoticed. However, at a restaurant famous for serving soul food, the patrons were very familiar with the rap artists and their clothing. The fact that the host also recognized the jacket resulted in preferential treatment: The women were treated like celebrities.

High-Brow, Low-Brow, and Omnivores

Four themes exist within the sociology of culture: production, consumption, stratification, and social-boundary making. Although sociologists generally separate these topics to study each with precision, the divisions are only rhetorical. In fact, production, consumption, and boundary making each stratify groups.

Culture is a motivating factor for many behaviors, and "culture influences action not by providing the ultimate values toward which action is oriented, but by shaping a repertoire or 'tool kit' of habits, skills, and styles from which people construct 'strategies of action'" (Swidler 1986: 273). As discussed in previous chapters, social structure configures our life. If the occupational hierarchy shifts dramatically, many workers are displaced or more may enter the workforce who had previously been denied access. Structure dictates the degrees of freedom that social actors have – that is, the number of possible actions to take. Culture dictates the strategies of action within the social structure.

Consider the distinct cultural differences between high and low socioeconomic groups (Bourdieu 1984) (see Chapter 4). Studies show that those in the upper class are generally engaged in *high-brow culture*, whereas those of more humble means engage in *low-brow culture*. Consider two live performances: the opera and a heavy-metal concert. Whereas some music lovers, known as *omnivores* (Peterson and Kern 1996), enjoy both high- and low-brow genres, operas generally are attended by those in the upper classes and heavy-metal concerts by the working class. However, not all members of the working class enjoy listening to heavy metal and rap – in fact, these genres are highly divisive due to the media's framing of them as dangerous (Bryson 1996).

What does the social exclusion of music genres mean in terms of interaction among groups? In other words, how are symbols used to create social space among people? First, people identify personally with art forms and some even develop their personal style around art forms, such as heavy metal and rap. Second, these art symbols hold meaning that is accepted as real and essential. In other words, rap means something and there is some consensus on its meaning. In the 1990s, the mass media bemoaned that rap was nefarious; does this actually mean that all rap music is immoral or wicked? No, but clearly some groups (e.g., the white media) associated rap with immorality and harm. Third, divisions in the art world may correspond with social exclusion among groups that either exist prior to the production of the art form or cause divisions among groups.

The hip-hop culture is a prime example of low-brow culture and we examine its power to create social exclusion. Economic inequality promotes the production of art (Blau, Blau, and Golden 1985) and many scholars have shown that hip hop was an extension of deindustrialization, hyper-ghettos, and racism (Southgate 2008; Spiegler 1996; Sullivan 2003). Hip hop started in the Bronx in the late 1970s as deindustrialization left urban areas devoid of opportunity, jobs, and civic services. In the 1970s, the Bronx lost 600,000 manufacturing jobs, which corresponds to a 40 percent decline in the local job market. Underground economies grew in response to economic plight; one such economy was arson. As owners lost renters who could not pay rent due to unemployment and mass layoffs, they hired local "thugs" from the neighborhood to burn down their buildings. This allowed the owner to collect insurance, which prompted New York journalists Joe Conason and Jack Newfield to write: "In housing, the final stage of capitalism is arson" (Southgate 2007: 168). In some of the forgotten properties (e.g., the old Edison Building), the electricity had not been disconnected. Artists had set up turntables and "toasted rhymes" (i.e., rapped) over "beats" created by playing previously recorded music – mostly the funk music of James Brown and Parliament/Funkadelic (Lena 2004).

A similar production process occurred on the West Coast when artist Too $hort recorded individualized rap music for colleagues in high school and subsequently sold tapes out of the trunk of his car in the late 1980s (Southgate 2008). The mainstream music industry, dominated by white males, was not interested in this new form of music (Negus 1999), which forced rap artists to develop their own means of production and distribution. It was not until the early 1990s when Too $hort earned more than $500,000 selling direct to market – without the aid of a record company – that Jive Records took interest in and subsequently signed him.

Hip hop was created by the working class; many rappers lived in abject poverty in urban areas across America. To these early pioneers, rap was a force of political resistance (Cross 1994). It also was a path of social mobility that few in the inner city had ever imagined. In 2002, at the height of the commercialization of rap (i.e., when the record majors embraced the genre), two rappers appeared in Fortune's *America's 40 Richest People Under 40*: Jay-Z, worth $286 million, and Sean Combs (a.k.a. Puff Daddy and P-Diddy), worth $315 million (Fortune 2002). Figure 12.1 compares the share of total

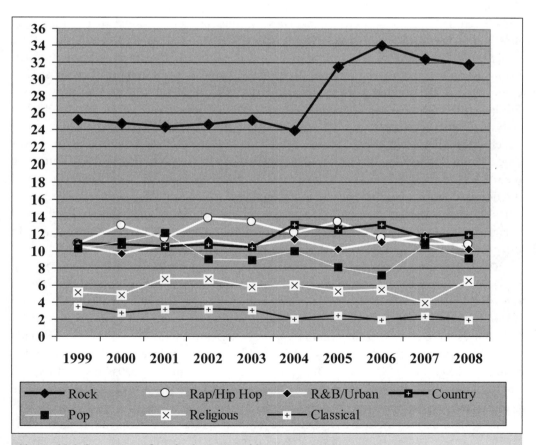

Figure 12.1 Percentage of total sales captured by genre, 1999–2008.
Data Source: Recording Industry Association of America (2009). 1999–2008 Music Consumer Profile.

sales by genre. Given the infancy of rap compared to genres with longevity (i.e., jazz, blues, and classical), it is impressive that within less than a decade, rap sales surpassed all other genres except rock.

The media's label of rap music as nefarious disregards the cultural elements of low-brow music. The media, as discussed herein, is an institution with a high concentration of ownership. The tenets of early rap music did not necessarily align with those of the corporate community. Rap producers circumvented the mainstream production process that initially had denied them access. The low-brow music of rap developed an alternative music industry that in many ways mirrored jazz and the blues industries.

Racism in the United States created segregated social spaces within art communities. Whites enjoyed listening to black music; however, black artists were not allowed to participate in what was then white social space. Black musicians could play in white-owned nightclubs, ballrooms, and theaters frequented by whites but they could not walk through the front door, eat or drink in the establishment, or sit with the audience. Despite the racial segregation of the twentieth century, black artists created their own social spaces and opportunities to perform. One network was called the *Chitlin' Circuit* (George 1988) – a collection of nightclubs, honky-tonks, theaters, and other venues considered safe for black performers. These venues became famous for debuting acts that would become top-rated celebrities in the white public domain. The Cotton Club and Apollo Theater in Harlem, New York, and the Howard Theater in Washington, DC (to name only three) allowed blacks access to a stage and an audience. The artists became part of an American music legacy including Count Basie, Cab Calloway, Duke Ellington, Dorothy Dandridge, James Brown, Aretha Franklin, Wilson Picket, and The Isley Brothers.

As rap production matured, so did a business model that was structured by previous black art production. By the 1990s, black-owned production was on the rise: There were record labels; production houses; cadres of producers and artists; and supporting staff including dancers, choreographers, and stagehands – all producing rap music. The strategies of action learned through previous racial segregation of black artists from white social spheres were applied in the 1990s and an industry was born – one that was in direct competition with the mainstream entertainment industry.

Despite the great efforts and immense success of rap music and the accompanying hip-hop culture, some consumers do not see value in this genre. Indeed, the media repeatedly uses the word *nefarious* when discussing rap. The hip-hop culture, which began in the inner city, spread to the dominant culture of America where previous social boundaries were blurred. Today, many young Americans identify with the hip-hop culture, particularly whites from the suburbs and heartland of America who consume the majority of rap music (Spiegler 1996). Moreover, a revival of the 1970s black culture has greatly impacted the dominant culture of today, bringing to the fore of youth culture the aesthetic of *ghetto chic* (Demers 2003).

The debate about whether music can be good or bad is an ethical rather than a scientific question, which conceals the deeper question: How much does music (or art in general) affect an audience? Did Elvis destroy the morals of America by dancing like the people in the 1950s honky-tonks? Perhaps not but this was a major concern of many in the public sphere.

The concern about the influence of cultural forces on society has long existed and rap is the most recent music genre under scrutiny. At the center of one heated debate in the United States is the Parents Music Resource Center (PMRC), organized by the wives of powerful men in Washington, DC: Tipper Gore (wife of Senator and later Vice President Al Gore); Susan Baker, wife of Treasury Secretary James Baker; and Nancy Thurmond, wife of Senator Strom Thurmond. According to a legal brief written by the ACLU under the Art Censorship Project (ACLU 2006), the PMRC began as a collective of fundamental religious and parental groups (e.g., the American Family Association) to "wage a persistent campaign to limit the variety of cultural messages available to American youth by attacking the content of some of the music industry's creative products" (2006: 1). The PMRC influenced the courts to prosecute artists, record companies, and store owners for distribution of obscene material.

In 1990, the PMRC won on two fronts. First, a Florida court ruled in its favor, resulting in the censorship of the band 2 Live Crew; and second, the Recording Industry Association of America (RIAA) agreed to create stickers with the logo "Parental Advisory – Explicit Lyrics" for use on rock and rap products. Again, industry personnel testified against this action on the grounds that it was a bigoted policy that impacted predominantly black artists. Artists including Frank Zappa argued that no standard was offered that defined obscenity and that the stickers were designed for placement on only two genres: rock and rap. Stickers, many argued, were not required for use on comedy, country, or opera records, even though many of their themes are as controversial as those articulated by proponents of the PMRC. This treatment was perceived in the music-production industry as uneven and racist.

Production and Consumption

Cultural sociologists are particularly interested in symbolic production and cultural consumption. Production studies generally focus on industries in which symbols are created and, subsequently, through consumption are adopted by the general public. Some industries include art, music, film, theater, and dance. Consumption patterns of art worlds (Becker 1984) also are of interest because they indicate the level of cultural dissemination. Moreover, sociologists study the mediators between production and consumption – that is, the mass media.

Cultural hegemony is a theory that explains how one social class rules over other classes within society through a monopoly of mass media and cultural production (Gramsci [1971]1990). Formulated by Italian sociologist Antonio Gramsci (1891–1937), the theory explains why Marx's revolutionary predictions did not come to fruition. By controlling the production of culture, the dominant class subordinates others by presenting inequality as natural. Moreover, the acceptance of domination is perpetrated through an *echo chamber*, a feedback loop between production and consumption.

To illustrate, have you ever listened to the radio and heard the same artists being played repeatedly or found music to sound generally the same? Is this a true reflection of the current state of music, what musicians are producing? Or could this be an artifact of the music industry, those who control the means of production? Scholars who study structural relationships in cultural production examined the relationship between market concentration and musical homogeneity – that is, how similar musical projects are to one another – based on who owns the means of music production. During times of heavy concentration, when there are but a few owners, music is homogeneous; there is musical diversity when ownership is dispersed (Dowd 2003; Peterson and Berger 1975). In the early 1980s, prior to rap music's acceptance by the major record labels as a profitable genre, there was great diversity in rap music. However, by the 1990s, that diversity had disappeared as production ownership became concentrated and many in-dependent record labels were purchased by the majors (Rose 1994).

The music industry was not the only art world to experience such control by so few. The business model of the entertainment industry and those who broadcast their messages prompted the *Wall Street Journal* to call the heavy concentration of ownership in the mass media an oligopoly (Pascal 1999). In recent years, all symbol industries and production houses experienced a concentration in ownership; consequently, a small group controls the mass media. In the film industry, six giants dominate the box office: Disney (owned by Walt Disney Corporation), Paramount Pictures (owned by Viacom), Sony Pictures (owned by Sony), Twentieth Century Fox (owned by News Corporation), Universal Pictures (owned by Seagram), and Warner Brothers (owned by Time Warner) (Compaine and Gomery 2000). The music industry has five giants: Universal/PolyGram, Warner Music, Sony Music, EMI Group, and BMG Entertainment. Combining the sales of all music genres, total sales of music in America in 2008 were more than $8 trillion (Recording Industry Association of America 2009).

Although this figure likely seems high, the fact is that the entertainment industry is suffering immensely from digital innovation. Figure 12.2 shows the decrease in revenues across genres between 1999 and 2008. The decline in the music industry is paralleled by the decline in radio listenership. Despite the decline, in 1996, the Telecommunications

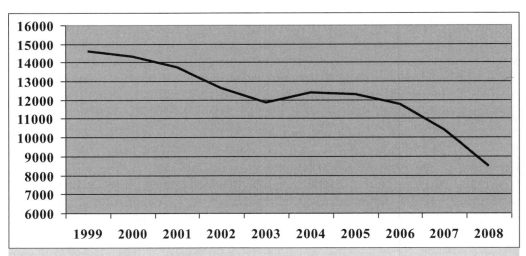

Figure 12.2 Total sales across music genres, 1999–2008.
Data Source: Recording Industry Association of America (2009). 1999–2008 Music Consumer Profile.

Act resulted in a concentration of radio ownership not seen since the 1940s (Gomery 2000). The bill allowed owners to group together large market shares of radio stations that previously had been outlawed as an infringement of antitrust laws.

Each media giant diversifies and dominates social space. Gramsci's hegemony theory can be understood more easily in light of this. The corporate-concentrated control over symbol production means that (1) those who are not members of the in-group have difficulty getting their products into the global market; and (2) broadcasts are legitimized in the marketing process. Members of the in-group include those with corporate sponsorships from media giants.

Although some cultural agents have had success going direct to market through the Internet, the majority have had little success without allowing their products to be sold through iTunes, owned by Apple Incorporated. Social-networking sites allow consumers to download music, yet even this turns a profit for the media giants. For songs purchased via the Internet, iTunes collects 100 percent of the song purchase price and then returns about 30 percent to the record company, which pays the artist 10 to 15 percent (Bragg 2006). For those who do not have record-company representation, there is little hope of being carried by iTunes. In one instance, MTV offered unsigned artists the opportunity to upload music to its new Web site – the songs that consumers voted for would be played on MTV. However, the small print contracted control over the music: "[U]sers have to grant MTV the right to transmit their material on the network 'in perpetuity and gratis'" (Bragg 2006), meaning forever and for free. We have seen how the mass media maintains control over media outlets; we now look at how hegemonic culture can influence people to accept inequality as natural.

We previously examined the status of women in America and the world. The gains that women made throughout the twentieth century increased their status, yet they still are paid less, do more housework, and have lower rates of political representation compared to men. Another dimension of inequality that men do not experience is called the "beauty myth."

Beauty Myth

The *beauty myth* is a socially constructed value system that measures the quality of women by their beauty. Generations have grown up watching TV, films, and commercials that show women as tall, thin, young, clear-complexioned, proportioned like a model, and – until recently – white. Yet, even models do not fit these ideals of beauty because their images are "fixed" or touched up in postproduction. The average American woman certainly does not fit this description: she is 5 feet 4 inches tall and weighs 165 pounds with a 37-inch waist (Centers for Disease Control and Prevention 2009). Yet, images of idealized beauty dominate the media. As women internalize the beauty myth that they are measured by their beauty and those who are not beautiful are somehow "less of a woman," social problems arise. These social problems are evidenced in the stratification of women, eating disorders, and cosmetic surgery (Wolf [1990]2002).

Idealized images of female beauty cause harm to women. Eating-disorder experts generally agree that the disorders are a result of social pressure or *supercultural* standards of thinness (Hesse-Biber 1989) – that is, a culture that overrides all other subcultures and distinctions. In America, about 3 percent of women have or have had an eating disorder. Because instances of eating disorders often go unreported, it is estimated that between 0.5 and 3.7 percent of women, approximately 4 million, have *anorexia nervosa* – a condition in which a woman limits the amount of food she ingests, often resulting in death. About 7 million women, 1.1 to 4.2 percent, have *bulimia* – binge eating and then engaging in compulsory behaviors like induced vomiting or the excessive use of laxatives. Between 2 and 5 percent, about 10 million women, have had at least one incident of binge eating within any given six-month period (National Institute of Mental Health 2009).

The media's continual use of the idealized woman creates objectification and commodification of women in society. Women are perceived and perceive their bodies as objects to be perfected, that they are commodities or a good to be supplied in a market. Measuring their worth only in terms of beauty, women purchase beauty aids, cosmetics, diets, and medical procedures to build a better model, to make a better product. Health issues are only one part of the problem; women's negative social relationships comprise the other. The ideal girl, according to junior and senior high school students, looks like a Barbie doll: 5 feet 6 inches tall, 110 pounds, and size 5 (Nichter and Nichter 1991).

Body image is significantly more negative for women after viewing supercultural media images of thin women than after viewing images of average or plus-size models or inanimate objects (Groesz, Levine, and Murnen 2002). A negative body image exacerbates gender inequality twofold. First, women with low self-esteem are more likely to have poor social relationships (McCaulay, Mintz, and Glenn 1988) and become isolated (Roberts et al. 2000). Second, men include attractiveness and thinness in their description of idealized partners (Jackson, Hunter, and Hodge 1995). For those women who do not meet the beauty standard, there is negative social feedback. Men feel pressured to date thin women so as not to be embarrassed by friends (Hesse-Biber 1997), although they do not live up to a similar standard. We may ask whether it is unnatural for women to be isolated when they do not meet this beauty standard. In fact, Finnish scholars showed that female obesity is not related to social isolation in Finland as it is in the United States (Sarlio-Lahteenkorva and Lahelma 1999).

The beauty myth is an example of hegemony – that is, it seems natural for a woman to be thin and beautiful. Many women internalize this and exhibit eating disorders, dissatisfaction with their bodies, and low self-esteem. In 2002, a group of young women approached magazine editors to lobby for the use of what they called "real girls" in magazines; they were met with great resistance. The young women asked the editors to include images that were not airbrushed or computer-altered and to use normal size 12 women – which is the size of the average American woman. The editors legitimized images of unrealistic women by claiming that they would like to use more realistic images but they cannot because of the following objections: Young women view magazines as fantasy; the average reader understands that the images are not real; and the photographers' reputations are linked to the models – if the editors use *ugly* or *fat* models, the photographers will suffer. It is interesting that the inclusion of real women was not intended to be fat and ugly models; however, that is how the editors interpreted the group's request (Milkie 2002). Ultimately, the editors felt as though they were powerless to change how Americans view women. However, in Spain, after the death of a fashion model due to anorexia nervosa, a new fashion-industry standard was enacted: no models with a body mass of less than 18.5; that is, for a 5-foot-9-inch woman, her weight must be at least 125 pounds.

How Does Hegemony Work?

Sociologist Herbert Marcuse (1898–1979) studied cultural hegemony (Marcuse 1964). He showed that hegemonic culture is intrusive of a person's inner space – of reason – and that force that allows the questioning of the status quo. For example, instead of questioning why women are expected to be unnaturally thin, hegemonic culture allows the general public to accept unnatural thinness as a *natural* fact. This is reinforced by magazine editors who, in an echo chamber of social action and reaction, feed back these images to the public. Marcuse argued further that all products in advanced industrial societies "indoctrinate and manipulate" (1964: 288); that is, ideology is in production.

Production of culture is a powerful social force because it influences many people. Of course, this does not apply to all cultural production: For example, it does not apply to a song when it is sung in an empty room or a story told to a child. Rather, cultural production is hegemonic when it is controlled as an industry and is produced en masse. The cultural production of today is global and affects most people. Consider Michael Jackson's *Thriller* (Epic Records 1982): No other album had ever sold so many or so widespread. In 2007, *The Guinness Book of World Records* cited sales at 65 million worldwide (Guinness World Records 2007).

Whereas artists create cultural artifacts, others mediate the relationship between production and consumption. Sociologist C. Wright Mills used the phrase *the cultural apparatus* to describe the decision-making brokers who broker the producers of culture. To illustrate how the cultural apparatus mediates the relationship between production and consumption, we examine the TV industry and the process of creating new TV series (Bielby and Bielby 1994).

Writers and producers shop pilots (i.e., new TV shows) to network executives who have the final say as to which will be "picked up" and which will not. The production logic is organized around institutionalized decision making. The cultural apparatus consists of network executives who make decisions that hedge against ambiguity about what a successful TV series should look like and uncertainty (of market appeal). In other words, they try to anticipate a "hit show."

Network executives tout innovation and "fresh blood" in programming but rely on prior production logic to produce new cultural products – especially hinging new series to "old blood" (particularly producers). Instead of risking failure by producing a series that is completely different from other series, decision brokers use ideas that, to them, predict the probable success of a pilot. The decision-making brokers frame their discussions of potential success on reputation, imitation, and genre to convince colleagues that their decisions about choosing a TV show are "appropriate, legitimate, and rational" (Bielby and Bielby 1994: 1310). The rhetorical devices that executives use include links to a previously successful producer, celebrity, series, or other media, or else no linkages. In this study, the variations in decision making were examined among the four major networks in 1991–1992: ABC, NBC, CBS, and FOX. The only sitcoms chosen for mass production were brokered with frames adhering to industry standards of success in terms of genre, reputation, and imitation – that is, there is social reproduction of cultural symbols.

The Stratifying Nature of Culture

Most of us are familiar with the term *capital* being used to describe money, credit, or property. In Chapter 4, *capital* in the social sciences also consists of intangibles – that which cannot be seen but can be measured empirically. Sociologists are particularly interested in two forms of capital: social and cultural.

To review, *social capital* is defined as "the aggregate of the actual or potential resources which are linked to possession of a durable network of more or less institutionalized relationships of mutual acquaintance or recognition" (Bourdieu 1985: 248). To summarize, it is not necessarily *what* but rather *who* you know.

Sociologists who study social networks show that the benefit of having large social networks lies in the diversity of connections or "the strength of weak ties" (Granovetter 1973). Job seekers, for instance, often find jobs through their associations with others who are not necessarily close friends. This occurs through at least one of four cultural associations within the social network: value interjection, bounded solidarity, reciprocity exchanges, and enforceable trust (Portes 1998).

Value interjection links people through their value system. Religious affiliation, for example, emphasizes values. If two individuals share values, say are of the same faith, they are likely to share social capital. *Bounded solidarity* ties people together through a sense of togetherness or fellowship. A group shares traditions, goals, and purpose and is linked even across time to other members. *Reciprocity exchanges* can best be described in the idioms "You scratch my back and I will scratch yours" and "*quid pro quo*" (i.e., "this for that"). Capital is accrued between people who provide favors for one another. *Enforceable trust* allows members to sanction other members who do not follow according to the shared ethics – that is, the culture of the group.

Power resides in symbols as well as people. Consider the White House, the Lincoln Memorial, a crucifix, the Star of David, or another religious item. Each holds power in meaning – that is, the sentiments that people afford these symbols imbue the symbols with power. French sociologist Emile Durkheim (1858–1917) studied symbols and man's relation to them. He noted that cultural artifacts could be either sacred or profane. Profane items are the mundane, everyday tools and materials with which we surround ourselves, including the TV, computer, pots and pans, and automobile. Sacred items, which Durkheim called *totems*, are those artifacts that hold deep meaning to humans including animal fetishes of native populations and religious and national symbols. In explaining the sacred, Durkheim discussed a fallen soldier who "died for his flag." Certainly, this does not mean that the soldier gave his life for a piece of cloth; rather, the flag holds sacred meaning to members who share a culture.

Cultural capital arises from that which is symbolically powerful. It can take three forms: embodied, objectified, and institutionalized (Bourdieu 1986). *Embodied capital* is defined as "long-lasting dispositions of the body and the mind" (1986: 98); *objectified capital* is defined as cultural products (i.e., books, music, artwork, and instruments); and *institutionalized capital* is a form of objectified capital that is legitimizing (i.e., a credential, college degree, or honorarium).

French sociologist Pierre Bourdieu's (1930–2002) cultural-capital theory explains how variations in culture among groups of people can advantage some but disadvantage others. As discussed in Chapter 4, one way that this happens is when students who exhibit behaviors associated with high-brow dominant culture academically surpass those students who do not exhibit this culture. Sociologist Paul DiMaggio (1951–) observed cultural capital and education and found support for Bourdieu's theory in the United States (DiMaggio 1982) in that students who participate in the high-brow arts perform better academically than those who do not.

How music affects students is controversial. Evidence suggests that the positive effect of music on academic achievement is biological. The study known as the *Mozart Effect* showed that students who listened to Mozart prior to taking a paper-and-pencil test performed at a higher level than those who did not listen. The effect was short-lived, lasting only about 5 minutes. Subsequent studies tested whether the effect was present for other types of relaxing music; no effect was observed, but the Mozart effect was durable.

In 2009, scholars approached the issue from a sociological perspective. Using a status-attainment model to test the relationships among music in school, out of school, and whether parents participated in the arts, they first measured which groups received musical training. Families with more economic and educational resources had higher rates of participation; Asians and whites had higher rates than blacks and Hispanics. As to the issue of whether music participation affects academic ability, they found that it reduces the achievement gaps due to socioeconomic status. That is, children from lower-income homes reap the most benefit from music participation (Southgate and Roscigno 2009).

This finding supports the theory of cultural capital, which suggests that students born in upper-class homes accrue the type of capital from symbols from the day they are born; they are, in essence, culture-rich. By the time these students reach high school, they have little to gain in terms of culture; they already have it. However, students who did not come from a rich cultural background will benefit from exposure to the arts in high school.

Consider the topic of education. The general public assumes that an education at an Ivy League school is far superior to that at a community college. Is the reason for that distinction based on educational substance or are other criteria considered? Although we would have to measure the facts precisely to provide a definitive answer, we can state with certainty that an Ivy League education provides more social and cultural capital than other schools. To be admitted to an Ivy League school, a student generally must have high grades, but some students are admitted with a less than stellar academic record. The reason for this is social capital; many elite students follow in their parents' footsteps – that is, they are admitted because their parents graduated from the same school. Again, we can see the importance of social reproduction in the intergenerational transmission of social class.

Sociologists show that elite activities form the mechanisms that create and support social stratification. Specifically, those students from families with legacies produce future legacies – creating an intergenerational cycle of privilege through cultural membership. Memberships, in turn, create social boundaries – that is, divisions between groups of people that create a dichotomous categorization of in- and out-group, or "us and them."

Memberships increase the social and cultural capital of its members by linking them to one another through time-honored traditions. We now look at how this occurs in schools and class societies within schools.

Social-Boundary Making

Culture often defines social boundaries. For example, the upper class most often educates its children in private preparatory schools (i.e., prep schools) (see Chapter 5). These schools have rich cultures that are passed from one generation to the next (Cookson 1997). After prep school, many elite students attend Ivy League colleges, where they are again immersed in a historical legacy of nonmaterial culture through attitudes, behaviors, rituals, and material culture – buildings, clothing, and food. Within these scholastic interactions, new members are socialized into an elite culture (Domhoff 1970; 2002). One way that this happens is through club memberships known as *senior societies*.

It is a familiar scenario that has been in existence for well over 100 years: Late at night, in the dark recesses of campus dormitory life, a group of students gather around the bed of a sleeping senior to deliver a message: "You have been tapped." The student is being asked to join a senior society. Some describe the event as frightening – hooded strangers place blindfolds on the inductees, rip them from their bed, and march them to an ominous place wherein they will be ritualistically tested. Other rituals are less dramatic, such as Ohio State University's SPHINX honorary society. Students congregate in the courtyard before University Hall, a campus landmark, and are initiated with speeches of encouragement that emphasize service (SPHINX 2009). Those who are tapped into societies become brothers and sisters in a time-honored tradition in colleges and universities across America.

Senior societies once were known as *class societies* because they were available only to the upper class. Class societies take various forms and have existed in the United States since the early days of education. Phi Beta Kappa, the first American class society, was established in 1776 at the College of William and Mary. Lesser known societies often are secretive, including the Sphinx Head (1890) and Quill and Dagger (1893) at Cornell University; The Order of Skull and Bones at Yale University; Seven Society (1905) at the University of Virginia; and Michagamua (1902) at the University of Michigan. There are literally hundreds of societies on American campuses, each with a distinct intergenerational culture maintained through membership.

Class societies began what is commonly known as the *Greek system* – social clubs with sponsored membership; that is, no one may join without the approval of the members. The oldest societies have existed since the College of William and Mary was established in America in 1693. Although many modern films have been constructed around secret societies – or societies with secrets, as some say – the fact is that small groups of students enter into a hierarchy of prestige where other students cannot. An important sociological question is: "Who is asked to join class societies?" Legacies matter – those students whose fathers and, more recently, mothers were members have a higher likelihood of being asked to join. Other reasons for inclusion, according to the charters, are leadership qualities, outstanding academic and athletic abilities, and even physical appearance – although many students who seemingly fit this description are not asked to join.

Conspiracy theorists attribute these social clubs with dubious intentions; however, sociologists offer a more scientific explanation. German sociologist Georg Simmel (1858–1915) studied secret societies and determined that they flourish when there is access to influence the distribution of power. Resources are scarce in society – not everyone can become a doctor or a lawyer – but doctors and lawyers hold high prestige in society. As groups compete for these resources, patterns of ownership and control emerge.

Consider Dartmouth College. Although we might extend its reputation as a prestigious school to include many famous alumni, one class society called Casque and Gauntlet, established in the 1800s, produced renowned celebrities such as Nelson Rockefeller, David T. McLaughlin, Robert Reich, and Theodor Seuss Geisel (better known as Dr. Seuss).

Sociologist Richard Zweigenhaft set out to test directly whether an elite education advantages those fortunate enough to attend a prep school prior to attending Yale University. Drawing on previous research and on Bourdieu's theory of social reproduction, he hypothesized that Yale graduates who had attended a public secondary school would be more likely than those who had attended a prep school to accumulate what Bourdieu called "cultural capital." However, Yale graduates who had attended a prep school would be more likely than their public-school counterparts to accumulate what Bourdieu called "social capital." A study of the life experiences of the Yale Class of 1963 in the 25 years after graduation supported this general expectation. There also was support for a series of more specific expectations about postgraduate educational achievement, occupational choices, and behavioral indices of loyalty to Yale (Zweigenhaft 1992). Social-class membership in a prep school sets those apart from others at Ivy League colleges – social boundaries (and exclusion) are created as in- and out-groups are defined.

According to their own literature, one-fourth of Dartmouth students are affiliated with one of eight senior societies: Abaris, Casque and Gauntlet, Cobra, Dragon, Fire and Skoal, Gryphon, Phoenix, and Sphinx. In addition to senior societies, memberships may include a fraternity or sorority in the Greek system, such as Psi Upsilon, which resulted from the class societies. Each organization has a unique culture that is passed from one cohort to another, as defined by the fraternity Psi Upsilon (Trustees of Dartmouth College 2009):

> Psi Upsilon is a way of life....Although the experience may differ, Psi Upsilon itself, as defined by its values, is constant. It is the fundamental nature of these values which has given Psi Upsilon the strength to flourish since its inception in 1833.

This citation emphasizes the continuity of values spanning more than 170 years – that is, the culture of Dartmouth students across generations.

Sociologists have long been interested in how social-club memberships create community cohesion and affect influence over others. Perhaps no other class society has received as much interest as Skull and Bones at Yale. Indeed, many famous individuals are Bonesmen, including some who hold public office: former Presidents George W. Bush and George H. W. Bush, former Vice President Dick Cheney, and Senator John Kerry. Social-club memberships extend well past college. We have seen how the middle class arose from guilds and unions, and party affiliations – as Weber called them – constitute one dimension of social status. One club, The Bohemians, has received particular attention by sociologists.

The Bohemians is a private club in San Francisco chartered to bring together wealthy and influential West Coast men. Once a year, members meet for a retreat called the Bohemian Grove, which is open to men only. During the retreat, an opening ceremony is performed with more than 350 cast members. The Bohemian Grove is well attended. Since the late 1800s, this group of wealthy and predominantly white men has gathered to relax and – although there is no official business – the retreat serves as a social space where members can meet, interact, and network with others of similar power and to influence other wealthy members of the elite class. Since 1890, "every Republican president of the twentieth century was a member or guest at the Bohemian Grove" (Domhoff 2002: 52). Indeed, many of the Bohemians also are members of Skull and Bones and other elite social clubs.

Religion and Strategies of Action

Nonmaterial culture is found not only within art worlds, consumption, and the time-honored traditions of elite families and through the education system; it is also the foundation of religious differences. One of the most influential works on this topic was written by German sociologist Max Weber.

Weber studied world religions and how they affect social interactions. One question that Weber strove to answer, which had eluded social scientists, was why capitalism developed in Northern Europe and America but not in other regions of the world, such as India and China. All of these regions are rich in resources and manpower, yet capitalism never developed beyond Europe and America. By using a cross-national analysis of possible cultural and structural influences, Weber found a fascinating link between capitalism and religion. Although it is only one segment of a larger theoretical development, Weber hypothesized that Protestantism deeply affected social action, which in turn fostered capitalism. He called this the *Protestant work ethic.*

In Northern Europe and certainly America, Protestantism (particularly Calvinism) set forth values of work and thrift, which are evidenced in Benjamin Franklin's *Poor Richard's Almanac* – for example, "Early to bed, early to rise makes a man healthy, wealthy, and wise" and "A penny saved is a penny earned." These adages convey the importance of being industrious. Other religions do not have this same value system. Indeed, comparing Catholicism to Protestantism reveals that Catholics were assured of salvation through the acceptance of Church doctrine; Protestants were not. Instead, Protestants (especially Calvinists) believed in predestination: God preordained a person's afterlife regardless of his or her acts on earth. To show faith in God's infallible wisdom, Protestants lived life as though they were the chosen ones because anything less would be denying God's will. How could Protestants *know* if they were one of the chosen? The level of one's wealth contributed to the sense of Godly benevolence. This strategy of action did not create capitalism per se; however, it did create a culture wherein work and thrift became important cultural values.

Religious-based social relationships have been a focus in sociology since the early days of the discipline (Durkheim [1912]1954; Simmel 1905; Sombart 1911; Weber [1905]1930), and scholars recently have begun to explore the modern significance of these connections. There is evidence that religious-based social connections can improve outcomes (e.g., emotional and physical health) and can promote life satisfaction, psychological coping, and positive behaviors among adolescents (Ellison 1991; Ellison, Gay, and Glass 1989; Ellison and Levin 1998; Krause et al. 2001; Levin 1994; Smith 2003b).

Today, religion is a central force in the life of many people, articulating strategies of action and creating networks of people within which social capital is shared. One way that religion matters is in wealth accumulation (Keister 2003). Religion affects wealth indirectly by shaping demographic behaviors. Religion often dictates sexual and reproductive practices, birth control, the acceptable age of first birth, and the number of children considered appropriate. The addition of children to a family generally decreases wealth and educational outcomes of each child. The percentage of children, age at first birth, and number of children by selected religions is reported in Table 12.1.

Americans that followed "other religions" in childhood have fewer children; black Conservative Protestants (CP) have children, on average, at age 22, the youngest age for first births in the sample; Hispanic Catholics have more children compared to other groups.

Table 12.1 Childhood Religion and Fertility (%)

	Have any children (%)	Age at first birth	Number of children
White Conservative Protestant (CP)	81.82	24.04	1.89
Black Conservative Protestant (BP)	80.33	21.95	2.07
Mainline/Liberal Protestant (MP)	78.05	26.49	1.72
Catholic	80.26	25.93	1.90
White	79.92	26.64	1.82
Hispanic	81.03	23.44	2.25
Black	85.00	23.18	1.80
Jewish	76.27	30.44	1.64
Mormon/LDS	71.43	25.52	1.74
Other Religion	67.21	26.63	1.48
No Religion	76.81	23.69	1.80
All Respondents	79.70	25.11	1.86

Data Source: Bureau of Labor Statistics (2009).
Notes: Author's estimates from the NLSY79. Total $n = 6,092$ (excluding 19 cases with missing data for childhood religion). Age at first birth only recorded for females ($n = 3,100$, excluding 8 cases with missing data for childhood religion). Sample percentage refers to the total sample (i.e., males and females).

The positive effect and self-reinforcing nature of religious-based social relationships can extend to wealth ownership. For example, people who are members of religious groups in which others have accumulated significant assets are more likely to learn the skills needed for wealth accumulation. These contacts also may provide information and financial resources that lead to wealth ownership.

Education directly affects a person's income, lifestyle, and culture. More education corresponds to more opportunities throughout life. Religion, in part, directs and organizes our world through the inculcation of action strategies that directly impact the educational process.

Table 12.2 shows that Jews have higher rates of education than Protestants, Catholics, Mormons, and others represented in the sample. On average, they earn at least a college degree, and more than one-third have earned an advanced degree (e.g., Ph.D., MD, or JP). Table 12.3 demonstrates the impact that religious affiliation has on wealth and education by comparing parental median income, the percentage of respondents whose parents earned a bachelor's degree, and the percentage who ever received an inheritance by selected religion.

A strong association exists between income and education (see Chapter 7). By separating religious groups, we can see the effect that strategies of action and social capital has on an important aspect of daily life: wealth. Using Table 12.3, we also can measure the educational attainment between fathers and mothers (in traditional male/female families). In the majority of sampled religions, more men have earned at least a bachelor's degree compared to women. Of the religions in which the opposite is true where more women earn college degrees compared to men (i.e., Jewish, black CP, and other religions), only in the Jewish religion do women show a significant educational advantage.

Unfortunately, religious-based social relationships also can reinforce negative attitudes, orientations, and behaviors. For instance, in faiths in which the majority of social contacts are asset-poor, the skills that are passed along may inhibit saving and wealth accumulation.

Table 12.2 Childhood Religion and Educational Attainment

	Years of education	Has advanced degree (%)
White Conservative Protestant (CP)	13.07	10.02
Black Conservative Protestant (BP)	12.72	3.89
Mainline/Liberal Protestant (MP)	14.21	18.28
Catholic	13.57	10.86
White	13.83	12.02
Hispanic	12.50	6.90
Black	13.48	5.00
Jewish	16.05	35.59
Mormon/LDS	13.94	11.43
Other Religion	14.67	24.59
No Religion	12.62	9.18
All Respondents	13.51	12.11

Data Source: Bureau of Labor Statistics (2009).
Notes: Author's estimates from the NLSY79. Total *n* = 6,092 (excluding 19 cases with missing data for childhood religion).

Table 12.3 Childhood Religion and Parents' Socioeconomic Status

	Parents' income (median)	Father had a BA (%)	Mother had a BA (%)	Ever inherited (%)
White Conservative Protestant (CP)	$14,000	6.54	4.84	42.32
Black Conservative Protestant (BP)	$8,840	3.16	3.63	22.45
Mainline/Liberal Protestant (MP)	$19,000	14.39	10.48	56.74
Catholic	$19,975	12.14	6.46	46.00
White	$21,975	13.88	7.25	51.89
Hispanic	$8,000	4.22	3.63	22.48
Black	$11,074	12.82	2.17	41.18
Jewish	$32,500	25.97	38.27	71.95
Mormon/LDS	$13,800	19.15	8.70	46.94
Other Religion	$14,000	13.79	14.12	59.57
No Religion	$12,000	9.78	9.17	43.02
All Respondents	$15,200	10.69	7.40	45.50

Data Source: Bureau of Labor Statistics (2009).

Notes: Author's estimates from the NLSY79. Total n = 6,092 (excluding 19 cases with missing data for childhood religion).

Poor saving habits, excess consumption, accumulation of debt, and other problematic behaviors can be passed along as easily as positive behaviors. Moreover, people do not simply "happen" on their social relationships, and recent research suggests that some religious groups deliberately and detrimentally restrict their social ties. In particular, CPs tend to have relatively narrow or consolidated social networks, populated largely by others from similar faith communities (Sherkat 2009; Smith 2003a). In these communities, there is a risk that narrow social networks will exacerbate the reinforcing effect of social relationships on negative behaviors. Sherkat (2009) showed a detrimental effect of consolidated social networks on education-related outcomes (e.g., verbal ability), and educational deficits ultimately will feed into wealth. It also follows that closed social networks may exacerbate any direct, negative effect that faith has on wealth by reinforcing negative saving and consumption behaviors. In communities in which wealth is historically low, the added effect of deliberately restricted social networks may contribute to wealth remaining low over time.

Summary

(1) Culture is a complex system of behaviors, attitudes, preferences, values, and material goods. It takes two forms: material and nonmaterial.
(2) Cultural membership stratifies by creating in- and out-groups. In-group members show preference to other members; out-groups members have no preference. This exacerbates social inequality.

(3) In addition to a dominant culture that is experienced by a majority of the population, groups create subcultures to share commonalities. When these commonalities break away from or reject the dominant culture, the subculture is known as a counterculture or oppositional culture.

(4) Culture is a complex system of social interactions that creates strategies of action.

(5) High-brow culture is that of the upper class and low-brow culture is found in the middle and working classes.

(6) High-brow culture most often is learned through a person's social background, particularly in the family and at school. Those who recognize and emulate high-brow culture navigate through social experiences with greater ease than those with low-brow culture.

(7) When high-brow culture benefits its possessor, that person is said to own cultural capital.

(8) Culture affects people's paradigm. Hegemonic culture is a theory that explains how one social class may dominate a much larger social class through the control of symbolic production.

(9) One form of hegemonic culture is the beauty myth, which measures the quality of a woman in terms of her "beauty" as defined by some group. In Western industrialized nations, that corresponds with being hyper-thin, youthful, tall, and white.

(10) The current control of symbolic production is in the hands of a highly concentrated media industry. Those who work within the industry are called the cultural apparatus. These decision brokers reproduce culture for their own commercial benefit.

(11) Religion is a type of nonmaterial culture that greatly impacts all aspects of social life. It structures decision making by linking people and ideas, which in turn affect education, coupling, reproduction, sex and gender roles, wealth accumulation, and even political forms (e.g., capitalism).

Box 12.1 Who's the Mack: Why Are Pimps Portrayed as Cool?

Culture consists of codes that hold meaning to in-group members. One code often used in the popular art of African Americans is the word *Mack*. Perhaps from the French *maquereau*, which means using words to hustle or trick, the meaning behind the *Mack* is complex and has been shown to be a residual of the African Diaspora, which Quinn (2000) traced back to the "Signaling Monkey" folktale. Three characters comprise this tale: a Monkey, a Lion, and an Elephant. The Lion is the ruler and unjust. The Monkey lies to the Elephant (a neutral – albeit powerful – third party) that the Lion is talking badly about the Elephant. This lie motivates the Elephant to bully (and threaten to kill) the Lion. Through wit and clever weaving of language, the Monkey resists the will of the Lion and, indeed, injects his own will, thus wielding power in a situation in which he was seemingly powerless. The Lion signifies the dominant forces (often referred to as "The Man"), the Monkey is the black trickster, and the Elephant is the medium by which the Monkey gains advantage over the Elephant.

   The trickster has deep meaning in the black community because it relates directly to the African trickster deities Esu, Legba, and Anansi. These tricksters are heralded throughout African American culture and are seen in other characters (e.g., Brer Rabbit) as weaving language in

Box 12.1 (*continued*)

clever ways, spinning illusory tales to exert power and gain control in situations in which one has no control. This trickster who gains control over others manifests in the form of a *pimp*, also called a *Mack* – that is, someone who exploits others for his own gain.

Max Julien was the star of the 1973 movie titled *The Mack*, which was one in a series of films called "blaxploitation." This genre celebrates the virile black hero who – through cleverness, wit, and skill – triumphs over adversity in an urban community. In this film genre, the police are portrayed as enemies who fail to protect individuals in the community, who are most often poor and black. The hero also battles other hostile influences from within the community: illegal organizations (e.g., The Mob), crooked preachers, women of ill repute, and other desperate individuals exhibiting deviant behaviors. The films underscore the importance of personal effort to overcome adversity, a role not afforded to blacks on film in the past. They also use funk music for soundtracks.

Arguably, one of the first films in the genre was *Sweet Sweetback's Baadasssss Song* (VanPeebles 1971); according to the promotional poster, it was "rated X by an all-white jury" and stars "the black community." Sweetback, the hero, killed two police officers who were beating a black community member who had voiced political resistance to the dominant culture. Throughout the film, Sweetback runs away from The Man, always one step away from danger – yet, he triumphs in the end. While the action on the screen keeps the audience entertained, the score playing behind the film articulates the struggle, the hope, and the despair seen on the screen. The score is funk music from the record company Stax with titles including "The Man Tries Running His Usual Game But Sweetback's Jones Is So Strong He," "Won't Bleed Me," and "Sweetback Getting It Uptight and Preaching It So Hard the Bourgeois Reggin." These songs, which are all instrumentals, were written by Van Peebles, the director and star of the film. However, he did not play music; instead, he hired a *pickup band*[1] to create this project. Afterwards, the band became Earth, Wind, and Fire, a top-selling funk band. The trickster, one who wins the contest, triumphed yet again. This film helped to set the standard by which others followed. It offered employment opportunities to black musicians of the day and brought positive black role models to the public.

The Mack (Campus 1973), starring Max Julien, followed a similar story line three years later. However, the hero was not running from The Man but instead was a pimp – a man who had "turned the game around" and rather than being exploited was now the exploiter. Using the African metaphor, he was the signaling monkey.

More than a decade later, in 1988 after meeting Max Julien, Too $hort titled his album, *Born to Mack*. In 1999, more than 25 years since the original film, Rappin' 4-Tay released *Introduction to Mackin'*. Julien was a regular visitor to the studio during the recording of the 1999 Rappin' 4-Tay project.

Using a production logic similar to that described by Bielby and Bielby (1994), the producers invoked genre, reputation, and imitation. Julien embodies the very essence of *Mack* (Quinn 2000); indeed, the trickster is the *Mack*. He is a strong and active member in the perpetration of meaning. The Mack is masculine, adaptable, and wins. Julien's film portrayal as the Mack is part of a legacy embodying meaning, and the use of the word *Mack* invokes this meaning.

Sources: 4-Tay, Rappin. 1999. "Introduction to Mackin." Celeb Ent.

Bielby, William T., and Denise D. Bielby. 1994. "'All Hits Are Flukes': Institutionalized Decision Making and the Rhetoric of Network Prime-Time Program Development." *The American Journal of Sociology* 99:1287–313.

Campus, Michael. 1973. "The Mack." USA: Cinerama Releasing Corporation.

Quinn, Eithne. 2000. "'Who's The Mack?': The Performativity and Politics of the Pimp Figure in Gangsta Rap." *Journal of American Studies* 34:115–36.

VanPeebles, Melvin and Jerry Gross. 1971. "Sweet Sweetback's Baadasssss Song." 97 minutes. USA: Cinemation Industries.

---

[1] A pickup band is created for the sole purpose of creating a musical project. The participants in this formation typically have no intention of remaining as a cohesive working collective.

Box 12.2 Culture or Torture: A Lesson in Diversity

Female genital mutilation (FGM) affects not only fertility, infertility, and mortality but also the dependency ratio of nations. Globally, it is estimated that 130 million females have undergone some form of FGM with approximately 2 million annual and 6,000 daily procedures (Dakenoo 1993). In Africa alone, 75 million to 85 million females 14 years of age and younger have undergone FGM. According to Nakalema (1990), "[E]thnic groups who practice it, including the Kikuyu, Kamba, Kisii, Kalenjin, Maasia, and people of Somali origin, have a death rate of 170 per 1,000 of their female population. Approximately half of these deaths are the result of FGM, a practice which also contributes to the poor health of mutilated women." A conservative crude mortality rate of 85 per 1,000 females does not consider the age distribution of these females' deaths. Because data are difficult to gather in underdeveloped regions, many figures cannot be well estimated. The fact remains that women may be dying at even higher rates due to lifelong complications from FGM, and estimations of these occurrences are rarely considered. Because country-level data are difficult to collect, statistics and demographic data describing the African regions that both engage in FGM and discuss global policies meant to treat FGM are used.

The areas most affected are in Africa, but FGM also occurs in the Middle East – Egypt, Oman, Yemen, and the United Arab Emirates – and cases have been reported in Central and South America but no data are available. It has become a global issue because immigrant communities in Western Europe, Canada, and the United States are impacted by the influx of women who have been exposed to this practice. Most of the countries associated with FGM face high fertility and mortality rates as well as high rates of HIV/AIDS.

Physical problems associated with FGM include chronic urinary-tract infections, stones in the bladder and urethra, kidney damage, reproductive-tract infections resulting from obstructed menstrual flow, pelvic infections, infertility, excessive scar tissue, keloids (i.e., raised, irregularly shaped, progressively enlarging scars), and dermoid cysts. Prior to sexual intercourse, many men must cut the infibulated tissue to penetrate the vulva (e.g., these cases are estimated at 15 percent in Sudan) (Lightfoot-Klein 1989). This often introduces the risk of infection because sanitary instruments are rarely used. Additional scar tissue often forms that can inhibit basic bodily functions such as menses and urination. The overall risks of this cultural practice have caused many agencies to enact policy in the hope of eradicating FGM worldwide.

The Federal Prohibition of Female Genital Mutilation Act of 1995 prohibits FGM in the United States and is punishable by up to five years in prison. However, it affects only minors – females younger than 18 years of age. It prohibits the procedure on ritualistic or cultural beliefs. It charges the U.S. Secretary of Health and Human Services to collect data on the number of females who have been affected by FGM and also informs all immigrants that the United States has strict laws against the practice. This law also enables local agencies to locate and provide outreach services to circumcised women and to educate those communities about the mental and physical risks. The Act also addresses the need to educate Western health-care professionals in the correct treatment of this population – especially to be informed of the risks that the women face throughout their life course.

Some U.S. states have more prohibitory policies regarding the practice of FGM. By 1991, four states – Illinois, Minnesota, Rhode Island, and Tennessee – had outlawed FMG for females of all ages. In six states – Colorado, Delaware, Maryland, New York, Oregon, and West Virginia – parents and legal guardians are held liable if they consent to FGM. California punishes both the doctor who performed the procedure and the parents of the girl; they also charge the parent for child endangerment.

A female who has FGM is seen as virginal, pure, and aesthetically pleasing. This intertwines with moral codes that predict a female's potential attraction for marriage. Those who are not "mutilated" are seen as pariahs. In regions touched by HIV/AIDS, famine, loss of labor force, and an increase in dependency ratios, females must submit to FGM or face isolation or death. Also not considered empirically is the function that infibulation serves in reducing fertility. FGM may offer women some control over their bodies, although this function is obscured by Western views of the practice. Proponents claim that FGM reduces rape and adolescent pregnancies.

Box 12.2 (*continued*)

Without data to confirm or deny these claims, the full impact of FGM on the demography of a nation can only be estimated (Larson and Yan 2000). Findings are equivocal about the impact of FGM on regional fertility and infertility rates. Discrepancies are associated with region and nationality but these differences may be due to inadequate data collection. The cultural practice of FGM has been correlated with patriarchy and honor codes. Infibulation has been compared to Chinese foot-binding, which is not religious in nature yet has the ritual effect of increasing group identity by providing community cohesion and boundary maintenance (Mackie 1996). However, few scholars link this practice to male circumcision. Worldwide, only 25 percent of men are circumcised for religious, cultural, or parental-preference reasons (Moses, Bailey, and Ronald 1998).

Policies now focus on education and outreach to at-risk communities. In a recent discussion of cultural identity, an African man warned agencies to allow people to define their own treatment, meaning that culture must be preserved and honored if this delicate transition is to succeed (Yankah 1992). He pointed to songs and fables that are used by locals to pass along symbolic cultural meaning and reiterated that policies can only suggest behaviors; it is through rituals that behaviors and then cultures may change.

Source: Yankah, Kwesi. 1992. "Traditional Lore in Population Communication: The Case of the Akan in Ghana." *Africa Media Review* 6.

Key Concepts

Beauty myth	In-group/out-group
Counterculture	Material culture
Cultural apparatus	Nonmaterial culture
Cultural artifacts	Oppositional culture
Cultural capital	Protestant Work Ethic
Cultural hegemony	Senior/class societies
Culture	Social capital
Culture wars	Social reproduction
Dominant culture	Strategies of action
Echo chamber	Subculture
Greek system	Supercultural
High-brow/low-brow	

Questions for Thought

1. What makes cultures different? Are there particular elements that change according to the culture or are some elements similar across cultures?
2. Historically, certain groups advocated for censorship of cultural products. Which products are regularly targeted? Why?
3. Countercultures often have an impact on mainstream society. How can a small number of people affect society at large? How would Marx and Weber reconcile this?
4. Hegemonic culture is in part a function of media concentration. Should there be policies regulating the media or art industries? How would that impact the production of culture?
5. Images of women in the media are harmful. Why have steps not been taken to reduce the harm? What steps could be taken?

6. Marcuse argued that all products in advanced industrial societies "indoctrinate and manipulate." Do you agree with his statement? Why or why not?

Exercises

1. *Garfinkel your family and friends.*

   Sociologist Harold Garfinkel studied the social construction of everyday life. His research focused on how people perform roles. An aspect of role-play is culture. Do you wash your hands before you eat a meal with family? Do you have specified seats at the dinner table? When you enter an elevator, do you look forward and divert the gaze of others? Try adopting a new culture in these familiar settings. What happens when you stand and face the "wrong way" in an elevator? Spend an afternoon Garfinkeling and keep a journal of the responses you receive. How do cultural expectations mediate these situations?

2. *Culturally relative examinations.*

   In 1973, Robert Williams created *The Black Intelligence Test of Cultural Homogeneity*. On this "exam," he listed questions that would be difficult for anyone not familiar with the black subculture to answer. The point of his work was to illustrate how cultural standards can affect measures of intelligence. Break into small groups in class and have each group make a list of questions similar to Williams's. Together as a class, see how well you do in answering them.

3. *Social boundaries in art.*

   Play a piece of music from a different culture – perhaps Indian or Chinese. Describe what you hear and your preferences regarding this music. How does it sound? Is it enjoyable? Then, play part of an opera, a symphony, a folk song, or another genre to which you do not normally listen. What does it mean to you? Describe your reaction but do not use any other genre when describing what you hear. Compare your reaction to others in class.

4. *They aren't like us.*

   Compile a list of social characteristics from six nations in various parts of the world: life expectancy, infant mortality, average years of education, literacy, and number of people living in poverty. Then, compare these data to that in America. Did you find what you expected to find? Discuss the expectations regarding these nations.

Multimedia Resources

Print

Bourdieu, P., A. Darbel, and D. Schnapper. 1991. *The Love of Art: European Art Museums and Their Public.* Stanford, CA: Stanford University Press.

Bourdieu, Pierre. 1987. *Distinction: A Social Critique of the Judgment of Taste.* Cambridge: Harvard University Press.

DiMaggio, Paul. 1997. "Culture and Cognition." *Annual Review of Sociology* 23: 263–87.

DiMaggio, Paul, and Francie Ostrower. 1990. "Participation in the Arts by Black and White Americans." *Social Forces* 68: 753–78.

Dowd, Timothy J. 2003. "Concentration and Diversity Revisited: Production Logics and the U.S. Mainstream Recording Market, 1940–1990." *Social Forces* 82: 1411.

Durkheim, Emile. [1912]1986. "The Elementary Forms of the Religious Life." In *Emile Durkheim: An Introduction to Four Major Works*, edited by R. A. Jones (pp 115-155). Beverly Hills, CA: Sage.

Gramsci, Antonio. [1971]1990. "Culture and Ideological Hegemony." In *Culture and Society: Contemporary Debates*, edited by J. C. A. a. S. Seidman (pp. 47-54). New York: Cambridge University Press.

Keister, L. 2003. "Religion and Wealth: The Role of Religious Affiliation and Early Adult Asset Accumulation." *Social Forces* 82: 173–205.

Lena, Jennifer C. 2004. "Meaning and Membership: Samples in Rap Music, 1979–1995." *Poetics* 32: 297–310.

Negus, Keith. 1999. *Music Genres and Corporate Cultures*. London: Routledge.

Peterson, Richard A., and David G. Berger. 1975. "Cycles in Symbol Production: The Case of Popular Music." *American Sociological Review* 40: 158–73.

Peterson, Richard A., and Roger M. Kern. 1996. "Changing Highbrow Taste: From Snob to Omnivore." *American Sociological Review* 61: 900–907.

Roscigno, Vincent J., and William F. Danaher. 2001. "Media and Mobilization: The Case of Radio and Southern Textile Worker Insurgency, 1929 to 1934." *American Sociological Review* 66: 21–48.

_____. 2004. *The Voice of Southern Labor: Radio, Music, and Textile Strikes, 1929–1934*. Minneapolis: University of Minnesota Press.

Rose, Tricia. 1994. *Black Noise: Rap Music and Black Culture in Contemporary America*. Middletown, CT: Wesleyan University Press.

Southgate, Darby E., and Vincent J. Roscigno. 2009. "The Impact of Music on Childhood and Adolescent Achievement." *Social Science Quarterly* 90: 4–21.

Weber, Max. [1922]1993. *The Sociology of Religion*. Boston, MA:Beacon Press.

_____. 2002. *The Protestant Ethic and the "Spirit" of Capitalism and Other Writings*. NY: Penguin Group USA.

Internet

(1) http://www.cjr.org/resources/: "Who Owns What." Columbia Journalism Review. Allows the user to choose a corporation in the media and look at all its holding companies.

(2) http://www.lostworlds.org/: Native American History.

(3) http://www.history.com/video.do?name=culture: History Channel's Web site offers short vignettes on various cultural topics (e.g., Woodstock, Elvis, and drugs).

(4) http://www.history.com/content/kwanzaa: History Channel on Kwanza.

(5) http://www.marxists.org/history/usa/workers/black-panthers/: Web site devoted to maintaining documents from the Black Panther Political Party.

Films

This Film Is Not Yet Rated (Kirby Dick, 2006). This documentary examines the Hays Code and the Motion Picture Association of America – the agency that sets movie ratings.

The Merchants of Cool (PBS Frontline) (Barak Goodman, 2001). Teenage culture can be reduced to males = mooks and females = midriffs in this polished PBS Frontline episode. The film tackles MTV, corporate concentration, and consumption.

The Corporation (Mark Achbar and Jennifer Abbott, 2003). This documentary investigates the development of modern corporations and evaluates their power and influence over society.

Reverend Billy and the Church of Stop Shopping (Dietmar Post and Lucia Palacios, 2002). This documents the protests of Billy Tallon and the Church of Stop Shopping. Through his activism, he preserves the Edgar Allan Poe house in New York City and attempts to shift the American culture away from consumerism.

What Would Jesus Buy? (Rob VanAlkemade, 2007). Reverend Billy is once again at his social-theater best in this new version of stop-shopping consumerism culture.

The Greatest Silence: Rape in the Congo (Lisa F. Jackson, 2007). A documentary that chronicles the plight of women in the Republic of Congo where civil war and domination for resources have made men – foreign-aid workers, soldiers, and members of the community – turn against women in the most violent acts imaginable. The culture of war is shocking and this documentary exposes it.

A Century of Women: Image and Popular Culture (Sylvia Morales, 1994). Ideal beauty and how women see themselves is explored through a star-studded cast reading from ethnographic accounts of women in the twentieth century.

Forgotten Fires (Michael Chandler, 2001). The documentary follows a young member of the Ku Klux Klan and traces a news headline in South Carolina to expose historical, economic, and social context of church burnings in the 1990s.

Keep Her Under Control: Law's Patriarchy in India (Erin Moore, 1998). This documentary provides a fascinating look at the experience of a woman in India who refuses to live by the moral and legal codes of her country.

Killing Us Softly III: Advertising's Images of Women (Sut Jhally, 2000). The series of Jean Kilbourne's exploration of images of women in the media exposes the objectification of women through the beauty myth.

Works Cited

American Civil Liberties Union. 2006. "Popular Music under Siege." Washington, DC.

Becker, Howard S. 1984. *Art Worlds*. Berkeley: University of California Press.

Bielby, William T., and Denise D. Bielby. 1994. "'All Hits Are Flukes': Institutionalized Decision Making and the Rhetoric of Network Prime-Time Program Development." *The American Journal of Sociology* 99: 1287–313.

Blau, Judith R., Peter M. Blau, and Reid M. Golden. 1985. "Social Inequality and the Arts." *The American Journal of Sociology* 91: 309–31.

Bourdieu, Pierre. 1984. *Distinction: A Social Critique of the Judgment of Taste*. Translated by R. Nice. Cambridge: Harvard University Press.

_____. 1986. "The Forms of Capital." In *Handbook of Theory and Research for the Sociology of Education*, edited by J. G. Richardson (pp. 241–58). Westport, CT: Greenwood Press.

Bragg, Billy. 2006. "Who Owns the Music, MTV or Me? The Rise of Networking Websites Brings into Question the Role of Record Companies in the Age of the mp3." In *Guardian.co.uk*. London: Guardian News and Media Limited, 2009.

Bryson, Bethany. 1996. "'Anything But Heavy Metal': Symbolic Exclusion and Musical Dislikes." *American Sociological Review* 61: 884–99.

Bureau of Labor Statistics. 2009. National Longitudinal Survey of Youth 79. Washington, DC: United States Department of Labor, Bureau of Labor Statistics.

Centers for Disease Control and Prevention. 2009. "Body Measurements: Measured Average Height, Weight, and Waist Circumference for Adults Ages 20 Years and Over." Atlanta, GA.

Compaine, Benjamin M., and Douglas Gomery. 2000. *Who Owns the Media? Competition and Concentration in the Mass Media Industry*. Mahwah, NJ: Laurence Erlbaum Associates.

Cookson, Peter W. 1997. *Lessons from Privilege: The American Prep School Tradition*. Cambridge: Harvard University Press.

Cross, Brian. 1994. *It's Not About a Salary: Rap, Race and Resistance in LA.* New York: Verso.

Dakenoo, E. 1993. "6,000 Girls at Risk Every Day: Female Genital Mutilation, Although Illegal, is Still Widely Practiced." *Women's Health Newsletter* 20: 10–11.

Demers, Joanna. 2003. "Sampling the 1970s in Hip Hop." *Popular Music* 22: 41–56.

DiMaggio, Paul. 1982. "Cultural Capital and School Success: The Impact of Status Culture Participation on the Grades of U.S. High School Students." *American Sociological Review* 47: 189–201.

Domhoff, G. William. 1970. *The Higher Circles.* New York: Random House.

_____. 2002. *Who Rules America? Power and Politics* (4th edition). New York: McGraw Hill.

Dowd, Timothy J. 2003. "Concentration and Diversity Revisited: Production Logics and the U.S. Mainstream Recording Market, 1940–1990." *Social Forces* 82: 1411.

Durkheim, Emile. [1912]1954. *The Elementary Forms of Religious Life.* New York: The Free Press.

Ellison, Christopher G. 1991. "Religious Involvement and Subjective Well-Being." *Journal of Health and Social Behavior* 32: 80–99.

Ellison, Christopher G., David A. Gay, and Thomas A. Glass. 1989. "Does Religious Commitment Contribute to Individual Life Satisfaction?" *Social Forces* 68: 100–23.

Ellison, Christopher G., and Jeffrey S. Levin. 1998. "The Religion–Health Connection: Evidence, Theory, and Future Directions." *Health Education and Behavior* 25: 700–20.

Epic Records. 1982. Michael Jackson's "Thriller." New York: Epic Records.

Fortune Magazine. 2002. "America's 40 Richest People Under 40." Available at www.fortune.com/fortune/40under40/.

George, Nelson. 1988. *Death of Rhythm and Blues.* New York: Pantheon Books.

Gomery, Douglas. 2000. "Radio Broadcasting and the Music Industry." In *Who Owns the Media? Competition and Concentration in the Mass Media Industry*, edited by B. M. Compaine and D. Gomery (pp. 285-358). Mahwah, NJ: Laurence Erlbaum Associates.

Gramsci, Antonio. [1971]1990. "Culture and Ideological Hegemony." In *Culture and Society: Contemporary Debates (47–54)*, edited by J. C. A. a. S. Seidman. New York: Cambridge University Press.

Granovetter, Mark S. 1973. "The Strength of Weak Ties." *American Journal of Sociology* 78: 1361–80.

Groesz, Lisa M., Michael P. Levine, and Sara K. Murnen. 2002. "The Effect of Experimental Presentation of Thin Media Images on Body Satisfaction: A Meta-Analytic Review." *International Journal of Eating Disorders* 31: 1–16.

Guinness World Records. 2007. *The Guinness Book of World Records.* London: Guinness World Records Limited.

Hesse-Biber, Sharlene. 1989. "Eating Patterns and Disorders in a College Population: Are College Women's Eating Problems a New Phenomenon?" *Sex Roles* 20: 71–89.

_____. 1997. *Am I Thin Enough Yet? The Cult of Thinness and the Commercialization of Identity.* New York: Oxford University Press.

Jackson, Linda A., John E. Hunter, and Carole N. Hodge. 1995. "Physical Attractiveness and Intellectual Competence: A Meta-Analytic Review." *Social Psychology Quarterly* 58: 108–22.

Keister, Lisa A. 2003. "Religion and Wealth: The Role of Religious Affiliation and Participation in Early Adult Asset Accumulation." *Social Forces* 82: 173–205.

Krause, Neal, Christopher G. Ellison, Benjamin A. Shaw, John P. Marcum, and Jason D. Boardman. 2001. "Church-Based Social Support and Religious Coping." *Journal for the Scientific Study of Religion* 40: 637–56.

Larson, Ulla and Sharon Yan. 2000. "Does Female Circumcision Affect Infertility and Fertility? A Study of the Central African Republic, Cote D'Ivoire, and Tanzania." *Demography* 37: 313–21.

Lena, Jennifer C. 2004. "Meaning and Membership: Samples in Rap Music, 1979–1995." *Poetics* 32: 297–310.

Levin, Jeffrey S. 1994. *Religion in Aging and Health: Theoretical Foundations and Methodological Frontiers*. Thousand Oaks, CA: Sage Publications.

Lightfoot-Klein, H. 1989. "The Sexual Experience and Marital Adjustment of Genitally Circumcised and Infibulated Females in the Sudan." *The Journal of Sex Research* 26: 375–92.

Mackie, Gerry. 1996. "Ending Foot-Binding and Infibulation: A Convention Account." *American Sociological Review* 61: 999–1017.

Marcuse, Herbert. 1964. *One Dimensional Man*. Boston: Beacon.

McCaulay, Marci, Laurie Mintz, and Audrey A. Glenn. 1988. "Body Image, Self-Esteem, and Depression-Proneness: Closing the Gender Gap." *Sex Roles* 18: 381–91.

Milkie, Melissa A. 2002. "Contested Images of Femininity: An Analysis of Cultural Gatekeepers' Struggles with the 'Real Girl' Critique." *Gender & Society* 16: 839–59.

Moses, Stephen, Robert C. Bailey, and Allan R. Ronald. 1998. "Male Circumcision: Assessment of Health Benefits and Risks." *British Medical Journal* 74: 368.

Nakalema, R. 1990. "Moi Bans Female Circumcision." *New African* June 47 PMID:12293761 http://www.ncbi.nlm.nih.gov/pubmed/12293761

National Institute of Mental Health. 2009. "Eating Disorders." Washington, DC: U.S.

Department of Health and Human Services, National Institutes of Health.

Negus, Keith. 1999. *Music Genres and Corporate Cultures*. London: Psychology Press.

Nichter, Mark, and Mimi Nichter. 1991. "Hype and Weight." *Medical Anthropology* 13: 249–84.

Ogbu, John. 2003. *Black American Students in an Affluent Suburb: A Study of Academic Disengagement*. Mahwah, NJ: Laurence Erlbaum Associates.

Pascal, Zachary G. 1999. "Let's Play Oligopoly! Why Giants Like Having Other Giants Around." In *Wall Street Journal*. New York: Dow Jones & Company, Inc.

Peterson, Richard A., and David G. Berger. 1975. "Cycles in Symbol Production: The Case of Popular Music." *American Sociological Review* 40: 158–73.

Peterson, Richard A., and Roger M. Kern. 1996. "Changing Highbrow Taste: From Snob to Omnivore." *American Sociological Review* 61: 900–907.

Portes, Alejandro. 1998. "Social Capital: Its Origins and Applications in Modern Sociology." *Annual Review of Sociology* 24: 1–24.

Recording Industry Associaton of America. 2009. "1999–2008 Music Consumer Profile." Washington, DC.

Roberts, Robert E., George A. Kaplan, Sarah J. Shema, and William J. Strawbridge. 2000. "Are the Obese at Greater Risk for Depression?" *American Journal of Epidemiology* 152: 163.

Rose, Tricia. 1994. *Black Noise: Rap Music and Black Culture in Contemporary America*. Middletown, CT: Wesleyan University Press.

Sarlio-Lahteenkorva, Sirpa, and Eero Lahelma. 1999. "The Association of Body Mass Index with Social and Economic Disadvantage in Women and Men." *International Journal of Epidemiology* 28: 445.

Sherkat, Darren. 2009. "Religion and Verbal Ability." *Social Science Research* 10: 2–13.

Simmel, Georg. 1905. "A Contribution to the Sociology of Religion." *American Journal of Sociology* 11: 359–76.

Smith, Christian. 2003a. "Religious Participation and Network Closure among American Adolescents." *Journal for the Scientific Study of Religion* 42: 259–67.

———. 2003b. "Research Note: Religious Participation and Parental Moral Expectations and Supervision of American Youth." *Review of Religious Research* 44: 414–24.

Sombart, Werner. 1911. *The Jews and Modern Capitalism.* Translated by M. Epstein. New York: E. P. Dutton and Company.

Southgate, Darby E. 2007. "Review Author for 'Can't Stop, Won't Stop' by Jeff Chang." *Socialism and Democracy* 20: 166–9.

_____. 2008. "Rap Music." In *Encyclopedia of Gangs*, edited by L. K. a. D. C. Brotherton (pp. 201–). Westport, CT: Greenwood Publishing Group, Inc.

Southgate, Darby E., and Vincent J. Roscigno. 2009. "The Impact of Music on Childhood and Adolescent Achievement." *Social Science Quarterly* 90: 4–21.

SPHINX. 2009. "SPHINX Senior Class Honorary." Retrieved December 1; available at www. sphinx.org.ohio-state.edu/.

Spiegler, Marc. 1996. "Marketing Street Culture." *American Demographics* 18: 28–32.

Stevens, Jay. 1998. *Storming Heaven: LSD and the American Dream.* New York: Grove Press.

Sullivan, Rachel. 2003. "Rap and Race: It's Got a Nice Beat, But What About the Message?" *Journal of Black Studies* 33: 605–22.

Swidler, Ann. 1986. "Culture in Action: Symbols and Strategies." *American Sociological Review* 51(2): 273–286.

Trustees of Dartmouth College. 2009. "Senior Societies." *Greek Life and Societies.* Available at www.dartmouth.edu/ orl/greek-soc/societies/senior.html.

Van Peebles, Melvin and Jerry Gross. 1971. Sweet Sweetback's Baadasssss Song Distributed by Cinemation Industries.

Weber, Max. [1905]1930. *The Protestant Ethic and the Spirit of Capitalism.* New York: Harper Collins.

Wolf, Naomi. [1990]2002. *The Beauty Myth. How Images of Beauty Are Used Against Women.* London: Vintage Books.

Wolff, Janet. 1999. "Cultural Studies and the Sociology of Culture." *Contemporary Sociology* 28: 499–507.

Wuthnow, Robert, and Marsha Witten. 1988. "New Directions in the Study of Culture." *Annual Review of Sociology* 14: 49–67.

Yankah, Kwesi. 1992. "Traditional Lore in Population Communication: The Case of the Akan in Ghana." *Africa Media Review* 6.

Zweigenhaft, Richard L. 1992. "The Application of Cultural and Social Capital: A Study of the 25th Year Reunion Entries of Prep School and Public School Graduates of Yale College." *Higher Education* 23: 311–20.

13 Inequality across the Globe

So far, our discussion has been almost exclusively about inequality in the United States. Although inequality and stratification in the United States are clearly complex enough to warrant the space given them, it is important to remember that patterns of stratification and the processes leading to them are different in other countries. It also is informative to consider where the United States falls in the larger picture. There are no contemporary societies in which resources are equally distributed, but the degree of inequality varies dramatically among countries. In particular, the disparity between the very rich and the very poor often differs notably across countries. This is especially true when comparing developed countries (e.g., Australia, the United States, Canada, and the United Kingdom) with those that are still developing (e.g., Brazil, China, Hungary, India, and Mexico). Understanding how the United States compares to other countries puts in perspective the processes we encounter close to home.

This chapter explores how the United States compares to other countries in terms of inequality and stratification. We consider various dimensions of inequality starting with a comparison of the United States to other developed countries. We explore cross-national patterns of income, poverty, work, mobility, and other indicators of well-being, such as the nature of the welfare state and the ownership of housing and other forms of wealth. We then compare developed countries to countries that are still developing. We explore multiple dimensions of inequality to provide as complete a picture as possible. We conclude with a discussion of inequality in transition economies – those that have undergone a transformation in recent decades from socialism to more market-oriented economic systems. As we consider inequality in comparative perspective, a special caveat is in order: The data used to compare countries can vary in subtle but important ways. As we discuss how the United States compares, remember that minor differences in data collection and analysis can have significant implications for interpretation. As with all data, read with a critical eye and an understanding that no empirical evidence is perfect.

Inequality in the Developed World

Inequality in the developed world can be somewhat unique from that of the developing world and deserves special attention.

Income

A comparison of inequality levels in the United States to levels in other developed countries reveals an important pattern: U.S. inequality is among the most extreme in the developed world. Table 13.1 compares the *Gini Index* (i.e., a single measure that summarizes overall inequality) in the United States to other developed countries. It ranges from zero to 1, with higher numbers indicating higher levels of inequality. An income Gini Index value of zero suggests perfect equality (i.e., everyone has the same income), whereas a value of 1 suggests perfect inequality (i.e., one person receives all income). The Gini Index also can be calculated for wealth ownership and other measures of social stratification. As Table 13.1 indicates, the income Gini Index in the United States is 0.41. Another interpretation of this number is that 41 percent of all income would have to trade hands for complete equality. The table also shows the Gini Index for several other countries, ranked from high to low. Notice that inequality is lower in all other countries than in the United States; some countries have inequality levels that are considerably lower. For example, Italy and the United Kingdom have Gini Index scores of 0.36, Australia and Spain are slightly lower at 0.35, and Canada and France follow closely at 0.33. Also notice that several countries have low inequality relative to other developed nations. Northern European countries and Japan, for instance, have Gini Index scores lower than 0.30.

Table 13.1 Gini Index for Income: The U.S. and Selected Developed Countries

Country	Gini Index
United States	0.41
Italy	0.36
United Kingdom	0.36
Australia	0.35
Spain	0.35
Switzerland	0.34
Canada	0.33
France	0.33
Korea (Republic of)	0.32
Netherlands	0.31
Germany	0.28
Finland	0.27
Norway	0.26
Denmark	0.25
Japan	0.25
Sweden	0.25

Data source: World Bank, 2008

Poverty

Poverty is another important concept to consider in cross-national comparisons because it suggests the proportion of the population that is adversely affected by inequality. In other words, if there were high inequality in a country but everyone lived above the poverty line, we would be less concerned than if the country had low inequality but a very high percentage of the population living in poverty. Studying poverty cross-nationally also provides insight about the effectiveness of government policies for addressing the negative effects of living at low income levels because they vary markedly. Although measuring poverty across countries is important, it is particularly challenging because poverty can be a subjective concept. Most industrialized countries are concerned about the detrimental effects of living with low and inadequate income, but few nations have official poverty measures. Among the developed nations, only the United States and the United Kingdom regularly track poverty rates (Smeeding 2008). In other developed countries, discussion related to low-income individuals and families takes different approaches. For example, Northern European and Scandinavian countries do not calculate poverty rates and most acknowledge that their social programs ensure that relatively few people live with extremely low income. In these countries, rather than focusing on poverty, debate centers on the income level at which social benefits should be received (Atkinson, Cantillon, Marlier, and Nolan 2002; Smeeding 2008).

The limited research that compares poverty rates cross-nationally shows that there is more poverty in the United States than in other developed countries. Using the Luxembourg Income Study (LIS) – a unique database that includes income information for several countries – Smeeding created a poverty threshold for select developed countries to understand how poverty varies across them. He showed that relative poverty in the United States is extremely high (Smeeding 2008). To measure poverty, he calculated the percentage of households living with an income below 50 percent of the median for that

Table 13.2 Poverty Rates in Select Developed Countries

Country	% in Poverty
United States	**17.0**
Spain	14.3
Australia	13.0
Italy	12.7
United Kingdom	12.4
Canada	11.4
Germany	8.3
France	7.3
Netherlands	7.3
Sweden	6.5
Norway	6.4
Finland	5.4

Data source: Luxembourg Income Survey, 1999–2002. Poverty is defined as people with disposable incomes less than 50 percent of adjusted national disposable median income.

country. In the United States, 17 percent of households are in poverty by this measure. For comparison, Smeeding showed that 20 percent of Mexican households were living in poverty. By contrast, poverty rates in Europe are relatively low. Of the European countries, Spain has relatively high poverty, with 14.3 percent of households living below the poverty line. Similarly, 13 percent of Australian households, 12.4 percent of UK households, and 11.4 percent of Canadian households were in poverty at the time of the study. As expected, Northern European countries with strong welfare states have much lower poverty levels. Smeeding showed, for instance, that 7.3 percent of households in the Netherlands, 6.5 percent of Swedish households, 6.4 percent of Norwegian households, and 5.4 percent of Finnish households live in poverty. Smeeding showed that rates of poverty for children follow similar patterns. Nearly 22 percent of U.S. children (age 17 or younger) live in poverty, whereas in Sweden, Norway, and Finland, less than 5 percent of children fall below Smeeding's poverty cutoff.

There is intense debate regarding whether inequality is desirable. Some scholars argue that inequality provides an incentive for low-income people to work hard and improve their living conditions (Welch 1999). Uncomfortable conditions provide an incentive for people to do better than their parents and to improve their own well-being over time. Others argue that there is no evidence from history or current data that poverty or inequality has any positive effect on incentives or motivation (Burtless and Christopher 2003; Smeeding 2008). Those who are skeptical about the benefits of inequality note that the real incomes (adjusted for costs) of poor households in the United States are at or below the income that a typical poor household receives in comparable, industrialized countries with less inequality (Smeeding 2008). Empirical studies examining changes in poverty over long periods also suggest that there are no real benefits to poverty. There also is compelling historical evidence suggesting that higher levels of social spending (e.g., government-transfer payments such as food stamps) create higher levels of economic growth while it improves social well-being.

Work and Employment

Patterns of work and employment also vary significantly among developed countries, and globalization is contributing to changes in these patterns. *Globalization* refers to the economic, political, social, and cultural connections among countries that increasingly characterize the globe. The effect of globalization is not limited to work and employment, but its impact is particularly evident there. An important change to which globalization has contributed and that highlights cross-country inequalities is the general trend in industrialized countries away from traditional work arrangements and toward using *nonstandard work relations* (NSWAs). NSWAs are any work relations other than full-time, permanent work, including part-time, temporary, on-call/day labor, short-term employment, and contract work (Polivka, Cohany, and Hipple 2000). NSWAs include arrangements that favor workers (i.e., when they provide flexibility or jobs for those who might otherwise be unemployed) and arrangements that have negative consequences for workers (i.e., when they ultimately reduce the pay or benefits that workers receive for the same job they did under a traditional arrangement). One challenge that researchers face is identifying when NSWAs are beneficial and when they are harmful.

Because there is no single conclusion, it is not always clear that the increase in NSWAs is a problem.

What accounted for the increased use of NSWAs? There was no single cause but rather a combination of factors that apparently contributed to the diffusion of these practices among countries. First, economic conditions during the 1970s "set the stage" by creating incentives for many workers, work organizations, and countries to adopt NSWAs. Slow economic growth in the later part of that decade increased unemployment and made it clear that many economies could not produce enough jobs for available workers. Second, globalization as we know it today began to become apparent. Global competitiveness began to increase and put pressure on firms to increase efficiency to remain profitable. As a result, many companies located in developed countries began to outsource tasks to developing countries. At the same time, the economies of many developed countries began to shift from manufacturing to service, increasing numbers of women and older workers demanded greater flexibility in their work, and improved technology made nontraditional arrangements possible (e.g., working from home) (Kalleberg 2000). These and related processes created demand for flexible NSWAs in developed countries (Kalleberg 2003, 2006).

Although the use of NSWAs generally has increased, countries differ in the specific types of work arrangements. The extent to which particular NSWAs are prevalent in a country depends on legal structure, norms, and history. Kalleberg (2006), for example, showed that there are significant differences among countries in the use of part-time workers. In the United States, the most common NSWA is part-time work; approximately 20 percent of American workers are part-time. In contrast, rates of part-time work are closer to 15–16 percent in many Western European countries; notable exceptions include Sweden (24 percent), the Netherlands (30 percent), and Finland (10 percent). *Temporary work*, defined as work obtained through temporary-help agencies that do not supervise the work, also has grown rapidly in both the United States and Europe. Whereas only a small percentage of the population in most industrialized countries works in temporary positions (i.e., less than 10 percent), growth in this type of position is increasing rapidly. Moreover, positions found through temporary agencies are important for understanding inequality because these jobs are extremely sensitive to business cycles and changing economic conditions. *Contract work*, obtained through agencies that supervise the work (e.g., data entry and cleaning) and self-employment also have increased, but trends in these types of work vary dramatically among countries. Only about 3 percent of U.S. workers are in temporary positions and about 8 percent are self-employed (Kalleberg 2006). By contrast, 26 and 33 percent of Australian and Finnish workers, respectively, are in temporary positions, and nearly 20 percent of Spanish and Portuguese workers are self-employed.

The concern with NSWAs is that they offer less employment security, usually by definition. In addition, there is evidence that nonstandard jobs are lower quality, provide lower salaries and fewer benefits, offer more limited opportunities for training and career mobility, and reduce saving and wealth ownership for workers (Kalleberg 2000, 2006; McGrath and Keister 2007). Part-time jobs in the United States tend to be particularly low paid and low prestige; they also typically provide few benefits such as health insurance, other forms of insurance, and retirement benefits (Kalleberg, Reskin, and Hudson 2000).

In contrast, some countries legally require that employers treat full- and part-time workers equally. In Sweden, France, Belgium, the Netherlands, and Spain, for instance, part-time workers receive treatment equivalent to full-time workers (Kalleberg 2006). Other developed countries are more similar to the United States in their labor laws: the United Kingdom, Germany, and Japan, for instance, allow employers to differentiate between part- and full-time workers (Kalleberg 2006). Some scholars argue that this reduces the quality of part-time work (Kalleberg, Reskin, and Hudson 2000).

Education

Developed countries also are similar in their focus on and relative success in providing basic mass education. During the nineteenth century, most of today's developed countries began to create what are now modern systems of formal education. These systems were consolidated and strengthened in the twentieth century and – despite some remaining flaws – are now relatively effective in providing at least a basic education for most citizens. Education systems are highly institutionalized throughout the world today. The approaches that developed countries take to mass education are extremely similar and have become more similar over time. The reasons that so many countries developed universal, standardized mass education systems are not as universally accepted as the systems they try to explain. However, there is agreement that the need to socialize people to the accepted practices of the nation was an important cause (Meyer, Ramirez, Rubinson, and Boli-Bennett 1977). For example, primary and secondary schools teach students the basic facts needed to understand how to participate in civic behaviors (e.g., voting).

Regardless of the historic processes that led to mass education, throughout the developed world, universal primary and secondary education is the norm. Enrollment in primary education for age-appropriate students is 100 percent, or nearly so, in industrialized countries (UNESCO 2009). Enrollment in secondary education is high as well, exceeding 90 percent in most developed countries and 100 percent in many of those (e.g., Belgium, the Netherlands, Sweden, and Japan estimate that all age-appropriate students are enrolled in secondary education). Consistent with these high levels of primary-school enrollment, literacy rates in developed countries are extremely high. The adult literacy rate for a country indicates the percentage of the population older than age 15 that can read and write. Because most developed countries have high literacy rates, many no longer collect related data. However, international organizations such as UNESCO suggest that literacy rates are nearly 100 percent in these countries.

Enrollment in tertiary education, which includes college, university, and business and other technical schools, also is high in developed countries (UNESCO 2009). It has become a more important part of the education systems of developed countries as demand for more advanced training has increased among most industries. Enrollment in tertiary education has increased and exceeds 80 percent of the age-appropriate population in the United States, Canada, and Australia. However, there is considerable variation in tertiary enrollments, and some developed countries have rates below 50 percent (UNESCO 2009). Variations in availability of tertiary options, assistance with educational funding, economic conditions, education quality, and other cultural factors influence the rates.

One ironic consequence of increases in education in general and tertiary education in particular is *credential inflation*, which refers to the growth in credentials that occurs when more people complete more education. As more people finish secondary and tertiary educations, the value of their education is lower. Employers can require higher levels of education for jobs, and the amount of income that a given level of education can "purchase" drops (Collins 1979). Nearly all industrialized countries have experienced some degree of credential inflation.

Wealth

Because data on wealth (i.e., net worth) are even scarcer than data on income, it is difficult to compare wealth inequality among countries. The available data can be problematic because the distribution of wealth is skewed (i.e., a few very rich households own much of the wealth), and these problems are even more difficult in cross-country data because of differences in collection procedures. Yet, wealth is critical to understanding cross-national variations in inequality. Fortunately, the quality of wealth data in many countries has improved in recent years and cross-national data are becoming more available. A significant advance in the cross-national study of wealth is the creation of the Luxembourg Wealth Study (LWS), an international effort to collate wealth data collected in several countries (Brandolini, Smeeding, and Sierminska 2008). The LWS makes it possible to draw basic conclusions about how countries rank on wealth ownership and levels of wealth inequality. Table 13.3 uses LWS data to compare wealth-ownership patterns in select developed countries. The list of countries is brief because comparable data simply are not available for a larger group of nations.

Table 13.3 suggests that the distribution of wealth in the United States is even more unequal than in other wealthy countries. The first column compares the percentage of households in each country that has positive net worth (i.e., total assets less total debts greater than zero). It shows that 77 percent of Americans have positive net worth. The same percentage (i.e., 77 percent) of Canadians has positive wealth. In contrast, nearly 90 percent of Italians and more than 80 percent of Finnish and British households have positive wealth. At the other end of the spectrum is Germany, where only 63 percent of households have positive wealth. The second column shows the percentage of households in each country that has negative net worth (i.e., more debts than assets). In the United States and Canada, 20 percent of households have negative net worth. Although this is extreme, it is not the worst case of high indebtedness; in Sweden, nearly one-third of households have negative wealth. Italy and Germany (3 and 9 percent, respectively) have many fewer households with negative net worth. Taken together, the data in the first two columns show that a relatively high percentage of American and Canadian households are in the tails of the wealth distribution. That is, wealth inequality is similar in the United States and Canada, and the level of inequality is relatively high compared to other developed countries (Brandolini, Smeeding, and Sierminska 2008).

The extent to which wealth is unequally distributed in the United States becomes even clearer when we consider other indicators of wealth inequality. For example, in previous chapters, we use wealth ownership by the very rich to understand the distribution of wealth. Because this also is a useful way to compare countries, Table 13.3 includes the

Table 13.3 Wealth Ownership in Developed Countries

	Positive Net Worth (%)	Negative Net Worth (%)	Share Owned by Top 1% (%)	Gini Index
Canada	77	20	15	0.75
Finland	83	15	13	0.68
Germany	63	9	14	0.78
Italy	89	3	11	0.61
Sweden	68	27	18	0.89
United Kingdom	82	11	10	0.66
United States	77	20	33	0.84

Data source: Luxembourg Wealth Survey (2007).

percentage of wealth owned by the very wealthy (i.e., the top 1 percent). In the United States, the top 1 percent owns 33 percent of all household wealth – by far, the highest percentage among the countries included in the table. Sweden has the second-highest value on this variable; however, in that country, the top 1 percent owns only 18 percent of wealth. In Canada – which we know is similar to the United States on other measures of wealth ownership – the top 1 percent owns only 15 percent of total wealth. In the United Kingdom, the percentage owned by the richest households is only 10 percent. In other words, in the United States, a small number of households owns a comparably high percentage of all wealth. This is borne out in the last column of Table 13.3, which displays the Gini Index for wealth. For the United States, it is 0.84, which means that 84 percent of wealth would need to trade hands for all households to have the same wealth. The value is high, but the Gini Index in Sweden in even higher (i.e., 0.89), reflecting the large percentage of Swedish households that have negative net worth. Although it is tempting to conclude that conditions are less desirable in Sweden, there is evidence that wealth mobility is higher there than in the United States (Klevmarken, Lupton, and Stafford 2003). The Gini Index for the remaining countries is noticeably lower than in the United States and Sweden, ranging from 0.78 in Germany to 0.61 in Italy.

Inequality in Developing Countries

Inequality in developing countries assumes an enormous number of forms. Likewise, the differences between developing and developed countries are immense. We cannot address all of the factors with which developing countries contend; however, in this section, we discuss some of the major issues. We explore inequalities in income, work and employment, education, and wealth because we addressed these topics for developed countries. As we might imagine, however, any of the issues addressed in this book are relevant to understanding stratification in the developing world. For instance, gender, ethnicity, religion, and culture all are issues on which people are stratified in developing countries just as they are in the United States. In addition, other issues are either unique to developing countries or intensified in these countries, including population pressures, access to adequate health care, crime, and war. Students who have an interest in any of these topics can explore the issues using the many volumes written on the subjects.

Income

Inequality in developed and developing countries should be compared only cautiously. After all, drawing conclusions about patterns in countries that have vastly different sized economies is difficult at best and, at worst, could be misleading. Yet, comparisons of this type can be informative. In particular, it is useful to understand how inequality in the United States compares to inequality in developing countries. Data on household income are widely available; therefore, considering global income patterns is a logical place to start. Table 13.4 is the Gini Index for income for select developing countries and for the United States; the estimates suggest that inequality in many developing countries is much worse than in the United States. Inequality in many South American countries, for instance, is relatively high. Argentina, Bolivia, Brazil, Chile, Columbia,

Table 13.4 Inequality in the Developing World

Country	Gini Index	% in Poverty	% Literate
Sierra Leone	0.63	70.2	34.8
Bolivia	0.60	60.0	86.7
Columbia	0.59	49.2	92.8
Brazil	0.57	31.0	88.6
Chile	0.55	18.2	95.7
Niger	0.51	63.0	28.7
Argentina	0.51	23.4	97.2
Venezuela (Bolivarian Republic of)	0.48	37.9	93.0
China	0.47	8.0	90.9
Mexico	0.46	40.0	91.6
Uruguay	0.45	27.4	96.8
Iran (Islamic Republic of)	0.43	18.0	82.4
United States	0.41	12.0	99.0
Russia	0.40	15.8	99.4
Jordan	0.39	14.2	91.1
India	0.37	25.0	61.0
Estonia	0.36	5.0	99.8
Lithuania	0.36	4.0	99.6
Poland	0.35	17.0	99.8
Indonesia	0.34	17.8	90.4
Hungary	0.27	8.6	99.4
Slovakia	0.26	21.0	99.0

Data sources: Gini Index: World Bank, 2008. Poverty rates: Central Intelligence Agency's World Factbook, 2009. Literacy rates: United Nations Development Program Human Development Report, 2007–08. The poverty estimate for the United States is lower than the estimate reported in Table 13.3 because the CIA reports the percentage below the official poverty level. The Uruguay estimate is for households.

and Uruguay all have high levels of income inequality. Bolivia has one of the highest levels of income inequality in the world, with a Gini Index of 0.60. Income inequality also is high in many African countries.

Table 13.4 includes two extreme examples to illustrate inequality levels at the high end of the spectrum: The Gini Index is 0.63 in Sierra Leone and 0.51 in Niger. Of course, there also are countries with a relatively low level of inequality; in particular, the table indicates that income inequality is comparatively low in some former socialist countries: Estonia, Hungary, Lithuania, Poland, and Slovakia all have less income inequality than the United States and relatively low inequality compared to other developing countries. Low inequality in these countries reflects government policies that aim to promote equality, which were pervasive under socialism. As markets continue to develop in these countries, it is likely that inequality will grow (transition economies are discussed later in this chapter).

Another way to think about global income inequality and the well-being of developing countries is to consider the distribution of income and wealth *across* rather than *within* countries. That is, what proportion of the world's total resources are owned or received in developed versus developing countries? As expected, developed countries have much higher incomes, both nationally and individually, than developing countries. The human development report indicates that GDP per capita for rich countries is more than $33,000 per year (United Nations 2008). GDP per capita for all developing countries is just over $5,000 per year and about $1,500 for the least-developed countries. Although income inequality among nations is not contested, there is debate about whether it is growing. Some observers have argued or simply assumed that globalization led to increasing income inequality (Castells 1998); others counter that these conclusions are based on misleading data analysis. In a provoking study of global income inequality, for example, Firebaugh (2003) argued that many researchers falsely conclude that income inequality across nations is growing because income growth has been more rapid in rich nations than in poor nations. His own analysis showed that global income inequality increased for a time but then leveled off and began to decline toward the end of the twentieth century. Part of the difficulty in quantifying patterns in inequality among countries results from the data inconsistencies mentioned previously. One conclusion is certain: The debate regarding patterns of global income inequality will continue.

Poverty

The pervasiveness of poverty and international variations in inequality become clear when poverty levels are compared cross-nationally. To understand poverty variation among developing countries, we draw on World Factbook estimates (Central Intelligence Agency 2003), shown in Table 13.5.[1] The range of poverty levels is more extreme

---

[1] Recall that we used Smeeding's (2008) research to understand poverty in developed countries. His data and methods are highly reliable for the countries he studied, but he does not include developing countries in his work. World Factbook estimates are considered reliable for developing countries.

Table 13.5 Gini Index for Wealth: The U.S. and Selected Developing Countries

Country	Gini Index
World	0.89
United States	**0.80**
Brazil	0.78
Indonesia	0.76
Mexico	0.75
Argentina	0.74
Nigeria	0.74
Turkey	0.72
Thailand	0.71
Pakistan	0.70
Russia	0.70
Vietnam	0.68
Bangladesh	0.67
India	0.67
China	0.55

Data source: Davies, Sandstrom, Shorrocks, and Wolff (2009). The Gini Index for the United States differs slightly from the value reported in Table 13.3 because the data source is different.

than in developed countries; at the low end are Estonia, Lithuania, and Hungary, which were socialist until relatively recently. Poverty in the United States (12 percent) also is low compared to many of the developing countries included in the table. This is lower than the estimate reported in Table 13.3 because the World Factbook reports the percentage below the official poverty level, whereas Table 13.3 shows the percentage below 50 percent of the median income. The United States is noteworthy for high levels of inequality paired with a relatively low poverty rate (i.e., when developing countries are the comparison group). This pattern reflects the small number of very-high-income people in the United States, which leads to high inequality combined with government programs that are only somewhat effective at keeping poverty in check.

Indeed, poverty in the developing world is extremely high. In Sierra Leone, for example, an estimated 70 percent of the population lives in poverty. Although a comprehensive explanation for the enormous poverty is unavailable, it is worth mentioning as an example of an extremely poor nation and typical of the factors that contribute to poverty in other African countries. Sierra Leone is a Western African country bordering the North Atlantic Ocean. Geographically, it is smaller than the state of South Carolina; however, it has a relatively large population (i.e., more than 6 million) and a high fertility rate (i.e., 5.9 children per female). In contrast, the U.S. fertility rate is slightly higher than 2 children per female; in Hungary, it is 1.4, where poverty rates also are low. Sierra Leone is an agricultural nation with abundant natural resources; however, economic development is extremely difficult due to political instability.

China is another country worth contrasting to Sierra Leone. Table 13.3 indicates that 8 percent of China's population lives in poverty. There are important historical reasons for this remarkable contrast. China's population exceeds 1.3 billion, but a strictly enforced one-child policy has kept the fertility rate to 1.8 children per female. In addition, the country's political stability, history of redistributive economics, and thriving economy contribute to relatively low poverty.

Poverty also is relatively high in many Latin American countries: 60 percent of Bolivians, nearly 50 percent of Columbians, and 40 percent of Mexicans live below the poverty line for their respective countries. Bolivia is an extremely poor country, in part as a result of a devastating financial crisis during the 1980s and subsequent political instability and social protest surrounding the export of natural-gas resources. The country has not recovered from these challenges, which is reflected in the poverty rates (CIA World Factbook 2009). Columbia also has both high inequality and high poverty. In recent years, however, poverty in Columbia has begun to decline at least in part as a result of market-oriented reforms that have increased incomes for many citizens. Mexico has another story: Access to food is relatively high and, using a food-access–based definition of poverty, a much smaller number of people are below the poverty line (CIA World Factbook 2003). However, access to other necessities is not as high, at least in part as a result of political corruption, which has made poverty alleviation difficult to achieve.

Work and Employment

Different issues related to work and employment are more important in developing countries than in their developed counterparts. As in developed countries, the relevant issues in developing countries today stem from the changing nature of globalization. As Sernau documented effectively, globalization is not new; rather, it began when humans first left Africa (Sernau 2009). However, some of globalization's byproducts are quite new. Both *outsourcing* and *off-shoring*, for instance, are processes that cause globalization and its effects. These processes also have implications for inequality within and among developing countries. *Outsourcing* is a process of subcontracting manufacturing or services to a third party. *Off-shoring* refers to the movement of industrial production or services out of one country, usually a developed country, to another country, usually a developing country. For instance, when U.S. companies hire workers in China to manufacture its products, it is off-shoring. *Outsourcing* is a more general term, but the two are sometimes used synonymously given that outsourcing happens across national borders.

It is difficult to ascertain whether outsourcing and off-shoring are beneficial or harmful. These processes often are criticized because they can involve wealthier, developed countries exploiting workers in other countries. One measure of who wins and who loses is hourly compensation. In the United States, for instance, production workers in manufacturing earn an average of $30 per hour (Sernau 2009: 53; data are for 2006 from the U.S. Bureau of Labor Statistics). Workers in developing countries earn significantly less, of course, adding to the appeal of off-shoring. In parts of China and India, workers can earn less than the equivalent of $1 per hour. Wages are even lower in other parts of the world, consistent with the patterns discussed previously. In many African and Latin American countries, particularly those with high poverty levels, wages are very low. Naturally, these patterns vary even within a country, and the cost of living makes the wages more feasible than they would be in developed countries. Yet, global pressure to lower wages can mean that workers in developing countries live with inadequate income. Others argue that outsourcing and off-shoring have created a more level playing field in which workers in any part of the world can compete for the best jobs. For instance, Friedman (2006) argued that particularly for educated people, the ability to compete globally can be an advantage.

Another potential problem with outsourcing and off-shoring involves child labor. Most developed countries currently have laws that prohibit or restrict the work that children can do – which is not to say that developed countries never use child labor. On the contrary, children have worked on farms and in mines and factories for decades, and many of today's developed countries were able to industrialize – at least, in part – because of child labor. However, child labor is illegal in most developed countries today, whereas in developing countries, it is still common. As historically in the United States and other industrialized countries, children work on farms, in factories, in mines, and in service industries. Under the best circumstances, child laborers are treated well and receive wages that help their families survive. Too often, however, children are subjected to unsafe working conditions and otherwise treated badly. In the worst cases, children are kidnapped and forced into jobs that are illegal (e.g., prostitution and drug trafficking) or extremely dangerous (e.g., armed combat). International trafficking of children as slaves also is still rampant (International Labor Organization 2009).

Children are appealing as workers for many reasons, including that they can perform work that adults often cannot (e.g., fit in small places such as mine shafts), they typically receive lower wages, there is an ample supply particularly in developing countries where fertility rates are high, and they are less able to protest poor treatment and bad working conditions. Yet, there are numerous problems with using child labor, many of which are related to what makes them appealing workers. Fitting in small places can mean doing work that is extremely dangerous. Also, children's lack of power makes it easy to exploit and force them to work in unsafe conditions for minimal wages. Moreover, there are important opportunity costs of using child labor, including education. Children who work many hours in paid labor are less likely to attend school and complete higher levels of education. Being deprived of education has long-term drawbacks for children, their family, and their country.

Education

Mass education is much less the norm in developing than in developed countries. In fact, whereas literacy rates in developed countries approach 100 percent, large segments of the population in some developing countries cannot read or write. Literacy means more than simply reading books and writing letters; it is the key to participating effectively in society, politics, and economic activities. The UN estimates that 860 million adults throughout the world are illiterate and that more than 100 million children do not have access to school (United Nations 2010). As discussed in Chapter 8, a lack of education has significant long-term consequences for people and the society in which they live. Table 13.4 includes literacy rates for the select developing countries highlighted for comparison. Browsing the literacy rates, it is tempting to conclude that they are quite high. However, if we look more closely, we notice that some countries have very low literacy rates. These countries are representative of entire regions or continents. Sierra Leone is a major example: Only 34.8 percent of the adult population is literate, leaving a remarkably high 65 percent who cannot communicate in written form. Literacy is equally low in Niger. Bolivia, Brazil, and India have comparatively low levels of literacy as well, another indicator that they have large populations of poor people with limited access to many forms of communication that are increasingly important in today's modern world. The positive aspect of this table is that literacy rates are extremely high in many regions, exceeding 90 percent in China and Mexico and approaching 100 percent in many other countries.

Wealth

Developing countries have high levels of wealth inequality; however, it is remarkable that wealth inequality in the United States surpasses many developing countries. Table 13.5 shows the Gini Index for wealth in the United States and developing countries for which the data are available. These estimates are from a wide range of data sources, reported by Davies and colleagues (Davies, Sandstrom, Shorrocks, and Wolff 2009). The Gini Index estimates reveal that the distribution of wealth in these countries is more unequal than the distribution of income. To be convinced, we compare these estimates to Gini Index estimates for income inequality in Table 13.4. The estimates in Table 13.5 also show how the United States compares to select developing countries: Wealth inequality in the United States is higher than in all other countries included in the Davies research. The Gini Index for wealth in the United States is 0.80; the second highest level of inequality among countries included is in Brazil, which has a Gini Index of 0.78. Wealth inequality also is relatively high in other Latin American countries listed: The Gini Index is 0.75 in Mexico and 0.74 in Argentina. The comparatively poor Asian-Pacific countries – Russia, India, and Bangladesh – have slightly less inequality than the Latin American countries. By contrast, wealth inequality in China is very low, with a Gini Index of 0.55. As mentioned previously, low levels of inequality in former socialist countries reflect government efforts to create perfect equality under socialism. We address these issues in greater detail later in this chapter in the discussion of transition economies.

It is instructive to consider how wealth is distributed among countries (rather than within countries). It may not be surprising to learn that the richest people live in North America, the wealthy nations of the Asia-Pacific region, and Europe. Yet, we may be surprised about the degree to which wealth is unequally distributed across the globe. Table 13.6 draws on research by Davies et al. (2009) to show the percentage of the world's wealthiest households in various regions of the world. The first and second columns list the region and percentage of adults in the top 1 percent of wealth owners in all countries. We see that 39 percent of the world's wealthiest people live in the United States or Canada (i.e., North America). Another 32 percent live in the wealthy Asia-Pacific countries including Japan, South Korea, Taiwan, Australia, and New Zealand. More

Table 13.6 Global Wealth Distribution

	Adults in Top 1% in the World (%)	Share of World's Wealth (%)
North America	38.9	34.4
Rich Asian-Pacific	32.2	24.1
Europe	25.9	29.7
Latin America, Caribbean	2.3	4.3
Other Asian-Pacific	0.5	2.9
Africa	0.2	1.0
China	0.0	2.6
India	0.0	0.9
World	100	100

Data source: Davies, Sandstrom, Shorrocks, and Wolff (2009).

than 25 percent live in Europe. Together, these three groups account for 95 percent of the world's wealthiest people. It is tempting to dismiss this as most of the people in the world; however, virtually none of the richest people live in the most populous countries of the world, including all African nations, China, and India. Not only do most rich people live in a relatively small number of locations; the same wealthy countries also own the lion's share of the world's wealth. The third column in Table 13.6 shows the percentage of all wealth held in various regions. Again, North American, rich Asian-Pacific, and European countries own most wealth; together, they own about 88 percent of total wealth.

Inequality in Transition Economies

Large-scale changes in the global political and economic landscape led to the proliferation of transition economies in recent decades, and it is clear that inequality and stratification in them deserve particular attention. *Market transition* is the movement of an economy away from state socialism toward market coordination of economic activity. In a *redistributive state socialist economy*, all property (e.g., factories, land, and capital) is collectively owned, and government officials collect and reallocate goods according to a central plan. State officials make nearly all decisions about what factories should produce, they sell the products, they collect revenues from sales of the products, and they distribute (or redistribute) the revenues to workers (as salaries and wages) and firms (to reinvest). The Chinese and Soviet economies in previous decades were models of redistributive economies. In contrast, in a *market economy*, buyers and sellers bargain directly over price. Entrepreneurs, corporations, and other organizations decide when and how much of a given product or service to produce, sell the products in markets (or stores), assume the risk of offering their products and services in a market, and enjoy the rewards if sales are sufficient to cover costs. The U.S. economy is an example of a market economy.

In the late 1970s, many formerly redistributive economies began to transition away from socialism and became more market-oriented. A major transformation of this type realigns the interests of economic and political actors, introduces new actors including new types of firms and entrepreneurs, creates unique opportunities for economic participation and achievement, transforms labor relations between workers and the state, alters the personal characteristics and social relations that are recognized and rewarded, and otherwise changes incentives and reward structures. As a result, market transition alters the nature of social stratification and inequality in a country, often dramatically. Imagine, for instance, who benefited under the old system: Typically, people with strong political connections or power were able to reward themselves well. Once a transition begins, however, it is not clear whether the same people stay in power or a new group replaces them. Research on the implications of market transition for social stratification has been abundant in recent years. Indeed, the term *market-transition debate* is now synonymous with the debate about how market transition changes the nature of stratification and inequality in a country and who ultimately wins.

Sociologists have two opposing conclusions about who benefits most from a transition and, consequently, what happens to the distribution of rewards in the new system. The two sides agree that social structure in postsocialist countries will be considerably different than before the transition, but they dispute who will be the beneficiaries of the change as well as the mechanisms that will determine who benefits. One side emphasizes the importance of market processes in shaping stratification outcomes and predicts that those with *economic control* will increasingly benefit during transition. The opposing side counters that the enduring importance of political control and influence combined with the experience and skills that initially produced political capital will ensure that those who had power before the transition continue to have power. The two perspectives are summarized in the following sections.

Economic Control and Inequality

The first school of thought is rooted in Nee's *market transition theory* (Nee 1996; Nee and Cao 2002; Nee and Stark 1989), which initiated recent debate about stratification outcomes during transition. Nee argued that the old socialist guard will be displaced by a new group of people, which will gain control and power during economic transition. Market-transition theory includes three principal theses. First, the *market-power thesis* states that departures from state socialism create multiple means of gaining power and privilege. As markets begin to develop and private ownership of property increases, incentives and opportunities for economic actors change (Cookson 1989). The waning of redistribution reduces the control that government officials have over resources, and their power gradually declines. At the same time, actors involved in market activities (e.g., starting a business) have increasing control over resources and their power increases. In addition, as prices are determined by market-type interactions between buyers and sellers rather than through state planning and other redistributive mechanisms, direct producers gain control over the market exchange and can enhance the prices they receive for goods and services (including their own labor). Together, these processes result in an increase in power for direct producers relative to redistributors (Nee 1997).

Second, the *market-incentive thesis* indicates that expanding reliance on market-based transactions creates new incentives for producers that were lacking under state socialism, which contributes to expanding rewards for individual effort and human capital. In a redistributive economy, prices are set by bureaucrats and rarely respond to demand for products or performance differences among suppliers. This creates few incentives for producers to improve productivity or otherwise to distinguish their output. Markets allow producers to withhold products or their labor until they agree to a price with buyers, and producers retain a greater portion of economic surplus. Incentives for individual productivity increase, which increases both effort and rewards for human capital. Nee (1989) originally hypothesized that changing incentives would be manifested in increasing returns to education because it is an indicator of individual productivity and easily measurable. Likewise, other scholars have focused on changing rewards for education, both conceptually and empirically (Gerber and Hout 1995; Hannum and Buchmann 2004; Hannum and Xie 1994; Xie 1996). Yet, market-transition theory suggests that transition will increase rewards for all elements of human capital, including formal education and technical training, work experience, and other measures of productive skills and technical knowledge. The second thesis indicates that during transition, rewards for market-based activities and performance increase and that human-capital indicators become better predictors of advantage.

The third thesis, the *market-opportunity thesis*, begins with the observation that the growth of markets creates new potential for individual social and economic mobility outside of the redistributive sector. State socialism offered opportunities for power and mobility as well as a range of advantages in areas such as housing and neighborhood quality, job placement, work bonuses, and access to other resources and non-wage benefits (Bian 1994; Szelenyi 1983; Walder 1992). However, these advantages were restricted primarily to those who had control of redistributive processes. The emergence of markets generates new avenues for advancement that are outside of the state-redistributive hierarchy and that are manifested in salaries and wages rather than nonwage benefits and bureaucratic advancement. Opportunities such as entrepreneurship in the private sector, affiliations with foreign firms, and voluntary job change empower economic actors and create prospects for improving well-being that were absent under state socialism. That is, the emergence of markets alters the nature of opportunities available to actors, creating new possibilities for mobility and stimulating entrepreneurship.

Market-transition theory also predicts distributional outcomes (Cookson 1997). As the importance of redistributive control declines, previously privileged groups lose their advantage and newly advantaged groups enjoy more opportunities and rewards. Those with redistributive control garner fewer resources, whereas direct producers expand their share of surplus; workers in the redistributive sector enjoy fewer rewards relative to workers in the market sector; and regions with weak markets grow and develop more slowly than those with strong, active markets. As a result, market-transition theory predicts that inequality is likely to decline during transition – at least, in the short run.

Researchers generally agree that the nature of inequality in a country changes during transition, but they disagree strongly about who wins and who loses as a result of the changes. Market-transition theory may seem straightforward at first, but it has been the source of intense debate that is still unresolved. The most common critique is that the theory is somehow too simple and this simplicity causes problems in understanding its implications. Critics argue that the reality of transition is more nuanced than market-transition theory suggests. In particular, critics claim that market-transition theory overemphasizes the importance of market emergence and neglects other factors that also affect how power and advantages are distributed. Numerous changes occur during transition at varying times and paces, even in a single country. Walder summarized the reaction to market-transition theory when he stated that "markets per se are not the issue. What matters are the variable institutions and conditions that define markets, and our theory and research must put them at center stage" (Walder 1996: 1060–1).

The fundamental point of many critics of market-transition theory is that reform is not a continuous, unimpeded move toward market equilibrium or any definitive new form of organizing economic activity. They point out that variations within a single country, the nature of social networks before and during transition, and a host of other factors can affect when and how inequality changes. Walder (1996) used property rights as an example. Privatization of property happens at different rates and in different ways in transition economies, and the extent to which politicians continue to control property affects the distribution of power and rewards. Walder added that Nee's prediction that cadre power will decline does not address whether cadres are able to develop new sources of power by becoming (or remaining) involved in enterprises as brokers and middlemen or as consultants, or otherwise capitalizing on the skills and connections they created under state socialism. Parish and Michelson (1996) pointed out that the dense social networks that developed in socialist economies produced a culture of bargaining, and the loosening of central control during transition allowed bargaining to flourish. They proposed that this culture does not just disappear and those with access to it have advantages. Other scholars highlight sectoral, geographic, and urban–rural differences in transition economies and fault market-transition theory for not specifically addressing how they affect inequality during transition (Lin 1995; Rona-Tas 1994; Tang and Parish 2000; Walder 1992).

Political Control and Inequality

The debate about who benefits from market transition is definitely far from resolved, and an important indicator that the issue is still contested is the growing number of theoretical perspectives proposed. Whereas market-transition theory focuses on markets and economic relations in its explanation, the majority of other explanations emphasize the importance of politics and political connections. This group of explanations is usually called *state-centered* because of their focus on the government or the state. An example of a state-centered approach is Walder's *growing power of the state* proposal (1995). He used research on state-owned companies in China to argue that the role of local governments may not diminish during transition; rather, there is reason to believe that it increases. Contrary to what other observers said about China's rapid growth during the 1990s and contrary to market-transition theory's prediction that the role of government would wane, Walder argued that economic growth in the early stages of China's transition was led by state-owned companies. He argued that local governments and local state-owned companies worked together to create the growth that made transition possible. In this model, the state clearly has an important role that suggests that bureaucrats will retain power, privilege, and material rewards over time.

Other state-centered alternatives have emerged as well. One proposal focuses on the notion of *power conversion*, which emphasizes that state officials can convert the skills and privileges they had before transition into power and privilege during and after transition. For example, because personal connections continue to be important during transition, government officials and others with good connections will continue to enjoy benefits beyond what the market provides. A second state-centered proposal emphasizes that *sector differences* are important in understanding who benefits from transition (Tang and Parish 2000: 79). For instance, people who work for large state-owned companies received better rewards before reform than people who worked for other companies. This approach suggests that people in these key sectors will continue to benefit regardless of what happens to markets.

A third state-centered approach emphasizes the need to consider *timing* in thinking about the effects of transition (Zhou 2000; Zhou, Li, Zhao, and Cai 2003). This approach suggests that different groups will benefit at different stages of the transition, and it is over-simplistic to point to a single group that will win or lose. It may be, for instance, that former state officials are rewarded in the early stages of transition but, as markets develop, those involved in business gain power and ultimately receive more rewards.

We imagine that the way to resolve the debate about who benefits during economic transition is to collect data and see who is doing well and who is not. This is definitely the correct approach, and it is the one that researchers have taken. In fact, the amount of evidence produced regarding inequality and stratification during transition is immense. The problem is that deciding who is doing well turns out to be more difficult to determine than we might imagine. Nee's early proposal of market-transition theory included data providing support for his arguments. Other researchers immediately began to test the ideas on other data and in other ways. The controversy strengthened as authors amassed often-divergent empirical findings and disputed the interpretation of seemingly contradictory empirical evidence (Bian and Logan 1996; Gerber and Hout 1998; Parish, Zhe, and Li 1995; Rona-Tas 1994; Walder 1995; Xie and Hannum 1996). Rather than the typical resolution of the theoretical controversies, empirical studies on this issue intensified the debate as researchers continue to have nearly opposite conclusions and, in many cases, cannot agree how to interpret the same results. One reason that the data are difficult to understand is that the countries under study are changing so rapidly, even as the data are being collected. Although it has not been resolved, this debate is worth understanding because it demonstrates how differently award structures operate around the globe and how rapidly societies that are in flux can change.

Summary

(1) Comparing the United States to other countries – both developed and developing – puts inequality in perspective.

(2) Income inequality is high across developed countries, but it is particularly high in the United States.

(3) Comparing poverty rates among developed countries is difficult because few countries have official poverty measures. However, research suggests that poverty in the United States is high compared to other developed countries.

(4) Globalization has changed the nature of work and employment in both developed and developing countries. In developing countries, globalization has contributed to a trend toward using NSWAs such as part-time work, temporary work, and contract work. Although these work arrangements are more flexible, there is evidence that they offer lower quality work, lower salaries, fewer benefits, and more limited opportunities.

(5) Standardized mass public education is common in developed countries, where universal completion of primary and secondary school is the norm. Although enrollment in tertiary education is not universal, it is high and increasing. A side effect of high rates of educational completion in developed countries is credential inflation, which lowers the value of any education.

(6) Wealth inequality is high in most developed countries, but the distribution of wealth is more unequal in the United States than in other industrialized countries.

(7) Income inequality and poverty levels in many developing countries are extremely high, much higher than even in the United States and other developed countries. In extreme cases (e.g., Sierra Leone), the Gini Index exceeds 0.60 with 70 percent of the population living in poverty.

(8) Globalization also has changed the nature of work in many developing countries, but it is uncertain whether the changes are helpful or harmful. The unequal cross-country relations that characterize outsourcing and off-shoring can lead to exploitation of workers, including children. Yet, some argue that globalization also has "leveled the playing field" and allowed some workers to compete for the best jobs in the world regardless of where they live.

(9) Because mass education is much less the norm, illiteracy is still common in some developing countries. However, there is tremendous variation among developing countries; in some, literacy is approaching 100 percent and educational attainment otherwise is comparable with the developing world.

(10) Wealth tends to be unequally distributed in developing countries, but wealth inequality is still higher in the United States than in many developing nations.

(11) There has been a proliferation of transition economies in recent years, and inequality and stratification in those countries has changed dramatically. There has been intense debate regarding who benefits from the change: Some speculate that those involved in economic activity will benefit most; others argue that politicians are still poised to win. Because the rate of change in transition economies is high, data collection is challenging and empirical evidence has yet to resolve the debate.

Box 13.1 Microfinance and Global Poverty

Moving out of poverty is difficult, and it is even more difficult given that banks usually offer few incentives to help clients who have little or no cash income. Banks incur considerable costs in managing client accounts, both small and large. A small account generates so few revenues for a bank that managing the account often costs the bank more than it makes. This problem is common in the United States and other developed countries. Despite regulations designed to protect the poor, those with little income and wealth are more likely to borrow from informal moneylenders and to use pawnshops, check-cashing outlets, and other fringe-banking establishments.

Access to capital is even more difficult where poverty is widespread, extreme, and well entrenched. Imagine a person living in poverty in a rural part of a generally poor nation. Even if that person was highly motivated to find a way out of poverty, without access to any financial resources, change is virtually impossible. In this context, there may not be permanent financial institutions and, worse, the national financial system may not be reliable as a source of capital even for those with a high income.

Microfinance is a movement that attempts to address this problem. It is a general term referring to financial services for low-income clients. It may (and sometimes does) include loans, savings accounts, insurance, and other financial services. More specifically, however, microfinance has come to refer to the provision of loans and other financial assistance to poor and near-poor households with the aim of helping them find a way out of poverty. The underlying assumption is that many of the poor have skills and talents that are not being used effectively and, with the proper support and resources, they can help themselves and their country out of poverty.

One successful effort is the *Grameen Bank*, a microfinance organization and community-development bank founded in Bangladesh. It makes small loans to the poor without requiring collateral. Muhammad Yunus, a professor and Fulbright scholar, is credited with starting the Grameen Bank in 1976 with a research program designed to examine the effects of creating a credit system that would provide banking services to the rural poor. By 2008, the Grameen Bank had provided $7.6 billion in loans and operated at a profit since 1993 (grameenbank.com). The bank is owned by its poor borrowers, most of whom are women, and its effectiveness often is traced to the group-based approach. Social pressure and support from other group members encourage borrowers to be cautious in financial dealings and to ensure timely repayment. Yunus and the Grameen Bank received the 2006 Nobel Peace Prize for their efforts to aid the poor.

Source: bankerindia.com

Box 13.2 AIDS in Africa

Only about 12 percent of the world's population lives in the countries of sub-Saharan Africa, but Africa has nearly 70 percent of the world's people infected with HIV (i.e., the virus that can lead to AIDS); AIDS is the leading cause of death there. What happened and how is it related to inequality?

The World Health Organization (WHO) estimates that in 2007, 33.2 million people were living with HIV, 2.5 million were newly infected with HIV, and 2.1 million died of AIDS. Of those people, 68 percent of those living with HIV, 67 percent of the newly infected with HIV, and 76 percent of those who died of AIDS were from sub-Saharan Africa (World Health Organization 2007). The epidemic disproportionately affects women in Africa and, whereas most of those affected are adults, children are not immune from the disease. More than 60 percent of adults living with HIV in sub-Saharan Africa are women, and nearly 90 percent of the world's children living with HIV live there. The magnitude of the problem varies considerably throughout the region; Southern Africa is the most heavily affected. In eight countries, more than 15 percent of the adult population is HIV positive: Botswana, Lesotho, Mozambique, Namibia, South Africa, Swaziland, Zambia, and Zimbabwe.

Many factors contribute to the spread of the HIV virus in Africa, which – consistent with prevalence rates – are particularly problematic in Southern Africa. Researchers are not yet certain which factors are most important, but they point to several issues as likely causes, including widespread poverty, inequality, social instability, gender inequalities, the prevalence of other sexually transmitted diseases (which facilitate HIV transmission), and concurrent sex partners. In many parts of Africa, there also is a stigma attached to having HIV, which prevents people from seeking treatment when it is available. The link to poverty and inequalities is strong. The lack of education among many parts of the African population makes it difficult to disseminate information that might curtail the spread of the disease. Poor, rural people also move frequently in search of work, and they are candidates for spreading the disease across regions. Moreover, poor women are more likely to engage in commercial sex work, which has obvious implications for the spread of the virus.

A particularly challenging contributing factor is the stigma attached to using condoms in many African countries. It persists despite efforts of HIV/AIDS organizations to disseminate the critical information that condom use can prevent the transmission of the virus. Research from Malawi (where 12 percent of the adult population is HIV positive) suggests that condoms remove the essence of what sex is all about (i.e., "the sweetness"). Moreover, while Malawians recognize that condoms can prevent disease transmission, many believe that the condoms cause disease (including cancer) and, at the very least, can signify a lack of trust between sexual partners (Tavory and Swidler 2009). One respondent told researchers that if he were to suggest using a condom, his partner would say, "The way I am you say that you want to use a condom? What have you suspected in my body or what have you suspected in yourself?" (2009: 180).

Implications of the HIV/AIDS epidemic in Africa are enormous. The loss of life is overwhelming, and the number of children orphaned by the disease grows yearly. The epidemic has economic implications, including reducing the availability of workers and high treatment costs for already-poor governments. This exacerbates poverty and potentially contributes to the spread of the epidemic. Education also suffers because there are not enough teachers in some areas and ill parents are unable to ensure that their children attend school. Important political implications range from reduced availability of young adults to serve in the military in some countries and political instability associated with poverty and inequality.

Although the story from Africa is discouraging, some agencies are making progress in certain areas. For additional information about efforts to curtail the epidemic, refer to UNAIDS, available at www.unaids.org.

Key Concepts

Contract work

Credential inflation

Gini Index

Globalization

Grameen Bank

Market economy

Market transition

Market-transition theory

Microfinance

Nonstandard work arrangements (NSWAs)

Off-shoring

Outsourcing

Redistributive state socialist economy

Temporary work

Questions for Thought

1. Nations located in Northern Europe have relatively low inequality. Which factors contribute to this pattern? What are the benefits of low inequality? What are the costs?

2. Scholars studying poverty cross-nationally often give particular attention to the percentage of children living in poverty. Recall, for example, Smeeding's study. Why are researchers particularly concerned with children? What does child poverty suggest about the current and future well-being of households?

3. Some commentators argue that relatively high levels of inequality and poverty in the United States create incentives for people to work hard and improve their conditions. According to this argument, incentives are higher in the United States than other industrialized countries, leading to greater entrepreneurship and innovation. Is this a compelling argument? Defend your reasoning.

4. Legal requirements for the pay and benefits received by full- and part-time workers vary among countries. Should employers be required to treat workers the same regardless of their employment status?

5. How would you describe wealth inequality in the United States compared to other developed countries (see Table 13.3)? Which factors might account for the patterns identified? What problems are associated with the patterns? Are there advantages as well?

Exercises

1. Select two countries that interest you: one with a relatively high and one with a relatively low Gini Index for income. Use online and printed material to investigate the social, economic, political, historical, and other factors that contribute to inequality in these countries. What are the pros and cons of living in relative equality versus relative inequality? Which is better and for whom?

2. Go to the LIS Web site (www.lisproject.org/keyfigures/povertytable.htm) and explore poverty rates for the countries included in the survey. What patterns do you observe in poverty rates? Identify as many explanations for those patterns as possible.

3. Select three countries and learn more about their labor policies. Do the countries allow workers to treat part- and full-time workers differently? Do the countries require employers to provide maternity and/or paternity leave to expectant parents? How else do work and employment differ in the countries selected? How do the differences affect inequality in the countries?

4. Learn more about child-labor laws and practices in a country that interests you. What are the long-term implications of these practices for the country?

5. Using data from the World Bank or the International Data Base, analyze the economic conditions of a developing country. Hypothesize about the origins of poverty in the country or discuss factors that perpetuate this condition. Research the effect of International Monetary Fund and World Bank policies on the development of this country. Have these organizations contributed to the problem or the solution?

6. Although the Grameen Bank has been extremely successful in helping the poor in Bangladesh, it has been difficult to replicate this success elsewhere (see Box 13.1). Read more about the Grameen Bank and other microfinance organizations to develop ideas about why this approach does not always work.

Multimedia Resources

Print

Collier, Paul. 2008. *The Bottom Billion: Why the Poorest Countries Are Failing and What Can Be Done About It.* New York: Oxford.

Friedman, Thomas. 2008. *Hot, Flat, and Crowded.* New York: Farrar, Straus, and Giroux.

Sachs, Jeffrey. 2006. *The End of Poverty: Economic Possibilities for Our Time* (Foreword by Bono). New York: Penguin.

Smith, Philip and Eric Thurman. 2007. *A Billion Bootstraps: Microcredit, Barefoot Banking, and the Business Solution for Ending Poverty.* New York: McGraw-Hill.

Yunus, Muhammad. 2003. *Banker to the Poor: Micro-Lending and the Battle against World Poverty.* New York: Public Affairs.

Wallerstein, Immanuel. 1974. *The Modern World System: Capitalist Agriculture and the Origins of the European World Economy in the Sixteenth Century.* New York: Academic Press.

Internet

(1) www.worldbank.org/: Homepage of the World Bank, a source of financial and technical assistance to developing countries around the world. www.worldbank.org/data is the official source of developmental data from the World Bank and other international agencies.

(2) www.census.gov/ipc/www/idbnew.html: The International Data Base was created by the U.S. Census Bureau's International Programs Center. It is a source of demographic and socioeconomic statistics for 227 countries and areas of the world.

(3) www.prb.org: Homepage of the Population Reference Bureau. This site contains information on the world's population, health, and environment.

(4) www.fh.org: This is the official Web site of Food for the Hungry, an international relief and development organization.

(5) www.care.org: CARE is a humanitarian organization formed to fight global poverty through health and developmental education services and emergency relief programs.

(6) www.aworldconnected.org/: WorldConnected.org is a project of the Institute for Humane Studies at George Mason University. The site is a source of information on global poverty, free trade, and global inequalities.

(7) www.globalhealthfacts.org/: A companion site to www.globalhealthreporting.org, this site includes current country and region-specific data on key health indicators as well as other demographic and economic indicators. The site includes tables, charts, and color-coded maps.

(8) www.Grameenbank.com: This is the official Web site of the Grameen Bank (see Box 13.1).

Films

Ajit. 1996. This film tells the story of an eight-year-old boy who works as a domestic servant in a middle-class Calcutta, India, family. The documentary includes footage of his daily chores: cleaning, laundry, and childcare. Ajit explains that although he is unable to attend school because he needs to work, he is fortunate to have adequate food and wages.

Life and Debt. 2003. This movie contrasts the lives of vacationers and residents in Jamaica, underscoring the vast differences in lifestyle across countries. The film also highlights the role that international policy and history play in shaping the poverty that native Jamaicans face.

Maquila: A Tale of Two Mexicos. 2000. This film depicts the advantages and problems created by *maquiladoras*, companies located in the industrial border zone between the United States and Mexico. The documentary raises questions about the realities of economic growth resulting from free trade.

Through Chinese Women's Eyes. 1997. This film follows Chinese women through the twentieth century. It shows how women's status has changed dramatically from the pre-Mao era through the Cultural Revolution (1966–1976) and into the current age of commercialization.

Wedding Banquet. 1993. On the surface, this is a simple romantic comedy about a homosexual couple living in New York. The movie portrays a series of encounters between the main character and his parents who do not know that he is gay and who are expecting him to marry and have children. The film highlights cultural, sexual, and generational differences that underlie inequality both within and among countries.

Series: City Life. 2001. A series of films focusing on social and economic challenges, and resulting inequalities, in a range of countries. Example programs include the following:

(9) *A Fistful of Rice*. This episode is set in Nepal and demonstrates the challenges that extreme poverty and malnutrition create.

(10) *Holy Smoke: Cambodians Fight Tobacco*. An episode that takes place in Cambodia and explores the effect of aggressive marketing by multinational tobacco companies in developing countries.

(11) *My Mother Built This House*. A program set in South Africa that explores issues of homelessness.

Works Cited

Atkinson, Anthony B., Bea Cantillon, Eric Marlier, and Brian Nolan. 2002. *Social Indicators: The EU and Social Inclusion*. Oxford: Oxford University Press.

Bian, Yanijie. 1994. "Guanxi and the Allocation of Urban Jobs in China." *The China Quarterly* 140: 971–99.

Bian, Yanjie, and John R. Logan. 1996. "Market Transition and the Persistence of Power: The Changing Stratification System in Urban China." *American Sociological Review* 61: 739–58.

Brandolini, Andrea, Timothy M. Smeeding, and Eva Sierminska. 2008. "Comparing Wealth Distribution across Rich Countries: First Results from the Luxembourg Wealth Study." *Bank of Italy Research Paper No. A7*.

Burtless, Gary, and Jencks Christopher. 2003. "American Inequality and its Consequences." In *Agenda for the Nation*, edited by H. Aaron, J. M. Lindsay, and P. Nivola (pp. 61–108). Washington, DC: Brookings Institution.

Castells, Manuel. 1998. *End of Millenium*. Malden, MA: Blackwell.

Central Intelligence Agency. 2003. "World Factbook." Washington, DC.

Collins, Randall. 1979. *The Credential Society: An Historical Sociology of Education and Stratification.* New York: Academic.

Cookson, P. 1989. "Closing the Rift between Scholarship and Practice: The Need to Revitalize Educational Research." Pp 321-31 In *Schools and Society: A Unified Reader*, edited by J. Ballantine. Mayfield: Mountain View, CA.

Cookson, Peter W. 1997. *Lessons from Privilege: The American Prep School Tradition.* Cambridge: Harvard University Press.

Davies, James B., Susanna Sandstrom, Anthony Shorrocks, and Edward N. Wolff. 2009. "The World Distribution of Household Wealth." In *Personal Wealth from a Global Perspective*, edited by J. B. Davies (pp. 395–418). Oxford: Oxford University Press.

Firebaugh, Glenn. 2003. *The New Geography of Global Income Inequality.* London: Cambridge University Press.

Friedman, Thomas. 2006. *The World Is Flat: A Brief History of the Twenty-First Century.* New York: Farrar, Straus, and Giroux.

Gerber, Theodore P., and Michael Hout. 1995. "Educational Stratification in Russia during the Soviet Period." *American Journal of Sociology* 101: 611–60.

———. 1998. "More Shock than Therapy: Market Transition, Employment, and Income in Russia, 1991–1995." *American Journal of Sociology* 104: 1–50.

Hannum, Emily, and Claudia Buchmann. 2004. "Global Educational Expansion and Socioeconomic Development: An Assessment of Findings from the Social Sciences." *World Development* 33:333-54.

Hannum, Emily, and Yu Xie. 1994. "Trends in Educational Gender Inequality in China, 1949–1958." *Research in Social Stratification and Mobility* 13: 73–98.

International Labor Organization. 2009. *Yearbook of Labor Statistics.* Geneva, Switzerland: International Labor Organization.

Kalleberg, Arne. 2000. "Nonstandard Employment Relations: Part-time, Temporary and Contract Work." In *Annual Review of Sociology* 26: 341–65. Annual Reviews, Inc.

———. 2003. "Flexible Firms and Labor Market Segmentation." In *Work & Occupations* 30: 154. Thousand Oaks, CA: Sage Publications,

———. 2006. "Nonstandard Employment Relations and Labour Market Inequality: Cross-national Patterns." Pp 136-62 In *Inequalities of the World*, edited by G. Therborn. London: Verso.

Kalleberg, Arne L., Barbara F. Reskin, and Ken Hudson. 2000. "Bad Jobs in America: Standard and Nonstandard Employment Relations and Job Quality in the United States." *American Sociological Review* 65: 256–78.

Klevmarken, N. Anders, Joseph P. Lupton, and Frank P. Stafford. 2003. "Wealth Dynamics in the 1980s and 1990s: Sweden and the United States." *The Journal of Human Resources* 38: 322–53.

Lin, Nan. 1995. "Local Market Socialism: Local Corporatism in Action in Rural China." *Theory and Society* 24: 301–54.

Luxembourg Wealth Survey. 2007. Authors' estimates. http://www.lisdatacenter.org/our-data/lws-database/

McGrath, Donald, and Lisa A. Keister. 2007. "The Effect of Temporary Employment on Asset Accumulation Processes." *Work and Occupations* 35: 196–222.

Meyer, John W., Francisco O. Ramirez, Richard Rubinson, and John Boli-Bennett. 1977. "The World Educational Revolution." *Sociology of Education* 50: 242–58.

Nee, Victor. 1996. "The Emergence of a Market Society: Changing Mechanisms of Stratification in China." *American Journal of Sociology* 101: 908–49.

———. 1997. "Federalist and Local Corporatist Theories: A Comment on an Empirical Test." In *The Political Economy of Property Rights: Institutional Change and Credibility in the Reform of Centrally Planned Economies*, edited by D. L. Weimer (pp. 288–93). New York: Cambridge University Press.

Nee, Victor, and Yang Cao. 2002. "Postsocialist Inequality: The Causes of Continuity and Discontinuity." *Research in Social Stratification and Mobility* 19: 3–39.

Nee, Victor, and David Stark. 1989. "Remaking the Economic Institutions of Socialism: China and Eastern Europe." Stanford, CA: Stanford University.

Parish, William, and Ethan Michelson. 1996. "Politics and Markets: Dual Transformations." *American Journal of Sociology* 101: 1042–59.

Parish, William, Xiaoye Zhe, and Fang Li. 1995. "Non-Farm Work and Marketization of the Chinese Countryside." *The China Quarterly* 143: 697–730.

Polivka, Anne E., Sharon R. Cohany, and Steven Hipple. 2000. "Definition, Composition, and Economic Consequences of Nonstandard Workforce." In *Nonstandard Work: The Nature and Challenges of Changing Employment Relations*, edited by F. Carre, M. A. Ferber, L. Golden, and S. A. Herzenberg (pp. 41–94). Champaign, IL: Industrial Relations Research Association.

Rona-Tas, Akos. 1994. "The First Shall Be Last? Entrepreneurship and Communist Cadres in the Transition from Socialism." *American Journal of Sociology* 100: 40–69.

Sernau, Scott. 2009. *Global Problems: The Search for Equity, Peace, and Sustainability*. Boston: Pearson.

Smeeding, Timothy M. 2008. "Poverty, Work, and Policy: The United States in Comparative Perspective." In *Social Stratification: Class, Race, and Gender in Sociological Perspective*, edited by D. B. Grusky (pp. 327–39). Boulder, CO: Westview Press.

Szelenyi, Ivan. 1983. *Urban Inequalities under State Socialism*. Oxford: Oxford University Press.

Tang, Wenfang, and William Parish. 2000. *Chinese Urban Life under Reform: The Changing Social Contract*. New York: Cambridge University Press.

Tavory, Iddo, and Ann Swidler. 2009. "Condom Semiotics: Meaning and Condom Use in Rural Malawi." *American Sociological Reviewer* 74: 171–89.

UNESCO. 2009. "Education Statistics." Washington DC: UNESCO Institute for Statistics.

United Nations. 2008. *Human Development Report*. Washington, DC: United Nations.

United Nations. 2010. *Human Literacy*. Washington, DC: United Nations.

Walder, Andrew G. 1992. "Property Rights and Stratification in Socialist Redistributive Economies." *American Sociological Review* 57: 524–39.

———. 1995. "Career Mobility and the Communist Political Order." *American Sociological Review* 60: 309–28.

———. 1996. *China's Transitional Economy*. Oxford: Oxford University Press.

Welch, Finnis. 1999. "In Defense of Inequality." *American Economic Review* 89: 1–17.

World Health Organization and Joint United Nations Program on HIV/AIDS. 2007. *AIDS Epidemic Update*. Geneva, Switzerland: World Health Organization.

World Bank. 2008. *World Inequality*. Washington DC: World Bank Press.

Xie, Cichang. 1996. *The Complete Book of Enterprise Property Rights (Qiye Chanquan Shiwu Quanshu)*. Beijing: *Jingji Ribao Chubanshe*.

Xie, Yu, and Emily Hannum. 1996. "Regional Variation in Earnings Inequality in Reform-Era Urban China." *American Journal of Sociology* 101: 950–92.

Zhou, Xueguang. 2000. "Economic Transformation and Income Inequality in Urban China: Evidence from Panel Data." *American Journal of Sociology* 105: 1135–74.

Zhou, Xueguang, Qiang Li, Wei Zhao, and He Cai. 2003. "Embeddedness and Contractual Relationships in China's Transitional Economy." *American Sociological Review* 68: 75–102.

14 Public Policy and Social Stratification

Who makes the rules that others must follow? We recall from previous chapters in which the distribution of power was the outcome of interest that this question is perhaps the most pivotal in stratification. Although we have seen different theoretical approaches to finding the answer to "Who rules and why?," the fact remains that a small group of people has immense power over a much larger group.

In the United States, the process by which some are allocated the power to rule over others is found in a democratic system. That is, people are given the power to vote for candidates to fill various official offices from local to federal levels. Although not everyone may vote and many choose not to, this chapter discusses the fact that the process involved in official decision making is complex and driven by previously established relationships among social class, gender, and race.

We begin a review of how policies affect inequality by discussing the debate on social welfare in the United States. We then focus on the voting process, the electorates, and the elected. We introduce two groups involved in brokering policies; Political Action Committees (PACs) and lobbyists. We end the chapter by reviewing a sample of policies aimed at reducing inequality in America and focusing on the success of these policies through a critical lens.

How Do Political Systems Affect Inequality?

The unequal distribution of wealth and income is an important aspect of inequality. Generally, Americans agree that under capitalism, those who take risks and advance innovation should be rewarded. In addition to *risk/reward*, Americans believe in *meritocracy*: People who work hard make gains and those who fall behind did not try hard enough (see Chapter 7 about the undeserving poor). However, the structure of America's economy has been criticized for the inability of some to access resources so that they may work hard to advance and become upwardly mobile.

A debate exists about whether inequality is a result of *capitalism* and is therefore a necessary element within society. Examining this issue, social philosophers outlined the most poignant issues currently under a debate centered on *egalitarianism* (Paul and Miller 2002) – that is, equality for all. The first is whether *socialism* or a *welfare state* better serves its constituents than private charities. As discussed in Chapter 7, America has more than a million charities with more being added daily. Some argue that charity serves to redistribute wealth more efficiently than a welfare state (Shapiro 2002). State-sponsored redistribution, in their view, is coercive. However, missing in this debate is the allocation process so well known to sociologists. Although the charity system indeed helps those who are in need of assistance, those who control the resources also may choose whom to help. Recall that many charities set up to assist victims of Hurricane Katrina did not provide any assistance; instead, many diverted funds to personal projects and even locations outside of America without disclosing this information to those who donated. Second, some assert that the welfare state hinders the poor. Using this logic, providing assistance to the poor reduces the probability for long-term economic growth (Cowen 2002). Although most agree, the best assistance that a state may offer the poor is a job that results from economic growth. However, what some fail to consider is globalization and the loss of jobs in one nation as the economic relations dramatically reduce the number of available jobs, occupations, and industries. Egalitarianism is an ideal that cannot be obtained by policy, but policies can provide access to groups that have been denied access throughout history. Moreover, assistance in America does not only target the poor. Whereas there is public assistance for the poor, the middle class receives *social insurance* such as Medicare and unemployment insurance, and many in the upper class benefit from *corporate tax policies* and corporate assistance (Domhoff 1990) intended to maintain American companies. For example, in Wisconsin, corporate income taxes comprised 11.3 percent of the state revenue in 1979. By 1988, this form of revenue decreased to 8.8 percent and, by 2000, it was 5.6 percent – half of what it was in 1979 (Wisconsin Budget Project 2001).

Recently, the "Great Recession" threatened the existence of banks and other financial institutions. Some argued that if Americans did not "bail out" the banks, the nation – and, indeed, the global economy – would fail. The popular phrase, "too big to fail," was used to explain that the center of the global economy is the financial industry. The sentiment behind "too big to fail" is that some institutions are such an integral force of the American economy that if they fail, so would the economy due to loss of jobs, property, and business. The assistance given private industries by the government is hotly debated because it seems to be counterintuitive to free-market capitalism. Capitalism is founded on the principal of *laissez faire*, which in French means "let do" or to go without restriction – to let it be. Laissez faire economics – that which separates government from business – has been adopted as a fundamental tenant of private ownership of capital.

Despite the American value of capitalism, corporate welfare has a long history in the United States. For example, in 2008, the United States assisted private corporations with a total of $772.5 billion in loans and grants. Some of the recipients included Bear Stearns, American International Groups (A.I.G.), Chrysler/General Motors, and Citigroup. During the bailouts, the mass media ran stories of extravagant parties within these failing institutes and told of "the golden parachute" – that is, a clause in an executive's employment contract that guarantees a large benefit if the corporation is acquired and the executive loses his or her job, regardless of the quality of the executive's work. In the 1970s, the railroad companies struggled and were considered too big to fail; they were assisted with $676 million. Lockheed was given $1.4 billion in loan guarantees in 1971; from 1986 to 1995, the FDIC gave more than $124 billion to assist failing savings and loan enterprises; and, in 1995, the U.S. Treasury gave $25 million to assist the State of New York (Sasseen and Francis 2008). These corporations, and many others, are given *corporate welfare* to maintain a healthy economy and nation. Some scholars compare this to the social welfare of the poor, which generally costs much less.

Another form of welfare for the top social classes is *crop subsidies* and *land grants* to industry. The National Mineral Act of 1866 gave millions of acres to mining companies free of charge. Even today, claims may be made on public lands with no royalty fees paid to the public. Before 1998, the U.S. Forestry Service gave public trees to companies that built roads in forests – roads used primarily by logging companies (O'Toole 1987). Crop subsidies are funds paid to farmers to not grow crops so that market values remain stable. The 2002 Farm Bill provided $190 billion to subsidize American farmers. The distribution of these funds is of interest to scholars and activists alike, who demonstrate that there is bias in agricultural welfare. It is estimated that 10 percent of America's largest (and richest) farms receive 75 percent of federal subsidies (Carr 2007).

The decisions about who gets assistance, how much, and the terms of repayment are established by the government. In America, the government is an elected body of individuals represented at federal, state, and local levels. Governmental institutions, electoral rules, political parties, and previously established policies drive policy and set its limits and opportunities. During the nineteenth and twentieth centuries, policies were devised and reformed by socially active groups and reformers (Skocpol 1993). Given the amount of power the government wields and the ability for groups to influence the government in a democracy, we would assume that the average American is deeply engaged in the electoral process; this, however, is not the case.

Who Votes?

Policies are the result of a long and detailed political process. In America, that process begins with the election of a group of people intended to represent the interests of the nation, state, county, and city. The voting process, then, is an integral component of policy making (Conway 1991).

Voting is the mechanism of equal representation in democratic societies, yet certain groups historically have been denied the right to vote and not everyone currently takes advantage of this right. Who votes in democratic countries and which factors influence this decision?

Throughout American history, groups have been denied the right to vote. At various times, different status groups have been disenfranchised, including nonproperty holders, Jews, Catholics, women, felons, the poor, Native Americans, blacks, Hispanics, Chinese, Japanese, and nonwhites. Dominant groups often used violence to enforce their opinion that all people are not created equal. Today in America, some still lack access to voting.

The highly charged 2008 presidential election had one of the highest turnouts of voters since 1978. An African American ran for the highest office in the nation and the Republican and Democratic parties had divergent ideas on how to proceed with the rule of the land. Regardless of the heated nature of the election, Figure 14.1 shows that fewer than 64 percent of eligible voters in America actually cast a ballot. In previous years, the average number of voters electing a president was closer to 56 percent. If we review the years between presidential elections, represented by the white bars in Figure 14.1, the number of voters is even lower – on average, about 48 percent. If one of the American values discussed in Chapter 6 is democracy, why do so few Americans participate in the electoral process?

American elections have long attracted older white constituents. Also, naturalized citizens, particularly those with high incomes and educational levels, are more likely to vote than natives with similar backgrounds (Bass and Casper 2001). Until recently, young people and people of color voted in low numbers. Table 14.1 reports the percentages of voters in the 2008 election by race, age, and educational attainment.

Looking at the percentages of voters by race/ethnicity, we see that whites constitute 76 percent, blacks 12 percent, Hispanics (of any race) 7 percent, Asian/Pacific Islanders 3 percent, and Native Americans and multiracial each 1 percent. Whereas the percentage of nonvoters for whites and blacks is lower compared with the percentage of voters, the opposite is true for those who identify as Asian/Pacific Islander or Hispanic. More Asian/Pacific Islanders and Hispanics did not vote than did. By removing the *two-step voting process* – that is, registration first, then a subsequent vote – scholars believe that the Asian–white gap in voter turnout would disappear; scholars also expect this would have a positive effect on the turnout of other ethnic minorities (Xu 2004).

Age also affects who votes: About 17 percent of those younger than 30 voted in 2008, compared to 83 percent of those 30 years or older. Twenty-nine percent of nonvoters

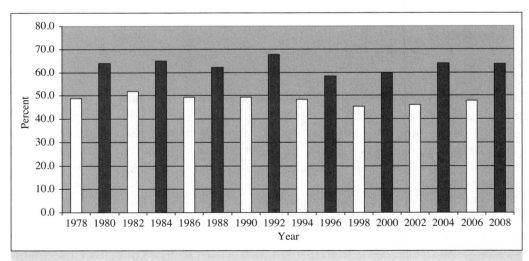

Figure 14.1 Percentage of voters in America, 1978–2008.
Data Source: U.S. Census, Current Population Survey (2010).

Table 14.1 Percentage of Voters by Race/Ethnicity, Age, and Education

	Adult Citizens	Voters	Unregistered	Non-Voters
Race	%	%	%	%
White	73	76	67	68
Black	12	12	12	11
Asian/Pacific Islander	4	3	6	5
Hispanic	9	7	13	13
Native American	1	<1	1	1
Multiracial	1	1	1	1
Age	%	%	%	%
Younger than 30	21	17	29	29
30 and Older	79	83	71	71
Education	%	%	%	%
High school degree or less	43	34	58	58
Some college or more	57	66	42	42

Data Source: November 2008 Current Population Survey (2009).

were younger than 30 and 71 percent were older than 30. Older Americans are more likely to vote than younger Americans. College-educated individuals are almost twice as likely to vote as those with less education, 66 and 34 percent, respectively. More than half of those without a high school degree are not registered to vote.

Additionally, of those who reported income, 15 million people earning less than $25,000 annually did not vote. If those at the bottom quintile of annual earnings had voted at the same rate as those in the top quintile, there would have been an additional 8.4 percent of low-income voters. Simply stated, the rich are more likely to vote than the poor (Beeghley 1986). If parity between voters had been reached, an additional 5,034 nonwhites, 5,665 unmarried women, 19,856 individuals with a high school diploma or less, 7,008 people under age 30, and 1,852 people with disabilities would have voted (Hess and Herman 2009).

The National Voter Registration Act (NVRA) of 1993 was enacted to allow voters easier access to voting and to maintain their registration across time. It allows the Federal Election Commission to provide states with information and guidance on the Act and the U.S. Department of Justice to bring civil action against parties who are in violation of the Act. However, the Act has had a negligible effect – there has been no impact in state-level turnouts and it appears to have exacerbated class and racial inequality in state electorates (Martinez and Hill 1999).

Why are so many Americans not registered to vote? Individual characteristics comprise part of the answer; that is, some lack interest in the political process. However, social scientists show that structural matters often block access to voter registration.

Scholars have demonstrated that some of the reasons for the variations in voter turnout include long-term political factors at the state level. Two principal determinants of registration levels are (1) party-elite ideology, and (2) restrictiveness of registration requirements (Jackson, Brown, and Wright 1998). *Party-elite ideology* refers to the number of party leaders that also are members of the elite social class – that is, the top 10 percent (some would argue the top 5 percent). When there are politically liberal elites dominating the party, more poor and undereducated voters are registered during any given election. The second determinant, *restrictiveness of registration requirements*, concerns the difficulty of registration by particular groups of people. In the 2008 election, for example, of the 75 million people who were eligible but did not vote, 60 million were not registered. How people register to vote differs by status group. Whereas the majority of Americans register at the Department of Motor Vehicles (i.e., about 26 percent), twice as many nonwhites, 12 percent, register through registration drives, compared with 6 percent of whites (Hess and Herman 2009). For those who do not drive, particularly those who cannot afford to drive, registering to vote can be an obstacle to political representation and equality. Moreover, people who relocate are disrupted and cannot register and therefore have lower participation rates (Highton 2000).

As discussed throughout this book, some groups repeatedly face difficulty in accessing resources. From the previous analysis, we know that resources are indeed allocated by status groups. As has been established, policies are created by elected officials. Who are these elected officials?

Who Are the Elected?

Elected officials come from the top 10 to 15 percent of the income distribution. Domhoff (1936–) studied the candidate-election process and described the social backgrounds of politicians. In his book, *Who Rules America? Power and Politics* (2002), he compared the rhetoric to the reality of early American presidents. He showed that George Washington was one of the richest men of the time; Andrew Jackson came from a wealthy slave-holding family; Abraham Lincoln was a corporate lawyer and married into a wealthy family from Kentucky; and many more current presidents also were from the upper class: Theodore Roosevelt, Franklin D. Roosevelt, George H. W. Bush, George W. Bush, John F. Kennedy, and Jimmy Carter. The list of presidents also exposes the way that race and gender affect political participation.

The majority of political power is held by men. Figure 14.2 shows that the percentage of male Congressional representation is more than four times that of female representation.

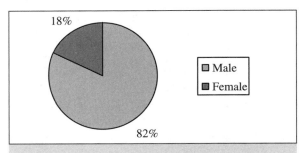

Figure 14.2 Percentage of the 111th Congress by sex.
Data Source: U.S. Office of the Clerk (2009).

Of the U.S. 111th Congress (2009–2011), 82 percent is men and 18 percent is women despite the fact that women comprise about 51 percent of the population at large. In both the Senate and the House of Representatives men comprise 82 percent of seats and women the remaining 18 percent. The division by sex is mirrored in the division of female membership by political party. Figure 14.3 shows that of the total number of female House Representatives, 22 percent are Republican and 78 percent are Democrat. Of the 18 female Senators, 22 percent are Republican and 78 percent are Democrat (U.S. Office of the Clerk 2009).

The number of women who have chaired committees in Congress also reflects the unequal distribution of political power in the United States. In the 111th Congress, three women chaired committees in the House of Representatives and three women in the Senate. The three women in the Senate chaired six seats: three seats by Dianne Feinstein (D-CA), two seats by Barbara Boxer (D-CA), and one seat by Mary Landrieu (D-LA).

How does America compare with other nations in terms of women as political leaders? The UN reports on the status of women's political representation (Commission on the Status of Women 2009). Globally, women represent one in five parliamentary positions. Today, female decision makers in the public sector occupy 18.4 percent of seats compared to 11.6 percent in 1995. Leading the world is the country of Rwanda, which elected women to 56 percent of its parliament. The spokesperson for the UN Development Fund for Women states that quotas contributed heavily to the increase in female representation. Despite the gains being made – even with the inclusion of quotas in many nations – it is predicted to take between 18 and 22 years for women to comprise 40 percent of all publicly held decision-making positions. Female political representation in the United States is comparable to the global average.

The majority of elected officials are white. Of the 435 members of the House of Representatives, 41 members are African American. Each of these Representatives is a Democrat; there are no black Republican Representatives. Senator Ronald Burris, (D-IL), whose predecessor Senator Barack Obama left the position to serve as President, is the sole black Senator. The replacement of Senator Obama was surrounded in controversy because it was the duty of the Illinois Governor Rob Blagojevich to fill the empty seat. Despite an investigation and pleas to repeal Blagojevich's decision, Senator Burris remains

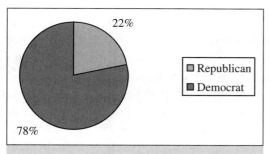

Figure 14.3 Percentage of females of the 111th Congress by political party.
Data Source: U.S. Office of the Clerk (2009).

the only black member of the Senate. Four African American Representatives chair House committees and there is no Senate committee chaired by an African American. Additionally, there are 28 Hispanic House Representatives, 3 Hispanic Senators, 9 Asian/Pacific Islander Representatives and 2 Senators, and 1 Native American in Congress, who is a member of the House of Representatives.

Elected state and local offices have seen an increase in women and ethnic minority participation. In 2009, there were 74 female office holders, compared to 73 the previous year. There were 1,787 females elected to state legislatures in 2009, up from 1,751 in 2008.

Who Influences the Political Process?

The power of *lobbying firms* continues to grow in the United States as different interests vie for the attention and control of the political process. Does lobbying amount to the bribing of elected officials, or is it a natural and healthy consequence of the democratic process? Scholars find that lobbying is not the same as a bribe; rather, it serves to open access for the lobbyist to be heard and be included in the political process (Barlett and Steele 1994). The effect of lobbyists in the public sphere led one scholar to write: "[D]espite much growth in the transparency and disclosure practices of many public and private institutions during the closing decades of the twentieth century, private efforts to shape public life are on the rise" (Walker 2009: 99).

In 2009, 13,426 lobbyists were currently shaping public life. We might ask whether this is an exact number. According to the U.S. Office of the Clerk Lobbyist Disclosure, in the second half of 2009, 354 potential noncompliant registrants were reported to the U.S. Attorney for the District of Columbia; that is, more than 300 potential lobbyists did not register. The amount of money spent by lobbying groups to affect the political process decreased to $2.5 billion in 2009 from $3.3 billion in 2007. The top lobbyists – that is, those who contribute the most to Congress – ranked in order of contributions were the U.S. Chamber of Commerce, American Medical Association, General Electric, AARP, American Hospital Association, Pharmaceutical Research and Manufacturers of America, AT&T Inc., Northrop Grumman, National Association of Realtors, ExxonMobil, and Edison Electric Institute (Center for Responsive Politics 2009).

In addition to lobbyists, the political process in America includes PACs, which are private groups organized to elect officials. There are a multitude of PACs organized by political parties, industries, corporations, and elected officials. The primary interest of a PAC is to support a candidate; however, they have been used increasingly for personal gain. In one public case, Representative Doolittle (R-CA) "paid ever-larger commissions to his wife's one-person company and spent tens of thousands of dollars on gifts at stores such as Saks Fifth Avenue and Tiffany & Co. and a Ritz-Carlton day spa" (Weisman and Birnbaum 2006: 1). Corruption within the political process, including some of the activities of PACs, has been shown to lower voter turnout (Cebula 2007). More recently the United States Supreme Court decided an important case in Citizens United v. Federal Election Commission (2010). The decision allows corporations unlimited funding of political broadcasts. Will this favor corporations over individuals or is part of democracy allowing access to the political process to all – including corporations?

The current political process – including low voting rates, lobbyists, PACs, corporate investment in political broadcasts and limited access for status groups, particularly women, the poor, and people of color – has some scholars questioning how well democracy works in America. A democracy is rule by the majority but, as seen in the previous analyses, it is only a minority that participates politically. Sociologist Robert Michels (1876–1936) theorized that democratic political parties inevitably become undemocratic and elitist. The *iron law of oligarchy*, as it is known, explains the process by which political parties create and maintain bureaucracies to obtain power. For grassroots leaders to gain political power, they must negotiate with officials – those already in power. Once upcoming leaders are in the social sphere of the political elite, they also divorce themselves of their proletariat roots, become interested in more power, and soon evolve into the elite class. Indeed, an analysis of the *corporate community* (i.e., the social network of corporate leaders) shows that newcomers adopt the manner of dress, speech, and recreational and charitable interests of the elite class (Domhoff 2002).

Is the political process more effective in other nations? Many nations do not have a two-step political process: A state identification card on voting day is all that is needed to vote, which results in higher voter turnout (Beckfield 2003).

Chapter 10 examines women and their changing roles in America. The issue of women's suffrage affected nations across the world (Paxton 1997). Despite women's right to vote and to hold office in 182 nations, some countries still do not allow female participation. Of those that do, the international average is still about 20 percent – that is, on average, women hold only 20 percent of all elected political positions in nations that allow them to do so. Using cross-national data, scholars studied the paths by which women gain political power. Three factors determine the success of women in making inroads in male-dominated politics: (1) social structure – the pool of available women; (2) political – the openness of political systems to women; and (3) ideology – the general impressions of women in politics and how visible they are as candidates and leaders. Of structure, politics, and ideology, research shows that the best predictor of national levels of female political participation is ideology. The ways that women are presented in the political process deeply affect how constituents view women leaders. During the demise of communism in the Soviet Union, women lost significant political representation as a result of government policies to maintain the perception that women were poor leaders. The public viewed women as less able and voted for fewer of them (Paxton and Kunovich 2003).

Democracy is highly valued in America, yet most Americans do not vote. Some turn away from a system that they feel is corrupt, others are turned away through the two-step voting process, and others do not vote because they think their vote does not matter. The political process moves by the hands of a selected few. Elected officials appear to be the dominant class in society: white, male, and elderly. However, this is changing as more power minorities enter politics at the federal, state, and local levels. Research shows that the political process is rife with groups that vie for power.

Do Policies Reduce Inequality?

Policies are deeply tied to those who write them. In the United States, the majority of Congress is economically privileged, white, elderly, and male. Policies are written to reduce inequality but they rarely do. They are met with resistance because they challenge the status quo, leaving groups and individuals to continue to act in ways that policies disallow. This is observed in the many attempts to open access to ethnic minorities, women, and the poor. Discrimination has been challenged by federal policies and, although gains have been made, there are still well-documented discriminatory practices in education, employment, and housing.

Calls to reduce inequality are often answered with claims that the American way of life will self-destruct. Individualism and freedom are valued highly and welfare often is considered an unfair system that gives some a free ride whereas others labor to survive. Structural barriers to wealth accumulation are not acknowledged and ethnic minorities, women, and the poor often are blamed for their lot in life.

Regardless of who writes the policies, how well do they work in reducing inequality? The following sections provide a sample of policies aimed directly at inequality.

Employment Policies

Several federal laws prohibit job discrimination. For instance, Title VII of the Civil Rights Act of 1964 prohibits employment discrimination based on race, color, religion, sex, and national origin. However, researchers have shown that discrimination is ongoing and difficult to prove (Kirschenman and Neckerman 1991; Roscigno, Garcia, and Bobbitt-Zeher 2007). The Equal Pay Act (EPA) of 1963 protects men and women who perform substantially equal work in the same establishment from sex-based wage discrimination, yet the gender gap still exists (Charles and Grusky 2004; Mandel and Semyonov 2005). Title I and Title V of the Americans with Disabilities Act (ADA) of 1990 prohibit employment discrimination against qualified individuals with disabilities in both the private sector and state and local government. Sections 501 and 505 of the Rehabilitation Act of 1973 prohibit discrimination against qualified individuals with disabilities who work in the federal government. However, Americans with disabilities still earn less than those who are not disabled (McNeil 2000).

Social Welfare Programs

Several social welfare programs have been designed and implemented in an attempt to eliminate poverty. Americans generally agree that poverty negatively affects the nation but they differ greatly on how to eradicate conditions that lead to it.

Two poverty policies that were met with resistance and controversy are Franklin D. Roosevelt's New Deal in the 1930s and Lyndon Johnson's War on Poverty in the 1960s. The New Deal prescribed structural treatments to reduce poverty through the Social Security Act of 1935. At the time, the unemployment rate was about 25 percent (higher in urban areas), and property values were rapidly shrinking as mortgages were foreclosed. As unemployment increased, so did the number of homeless and helpless. To combat this downward trend, federally funded initiatives and work programs were fostered across the nation, as well as the establishment of national parks. Medicare and Social Security, two major initiatives of the New Deal, targeted those in society who are most at risk of poverty: the ill and the elderly. Both programs remain an integral part of social services despite the controversial nature of social welfare in America.

The War on Poverty was enacted when the unemployment rate was about 19 percent. One successful program still in place today is Head Start, which is a federally funded program that focuses on early childhood – it provides food and education for the poor. Although the program's efficacy has been challenged, scholars are confident that children who have participated in Head Start score significantly higher in a majority of measures involving language, literacy, and some math skills compared to those 3 and 4 year olds who did not participate (IES 2010). The Head Start program feeds millions of children who would otherwise go to school hungry. Both policies, which aimed at increasing jobs and assisting Americans by providing opportunities, were criticized for being expensive, lacking in coherency, and expanding government (Russell 2003).

Aid to Families with Dependent Children (AFDC), established by the Social Security Act of 1935, was the largest federal program serving poor children of America. It allocated funds to states that, in turn, would provide assistance to needy children who had been deprived parental support through absence, disability, unemployment, or death. AFDC allowed states to determine need by setting their own poverty thresholds. In 1996, AFDC was replaced by Temporary Assistance for Needy Families (TANF) when Congress passed the Personal Responsibility and Work Occupation and Reconciliation Act. The Act replaced many social welfare programs including AFDC, Job Opportunities and Basic Skills Training (JOBS), and Emergency Assistance (EA). TANF, unlike AFDC, limited the amount of time a family may receive federal funds, increased work-participation requirements of the states, and allowed states to broadly design welfare programs. Moreover, funds may be used by a state in any way that aligns with TANF's four goals: "to provide assistance to needy families so that children can be cared for at home; to end the dependence of needy parents on government benefits by promoting job preparation, work and marriage; to prevent and reduce the incidence of out-of-wedlock pregnancies; and to encourage the formation and maintenance of two-parent families" (U.S. Department of Health and Human Services 2004).

Proponents of TANF argue that it has been effective in reducing poverty as evidenced in the declining welfare rolls (i.e., the number of people seeking assistance from welfare services). This could mean, however, that homeless and other populations are not being served rather than indicating that their numbers or proportion decreased (Lichter and Crowley 2002).

Today, new welfare policies are used in an attempt to stop further development of an underclass. Reforms have been met with criticism and mixed results. Within the first year of his election, President Obama signed into law the American Recovery and Reinvestment Act of 2009, which included the Homelessness Prevention and Rapid Re-Housing Program (HPRP). This program aims to reduce chronic homelessness across America. Philip Mangano was appointed by former President George W. Bush as homelessness czar and he continues to serve under President Obama. In 2000, Mangano designed a 10-year plan to eradicate chronic homelessness which has seen great success.

Although homelessness still exists, there has been a 12 percent decline in the national homeless rate. In the most recent report generated by the Los Angeles Homeless Service Authority (LAHSA), homelessness has decreased by more than 38 percent in the greater Los Angeles area – the city with the highest homeless rate in America (LAHSA 2009). However, according to Jeanette Rowe, Director of Emergency Response Team and Homeless Children and Families Program at LAHSA, the number of homeless people seeking services is lower as a result of many factors. First, "word on the street is that there is no money available for housing"; with a perception that assistance is not available, fewer clients seek services. Second, federal dollars from HPRP are so regulated that it is difficult for agencies to administer their allocation to the homeless. Third, methodological problems in counting render claims regarding the reduction of homelessness difficult to support (Southgate 2009).

Scholarly response to the change in the U.S. welfare system has been met with criticism. One UN human-rights investigator demonstrated that limiting levels of social welfare and social security in the last two decades, in combination with corporate welfare, contributed to what she called the "shameful neglect" of the homeless in one of the richest nations in the world (McGreal 2009). The investigator reported verbally to the U.S. State Department and provided the UN with a written report early in 2010. The lack of effective welfare policies in light of the wealth in America has prompted global consternation.

Race/Ethnicity Policies

One highly controversial policy meant to reduce inequality began in 1961 when President Kennedy ordered employers to take *affirmative action* to lessen discrimination by race, creed, color, and national origin. Affirmative action describes many policies aimed at equality in education (e.g., busing and desegregation); however, affirmative-action policies today generally target higher-education admissions.

The controversy was heightened in 1997 when two white Michigan students filed a federal lawsuit against the University of Michigan on grounds that they were denied entrance. They argued that students of color with lower test scores and grades had been admitted, which violated the constitutional right of equal protection for the white students. The U.S. Supreme Court upheld the university's decision in 2003, citing evidence from social scientists that a critical mass must be reached to allow diversity to flourish within the occupational structure of the United States. The only way to ensure access to upper-level positions is through the enrollment of people of color and women in colleges and universities. The system by which universities allocated points to applicants was scrutinized and the debate continues.

Critics of affirmative action policies voice concern that (1) individuals who benefit are not qualified to compete against white students with higher scores and grades – what is termed the *mismatch hypothesis*; (2) the policies create a *stereotype threat* by grouping all people of color into a lower status category; and (3) affirmative action is *reverse discrimination*. Proponents have shown that there is no evidence to support the mismatch hypothesis (Fischer and Massey 2007). Using longitudinal data to track students in selective colleges and universities, sociologists found that beneficiaries of affirmative action actually outperform others. There is support for the claim of stereotype threat; however, the effect is small and further reduced through academic performance. The claim of reverse discrimination is refuted by studies that show the long history of social reproduction in the United States.

Despite resistance, affirmative action has reduced inequality. Access to prestigious colleges and universities by people of color and women has increased since affirmative-action polices were enacted. Although legal actions at the state level have decreased the use of affirmative-action policies to assign points toward entrance for ethnic and racial minorities, the increased focus on test scores in higher education encourages the continuation of this policy (Alon and Tienda 2007).

Given that affirmative action is a political treatment for inequality, why is it so controversial? According to some sociologists, Americans have an idealized notion of justice (Crosby 2004). The ideal of justice includes awards based on merit and individual performance. However, discrimination in college enrollment has traditionally limited opportunities for people of color, women, and the poor. Generally, whites do not perceive their access as privilege; instead, many view affirmative action as reverse discrimination. From this perspective, affirmative action is perceived as placing less qualified minority individuals before more qualified whites. What is generally not considered is the system that universities use to choose students. In addition to SAT scores, many schools give advantages to legacies – that is, those students whose parents attended the school. Critics of affirmative action do not see this as unequal treatment.

Educational Policies

Chapter 9 describes the education system and discusses how access to resources for some led to a reproduction of social-class status. The intersection of social class and race is explored in Chapter 11. We learned that racial segregation in schools resulted in a change of federal policy. What began in the 1950s continues today as policy makers and constituents debate the merits, form, and implications of educational policy on lessening inequality and increasing access to education.

Title I

The issue of equity in education generated policies that often are controversial. One effort to increase equity in education is known as Title I of the Elementary and Secondary Education Act of 1965. It was recently amended to Title I: Improving The Academic Achievement of the Disadvantaged; the "[purpose] of this title is to ensure that all children have a fair, equal, and significant opportunity to obtain a high-quality education and reach, at a minimum, proficiency on challenging State academic achievement standards and state academic assessments" (U.S. Department of Education 2009). Under Title I, funds are appropriated to states, agencies, school districts, and school sites to improve the education of disadvantaged groups. Some Title I funds are used to increase the efforts of literacy programs (e.g., Reading First, Early Reading First, Even Start, and Improving Literacy Through School Libraries); assist in the education of migratory children; prevention and intervention programs for neglected, delinquent, or at-risk youth; comprehensive school reform; dropout prevention; school improvement; and state administration. Title I funds are not guaranteed but must be requested and then are allocated by federal administrators.

School Choice

Another educational policy aimed at reducing inequality was President George W. Bush's No Child Left Behind (NCLB) program. The NCLB policy institutionalized *school choice*. Instead of children being placed randomly in schools based on residence, parents with children in failing schools were given vouchers that allowed them to attend a different school of their choosing. Much controversy surrounds this arm of the policy because many see the beginning of the demise of the public-school system; that is, much-needed funds are redistributed to other schools that may not be part of the public-school system. The erosion of the public-school system is a concern of sociologists who fear that privatization of education will only increase inequality through social reproduction (Berliner and Biddle 1995).

Two forms of schools have emerged under school choice: *magnet schools* and *charter schools*. Magnet schools are decentralized, pooling students from various areas, often through a lottery process. They most often are subject-oriented, such as mathematics or performance arts. They have more autonomy than an average public school but remain under the bureaucracy of the public-school system.

More controversial are the charter schools. Both states and school districts charter schools to shift centralized decision making to the school level. The move toward *privatization of schools* allows charter schools to be exempt from state and local regulations; in return, they guarantee that students will pass standards-based examinations. If they do not meet the standards set out in the charter, it is revoked and the school is closed. Driven by political and institutional needs rather than achievement (Zhang and Yang 2008), the number of charter schools has increased in response to the demand in school choice. In 2004–2005, charter schools comprised 4 percent of all public schools in the United States and enrolled more ethnic minorities and children who received free or reduced-cost lunches (an indicator of poverty) than conventional public schools (National Center for Education Statistics 2007).

One characteristic of charter schools with inequitable implications is that they may refuse entrance to students, which public schools cannot. Recent attention has been given to the "dumping" of students with special educational needs or learning disabilities into conventional schools, which lifts the achievement aggregate score of choice schools. Others are concerned that charter schools are not required to report indicators such as dropout rates. Evaluating charter-school efficacy is challenging given the variety of charters and the lack of data; however, there is no current evidence that charter schools outperform conventional public schools (Carnoy, Jacobsen, Mishel, and Rothstein 2005).

Previous attempts at educational policy reform have failed because they refuse to question the basic structure of property and power in economic life. Some believe that the key to reform is the democratization of economic relationships: social ownership. Thus, educational reform is linked to the grand scheme of Marxist solutions – namely, socialism.

Despite the fact that education often has been used as a central instrument of liberal reformers, the range of effective educational policy (in the United States) has been severely limited by the role of schooling in the production of an adequate labor force in a hierarchically controlled and class-structured production system.

Can Inequality Be Lessened through Education?

Given the persistence of social inequality on education, how can public schools "level the playing field"? Jenks et al. ([1972]2001) argued that schools cannot level the playing field, that inequalities exist, and that Americans, in general – although they want to be believe in a meritocratic process – are content with thinking that if there is a chance for upward mobility, there is no reason for concern with stratification systems.

Is there a chance to overcome inequality? Most Americans assume that by applying themselves and working hard, individuals can raise their status beyond their original social location. However, in a cross-national analysis on academic outcomes, scholars confirm that social location matters more than school-level treatment[1] or personal effort (Blossfield and Shavit 1993). They find that equality exists in the relationships between socioeconomic status and educational opportunity and socioeconomic status and educational attainment in the Netherlands and Sweden, but persistent inequalities remain in the nine other industrialized countries they studied.

Social scientists believe that the reason the Netherlands and Sweden have reduced inequality to less than 5 percent is that the political systems are socialist and the culture of these nations has a rich history of class consciousness (Blossfeld and Shavit 1993). They devised education systems that value parental choice and allow vouchers. The difference between vouchers in these nations compared with the United States is that schools are neither allowed to choose students by ability nor are they allowed additional tuition. In this regard, public and private schools coexist with the same revenue. Schools are formed around pedagogic styles[2] rather than funding. The outcome is that students have similar opportunity, which translates into similar attainment. Finally, for our purposes, policies aimed at decreasing national levels of inequality are negligible. In fact, policies aimed at further decreasing inequality in the Netherlands and Sweden were enacted after the equality levels already had been achieved. Equality within society, therefore, is a function of opportunity that begins with education.

Education is an important institution that informs stratification in industrialized nations. Enrollments and corresponding matriculation rates reflect a nation's ability to compete in a growing global market. Those who fail to graduate or who attend schools that provide a poor education will rank among the lowest in a nation and require assistance to survive. Despite the need to maintain quality education and motivation among students, policies have had mixed results in contributing to school equality. Students of

---

[1] They review 11 nations that vary in terms of governmental organization: some are capitalist, some are socialist, most are somewhere between the two. These nations also differ in terms of institutional arrangements and national culture.

[2] Most popular pedagogic styles are Waldorf and Montessori.

color now attend schools that at one time admitted only whites; however, due to residential segregation and racial earning gaps, they are likely to be concentrated in schools with other students of color. In other words, although students of color have the right to access the same education as a white student, due to structural circumstances, they remain in schools with low levels of diversity.

Summary

(1) Inequality exists in all countries, but America has the highest level of inequality when compared with other industrialized nations.

(2) America's high level of inequality is a result of the economic structure of capitalism, which values a model of risk/reward as opposed to egalitarianism. Other political structures, such as socialism or welfare states, run on a model of egalitarianism.

(3) Social welfare occurs in all developed nations. In America, it is provided to corporations, farming industries, and other industries. In some cases, these are major industries and corporations; when they fail, they receive large bailouts because policy makers believe the death of the industry would have a negative impact on America's economy. Although this practice is against the economic model of laissez faire free-market trade, it is a recurrent phenomenon.

(4) Because America is a democracy, policies are determined by a small group of elected officials who are influenced by grassroots efforts, organized lobbying firms, and PACs.

(5) Despite the valuing of the democratic process, the majority of Americans do not vote. The NVRA was designed to lessen restrictions on voter registration; however, it actually increased the bias by white, rich, and elderly voters. Social scientists demonstrate that the way to increase voter turnout is through party-elite ideology and a less restrictive registration process (e.g., removing two-step voting).

(6) Michels's iron law of oligarchy explains how power over the many rests in the hands of so few in a democracy. Once outsiders infiltrate the power structure, they soon adapt and assimilate the ways of the powerful to maintain their own power position.

(7) Many laws have been aimed at reducing inequality and have been successful in that power minorities (e.g., women, people of color, and the poor) have more rights compared to their status before the policies. However, there is still residual inequality between groups, such as wage gaps, stereotyping, discrimination, and racial segregation.

Box 14.1 Policies Are Created by the Dominant Class: Workers Must Unite for Change to Occur

Karl Marx and Friedrich Engels wrote the *Communist Manifesto* in 1848 at the height of the European Industrial Revolution and a period of great political turmoil. The manifesto was composed for the Communist League, whose goal was to overthrow bourgeois society and establish a new social order without classes and private property. In the pamphlet, Marx and Engels established an intrinsic link between political and economic power.

Box 14.1 (*continued*)

Marx believed that the contemporary stratification system could be separated into two classes: the bourgeoisie and the proletariat. The bourgeoisie was that group of individuals who had access to the means of production; they owned the factories, the banks, and other instruments of economic and financial success. The proletariat lacked access to these modes of production and were instead forced to sell their labor to the bourgeoisie to survive. Because one class had access to the means of production and the other class was entirely dependent on them, Marx wrote that the two classes had opposing interests. The bourgeoisie sought to maintain the status quo, whereas the proletariat was interested in reorganizing society so that the wealth generated by the Industrial Revolution would be dispersed more equally among the entire population.

The *Communist Manifesto* declared that the political structure of society was simply the reification of the economic struggle between the two classes. The bourgeoisie did not only control the means of production, they also controlled the political system: "[T]he executive of the modern state is but a committee for managing the common affairs of the whole bourgeoisie." Their control of the process of "who gets what, when, where, and how" allowed the owners of the means of production to politically, economically, and legally continue their domination of the working class.

The intent of Marx's pamphlet was clearly stated in its opening lines: "A specter is haunting Europe – the specter of communism. All the powers of old Europe have entered into a holy alliance to exorcise this specter." Marx called for the Communist Party to "meet this nursery tale of the specter of Communism with a Manifesto of the party itself." Marx believed that the proletariat ultimately would become increasingly impoverished and alienated under the oppressive rule of the bourgeoisie. This would result in the development of a class consciousness among the workers and the ability to overthrow the bourgeoisie and create a new social order – a communist society. "The communists disdain to conceal their views and aims. They openly declare that their ends can be attained only by the forcible overthrow of all existing social conditions. Let the ruling classes tremble at a communist revolution. The proletarians have nothing to lose but their chains. They have a world to win. WORKING MEN OF ALL COUNTRIES, UNITE!"

Although the inevitability and plausibility of Marx's vision of the future have been questioned, the link that he drew between economic power and political power is noteworthy. The economic elite have an important role in the political process, and it would be unrealistic to assume that this power is not used to protect their own interests. The *Communist Manifesto* is one of the most important and widely recognized historical political pamphlets, and its significance is unmistakable. For this reason alone, it is worthwhile reading. Furthermore, the still-relevant insight about the political economy of capitalistic societies will contribute to a reader's understanding of the interplay between politics and social stratification.

Source: Marx, Karl, and Friedrich Engels. 1848. *The Communist Manifesto*. New York: Penguin Books.

Box 14.2 The Policy-Planning Network

How policies are developed and subsequently enacted into law is a complex social process. Sociologist William Domhoff studied this topic in depth and outlined the social interactions involved in the process of policy making. He applied the scientific method of social-network analysis to the study of elites and found that at the heart of the network is the corporate community.

Policy begins with both formal and informal interactions by the elite. Members of the upper class meet formally in boardrooms and informally in social clubs and through casual conversation when they discuss problems that need solutions. Ultimately, the solutions become policy through the official legitimation of the government at various levels: federal, state, county, and city. Between the beginning and ending, formal institutions are called on to direct the policy by providing information needed to steer decisions. Two formal institutions often complete this work: the *foundation* and the *think tank*.

(*continued*)

Box 14.2 (*continued*)

Foundations are tax-free organizations founded on a mission statement. They are created to grant funds, called *grants*, to individuals and nonprofit organizations for a wide range of activities. A familiar foundation is the John D. Rockefeller Foundation, which – according to its stated history: "Since its establishment in 1913, the Rockefeller Foundation has sought to identify and attack at their source the underlying causes of human suffering" (John D. Rockefeller Foundation 2009a). Two examples of the grants issued by the foundation that were aimed at policy creation include (1) $100,000 to the Initiative for a Competitive Inner City in Boston, Massachusetts, in November 2009 "toward the costs of its project to analyze the underlying causes of inner-city economic stagnation and recommend potential federal policy responses"; and (2) in December 2009, it gave Freedman Consulting, LLC, in Washington, DC, a grant of $155,000 "in support of providing technical assistance to select grantees of the Rockefeller Foundation's Campaign for American Workers initiative, focusing on positioning of policy proposals to be noticed by and useful to policy makers and other stakeholders." In November alone, the foundation granted more than $7.1 million to various recipients (John D. Rockefeller Foundation 2009b).

Think tanks comprise the second formal institution in the policy-planning network. "Think tanks are nonprofit organizations that provide settings for experts in various academic disciplines to devote their time to the study of policy alternatives, free from the teaching, committee meetings, and departmental duties that are part of the daily routine for most members of the academic community" (Domhoff 2002: 71). One think tank that generally garners bipartisan support and is highly cited is the Brookings Institute, where "more than 200 resident and nonresident fellows research issues; write books, papers, articles and opinion pieces; testify before congressional committees and participate in dozens of public events each year" (Brookings Institute 2009).

The policy discussions bring together "corporate executives, lawyers, academic experts, university administrators, government officials, and media specialists to talk about such general problems as foreign aid, free trade, taxes, and environmental policies" (Domhoff 2002: 71). Together, the network crystallizes priorities and creates strategies of action that ultimately become policy.

Sources: Domhoff, G. William. 2002. *Who Rules America? Power and Politics* (4th edition). New York: McGraw Hill.

Brookings Institute. 2009. "About Brookings." Retrieved December 7, 2009. Available at www.brookings.edu/about.aspx.

John D. Rockefeller Foundation. 2009a. "About Us." Retrieved December 7, 2009. Available at www.rockfound.org/about_us/about_us.shtml.

———. 2009b. "Rockefeller Foundation Grant Search." Retrieved December 7, 2009. Available at www.rockfound.org/grants/GrantSearch.aspx?keywords=&allDates=1&monthFrom=1&yearFrom=2004&monthTo=12&yearTo=2009).

Key Concepts

Affirmative action

Aid to Families with Dependent
    Children (AFDC)

American Recovery and Reinvestment
    Act of 2009

Americans with Disabilities Act of 1990

Bailout

Capitalism

Civil Rights Act of 1964

Corporate community

Corporate tax policies

Corporate welfare

Crop subsidies

Educational policies

Employment policies

Equal Pay Act of 1963

Golden parachute

Head Start

Homelessness Prevention and
    Rapid Re-Housing Program (HPRP)

Iron law of oligarchy

Laissez faire

Land grants
Lobbying firms
Medicare
Mismatch hypothesis/stereotype threat
National Mineral Act of 1866
National Voter Registration Act (NVRA)
New Deal
No Child Left Behind (NCLB)
Party-elite ideology
Political Action Committee (PAC)
Privatization of schools
Race/ethnicity policies
Rehabilitation Act of 1973
Restrictiveness of registration requirements

Risk/reward
Social insurance
Social Security
Social welfare programs
Socialism
Temporary Assistance for Needy Families
  (TANF)
Title I
"Too big to fail"
Two-step voting process
2002 Farm Bill
War on Poverty
Welfare state

Questions for Thought

1. What is the role of the government in shaping social stratification?
2. Does the U.S. political system truly represent the interests of all? Is this an equal representation?
3. Does a capitalist economic system founded on liberty and resulting in an unequal distribution of rewards contradict the equality goals of democracy?
4. What role do campaign finance contributions have in the voting decisions of elected representatives? Does this present a threat to democracy?
5. How important is it that women and minorities are equally represented in the political process? Does unequal material representation necessarily mean that their interests are not being voiced?
6. What drives the formation and longevity of a democratic form of government? Are these attributes found in all societies and countries? Must these be present for a democracy to function? Can a democratic form of government be forced on a country or is it necessary that the citizens initiate this particular form of government?

Exercises

1. *Media portrayals of politicians.*
   In small groups, collect a sample of 20 articles from newspapers, magazines or other sources that report on elected politicians. In the sample, have a balance between male and female politicians. Analyze the content of the articles looking specifically at the following topics: family, spouses, balancing family and work, appearance, experience, and education. In addition to these topics are the photographs similar or different? Are men and women treated similarly in the media? What do your results say about how power in America is treated?
2. *Who rules in your community?*
   Use the following Web sites as possible resources to identify the background and social and economic characteristics of legislators in national legislative bodies such as the U.S. Congress. Are these national patterns consistent with patterns in your home city and state? In groups, discuss possible implications of these patterns.
   www.congress.org
   www.house.gov
   www.senate.gov

3. *Do neighborhood policies reduce inequality?*
   Identify local grassroots organizations in your community. What do they lobby for and whom do they target? How successful are their efforts? Is there controversy surrounding their goals? Discuss how local-level politics affects inequality.
4. *Policy-planning network: foundations and think tanks.*
   Create a list of foundations and think tanks. What is the mission of each? In which activities is each engaged? Do the mission statement and activities align? How so or, if not, how do they differ?

Multimedia Resources

(1) www.sociology.ucsc.edu/whorulesamerica: William Domhoff's Web site is devoted to the study of the distribution of power in America today.
(2) www.guardian.co.uk/world/interactive/2008/jun/04/barackobama.hillaryclinton: *The Guardian* focuses on American voters in the 2008 election. The Web site allows viewers to choose a state to obtain information on voter demographics.
(3) www.npr.org/news/specials/election2008/2008-election-map.html#/president:
(4) NPR provides an interactive map of the 2008 election. Web sites of the U.S. government include:
   www.congress.org
   www.house.gov
   www.senate.gov
(5) http://clerk.house.gov:
   Office of the Clerk of the House of Representatives

Print

Ball, Steven J. 2006. *Education Policy and Social Class: The Selected Works of Stephen J. Ball.* New York: Routledge.

Bobo, Lawrence D., and Camille Z. Charles. 2009. "Race in the American Mind: From the Moynihan Report to the Obama Candidacy." *The Annals of the American Academy of Political and Social Science* 621: 243.

Caplan, Bryan Douglas. 2007. *The Myth of the Rational Voter: Why Democracies Choose Bad Policies.* Princeton, NJ: Princeton University Press.

Cooke, Lynn Prince. 2007. "Policy Pathways to Gender Power: State-Level Effects on the U.S. Division of Housework." *Journal of Social Policy* 36: 239–60.

Domhoff, G. William. 2002. *Who Rules America? Power and Politics* (4th edition). New York: McGraw Hill.

Jenkins, J. C. 2006. "Nonprofit Organizations and Political Advocacy." In *The Nonprofit Sector: A Research Handbook*, edited by R. S. Walter W. Powell (pp. 307–32). New Haven, CT: Yale University Press.

Kalev, Alexandra, Erin Kelly, and Frank Dobbin. 2006. "Best Practices or Best Guesses? Assessing the Efficacy of Corporate Affirmative Action and Diversity Policies." *American Sociological Review* 71: 589–617.

Klein, Naomi. 2007. *The Shock Doctrine: The Rise of Disaster Capitalism.* New York: Metropolitan Books.

Marx, Karl, and Friedrich Engels. 1848. *The Communist Manifesto.* New York: Penguin Books.

Mills, C. Wright. 1956. *The Power Elite.* New York: Oxford University Press.

Paxton, Pamela Marie, and Sheri Kunovich. 2003. "Women's Political Representation: The Importance of Ideology." *Social Forces* 82: 87–113.

Smeeding, Timothy M. 2008. "Poverty, Work, and Policy: The United States in Comparative Perspective." In *Social Stratification: Class, Race, and Gender in Sociological Perspective*, edited by D. B. Grusky (pp. 327–39). Boulder, CO: Westview Press.

Internet

www.congress.org: A private, nonpartisan Web site designed to facilitate civic participation. This Web site is sponsored by Capital Advantage and contains contact and background information on elected leaders in Congress, the White House, and state legislatures.

www.house.gov/: Official Web site of the U.S. House of Representatives.

www.senate.gov: Official Web site of the U.S. Senate.

www.govtrack.us: A free and comprehensive source of information related to the status of federal legislation, voting records, and campaign contributions.

www.opensecrets.org: The Web site for the Center for Responsive Politics. Its homepage is a good source of information on campaign finances and the role of money in politics.

www.whitehouse.gov: Official Web site of the White House and the President of the United States of America. This site contains current and relevant political news, policy information, and other information related to the current presidency.

www.thomas.loc.gov: The official Web site for the status of legislation at the Library of Congress. This site, along with the Senate and House Web sites, is the official source for congressional voting records and legislative information.

www.orgnet.com/lobbying.html: Interactive site from OrgNet that allows users to explore the social network of lobbyists in Washington, DC.

Films

Constructing Public Opinion: How Politicians and the Media Misrepresent the Public (2002). This video describes the use of polls by the mainstream media to reflect and construct American public opinion. It explores the alternative meanings of polls and politics and the role that the media plays in "manufacturing consent" for political elites.

Women, A True Story: The Power Game (1996). This video offers an analysis of the role of women in politics. Through discussions concerning women who have supposedly gained political power through their husband – a Brazilian senator, a corporate president, and a Turkish community activist – the program delves into the meaning of female political, economic, and social power.

The Power Game (1993). This film analyzes the acquisition and maintenance of political power following the Vietnam War. By interviewing political figures, the program documents how this process has changed and predicts future changes.

Chicano!: History of the Mexican American Civil Rights Movement (1996). This PBS TV series documentary consists of four one-hour episodes. The series offers an analysis of the history of the Mexican American Civil Rights Movement from the events that ignited the movement, the efforts of farmers to gain political power, to the emergence and creation of political parties and power.

Yuri Kochiyama: Passion for Justice (1994). The political and social video biography of an Asian American woman and humanitarian civil-rights activist, Yuri Kochiyama. She became politically active while interned in a World War II Japanese American camp and voiced the necessity of racial and ethnic cooperation in the fight to change the structure of political power in the United States.

Works Cited

Alon, Sigal, and Marta Tienda. 2007. "Diversity, Opportunity, and the Shifting Meritocracy in Higher Education." *American Sociological Review* 72: 487–511.

Barlett, Donald L., and James B. Steele. 1994. *America: Who Really Pays the Taxes?* New York: Simon and Schuster.

Bass, Loretta E., and Lynne M. Casper. 2001. "Impacting the Political Landscape: Who Registers and Votes among Naturalized Americans?" *Political Behavior* 23: 103–30.

Beckfield, Jason. 2003. "Inequality in the World Polity: The Structure of International Organization." *American Sociological Review* 68: 401–24.

Beeghley, Leonard. 1986. "Social Class and Political Participation: A Review and an Explanation." *Sociological Forum* 1: 496–513.

Berliner, David C., and Bruce J. Biddle. 1995. *The Manufactured Crisis: Myths, Fraud, and Attack on America's Public Schools.* New York: Addison Wesley Longman.

Blossfeld, Hans-Peter, and Yosi Shavit. 1993. "Persisting Barriers: Changes in Educational Opportunities in Thirteen Countries."

Brookings Institute. 2009. "About Brookings." Retrieved December 7, 2009. Available at www. brookings.edu/about.aspx.

Carnoy, Martin, Rebecca Jacobsen, Lawrence R. Mishel, and Richard Rothstein. 2005. *The Charter School Dust-Up: Examining the Evidence on Enrollment and Achievement.* Washington, DC: Economic Policy Institute.

Carr, Don. 2007. "As Congress Finalizes Farm Bill Deal; EWG Lists Recipients of Controversial Direct Payment Subsidies for 2007." Washington, DC: Environmental Working Group.

Cebula, Richard J. 2007. "The Political Economy of Politics PAC Congressional Election Campaign Contributions and Other Political or Economic Influences on the Voter Participation Rate." *American Journal of Economics and Sociology* 66: 399–412.

Center for Responsive Politics. 2009. "Lobbying Database." Retrieved November 30. Available at www.opensecrets.org/lobbyists/index.php.

Charles, Maria, and David B. Grusky. 2004. *Occupational Ghettos: The Worldwide Segregation of Women and Men.* Chicago: Stanford University Press.

Commission on the Status of Women. 2009. "Despite 'Record Year' Globally for Women Decision Makers in Public Sector, Road Was Long to Achieve Parity with Men." New York: UN Economic and Social Council, News and Media Division.

Conway, M. Margaret. 1991. *Political Participation in the United States.* Washington, DC: Congressional Quarterly, Inc.

Cowen, Tyler. 2002. "Does the Welfare State Help the Poor?" In *Should Differences in Income and Wealth Matter?* Edited by E. F. Paul, Fred D. Miller, and Jeffrey Paul (pp. 36–54). New York: Cambridge University Press.

Crosby, Faye J. 2004. *Affirmative Action Is Dead: Long Live Affirmative Action.* New Haven, CT: Yale University Press.

Domhoff, G. William. 1990. *The Power Elite and the State: How Policy Is Made in America.* New York: Aldine de Gruyter.

_____. 2002. *Who Rules America? Power and Politics* (4th edition). New York: McGraw Hill.

Fischer, Mary J., and Douglas S. Massey. 2007. "The Effects of Affirmative Action in Higher Education." *Social Science Research* 36: 531–49.

Hess, Douglas R., and Jody Herman. 2009. "Representational Bias in the 2008 Electorate." Washington, DC: Project Vote.

Highton, Benjamin. 2000. "Residential Mobility, Community Mobility, and Electoral Participation." *Political Behavior* 22: 109–20.

IES. 2010. **"Head Start Impact Study: Final Report"** What Works Clearinghouse. WWC Quick Review of the Report. Washington, DC.: Institution of Educational Sciences, U.S. Department of Education.

Jackson, Robert A., Robert D. Brown, and Gerald C. Wright. 1998. "Registration, Turnout, and the Electoral Representativeness of U.S. State Electorates." *American Politics Quarterly* 26: 259-87.

Jencks, Christopher, Marshal Smith, Henry Acland, Mary Jo Bane, David Cohen, Herbert Gintis, Barbara Heyns, and Stephan Michelson. [1972]2001. "Inequality: A Reassessment of the Effect of Family Schooling in America." In *Social Stratification*, edited by D. B. Grusky (pp. 403-10). Boulder, CO: Westview Press.

John D. Rockefeller Foundation. 2009a. "About Us." Retrieved December 7, 2009. Available at www.rockfound.org/aboutus/aboutus.shtml.

———. 2009b. "Rockefeller Foundation Grant Search." Retrieved December 7, 2009. Available at www.rockfound.org/grants/GrantSearch.aspx?keywords=&allDates=1&monthFrom=1&yearFrom=2004&monthTo=12&yearTo=2009.

Kirschenman, Joleen, and Kathryn M. Neckerman. 1991. "'We'd Love to Hire Them but...': The Meaning of Race for Employers." *Social Problems* 38: 433–47.

Lichter, Daniel T., and Martha L. Crowley. 2002. "Poverty in America: Beyond Welfare Reform." *Population Bulletin* 57: 36.

Los Angeles Homeless Service Authority. 2009. "2009 Greater Los Angeles Homeless Count Report." Los Angeles, CA.

Mandel, Hadas, and Moshe Semyonov. 2005. "Family Policies, Wage Structures, and Gender Gaps: Sources of Earnings Inequality in 20 Countries." *American Sociological Review* 70: 949–67.

Martinez, Michael D., and David Hill. 1999. "Did Motor-Voter Work?" *American Political Science Review* 27.

McDonald, Michael. 2009. "Turnout Data." *United States Elections Project.* George Mason University: Department of Public and International Affairs.

McGreal, Chris. 2009. "UN Investigator Accuses US of Shameful Neglect of Homeless." *The Guardian.* London: Guardian News and Media Limited. November 12, 2009. Retrieved December 7, 2009. Available at http://www.guardian.co.uk/world/2009/nov/12/un-investigator-us-neglect-homeless

McNeil, J. M. 2000. "Employment, Earnings, and Disability." In *75th Annual Conference of the Western Economic Association International.* Washington, DC: U.S. Bureau of the Census.

National Center for Education Statistics. 2007. "The Condition of Education 2007 (NCES 2007–064)." Washington, DC: U.S. Department of Education.

O'Toole, Randal. 1987. *Reforming the Forest Service.* Covelo, CA: Island Press.

Paul, Jeffrey, and Fred D. Miller. 2002. *Should Differences in Income and Wealth Matter?* New York: Cambridge University Press.

Paxton, Pam. 1997. "Women in National Legislatures: A Cross-National Analysis." *Social Science Research* 26: 442–64.

Paxton, Pamela Marie, and Sheri Kunovich. 2003. "Women's Political Representation: The Importance of Ideology." *Social Forces* 82: 87–113.

Roscigno, Vincent J., Lissette M. Garcia, and Donna Bobbitt-Zeher. 2007. "Social Closure and Processes of Race/Sex Employment Discrimination." *The Annals of the American Academy of Political and Social Science* 609: 16–48.

Russell, Judith. 2003. *Economics, Bureaucracy, and Race: How Keynesians Misguided the War on Poverty*. New York: Columbia University Press.

Sasseen, Jane, and Theo Francis. 2008. "The Financial System Bailout: Deal or No Deal?" In *Bloomberg Businessweek*. September 25, 2008. Available at http://www.businessweek.com/bwdaily/dnflash/content/sep2008/db20080925_596844.htm

Shapiro, Daniel. 2002. "Egalitarianism and Welfare-State Redistribution." In *Should Differences in Income and Wealth Matter?* Edited by E. F. Paul, F. D. Miller, and J. Paul (pp. 1–35). New York: Cambridge University Press.

Skocpol, Theda. 1993. *Protecting Soldiers and Mothers: The Political Origins of Social Policy in the United States*. Cambridge: Harvard University Press.

Southgate, Darby E. 2009. "Interview of Jeannette Rowe, Director of Emergency Response Team and Homeless Children and Families Program, Los Angeles Homeless Service Authority." Los Angeles: Los Angeles Homeless Service Authority.

U.S. Department of Education. 2009. "Title I: Improving the Academic Achievement of the Disadvantaged." Available at www.ed.gov/policy/elsec/leg/esea02/pg1.html.

U.S. Department of Health and Human Services. 2004. "Aid to Families with Dependent Children (AFDC) and Temporary Assistance for Needy Families (TANF)." Washington, DC: Office of Human Services Policy.

U.S. Office of the Clerk. 2009. "Women Representatives and Senators by Congress, 1917–Present." Washington, DC: U.S. Office of the Clerk.

Walker, Edward T. 2009. "Privatizing Participation: Civic Change and the Organizational Dynamics of Grassroots Lobbying Firms." *American Sociological Review* 74: 83–105.

Weisman, Jonathan, and Jeffrey H. Birnbaum. 2006. "Lawmaker Criticized for PAC Fees Paid to Wife." *The Washington Post, p. A01 July 11, 2006*. Washington, DC: The Washington Post Company.

Wisconsin Budget Project. 2001. "Tax Trends in Wisconsin: Tracking Corporations' Share of State Revenues." Madison: Wisconsin Council on Children and Families.

Xu, Jun. 2004. "Why Do Minorities Participate Less? The Effects of Immigration, Education, and Electoral Process on Asian American Voter Registration and Turnouts." *Social Science Research* 34: 682–702.

Zhang, Yahong, and Kaifeng Yang. 2008. "What Drives Charter School Diffusion at the Local Level: Educational Needs or Political and Institutional Forces?" *Policy Studies Journal* 36: 571–91.

Index